THE IMAGE OF AFRICA

THE
IMAGE OF AFRICA

British Ideas and Action, 1780–1850

PHILIP D. CURTIN

The University of Wisconsin Press
Madison, 1964

To Anne Gilbert Curtin

Published by
The University of Wisconsin Press
430 Sterling Court, Madison 6, Wisconsin

Copyright © 1964 by the
Regents of the University of Wisconsin

Printed in the United States of America by
George Banta Company, Inc., Menasha, Wisconsin
Library of Congress Catalog Card Number 64-10922

PREFACE

It was apparent during the 1950's that the West in general, and the colonial powers in particular, were unprepared for the emergence of Africa. The popular mental image of the "dark continent" lived on, in spite of the decades of government over Africans, stretching back to the 1880's and sometimes beyond. This image owed something to the superiority feelings of the conquerors over the conquered, the administrators over those whom they administered. Its roots, however, lie much further back in the history of Western ideas. An image began to emerge out of the haze of the unknown with the first voyages down the West African coast in the fifteenth century. It was strengthened by more frequent contact during the sixteenth century, strengthened still more by intensive commercial contact through the slave trade in the centuries from the seventeenth to the middle of the nineteenth.

The crucial period, however, was the early nineteenth century. Beginning in the 1780's, Europeans began to take a new look at Africa. Now that the slave trade was under sharp attack in England, France, and America alike, a new prospect appeared in Afro-European relations. For the British, this prospect was one of "legitimate" trade, which might soon replace the slave trade, and provide a radically new basis for Anglo-African commerce. From the 1780's, therefore, the British began to see Africa, not merely as it was, but as it might be, and with full consideration for the new Africa in the imperial scheme of things.

Since West Africa was the core-area of the old slave trade, it was the first part of Africa to attract attention; and the British image of "the African," and of African conditions generally, was initially concerned almost entirely with West Africa. South Africa entered the picture only in the 1820's, Central and East Africa only in the 1850's, and the Congo basin only in the 1870's. With each new dimension, the image spread and took on local variations, but for Britain itself the early-nineteenth-century image of Africa was, in fact, the image of West Africa.

The new view of Africa which began to emerge in the 1780's, drew some of its novelty from a new attitude on the part of Europeans, but even more from the flood of new data that began to pour in—first from coastal travellers, then from explorers into the interior (and the early nineteenth century was the great age of African exploration), finally from the refinement and synthesis of these data in the hands of stay-at-home scholars and publicists. As the decades passed, British ideas about Africa became more and more detailed and better publicized. By the 1850's the image had hardened. It was found in children's books, in Sunday school tracts, in the popular press. Its major affirmations were the "common knowledge" of the educated classes. Thereafter, when new generations of explorers or administrators went to Africa, they went with a prior impression of what they would find. Most often, they found it, and their writings in turn confirmed the older image—or at most altered it only slightly.

With the 1850's, British interest in West Africa began to taper off, until it reached a low point about 1865. It then rose gradually as the era of the new imperialism approached, and Britain entered fully into the scramble for Africa of the 1880's and 1890's. For convenience' sake, the period of limited missionary and commercial penetration up to the 1850's can be called the era of humanitarianism. The three decades from about 1850 to about 1880 mark a transition from this to the era of imperialism.

There is no need to enter the period of transition. The hardened image of Africa was complete by the 1850's. It was to change slowly in later years, but the later image of Africa was very largely drawn from Europe's first impressions, taken during the earlier and formative decades. It is not my concern here to trace the later course of these ideas, but it should be apparent that they lived on into the middle of the twentieth century—indeed, that they contributed substantially to the cross-cultural misunderstandings of the recent past.

The aim of the present work is to show how these ideas were formed and integrated with Western thought. The history of political events is therefore carried down to the reaffirmation of the anti-slave-trade blockade in 1850, the capture of Lagos in 1851, and the fall of the Russell Government in 1852. These three events together mark both the last important stand of humanitarian policies, the first step toward more active intervention along the Gulf of Guinea, and the fall of the last British Government that clearly belongs to the era of humanitarianism. The history of British thought about race and its meaning can stop conveniently with the publication of Darwin's *Origin of Species* in 1859. Economic thought and policy took a new direction from the passage of the Sugar Act of 1846 and the end of the Brazilian slave trade in 1850, while European medical technology also reached a new level of achievement at about 1850. Finally, the great age of West African exploration was rounded out by the first really successful steamboat entry into the Niger in 1854 and the emergence of Barth, the greatest explorer of West Africa, in 1855.

It is customary for historians of the British Empire to write about the history of British policy, and British policy can be most conveniently studied with reference to the explicit documentary record of the central administration. It has not usually been thought relevant or useful to consider anything so broad as the national "image" one people may hold of another.

Even from the narrow point of view of policy-formation, however, the broader history of ideas has some importance. Officials in the Colonial Office did not, in fact, write down all that they believed to be true about the world in which they lived or the regions they governed. Beyond the world of despatches, there was also a world of unstated assumptions. The more cohesive the society, the less need to bring these unstated assumptions into the open—and the ruling class of nineteenth century Britain was very cohesive indeed. Officials therefore wrote for other officials, who held very much the same set of beliefs, placed much the same values on their own culture (or on that of foreigners), or shared unstated assumptions about the nature of race and its role in history.

Any attempt to discover the roots of European policy in any part of the world must therefore take account of these unstated assumptions, and a great deal of light can be thrown on them by examining the attitudes, values, and sentiments present in European society at large. The history of European ideas about the African people, the African way of life, or the earlier course of African history, therefore, is something more than the history of African studies—though it is that too. These ideas were formed in a particular historical setting. They, in turn, helped to influence the course of future history.

It can, of course, be argued, that the prominence of an idea in British thought as a whole is no guarantee that any particular body of administrators were moved by it in their decisions. This is quite true: it is no *guarantee*. But it is extremely likely that people who share a common educational background and who are subject to common intellectual influences will share a common denominator of ideas and attitudes. In practice, those who dissented from the common attitudes of the day often said so in their despatches. The best verification, however, comes with the study of the official correspondence against the background of generally held ideas. Once the broader image of Africa is uncovered, it becomes obvious that this image—this combination of attitudes, values, and theory about the world—does in fact provide the set of unstated assumptions that lead rationally to the policies that did emerge.

On another plane, it has been customary for general historians to neglect the technical aspects of European relations with the world overseas. Matters like the history of tropical medicine, however, are more than a sidelight of importance only to historians of medicine. The inability of the Europeans to solve medical problems on the African coast—even to survive in reasonable proportion—was one of the basic determinants of Afro-European relations in any period before the First World War. The state of this problem at any moment in time set limits on the policies that were practicable. This is true not merely of correct knowledge, which led to medical progress: it is equally true of incorrect knowledge. Erroneous medical ideas, the *culs de sac* in the history of medicine, led men to die and policies to be abandoned on the coast of West Africa.

Nor was technical knowledge unrelated to other ideas and attitudes. As it turned out, incorrect information about racial immunities to disease became one of the strongest rational supports for pseudo-scientific racism in the early nineteenth century. Racism, in turn, colored British attitudes toward other peoples across the whole spectrum of thought, from the theory of history at one end to explicit provisions for African education at the other.

In short, the body of knowledge about Africa which influenced African history was much broader than mere "colonial policy." It was also interrelated in curious ways, which carry the investigator across many of the usual divisions of knowledge. By concentrating on the study of what one country thought about one part of Africa, investigation is drawn into many of the nooks and crannies of the history of British ideas themselves. It is hoped that this study, with its first concern for the role of British ideas in African history, will also add something to our knowledge of the way in which ideas originated in Western society, the ways they changed through time, and some of the uses to which they were put by those who tried to carry them into action. Even more, it is hoped that this study of the early origins of the image of Africa will help to illuminate present relations between Africa and the West, and through this example, will say something useful about the role of ideas in the confrontation of differing civilizations.

The trail of debt I have left in the preparation of this book is even more diverse than the material that has found its way into it. The library of the British Museum and the Memorial Library of the University of Wisconsin have been far more than ordinarily helpful. I am especially grateful to Miss Margarite Christensen of the Wisconsin library for searching out and procuring through inter-library loan the books which neither library held. In London, The Institute of Commonwealth Studies of the University of London was extremely generous in making its facilities available, and I am grateful for the intellectual stimulus of its staff and my fellow-visitors during several prolonged visits. In West Africa, I am especially indebted to Mr. Peter Kup, the archivist of Sierra Leone at the time of my visit, to Mr. J. M. Akita of the National Archives of Ghana, and to Dr. K. O. Dike, Mr. L. C. Gwam, and Mr. S. S. Waniko of the National Archives of Nigeria.

Among colleagues and friends, Mr. Christopher Fyfe was generous far beyond the call of duty in supplying citations and guideposts to the literature about Sierra Leone. Drs. David Kimble and J. F. A. Ajayi were kind enough to allow me to read their books on the Gold Coast and Nigeria respectively, prior to publication. Others were generous with their time in reading and commenting on sections of the manuscript. Among those to whom I am especially grateful are Thomas L. Hodgkin, Jeffrey Butler, J. F. C. Harrison, Paul J. Bohannan, Joseph H. Greenberg, Robert Stauffer, Jan Vansina, M. J. Coulbourne, T. H. Silcock, Gerald S. Graham, and Anne G. Curtin, the most exacting critic of all. Needless to say, none of these can be held responsible for those occasions where I may have persisted in error against their good advice, or where I have added error at a later stage of revision.

The Journal of the Historical Society of Nigeria and the *Journal of British Studies* have been kind enough to permit republication of material which first appeared in their pages in a different form.

Still another, and substantial, indebtedness is due to the Research Committee of the University of Wisconsin for generous support during research leaves from my teaching post, and to the Ford Foundation for a year of travel and study in West Africa and Great Britain.

Messrs. Randal Sale, Melvin Albaum, and Rodney Helgeland of the Cartographic Laboratory of the University of Wisconsin have been responsible for the preparation of the maps.

P. D. C.

Madison, Wisconsin
June, 1963

TABLE OF CONTENTS

xi

LIST OF FIGURES

xiii

LIST OF MAPS

KEY TO ABBREVIATIONS

IN THE NOTES

Ad. Mss.	Additional Manuscripts, British Museum
AG	National Archives of Ghana, Accra
ASP	Papers of the Anti-Slavery Society and the Aborigines Protection Society, Rhodes House, Oxford
BT	Board of Trade series, Public Record Office
CMSA	Archives of the Church Missionary Society, Salisbury Square, London. (Microfilm series also available at Memorial Library, University of Wisconsin.)
CO	Colonial Office series, Public Record Office
DNB	Dictionary of National Biography
HO	Home Office series, Public Record Office
H	Hansard
IA	Nigerian National Archives, Western Regional Repository, Ibadan
PP	Parliamentary Papers
PRO	Public Record Office, London
SLA	National Archives of Sierra Leone, Freetown
T	Treasury series, Public Record Office

PART I

*The "New World"
of Eighteenth-Century Africa*

WEST AFRICA:

THE KNOWN

AND

THE UNKNOWN

The decade between the Peace of Versailles in 1783 and the war with France in 1793 marked a phase of special importance in British relations with the world overseas. The loss of the thirteen American colonies closed an epoch, and seemed to close it decisively. Few in Britain looked back with nostalgia or wanted to found another family of settlement colonies like those in North America. Even fewer were willing to accept the military defeat as final. It was only a temporary decline of British fortunes, and it was met by rapid recovery, reform, and determination to regain some equivalent for the loss.

Britain was then in the middle of the late-eighteenth-century population explosion. The first great burst of industrial growth was just beginning. The way was open to some kind of new overseas activity. But the kind was still undecided, and its geographical focus still undetermined. There were only areas of preference or possibility. The temperate zone as a whole seemed unattractive: its products were competitive with those of Britain. The fur-producing regions on the northern temperate fringes were highly valued, but

Canada and the Hudson's Bay Company territories filled that particular need. The tropical world promised something better—greater material gains, complementary to Britain's own production and without the political inconvenience of managing thousands of importunate settlers.

Several possibilities were open. The trade of China and Southeast Asia was one, calling for the further development of trading-post enclaves in East Asia. (The British had, indeed, begun to show a greater interest in the further East beyond India since the end of the Seven Years' War.) India was a second, and here too British interests had been advancing since the 1750's. Recent decades had seen the transformation of enclaves and informal influence into *de facto* territorial sovereignty in Bengal. The new situation was recognized in North's Regulating Act of 1773 and Pitt's India Act of 1784, but the Indian Empire of the future was still only a very vague promise.

An equal or even greater promise lay in the lands on either side of the tropical Atlantic, where a variety of openings might be exploited. The most valuable form of overseas activity for any of the major European colonial powers was still considered to be the complex of long-distance trade and production centering in the Caribbean. This system as a whole had no contemporaneous name, but in retrospect it may be called the "South Atlantic System."[1] The goal was the production of tropical staples for the European market, and its ramifications stretched out in every direction. The West Indian slave plantations lacked a self-reproducing labor force. Continuous slave trade from Africa was needed to maintain the level of production. Many of the Caribbean islands were so heavily involved in cash-crop production that food supplies, as well as timber and other provisions, had to be imported in a continuous stream from North America or Ireland.

In the European theory of empire, from the later seventeenth century onward, it was thought desirable to have a balanced set of colonies, so that slaves, provisions, and shipping, as well as plantations themselves, could all be monopolized for the benefit of the mother country. Thus, in theory, there was not a single European South Atlantic System, but a series of systems, each completely

1. In naval usage, South Atlantic means the Atlantic south of the equator, but ordinary American usage, which places the South Atlantic more vaguely to the south of the Mason-Dixon line, serves best to describe the extent of the system.

separate from the others. In fact, it never worked out as the theory suggested. By the mid-eighteenth century only France and Britain held the theoretically essential set of colonies in North America and tropical America, plus slave-trade posts on the African coast. Dutch, Danes, Brandenburgers, Spanish, and Portuguese, however, had all participated to some degree or held incomplete sets of colonies. Furthermore, even the French and British sectors were often internally out of balance, having more slaves or more provisions than their own plantations could use, or less tropical production than the home market needed. As a result, the nationals of all countries traded widely, if illegally, between sectors, until the whole system had become most unsystematic. In fact, if not in law, it was a great international network of trade and production.

The South Atlantic System, though principally concerned with tropical agricultural production, had also come to be closely and illegally interlocked with the trade of Spanish America. The gold and silver of Mexico and Peru, mainly acquired by illegal trading on the part of north European nationals, had long since become essential to the monetary operation of the South Atlantic economy. For the British in particular, it was an ancient ambition of colonial policy to pry open a larger access to the trade of Spanish America— either by encouraging smuggling, by direct diplomatic pressure on Spain, or possibly by seizing all or part of the Spanish Empire, if the opportunity presented itself.

At the end of the American War, the British sector of the South Atlantic System was seriously damaged by the loss of the thirteen mainland colonies, and the French sector began to compete more efficiently than ever. The British saw it as a threat that might drive their sugar out of the Continental markets. If Britain were to recover its old position, two alternate possibilities were open. One was to push harder for entry into Latin America. The other was to concentrate on revitalizing the British sector itself. Each course had its advocates, but each had its dangers. Illicit trade with Spanish America was valuable, but to extend it might mean a clash with Spain. The West India interest in Britain preferred government support for their own plantations in the British Caribbean. But the West India interest was narrow and particular, and it was beginning to meet opposition from the anti-slave-trade movement. Humanitarian publicity both underlined moral defects of the South Atlantic System, and pointed out a third possibility. Tropical development might also be encouraged on the eastern shore of the South Atlantic. No other power was so well supplied with African trading posts, and no potential European ally would be alienated by the spread of tropical agriculture in the hinterland of these posts. In the decade after 1783, therefore, the alternative of developing tropical Africa began to have a following.

When Britain or any other European power turned to Africa in the eighteenth century, it was West Africa that counted. Without the Suez Canal, the east coast was far away in the sphere of the Indian "country trade." The Cape was Dutch, and little more than a way station on the route to India. The region of commercial promise was that of the existing slave trade—"the Coast," extending from Benguela in Angola to St. Louis at the mouth of the Senegal. In the later 1780's, all European nations together exported about 75,000 slaves a year from this part of Africa, about half of them carried by British merchants. The annual average "official" value of British exports to Africa in 1783–87 was £691,000, representing 4.4 per cent of the total value of British exports.[2] Export values, however, are misleading by themselves. The importance of the African trade was not merely in the value of goods sold in Africa. The gross income from the sale of slaves in America was nearly twice the value of exports to the Coast, being in the neighborhood of £1,000,000 a year.[3] More important still, West Indian planters depended for their own prosperity on a steady supply of slaves.

But those who favored African development were not concerned with its role in the South Atlantic System. They looked ahead to projected economic growth of astronomical proportions within a few years or decades. As it turned out, they were wrong. West Africa was never again so important to the British sector of the

2. Great Britain. Privy Council. *Report of the Lords of the Committee of Council for . . . Trade and Foreign Plantations . . . Concerning the Present State of Trade to Africa, and Particularly the Trade in Slaves . . .* (London, 1789), Part IV. These figures give a rough indication, but in the 1780's they no longer corresponded to the actual market values of the goods exported. (See Albert Imlah, *Economic Elements in the Pax Britannica* [Cambridge, Mass., 1958], pp. 20–41.)

3. Assuming that British merchants landed about 30,000 slaves annually in the Americas and sold them for the average West Indian price for the period, or about £35 each.

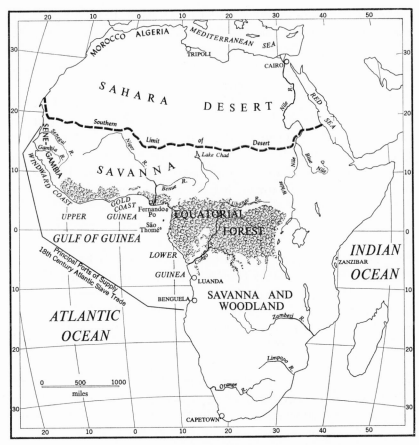

Map 1. West Africa and the Slave Trade

world economy as it was in those last few decades before 1807, but no one could know this at the time.

Britain had no more than a shadow of sovereignty over any part of the Coast, though the Portuguese at Luanda and the French at St. Louis had tiny enclaves. Elsewhere, the relations between African political authorities and Europeans trading on the Coast were generally those of equal partners in a commercial transaction. The question of political sovereignty was seldom raised in the technical sense of European usage. There were some trading forts on shore, but the relative power of the European traders and the African states was roughly in balance. A trading fort did not necessarily imply a sphere of European influence over its hinterland. In most places, the forts were allowed by the Africans as a mutual convenience for African and European merchants alike; and the Europeans paid for the privilege of trade, either in the form of ground rent for the land occupied by the fort or as a gift in return for good will.

For that matter, British trade was not necessarily centered around the forts, and it was distributed unevenly along the length of the Coast. The region north of the Gambia had been abandoned to France at the end of the American war. Lower Guinea, south of the equator, had traditionally been the special sphere of the Portuguese in their slave trade to Brazil; but the British merchants were active even there, whenever the supply of slaves was plentiful. All along the Coast, indeed, the supply of slaves shifted from time to time with the changing patterns of war or peace in the interior of the continent. Forts and factories, on the other hand, were relatively immobile.

Some British forts were considered to be national property and maintained by grants from the royal government. These were narrowly concentrated along 200 miles on the Gold Coast. The only exceptions were a fort at James Island in the Gambia and a factory at Ouidah (then called Whydah) in Dahomey. All of these were administered by the Company of Merchants Trading to Africa and managed by its elected committee of merchants, informally called the African Committee. A firm trading to Africa was obliged to join the Company, but the membership fee was low and the Company did not engage in trade on its own account.

There was, however, no obligation to trade through the Company's forts, and most trade went elsewhere. Any firm that chose to do so could maintain its own factory wherever it could make suitable arrangements with an African ruler. The circumstances of these private factories varied enormously. In some places a factor was simply left on shore in African territory to purchase slaves between calls from ships. In other places, and especially where African political authority was highly fragmented, a European slave trader with a few hundred armed African followers could set himself up as an authority with power equal to that of the surrounding rulers. In these cases he became a petty king by *de facto* African recognition but not in European international law. Small posts of this kind were most numerous on the "Windward Coast" which is now Portuguese Guinea, the Republic of Guinea, Sierra Leone, and parts of Liberia.[4] To the east of the Gold Coast, however, in the Bights of Benin and Biafara, ships called at established African trading towns and dealt directly with the African merchants, without the permanent European posts, either official or unofficial.

Other European holdings fell into much the same pattern as the British. Along the Gold Coast, where the British forts were most numerous, Dutch and Danish forts were also plentiful; and they were interspersed without regard for nationality. In Accra, Dutch, English, and Danish forts were all within sight of one another and the principal Dutch fort at Elmina was only eight miles from the British administrative center at Cape Coast.

This form of European contact, strictly limited to the coast and a few navigable rivers, was admirably suited to the conditions of the slave trade. European merchants were in no position to go inland to buy or capture slaves, and they were content to let the African middle-men handle that part of the trade. By the later eighteenth century, each of the major partners understood his own function and was supported in it by a body of custom now become traditional. The pattern of commerce, therefore, was not one that could respond rapidly to a flow of new products from Europe or a new economic demand for African products at the coastal ports. If the British in the 1780's hoped to do more in Africa than simply extend the slave trade, some new relationship would have to be worked out between Britons and Africans on the coast; but any assessment of possibilities depended on the existing information about Africa, and theoretical propositions derived from it.

The pattern of empirical information about Africa was itself a product of the peculiar relations built up during the centuries of the slave trade. A great deal was known about the coast in ways that were intimate, detailed, and highly specialized. Almost nothing was known through direct contact with the far interior, but then very little was known about the interior of North or South America or about Central Asia. The image of "darkest Africa," either as an expression of geographical ignorance, or as one of cultural arrogance, was a nineteenth-century invention. Relative to their knowledge of

4. For the variety of slave-trading posts on the Windward Coast, see C. Fyfe, *A History of Sierra Leone* (London, 1962), pp. 1–10.

the world in general, eighteen-century Europeans knew more and cared more about Africa than they did at any later period up to the 1950's.

This knowledge was available in England from a number of sources, often derived from different periods of time, and coming into British consciousness by a variety of routes. Virtually all knowledge about the Western Sudan, the savanna country lying between the forest and the Sahara, came by way of North Africa. This was only to be expected. The centuries-old caravan trade across the desert linked the Maghrib with Sudanese cities like Jenne, Timbuctu, and Gao. The more surprising fact about this source of knowledge is its narrow range of origin in time. The trans-Sahara trade had begun in the very distant past and continued through the nineteenth century; yet the reports of the Western Sudan, transmitted by the Arabs and available in Western Europe at the end of the eighteenth century, dated almost entirely from the period between the tenth century and the early sixteenth.

It was during this period that the great tradition of Arabic geographical studies flourished in the Maghrib, Egypt, and Southwest Asia. Ibn-Hawqal brought back the first surviving Arabic account of the Western Sudan in the tenth century.[5] From that time onward, Arabs crossed and recrossed the desert over a variety of routes, and scholars built up a body of systematic knowledge. Some of the important Arabic manuscripts were available in Western libraries, but the scarcity of Western scholars of Arabic kept them below the intellectual horizon. Neither al-Bakri's geography, ibn-Battūta's travels, nor ibn-Khaldūn's history was available in translation, though much of the substance of Arabic geography and history of the Western Sudan was known through other sources.

Only a few of the major works were known. One of the most important was the *Kitab Rudjar* of al-Idrīsi (c. 1100–1166), completed in 1154 at the court of Roger of Sicily. The sections dealing with Africa were published in Paris in 1619 in both Arabic and Latin, and a further abridged and annotated Latin version appeared in Göttingen in 1796.[6]

5. See E. W. Bovill, *The Golden Trade of the Moors* (London, 1958), pp. 60–65; G. H. T. Kimble, *Geography in the Middle Ages* (London, 1938), pp. 44–68.

6. *Geographia Nubiensis* (Paris, 1619), translated and edited by Gabriel Sionita and Joannes Hesronita; *Africa* (Göttingen, 1796), translated and edited by Joannes Melchoir Hartman.

Al-Idrīsi was not a traveller, but a geographical scholar, working with original travel accounts that have since been lost. Only one good travel account of this kind was available. This was the *Description of Africa* of Leo Africanus, which became the most popular of all the Arab works known to Western Europe. Leo Africanus was a Maghribi who had travelled widely in the Western Sudan before his capture by Christian ships in the Mediterranean. He wrote his original narrative in 1526, in defective Italian using Arabic notes. It then appeared in a more literary Italian version in 1550 and was translated into English in 1600. Its eighteenth-century vogue in England came from the fact that Samuel Purchas published certain portions in his enormous seventeenth-century collection of travels.[7]

A third source of Arabic knowledge was Luis del Marmol Carvajal, who wrote a history of North Africa in Spanish toward the end of the sixteenth century, taking a great deal of his material from the work of Ibn Khaldun.[8] Thus something of the Arabic historical tradition joined the geographical.

After Marmol and Leo Africanus, there were only rumors and occasional reports picked up in the North African ports. This piecemeal information might have been systematically collected and used, but it was not. Thus, the interior of western Africa was known at second hand, and the latest solid and systematic information available in the 1780's was already almost three hundred years old.

The sixteenth century, which brought the last of the detailed Arabic accounts of West Africa, also brought the first direct European reports. The Portuguese began sailing down the African coast in the fifteenth century, and they were followed shortly by other Europeans. From the mid-fifteenth to the mid-eighteenth century, several hundred different travellers left some account of their voyage to Guinea. Many of these journals and reports had dropped from sight by the 1780's, but about twenty different works had come to be accepted as a canon of West African knowledge.

These works were easily accessible to the educated English public, in spite of the fact that they had been written in a variety of European languages and sometimes dated from the distant past. Pub-

7. See introduction to recent critical edition: A. Epaulard (Translator and editor), *Description de l'Afrique, par Jean Léon l'Africain*, 2 vols. (Paris, 1957).

8. Luis del Marmol Carvajal, *La descripción general de Affrica, con todos los successos de guerras que a avido . . . hasta el año del Señor 1571*, 3 vols. (Granada and Malaga, 1573–1599).

lished collections of travel accounts had appeared regularly ever since Hakluyt's *Principal Voyages Traffiques & Discoveries of the English Nation* in 1599. The later multi-volume collections of Purchas and Churchill kept the older travellers in print and added the more recent ones. Major publications of world-wide scope were supplemented by local or regional collections, some of which were designed to serve as a systematic source book for an individual part of the world. Father J. B. Labat covered the African coast in this way by gathering both published and unpublished accounts and stringing them together in a scissors-and-paste compilation. One set of five volumes, based mainly on the notes of La Brue, dealt with the Senegambia and the coastal region from Cape Blanc in Mauritania to Sierra Leone. A second set of four volumes, derived more narrowly from the voyages of Des Marchais, carried on from Sierra Leone to Dahomey and across the ocean to French Guiana.[9]

This form of presentation was taken up in England by the publisher, Thomas Astley, whose editors produced the *New General Collection of Voyages and Travels* between 1745 and 1747. Its scope was world-wide, but a quarto volume of some six hundred pages in double columns was devoted to Africa alone. Astley's *Voyages* absorbed both English works and French accounts, arranging the excerpts so as to omit the tales of adventure and emphasize geographic and ethnographic information. All the authorities on any section of the coast were brought together, reprinted in their own words where possible, but otherwise rewritten as necessary and supplied with connecting passages to present a comprehensive account. Here, in short, was the whole canon of travel literature, presented in one place. It became the inevitable mine of information for anyone concerned with African affairs during the second half of the century, serving that generation as Lord Hailey's *African Survey* was to serve another generation some two centuries later.[10]

Alongside the collected travel reports, competent works of synthesis were also available. The most ambitious of these was the great *Universal History* published between 1736 and 1765 in sixty-five octavo volumes, or in a special luxury edition of twenty-three folio

9. J. B. Labat, *Nouvelle relation de l'Afrique occidentale,* 5 vols. (Paris, 1728), and *Voyage du Chevalier des Marchais en Guinée, Isles voisines, et à Cayenne, fait en 1725, 1726, et 1727 . . .*, 4 vols. (Paris, 1730).

10. Thomas Astley (Publisher), *A New General Collection of Voyages and Travels,* 4 vols. (London, 1745–1747).

volumes.[11] It was designed to be an epitome of world history and geography, and its balance of emphasis is some indication of the range of British interest. Nearly half the total was allotted to the history of the non-Western world—a generosity toward other peoples' history that would be hard to find in similar publications of the twentieth century. Africa also figured much more heavily than it was to do in future works. Two of the sixteen folio volumes of the Modern History section were devoted to Africa—one-eighth of the total, or the same space given to East, Southeast, and South Asia together. The treatment of individual African countries included a short sketch of European activities; but the body of the work was concerned with the history, manners, and customs of the Africans themselves, and a quarter of the Africa section was given over to West Africa.[12] Measured against modern knowledge, the presentation was not always accurate, nor was it free of ethnocentric prejudice. It was, however, a serious and ambitious effort to understand the African world with a tolerance and interest that was to be slowly eroded away during the course of the nineteenth century.

The established body of knowledge constantly absorbed new information. One source was the movement of individuals back and forth between Africa and Europe. The African posts were highly manned, but there were always a few ex-officials, merchants, or military officers in England who could claim personal knowledge of the Coast, and some of these were eager to make their knowledge available.[13] The age of the "expert" witness had already come, and committees of Parliament or the Privy Council could always round up a dozen or so, who willingly gave their various and contradictory opinions about the present situation and future possibilities. Many of these specialists were, in fact, professional or interested publicists ad-

11. Authors attributed by the Library of Congress catalogue are George Sale, George Psalmanzar, Archibald Bower, George Shelvocke, John Campbell, and John Swinton.

12. This relatively heavy concentration on Africa was typical of other works of the period as well. C. T. Middleton's *New and Complete System of Geography*, 2 vols. (London, 1779), for example, gave Africa more space than it gave to all of Asia, and three times as much space as the Americas. West Africa alone received more detailed treatment than India.

13. F. L. Bartels, "Philip Quaque, 1741–1816," *Transactions of the Gold Coast and Togoland Historical Society*, I, 153–77 (Achimota, 1955); John Adams, *Remarks on the Country Extending from Cape Palmas to the River Congo* (London, 1823), p. 144; Matthews, Penny, and Norris to John Tarleton, 16 April 1788, in Privy Council, *Report on the Trade in Slaves*, Part I, Detached pieces, no. 4. See also Kenneth Little, *Negroes in Britain* (London, 1947), pp. 165–94.

vocating particular forms of action or inaction in West Africa. They
were joined by the ever-present group of absentee West Indian proprietors, whose source of labor was in Africa, and who believed they
knew a good deal about the Africans, if not about Africa.

There were also several hundred Africans resident in England.
They rarely supplied information on their own initiative, but they
would often do so if asked; and their information was more or less
reliable according to the length of time they had been away from
home and their level of acculturation. Some of these were the "black
poor," African servants who came to England by way of West Indian
slavery, discharged sailors and soldiers from the American war, and
other Negroes who had become permanent residents in Britain.

As informants, they were not nearly so trustworthy as a second
group of transients direct from Africa. The long contact with the
Europeans had already produced in Africa a need for literacy in
English and for other Western skills. A small group of educated
Africans was to be found at many points along the Coast. There were
a few schools, such as one in Bonny conducted by English-educated
schoolmasters, but most well-to-do Africans who wanted an education for their children had to send them to Europe. At least one of
these, Philip Quaque of Cape Coast, had completed a formal education in Britain and returned to the Coast in 1765 as an ordained
minister and chaplain at Cape Coast Castle. Most had the more modest aim of learning to read and write and do a little commercial arith-
metic. They were usually sent in the charge of English traders who
assured them of some care and supervision. In the later 1780's, about
fifty of these trainees were to be found in and around Liverpool.

In addition to those who travelled in line of business, a new kind
of reporter appeared in West Africa during the latter part of the
eighteenth century. Some Europeans began to travel for the sake
of gathering information. People had, of course, travelled out of
curiosity before this time, but now they were after specific bodies of
knowledge—something to fill in a corner of an intellectual puzzle,
part of which was already known. It was not yet "scientific" investigation but it was heavily influenced by the rationalism of the Enlightenment. At the very least it was scholarly field work, and the
scholarship was up to the best intellectual standards of the time.

Two general ways existed for organizing the flow of data from
overseas for scholarly ends. One method, in occasional use for cen-

turies, was to send a questionnaire to people who were already there. The Spanish Council of the Indies had done this as early as 1517, hoping to base their "native policy" in Hispaniola on systematic ethnographic knowledge. An eighteenth-century variant on a more ambitious scale was organized by Professor Johan Michaelis of Göttingen, a Biblical scholar and linguist. He proposed an expedition of five scholars to the Red Sea to act as emissaries from the "Republic of Letters" in Europe. Through correspondence, Michaelis prepared a questionnaire based on the desiderata of scholars in many fields and from many countries. Fauna, flora, ethnography, medicine, linguistics, economic and commercial matters were all included. The questionnaire itself was published as a book of nearly five hundred pages, and the project received the patronage of the Danish court. There were obvious flaws in this kind of project as a technique of scholarship, but it marked a transitional stage between dependence solely on whatever travellers might choose to report, and scholarly investigation on the spot.[14]

The second alternative was to send junior researchers with specific objects in mind. The naturalists were the first to experiment on a considerable scale with this technique. Karl Linnaeus began sending botanical expeditions from Upsala in the 1740's. His emissaries went first to the coast of China, later to America, Java, and Egypt. In 1771, Andreas Berlin was sent to West Africa to make a botanical collection, though he died of disease shortly after his arrival.[15] Meanwhile, Sir Joseph Banks followed the same method from his base at Kew Gardens. He had worked overseas himself on Captain Cook's voyage round the world in 1768–71, and later in North America and Iceland. To fill in the botanical picture of Africa, he sent Francis Masson to the Cape of Good Hope and Henry Smeathman to West Africa.

Whether on specific missions from Linnaeus and Banks, or as independent travellers, the naturalists were also the first of the enlightened travellers to visit West Africa, and they came with a curiosity that extended broadly beyond their immediate botanical or zoological objectives. Michel Adanson, who spent the years 1749 to

14. J. D. Michaelis, *Receuil de questions proposées à une Société des savans* . . . (Frankfurt-a.-M., 1763); *Colleción de documentos inéditos relativos al descubrimiento, conquista y organización de las antiguas possessiones españolas,* 42 vols. (Madrid, 1864–1889), XXXIV, 201–29.

15. A. A. Boahen, "British Penetration of North-West Africa and the Western Sudan, 1788–1861," (Unpublished Ph.D. thesis, London, 1959), p. 17.

1757, in Senegal, was mainly a naturalist, but he also made the first consciously "scientific" effort to carry out ethnographic field work in West Africa. He stayed within the region already known through the slave trade, but he learned Wolof and he made a systematic study of the manners and customs of the people.[16] His successors were mainly Scandinavians, who drew on the combination of Linnaean interest and Danish commercial establishments on the Gold Coast. Ludevig Ferdinand Römer published in 1760 a highly ethnographic account of the region around the Danish forts.[17] Between 1783 and 1787, Paul Erdman Isert, another Danish naturalist, tried consciously to broaden his subject to include the "natural history of man," being especially anxious to record the "manners and customs of savage peoples" before they should be lost or submerged in the advance of civilization.[18]

Still other expeditions bridged the gaps between natural history, ethnography, and a more active interest in African affairs. Banks' emissary, Henry Smeathman, went to the Banana Islands off Sierra Leone in 1771. He settled down for several years and made the first substantial collection of West African plants and insects. In addition to his work for Kew Gardens, Smeathman conducted his own research on termites and followed an interest in ethnography, though he never published in that field. Instead, his experience in Africa led him ultimately to become the first promoter of the English settlement at Sierra Leone.[19]

A Swedish expedition of Arrhenius, Sparrman, and Wadström set out in 1787 with mixed objectives. Sparrman and Arrhenius were naturalists, and Sparrman was a veteran enlightened traveller with ex-

16. M. Adanson, *Histoire naturelle du Sénégal* (Paris, 1757); English translation, *Voyage to Sénégal* (London, 1759). See also A. Chevalier, *Michel Adanson, naturaliste et philosophe* (Paris, 1934). Although Adanson was long an obscure figure in the history of biology, his botanical work in Senegal has recently been recognized as having a place of the first importance in the history of that science. For this rehabilitation, see Bentley Glass, "Heredity and Variation in the Eighteenth Century Concept of the Species," in B. Glass and others, *Forerunners of Darwin, 1745–1859* (Baltimore, 1959), pp. 151–57.

17. L. F. Römer, *Nachrichten von der Kuste Guinea* (Copenhagen and Leipzig, 1769). First published in Danish, Copenhagen, 1760.

18. P. E. Isert, *Reise nach Guinea und den Caräibischen Inseln* (Copenhagen, 1788). See also C. D. Adams, "Activities of Danish Botanists in Guinea, 1783–1850," *Transactions of the Historical Society of Ghana*, III, 30–46 (1957).

19. Henry Smeathman to J. C. Lettsom, 19 October 1782, in J. Fothergill, *The Works of John Fothergill, M.D.* . . . , 3rd ed. (London, 1784), pp. 575–82.

perience in Cook's second voyage and in South Africa. Karl Bernhard Wadström, the third member, was a Swedenborgian, an enthusiast for colonization, and something of a *philosophe* with an interest in "contemplating human nature in simpler states." All three hoped to penetrate into the Western Sudan by way of the Senegal, but they were held up at Gorée by warfare on the mainland and returned to Europe the next year. Arrhenius died, Sparrman went off alone on a new expedition to South Africa, and Wadström followed Smeathman into a quixotic career as a colonial projector in both England and France.[20]

Sir Joseph Banks was meanwhile working toward an even more systematic organization of enlightened travel in Africa. In 1788 he founded the Association for Promoting the Discovery of the Interior Parts of Africa, and he dominated its operations until 1805 from the post of Treasurer. The organization was commonly called simply the African Association, causing a certain amount of confusion both then and later. There was already an African Committee, which administered the Gold Coast forts, and an African Institution was founded in 1807 to promote humanitarian policies. These three bodies were respectively scientific, mercantile, and Evangelical-humanitarian. Each worked within its own circle of interest, though individuals could and did belong to two or more of them. They continued into the 1820's as important but distinct pressure groups acting in Africa, as well as influencing British policy.

The object of the African Association was exactly what its full name suggests, to send enlightened travellers into the interior of Africa to report on geography, ethnography, and natural history. Three explorers, Ledyard, Lucas, and Houghton, were sent to try an entry of the Western Sudan from three different directions. Ledyard went to Cairo to attempt a westward crossing from the upper Nile. He died there in 1788 before he had moved inland. Lucas went to Tripoli, hoping to move south into Fezzan, then across the desert and west to the Gambia. He reached Murzuk in Fezzan, but then he re-

---

20. C. B. Wadström, *Observations on the Slave Trade* . . . (London, 1789); *An Essay on Colonization* . . . 2 vols. (London, 1794–1795), I, i; [J. Leyden], *A Historical and Philosophical Sketch of the Discoveries and Settlements of Europeans in Northern and Western Africa at the close of the Eighteenth Century* (Edinburgh, 1799), pp. 107–11.

treated to the coast. Houghton was to move east from the Gambia, but he died somewhere beyond Bambuk in 1791.[21] Thus the triple effort of the first years became a triple failure, though Houghton and Lucas produced some new evidence; but the general effort was only delayed, not abandoned.

In all, British scholars of the later eighteenth century were reasonably well supplied with data, even though the data varied greatly in relative reliability. Geographers found themselves dealing with three different zones of evidence. The first was the coastal zone of constant contact, plus the navigable Senegal and Gambia Rivers. European ships could go as far as the falls of Baracunda on the Gambia, about 200 air miles toward the heart of the Western Sudan. The Senegal was more difficult for ocean shipping, but here the head of navigation was nearly 350 miles inland. The coastal waters had been described since 1701 by the appropriate volume of the *English Pilot*, predecessor of successive pilot guides published by the Hydrographic Office. Its sectional charts showed each stretch of the coast, with soundings, advice on trade and navigation, and sketches of the seaward appearance of prominent headlands.[22] This zone of coastal knowledge, however, was extremely narrow. Detailed data rarely existed for regions more than twenty miles or so inland.

Beyond, there was a second zone of occasional and unsystematic hearsay evidence. African merchants went inland for slaves. Arab travellers from the Maghrib occasionally came south across West Africa to the Guinea coast. Muslim Africans from as far west as the Gambia travelled eastward to Mecca. Any of these African travellers could have filled in pieces of information, and these pieces could have been fitted into a whole—but the Africans were often unwilling to tell what they knew, and the coastal Europeans were unwilling to spend time collecting and collating such evidence. Commercial routes into the interior were a form of trade secret. Most Europeans on the coast were not sufficiently interested in knowledge for its own sake to report all they picked up by hearsay. Even those European travel-

21. Boahen, "British Penetration of North-West Africa," pp. 3–14, 32, 41–43; A. A. Boahen, "The African Association, 1788–1805," *Transactions of the Historical Society of Ghana*, V, 43–64 (1961); Association for Promoting the Discovery of the Interior Parts of Africa, *Proceedings* (London, 1792).

22. J. Seller and C. Price, *The Fifth Part of the General English Pilot . . . Describing the West-Coast of Africa: From the Straits of Gibraltar to the Cape of Good Hope* (London, 1701).

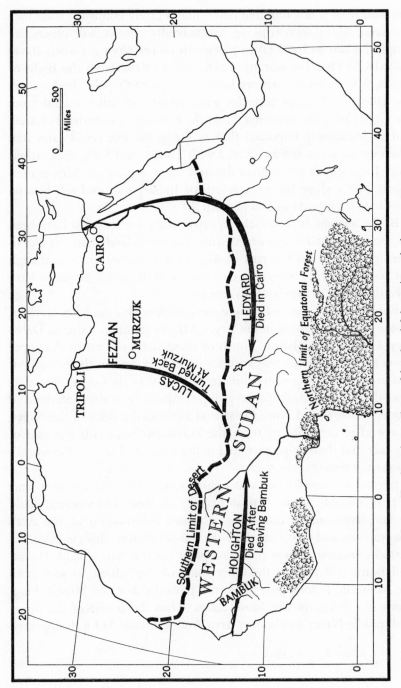

Map 2. Explorations planned by the African Association, 1788–1791

lers who went a few hundred miles inland rarely published what they had seen. Many such trips are undoubtedly unrecorded; others are simply known to have taken place. An officer from a French slaver visited Old Oyo (or Katunga), 180 miles inland from the Bight of Benin, a full quarter century before Clapperton's publicized visit in the 1820's.[23] Another traveller went about 120 miles inland from the Gold Coast and reported, "that the Country, was entirely cleared, and so immensely Populous that as far as the Eye could carry him wherever he went, it was covered with Towns, and Villages. Furthermore India goods are in great demand there, so that the African merchants buy a slave for 22 s. worth of India goods and sell him on the Coast for a profit of 400 per cent."[24]

If the account is accurately reported, the traveller must have been on the northern fringes of Ashanti, further inland than any publicized penetration of this part of Africa for a century to come, though not so far as the Portuguese embassy to Mali, which seems to have used this route in the sixteenth century.

Europeans on the coast were nevertheless able to keep track of major political changes in the larger African states—in Ashanti, Dahomey, Oyo, or Futa Jallon. North of these states or east of the upper Senegal, the evidence was very scanty indeed, and in the latitude of the present-day Nigerian "middle belt" it was almost nil. But even near the coasts it could be very slight, especially in the hinterland of modern Liberia and Ivory Coast, and again in the delta of the Niger, where after centuries of trade the Europeans were still ignorant of the fact that their ships anchored in the mouths of one of the world's great river systems.

Beyond the middle belt was a third zone, where information came in part through North African hearsay evidence, but where it could be supplemented by the older published information of the Arab geographers and travellers. Like the coastal sources, this evidence was spatially limited. It was most complete for the Niger bend, Hausa, and Bornu—in a sense the other shore of the Sahara, as seen from the Maghrib. It told little about the powerful but non-Muslim kingdoms like Jukun or the Mossi states. Thus the course of the upper and middle Niger was known from Arab evidence, but it disappeared

23. J. Adams, Remarks, pp. 93–94.
24. Lt. Clarke to William Pitt, 17 March 1785, PRO 30/8/363.

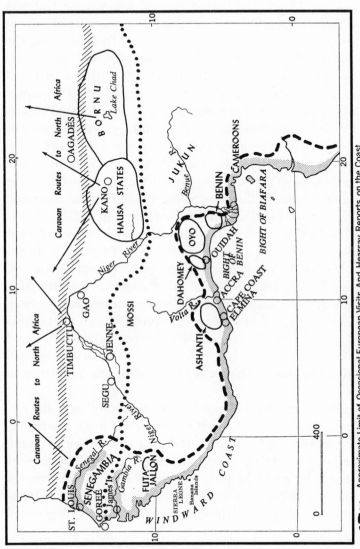

Caravan Routes to North Africa

ST. LOUIS
SENEGAMBIA
Senegal R.
GOREE
James I.
Gambia R.
FUTA JALLON
SIERRA LEONE
Banana Islands
WINDWARD COAST

TIMBUCTU
GAO
JENNE
SEGU
MOSSI
Niger River

Niger River

ASHANTI
Volta R.
ACCRA
CAPE COAST
ELMINA
DAHOMEY
OYO
OUIDAH
BIGHT OF BENIN

BENIN
JUKUN
Benue R.
CAMEROONS
BIGHT OF BIAFARA

KANO
HAUSA STATES
OAGADES
Caravan Routes to North Africa

B O R N U
Lake Chad

Caravan Routes to North Africa

Approximate Limit of Occasional European Visits And Hearsay Reports on the Coast
Approximate Southern Limit of the Sahara Desert
Area of Detailed Knowledge
Approximate Southern Limit of Detailed Reports From the Maghrib

0   400

Map 3: European Knowledge of *Africa, c.* 1780

21

over the horizon of systematic Maghribi knowledge when it flowed south into the "middle belt" beyond Nupe.

In spite of the fact that neither the Europeans on the Guinea coast, nor those in the Maghrib, collected the full information that was surely available to them, the geographers in Europe were already at work collating whatever reports they could gather from overseas. The rational and critical spirit of the Enlightenment appeared successively in the geographical work of Guillaume Delisle (1675–1726) and J. B. Bourguignon d'Anville (1697–1782) in France. Both attempted a scholarly reconstruction of the map of Africa, and the final version by d'Anville became the basis on which English geographers were to work. It was remarkably accurate, given his sources. Desert cities such as Agadès were located. The Niger was shown flowing from west to east (correctly enough), but flowing into Lake Chad instead of the Gulf of Guinea. Some of the cities of the Western Sudan appeared, though Kano was confused with the ancient kingdom of Ghana.[25]

D'Anville's British successor was James Rennell, who had been Surveyor-General of Bengal. After his return to England, he began work on a historical reconstruction of the geography of Herodotus, which carried his interest into Africa. In collaboration with the African Association, he became the principal analyst of new reports from Africa, taking account of Houghton's information from the Gambia and Lucas' reports from Fezzan. Rennell incorporated these data and other new information from North Africa into a series of maps and commentaries, the first of which was published by the Association in 1790.[26]

Ethnographic reporting and synthesis necessarily followed the pattern of geographical evidence, but the contrast was much sharper between the relatively well-known coastal area and the virtually unknown interior. Mountains, rivers, and even the vague outlines of political geography could be picked up by hearsay. More complex information about culture was harder to come by, and harder to transmit without the written word. The quality of cultural reporting varied

25. J. B. Bourguignon d'Anville, "Mémoire concernant les Rivières de l'interieur de l'Afrique," *Recueil des Mémoires de l'Académie des Inscriptions et Belles-Lettres,* XXVI, 64–81 (1759). See also J. D. Barbie de Bocage, *Notice sur les ouvrages de M. d'Anville* (Paris, 1802).

26. African Association, *Proceedings* (1792); James Rennell, *Elucidations of the African Geography* (London, 1793); C. R. Markham, *Major James Rennell and the Rise of Modern English Geography* (London, 1895), pp. 122–45.

enormously, even in the coastal regions. Adanson, Römer, and Isert made an effort to understand Akan, Ga, and Wolof culture and to see African society as a functioning whole, but of these authors only Adanson was translated into English. Even the more serious enlightened travellers tended to see Africa through a cultural filter, and the filtering process was even more selective with the non-scholarly travellers whose works made up the bulk of the canon.

Since Europeans mainly came to the Coast for trade, they reported with an eye to matters of commercial importance. An elementary knowledge of political structure was essential for traders, who had to deal with the African authorities. Certain aspects of material culture and the African economic systems were equally crucial, especially when they concerned the slave trade into the interior or the market demand for European goods. With the growth of the anti-slavery movement in Britain, more attention was paid to the place of slaves in African society, and especially to the question of how an individual might be made a slave in the first instance. Social structure as a whole, however, was ignored, and there was little notice that the institution of slavery was part of a wider net of family and group relations. The European concept of slavery, derived ultimately from Roman law, stood in the way of understanding what slavery meant in Africa. Most of the more subtle differences between distinct African cultures were also lost. The fact that all were strikingly different from that of Europe made them seem much the same. But some "tribal" distinctions had to be recognized as a matter of practical necessity—not only on the Coast but in the West Indies, where the planters believed that the African-born slaves had various "national characteristics," and that their market value varied accordingly.[27]

The European travellers wrote to please their audience as well as to inform. Religious beliefs were of no interest: they were mere "pagan error." But spectacular festivals, human sacrifice, judicial ordeals, and polygyny were "curiosities," and were therefore recounted at length. Thus the reporting often stressed precisely those aspects of African life that were most repellent to the West and tended to submerge the indications of a common humanity. This love of the extraordinary was partly the reflection of a much older European interest

27. Bryan Edwards, *The History, Civil and Commercial, of the British Colonies in the West Indies,* 2nd ed., 2 vols. (London, 1794), II, 60–79.

in the exotic—an interest blending genuine intellectual curiosity with
a libidinous fascination for descriptions of other people who break
with impunity the taboos of one's own society. Part of this interest
came with the romantic movement. In the later eighteenth century,
there was an increasing tendency to look whenever possible for diversity in experience as in literary expression. Lovejoy has called this
tendency "diversificationism," replacing the "uniformism" which
dominated the earlier, or Newtonian, phase of the Enlightenment.[28]

This tendency influenced both the first-hand reports and the work
that might be called ethnographic scholarship. Astley's *Voyages* and
the *Universal History* both abstracted or condensed descriptive passages with an eye to the exotic. Other choice bits were gathered together in popular manuals, like the Reverend John Adams' *Curious
Thoughts on the History of Man*.[29] Historical works showed a similar
emphasis. Robert Norris' *Memoirs of the Reign of Bossa Ahadee* was
a vitriolically anti-African history of Dahomey during the middle
decades of the eighteenth century, and it was largely incorporated in
the more inclusive *History of Dahomey* compiled by Archibald Dalzel, the Governor of Cape Coast Castle, to show the savagery of the
Dahomeans as a justification of the slave trade.[30] In spite of their bias,
these two works were the first English attempt to write the history
of any African state south of the forest. At the very least, they represented an admission that African states had a history, a generous attitude compared with the prevailing view a century later.

The scholarly study of West African languages was also in its
infancy in the later eighteenth century. (Perhaps because the *linguae
francae* on the Coast were English and Portuguese, African languages
were not essential as a tool of the trade.) Travellers occasionally
gave a word list in some language they encountered. A vocabulary of
Fetu, one of the Akan languages of the Gold Coast, had been published in Nuremberg as early as 1675, but the only recent result of
linguistic research was a brief study of Fante and Ga grammar by
Christian Protten, a Danish visitor to the Gold Coast.[31] The most ex-

28. A. O. Lovejoy, *The Great Chain of Being: A Study of the History of an Idea*
(Cambridge, Mass., 1936). See pp. 233–311 for a detailed discussion of this tendency.
29. J. Adams, *Curious Thoughts on the History of Man* . . . (London, 1789).
30. R. Norris, *Memoirs of the Reign of Bossa Ahadee, King of Dahomey* (London,
1789); A. Dalzel, *The History of Dahomey* (London, 1793).
31. C. Protten, *En nyttig grammaticalsk indledese til tvende hindindtil gadanske
ubekiendte sprog, Fantiesk og Acraisk* (København, 1764). For a brief history of
African linguistic studies, see: R. N. Cust, *A Sketch of the Modern Languages of Africa,*
2 vols. (London, 1883), pp. 24–38.

tensive collection of comparative African vocabularies was also the work of a Dane, Christian Oldendorp, a missionary in the Danish West Indies who compiled a list of numbers from one to ten, plus thirteen common words, in twenty-six different African languages. This work was carried out in the spirit of enlightened travel, and Oldendorp went further still and pieced together a picture of African religion and customs from his slave informants.[32] Even though Oldendorp's investigation was conducted in the New World rather than the Old, it was the only recent source of published information about the peoples of the interior.

Otherwise, information about the Western Sudan was so vague, ancient, or unsupported that it was possible to believe almost anything. Fact–even the often-erroneous "facts" reported about the coast–gave way to myth and legend. Some supporters of the slave trade claimed the people of the interior were even more "degraded" than those of the coast.[33] (Since slaves for export were largely from the interior, the more "barbarous" they were, the more they would gain by transportation to the West Indies.) But this view of a savage interior was relatively rare.

The main line of speculation dwelt on the great unknown cities and civilizations, the known fact that gold flowed across the Sahara to North Africa in the caravan trade, and the reports of the Arab travellers, in particular Leo Africanus. Even further back in the European past there had been the shadowy figure of Prester John, the supposedly powerful Christian Prince in the heart of Africa. By the eighteenth century, Prester John was identified with Christian Ethiopia, but James Bruce's account published in 1790 was the first really detailed report from that part of the world since the early seventeenth century. Even before its actual publication, knowledge of his travels and discoveries lent color to the possibility of an equivalent civilization further west.[34]

The possibility was further supported by a variety of reports from the fringes of European activity in West Africa. La Brue wrote a glowing description of the country beyond the upper Senegal, which

---

32. C. Oldendorp, *Geschichte der Mission der Evangelischen Brüder auf den Caraibischen Inseln S. Thomas, S. Croix, und S. Jan* (Barby, 1777), pp. 270–347.

33. John Matthews, *A Voyage to the River Sierra-Leone* . . . (London, 1788), pp. 93–94.

34. Bruce returned to Europe in 1773, and the general findings of his journey were immediately publicized. The full account first appeared as *Travels to Discover the Source of the Nile,* 5 vols. (Edinburgh, 1790).

was printed by Labat in 1728 and reprinted by Astley. The promise of the interior could be taken upon several sides—by merchants who had come to suspect the rate of profit made by African middle-men in the slave trade, or by humanitarians who wished, at least in some moods, to show that Africa was capable of civilization. Among these, John Wesley himself painted a very favorable picture of the West African interior, and Wesley was widely read by the faithful.[35]

The strongest religious interest in the Western Sudan, however, was shown by Emanuel Swedenborg. His information ostensibly came by direct divine revelation, rather than human agency, but it was important in directing European efforts to West Africa in the 1780's and 1790's. According to Swedenborgian doctrine, God had created not one church but a series of "true churches," each of them founded in whatever part of the world men have the most perfect knowledge of God. Each church in turn declined from its original purity. As this happened, each in turn was "consummated" and underwent its "last judgement." A new "true church" was then founded among another, previously heathen, nation. Swedenborg held that, up to the eighteenth century, there had been four churches, the "Adamical Church," the "Noahtical Church," the "Israelite Church," and the Christian Church as it was known in Europe. Having fallen into decay, the European Christian Church had undergone its "last judgement" in 1757, and God was even then in the process of founding a new church.[36]

There was a strong presumption in Swedenborg's writings that this church would be in Africa. He praised the Africans of the interior regions for thinking "more internally" than other people and living a more spiritual life. He even reproduced a map of Africa showing the "celestial" region at the center and the corrupted nations surrounding it. The worst of these corrupt people were shown in Egypt, those at the Cape were a little less corrupt, and those who lived in the east toward Asia still less so. There was no specific mention of the West coast, but it was a possible inference from corruption elsewhere that the best approach to the interior would be from that side.[37] Many

35. John Wesley, "Thoughts upon Slavery," in *Works* (London, 1872), XI, 59–79. First published 1774.

36. "That the Lord now establishes a Church in Africa," *The New Jerusalem Magazine* (London, 1890), pp. 181–82. For a guide to Swedenborg's references to Africa see J. F. Potts, *The Swedenborg Concordance*, 4 vols. (London, 1888), I, 99–100.

37. E. Swedenborg, "Continuation of the Last Judgement," in *The Last Judgement* (London, 1951), pp. 103–5. First published 1763.

Swedenborgians both then and now reject the view that the new church was being raised in Africa and only in Africa, but some did not. Spelled out, their view came to this:

According to Swedenborg, all the nations who live in the earth may be reduced to two general species, the white and the black, the habitation of the former is chiefly in Europe and corresponds with the spiritual kingdom of the Lord. The latter dwell in Africa and correspond to the celestial kingdom of the Lord. The whites have cultivated only their understanding, but the blacks have cultivated their will and affections; the ancient Christian Church being a spiritual church, was instituted among the European nations; but this New Church being celestial cannot easily be established in Europe, by reason that the nations of which Christendom is now composed, are in a very great degree worse than the nations which do not belong to the Christian world, and whom we call Heathens; of which the Africans are the best of all; therefore the Church of the New Jerusalem becomes established among those who are situated in the interior parts of Africa.[38]

This view went beyond the present condition and possibilities of Africa. By introducing the concept of two separate species of man it went beyond the conclusions possible from current observation, and on to those that might be derived from a consideration of assumed and innate racial qualities. The Swedenborgian speculations about the interior of Africa thus merged with another and intricate body of European thought about the Africans' place in nature.

38. *New Jerusalem Magazine*, p. 183. See also Henry Serventé to James Glen, 12 August 1805, printed in *Monthly Observer, and New Church Record*, I, 313 (London, 1857); Sten Lindroth, "Adam Afzelius: A Swedish Botanist in Sierra Leone, 1792–1796," *Sierra Leone Studies*, I (n.s.), 196 (June 1955).

2

THE AFRICANS'
"PLACE IN NATURE"

The terms "racism" and "racist" have become highly emotive since the 1930's, when a special variety of racism was taken up and carried to power in Germany by the National Socialist Party. The atrocities committed during the 1940's in the name of pseudo-scientific racism give special overtones to any discussion of the history of Western thought about race differences. Race prejudice, racial consciousness, and racism can mean many things. At one level, there is the simple and unavoidable fact that major racial differences are recognizable. In every racially mixed society, in every contact between people who differ in physical appearance, there has always been instant recognition of race: it was the first determinant of inter-group social relations.

Beyond this point of recognition, the further interpretations have varied enormously. These variants have all felt the weight of a second factor—that of plain xenophobia. People tend to fear and dislike the strange and the unknown, and racial difference immediately brands the individual of another race as a stranger, and as a member of an alien group. When this happens, racial recognition may lead naturally to the assumption that such a person will have all the characteristics imputed to his group. To this extent, race difference has always played a role in history and surely will continue to play a role.

But beyond these underlying constants of race relations, more elaborate sets of ideas about race have also played an important part in history. Some people, perhaps most people, have been conscious of their own racial type. Some have assummed that they were a "chosen people," especially favored by God. Some have assumed that they, and they alone, were human. Most have preferred their own type as the esthetic standard of human beauty. Most have assumed that people of their own type were physically or mentally or culturally superior to other races.

Any of these views may be labelled "racism" of some variety, but they need to be kept separate from the full-blown pseudo-scientific racism which dominated so much of European thought between the 1840's and the 1940's. The difference lay in the fact that "science," the body of knowledge rationally derived from empirical observation, then supported the proposition that race was one of the principal determinants of attitudes, endowments, capabilities, and inherent tendencies among human beings. Race thus seemed to determine the course of human history.

These rationalized and elaborate theories about race difference were not "pseudo" in their beginnings. They were the teachings of science at its best for its own time. In the twentieth century, when earlier science is recognized to have been mistaken, they have continued as truly pseudo-scientific. That is, they claim the backing of science for propositions which the consensus of authoritative science denies, and in the face of overwhelming evidence to the contrary. It is more difficult to assess the degree of pseudo-science in the racial doctrines of the eighteenth and nineteenth centuries. Many were stated by men who pursued truth for its own sake. Others were stated by men who pursued political ends, wished to find support for their prejudice, or were merely misled by a little learning into wild speculations which the best science, even of their time, would not sustain on the basis of reason and evidence. For us, it makes little difference whether error followed the pursuit of truth or the pursuit of other ends. It received, in time, the backing of Western science, and it was, perhaps, the most disastrous error scientists have ever made.

Even today, when rationalized, "scientific" racism is no longer tenable, many people of middle age half remember the teachings of their early training and half believe, if only at an emotional level, that physical race is an outward sign of other inborn characteristics. In addition, today as in the eighteenth century, many people are subject to a variety of xenophobic feelings about people who are racially different from themselves. In this same emotional sense, the recognition of racial difference dominated European thought about Africans even before the rise of scientific and pseudo-scientific racism. If "racism" can be defined as any of the various doctrines holding that human culture and behavior are strongly influenced by physical race, then even this vague xenophobic sentiment is a form of racism. It should, however, be distinguished from the rationalized racial theories attempting to explain the nature of society in racial terms, and even more sharply distinguished from the extreme political creeds which hold that "racial inferiority" justifies inequality of treatment, enslavement, or genocide for the "inferior races." These things may follow from racism, but they are not a necessary part of racist beliefs as such.

Europeans in the later eighteenth century had already had several centuries of contact with Africans, both with the sellers of slaves on the African coasts and with the slaves in the New World. Whatever their views in detail, one assumption was almost universal. They believed that African skin color, hair texture, and facial features were associated in some way with the African way of life (in Africa) and the status of slavery (in the Americas). Once this association was made, racial views became unconsciously linked with social views, and with the common assessment of African culture. Culture prejudice thus slid off easily toward color prejudice, and the two were frequently blended in ways that were imprecise at the time—and even harder to separate after the passage of almost two centuries.

There is a further problem here. Even today, when pride of race has weakened in the West, pride of culture has continued. Many otherwise well informed people continue to think of pre-colonial Africa as a series of "primitive" societies, still in the stone age or only just emerging from it under the impact of Europe. They tend to accept an older historical tradition, which held that Africa was static, while Europe and, to a lesser extent, Asian and American civilizations advanced during the past few millennia. This view derives some of its continuing force from the general Western ignorance of the African past. It draws as well from our tendency to emphasize technology as the principal measure for the "advancement" of any society. Technology is, indeed, the one field of human culture where it is legitimate to make value judgments of general validity. (A repeating rifle is clearly superior to a bow and arrow for its purpose in hunting and warfare, but no such certainty is possible in comparing artistic culture—the bronze heads of Ife with Greek sculpture, for example.)

In technology, then, it was obvious that nineteenth-century Europe was far ahead of nineteenth-century Africa, but to see this fact alone gives too much emphasis to the short run of history. Pre-colonial Africa had long been within the iron age. Perhaps as many as a third of the people south of the Sahara lived in societies that were literate in the sense that Europe was literate during the middle ages—that is, at least a class of scribes could read and write. While there was certainly a technological lag between Africa and the West, it has to be seen against the perspective of human history. If Africa was behind, it was hardly more than a thousand years behind. The technology of most African societies of about 1750 A.D. had reached and in some respects passed the level of technology prevalent in northwest Europe in 750 A.D. If the line of comparison is pushed back further still, and centered specifically on Britain and the Western Sudan in 750 B.C., the two societies were very much on a par.

A similar comparison can be set in broader, and somewhat different, terms. Robert Redfield has made a distinction between the "little community" and the larger society of which it may form a part. This distinction can be made in Africa, separating the peasant village of the forest or savanna from the centers of learning and commerce in the towns or the courts of rulers in Abomey, Jenne, Kumasi, or Kuka. It can also be made in Europe, where peasant culture, peasant values, and quality of peasant life were historically sharply different from those of the upper classes. Taking one European century with another, from the middle ages through the seventeenth century, European peasant life did not change very radically. Neither did African peasant life change very radically from the middle ages to the end of the nineteenth century. Nor were the conditions of peasant life in Africa very markedly different from the conditions of peasant life in Europe. Both were subordinate communities, suffering from peace and war, famine and plague, and other external factors that were the normal lot of mankind. There were, of course, differences within

Africa and differences between Africa and Europe; but both shared, at the level of the "little community," the conditions common to all little communities between the invention of settled agriculture and the coming of the industrial revolution.[1]

The cultural difference between the great communities is another matter. For Europe, much is known about the life of the great communities at many periods in the past: they have too often been the sole object of historical investigation. For Africa, almost nothing is known about the distant past—about the life and thought of Ife, for example, at the period when the bronzes were cast. Comparisons are therefore difficult, but it is clear that the European great community entered a period of unusual creativity about one millennium ago. This in turn was based on a period of similar creativity in the Mediterranean basin stretching back about two millennia further. Even if we assume no such creativity in African great communities during these three millennia, three millennia are a relatively short period in the whole of man's history, and African society was far from static.

Eighteenth-century Europeans, however, were not able to look at the world with this perspective. Their ignorance of Africa was enormous, and they were only beginning the serious study of early human history. Most of their thought on the matter was still set in a Biblical frame of reference, carrying back about six thousand years. European contacts with non-Western societies outside of the Mediterranean basin were not yet really extensive. They had been increasing for the past three hundred years, but they were still contacts on the periphery. The only Europeans who had yet tried the experiment of ruling over a non-Western society were the two Hispanic powers.

The Spanish theorists and administrators had faced in the sixteenth century a whole series of questions about their proper relations with the Middle American and Andean Indians. Among these were problems of the right of Christian conquest, the nature of the Indians in law and religion, and the practical means Christians should use in dealing with them. During that century the Spanish had gathered information, quarrelled over its meaning, and beat out a "native policy" in both theory and practice. Their conclusions were further supported by the authority of the papacy. Paul III in the bull *Sublimis Deus* of

1. R. Redfield, *The Little Community and Peasant Society and Culture* (Chicago, 1960).

1537 condemned as heretical the opinion that American Indians were not rational or were incapable of receiving the True Faith, and this position was confirmed and repeated in various forms in later centuries. By extension, whatever else might be said of non-Westerners, they were officially human beings and potentially Christians with full spiritual equality.[2]

Because of the religious difference, this position did not necessarily extend to Protestant Europe. Nor did English overseas activity from the sixteenth century to the mid-eighteenth involve them in practical situations where these questions had to be met as they were by sixteenth-century Spain. The English trading posts in the East had an indigenous population, but the principal purpose was commercial, and there was no serious concern with the way men of a different culture should be ruled. In the West Indies the dominant social form by the middle of the seventeenth century was the slave plantation. Uprooted individuals from Africa were forced into a social mold that was not distinctly English—and certainly not African. In this case, the English simply took over the social forms created in the Mediterranean, and developed further in Brazil and the Hispanic West Indies. There was no need to innovate, and hence no need to consider seriously what policy to follow. Even in North America, the confrontation of the English and the Indians was not so much a "native problem" as a "frontier problem." The relatively sparse Indian population was pushed westward, rather than being absorbed into the settlers' society. Before the 1780's, it was only in Ireland that a persistent and troublesome "native problem" had developed, and here the racial and cultural difference between the metropolis and the empire was much less than that between the overseas world and the West.

In any case, the British Empire before 1783 was loosely organized. The North American settlers on one hand and the West Indian planters on the other were allowed to make their own internal policy without metropolitan interference. It was only when imperial control began to tighten in the reign of George III that British imperial theory had to take account of the questions discussed in Spain some two cen-

2. See J. H. Parry, *The Spanish Theory of Empire in the Sixteenth Century* (Cambridge, 1940); S. A. Zavala, *New Viewpoints on the Spanish Colonization of America* (Philadelphia, 1943); L. U. Hanke, *The Spanish Struggle for Justice in the Conquest of America* (Washington, 1949).

turies earlier. Especially after 1783, in the shadow of the lost war and in a spirit of general reform, British publicists began to consider the Africans' "place in nature" and its bearing on imperial policy.

In its early stages, with little background in conscious or rationalized theory, British consideration of African race and African culture was highly dispersed. It was not a central problem discussed as such, but a peripheral question that had to be taken into account by several groups of writers. "The Negro's place in nature" naturally had a role in whatever reporting came from Africa or the West Indies. It was discussed from another point of view by biologists, who were just then concerned with the problem of explaining human varieties. In quite another context, men of letters used the convention of the "noble savage" for their own purposes. Finally, the anti-slavery writers of a dominantly Christian and humanitarian turn of mind were forced into a discussion of race by their efforts to reform imperial policy.

Of these four groups, only the travel writers had adequate access to empirical data. Their information, therefore, had to serve the others as a store from which they could draw as it suited their needs and interests. Travel reports contained something for everyone, with accounts varying from the most bitter condemnation of Africans and their way of life to an equally broad-minded tolerance. If there was a principal thread running through the whole body of information, it was one of moderate xenophobia. Slave traders, officials, and planters were all men sent out to live in dangerous tropical conditions. They were there to do a job, and one that necessarily brought them into contact with alien peoples whose culture they did not understand. Their resentments were those of foreign visitors in any country. In Africa they often thought they were cheated, and they disliked the strangeness of African customs. In America they took the slaves to be obstinate, rebellious, thievish, and lazy—which they probably were: these are the expected attributes of slaves in any society.

But for all their xenophobia, the travellers were unusually free of racial antagonism. Most men connected with the slave trade, and even the West Indian planters (to say nothing of the enlightened travellers with their ethnographic and humane interests), were less inclined to emphasize racial factors than those who stayed in England. This was especially true of their accounts of day-to-day dealings with the Africans. In 1789, for example, sixteen recent visitors to

West Africa reported to a Privy Council Committee on the African trade. While most of them had been concerned in one way or another with the slave trade, none mentioned an assumed African racial inferiority as a bar to future development.[3] They had little respect for the African way of life, but those who belonged to the Company of Merchants Trading to Africa had in Philip Quaque, their official Chaplain at Cape Coast, an African who was later the most highly paid man on their staff, except the Governor himself.

The travellers often condemned individual Africans as bad men— or all Africans as savage men—but they left the clear impression that Africans *were* men. The African way of doing things might be curious or unpleasant, but individual Africans were shown with abilities, faults, and virtues in much the same proportion as Europeans. Merchants on the African coast (in contrast to planters in the West Indies) dealt with Africans as partners in trade—not, perhaps, equal partners, or the partners an Englishman might choose, but nevertheless men of substance whose views could not safely be ignored.[4] Thus the image of Africans in America was radically different from the stereotype of the servile Africans of the Americas.

Moderate xenophobia, with emphasis on the fact of moderation, was reproduced in the popular attitude toward Africans in England, especially among those in day-to-day contact. Negro servants who came to England from the colonies were popular with their masters and were often valued by the aristocracy in preference to white servants. They were also popular with their European fellow-servants, and with members of the English working class who came to know them. Some racial tension was present, but it came from the normal distrust of strangers, from sexual competition or the belief that Negroes took away employment from Englishmen.[5] However wrongheaded these attitudes might be, either on the Coast or in England,

3. Great Britain. Privy Council. *Report of the Lords of the Committee of Council for . . . Trade and Foreign Plantations . . . Concerning the Present State of Trade to Africa, and Particularly the Trade in Slaves* . . . (London, 1789), Part I.

4. The most accessible sample of mid-eighteenth century attitudes is T. Astley (Publisher), *A New General Collection of Voyages and Travels*, 4 vols. (London, 1745–1747). For representative later works see: William Snelgrave, *A New Account of Guinea and the Slave Trade* (London, 1754); Bryan Edwards, *The History, Civil and Commercial, of the British Colonies in the West Indies*, 2nd ed., 2 vols. (London, 1794); John Matthews, *Voyage to the River Sierra-Leone* . . . (London, 1788), esp. pp. 91–94. See also B. Davidson, *Black Mother* (London, 1961), pp. 101–2.

5. J. J. Hecht, *Continental and Colonial Servants in Eighteenth Century England* (Northampton, Mass., 1954), pp. 33–36, 45–47.

they arose from the practical concerns of one people dealing with another. As such, they were in touch with social reality. Race as such was a *mark* identifying the group—not a *cause* of the group's other characteristics.

A different kind of attitude emerged when the travellers abstracted from qualities of individuals and began to talk about the group— not individual men but the collective "Negro." Reporting of this kind became increasingly common in the 1780's, as the Africa interest felt itself threatened by the rise of the anti-slave-trade movement. Several writers began to project a double image, relatively friendly to in- dividual Africans but unfriendly to the collective African. Individuals in Norris' *Memoirs of the Reign of Bossa Ahadee,* for example, are clearly living portraits of men not especially different from men else- where, while "the African" in his collective image is an inhuman savage.[6]

As the element of political purpose made its appearance, so did a certain degree of circularity between the works of travellers to Africa and those of theorists in Britain. Lt. John Matthews, the pro- slavery author of an account of the Coast in 1785–1787, wrote from what were ostensibly his own observations. Some parts of his works were in the matter-of-fact tradition of earlier reports, but some were clearly derived from Edward Long, an early "scientific" racist resi- dent in Jamaica, who had never visited Africa. Long's low assessment of "the Negro's place in nature" thus found its way into Matthew's book, where it could later be picked up as a piece of first-hand evi- dence from Africa.[7]

The tendency to write about the abstract and collective "Negro" was strongest among biological writers, whose business it was to deal with abstractions of this kind. Where the travellers set out to report what they saw, without the necessity of building their evidence into a sys- tem, the eighteenth-century biologists began with a system and used empiricism to make it as accurate as they could. Their principal aim was to examine, classify, and arrange the whole order of nature in a rational pattern.

6. R. Norris, *Memoirs of the Reign of Bossa Ahadee, King of Dahomey* (London, 1789).

7. Matthews, *Voyage to Sierra-Leone,* pp. 158–59; Edward Long, *History of Jamaica,* 3 vols. (London, 1774), II, 373–74.

This emphasis on the creation of a large-scale system tended to distract attention from the systematic study of man. The first concern of naturalists like Linnaeus and Banks was the world-wide collection of specimens to build up a picture of botany and the zoology of the "lower animals," which made up the largest part of the whole order of nature. No individual or group of scholars was concerned with anthropology, defined a century later as "that science which deals with all phenomena exhibited by collective man, and by him alone, which is capable of being reduced to law."[8] The physical structure of man belonged institutionally to anatomical studies, as a branch of medicine. Data about human culture and society outside of Europe was collected by whatever travellers happened to have the interest to write down what they saw. Analysis of these data was mainly left to a rather vague and still-undifferentiated social science, most often under the rubric of "moral philosophy." The scientific study of human varieties therefore fell by default to the biologists, as a kind of appendix to their general systems of nature.

The major eighteenth-century classifications of nature began with Linnaeus' *Systema Naturae,* first published in 1735, and later revised with additions. This work and its successors formed the basic framework of modern biological classification, and they were decidedly set in the eighteenth-century modes of thought. One of the important items of intellectual lumber common to educated men was the ancient belief that God (or Nature, according to taste) had so organized the world that all creation was arranged in a "Great Chain of Being"— that all living things could be classified and fitted into a hierarchy extending "from man down to the smallest reptile, whose existence can be discovered only by the microscope."[9]

Since man had a place as the highest term on the scale, the varieties of mankind had also to be taken into account, and the biologists assumed from the beginning that they too could be arranged in hierarchic order. Linnaeus himself included a racial classification, which changed slightly in different editions of his work. Initially it was a simple system based on skin color, with a white, red, yellow, and black race, each of them placed on one of the four major continents.

8. T. Bendyshe, "The History of Anthropology," *Memoirs Read Before the Anthropological Society of London,* I, 335 (1863–1864).

9. Charles White, *An Account of the Regular Graduations in Man* . . . (London, 1799), p. 1. See also A. O. Lovejoy, *The Great Chain of Being* (Cambridge, Mass., 1936).

In 1758 he divided *genus homo* into two species to make room for orang-outangs and certain rumored wild men without speech.[10] This later division seemed to be called for by another assumption implicit in the Great Chain of Being: since God in His perfection must have created a perfect hierarchy of living things, the gap between any two creatures was not expected to be very great—not, certainly, so great as that between man and the higher apes.

Other authorities used a four-fold classification like that of Linnaeus, or else dropped back to the ancient and familiar Biblical distinction between the descendents of Ham, Shem, and Japhet, and thus to a three-fold division. Or, the three-fold division could be extended to five by introducing mixed races. J. F. Blumenbach of Göttingen worked with three primary races, the Caucasian, Ethiopian, and Mongolian. American Indians were taken to be a mixture of Caucasian and Mongolian, and a Malay race was supposedly a mixture of Mongolian and Ethiopian. Blumenbach's term "Caucasian" for the European variety lasted into the twentieth century, but later authorities using the five-fold system adopted their own variants. Thus, John Hunter in England took the European, American, and African to be three primary varieties, with two other mixed races to fill out the scheme.[11] By any of these systems of classification, the African variety was always considered a primary stock, if only because of its skin color, so strikingly different from that of Europeans.

Whatever the number of races, the second problem was to arrange them in order of quality. Since there is no strictly scientific or biological justification for stating that one race is "higher" than another, the criteria of ranking had to come from non-scientific assumptions. All of the biologists gave some order of classification, but few of them stated their basis for doing so. Their unstated assumptions, however, were clear enough, even when they were not explicit. All of them began by putting the European variety at the top of the scale. This was natural enough, if only as an unthinking reflection of cul-

10. A. C. Haddon, *History of Anthropology,* 2nd ed. (London, 1934), p. 71.
11. J. F. Blumenbach, "On the Natural Variety of Mankind" (1775 and 1795), p. 264; John Hunter, "An Inaugural Disputation on the Varieties of Man" (1775), pp. 366–67. Both translated in T. Bendyshe (Ed.), *The Anthropological Treatises of Johann Friedrich Blumenbach* (London, 1865). This John Hunter, a physician (d. 1809) should not be confused with his more famous namesake, the anatomist (1723–1793). See DNB biographies. It is an interesting commentary on the staying power of these first formulations that Blumenbach's terminology and the substance of his classification was still in use by the United States Immigration Service in 1961.

tural chauvinism. It could be held to follow from their assessment of European achievements in art and science, or even from the "fact" that God had given the One True Religion to the whites. It was taken for granted that historical achievement was intimately connected with physical form—in short, that race and culture were closely related.

The first term of the series was thus accepted by common agreement. Disagreement came only with the ranking of the others. One solution was to concentrate on skin color. If whiteness of skin was the mark of the highest race, then darker races would be inferior in the increasing order of their darkness. On this basis, and with no further evidence, Africans could be put at the bottom. Esthetic judgements could also be introduced. Blumenbach, who became in his later years a champion of the Negro, fell into this form of racio-esthetic pride. He described Caucasians as having, "in general the kind of appearance which, according to our opinion of symmetry, we consider most handsome and becoming." His description of Africans was less flattering:

Ethiopian variety. Colour black; hair black and curly, head narrow, compressed at the sides; forehead knotty, uneven, malar bones protruding outwards; eyes very prominent; nose thick, mixed up as it were with the wide jaws; alveolur edge narrow, elongated in front; upper primaries obliquely prominent; lips very puffy; chin retreating. Many are bandy-legged. To this variety belong all the Africans, except those of the North.[12]

This description was hardly accurate, and even where it was accurate it took the European type as a standard of comparison. Blumenbach, however, was more kind to the Africans than his colleagues. He gave primacy to the "Caucasian" variety, but he placed the others below it on the same level. Here at least, Negroes were not automatically put at the bottom of the human family. Blumenbach was also conscious that qualitative descriptions of this kind were not sufficiently precise, and he experimented with head shape as a possible basis for a more accurate system of classification.

The most important of the eighteenth century attempts to quantify racial distinctions, however, was the work of Pieter Camper (1722–1789) in Holland. "Camper's facial Angle," as it was later called, was essentially a measurement of prognathism, derived by looking at a human head in profile. One line was drawn from the meeting of the lips to the most prominent part of the forehead, and another

12. Blumenbach, "Varieties of Mankind," pp. 265–66.

from the opening of the ear to the base of the nose. The crucial angle was formed where these two lines met. Presumably, the wider the angle, the smaller the degree of prognathism, and prognathism was suggestive of the headshape of animals. A wide angle was also supposed to indicate a higher forehead, a greater skull capacity, a better esthetic appearance, and greater intelligence. Camper claimed that, if this angle were measured for men of various races (or even for animals), the measurements would fall into an ordered series, from Greek statuary as the ideal form, through the European races, to Negroes as the lowest human variety, and finally to the "lower animals."[13] After a vogue of popularity in the later eighteenth century, Camper's angle died out of respectable usage, principally because it was extremely difficult to measure accurately. But the suggestion that skull shape had something to do with ability was to have a long future.

The attempts to classify and grade human races were damaging enough to the reputation of Africans, but the efforts to explain the origin of race were more serious still. The traditional and orthodox view was that of Christian revelation: God created man, a single pair, at a finite time in the not-very-distant past. Scientific versions of this belief in a single creation came to be known as "monogenesis." If the basic tenets of monogenesis were accepted, all the biologist had to do was explain the origin of later variations among Adam's descendants.

There were many suggestions. Moreau de Maupertuis believed the original creation included the creation of all the racial varieties to emerge later in time. They were latent in the original female egg and the original male sperm given to Adam and Eve, though Adam and Eve were themselves of the white race. When Negro variants appeared, the "normal" part of mankind drove them off into Africa, a less desirable part of the world. Once there, they continued to breed true to their Negro form and color, though it was still possible that they might one day change back into their original European race.[14]

A more common view held that African form and color were acquired traits, strengthened through generations of life in the tropics,

---

13. Haddon, *History of Anthropology*, p. 16: W. E. Mühlmann, *Geschichte der Anthropologie* (Bonn, 1948), p. 60.

14. P. L. Moreau de Maupertuis, "Venus Physique" (1745), II, pp. 106–10, 129–30, in *Oeuvres de Maupertuis*, 4 vols. (Lyon, 1756).

not unlike a heretable and constantly deepening suntan. This was authoritatively restated in Buffon's *Histoire naturelle,* which began to appear in 1749, and it was repeated by later monogenists like Blumenbach and John Hunter.[15] Kant's position was midway between this and the opinion of Moreau de Maupertuis. He thought that Negro features and skin color were not simply acquired characteristics. They were latent in the original stock and appeared when it was subject to heat and humidity.[16]

The unconscious assumption in all these ideas was that God had created man "in His image," which was necessarily the image of the biologist. Other varieties must therefore be worse varieties, and thus "degenerations" from the original stock. Even at its worst, however, the usual monogenetic view allowed all races a place in humanity, and peoples who had "degenerated" in a few thousand years might well "improve" again in a relatively short time.

The opposing theory of polygenesis was less favorable. It held that each race was a separate creation, distinct from the children of Adam and permanently so. Although polygenesis was a minority position in eighteenth-century Europe, it has probably been the most common explanation of race throughout human history. Several European suggestions to this effect had appeared from time to time, in spite of the open contradiction of the Bible. One of the most widely read was Isaac LaPeyrere's *Prae-Adamitae,* published in 1655, which held that Adam and Eve had been the last of a series of special creations, and some of the living non-Europeans were descended from the earlier pre-Adamites. Another possibility was that of the anonymous *Co-Adamitae* of 1732, which held that all races were created simultaneously but not endowed with equal ability. The idea was specifically applied to Africans in 1734 by John Atkins, a naval surgeon who had visited the Coast.[17]

Polygenesis was especially attractive to the eighteenth century *phi-*

15. Blumenbach, "Varieties of Mankind," pp. 209–13; Hunter, "Inaugural Disputation." See also J. C. Greene, "Some Early Speculations on the Origin of Human Races," *American Anthropologist,* LVI, 33 (February 1954).

16. E. W. Count, "The Evolution of the Race Idea in Modern Western Culture during the Period of the Pre-Darwinian Nineteenth Century," *Transactions of the New York Academy of Sciences,* VIII (2nd series), 143–45 (February, 1946); A. O. Lovejoy, "Kant and Evolution," in B. Glass and others, *Forerunners of Darwin, 1745–1859* (Baltimore, 1959), pp. 186–87.

17. Bendyshe, "History of Anthropology," pp. 345–49; Count, "The Race Idea," p. 158; John Atkins, *Navy Surgeon* . . . (London, 1734), pp. 23–24.

losophes who were concerned to find a plausible and systematic explanation of the world, and not especially concerned either with religious orthodoxy or with the kind of evidence they used. Both Voltaire and Rousseau suggested that Negroes were naturally inferior to Europeans in their mental ability. David Hume argued that, "There never was a civilized nation of any other complexion than white, nor even any individual eminent either in action or speculation. No ingenious manufactures amongst them, no arts, no sciences. . . . Such a uniform and constant difference could not happen, in so many countries and ages, if nature had not made an original distinction betwixt these breeds of men."[18] He thus incorporated the two key assumptions—that white Europeans had a superior culture, and that race and culture were causally connected.

New evidence for polygenesis was brought to light by the publication of Buffon's *Histoire naturelle,* even though Buffon himself was a monogenist. His comparative anatomy showed that there were amazing similarities in physical structure between all animals, and especially between men and certain apes. This information fitted in with the Great Chain of Being and the expected close gradation between species. As early as 1713 naturalists began looking for a "missing link" between men and apes and speculated on the possibility that Hottentots and orang-outangs might be side by side in the "scale of life," separated only by the fact that orang-outangs could not speak.[19]

By the mid-century anatomical knowledge was improving and the structural similarities seemed even clearer. Linnaeus changed his classification in 1758 to allow for lower species of *genus homo.* In 1773 James Burnet, Lord Monboddo, stretched the classification still further and included men and orang-outangs in the same species. The following year, his friend, Lord Kames, published *Sketches of the History of Man,* where he developed a fully fledged polygenist theory. Kames held that God had created the varieties of men in order to adapt each to a particular climate. But neither Monboddo

18. David Hume, "Of National Character," *The Philosophical Works of David Hume,* 4 vols. (London, 1898), III, 252. The essay was first published in 1742, but the passage quoted was added as a footnote in the edition of 1753–54. See also M. Cook, "Jean Jacques Rousseau and the Negro," *Journal of Negro History,* XXI, 294–303 (July, 1936).

19. Lovejoy, *Great Chain of Being,* pp. 233 ff.; A. O. Lovejoy, "Some Eighteenth Century Evolutionists," *Popular Science Monthly,* LXV, 327 (1904).

nor Kames were biologists. Monboddo merely wanted to cite an example of a human society without language, and Kames was struck by the distinct physical appearance of Europeans and Africans. Neither statement was well supplied with evidence that could pass for "scientific," and both were shocking to orthodox Christians.[20]

Another work of 1774 was to be immensely more important in giving a pseudo-scientific base to polygenist theories already in the air. This was the *History of Jamaica* by Edward Long, who, as a resident of the island, was in a position to bring forward "evidence" about the African slaves. In spite of the title, the book was a multi-volume compendium of history and description, and a guide to future British policy in Jamaica. In a key section, Long tried to assess the place of the Negro in nature, drawing partly on Buffon and partly on the xenophobia natural to his home, where lines of caste and race ran parallel. Africans, in his opinion were "brutish, ignorant, idle, crafty, treacherous, bloody, thievish, mistrustful, and superstitious people." Their skins were dark, their features different, and they had "a covering of wool, like the bestial fleece, instead of hair." They were inferior in "faculties of mind," had a "bestial and fetid smell," and were even parasitized by black lice instead of the lighter-colored lice of the Europeans.[21] All of this was the common prejudice of the West Indies.

Long's importance in biological thought was not simply his restatement of old prejudice, but the fact that he gave his prejudice the backing of technical biological arguments. He claimed that Europeans and Negroes did not belong to the same species. Since species were generally held to have been created in the beginning by God, while varieties were produced after the creation, it was a distinction of some importance. Species also had a technical meaning that still persists: individuals that can breed together and produce fertile off-spring are considered to be of the same species.

Long tried, among other things, to associate Negroes with animals by claiming that Negro children, like animals, mature more rapidly than whites. According to him, Negro women bear children after

20. A. O. Lovejoy, "Monboddo and Rousseau," *Modern Philology*, XXX, 275–96 (February, 1933); James Burnet, Lord Monboddo, *The Origin and Progress of Language*, 8 vols. (Edinburgh, 1773–1792), I, 279–90; Henry Home, Lord Kames, *Sketches of the History of Man*, 2nd ed., 4 vols. (Edinburgh, 1788), I, 11–13, 36–40.

21. Long, *Jamaica*, II, 353–56.

only brief labor and practically without pain. This point could be taken to "prove" that Negro women escaped the Divinity's curse on Eve's female descendants. (It might equally well have "proved" that Negroes were without original sin, but Long went no further in his theological speculations.) Finally, as the key argument, Long claimed that mulattoes were unfertile hybrids. This particular point was a little difficult to sustain in the face of evident race mixture in the West Indies, but most of his readers had no access to the evidence, and his specific argument was subtle enough to pass with people who might otherwise know better. He admitted that Europeans and Africans could breed together in the first generation and produce fertile children, but the mulatto children would only be fertile when breeding with one or the other of the "pure" races. Mulattoes breeding with other mulattoes could not in his opinion, produce a permanent mixed race.[22]

On this basis, Long divided *genus homo* into three species: Europeans and similar people, Negroes, and "orang-outangs." This last group included not only the real orang-outangs of Southeast Asia, but also the larger African tailless apes, such as chimpanzees. Using the evidence from Buffon that so impressed Lord Monboddo, he argued that these "orang-outangs" differed from other men only in the formation of the feet and the *os ilium,* and in their inability to speak or reason. But this failing was only a matter of education. The apes would be able to talk and think well enough, if only they were properly trained.[23]

Long's system also met the demands of the Great Chain of Being. There were three species of man, with many gradations within the species. He arranged Africans on an ascending scale from the half-legendary Jagas of Angola upwards through Hottentots, Fulbe and Mandinka peoples of West Africa, to the Wolof and Ethiopians, the highest type of African man.[24] He could thus claim a certain credibility on grounds of symmetry alone: "The system of man will seem more consistent, and the measure of it more complete, and analogous to the harmony and order that are visible in every other line of the world's stupendous fabric. Nor is this conclusion degrading to human nature, while it tends to exalt our idea of the infinite perfections

22. Long, *Jamaica,* II, 336–37, 380.
23. Long, *Jamaica,* II, 358–71.
24. Long, *Jamaica,* II, 373–74.

of the Deity; for how vast is the difference between inert matter, and matter embued with thought and reason."[25]

Long's ideas on race are so obviously nonsense by any modern standard, their importance has sometimes been neglected. He was widely read by the naturalists of his time, and his thought had a place in the background of the theory of biological evolution. Even though he published later than Monboddo and knew about Monboddo's theory, he seems to have "discovered" the human qualities of the orang-outang independently, and he stated his case with more "scientific" care than Monboddo had done. Long's West Indian background also gave a note of authority, even though the "facts" he claimed to have observed himself were often false. Where Monboddo was laughed at for thinking that apes were men, Long was not laughed at for saying that Negroes were less than men. The idea fitted all too well into the pattern of racial and cultural pride already prevalent in English thought.

Long's greatest importance was in giving an "empirical" and "scientific" base that would lead on to pseudo-scientific racism. The part of the *History of Jamaica* dealing with race was reprinted in America in the *Columbia Magazine* of 1788, where it became a support for later American racism.[26] It was used again and again for three-quarters of a century by British and Continental polygenists of scientific repute, and it provided a set of ready made arguments for any publicist who wanted to prove the "fact" of African inferiority.

Long was more of a pro-slavery publicist than a scientist, but his views influenced even those scientists who believed in a more liberal social policy. One of the more important restatements of the polygenist case toward the end of the eighteenth century was that of Charles White, a Manchester physician. White favored the abolition of slavery throughout the world—an advanced position for his day, when only the slave trade was under direct attack in Parliament—but his attention was drawn to the similarities between human and animal skulls by the lectures of John Hunter on comparative anatomy. Hunter himself was a monogenist, but White discarded that position largely on the strength of Long's evidence. Like many of his contemporaries, he was also impressed by an inordinate admiration for European

25. Long, *Jamaica*, II, 371.

26. J. C. Greene, "The American Debate on the Negro's Place in Nature, 1780–1815," *Journal of the History of Ideas*, XV, 387 (June, 1954).

physical beauty and the expectation of a symmetrical and graded order of nature.[27]

White's thesis was first presented in 1795, and new biological work over the two decades since Long had published made it possible for him to clear up some of Long's patent inaccuracies. He straightened out the difference between chimpanzees and orang-outangs. By reference to Camper's dissection of apes, he showed that they could never be taught to speak. Thus the "orang-outangs" were down-graded and sent back to become two different species of *simiae*. But the greater care and precision merely made polygenesis scientifically respectable, without saving the reputation of the Africans. Indeed, new "evidence" had been produced by S. T. von Soemmering in Germany, whose comparative anatomy of Negroes and Europeans showed striking physical differences between the two races.[28] Soemmering's work had been badly done, but it was enough to satisfy White, who checked it by measuring a single Negro skeleton. He was even more impressed by the alleged mental inferiority of the Africans—a "fact" which he accepted on the authority of Thomas Jefferson, Edward Long, and a single visitor to the East Indies. His conclusion was to produce a new division of mankind into four separately created species. In descending order, these were the European, Asian, American, and African. The one saving grace was that all four species had souls.[29]

It is clear that the biologists, as well as the travellers, were influenced by the tendencies of "diversificationism." They were actively looking for differences between human races. On one hand, this tended to blind them to similarities. On the other, it made them more willing to accept popular myths. There was, for example, a belief going back to antiquity, that southern people are more lascivious than northerners. It was sometimes re-expressed in racial terms, and Negroes were given credit for extraordinary sexual prowess. In the guarded language of a popular pamphlet of 1772: "The lower class of women in *England,* are remarkably fond of the blacks, for reasons too brutal to mention. . . ."[30] The biologists were less timid.

27. White, *Regular Gradations in Man,* pp. iii, 1, 125–29, 134–35.
28. S. T. von Soemmering, *Über die Köperlich Verschiedenheit des Negers vom Europäer* (Frankfurt am Main, 1785).
29. White, *Regular Gradations in Man,* pp. 26–29, 41–44, 63–66, 83–85, 125–33.
30. *Candid Reflections Upon the Judgement Lately Awarded by the Court of King's Bench in Westminster-Hall, on What is Commonly Called the Negro-Cause, by a Planter* (London, T. Lownes, 1772), p. 49.

Both monogenists and polygenists thought the penis of Negro men was larger than that of Europeans, and that Negro women were sexually more desirable for physiological reasons left unexplained.[31] Thus a great deal of the popular xenophobia already prevalent on the fringes of Empire came to be expressed in terms of race difference and endowed with "scientific" authority.

There were only occasional efforts to redress the balance and recall the unity of mankind. Adam Smith pointed out the relativity of physical beauty: "What different ideas are formed in different nations concerning the beauty of the human shape and countenance? A fair complexion is a shocking deformity on the coast of Guinea. Thick lips and a flat nose are a beauty."[32]

John Hunter held that, "Travellers have exaggerated the mental varieties far beyond the truth, who have denied good qualities to the inhabitants of other countries, because their mode of life, manners and customs have been excessively different from their own."[33]

But only Blumenbach among the biological writers made a serious effort to correct the dominant tendencies of the science as a whole. In some of his later writings he not only moderated his own earlier racial chauvinism but tried to make a reasoned case for Negro equality. His defense significantly stressed the non-biological factors which had contributed so heavily to the ranking of human races. Since the Negro race was so often condemned by reference to African culture, Blumenbach compiled brief biographies of Africans who had made a name for themselves in European society. His list of notable Negroes included an author of Latin poetry, a Prussian counsellor of state, a meteorologist, and a variety of literary figures.[34]

Blumenbach's authority was undoubted, and his work was enormously influential far into the nineteenth century, especially with English anthropologists like Prichard and Lawrence. His positive and scientific anti-racism was therefore of the greatest importance in stemming the eighteenth-century tendencies toward pseudo-scientific racism, even though his was a minority voice in his own time—in much the same way that full-scale polygenesis was a minority position on

31. Long, *Jamaica*, II, 383–84; Blumenbach, "Varieties of Mankind," p. 249; White, *Regular Gradations in Man*, p. 61.

32. A Smith, "The Theory of Moral Sentiments," *Essays* (London, 1869), p. 175. First published 1757.

33. Hunter, "Inaugural Disputation," p. 392.

34. J. F. Blumenbach, "Observations on the Bodily Conformation and Mental Capacity of the Negroes," *Philosophical Magazine*, III, 141–47 (1799).

the anti-Negro side. The majority view of the biological writers was still monogenesis, but monogenesis with strong overtones of racial pride.

While the reputation of the Africans lost something in the chance tendencies of eighteenth-century biological thought, it gained from the literary convention of the "noble savage." The alien or savage literary hero began to appear as a stock figure of English *belles lettres* toward the end of the seventeenth century and reached a kind of peak of popularity toward the end of the eighteenth.

This literary African had some characteristics of the biological African of the same period. He was just as much an abstraction, and drawn just as much from the needs of European thought without concern for the empirical evidence. The noble savage as a literary hero was not only removed from reality, he was necessarily so. Any literary hero of this period was something of an abstraction, designed to point moral lessons. His exceptional qualities of strength, intellect, or virtue reflected, while at the same time they reinforced, the ethical standards of the age. From the later seventeenth century onward, some heroes were drawn for the purpose of criticizing the artificialities of European civilization. It was the fashion to show virtue or nobility springing from nature itself, rather than from training or birth. The hero's origin was of little consequence, as long as he was alien to the social class of the reading public. He could be from the lower orders, by preference from the peasantry and thus close to the soil. He could be from an exotic overseas society, in which case the author could indulge the romantic taste of the public in still another way.

The exotic hero drew on several aspects of European thought. It was an ancient device of social criticism to describe a golden age—a time and place infinitely better than the real world, necessarily beyond the view of the audience, either in the past, the future, or a far country. European explorations in the sixteenth century had opened the possibility of setting all manner of utopias in the half-known lands of the non-Western world. Even before the discoveries, some European traditions had associated simplicity and moral excellence. The medieval Franciscans laid great stress on the value of unadorned nature, apostolic poverty, and a simplicity that was thought of as "primitive."[35] Perhaps because they expected to find a golden age of

35. J. L. Phelan, *The Millennial Kingdom of the Franciscans in the New World* (Berkeley, 1956), pp. 64–65.

primitive simplicity overseas, the travellers' reports often described
the moral superiority of savage life. Not all, of course, were en-
chanted by the world beyond Europe, but the belief in actual "good
savages" was strong enough in the eighteenth century to support such
visions as Swedenborg's dream of a new Church to be founded in the
heart of Africa. All the more reason to draw the literary hero from
a "savage" society.[36]

The first popular African hero appeared in English literature with
Aphra Behn's *Oroonoko,* before the end of the seventeenth century,
but he was merely the standard hero in fancy dress. The fully con-
ventionalized "noble savage" made his entrance only in the second
half of the eighteenth century along with the cult of nature. Rousseau's glorified "state of nature" was widely misunderstood, but it
gave color to the alleged virtues of savage society.[37] The savage himself became more and more like Pope's poor Indian,

> . . . whose untutor'd mind
> Sees God in clouds, or hears him in the wind;
> His soul proud Science never taught to stray
> Far as the solar walk, or milky-way;
> Yet simple Nature to his hope has giv'n
> Behind the cloud-topt hill an humbler heav'n; . . . .[38]

By the 1760's the literary fad was fully developed in England, with
pride of place going to the American Indian, the noble savage *par
excellence.* The publicity attending Cook's voyages added the Polynesians, and Africans came in especially with the 1770's, as the anti-
slavery movement enlisted the sympathy and talents of literary men.[39]

Beyond any doubt, the use of the savage hero as a literary device
helped to create a much more favorable emotional climate for
Africans than they would otherwise have enjoyed, but it was not so
wholly favorable as might appear. The writers in this vein had no
intention of suggesting that Africans were better than Europeans, or
that their culture, on balance, measured up to the achievements of

36. For the theme of the noble savage, the best general treatment is H. N. Fairchild,
The Noble Savage (New York, 1928), on which much of the following account is
based.

37. A. O. Lovejoy, "The Supposed Primitivism of Rousseau's Discourse on Inequality," *Modern Philology,* XXI, 165–86 (November, 1923); Cook, "Rousseau and
the Negro."

38. Alexander Pope, *Essay on Man* (1732), Epistle I, lines 95–104.

39. For a discussion of this literature see Wylie Sypher, *Guinea's Captive Kings*
(Chapel Hill, 1942) and E. B. Dykes, *The Negro in English Romantic Thought* (Washington, 1942).

Europe. A poet, such as William Roscoe, might lavish praise on African art:

> The sable artist; to the jav'lin's shaft,
> The ebon staff; or maple goblet, gave
> Fantastic decorations; simply carv'd
> Yet not inelegant: beneath his hand,
> Oft too a cloth of firmer texture grew,
> That steep'd in azure, mocks the brittle threads,
> And fleeting tincture, of our boasted arts.[40]

But Roscoe's sentiments should not be mistaken. He was not suggesting that Europeans should import African textiles or buy African carvings. Neither he nor his audience believed for a moment that Africans had a superior art. He merely points with slight wonder to the fact they had any art at all. In the same way, the nobility of the savage hero was not a greater nobility than might well be achieved by a European. The lesson to be drawn was that *even* a savage could rise to nobility of action because he was close to nature. The attitude was mildly patronizing, and the impact of the literature depended in part on the superiority feelings of the audience. It did not even imply liberal views about race or social policy on the part of the author. Racists and defenders of West Indian slavery could and did use the device of the noble Negro in their literary work.[41]

When the theme of the noble savage merged with Christian humanitarianism of the anti-slavery movement, the patronizing attitude persisted. Christians could not very well depict people without knowledge of God's word as equal in all respects to themselves. Spiritual equality, they certainly had, but even so Christian and humanitarian a poet as William Blake could couple a belief in spiritual equality with pejorative references to the dark skin of the Africans.

> My mother bore me in the southern wild,
> And I am black, but O! my soul is white;
> White as an angel is the English child,
> But I am black, as if bereav'd of light.[42]

The mixture of attitudes in the anti-slavery poets varied widely. In Day and Bicknell's *Dying Negro,* one of the earliest and most popular of the longer poems, the theme is that of superiority to

40. *The Wrongs of Africa, a Poem* (London, 1787), p. 10.
41. Sypher, *Guinea's Captive Kings,* pp. 6–7.
42. From "Songs of Innocence and of Experience," in *Poetical Works of William Blake* (London, 1914), p. 68. First published 1789.

circumstances drawn from nature, but equality drawn from God. The combination is summed up in the authors' picture of Africa:

> There too Heav'n planted man's majestic race;
> Bade reason's sons with nobler title rise,
> Lift high their brow sublime, and scan the skies,
> What tho' no rosy tints adorn their face,
> No silken ringlets shine with flowing grace?
> Yet of etherial temper are their souls,
> And in their veins the tide of honour rolls;
> And valorous kindles there the hero's flame,
> Contempt of death, and thirst for martial fame.[43]

Here the portrait of the noble African was at its most favorable, as might be expected from an author trying to make a political argument as well as a work of literature. But even here he took for granted an esthetic prejudice in favor of "silken ringlets" and "rosy tints." The contrast on which this literary effect depends is still (though less skillfully used) the same as Blake's.

After its phase of greatest popularity in the last three decades of the eighteenth century, the theme of the noble Negro died out slowly, with an occasional re-appearance throughout the first half of the nineteenth. Its importance for English thought about Africa is very difficult to assess. It certainly helped to form a vague and positive image of the "good African," and it was widely used by the anti-slave-trade publicists for exactly this purpose. On the other hand it was very much a literary convention, not a rationally supported affirmation about savage life. Aside from those who used it for polemic anti-slavery ends, literary men had no intention of speaking as ethnographic popularizers. They were principally social critics of their own world. As Fairchild put it, "The true Noble Savage arises from a combination of disillusion about the here and now and illusion about the there and then."[44] In some instances, at least, the illusion was consciously an illusion, which the author himself considered a form of poetic license, though many readers probably mistook poetry for reality. Curious assumptions about the nobility of savages recur during the next half century in unexpected quarters outside the field of *belles lettres,* as though the writers were still echoing a belief picked up in casual reading when young.

43. Thomas Day and John Bicknell, *The Dying Negro* (London, 1775), pp. 7–8. First published 1773.
44. *The Noble Savage,* p. 127.

Just as literary men who used the convention of the noble savage were not principally concerned to describe Africa or Africans, humanitarians of the anti-slavery movement were not principally interested in "the Negro." Their own aim was to eradicate evil as they saw it from the world. The more emotional Christianity of the later eighteenth century, especially the Wesleyan movement and its counterpart, the Evangelical wing of the Church of England, made new moral demands on Christians. It was not enough for them, to live by a negative code—to abide by the "Thou shalt not's" and be present once a week at Church services. The Christian life included positive responsibilities. Whatever talent, wealth, or training a Christian might have was not his alone. He was obliged to dispense some part of it for the relief of his fellow creatures, and he was accountable to God for the use he made of it.[45]

The African slave trade was one of the first evils to catch the attention of the humanitarians. It was perfectly evident that the trade produced suffering in Africa, more loss of life in transit to the Coast and to America, and still further cruelty on the American plantations. The Religious Society of Friends had opposed both slavery and the trade on moral grounds since the seventeenth century. The secular rights-of-man philosophy of the eighteenth century added another thread of opposition. The continuing body of travel literature from West Africa and the West Indies called attention, often unconsciously, to the amount of human suffering necessarily involved in the customary form of labor supply to the South Atlantic System.[46]

Whatever the source of opposition, there was no need in the beginning to enquire what *kind* of men the Africans were. For secular reformers, they were simply men, entitled as such to their natural rights. For Christians they were "fellow creatures." (Even the most anti-Negro racist could hardly deny this minimum claim and still remain a Christian.) In either case, it could be argued that Africans were entitled to the benevolence and protection of the "civilized

---

45. Thomas Clarkson, *History of the Rise, Progress, and Accomplishment of the Abolition of the African Slave Trade by the British Parliament,* 2 vols. (London, 1808), I, 7.

46. For the varying points of view on the anti-slave-trade movement, see, in addition to Clarkson: R. Coupland, *The British Anti-Slavery Movement* (London, 1933); R. Coupland, *Wilberforce: A Narrative* (Oxford, 1923); F. J. Klingberg, *The Anti-Slavery Movement in England* (New Haven, 1926); G. R. Mellor, *British Imperial Trusteeship 1783–1850* (London, 1951); Eric Williams, *Capitalism and Slavery* (Chapel Hill, 1944).

world"—at the very least, against the evils caused by Christian and civilized men. The initial issue was thus that of slavery as such, without concern for racial status, the supposed barbarism of African culture, or the place of Africans on the Great Chain of Being.

Individual reformers came into the movement with a variety of opinions about the Africans, or with no opinion at all. Granville Sharp, the principal leader of the fight against slavery in England itself, rested his initial case on purely legal arguments. The laws of England took no account of slavery, therefore any slave brought to England should automatically become a free man.[47] This view already had some support in judicial decisions, and it was sustained in 1772 by Lord Mansfield.[48] Even as late as this first victory, Sharp himself was uncertain about the nature of the Africans. He wrote to Jacob Bryant, the antiquarian, asking for information and saying: "I am far from having any particular esteem for the Negroes; but as I think myself obliged to consider them as *men,* I am certainly obliged also to use my best endeavours to prevent their being treated as *beasts* by our unchristian countrymen; . . ."[49]

Bryant answered that Negroes were human, descended from Adam through the line of Ham, like all dark-skinned peoples. This was clear enough to satisfy the needs of the moment, but it was not the only image of "the African" reflected in Evangelical thought. John Wesley himself was, at best, ambivalent in his attitude toward Africans and their culture. Through the bulk of his printed work, he treated "savages" in general as a moral lesson—an example of the influence of untrammeled original sin on corrupt mankind. African culture was thus degenerate, showing the common lot of man without Christianity.

On the specific issue of the slave trade, however, Wesley joined the general humanitarian hue and cry. He borrowed freely from the common stock of abolitionist arguments. Since the slave traders claimed African life was so "degraded" that even slavery in the West Indies was preferable, the humanitarians had to provide an answer. In Wesley's case, the answer was taken from the works of the enlightened travellers, from which the favorable passages could be

47. Granville Sharp, *A Representation of the Injustice and Dangerous Tendency of Tolerating Slavery in England* (London, 1769).

48. Hecht, *Continental and Colonial Servants,* pp. 37–39.

49. G. Sharp to J. Bryant, 19 October 1772, quoted in Sharp, *The Just Limitation of Slavery in the Laws of God . . .* (London, 1776), pp. 44–46.

abstracted. Wesley claimed, for example, that Africans were "far more mild, friendly, and kind to strangers than our forefathers were."[50] Other humanitarians took up the same case in greater detail, especially the Quaker Anthony Benezet in *Some Historical Account of Guinea*.[51] Here the literary figure of the noble savage, so often painted in fiction, reappeared as "fact."

Granville Sharp also began to interest himself in the facts of "savage" culture. He made it a point to meet whatever specimens of noble savagery might turn up in England, such as Omai, a Polynesian visitor in 1776. Through his conversations with Omai, Sharp became convinced that "natural man" could be made to understand civilized morality through reason alone. By the later 1780's he was convinced of the high natural endowment of Africans; but he was never a cultural relativist. He continued to believe, for example, that Hindu religion and Hindu law were quite literally the devil's work.[52]

Many of the prominent anti-slave-trade leaders kept to the adverse opinion of African culture throughout the 1780's. Wilberforce in particular argued that Africans were men, but "fallen men," degraded by their savagery and by the equally savage Christians that carried out the slave trade. He was supported in this line by both Burke and Pitt, though something of Wesley's ambivalence was present too. If only to counter the accusation that "degradation" was the natural state of the Africans, Wilberforce occasionally came to the defense of at least some aspects of African culture, pointing to the relatively benign system of household slavery in Africa—and to the cheerfulness, love of peace, and hospitality to strangers.[53] By the 1790's some such mild defense had become a usual part of the humanitarian case, though not inevitably so.

The humanitarians' treatment of race followed much the same course as their treatment of African culture. They began with little

50. John Wesley, "Thoughts upon Slavery" in *Works* (London, 1872), XI, 65. First published 1774; M. T. Hodgen, "The Negro in the Anthropology of John Wesley," *Journal of Negro History*, XIX, 308–23 (July, 1934).

51. *Some Historical Account of Guinea,* new ed. (London, 1788), esp. pp. 2, 81–87.

52. Prince Hoare, *Memoirs of Granville Sharp,* 2nd ed., 2 vols. (London, 1828), I, 221–22, 224–26; Sharp, *A General Plan for Laying out Towns and Townships, of the New Acquired Lands,* 2nd ed. (London, 1804), pp. 21–23. First published 1794.

53. William Wilberforce, Commons, 12 May 1789, *Parliamentary Register,* XXVI, 147; 18 April 1791, *Parliamentary Register,* XXIX, 184, 196–97; Edmund Burke, Commons, 21 May 1789, *Parliamentary Register,* XXVI, 201; Coupland, *Wilberforce,* pp. 170, 292–93.

more than the vague belief that Africans were men, but the growing theory of polygenesis was a double threat. It could be used to "prove" that Africans were separately created by God, specifically to serve the children of Adam as slaves. More serious still, it seemed to deny the truth of revelation and thus strike at Christianity itself. In this case, the first line of defense was the Bible. By his own word, God had made all men "of one blood" (Acts 7:26). Granville Sharp in particular undertook the detailed examination of the legal and scriptural case against the slave trade and in favor of the equality of man.[54]

But this appeal to authority would only be valid for those who accepted the authority itself. By the later 1770's, Sharp was searching for counter arguments to meet polygenesis on its own ground, looking into such matters as the alleged infertility of one mulatto breeding with another. The most comprehensive humanitarian effort in this direction, however, came from another source. After nineteen years on St. Kitts, the Reverend James Ramsay returned to England with a claim to speak from personal knowledge. His principal work, *Essays on the Treatment and Conversion of African Slaves in the British Sugar Colonies,* published in 1784, was the best anti-racist tract of the eighteenth century.

Ramsay used the arguments from revelation, but he went on to counter the biologists with biological arguments, and at several points at once. He attacked the assumption that "the Negro" could be considered a valid abstraction by showing that, even in their physical features, Africans were a diverse lot. Furthermore, the biologists had not really established a definite relationship between physical form and ability, or between ability and climate. Until they did so, their arguments would have to be set aside. On the more detailed anatomical points, he showed that, even if Negro skulls could be proven to stand between those of Europeans and those of apes, there was no evidence that skull shape or size had any relation to intelligence or any other quality. Even if it could be shown that the cranial capacity of Negroes was smaller than that of other people, there was still no proof that this characteristic was permanent and independent of such factors as mental exercise. He contradicted Long's assertion that

54. G. Sharp, *Just Limitation of Slavery;* Sharp, *The Law of Liberty* . . . (London, 1776); Sharp, *The Law of Passive Obedience* . . . (London, 1776); Hoare, *Granville Sharp,* II, xiii–xvi.

mulattoes were relatively infertile from his own observations in the West Indies. Finally, even if Negroes could be proved to be a distinct race or even a separate species, there was no proof that they were inferior. If they could be proved to be both distinct and inferior *as a group,* there was no proof that individual Africans were inferior to individual Europeans. Even if *all* were inferior, there was still no moral case for their enslavement.[55] All in all, Ramsay used the critical rationalism associated with science in a way the "scientists" had neglected to do.

Ramsay's essay was especially effective for catching a maximum following for the anti-slavery cause. On questions of race there were many stopping places, and the alignment of anti-slavery and anti-racist opinion was never complete. Humanitarians in general were less overtly arrogant in their writings than the defenders of the slave trade, but the possible variety of opinion was enormous. As a minimum common denominator, all humanitarians believed that Africans should not be carried to the West Indies against their will. Beyond this point, views ranged from Ramsay's own egalitarianism through to Charles White's belief that Negroes were a distinct species and the lowest species of man—and yet ought not to be enslaved. Most humanitarians, however, believed in the spiritual equality of all men before God. Perhaps a majority believed that Africans might achieve equality with the Europeans on this earth as well, but only a very few saw much value in African culture as it was.

Within any one of the four distinct traditions of thought about the Africans there was a similar range of opinion. Most biologists were within the pale of orthodox monogenesis, even though some were laying the foundations of "scientific" racism. Among those who used the theme of the noble savage, some believed "the African" was "natural man," yet others simply wrote within a literary convention. Among those who defended the slave trade, several were relatively free of racial prejudice, yet racists could also be humanitarians. Taken as a group, the travellers to Africa were less prejudiced than those who stayed at home. They were often annoyed in petty ways by contact across cultures in the tropics, but they also came closest to an understanding of Africans as men like themselves with an integral

55. James Ramsay, *Essay on the Treatment and Conversion of African Slaves in the British Sugar Colonies* (London, 1784), pp. 179–263.

culture that was more than mere savagery. As a group they were less anxious to reduce individual Africans to an inhuman and abstracted "African." Many of the travellers, however, were in the slave trade, and they defended it before their countrymen in Britain. But the defense they found most convincing to themselves was not race difference. It was, instead, the intractable and unfamiliar conditions of tropical life.

3

THE PROMISE

AND THE TERROR

OF

A TROPICAL ENVIRONMENT

For eighteenth-century Europe, the
world between the tropics was much more a "New World" than
North America had ever been. In its newness it held out both promise
and terror—the promise of tropical wealth and the terror of the unknown. Even though Englishmen had been sailing southern seas
since the reign of Elizabeth I and had settled on Barbados in the
reign of Charles I, the tropical environment was still alien and forbidding and barely understood. But the most crucial fact *was* known:
Europeans died there with considerably greater frequency than they
did in Europe. Whatever else it held out, a visit to the tropics meant
running the gauntlet of disease and death.

Add to this the factor of sheer unfamiliarity. North Europeans,
then as now, preferred being a little cold all the time to being a
little warm all the time, and a temperature of eighty-five degrees
Fahrenheit seemed an uncomfortable extreme of summer heat. Plants,
animals—even the feel of the wind was different. If the tropical
world broke in some respects the expected pattern of natural behavior, who could tell how far and in what ways natural law was

set aside? Something of the medieval legends of intolerable heat, monstrous animals and plants, strange diseases, and strange people remained in the popular imagination. Even though some Englishmen had spent most of their lives in the tropics, their specialized knowledge did little to correct the apprehension of those who stayed at home. Travellers, as much as any, helped to preserve the mixture of legend and fact. With no rational limit to the credulity of their listeners, one generation after another of "Old Coasters" told their stories. They could still be heard in the middle of the twentieth century on the verandah of the European club or in the smoking room of a ship outward bound from Liverpool to West African ports.[1]

On the other side, in the popular belief of the eighteenth century, the tropical world was a place of immense wealth, from which the "Nabobs" and the absentee West Indian planters drew the funds to buy their country houses and their seats in Parliament. Popular imagination had also been caught by the discoveries of Captain Cook in the South Seas, just as more learned circles were taken with a new curiosity about natural history beyond Europe. The trend of awakening interest was heightened by the romantic movement. As the exotic in all forms came into vogue in Europe, what part of the world could be more exotic? Untouched and unfamiliar natural beauty met the new esthetic standard. The supposed "primitive simplicity" of "savage" life offered a much advertised contrast of the artificiality of Europe.

Enlightened travellers from Michel Adanson onward felt this lure of the tropics especially keenly. Once arrived in West Africa, they found what they were looking for. Henry Smeathman caught the mood of the times as he looked back on his three years of botanical work on the Banana Islands:

Pleasant scenes of vernal beauty, a tropical luxuriance, where fruits and flowers lavish their fragrance together in the same bough! There nature animates every embryo of life; and reigning in vegetable or animal perfection; perpetually glows in wild splendour and uncultivated maturity!

I contemplate the years I passed in that terrestrial Elysium, as the happiest of my life. The simple food, which my solitude usually afforded, was sweetened with rural labour; and my rest was not broken by those corroding cares and

1. For a recent and effective use of environmental xenophobia to create "atmosphere" see Graham Greene's novel, *The Heart of the Matter,* set in Freetown at the period of the Second World War.

perplexing fears, which pride and folly are ever creating in the ambitious emulations of populous communities.[2]

The dream of tropical wealth was much older, going back to the fabulous profits of the sixteenth-century spice trade, or to the gold and silver of New Spain and Peru. By the eighteenth century it centered on the South Atlantic System and the production of tropical staples. The very success of the West Indian plantations reinforced an early and serious European misconception about the wet tropics. When they first saw the exuberant growth of vegetation in the West Indies and coastal Brazil, European explorers thought they had encountered a new relationship between man and nature. Nature seemed to supply the necessities of life freely, and human labor was not needed. As Sir Walter Raleigh reported of the Orenoqueponi: "They never eat of any thing that is set or sowen; and as at home they use neither planting nor manurance, so when they come abroad, they refuse to eat of aught, but that which nature without labour bringest forth."[3]

Similar quotations about many parts of the tropical world could be strung out from the sixteenth century into the twentieth. By the eighteenth century a full-fledged myth of tropical exuberance had been created. In fact, some tropical soils could support very dense populations, even at existing levels of technology, but all tropical soils were not that good. The exuberance of tropical foliage was no true indication of possible agricultural wealth, and quick growth by no means released man from labor, even in the best of circumstances.[4] But appearance was more striking than reality, and eighteenth-century travellers or publicists described the Guinea Coast in rapturous terms. John Wesley believed it was "one of the most fruitful, as well as the most pleasant countries in the known world," a place where: "the soil is in general fertile, producing abundance of rice and roots. Indigo and cotton thrive without cultivation; fish is in great plenty; the flocks and herds are numerous and the tree loaden with fruit."[5]

Or, as Henry Smeathman reported in his famous description of

2. H. Smeathman to J. C. Lettsom, 19 October 1782, in J. C. Lettsom (Ed.), *The Works of John Fothergill, M.D.,* Rev. ed. (London, 1784), p. 577.

3. Quoted in H. N. Fairchild, *The Noble Savage* (New York, 1928), p. 21.

4. See Pierre Gourou, *The Tropical World* (London, 1953), pp. 13–24.

5. John Wesley, "Thoughts Upon Slavery" in *Works* (London, 1872), XI, 61. First published 1774.

Sierra Leone, "the woods and plains produce spontaneously great quantities of the most pleasant fruits and spices, from which may be made oils, marmalades, wines, perfumes, and other valuable articles, to supply the markets of Great Britain and Ireland."

And he continued: "Such are the mildness and fertility of the climate and country that a man possessed of a change of cloathing, a wood axe, a hoe, and a pocket knife, may soon place himself in an easy and comfortable situation. All the cloathing wanted is what decency requires; and it is not necessary to turn up the earth more than two or three inches, with a light hoe, in order to cultivate any kind of grain."[6]

Similar ecstatic reports figured in the works of almost every traveller to West Africa, and the witnesses before the Committee of Privy Council in 1789 told the same story of agricultural wealth.[7] The most obvious implication was perfectly clear. Britain at the dawn of the Industrial Revolution would need more tropical products, and West Africa could supply them in an endless stream, to the profit of those Englishmen who took part.

This implication was not the only one, nor the first to be drawn by the theorists of Europe. From the earliest times, exuberant vegetation of tropical America had seemed to confirm the medieval legend of an earthly paradise in the Fortunate Islands. Men who lived without labor ("strangers alike to luxury and toil," as William Roscoe called the Africans)[8] could hardly help creating a good society. Thus the legend of tropical exuberance lay behind many early reports of the "good savage" and led on to the "noble savage" of literature.[9]

Most eighteenth-century social theorists continued to believe that some intimate relationship existed between tropical vegetation and tropical society; but the paradisaic view of the earlier period gave way to a new interpretation, which was to dominate European thought about tropical environments for more than a century to come. The new view in typical form was laid down in 1770 by James Steuart as a law of tropical society: "If the soil be vastly rich, situated

6. Henry Smeathman, *Plan of a Settlement to be Made Near Sierra Leone* (London, 1786), pp. 8–9.

7. See especially John Matthews, *A Voyage to the River Sierra-Leone . . .* (London, 1788); Great Britain. Privy Council. *Report of the Lords of the Committee of Council for . . . Trade and Foreign Plantations . . . Concerning the Present State of Trade to Africa, and Particularly the Trade in Slaves . . .* (London, 1789), Part I, Produce.

8. William Roscoe, *The Wrongs of Africa, a Poem* (London, 1787), p. 9.

9. See Fairchild, *Noble Savage*, pp. 1–22.

in a warm climate, and naturally watered, the productions of the earth will be almost spontaneous: this will make the inhabitants lazy. Laziness is the greatest of all obstacles to labour and industry. Manufactures will never flourish here. . . . It is in climates less favoured by nature, and where the soil produces to those only who labour, and in proportion to the industry of every one, where we may expect to find great multitudes."[10]

Thus tropical exuberance was a curse rather than a blessing. Far from causing the nobility of the noble savage, it caused his savagery; and his savagery was far from good.[11] The crucial change was the value set on labor. In the Bible man had been cursed and driven from the Garden of Eden to earn his bread by the sweat of his brow (Genesis 3:19). In this view, as in that of sixteenth-century Europe, work was an unpleasant necessity. Eighteenth-century theorists, however, began to see labor as good in itself, even as the mother of civilization and of all progress.

Max Weber and others have traced a similar attitude to the influence of the Protestant ethic and especially to the Calvinist form of Protestantism. It is therefore of some interest that the proposition was stated with special emphasis, but without theological reference, by the Scottish moral philosophers and the Evangelicals in England. Both these groups had a background of Calvinist influence. Economic thought in the later eighteenth century also stressed the value of labor, and the tendency led in time to the central role of the labor theory of value in classical economics. All of these cross-currents, plus the less explicit sense of a need for disciplined and regular wage labor in the new British industries, played their role in producing, by the 1790's, an attitude that was virtually universal. In its most simple form it could be expressed as an equation: labor equals civilization.

The discussion of tropical exuberance and its consequences was only one among a number of points where European social theorists

10. Sir James Denham Steuart, "An Inquiry into the Principles of Political Economy," (1770) in *The Works, Political, Metaphisical, and Chronological of the late Sir James Steuart* (London, 1804), I, 44.

11. See James Burnet, Lord Monboddo, *The Origin and Progress of Language,* 8 vols. (Edinburgh, 1773–1792), I, 252; *Candid Reflections Upon the Judgement Lately Awarded by the Court of King's Bench in Westminster-Hall, On What is Commonly Called the Negro-Cause, By a Planter* (London, 1772), pp. 64–65; Robert Norris, *Memoirs of the Reign of Bossa Ahadee, King of Dahomey* (London, 1789), pp. 145–47; and works cited in note 7 above.

were beginning to think more broadly about the world beyond Europe. The proper study of mankind, especially in the wide ranging reports of the travellers, could take in all kinds of men, and it could be approached from a variety of different backgrounds. There was still no specialized body of ethnological theory, except within the broad realm of moral philosophy. Before the days of ethnographic field work, armchair speculations were open to any educated man who cared to try his hand at amateur scholarship. Some began, as the enlightened travellers in West Africa had commonly done, searching for diversity in human culture through the study of "primitive peoples." Others, like Sir James Mackintosh at the end of the century, sought the least denominator common to all mankind: "under the most fantastic multitude of usages and rites which have prevailed among men, the same fundamental, comprehensive truths, the sacred master-principles which are the guardians of human society, recognized and revered (with few and slight exceptions) by every nation on earth. . . ."[12]

In either case, whether diversity or uniformity was the goal, important subsidiary questions followed in very short order—questions of environmental influence on human culture, the possibility and mode of cultural diffusion, and the nature of human progress. Before they were finished, the eighteenth-century philosophers had raised and given rudimentary answers to many of the problems that still concern social scientists. Most of these discussions were not directly concerned with African affairs, but they set the patterns of British thought. Hence they gave the starting point for any consideration of tropical life.

One of the most common assumptions even then was to hold that non-Western civilizations represented earlier stages in human progress, frozen, as it were, while the European world advanced. If so, it might be possible to explore the earlier stages of man by taking the overseas world as a kind of living museum of human cultures. Some eighteenth-century writers, like Jean Jacques Rousseau in his *Origins of Inequality,* were willing enough to describe the earliest ages of human history without benefit of empirical data, but the more common course was to begin with deductive reason, then to add examples from a convenient compendium like the *Universal History.*

12. Sir James Mackintosh, *A Discourse on the Study of the Law of Nature and Nations* (London, 1799), p. 27.

The most active British theorists in this line of effort were the Scottish moral philosophers. Like their counterparts in England or on the Continent, they sketched the outlines of human history as a story of progress, passing through a series of stages. The number of stages might vary from one philosopher to another, but the nature of the schema was remarkably consistent. The Scottish school were especially attached to the economic system as the principal touch-stone for assessing the stage reached by any society.

Among a welter of variants, the common tendency is well repre-sented by John Millar's influential four-stage pattern. For Millar, the earliest men were hunters and gatherers, who moved on to the second stage of pastoralism. From there, they rose to settled farming, and finally to the fourth level of commerce and manufacture. These four stages were thought to parallel a similar four stages of political organization from (1) the family alone, to (2) the tribe or village of several families, to (3) the federation of smaller units or the imposition of a feudal control from above, and on to (4) the further elaboration of the modern stage. Millar, more than others, laid spe-cial stress on the position of women as an additional guide to the level reached by a society. The course of progress in this respect began with women merely as servants, reduced to this status by the greater physical strength of men. It then passed through a series of gradual improvements until, at the fourth stage, women were espe-cially valued for their alleged special ability to acquire the arts and graces.[13]

Others might arrange the stages in slightly different ways, some-times having only three instead of four. In this case, savagery, bar-barism, and civilization could be technical terms for a three-part schema, but the progression of hunting, pastoral, agricultural, and commercial was the normal pattern. African societies did not fare badly by this scheme of things. They were mainly agricultural rather than hunting or pastoral peoples. Thus they were near the top and generally assessed as "barbarous" rather than "savage" in a technical sense.[14]

---

13. John Millar, *Observations Concerning the Distinction of Ranks in Society* (London, 1771). For the Scottish moral philosophers see Gladys Bryson, *Man and Society: The Scottish Inquiry of the Eighteenth Century* (Princeton, 1945); W. C. Lehman, *John Millar of Glasgow* (Cambridge, 1960).

14. See, for example, Montesquieu, *The Spirit of Laws,* 2 vols. (New York, 1949), Bk. XXI, pt. 2. First published 1748.

But the establishment of a pattern and series of stages for advancement was only a preliminary step. The crucial question was to explain
why some societies advanced more rapidly, while others seemed relatively static. One answer was implicit in Steuart's analysis: the lag in
tropical social development came from the environment, but indirectly so, out of laziness by way of tropical exuberance. West African
"barbarism" was most often explained in this way, but other and
more direct environmental explanations were also popular. Among
these, Montesquieu's belief that climate acts directly on the human
psyche was most influential. Montesquieu said little about West
Africa, being specifically concerned with "national character" within
Europe; but his theory that northerners were generally more active in
mind and body, while southerners were more sensitive in soul and
spirit, had broader possibilities and echoed an ancient belief.[15]

It was very widely spread by the 1780's and repeated on every
side, even being reported back by visitors to the tropics as a piece of
empirical information. Dr. Benjamin Mosely, for example, who practiced medicine for twelve years in the West Indies, claimed that Europeans "degenerated" after a long residence in that part of the world,
if not in actual mental powers at least in mental activity. "There is,
in the inhabitants of hot climates, unless present sickness has an absolute control over the body, a promptitude and bias to pleasure, and
an alienation from serious thought and deep reflection. The brilliancy
of the skies, and the levity of the atmosphere, conspire to influence
the nerves against philosophy and her frigid tenets, and forbids their
practice among the children of the sun."[16]

If this were the result for a people of northern origin, it was natural to use Montesquieu's ideas even more systematically to explain
human societies native to the tropics. Adam Ferguson and especially
William Falconer brought non-European societies more decidedly into
the picture. In Falconer's view, both the far north and far south
produce unpleasant extremes. Northerners are insensitive, but southerners are overly passionate. Northerners are too kind, while southerners are vindictive. Northerners are brave to a fault, while southerners are timid. Northerners are active, while southerners are indolent. In each case, the northern quality was described in terms a
little less pejorative than the southern equivalent. The conclusion is

15. Montesquieu, *The Spirit of Laws,* Bk. XIV, pts. 1-3.
16. Benjamin Mosely, *A Treatise on Tropical Diseases; and on the Climate of the
West Indies* (London, 1787), p. 48.

easy to foresee. In Falconer's opinion, the best possible balance of human qualities is to be found near the northern edge of the temperate zone—in short, in Britain.[17]

Social theories of direct environmentalism, whether in the version of Montesquieu, Falconer, or Ferguson, were not very favorable to the prospects of a rapid African advance toward "civilization." Whatever the Africans' other faults or virtues, they were, for the environmentalists, timid, lazy, oversensitive, and oversexed. But the possibility remained that these faults could be overcome. In their specific discussions of West Africa, Falconer and Ferguson allowed for the possible influence of diet, soil, and location. Montesquieu explained the lag in African development by the lack of easy commercial contact across the Sahara: Africa had been cut off from the main trade routes of the Eurasian land mass, but this failing could presumably be remedied by introducing sea-borne trade.[18]

Opposition to direct environmentalism came principally from the polygenists, and especially from the white West Indians. As a tropical people themselves, they resented the implication that they were cowardly (though Bryan Edwards of Jamaica admitted that his fellow West Indians did tend to be lazy). More important still, they preferred to view the "faults" of African society as the congenital faults of the African race as such. Thus the racial and environmental explanations of African "backwardness" were to some extent rivals, though the two views might be squared in the light of recent scientific knowledge.[19]

The most enterprising effort in this direction was made by Alexander Wilson, who was impressed by Priestley's recent chemical investigations. He took up the discovery that respiration and combustion had much the same chemistry, pointing out that animal respiration produced "phlogiston," the material or principle of fire. Living vegetable matter, in turn, needed "phlogistonated air" in order to survive, while at the same time it purified the air for reuse by ani-

17. W. Falconer, *Remarks on the Influence of Climate* . . . (London, 1781), especially pp. 6–24.

18. Montesquieu, *The Spirit of Laws*, Bk. XXI, pt. 2; Falconer, *Influence of Climate;* Adam Ferguson, *An Essay on the History of Civil Society* (Edinburgh, 1767), pp. 171, 177.

19. Edward Long, *History of Jamaica*, 3 vols. (London, 1774), II, 277; Bryan Edwards, *The History, Civil and Commercial, of the British Colonies in the West Indies,* 2nd ed., 2 vols. (London, 1794), II, 6–15; David Hume, "Of National Character," *The Philosophical Works of David Hume,* 4 vols. (London, 1898), III, 249 and 252 n.

mals. The decomposition of organic bodies was also thought to be a source of phlogiston, while water had the capacity to absorb it.[20]

With these elementary "facts" as a starting point, it seemed obvious that greater heat in the tropics speeded the process of decomposition, thus producing highly phlogistonated air. As the air approached the point of saturation with phlogiston, it was less able to absorb phlogiston produced by human respiration. Europeans and others unaccustomed to the tropics were therefore unable to throw off enough phlogiston, while Negroes and other tropical peoples had acquired the ability to get rid of phlogiston through more profuse perspiration. But they paid a price for their physical adjustment. According to Wilson, this price was a weaker power of the mind plus an extreme tendency to indolence. Therefore, no high civilization had ever occurred, nor was one possible, in any part of the tropical world, though the agricultural riches of the tropics were themselves a result of the same highly phlogistonated air that made tropical civilization impossible.

The more pessimistic views of Africa's future came from "natural philosophy," while "moral philosophy" held out a little hope. The most optimistic of all was the view that African faults were merely institutional failings. Henry Smeathman, for example, admitted that Africans were "indolent," but added:

Whatever may be said of the effects which local situation and extremes of heat and cold have on the human body, it will probably be found hereafter, that all men in regard to their dispositions and conduct in life are formed more on artificial than natural causes, by the laws which impel and the education which trains them, in short by custom and habit. A very singular jurisprudence, and customs, which in some respect are wise, but in this pernicious, operate [at Sierra Leone] like enchantment upon the inhabitants of this part of the globe, and till the charm is broken, must continue to keep them in indigence, indolence, and contempt.[21]

He went on to say that the hold of custom discourged enterprise,

20. A. Wilson, *Some Observations Relative to the Influence of Climate on Vegetable and Animal Bodies* (London, 1780). Wilson's theory of the origin of the Negro race seems to be derived from the similar theory published by Kant in 1775, and amplified in 1785. Kant, however, did not draw out the implications about racial inferiority which Wilson suggests, and both were decisively contradicted by Lavoisier's discovery of oxygen, announced in 1777, and amplified in 1783. (See A. O. Lovejoy, "Kant and Evolution," in B. Glass and others, *Forerunners of Darwin, 1745–1859* [Baltimore, 1959], pp. 186–87.)

21. Smeathman to Knowles, 21 July 1783, printed in *New Jerusalem Magazine*, I, 286 (1790).

innovation, and reform, but that these weaknesses could be corrected by a new form of government and better education.

Each of the various theories about the cause of African "backwardness" implied its own form of cure. Those who believed African indolence came directly or indirectly from the climate, or from basic racial endowment, already had an answer. Their remedy was the slave trade itself, which transported the "indolent" Africans to the West Indies. They could be put to work there under coercion, which alone makes possible a productive tropical society.[22] The idea occurs again and again in the defense of the slave trade and later of slavery: they were illicit in temperate regions, but necessary in the tropics.

In answer, the humanitarians came increasingly to the defense of African society, showing first that its faults were not insuperable and, second, that the slave trade itself was to blame. Wilberforce argued in Parliament that the Africans could hardly be very lazy, seeing the efforts they made to catch one another for the slave trade. Their activities were merely misdirected.[23] Thomas Clarkson made a large collection of African products. It included some twenty polished specimens of tropical woods, pepper, ivory, musk, gum, spices, tobacco, indigo, food crops, and a further selection of manufactured articles such as cotton cloth, pottery, iron, and leather work. He carried this display around to government committees, "that they might really know what Africa was capable of affording instead of the Slave-trade, and that they might make a proper estimate of the genius and talents of the natives."[24]

The humanitarian panacea for improving Africa grew partly from the attack on the slave trade. If the trade were to blame for African barbarism, its abolition would be the first step in bringing about the cure. The humanitarians' further case rested on existing social theory. If the Africans had reached the "agricultural stage," then commerce was the missing element to raise them another step. If, as Montesquieu had suggested, lack of commerce held Africa back, then the introduction of commerce could push her forward. Admiration of commercial life had grown with the expansion of British trade. Most

22. *Candid Reflections* . . . , pp. 64–65; Wilson, *Observations on Climate*, pp. 278–80.
23. William Wilberforce, Commons, 12 May 1789, *Parliamentary Register*, XXVI, 148.
24. Thomas Clarkson, *History of the Rise, Progress, and Accomplishment of the Abolition of the African Slave Trade by the British Parliament*, 2 vols. (London, 1808), II, 13–16.

writers took for granted the superiority of a commercial society, and William Falconer explained in detail why they were right in doing so. He held that commerce not only encourages the desirable qualities of frugality, peacefulness, justice, and honesty; it also improves the mind: "A commercial life may, in several respects, be accounted favorable to the intellectual faculties. Thus it tends to exercise, and consequently to improve, the memory; it introduces a methodic arrangement into the business of life, which facilitates it greatly, by instructing us to apply our abilities separately to their proper purposes. Commerce also enlarges the ideas, teaches nations their true interests, and is a cure for the most pernicious prejudices."[25]

Against this background, it was only natural to call for the substitution of "legitimate commerce" in place of the slave trade. Wilberforce in particular publicized legitimate commerce as the hope of Africa. What he had in mind was quite clearly a system of enterprise largely in African hands, at least in its African aspect. The European traders would come to Africa with their manufactures and take off the African raw materials, much as the slave traders in the past had worked with and through the enterprise of African middlemen. Such a system would not only help Africa. As Wilberforce told the House of Commons, "we shall find the rectitude of our conduct rewarded, by the benefits of a regular and growing commerce."[26] Legitimate traders, in short, would reap the reward for their morality in the form of higher profits. This in turn rested on a tacit assumption of many Calvinists and Evangelicals—that virtue would be rewarded, both in this world and the next.

Others saw African economic development in terms of temporal rewards alone. It required no feat of economic reasoning to see that the South Atlantic System was to some extent wasteful. It carried labor to the American tropics, whereas, in the light of tropical exuberance in Africa, it might be employed just as effectively at home. As early as the 1680's, the Royal Africa Company had experimented with indigo plantations on Bance Island in the Sierra Leone River, and corn for the supply of slave ships became a regular export of the Gold Coast at about the same period. From the middle of the eighteenth century, suggestions for still more extensive development of

25. Falconer, Influence of Climate, p. 415.
26. William Wilberforce, Commons, 12 May 1789, Parliamentary Register, XXVI, 150. K. G. Davies, The Royal African Company (London, 1957), pp. 220–21 and 228.

African agriculture began to appear. Malachy Postlethwayt became a kind of apostle for the relocation of British enterprise in the tropics. In Africa, he argued: "the fruitful soil lies waste, a very extended country, pleasant vallies, banks of the fine rivers, spacious plains, capable of cultivation to unspeakable benefit, in all probability remain, fallow and unnoticed: Why do not the *Europeans* enclose such lands for cultivation, as by their nature and situation appear proper for beneficial production?"[27]

Postlethwayt's suggestions were significantly different from those put forward by the advocates of legitimate trade. Where the legitimate traders merely wanted to substitute one kind of commerce for another, keeping the basic forms of African commercial organization, Postelthwayt looked to the more drastic innovation of setting Europeans ashore in West Africa in a managerial capacity. They would then be able to apply the considerable European skill and experience in tropical agriculture.

During their centuries of activity in the West Indies, the English had developed the production of certain tropical crops to a high point of efficiency. Especially in the major staples of sugar and coffee they were technologically well ahead of the West Africans, and they could call on a considerable body of published technical literature, as well as the practical knowledge of the West Indian planters. Among the several manuals on sugar or coffee planting, James Granger produced something of a tour de force in 1764 in the form of a planter's guide entirely in verse, and Labourie's *Coffee Planter of Saint Domingo* outlined a technique so developed that it was still in use into the twentieth century.[28]

But these specialized skills also had their limitations. They had been developed mainly in the West Indies and in the light of West Indian conditions. They were not necessarily transferable to the different soils and different plants of the African tropics. Next to the misjudgment of tropical exuberance, perhaps the most serious and common mistake of eighteenth-century European thought about the

27. M. Postlethwayt, *The Importance of the African Expedition Considered* . . . (London, 1758), p. 93. See also, "Africa" in his *Universal Dictionary of Trade,* 2 vols. (London, 1774) and Postlethwayt, *The National and Private Advantages of the African Trade Considered* (London, 1746).

28. J. Grainger, *The Sugar Cane* (London, 1764); P. J. Labourie, *The Coffee Planter of Saint Domingo* (London, 1798). For further references to this literature see L. J. Ragatz, *A Guide to the Study of British Caribbean History, 1763–1834* (Washington, 1932), pp. 239–338.

possibilities of African agriculture was to see West Africa as potentially a second and larger West Indies.

Tropical medicine, however, was far more important than tropical agriculture as an essential technique for the mastery of the African tropics. West African mortality figures were not widely publicized or given statistical precision, but the region's general reputation for having a "deadly climate" rested on a basis in fact. Somewhere between 25 and 75 per cent of any group of Europeans newly arrived on the Coast died within the first year. Thereafter, the death rate was much less, perhaps on the order of 10 per cent per annum, but still substantial. Any European activity demanded a price in European lives that was not only intrinsically high, but considerably higher than the cost of similar activity in the West Indies or South Asia. Slightly later calculations of military mortality over twenty years show a loss of 483 per thousand mean strength among European troops in West Africa, against only 78.5 per thousand in the West Indies. Civilian life insurance premiums charged by British firms for different tropical regions tell a similar story: European mortality was roughly four times as high in West Africa as it was in India or the West Indies.[29] Even though these facts were not emphasized, nor even quantitatively understood at the time, they suggest a perfectly valid reason for maintaining the South Atlantic System and one of the probable reasons for establishing it in the first place.

The facts of tropical mortality were not, however, something the Europeans accepted as beyond their control. Their study of tropical medicine went back to the first expansion into the tropical world. By the middle of the seventeenth century, there were important medical studies by Garcia da Orta based on Goa, Nicholas Monardes on the American tropics, and Bontius on Southeast Asia. Further medical studies followed, especially in Britain where the problem of tropical survival took on military implications during the eighteenth-century wars for empire.

All of these works were solidly set in the theoretical framework of medicine inherited from classical antiquity, re-expressed in the eighteenth-century tendency to build medical systems. The essence of any of these systems was to see all pathological conditions as the result of some single cause. Thus the eighteenth-century re-expression

29. PP, 1837–38, xl (138), p. 5; PP, 1840, xxx [C. 228], p. 7; North British Insurance Office to Macgregor Laird, 27 June 1842, in PP, 1842, xi (551), p. 585.

of the classical humoral pathology considered all disease to be the result of an imbalance or impurity of the bodily fluids. Treatment therefore aimed at readjusting the liquid balance by bleeding, purging, or some other general treatment. A second kind of system concentrated instead on the "tone" of the nervous system. In this case the cure consisted of stimulating or relieving tensions. Thus, if the body were "overstimulated" by heat, diet, or mental exertion, stimulation could be reduced by bleeding, purging, or tonics of various kinds. In either case, the treatment was much the same.[30]

By any modern standard, the whole of medical theory was completely erroneous, but improvements in medical practice were possible none the less. Critical standards of observation were improving gradually throughout the eighteenth century, following the tradition of Thomas Sydenham (1634–1689). The clinical description of tropical disease was increasingly accurate, and any of the systems allowed a good deal of latitude to the skill and knowledge of the individual practitioner. Warfare in the tropics gave many European doctors a field training that would otherwise have been impossible, and this experience was passed on through a growing body of literature.[31] By the 1780's the most authoritative summary of British tropical medicine was the work of James Lind (1716–1794), who had served on the Guinea coast as a naval surgeon. He is better known today for his *Treatise on Scurvy* (1754); but his *Diseases of Hot Climates* was equally important in its own time, passing through five editions between 1768 and 1808.[32]

When it came to the specific problems of West Africa, the medical

30. R. H. Shryock, "Nineteenth Century Medicine: Scientific Aspects," *Journal of World History,* III, 881–82 (1957); T. Trotter, *Medica Nautica,* 3 vols. (London, 1797–1803), I, 334–44.

31. The following may be considered representative of the literature as a whole: John Atkins, *Navy Surgeon* . . . , (London, 1734); J. Huxham, *An Essay on Fevers* (London, 1750); Sir John Pringle, *Observations on the Diseases of the Army in Camp and Garrison* (London, 1752); W. Hillary, *Observations on the Changes of the Air and the Concomitant Epidemical Diseases in the Island of Barbados,* 2nd ed. (London, 1766); C. Bisset, *Medical Essays and Observations* (Newcastle-upon-Tyne, 1766); Philippe Fermin, *Traité des maladies les plus frequent à Surinam* . . . (Masstricht, 1764); James Lind, *Essay on the Diseases Incidental to Europeans in Hot Countries* (London, 1768); L. Rouppe, *Observations on Diseases Incidental to Seamen* (London, 1772); J. P. Schotte, *A Treatise on Synochus Atrabiliosa, A Contagious Fever which Raged in Senegal in the Year 1778* (London, 1782); B. Mosely, *A Treatise on Tropical Diseases; And on the Climate of the West Indies* (London, 1787).

32. For Lind's career and contribution, and for naval medicine in general during this period, see: C. Lloyd and J. L. S. Coulter, *Medicine and the Navy 1200–1900. Volume III, 1714–1815* (Edinburgh and London, 1961).

men of the eighteenth cenutry concentrated their attention on "fevers." Malaria, yellow fever, typhus, typhoid, and minor fevers like dengue were all present, but the undifferentiated "fevers" of the Coast were in fact mostly malaria. Virtually the whole of West Africa was and is still an extremely favorable environment for the mosquitoes, *Anopheles gambiae* and *Anopheles funestus*. Both are among the most effective vectors for carrying plasmodial parasites from one individual to another, and their presence is the most important reason why mortality in West Africa was high compared with other tropical areas. *Plasmodium falciparum,* the prevalent West African parasite, is also especially dangerous, since it often kills in the first attack, while the *P. vivax* of the West Indies is more often enervating than fatal.

Even today West Africa is classified as a hyperendemic area for *P. falciparum.* The chance of an individual living there as long as a year with out receiving an infective mosquito bite is negligible. In some areas the average number of infective bites may range upward to one hundred or more. This fact implies different conditions for different groups of people. For the local population, a child is normally infected shortly after birth. During the first years of life it fights a perilous struggle with the parasites, and the rate of infestation is close to 100 per cent of the population under five years of age. Infant mortality from this cause is extremely high, but those who survive attain an apparent immunity in later life. This immunity, however, is not completely effective, either against other kinds of malaria or even against other strains of *P. falciparum.* It can also decline unless the individual is reinfected at frequent intervals. But, if the rate of reinfection is high, there will be no clinical symptoms of the disease; and even if the rate of reinfection drops, the clinical symptoms will rarely be more serious than chills and a slight fever. An absence of several years spent in a non-malarial area, however, may weaken or even destroy the immunity.[33]

Europeans coming to West Africa for the first time had no such

33. A distinction is sometimes made between holoendemic areas, where the rate of reinfestation is so great that adults rarely show clinical symptoms, and hyperendemic areas, where symptoms are more frequent. For historical discussion, this distinction is too fine to be useful, and the term hyperendemic will be used for all areas of high malarial infestation. For recent studies of malariology in West Africa see M. F. Boyd (Ed.), *Malariology,* 2 vols. (Philadelphia, 1949) ; F. B. Livingstone, "Anthropological Influences of Sickle Cell Genes in West Africa," *American Anthropologist,* LX, 533–62 (June, 1958); M. J. Colbourne and F. N. Wright, "Malaria in the Gold Coast," *West African Medical Journal,* IV, 3–17, 161–74 (1955), and works there cited.

immunity, even though malaria was endemic in some parts of the
Mediterranean basin and in the fen country of England itself. In
Europe or the West Indies they were accustomed to other types of
plasmodia, or to other strains of *P. falciparum* which gave little or
no protection in West Africa. Thus they paid the same kind of price
in adult mortality that African populations paid in infant mortality.
After a few years on the Coast, Europeans too acquired an apparent
immunity, perhaps not quite so effective as the childhood immunity
of the Africans, but sufficient to establish a pattern for newcomers—
either a speedy death, or else a reasonable chance of survival over
years or decades.

This pattern of disease can be seen clearly in retrospect from the
eighteenth-century reports, but it was not so clearly perceived at the
time. Neither was the disease itself well understood, though Europeans had been familiar enough with their own kind of malaria for
millennia. It was described by Hippocrates, who distinguished the
different types according to periodicity, dividing them into quotidian,
tertian, and quatran varieties. The enlarged spleen, typical of chronic
malaria, was also known to the ancients, and it was commonly associated with marshes and stagnant water.[34] All of this was substantially correct observation, but the problem came from another direction. European pathology still confused the disease and the symptoms. Thus "fever" was thought of as a generic term for a pathological condition. Lind defined it as "an indisposition of the body, at-
tended commonly with an increase of its heat, a thirst, often a head-
ache, and oftener a remarkable quietness of the pulse; or at least a
great change from its natural state; accompanied, for the most part,
with other symptoms of distress; and which in a few days, will certainly terminate, either in recovery, in a remission, or the death of
the patient."[35]

This description would cover not only malaria, but a fair proportion of the other ailments known to man. Sub-classification was therefore necessary, and it took the direction of describing the symptoms
with greater accuracy. The ancient Greek classification was still one
of the most common, dividing fevers roughly according to the apparent degree and duration of the patient's increased body temperature. There were *ephemera,* or fevers lasting less than twenty-four

34. P. F. Russell, *Man's Mastery of Malaria* (London, 1955), pp. 7–8.
35. Lind, *Diseases in Hot Countries,* pp. 17–18.

hours; *synochus non putris,* or a mild continual fever; *synochus putris,* or a more critical fever; and *causus,* a very high fever which commonly killed the patient in the third or fourth day. (Serious fevers were called putrid because of the association between heat and decay.)

A second form of classification was more suitable for tropical fevers, since it stressed the periodic peaks of high temperature typical of malaria. Lind used this system, with a three-fold distinction between continual fevers, remitting fevers which were irregular in their periodicity and might leave some clinical symptoms during remissions, and intermitting fevers which returned regularly. The intermitting fevers were further sub-divided into the old classes of quotidian, tertian, and the like. Any of the three major classes could be bilious or non-bilious, mild or malignant.[36]

Variants of this classification were used throughout the nineteenth century, and the confusion they caused was not merely a question of terminology. Malaria could be fitted into the scheme at several points. It was, of course, intermittent, but it was also remittent in the sense that the series of closely spaced peaks of fever would die away, only to return weeks or months later without subsequent reinfection. It might also appear to be bilious, on account of jaundice and vomiting which sometimes accompanies the disease, or non-bilious in its milder forms. Thus even a single type of malaria. like *Plasmodium falciparum* would be identified as two or three different kinds of fever, each of which might well be treated in a different manner. In addition, typhus and even typhoid fever could easily be mistaken for malaria, though in West Africa the most serious confusion occurred between malaria and yellow fever.

Yellow fever was also common on the Coast, but its behavior and social consequences were very different. Its vector is another mosquito, *Aedes aegypti,* which ultimately turned out to be more easily controlled than *Anopheles gambiae.* Instead of giving the victim a long struggle that might result in apparent immunity, the disease either kills within five to seven days or allows the victim a rapid recovery followed by life-long and complete immunity to further attacks. Once immune, the victim cannot even serve as an intermediate host for the parasite. Since the disease is also much less serious for

36. Rouppe, *Diseases Incidental to Seamen, passim;* Lind, *Diseases in Hot Countries,* pp. 10–14.

children than for adults, it was possible for an entire tropical population to acquire immunity in childhood. When this happened, the disease might die out for a time, even though the vector was still present. Thus, among a stable population an entire generation of non-
immunes might grow up and be subject to a devastating epidemic if
the parasite was reintroduced from the outside. This had already happened several times in the medical history of the West Indies, but in
West Africa it appears that infection of the African population, and
hence its immunity, was maintained at most times. Non-immune
strangers, however, were extremely susceptible to the parasite normally present among the African children. The disease would appear
periodically as an epidemic passing rapidly among the European population before it died out again to await the arrival of a new group
of non-immunes from Europe. The chance appearance of these epidemics accounts for a great deal of variability in European mortality
rates in West Africa.[37]

Like malaria, yellow fever was classified by medical men along
with the other fevers, but certain occurrences were recognized as a
specific type of fever and the name, yellow fever, was already in use.
Both diagnoses and terminology were nevertheless extremely confused. It was very easy to mistake yellow fever not only for malaria
but also for scurvy, the relatively harmless dengue fever, and a number of other diseases. Very commonly, both yellow fever and some
forms of malaria were called "bilious remittent fever, even though
the epidemic quality of the former was already recognized and a good
clinical description of the disease in West Africa was published by
Schotte in 1778. In this case the terminology was even further confused by Schotte's insistence on calling yellow fever *Synochus atrabiliosa* and reserving the name "yellow fever" for what is now called
malaria.[38] It followed from both the confusions of clinical description and terminology, and from the prevalent systems of one-
cause pathology, that any and all of these various fevers were attributed to the same set of causes.

In seeking the cause of fevers, eighteenth-century medical men had
two salient facts on which all were agreed. First, they "knew" that
men came down with fevers more readily in wet or marshy areas

37. Henry H. Scott, *A History of Tropical Medicine,* 2 vols. (London, 1939), I,
322–23; P. M. Ashburn, *The Ranks of Death* (New York, 1947), pp. 135–36.
38. Schotte, *Synochus Atrabiliosa, passim.*

than in dry areas. This point was reasonably accurate for most malarial areas, since most mosquitos breed in marshes. It was not especially the case for West Africa, however, since *A. gambiae* can breed in any tiny pool or puddle and was thus found virtually everywhere and not simply near swamps.

Second, they knew that men came down with fevers more readily in the tropics than they did in Europe. This point was quite accurate, but it led to a serious and persistent confusion. Since the prevalence of disease altered with the climate, the climate was thought to be in some way the cause of the disease. Thus, the expression, "a bad climate" came to mean a place where the mortality rates were high, and not necessarily a place where it was physically uncomfortable to live. At the same time, talk of a "bad climate" between the tropics conjured up a picture of burning heat and great physical discomfort. Some travellers tried to correct the impression. Long pointed out, quite correctly, that summer in Jamaica is not so hot as summer in New York, and others made the same point in regard to West Africa; but the false impression of West Africa as a kind of humid oven beyond all experience in temperate lands lived on.[39] From the start, then, the visual picture of West Africa in the mind of the British non-traveller was false, but it colored a great deal of British thinking about West Africa.

In the serious medical works, the nature of climatic influence was more precisely considered. Marshes were thought to be the point of origin for some form of poison which found its way into the air. For some authorities the poison came from water vapor itself. For others, it was a product of the soil or of wet vegetation. Thus one emphasized the dangerous dampness of tropical air, or its saturation with phlogiston, while another would stress the stink of the mangrove swamps, and still a third the "thickness" of tropical air compared with the air of England. Atkins had even explained that the "thick" air of the African coast was the very factor that kept Guinea from being unpleasantly hot, in spite of its equatorial location.[40]

Most authorities tried to associate the poison and the climate by considering malarial poison an "exciting cause" of fevers, after the body had already been prepared by "predisposing causes." These

39. Atkins, *Navy Surgeon*, p. 2; Lind, *Diseases in Hot Countries*, p. 46; Long, *Jamaica*, I, 363–75.
40. Atkins, *Navy Surgeon*, p. 2.

were, of course, the heat and humidity of the tropics, acting according to one of the more popular medical systems, or a combination of several. Ludovicus Rouppe's explanation of heat as a predisposing cause of disease illustrates the line of argument.

> It is a physical truth that heat rarifies all bodies, excepting some few not necessarily to be mentioned here; by getting into their most secret recesses, it separates the parts from their mutual contact, and increases their porosity, whence we daily observe that bodies increase by heat, and decrease by cold; but by this diminishing and cohesion of the parts, it not only relaxes the solid parts of our body, and weakens them, but expands the fluids and increases their compass; it diminishes the force of cohesion of the globules, by which means they become looser and more slippery; but when it proceeds to act upon the moist parts of the body, they resolve into vapours, and the intestine motion is greater, by which means the thinner parts of the blood are too much thrown off, and the glutinous part which nourishes the body is too much divided and dissipated.[41]

Others would have agreed with the main points of this analysis, that heat relaxes the "animal fibres" and thins the blood.[42] The belief led naturally to a vital concern with the liquids entering and leaving the body—especially with the intake of wine and spirits and the output of perspiration. This was a crucial point. Even in England perspiration brought on by hard exercise might well be the cause of ephemeral fevers. That, at least, was the obvious suggestion of the humoral pathology. In the tropics, fevers were empirically associated with heat. Heat was an obvious cause of a changed liquid balance through perspiration. Thus, if liquid balance was the key, then perspiration was also the key to the understanding of tropical fevers, and Alexander Wilson merely echoed the common understanding in stressing perspiration in his phlogiston theory.[43]

From this point, speculation could lead out in several directions. One possibility was to show the special dangers of quick change in temperature. Mosely, for example, held that the body could become accustomed to heat by increasing the quantity of perspiration, but then it became especially sensitive to "the slightest impression from cold," and "cold is the cause of almost all diseases of hot climates."[44]

41. Rouppe, *Diseases Incidental to Seamen*, p. 382.
42. See, for example, Hillary, *Changes of the Air*, p. vii.
43. Huxham, *Fevers*, pp. 2–4; Rouppe, *Diseases Incidental to Seamen*, pp. 371–72, 390–91; Hillary, *Changes in the Air*, p. 146.
44. Mosely, *Tropical Diseases*, pp. 38–47. See also Bisset, *Medical Essays*, p. 38.

Another principal concern was physical exercise, since this too increased perspiration. Still another was the question of drink.

All of these could be referred back to the humoral theory, and they led in turn to a somewhat diverse set of rules for a healthy tropical life. The rules agreed in stressing the importance of perspiration, exercise, temperature change, and diet, but the specific recommendations varied greatly. Edward Long of Jamaica described the dangerous habits imported into that Island. "The European keeps late hours at night, lounges abed in the morning; gormandizing at dinner and supper on loads of flesh, fish, and fruit; loves poignant sauces; dilutes with ale, porter, punch, claret, and madeira, frequently jumbling all together; and continues this mode of living till, by constantly manuring his stomach with such a heterogeneous compost, he has laid the foundation for a plentiful crop of ailments."[45]

For Long, the safer course would be to drop these ways and take plenty of light exercise, bathe frequently, stay out of fogs and damp, especially in the evening, and keep a fire going or smoke tobacco in order to purify the air. The European should also keep himself psychologically fit by avoiding "strong passions," a way of preserving the proper tone of the nervous system. He should use spirits only moderately, properly aged rum being especially recommended. His clothes should be light in weight and color and loose fitting, and his diet should contain more vegetable and less animal food than it did at home.[46] Mosely gave another set of West Indian rules, recommending as little exercise as possible, the avoidance of cold baths, of all spirits, and especially of rum. Light wines and water were, however, permitted.[47]

Each authority thus had his own set of taboos—except James Lind, who showed that neither drinking water, nor diet, nor excesses of food and drink correlated very well with the pattern of fever. Fevers came seasonally, and when they came they struck down the most moderate of men along with the gluttons and drunkards.[48] While Lind was certainly correct in thinking that personal excesses could be nothing more than minor contributing causes of disease, he was

45. Long, *Jamaica*, I, 375.
46. Long, *Jamaica*, II, 505–70.
47. Mosely, *Tropical Diseases*, pp. 49–51. See also Schotte, *Synochus Atrabiliosa*, pp. 158–62 for another detailed code of conduct.
48. Lind, *Diseases in Hot Countries*, pp. 6–7.

not followed in this respect by later writers. It seems to have been a psychological necessity to have some set of rules for personal hygiene. Especially in the high-mortality posts like those in West Africa, to think that life and death were pure chance beyond human knowledge would have been intolerable. It was much more satisfying to believe the dead had broken one or another of a numerous and complex system of taboos.

A second set of rules for tropical conduct were topographical rather than personal, and they depended more heavily on actual experience and observation. The Europeans had already gained a certain amount of experience in trying to pick a healthy spot for a trading post or a settlement. By general agreement, high, dry places, exposed to the wind were preferred. Winds blowing off shore were more dangerous than sea breezes, presumably because they picked up moisture and "noxious vapours" from the land over which they passed. Marshes were, of course, dangerous, but if one had to live near them, it was better to live on the windward than the leeward side. Places where insects were common were also considered dangerous, and bush and forest were more dangerous than cleared and planted fields. Barbados' freedom from malaria was sometimes thought to be caused by its much greater degree of cultivation than other West Indian islands or the Guinea coast. Lind placed the greatest emphasis on following these rules and would have preferred never to let Europeans go ashore in West Africa if it could possibly be avoided. At the very least, they should stay away from the shore in the evening and early morning, and avoid the forest country during the rainy season.[49]

Most of these suggestions were based on experience in the Americas, but they could also be justified by reference to Alexander Wilson's phlogiston theory. Phlogiston, as a product of decay, was naturally produced most abundantly in swamps. It was carried by the winds; but, since water could absorb it, passage over water cleared the air. Islands and ships at sea were therefore relatively healthy. Cleared and cultivated lands were also safe, because living vegetation absorbed phlogiston in the presence of sunlight. In wooded country, however, the phlogiston produced by decay in the undergrowth was too great for the absorptive capacity of the sunny treetops. Cutting

49. Fermin, *Traité des maladies,* pp. 4–5; Bisset, *Medical Essays,* p. 11; Lind, *Diseases in Hot Countries,* pp. 51–52, 127–28, 132–42, and 159–63; Long, *Jamaica,* II, 506.

the tall trees would admit the sunlight and purify the air; and experimental proof was available in North America, where clearing and cultivation had been followed by the decline of fever.[50]

Both the rules of medical topography and the suggestion of clearing the brush in order to improve the climate were substantially correct for America, and they undoubtedly did reduce European mortality in North America, where the common vector was *Anopheles quadrimaculatus*. *A. gambiae*, however, would not have been appreciably disturbed by these changes. It breeds in small natural collections of water exposed to sunlight, especially small pits, drains, pools made by hoofprints, receding rivers, or rain water collections in small depressions. Its most important breeding places are those made by men, and it stays close to human habitation and outside of the deep forest.[51] Clearing and cultivation were therefore precisely the measures most likely to increase its numbers, but the ubiquity of infective mosquitos in West Africa made the situation there very different from North America. It is unlikely that any preventive measures, short of staying aboard ship well offshore, could have done more than delay the first attack of malaria by a few months.

The treatment of fevers in the later eighteenth century followed the indications of the medical systems, and it varied greatly with the individual practitioner. It generally consisted of some combination of bleeding, blisters, purges, hot or cold baths, diaphoretics, and chinchona bark, each of them "exhibited" at some particular phase of the disease. Of these treatments, chinchona bark (*Cortex peruvianus*) had real therapeutic value. Quinine and some of the other alkaloids derived from it have been until recently the best of the known antimalarial drugs. Even in its raw form, "the bark" could be effective, both for treatment of the disease and for prophylaxis against an expected attack. Taken regularly and in sufficient quantities it built up a resistance to plasmodial parasites that could greatly reduce both morbidity and mortality.

Thus a genuinely valuable form of treatment was known, and had been known in England since the 1670's. But it was not univer-

50. Wilson, *Observations on Climate*, pp. 21–22, 272–76.
51. E. H. Acherknecht, *Malaria in the Upper Mississippi Valley 1760–1900* (Baltimore, 1945), pp. 75–78; B. Rush, "An Inquiry into the Causes of the Increase of Bilious and Intermitting Fevers in Pennsylvania. Read in the American Philosophical Society, December 16, 1785," *Medical Inquiries and Observations*, II, 265–76 (1797); Boyd, *Malariology*, I, 380 and 458.

sally respected as a proper treatment for fevers, and its use went through phases of popularity followed by neglect. These shifts occurred because chinchona is a specific only for malaria, and malaria was not yet clearly distinguished from other fevers. A few failures would turn an experimenting physician back to the traditional purgatives and bleeding, with the occasional addition of mercury and arsenics. When negative results were widely reported by a prominent doctor, the drug could fall into general disuse for decades.[52]

In the 1780's chinchona bark was passing through a phase of relative popularity. The great Sydenham had disapproved of it in the seventeenth century, but in the middle of the eighteenth it received the backing of Fothergill and especially of Lind. Even then, it was not unanimously favored, and some doctors thought that heavy dosages might lead to madness.[53] Lind himself gave the bark along with emetics and blisters, though he advised against bleeding. In the general practice of tropical medicine, the bark seems to have been used widely by British doctors, but not in the way that would have been most effective. In particular, prophylactic treatment with bark was not common, though it was an occasional preventive measure among others of less value. Lind, for example, advised people in malarial areas to smoke tobacco, wear a bit of garlic or camphor sewed in a piece of linen, to take light laxatives regularly, and, "For further prevention, a wine glass of an infusion of the bark and orange peel in water, or what will prove more effectual, a table spoonful of a strong tincture of the bark, in spirits, diluted occasionally with water, may be taken every morning before breakfast."[54]

If this practice were regularly followed, it would certainly have been helpful, more or less so according to the quality of the bark available. Other variants, however, recommended prophylactic bark to be taken only at each change of the moon and before the full moon, a practice that lacked the special benefits of regular treatment.[55]

Eighteenth-century doctors also recognized that those who had lived for some time in the tropics were more resistant to disease than

52. Russell, *Man's Mastery of Malaria*, pp. 97–104.

53. J. Fothergill, *Works* . . . (London, 1781), pp. 268–69; Lind, *Diseases in Hot Countries, passim,* esp. pp. 38 and 55–67; Hillary, *Changes of the Air,* pp. 156–64; Mosely, *Tropical Diseases,* pp. 115–18, 416–56.

54. Lind, *Diseases in Hot Countries,* p. 286. See also Russell, *Man's Mastery of Malaria,* pp. 132–33.

55. Wilson, *Observations on Climate,* pp. 190–91.

newcomers were. They were thought to be "acclimatized" or "seasoned." One school believed that the first sickness, or the "seasoning sickness," was the necessary hurdle. Once the patient had lived through this he was relatively safe. In this belief they were, of course, quite correct, but it was no solution to the problem of avoiding high initial mortality. Various forms of prophylaxis to produce the same effect were therefore suggested. One very old practice was to bleed newcomers periodically. The Portuguese had long before justified this measure by assuming that immunity was connected with diet. Blood manufactured by the body from local food was supposed to be resistant to local diseases. They therefore removed the European blood a little at a time to allow for its replacement by the local product. British doctors often followed the same practice with a different justification drawn from the humoral pathology. If increased heat made the blood expand, the unaccustomed pressure could be relieved with occasional use of the lancet.[56]

The apparent immunity of Africans was even more striking than that of the "acclimatized" Europeans. Africans not only lived in health where the Europeans died of fevers, they also seemed to have diseases of their own which Europeans rarely contracted. Among these, sleeping sickness, yaws, and Guinea worm were all recognized and described by Atkins as early as 1734. They were a common problem both for the surgeons on the slavers and those on West Indian plantations, whose job it was to care for the health of the slaves. Negroes were known to suffer from the "vice," as it was considered at the time, of "dirt-eating," now recognized as a symptom of infestation with hook worm (*Necator Americanus*). They were also mysteriously susceptible to "dry belly-ache," especially on the slave ships and shortly after their arrival in America. In all probability, this complaint was lead poisoning from the white lead used to treat slaves for worms. Elephantiasis and several varieties of leprosy were also considered peculiar to the Negro race.[57]

Medical opinion was divided on the question of race and its relation to disease. Some believed there was an absolute racial immunity, which saved Africans from the European diseases and Europeans from those of the Africans. Others thought the immunity was merely

56. Lind, *Diseases in Hot Countries*, pp. 4–5 and 146; Long, *Jamaica*, II, 517–18.
57. Atkins, *Navy Surgeon*, Appendix, pp. 19–28; Hillary, *Changes of the Air*, pp. 182–85; Ashburn, *The Ranks of Death*, pp. 36, 168–70.

relative. The consensus of West Indian opinion was in this direction: apparent racial tendencies toward certain kinds of illness were recognized, but Africans were held to suffer from all tropical diseases.[58] No authority of importance believed that all races were equally endowed in respect to immunity. The different racial mortality rates on the African coast alone were too striking, and men of the time had no way of knowing the real causes. James Lind gave the idea of racial immunities the prestige of medical opinion. John Wesley added the sanction of humanitarian theology. Anthony Benezet claimed it was part of the divine plan—that God had endowed Africans with immunity to fevers so they could live their lives in their own way without interference. In his view, the slave trade was a special sin against the divinely ordained geography of race.[59] Thus the humanitarians, who generally defended the racial equality of all men, accepted the unanimous evidence that, at least in resistance to disease, racial difference was significant. In the end this "fact" rebounded to the favor of the polygenists, and they used it as the one clear argument on which all had to agree.[60] In this way the misunderstanding of the medical men came ultimately to be enshrined at the core of "scientific" racism.

Meanwhile, medical writers tried to explain the differential immunities, occasionally giving a role to custom as well as race. It could be held that Negroes avoided the Europeans' fevers because they

58. Privy Council, *Report on the Trade in Slaves,* Part III. The possibility of a degree of racial immunity is still held open by some authorities, but recent investigations indicate that it is either unlikely or insignificant. Recent studies in serology, however, show that some hemoglobin characteristics in human blood improve the individual's chance of successfully resisting certain diseases. Some of these traits might be thought of as "racial characteristics," since they are inherited; but they do not parallel the recognizable physical features of the major racial stocks. The most widely investigated so far has been the sickle-cell trait, which seems to improve childhood resistance to *Plasmodium falciparum.* [See A. B. Raper, "Malaria and the Sickling Trait," *British Medical Journal,* II 1955), 1186–89 (24 May 1955).] Some West African peoples have a very high incidence of this trait, while others have a very low one. It also occurs in Greece and some other parts of the Mediterranean basin. [See Livingstone, "Anthropological Influences of Sickle Cell Genes in West Africa."] It is probable that further studies in serology will reveal other blood characteristics which may also have the effect of producing relative immunities. Meanwhile, the answer is sufficiently clear for historical purposes. The really important immunities apparent in eighteenth and nineteenth-century West Africans were acquired in childhood, and not inherited.

59. Lind, *Diseases in Hot Countries,* pp. 224-25; Wesley, "Thoughts upon Slavery," p. 61; A. Benezet, *Some Historical Account of Guinea,* Rev. ed. (London, 1788), pp. 3–4.

60. See, for example, Charles White, *An Account of the Regular Gradations in Man. . . .* (London, 1799), pp. 73–79.

lived in "happy Want and Ignorance of luxurious living." Or it was possible that Negro slaves in the West Indies were more susceptible to their own ills because they were worse fed, clothed, and housed than their masters.[61] The more common explanation returned to the question of bodily fluids and the greater Negro capacity for perspiration. Schotte in particular seized on the difference between African and European body odor and suggested that Negroes were better able to throw off "foul and nasty vapours" which poisoned the European body.[62] Most authorities, however, simply took it for granted that in some way or other the Africans were differently constituted.

These medico-racial considerations were crucial to any planning for European activity in tropical lands. They had been a matter of practical experience ever since the early-seventeenth-century attempt to colonize Barbados with European settlers. The dominant view of the West India interest in the 1770's and 1780's was the solidified opinion that whites could not settle in the tropics except as a managerial class. Some believed that whites could not even do hard labor as far north as South Carolina. In the West Indies, physical work for Europeans was considered to be certain death.[63]

To an uncertain extent, however, this position was merely a justification for continuing the slave trade. Earlier in the century, when the facts of mortality were equally well known, most West Indian colonies had been anxious to have a high proportion of European overseers and had encouraged immigration from Britain as best they could. In 1774, Edward Long had put forward a complex scheme for settling white farmers in Jamaica. He believed the island suffered from a lack of provisions that might be raised by yeoman farmers, and the central highlands seemed both healthy and unused. His plan called for a settlement scheme managed by the island government. It should acquire tracts of land, divide them into townships, and lay them out in plots of twenty acres for each farming family, or five acres for artisans. The size of these plots could be smaller than was common in North America, since the special exuberance of the tropics would make the land more productive. Each community was to be a

61. Atkins, *Navy Surgeon*, p. 17; Hillary, *Changes of the Air*, p. 206.
62. Schotte, *Synochus Atrabiliosa*, pp. 104–5.
63. *Candid Reflections*, p. 21; Privy Council, *Report on the Trade in Slaves*, Part III.

balanced group of twenty-eight farming families and sixteen artisans. The land was to be cleared and prepared in advance, and each settler was to receive one male mulatto slave in return for a fixed annual rent. Once the state had been repaid for its outlay on slaves, they would become free and constitute a class of farm laborers.[64] Nothing came of Long's plan, but it foreshadowed later West African projects in both conception and detail. It shows, moreover, that some informed West Indian opinion still favored European settlement in spite of the known dangers of mental "degeneration" and disease.

There were no equivalent plans for West Africa before 1783, and it was known in any case that West Africa was much more dangerous than the West Indies. The best medical opinion was, indeed, opposed to the kind of establishment that already existed there. Lind argued that European garrisons for the West African posts should be reduced to the smallest possible numbers and moved to hulks anchored off shore. As much work as possible should be entrusted to Africans, trained for commercial positions. These men "should be naturalized; should be entitled to rise to a certain rank in the government or army; and they should be entitled to the other privileges of British subjects."[65] Lind's precedent was the earlier assimilationist policy of the Portuguese along the Guinea coast, and the idea returned again and again in other hands during the century that followed.

No matter how discouraging Lind might be about the dangers of West Africa, he himself suggested the possibility of a contingent and limited safety for Europeans. Just as Long assumed that the Jamaican highlands would be safe enough, Lind pointed out that most parts of the Coast had their healthy seasons. Some places were thought to be healthy all year round. Among these were the Banana Islands and the "high hills of Sierra Leone, upon whose summits the air is clear and even, while thick mists and noisome vapours overspread the lower grounds."[66] Thus some few healthy spots were "known," while others could be guessed at. Even as the African Association reported the mediocre results of its first explorations, it added a sanitary element to the myth of the better interior by supposing that, "the long descent of the rivers is a proof that the elevation of the inland country is raised above the level of the coast, and consequently that the

64. Long, *Jamaica*, II, 404–32.
65. Lind, *Diseases in Hot Countries*, pp. 224–25.
66. Lind, *Diseases in Hot Countries*, pp. 52–53, 151, 225–26.

climate is much more temperate, and probably more salubrious."[67]

While the British thus knew both the promise and the dangers of the West African tropics, neither the one nor the other was well enough known to be a cause for unqualified optimism or complete discouragement. The practical difficulties of exploiting African resources were hardly suspected, while the dangers were recognized in a way that still gave room for hope.

67. Association for Promoting the Discovery of the Interior Parts of Africa, *Proceedings* [1790], (London, 1792), p. 206. In fact, they were quite wrong on this point. Recent studies indicate that the incidence of infective bites by malaria-carrying mosquitos is, if anything, higher in the more open savanna country of the interior than it is on the coast or in the forest belt. [Colbourne and Wright, "Malaria in the Gold Coast," (1955), p. 167.]

4

NEW

JERUSALEMS

It was clear by 1781 that Britain
was losing the American war, and, as the old empire crumbled, it was
equally clear that some basic adjustments would take place in her relations with the overseas world. Many of those with a special interest
in Africa began to turn their attention to specific projects or suggestions for a new African policy. After a period of gestation in the
first years of peace, the projects began to appear in quantity. Between
1788 and 1793 (and the new war with France) a few actually materialized in a series of attempts to colonize the West African coast.

The planning and promotion took place against a background of
shifting British attitudes. In the first postwar years, the pressing problem seemed to be the rivalry with France, and it led to the hope of re-
dressing the balance of the lost American colonies by creating a new
empire in Africa. As time passed, and the lost war slipped further
behind; a more optimistic mood set in. Those who believed in empire
could then begin thinking not merely of a new empire but of a better
empire. Pitt's Government showed a spirit of moderate reform at
home, even among the ruling classes. On the fringes of political life,

still more radical reformers wanted to move with the spirit of the revolution which had just shaken America and would soon shake France. The eighteenth-century faith in man's potential achievement reached its British peak in this decade. It seemed, in the light of reason, that men could both remove the evils of the world around them and build anew on better foundations.

For Africa, this meant first of all the abolition of the slave trade, and the anti-slave-trade movement very nearly succeeded in the early 1790's. It also meant that new plans for Africa could be drawn on a clean slate, designed from the beginning to produce both wealth and a degree of human happiness which would be harder to achieve in the corrupt "Old World" of Europe. Africa was thus peculiarly open to utopian dreaming of a sort that fastened on America in other decades.

The planning of utopias was not merely an exercise for the radical fringe, though it was most common there. Respectable and practical people accepted some elements of utopianism. In spite of the knowledge in the hands of medical men, the general public had not yet formed an image of West Africa as the "white man's grave." The Africans themselves were thought of as a malleable and oppressed people, who would accept with gratitude whatever might be done for them. (The slave rebellion on Saint Domingue in 1791 had not yet destroyed France's richest plantations and created the first independent ex-colony ruled by non-Europeans.) The reform movement in Europe had a broad momentum, unopposed as yet by the backwash from the French Revolution and the Jacobin scare of the 1790's.

The first new project for West Africa, however, came directly out of the pressing problems created by the wreckage of the old empire. Convicts sentenced to transportation were crowding English jails. The dumping ground in America was closed, and some alternative had to be found. It was accepted on grounds of custom, conviction, and economy that transportation was preferable to building more prisons in Britain. No important body of opinion doubted the wisdom of this policy. For some, transportation was simply a cheap form of punishment. The convicts atoned for their crimes, and their suffering supposedly acted as a deterrent for others. Transportation could also be defended as a scheme for rehabilitation. In a new social setting, it was possible that some of them would start afresh and be-

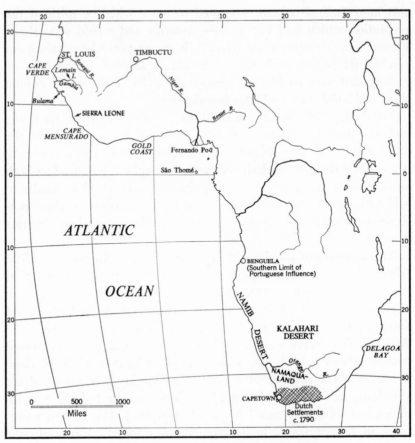

Map 4. Africa in the Late Eighteenth Century

come useful members of society. There was also an economic argument. The convicts were a source of labor, and it was better to use
their labor in some part of the King's dominions where labor was
scarce. But for most people, the real advantage of transportation was
the simple fact that it removed undesirable people from Britain.

For a number of reasons, Africa seemed to provide a suitable alternative to America. If it were a question of removing undesirables,
the African "climate" would make quick work of them. With potential riches in a region where Europeans might not go of their own
will, convict labor seemed an easy solution. Convicts would be especially useful during the assumed dangerous period at the beginning
of any settlement, before clearing and cultivation had improved the

"climate." At the same time, Africa was something of a land of opportunity. It was still possible that some of the convicts sent there
would reform and find an honorable place in a colonial society.

Small-scale convict shipments to West Africa had begun during the
American War itself, thus creating a precedent, however unhappy.
The Home Office had provided involuntary convict recruits to the
military forces both in the royal colony of Senegambia and the forts
controlled by the African Committee, but the scheme was not a success. Out of 350 men sent to the Gold Coast in 1782, only seven
were alive and on duty in 1785. The rest had either gone over to
the Dutch, escaped and turned pirate, or died of disease—mostly the
latter.[1]

But further requests for convicts came from the officials in Africa.
In 1776, Governor MacNamara of the Senegambia recommended
Bintang on the Gambia as a desirable place for convict settlement.
Others suggested a point further up the river at Nyanimaru.[2] At the
end of the war, Chief Justice Morse sent in a more elaborate scheme
with an emphasis on economic development. In his opinion, "The
River Gambia is universally allowed to be the richest spot in Africa.
It produces Bees Wax, Ivory, Gold, Rice, Castor Oil, Dye Woods,
Mahogany equal to that of Jamaica, Sugar Canes, Indigo, Cotton,
Balsam, Tobacco, and many other articles; Indian and Guinea Corn
of various sorts and variety; the Vine, Coffee, Cocoa, Ginger, and
Aloe. . . ."

Surely, here was wealth worth developing, and Morse thought it
could be done in a way that met the problems posed by the post-war
situation in Europe and America. He hoped to develop the Gambia
as a route into the interior. New posts at Nyanimaru and Fattatenda
would reach into the hinterland otherwise served by a French post in
Galam, thus destroying the value of the Senegal, returned to French
control in 1783. Development along the Gambia itself could concentrate on indigo and rice to replace the old supplies from South
Carolina and Georgia. Timber, slaves, and plantation provisions from
the Gambia would also shore up the West Indian economy and replace North America's functions in the South Atlantic System. The
convicts were needed to man the posts and plant the new crops, but

1. Evidence given the Parliamentary Committee on Transportation, 1785, *Commons Journals*, XL, 959.
2. J. M. Gray, *A History of the Gambia* (Cambridge, 1940), p. 277.

they were not to be under punishment after they arrived. Instead, Morse hoped to settle a select group of convicts mixed with free immigrants in ordinary civil society, thus creating a true colony of Britons in Africa.[3]

The home government began to move in 1784. It first obtained an Act of Parliament giving the Crown authority to select a place overseas for the reception of convicts.[4] The initial plan was to use the Gambia, though not quite as Morse had suggested. It was a mixture of dumping, pure and simple, along with some hope for the development of tropical agriculture. John Barnes, an Africa merchant, supplied the detailed suggestion and urged the Gambia partly to keep undesirable convicts away from the other centers of African trade.

As developed further at the Home Office, the plan took on some curious utopian overtones. Lemain Island (later MacCarthy Island) was selected as the best site, situated as it was about 125 air miles inland from the coast. A first contingent of about 200 convicts were to be left there with tools and six-months' provisions. The guards would then retire downstream to Nyanimaru, where they could live aboard an armed ship and prevent escape by river. The convicts themselves would be left on their own, under an elected chief and council, to form their government and fare as they could. It was assumed that a great many would die, but new contingents could be landed from time to time until the island reached its estimated potential population of 4,000.[5] As a result, agriculture would flourish and soon Britain would have a rich trade. Nor were the possibilities of rehabilitation discounted. As the Home Office memorandum put it: "in a very few years they would become Planters, and take those who might be sent out hereafter into their Service—as they grow rich they naturally grow honest."[6]

A preparatory mission was sent up the river to negotiate with the African authorities. In February 1785, it purchased Lemain Island for Britain at a total cost of £579 in bribes and gifts and the promise of a future annual tribute.[7]

3. "Sketch of a Plan for Erecting a Colony in the Territory Belonging to the River Gambia in Africa," enclosed in Edward Morse to Lord Sydney, 26 April 1784, CO 267/8.

4. 24 George III, c. 56.

5. In fact, the population of MacCarthy Island only reached 1,786 at the census of 31 December 1960.

6. Undated memorandum, enclosed with Lord Sydney to Lords of the Treasury, 9 February 1785, HO 35/1.

7. Gray, Gambia, p. 278.

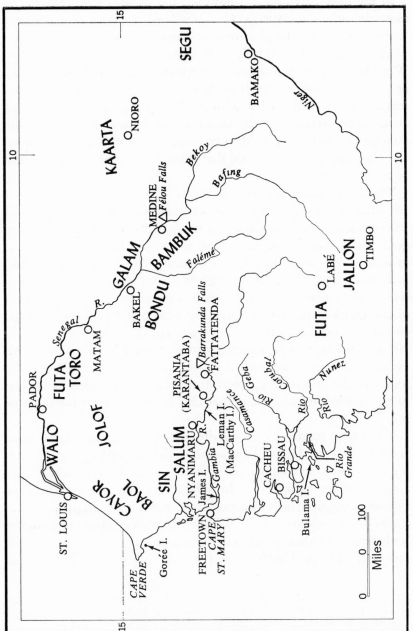

Map 5. Senegambia in the 1780's

93

In the early part of 1785, however, the Gambia scheme began to meet difficulties in Britain. Criticism built up from two different sources. On the one hand, enthusiasts for other parts of Africa began to enter their claims. Edward Thompson, the naval commander in West African waters, disliked the site and thought São Thomé should be purchased from Portugal in its place.[8] His first plan was not accepted, but he followed it with a glowing report of the coast of South West Africa near the mouth of the Orange River. Here the promise of wealth was held to be greater even than at the Gambia, and the "climate" was so good that voluntary European settlers could be easily recruited.[9]

Thompson had never been to South West Africa, but his report fell in with a flurry of European excitement about the prospects of settlement north of the Cape and south of Angola. The Portuguese governor at Luanda sought to push south with European settlement in what is now southern Angola. From the Dutch side, Henrik Hop had travelled north of the Orange in 1761–62 and investigated the copper of Namaqualand. Francois le Vaillant explored to the north of the Dutch settlements in the early 1780's, and published in 1790 an extravagant and partly fictitious account of what he found there. He returned to Europe in 1784, and it is possible that some of his exaggerations had become common knowledge.[10] Whatever the source of the information, the British government shifted its interest to South West Africa, but it kept that interest a secret for the time being.

The second source of criticism directed at the Gambia scheme came from Parliament. Edmund Burke protested in April 1785 that sending convicts to the Gambia meant imposing the death penalty, "after a mock display of mercy."[11] In May a Committee of the House of Commons began to hear evidence. Some was humanitarian. Some was the *ex parte* testimony of the West Africa traders, afraid of a convict settlement near their posts. The stream of expert witnesses agreed, however, that the Gambia was too unhealthy for settlement, that

---

8. Edward Thompson to Secretary of State, 15 February 1785, CO 267/9.

9. "Some Account of the Country on the West Coast of Africa between 20° and 30° of South Latitude, well calculated for the reception of the loyal Americans and where Convicts of Britain may be made useful to the State," 9 March 1785, CO 267/9.

10. F. C. C. Egerton, *Angola in Perspective* (London, 1957), pp. 50–51; H. Vedder, *South West Africa in Early Times* (London, 1938), pp. 21, 31.

11. *Cobbett's Parliamentary History*, XXV, 431.

Europeans could never work in the tropics and survive, that the Africans would kill any settlers the "climate" spared.[12] The virtues of South West Africa were also expounded, and Sir Joseph Banks, who had been to Australia with Cook, suggested still another possibility—Botany Bay in New South Wales.[13]

The Committee's conclusion was anti-Gambia and against the scheme of letting convicts run their own government while some were becoming rich and honest. It approved the substance of Thompson's report and recommended South West Africa as the best site, especially since it might serve for the relocation of North American loyalists as well as British criminals.[14] All that remained was to send a survey party to examine the coast itself. After some delay *Nautilus* sloop returned with a discouraging account—the entire coast from 15° to 33° South Latitude was barren and sandy. It was, in fact, the Namib Desert. With this, the South West Africa boom collapsed. The Home Office gave up all thought of Africa and ordered a fleet prepared for Botany Bay instead.[15] Thus the first post-war effort to develop West Africa ended in the foundation of Australia.

In spite of the final outcome, the Gambia project has some interest as an indication of British official thinking in the 1780's. The picture of tropical wealth had been accepted without question, and even the terrible mortality was not enough to rule out West Africa as a possible site for a colony. A certain carelessness with the selection of a distant place on scant or uncertain information was also evident. If responsible and practical officials like Lord Sydney and Commodore Thompson could indulge in thoughtless and optimistic planning of this kind, others, less practical and more enthusiastic, might find support for utopian settlements.

Two outlines for a project in West Africa emerged in the year of the peace, and in time they merged to serve as the basis for an actual attempt at settlement. One was the work of Henry Smeathman, the naturalist. When he returned from his collecting trip in the Banana Islands, he was anxious to help the African people, and in 1783 he wrote to a prominent Quaker, offering his services to the Society of Friends. He saw an opening for humanitarian good works in the po-

12. *Commons Journals,* XL, 954–59.
13. Minutes of Evidence in HO 7/1.
14. *Commons Journals,* XL, 1163–64.
15. Unsigned draft addressed to Lords of Treasury, 18 August 1786, HO 35/1.

litical order then prevalent on the Windward Coast around Sierra
Leone. The African nations in this region had only a rudimentary
political organization. The way had long since been open for European slave dealers and their mulatto descendents to create virtually
sovereign enclaves. Armed with guns, any man who could gather a
few hundred followers and slaves was a law to himself. The Banana
Islands, where Smeathman had lived so happily, were ruled in
this way by the Afro-English Caulker family. Smeathman sensed
that if a state could be founded by an ill-educated slave dealer it
could also be done by an educated European. A properly sponsored
and conducted expedition might found a "true commonwealth" on
the African coast, beyond the sovereignty of any European power.

The scheme was backed by the economic calculation already publicized by Postlethwayt and others. With the potential wealth of
African agriculture, tropical products could be supplied more cheaply
with free labor in Africa than with slave labor in America. By founding a settlement in Africa, Smeathman believed the West Indies could
be driven from their place in world markets. They would lose their
supply of slaves, since a demand for labor in Africa would raise the
cost of slaves to prohibitive levels. African labor would stay in Africa,
and the whole South Atlantic System would collapse of its own inefficiency. Furthermore, the promoters would gain wealth for themselves
in return for their good deeds.[16] It was a combination of ideas based
squarely on the accepted British beliefs about West Africa, and it
lived on to become the basis for countless projects in later decades.

Smeathman's original project had a social as well as an economic
program. He was consciously interested in creating a new and better
society, but he reasoned that such could not be founded with men
already set in their ways, especially if they were drawn from a single
culture. European settlers would merely create a little Europe. He
hoped, therefore, to begin with men intentionally chosen for the
variety of their cultural background. Poor Negroes stranded in England in the aftermath of the war, British artisans, slaves purchased in
Senegal, and volunteer settlers from the Canaries and Madeira would
be amalgamated together with slaves and voluntary recruits from the
immediate vicinity of the new colony. With such a mixture, there
would be no established institutions to combat, and a truly new society

16. Smeathman to Knowles, 21 July 1783, printed in *New Jerusalem Magazine*,
I, 179, 281–93 (1790).

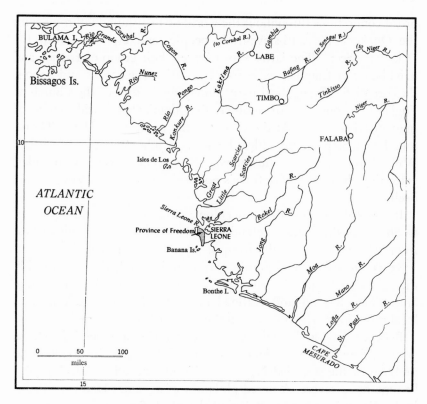

Map 6. Part of the Windward Coast

could be molded under the forms of democratic liberalism. Political freedom, elective office, and a color-blind constitution would attract still more settlers, and a true commonwealth could grow. "In short, if a community of 2 or 300 persons were to be associated on such principles as constitute the prosperity of civilized nations, such are the fertility of the soil, and the value of its products, and the advantage of such an establishment, that it must, with the blessing of the Almighty, increase with a rapidity beyond all example; and in all probability extend its saving influence in 30 or 40 years, wider than even *American Independence.*"[17]

The second sketch of an African utopia prepared in 1783 came from the hand of Granville Sharp, for more than a decade past the unofficial protector of Negroes in Britain. Sharp was a man with

17. Smeathman to Knowles, 21 July 1783, *New Jerusalem Magazine*, I, 293.

broad connections throughout the world of British philanthropy, with the Quakers, the anti-slave-trade people, and especially with the "Clapham Sect." The latter was a loosely knit group of friends and neighbours in Clapham who formed, during the 1780's and 1790's, the core of the Evangelical party among the laymen of the Church of England. In one way or another, they dominated a wide range of humanitarian causes. At the center of the group were Henry Thornton, James Stephen the elder, Henry and John Venn, and William Wilberforce, but its ramifications and connections were much wider, extending through Wilberforce's political activity to the government itself.

It was only natural that any colonization project would be shown to Sharp, as the known defender of the Africans. His own earliest recorded response took the form of a memorandum dated 1 August 1783, commenting on the outlines of a project he had seen, probably the Smeathman plan. In any event, Sharp's document took up where Smeathman left off and outlined more detailed constitutional and legal provisions to be followed at the new settlement.[18]

Between 1783 and 1786, plans were maturing in several directions at once. Smeathman continued to agitate his project. In London, the problem of the stranded Negro Americans, and other "black poor," became more severe. A noted philanthropist, James Hanway, organized a Committee for the Relief of the Black Poor, including among its members some of Sharp's Evangelical friends. Sharp both supported the organization and continued his private patronage of Negro clients. Early in 1786, Smeathman's project had been taken up by Sharp and the Committee and shifted slightly to become that of a colony principally, but not exclusively, for the purpose of settling the "black poor" in Africa. A Prospectus was issued over Smeathman's signature. It offered the privilege of enrolling for the sum of £5 to, "Any person desirous of a permanent and comfortable establishment, in a most pleasant and fertile climate, near SIERRA LEONE, where land may be purchased at a small expense, . . ."

Emigrants were to receive all the land they could cultivate, passage to Sierra Leone, and supplies for three months after landing. A clergyman for their spiritual comfort, a schoolmaster for their children, and a "physician skilled in tropical medicine" were to accom-

---

18. Memorandum of 1 August 1783, printed in Prince Hoare, *Memoirs of Granville Sharp*, 2nd ed., 2 vols. (London, 1828), II, 11–15.

pany the party.[19] The government also contributed a subsidy of £12 for each settler. By the early part of 1786, the expedition was preparing to leave under Smeathman's direction, but with varied support from other individuals and groups.[20]

At this juncture, Smeathman died. The project passed definitively into the hands of Granville Sharp and the Committee for the Black Poor, though Sharp assumed the principal responsibility. After a hurried reorganization, an expedition actually sailed early in 1787 with 411 passengers under the command of Captain T. Boulden Thompson of the Navy. In May, it arrived in Africa and founded the "Province of Freedom," under circumstances that made it one of the oddest of all efforts to create human happiness in Africa.

Captain Thompson bought a tract of land from the African authorities in the King's name—not on the Banana Islands as Smeathman had planned, but on the Sierra Leone peninsula near by. Most of the settlers were "black poor" recruited in London, though about sixty English prostitutes were also recruited to provide wives for the settlers. Thompson's command of the expedition was simply a temporary expedient. Once the settlers were landed, he withdrew and left them to govern themselves.[21] The motives of the principal sponsors were clearly humanitarian and altruistic, but others simply wished to rid England of people they thought undesirable. At this level, there was an element of similarity to the Gambia convict project.

Sharp's own intention was quite different. He wanted not only to help the black poor but to experiment in social engineering. He equipped the expedition with an elaborate code of regulations, built on Smeathman's scheme and modified by ideas Sharp himself had been maturing since 1783. The constitution of the new state was modelled on what Sharp understood to have been that of ancient Israel, modified by that of medieval England. Ultimate power in political affairs was given to a common council, made up of all house-

19. Henry Smeathman, *Plan of a Settlement to be made near Sierra Leone* (London, 1786).

20. See C. Fyfe, *A History of Sierra Leone* (London, 1962) for the authoritative account of the Sierra Leone settlement. Fyfe (pp. 14–15) gives a slightly less favorable view of Smeathman's project and character.

21. The legal status of the colony was not precisely defined, but it was clearly not sovereign British territory at this stage, nor do the settlers appear to have been considered British subjects. In English law, the colony itself might have been held to be a sovereign entity, or, more likely, under the authority of Naimbana, the King of the Koya Temne. See Fyfe, *Sierra Leone*, pp. 16, 19–20, and 24–25.

holders gathered together. Actual administration was left to elected magistrates—"tythingmen" elected by each twelve householders and "hundredors" to represent each eight tythings, or ninety-six households. All males between sixteen and sixty years of age were to serve in rotation as a militia for defense and police.

In spite of its representative government, the Province of Freedom was not designed to be a classless society. The householders were to be a kind of yeoman class with two inferior groups. One of these was a class of indented servants, serving up to five years for adults or eleven for children before they attained equality of rank. Still lower on the social scale, slaves purchased in neighboring countries might be introduced into the colony. Slave-holding was prohibited for individuals, but slaves were permitted as state property under an arrangement that allowed them to earn their redemption by five years' labor at public works.[22]

Sharp's regulations also called for some radical economic experiments. He began with the proposition that, "HUMAN *Labour* is more essential and valuable than any other article in new settlements, which chiefly depend on the cultivation and produce of the earth for their subsistence and commercial profit."[23] Hence the medium of exchange should be based on labor rather than gold or silver. The device chosen was a labor tax, due from each male citizen at the rate of 62 days a year, or 20 per cent of each man's working time. At the first of each year, each man was to sign a series of labor indentures in favor of the government, in denominations of five, ten, or more days of work. These indentures were transferable. As the government sold them, they became a circulating medium, based on an article of real value. Taxation was also progressive. "Gentlemen" were to pay triple taxes and skilled workers double, though their actual service would be done by unskilled deputies.[24]

Land values were also tied to the system of labor-currency. The original settlers had been promised free land, but later settlers or young men coming of age would have to purchase an allotment with four years' service to the state, paid in the form of labor-currency indentures. The scheme of allotments also tried to take account of

22. Granville Sharp, *Short Sketch of Temporary Regulations . . . for the Intended Settlement on the Grain Coast of Africa, near Sierra Leone* (London, 1786), pp 1–11, 22–32.
23. Sharp, *Temporary Regulations*, p. 13.
24. Sharp, *Temporary Regulations*, pp. 13–15, 56–67.

Adam Smith's recent discussion of rents. Each householder was to receive a town lot plus a farm, the farms varying in size according to distance from town, 20 acres if it were only three miles from town, up to 200 acres twelve miles away.

Finally, an element of state enterprise was added. Sharp intended the government to keep 30 per cent of the land in its own hands, to be worked through the "investment" of part of the labor tax. Income from both its own farms and the labor tax should have provided very generously for financing education and other government services.[25]

On the whole, it was an ingenious plan, foreshadowing utopian socialism and based squarely on the eighteenth-century faith that rational planning could produce a "good society" on earth—so much so that some of Sharp's close friends and admirers thought he had gone too far.[26] In retrospect they were certainly correct, and Sharp appears exceedingly naive to have expected utopia from human material drawn so largely from the outcasts of London slums. In fact, Sharp did not intend to create quite the kind of colony that took shape. He hoped to form a multi-racial settlement and to send out a broader cross section of English society. European settlers were especially encouraged by large land grants, and some individuals were to be given free land in return for their special contribution of skill or intellect. Early in 1788, lots were reserved for Thomas Clarkson, the anti-slavery leader, his brother John, then a naval officer, and twelve Swedenborgians anxious to reach the interior of Africa.[27]

Sharp himself was well pleased with his regulations, and he wrote some months after the expedition sailed: "The Code of Regulations which I drew up for the settlement, not being objected to by the Government, was adopted by the Settlers before they sailed: and, if they would be careful to maintain it, they would become the freest and happiest people on earth; because the poor are effectually provided for, and their rights secured. . . ."[28]

In practice, the regulations were not applied, but the failure was not so much Sharp's utopianism as the more basic errors he shared

25. Sharp, *Temporary Regulations,* pp. 32–53, 56–73.

26. G. Sharp to inhabitants of the Providence of Freedom, 16 May 1788, printed in Hoare, *Memoirs of Granville Sharp,* II, 104.

27. Hoare, *Memoirs of Granville Sharp,* II, 11.

28. G. Sharp to a New York Lady, 12 January 1788, printed in Hoare, *Memoirs of Granville Sharp,* II, 85.

with other Britons of his time. The soil was poor, and the crops
failed. Mortality was well within the range that should have been
expected. Even though the settlers were mainly Negro, half died
between May 1787 and November 1789.[29] At the end of 1789 a
minor chief attacked and dispersed the settlers in retaliation for in-
juries done him by other Europeans. By then the Province of Freedom
was already a failure.

While plans for the Province of Freedom were maturing in humanitarian quarters, other outlines and projects had been advanced.
Many of them came to nothing, but they indicate some of the vast
possibility open to European activity—ranging from the Province of
Freedom on one hand to the Gambia convict scheme on the other.
One scheme, proposed in a private letter to William Pitt in 1785,
centered on the Gold Coast. Its author, a Lt. Clarke of the Army, was
concerned about the need to recover from the American losses in the
late war. He saw the golden opportunity where there were already
British trading forts. All that was needed was to shift from commerce to agriculture. The land was "rich beyond conception," given
proper organization and manpower. The organization, according to
Clarke's scheme, would come with the appointment of Crown Commissioners to replace the African Committee. Two hundred soldiers
could protect the settlement, while three hundred convicts could be
sent out as settlers. Other manpower would come through the institution of forced labor for Africans, though limited to six hours each
day. Still more labor could be obtained from slaves, and Clarke
thought slaves would be available in large numbers if the export
slave trade to America were forbidden. Thus the accustomed slave
trade from the interior would be held and used on the Gold Coast
itself.[30]

Still other plans were laid for the vicinity of Sierra Leone. One
centered on Smeathman's chosen Banana Islands, hoping to make
them into another and more successful plantation colony on the West
Indian model.[31] Another chose the Sierra Leone mainland.[32] Some of
the slave merchants in the Sierra Leone River actually began about
this time to grow plantation crops on Tasso Island as a side line to

29. See Appendix.
30. Lt. Clarke to W. Pitt, 17 March 1785, PRO 30/8/363.
31. W. H. [William Halton?] to Duncan Campbell, undated, CO 267/10.
32. J. Matthews, *A Voyage to the River Sierra-Leone* . . . (London, 1788),
pp. 21–23, 52–59, and 63.

their commercial operations. Still other projects kept to the European-managed plantation as the expected economic form, but incorporated some of the anti-slavery aspects of the Smeathman scheme.[33] Many of these plans were sketchy and perhaps only half serious. Others were not only seriously projected but were brought forward again and again over a decade or more in the face of real discouragement.

One of the most energetic, if erratic, of the colonial enthusiasts was Carl Berns Wadström, a Swedish explorer and promoter who first made his appearance in England in 1788. He was an engineer by profession, a Swedenborgian by religion, and he came to England with an interest in colonization that dated back to 1779. His original idea was to set up a utopian community of Swedenborgians some-where in Europe, but he and his supporters soon shifted the scene of their project to Africa—in part, certainly, because of Swedenborg's African doctrines.[34] Their plans were held up at first by the American War. Then, after they had obtained a charter from the Swedish Crown and had begun to organize a Swedish colony in West Africa, religious dissension broke out in the group. Wadström himself, who had been president of the Swedish colonization society, left Sweden in 1787. His first objective was to explore Africa and find a site for the colony he might sometime found. He therefore joined Sparrman and Arrhenius on their unsuccessful reconnaissance expedition to Gorée. On his return to Europe, Wadström made for England where the growing anti-slavery movement, the launching of the Province of Freedom, and the rise of interest in Africa suggested that he might find backing for a new effort. Further Swedish support was out of the question in any case, not only because of his old Swedenborgian quarrels but also because of the outbreak of war with Russia.

Once in England, Wadström got in touch with Thomas Clarkson, gave information about the slave trade, and talked with Granville Sharp about the possibility of merging the Swedenborgian venture with the Province of Freedom. It was then that he got permission for himself and eleven other Swedenborgians to sail with the relief ship due to leave in the summer of 1788. Something went wrong, as things usually did with Wadström's schemes, and the ship sailed

33. Henry Gandy to C. B. Wadström, 17 August 1788, printed in *New Jerusalem Magazine*, I, 165 (1790).

34. See obituary by Helen Maria Williams, *Monthly Magazine*, VII, 462–65 (1799); C. B. Wadström, *An Essay on Colonization, Particularly Applied to the Western Coast of Africa* . . . 2 vols. (London, 1794–1795), II, 179–181.

without them. After this break with Granville Sharp, he turned to other sources of help and obtained permission to sail again for Africa on a British naval vessel. This time the ship was ordered off on other duty following the Nootka Sound crisis, and Wadström was still left stranded in England.[35]

He swallowed his disappointment and settled down as a publicist and colonial projector. With the aid of Augustus Nordenskiold, a friend and supporter in the old Swedenborgian quarrels, he gathered a group of English Swedenborgians, and together they published a prospectus for a new West African colony. It was to be located at Cape Mesurado, where Monrovia now stands, entirely under Swedenborgian religious control, and beyond the sovereign power of any European state. The goal was still much the same as that of the original Swedish group—escape from Europe as it was. Africa offered itself as a "place out of the bounds of Europe, where the natives shall be found in a simple state of nature, comparatively innocent, because uncorrupted with the vices which have hitherto sprung from a disordered circulation."[36]

The design for this particular utopia was partly based on the pseudo-ethnography of the "noble savage," and partly on Swedenborgian theology. The political constitution, unlike that of the Province of Freedom, was calculated not to free men from the trammels of an old society, but to protect the faithful from deviation. All office holders were to be members of the Church of the New Jerusalem, and a complex set of regulations assured a Swedenborgian theocracy.

But the new society was not projected for Swedenborgians alone, nor exclusively for Europeans. Europeans, according to Wadström were morally bound to invite Africans into the settlement. In his view, human cultures were divided into the civilized and the uncivilized. In civilized society, understanding is elevated above will and passion. In uncivilized societies, will and passion dominate. This

---

35. Wadström, *Colonization*, II, 185–95, 399; R. L. Tafel, *Documents Concerning the Life and Character of Emanuel Swedenborg*, 2 vols. (London, 1875–1877), I, 640; T. Clarkson, *History of the Rise, Progress, and Accomplishment of the Abolition of the African Slave Trade by the British Parliament*, 2 vols. (London, 1808), I, 488.

36. *Plan for a Free Community Upon the Coast of Africa Under the Protection of Great Britain, but Entirely Independent of All European Laws and Government* (London, 1789), p. 43. See also C. B. Wadström, "Letters of a Voyage to Africa," *New Jerusalem Magazine*, I, 70–73, 125–32, 157–74 (1790).

situation could and should be corrected through education. Just as the individual is morally committed to educate his children, civilized people are morally committed to promote the "happiness of the barbarous and uncivilized."

The moral obligation also carried concomitant rights. Among these, Wadström found the right of European peoples to rule over the Africans: "If the tutelage of children be regarded as a period of slavery, I allow that civilized nations have some right to exercise a certain dominion over the uncivilized, provided that this happy dominion be confined as a paternal yoke, and that the duration do not exceed the period of a child's maturity."[37]

It followed therefore that Africans would be recognized as fundamentally equal to the European settlers; but initially they would have to accept a status of "gentle servitude," from which they could gradually redeem themselves by work and education. Ultimately they would advance to full membership in society and intermarry with the colonists from Europe.[38]

As might be expected from the narrowly exclusive religious base, nothing came of the Mesurado project. There were very few Swedenborgians in England. Wadström had nevertheless detailed a version of Christian paternalism that was uncommon in eighteenth-century England, though basic to many nineteenth-century concepts of the proper relations between differing societies. His intellectual justification, however, was not completely new: much the same kind of thing had been said again and again in sixteenth-century Spain.

Wadström would be heard from again. Meanwhile he drifted off to Manchester, ostensibly to learn the textile industry so that he could introduce it into his new colony whenever it should be established. He was quiet for a time after 1790. Those of his followers who were determined to reach Africa went there under other auspices.

The most significant colonization project of 1789 and 1790 came, instead, from Granville Sharp's Evangelical and humanitarian friends. "The Province of Freedom" was clearly a failure, as Sharp himself recognized by the middle of 1789. It was necessary to save what might be saved, but Sharp, who had put nearly £2,000 of his own money into it, was not able to carry on alone. The potential profits

37. C. B. Wadström, *Observations on the Slave Trade* . . . (London, 1789), pp. 58–61; p. 60 for quotation.
38. *Plan for a Free Country*, esp. p. 50.

of legitimate commerce were well advertised. He therefore appealed to friends with business connections, hoping to use the Province of Freedom as a base for commercial operations.[39] Through William Wilberforce, he appealed to the government for a charter. At the end of 1789, with the aid of Henry Thornton, the Evangelical banker, the St. George's Bay Association was formed. By then, the original settlers had been dispersed, but plans went forward and the Association received a Parliamentary charter in July 1790 as the Sierra Leone Company.

In sharp contrast to the other African projects of the period, the Sierra Leone Company began without a blueprint for utopia, or even a very clear idea of what should be done. It appears that Sharp only intended to add a commercial adjunct to the utopian colony, but in fact he lost control altogether. His financial interest in the new firm was that of a minor stockholder along with two thousand others. While he was given a place on the committee, control passed to Henry Thornton as chairman. The Sierra Leone Company gradually abandoned the goals of the Province of Freedom, and Sharp became a somewhat embittered critic watching from the sidelines.[40]

The Company was given control of the land originally purchased in Sierra Leone for Sharp's settlement, to be used as a trading post. In the words of the charter, it was to serve as a place "where they may form a Factory or Settlement for their Servants, a secure Depository for their Goods and Merchandize, and a safe Harbour for their Shipping."[41] The principal goal was clear enough. It was to work in the spirit of Wilberforce's belief that Africa should be civilized through the influence of "legitimate trade," not colonization for its own sake.

Before an expedition could be launched, however, the scope and nature of the project began to change. A secure profit from trade depended on the grant of a Parliamentary monopoly excluding other British merchants from the Sierra Leone River and its hinterland. When the Company's request for such privilege failed—as it did at an early stage through the opposition of the Company of Merchants

39. Hoare, *Memoirs of Granville Sharp*, II, 124, 136–40.
40. [G. Sharp], *Free English Territory in Africa. An Account of the District Purchased for the Settlement at Sierra Leone* (London, 1790); Hoare, *Memoirs of Granville Sharp*, II, 82, 157–59, 172–82.
41. 31 George III, c. 55.

Trading to Africa—the promoters were forced to consider other alternatives.[42] The idea of free-labor plantations came naturally to mind. Lt. John Matthews' glorious picture of tropical luxuriance at Sierra Leone gave a nudge in this direction.[43] Through the latter part of 1790 and early 1791 the Company thought in terms of sending out "a hundred or so enterprising Englishmen" to lay out plantations worked by local African labor. Lt. Henry Hew Dalrymple was engaged to lead the expedition. He was a warm advocate of the plantation form of enterprise, and he had served at Gorée during the American War. The Company still planned to engage in trade on its own account, and it hoped for a *de facto* monopoly over the trade of its own settlement; but the principal revenue was to come from land rents. This was the second phase of the project.

Toward the middle of 1791 the plan again changed. Dalrymple was a difficult man to deal with, both on grounds of personality and of policy. The Company requested his resignation, and with it many of his associates also resigned. The directors were also disappointed with the would-be European settlers who were often men without capital, character, or experience. The Company learned, about this time, that several thousand Negro loyalists from the thirteen lost colonies were stranded in Nova Scotia and might be willing to emigrate to Africa.[44] The project was hurriedly readjusted. White settlers were now discouraged, and the Company's servants were to be the only Europeans allowed in the colony. The Company still intended to run plantations of their own, but the economic base would be peasant cultivation by the "Nova Scotians."[45] Plans went ahead on this basis. About 100 Europeans went direct from England to organize a settlement. They were joined in March 1792 by 1131 Negroes from Nova Scotia and later on by some 64 survivors of the Province of Freedom, who had been living precariously in the vicinity.

The political constitution of the new colony carried remnants of

42. Williams to Schoolbred, 23 April 1790; Schoolbred to Williams, 28 April 1790, BT 6/8.

43. *Sierra-Leone*, 21–23, 52–59, and 63.

44. For the earlier history of these loyalist refugees, see B. Quarles, *The Negro in the American Revolution* (Chapel Hill, 1961), esp. pp. 158–181.

45. H. Thornton to John Clarkson (Private), 30 December 1791, Ad. Mss. 41262A. Sierra Leone Company, *Report of the Court of Directors of the Sierra Leone Company to the General Court*, 7 vols. (title varies) (London, 1791–1808), I (1791), 21–28.

all the planning stages through which it had passed, and a good deal of continuing uncertainty as well. As Henry Thornton later wrote: "Who were to be the governed party at Sierra Leone, we knew not—whether many or few, blacks or whites, whether natives who might migrate thither, or Nova Scotians, or Europeans in general, or British, and if British, whether servants of the Company or independent settlers of all ranks, and degrees.—Nothing in the world could be more uncertain than the speculation; who were to be the governed part of the new colony, at the time it became necessary for us to fix some government."[46]

The directors therefore began with a Governor and Council of eight members, modelled on that of the East India Company in the time of Warren Hastings. The powers of the councillors were independent of the governor. It was a system designed for governors in whom the home authorities had little confidence—in short, for H. H. Dalrymple. In fact, the first Governor was John Clarkson, brother of the anti-slavery leader and much closer to the directors than anyone else in the colony. He thus began with uncertain authority, and political squabbles among the Council made a clear line of action difficult.

In time, the directors straightened out the upper reaches of the constitution, giving John Clarkson full authority as Governor along with authority to settle constitutional details on the spot. The final shape of the political and economic structure was therefore hammered out in Sierra Leone itself, based on official advice from Henry Thornton and unofficial suggestions from the Clapham Sect and their friends.

Thornton himself had no strong views on the government of colonies, though he was a Tory in politics and distrusted the Nova Scotians as a possible electorate. Thomas Clarkson and Granville Sharp, on the other hand, wanted to preserve the radical democracy of the Province of Freedom. The result was a compromise. The offices of Tythingman and Hundredor were retained, but without their old function as a magistracy. They were merely constables with the power to advise the government on matters of common concern. Executive and judicial power remained with the Company's servants, but with safeguards such as trial by jury and a guarantee of equal

46. H. Thornton to J. Clarkson, 14 September 1792, Ad. Mss. 41262A, f. 166.

rights regardless of race. Sharp and his friends had managed to salvage the representative forms, but little else.[47]

There were equivalent cross currents of opinion about what ends these political means should serve. Thornton was anxious to recover some of the stockholders' investment by the collection of rents. Sharp wanted to recreate as much as possible of his old utopia. Thomas Clarkson was anxious to use Sierra Leone as an outpost in the battle against the slave trade. He had little faith in the efficacy of "legitimate trade," or any other kind of trade, in civilizing Africa. Instead, he thought of the colony as a kind of bridgehead on the African continent, from which "civilization" could be extended by persuasion. To this end, he urged his brother to create three committees of council. One was to work at persuading African kings to give up the slave trade and shift to agricultural production. A second was to work for the abolition of African slavery by persuasion and by "ransoming" young slaves to serve on the Company's plantations. The third was to work for the eradication of "superstition."[48]

William Wilberforce meanwhile kept up pressure for his own panacea of "legitimate trade," and especially trade into the distant interior where the existence of "considerable towns" was known or suspected. He had the support of Henry Thornton and the possibility of working with the African Association, which also hoped to open up the trade of the interior through exploration. A trading post on the Gambia was planned in co-operation with the government and the African Association, but the plans never materialized. In the end, the African Association acted alone and sent a single explorer, Mungo Park, inland from the Gambia in 1795.[49]

An even more promising prospect opened briefly in the spring of 1792, when it appeared that the abolition of the slave trade might well pass the House of Commons. Pitt intimated privately that, with abolition, all British West African posts might be turned over to the

47. H. Thornton to J. Clarkson, 14 September 1792; T. Clarkson to J. Clarkson, 17 July 1792; G. Sharp to J. Clarkson, 24 July 1792, Ad. Mss. 41262A. Sierra Leone Company, *Account of the Colony of Sierra Leone From its First Establishment in* [*sic*] *1793* . . . (London, 1795), pp. 74–76.

48. T. Clarkson to J. Clarkson, 28 August 1791 and January 1792, Ad. Mss. 41262A.

49. W. Wilberforce to J. Clarkson, 28 December 1791 and 27 April 1792; H. Thornton to J. Clarkson, 6 June 1792, Ad. Mss. 41262A. Undated draft of instructions to James Willis, CO 267/10. Association for Promoting the Discovery of the Interior Parts of Africa, *Proceedings* (London, 1790), p. 204; Gray, *Gambia*, p. 283.

Sierra Leone Company, along with the £13,000 annual subsidy for their upkeep.[50] With this support, the Company could have returned to its original commercial basis, but abolition failed in Parliament. The beginning of the new war with France early in 1793 ended further opportunities for extension. Sierra Leone then settled down to live its life as the turn of events had created it—a settlement of Negroes under a Chartered Company, which also participated in trade.

Even before the Sierra Leone expedition had left England, the very fact that a colony was to be established in Africa, and with substantial support from commerce and government, encouraged other projectors. Among those left out of the Sierra Leone venture were the associates of H. H. Dalrymple, displaced from the Company toward the middle of 1791. Many were half-pay officers from the forces, and the most active of these was Lt. Philip Beaver, a former shipmate of John Clarkson and a man of liberal views. Dalrymple and his friends formed their own colonization committee and gained a little support in the City, notably from Paul Le Mesurier, then a Member of Parliament and later Lord Mayor of London. C. B. Wadström took an interest in the scheme, bringing in further support from Manchester and from Swedenborgians generally. By the end of 1791 this ill-assorted group of speculators and philanthropists formed the Bulama Island Association, with the intention of founding a colony on what is now Bolama Island in Portuguese Guinea.[51]

The essential elements of the project were those cast aside by the Sierra Leone Company at the time of Dalrymple's dismissal. It was to be a colony of European settlers operating plantations of sugar and other tropical staples in competition with the West Indies. The main purpose was to make the settlers rich, but the group had other philanthropic objects for the Africans: "To purchase land in their country, to cultivate it by free natives hired for the purpose; and thereby to induce in them habits of labour and industry, it was thought might eventually lead to the introduction of letters, Religion, and civilization, into the very heart of Africa."[52]

The object was clearly to be agriculture and not commerce (though

50. H. Thornton to J. Clarkson, 3 May 1792, Ad. Mss. 41262A.
51. Philip Beaver, *African Memoranda* (London, 1805), pp. xiii–xiv; Wadström, *Colonization*, II, 133–34.
52. Beaver, *African Memoranda*, p. 3.

some of the individual settlers hoped for commercial profits as well).
Instead of selling shares, the Association sold land—at the rate of
£30 for each 500 acres to actual settlers, and £60 per 500 acres to
absentees. These were generous and attractive terms, as well they
might be for land the promoters did not own and had never seen.
The scale was designed for large plantations, and some absentee
subscribers took up 2000 acres or more.[53]

In other respects the project fell short of its first hopes. Some of
the subscribers, being self-chosen as colonists, were badly chosen.
William Bant, a Quaker who had an unsavory reputation in the City,
alienated some of the potential financial support. The powerful interests of the Sierra Leone Company and the West Indian planters were
equally opposed, and the Government seems to have concluded that
the Association was under-capitalized at a mere £7,000, where
£25,000 or more would have been realistic.[54] Whatever the inspira-
tion, the Government refused its recognition and support. The Association nevertheless went ahead with its plans and mounted an
expedition. Two hundred and sixty-nine settlers including women and
children sailed from England in April 1792 in two parties commanded by Dalrymple and Beaver respectively.

The legal problem of non-incorporation and the lack of any authority to found a colony were settled after departure by drawing up
a written constitution in radical democratic terms. Sovereignty was
held to reside with the people, represented in a thirteen-member
legislative council, elected annually by adult male suffrage, and subject to impeachment and recall by the voters. The legislative council
in turn elected the president or governor. Slavery, the slave trade, and
a public debt were equally prohibited. The liberties of the individual
were guaranteed, with trial by jury and the rights of free assembly,
consultation, address, petition, and remonstrance. The only defense
force was to be a militia of all able-bodied males who had no religious objections against military service, and the militia officers
were to be elected.[55]

When the settlers arrived on the Coast in June 1792, they had a
brief military encounter with the African owners of their prospective

53. H. H. Dalrymple, Memorandum of 2 November 1791, CO 267/9; Wadström,
Colonization, II, 359–62.
54. Unsigned, undated memorandum in CO 267/9.
55. "Memorandum of Agreement," 9 March 1792, CO 267/9. Also printed in
Beaver, *African Memoranda*, pp. 425–32.

territory. After a slight delay, however, they managed to buy Bulama Island twice over from different claimants. The discomfort of the rainly season and a series of personal quarrels further discouraged many of the party. Their actual mortality was exceptionally low, with only nineteen dead by the middle of July, but even this was more than they had expected. Dalrymple and about 150 of the would-be colonists abandoned the project and sailed for Sierre Leone, where a third of them died of fever during the six weeks their ship lay in harbor waiting to leave for England.

Philip Beaver and 91 others remained on Bulama to salvage what they could of the original plan. They set to work with hired African labor to build a blockhouse for protection and clear the ground for planting. The following sixteen months were an epic of achievement in the face of obstacles, but it ended in failure. The blockhouse was built, the ground cleared and planted, but two-third of the settlers died of fever and others deserted or returned to England. At the end of November 1793, only Philip Beaver and eight others remained, and they decided they were too few to carry on alone.[56]

Beaver's enforced return to England was discouraging enough. In addition, war with France had begun in January 1793, and Beaver was recalled to the Navy. The original investment had been dissipated. By 1794 the Association's resources were reduced to something less than £1,000 in credits of doubtful value. But there was still a fund of optimism among some of the original promoters, not least with Beaver himself. They tried again to raise a public subscription, this time £10,000, but without any evident success. They continued nevertheless to memoralize the government, asking for a charter, and as late as 1796 were still pleading for government support in the re-establishment of their colony.[57]

Instead of retiring from their advanced political views, as might be expected in these years of the Jacobin fear in England, the new Bulama project of 1794–95 was, if anything, more utopian than the first. C. B. Wadström, who had been merely a peripheral supporter

56. Beaver's journal for his period in command is reproduced in *African Memoranda*, pp. 89–283. There are slight variations in different accounts of the number of settlers present at any time.

57. Wadström, *Colonization*, II, 168; Bulama Association to Dundas, 27 January 1794; Paul Le Mesurier to John King, 16 August 1796, CO 267/10; Andrew Johansen, *Description of Bulama Island* (London, 1794).

now became a principal publicist for the Association. His two fat volumes on the history and theory of African colonization reviewed the past attempts and put forward his outline for another try.

If earlier projects can be divided according to emphasis on commerce or agriculture, Wadström's new plan was far over toward the side of agriculture. His theoretical defense was based on the arguments of the physiocrats—"Commercial colonies tend to slavery, agricultural to liberty." There were, according to Wadström, two kinds of commerce. Good commerce was "commission commerce," where goods and monetary metals move freely according to their "natural" values. "Speculation commerce," on the other hand was dangerous. Under this form, paper money, coined metals circulating as fiat money, and monopolies open the way to the anti-social greed of the merchants, speculators, and money-jobbers. Speculation commerce was therefore to be controlled in the new colony by adopting Sharp's labor-currency, ending imprisonment for debt, allowing the free coinage of monetary metals and avoiding a monopolized trade in the hands of the company itself. Land tenure also followed Sharp's scheme, as adjusted by Paul Le Mesurier to favor large planters rather than peasant proprietors. The basic division was a district of 50,000 acres, subdivided into tythings of 5,000 acres, and lots of 500 acres each.[58]

The dominance of agriculture was to be further assured by political safeguards. Colonists were divided into three estates according to economic function. In the first estate were the producers of raw materials; in the second, manufacturers; and in the third, merchants. Producers alone would have the right to vote, and a system of progressive taxation would fall most lightly on planters, somewhat more heavily on manufacturers, and more heavily still on merchants. The strictly Swedenborgian aspects of Wadström's earlier plan were quietly dropped, and the colonists were promised full religious freedom, except for Roman Catholics, whose belief in a celibate clergy ran counter to the Swedenborgian emphasis on "conjugal love."[59]

It was futile to hope that government or private capitalists would support a scheme of this kind, much less in wartime, and less still after a destructive French raid on Sierra Leone in September 1794.

58. Wadström, *Colonization*, I, 66–72, 85–92, 103–05, 117.
59. Wadström, *Colonization*, I, 95–96, 118–19.

Wadström himself gave up the effort to secure support in England and skipped across the Channel in 1795, leaving a debt of £126 to the man who helped him compile his *Essay on Colonization*.

The last four years of Wadström's life were spent in France, and they form an illuminating postscript to his ubiquitous activities as a colonial promoter. In this phase, he began to work out suggestions for an international trusteeship over the "uncivilized" peoples of Africa. In one proposal to the Directory he suggested that France and Britain should join together when the war ended and found a new international association for the civilization of Africa and the end of slavery and the slave trade. Member states would reform their own colonial systems and then bring pressure to bear on non-members, mainly through an international naval squadron blockading the West African coast. Each of the associated states would also indicate some part of the African coast as its own sphere of influence and responsibility for civilizing Africa, and slavery would be prohibited in all African colonies. Sierra Leone and Bulama, as humanitarian colonies, were to be given a special status, including neutrality in war time.[60] It was an odd twist of fate that these suggestions, unrealistic as they were in their own time and place, prefigured more that was actually to happen during the coming century than any of Wadström's other projects.

Even as a colonial projector, Wadström was more warmly received in France than he had been in England. A commission of the Assembly reported favorably in 1798 on his last colonial blueprint, the only one of his many projects that was ever attempted. By the time it materialized, however, Wadström was dead, and the project was altered beyond recognition. Its setting was shifted from West Africa to Egypt, where it took the form of Napoleon's drive to the east.[61]

By the later 1790's the first scramble for Africa was over. The brakes were first applied at the beginning of the Anglo-French war

60. C. B. Wadström, *Adresse au Corps législatif et au Directoire exécutif de la République française* (Paris, 1795). There was other interest in African colonization from France in these same years, including one project to revive the Bulama idea under French sponsorship. See Charles Le Clerc de Montlinot, *Essai sur la transportation comme recompense et la deportation comme peine* (Paris, 1797).

61. C. L. Lokke, *France and the Colonial Question: A Study of Contemporary French Opinion, 1763–1801* (New York, 1932), pp. 174–82; Eschasseriaux, aîné, *Rapport au nom de la commission chargée d'éxaminer l'ouvrage presenté au Conseil par le citoyen Wastrom [sic] . . .* (Paris, 1798).

in 1793. For a year or so the movement ground along under its own momentum. By 1795 it had come to a stop. Only Britain had unrestricted access to West Africa, and any British resources that could be diverted from the European war would go to the seizure of existing French and Dutch colonies, not to doubtful projects for founding new ones.

Examing the dozen or so British projects for West Africa during the decade of peace, their outstanding characteristic is the apparent lack of contact with reality, at least with African reality. They were based firmly enough on the European attitudes and theories of the day, but the actual setting was something of a dream world. In spite of the Europeans' detailed knowledge of the coast, sites were selected with an amazing nonchalance. Two of the expeditions planned for West Africa ended in Australia and Egypt respectively. Other locations were picked for superficial appearance, or on information long out of date. Sierra Leone attracted attention by its spectacular terrain. (The mountains of the peninsula stand alone like a high island barely attached to a flat shore, the most impressive landmark along the whole coast from the Senegal to the Cameroons.) It satisfied the romantic love of natural beauty, but its value for agriculture was slight. Dalrymple and his associates selected Bulama Island sight unseen from a description written ninety years earlier by Sieur de la Brue. Wadsröm picked Cape Mesurado from a similar description by Des Marchais. Even the Swedenborgian myth of the interior and the centuries-old Arab accounts of the Western Sudan played a role in drawing some optimistic planners toward the commercial penetration of the interior.

Ethnographic information was either ignored or buried under largely imaginary concepts of man-in-general, "the barbarian," or "the savage." Specific customs of specific peoples counted for much less than their cultural difference from Europeans. For all the projectors, Africa was barbarism confronted by civilization. Some may have chosen Africa because of its reputation for untapped wealth, but the utopian planners were also attracted by the lack of "civilization." They followed the unconscious assumption of popular culture theory that a lack of civilization meant a lack of culture. African society therefore lay there, a *tabula rasa* ready and waiting for the utopian inscription. All planners, utopian and otherwise, took it for granted that Africans had little but unskilled labor to offer the new settlements. Many assumed what Wadström made explicit—that the absolute superiority of Western culture implied a moral obligation to change African culture. This obligation in turn gave a moral sanction to colonization, which was contested only by the West Indian planters and the slave traders. Even these opponents often accepted the ideal of the culture bearer as a moral goal. They merely thought the job was too difficult to be worth trying, or else impossible on account of the irremediable "racial inferiority" of the Africans.

Compared with their opponents—or with most nineteenth-century advocates of African colonization—the eighteenth-century projectors were remarkably free of overt racism. With the exception of those who simply wanted to set up West Indian slave plantations in West Africa, they accepted the goal of an integrated and multi-racial society; but, for most, the equality of races was potential and not actual. Even the Province of Freedom discriminated by giving larger land grants to Europeans. Almost all the projectors assumed a racial division of labor even when it was not explicitly stated: the blacks would do the work and the whites would supervise. This had been the pattern of tropical colonization in the past, and it was the teaching of medicine that Europeans could not do field work in the tropics. Only Smeathman clearly had in mind a multi-racial society where whites might be found at all social levels, but he alone believed in hard work as the best way to keep alive in West Africa.

Another curious element, perhaps connected with a degree of latent racism, was a common tolerance for some form of forced labor. This appears in projects ostensibly tied to the anti-slavery movement and utopian in their political forms. Only Philip Beaver believed unreservedly in free labor for wages, with no other form of control than the market price. Wadström's early project ordained a "gentle servitude" for Africans. Sharp allowed a class of indented laborers and another of ex-slave redemptionists in state service. Smeathman also allowed temporary slavery as a means of redemption. The Sierra Leone Company enjoyed its own kind of dominance as the only sizeable employer of labor and set wage rates as it chose. It is uncertain how far this pattern merely reflected customary relations between masters and servants in eighteenth-century England, and how much it may have drawn on the expectation of laziness caused by tropical exuberance.

All the projectors believed in tropical exuberance. It was the basis for their dreams of wealth. They mainly differed in their ideas of how that wealth should be tapped. One division of opinion was clearly that between an emphasis on trade and African proprietorship, as against one on European-managed agriculture. Both sides had the support of a considerable body of theory. Wilberforce and other followers of the commercial ideal could draw on social theory that glorified the "commercial stage" of civilization. They could also find economic justification in Adam Smith's belief that the division of labor was the key to economic progress: exchange was therefore the key to economic development. On the other side, Wadström and the agriculturalists in general could draw on the popular *mystique* of land as the only real source of wealth, fully developed in theoretical form by the physiocrats.

In other respects, the projectors were curiously fuzzy in their economic thinking. Adam Smith had pointed out in *The Wealth of Nations* that land is cheap in new countries and labor is dear. Sharp's labor-currency was, indeed, a recognition of this principle. But the Sierra Leone Company, the original Bulama project, and Wadström's project of 1794 all put their faith in a prospective inflation of land values. They brought land from the Africans for very little, and then hoped to sell it immediately at many times the price they had paid. Having given less than £100 for Bulama Island, the Association was trying in 1794 to raise subscriptions of £100 for a mere 400 acres.[62] If the promotors themselves had not been the principal subscribers, one would suspect them of fraud. As a more probable explanation, they were accustomed to thinking of land in English terms, as intrinsically valuable, not merely subject to the market like other commodities.

Still another carelessly handled subject was the question of sovereignty and international law. Some might, like Wadström, try to prove the Europeans' moral right to dominion in Africa. Or they could do as Smeathman did, and simply observe that *de facto* petty Afro-European states had been created on the coast. If it had been done before, it could be done again. But the land purchases at Sierra Leone, Bulama, and Lemain Island were made in a way that confused property rights with soverign political dominion. It is extremely unlikely that any of the African sellers had a legal right to sell sovereignty over the ceded territory, or that they understood the treaty in these

62. Johansen, *Bulama Island,* pp. 7–9.

terms.[63] In effect, sovereign control was acquired as Smeathman had said it could be done—by *de facto* usurpation in a social setting where the European concept of sovereignty simply had no meaning.

But the handling of sovereignty was curious even in relation to Europe. The convict colony at Lemain Island and the Province of Freedom were both to be recognized in some vague sense as British territory, but in fact the government had not the slightest intention of carrying out the normal obligations of a sovereign in either of them. Though chartered, the Sierra Leone Company had no legal right to the judicial functions its officers carried out on an *ad hoc* basis from 1792 to 1800. More anomalous still, Beaver's Bulama settlement, Smeathman's project, and Wadström's Swedenborgian project would have been new states founded by men already subject to recognized European rulers. Yet none of these writers seemed to be seriously concerned about the problems this might raise. In fact, though not in theory, European international law did not fully extend to tropical Africa.

Compared with their unconcern with external relations, the projectors were deeply concerned about the political constitutions appropriate to new settlements. The American Revolution and the Parliamentary reform movement had already popularized the tenets of political liberalism, with a special stress on representative government and written constitutions. Some projects clearly reflected this influence, but not all projects were democratic or even liberal. They can, indeed, be arranged along a spectrum from complete democracy at one end to complete autocracy at the other. On the side of democracy, the extreme form of primitive democracy foreseen for the Lemain Island convicts would have to be counted the most radical of all. The Province of Freedom was hardly less democratic, but its democracy was guarded by a constitution protecting the rights of the individual. Wadström's projects ran to oligarchy, either of "producers" as in the 1794 version, or of Swedenborgians in that of 1789. The Bulama constitution of 1792 was also an oligarchy of European planters, since

63. The custom along most of the Coast had been for slave dealers to make regular payments to the African authorities, which might have been interpreted either as tribute or rent. In most cases, the Africans seem to have assumed, on the precedent of earlier dealings with Europeans, that they were now entering into a similar arrangement. The Sierra Leone settlement, for example, rested on two treaties of 1787 and 1788, neither of which was legally sound. (Fyfe, *Sierra Leone*, pp. 19–20, 22, and 24–25.)

no representation was planned for the African workers attracted to the settlement.

Toward the other end of the spectrum, Smeathman's scheme called for enlightened despotism, but with liberal institutions and freedom for all. The Sierra Leone Company was, in fact, a despotism in the hands of the company's officers, but controlled from above by the Directors in London, and capable of being checked from below by elected minor officials. Finally, at the extreme of despotism, the convict settlement destined for South West Africa (and actually founded in New South Wales) was an autocracy on the spot, even though it might be controlled by the ultimate power of the British Parliament. If any field of thought was neglected in planning for human happiness in Africa, it was certainly not political theory.

In fact, no important body of European theory was left out of account. The failures were not failures in theory, but in practice based on wrong or incomplete information. Some information—anything, for example, that might have corrected the belief in tropical exuberance—was simply not available at the time. Other information was available but not used. This was most serious in regard to health precautions. Lind and others with experience on the coast had made the dangers abundantly clear, but they were either disregarded or passed over in the hope that clearing and cultivation would "improve the climate." The utopian plans would probably have failed in any case, but they had no chance. Mortality alone was enough to ruin the Province of Freedom and the Bulama settlement, and it very nearly ruined Sierra Leone as well. But Sierra Leone was not ruined. For a decade, when more grandiose projects were impossible, it continued unhappily as the first true British colony on the Coast. It was, therefore, a base for gathering new information and experience to serve a new generation of policy-makers—and perhaps to bring success where lack of knowledge had so clearly brought failure.

PART II

The Age of Exploration and Disappointment
1795–1830

5

SIERRA LEONE:
THE
LESSONS OF EXPERIENCE

The world-wide strategy of British affairs began to alter markedly in the mid 1790's. As the possibility of a quick victory over Revolutionary France faded, the global strategy of the eighteenth-century wars for empire was re-established. Where, in the decade of peace from 1783 to 1793, undeveloped regions like West Africa seemed at least potentially valuable, they were now pushed into the background. Old settlements of known value were available for the taking, and their capture could be justified as part of the military effort against France. French colonies in the West Indies and India, Dutch colonies at the Cape of Good Hope and Java—these were the principal objectives. The minimum requirement for West Africa was the protection of the British slave-trade factories and the interception of French shipping. Resources could be diverted to the capture of the French posts or the exploration of the interior only when other circumstances permitted.

In this situation Sierra Leone remained as the one permanent product of the earlier African enthusiasm, and that enthusiasm was fading. It was pushed aside, on one hand, by the rally of British conservatism and the hysterical fear of "red Jacobinism" in 1793 and 1794. In addition, it was simply overshadowed by other and more pressing concerns.

But Sierra Leone, unlike the other posts, was a miniature society with a resident population of African descent, however small. As such, it continued to serve as the sole enduring example by which to measure any and all of the utopian projects of the 1780's. It was mainly coincidence that the least single-minded and theoretically planned of these projects should be the one to stand the test of maintaining itself. The Bulama experiment was too short-lived to prove much. The Province of Freedom was forgotten or absorbed, in popular view, by its more permanent successor.

Sierra Leone, however, was neither a just example of the other projects, nor a fair test of the Directors' original intentions. The wars themselves changed the objective conditions on which the Sierra Leone Company had based their hopes. They had anticipated high trading profits, partly because they expected the slave trade to be made illegal for British subjects. Abolition had, indeed, been carried in principle in the House of Commons in April 1792, only to be lost through the delaying action of the House of Lords. With the growing impact of revolution in France, war in Europe, and slave revolt in Saint Domingue, the marginal supporters of abolition fell away and the measure was delayed till 1807. The Company was therefore forced to operate in direct competition with the slave trade.

They were also forced to operate under wartime conditions, and this was probably the more serious disadvantage. Insurance rates went up, and the Royal Navy was unable to provide constant protection against commerce raiders. A hit-and-run raid on the colony itself by a small French fleet in September and October 1794 was nearly fatal. During a fortnight's stay in the Sierra Leone River, the French destroyed or removed the buildings, furniture, equipment, and trade goods that could not be carried away into the forest for safety. The Company set their losses at almost a quarter of their capital. They were undercapitalized in any case, and the raid forced a policy of retrenchment, inhibiting any real effort to carry out the original plans for development.

Whatever their other motives, the Directors were running a commercial concern. However much they intended to help humanity, their first obligation was to achieve financial success. Otherwise they could only admit failure and liquidate. Even before the French raid, it was obvious that their calculations of agricultural production had been over-optimistic. At least in Sierra Leone, the expected wealth burgeoning from the tropical soil was simply not forthcoming. The Directors admitted in 1794 that they had been misinformed in this respect, and they placed the blame on Lt. Matthews of the Navy, whose report they had trusted. (This was, perhaps, a little sly on their part, since Matthews' was not the only report they trusted; but he was a pro-slavery man, and thus a political opponent.) One early lesson was, therefore, a revision of emphasis. Freetown, the new capital of the colony, was again thought of principally as a commercial station, supplemented by the agriculture of its environs.[1]

The Directors were thus thrown back to their initial plan to civilize Africa through "legitimate trade." Most supporters of the Company at any time would have agreed with their Chairman, that "trade is the great engine by which towns are made to rise up, and industry excited in all civilized countries."[2] The expected competitive relation of their trade to the slave trade, however, was not always clear in the Company's early statements. Their first and most optimistic hope appears to have been that legitimate trade would prove more economic than the slave trade, driving it out like a commercial Gresham's law in reverse. But this optimism was not universal, even before the founding of Sierra Leone. Another school of thought held that legitimate trade could not compete without help. It needed either government suppression of the slave trade, or else its own plantations from which to draw African products.

In the event, legitimate trade in the hands of the Sierra Leone Company was not a success. Whether the French wars, the slave trade, mismanagement, or some other factor was the principal cause, the Company placed the blame squarely on the slave trade. This view was most useful. It excused the Directors for their original over-optimism, and it could serve their immediate political needs. Even though the slave trade was an important branch of British commerce,

1. Sierra Leone Company, *Report of the Court of Directors of the Sierra Leone Company to the General Court,* 7 vols. (title varies) (London, 1791–1808), II (1794), 15. The most authoritative general history of Sierra Leone is C. Fyfe, *A History of Sierra Leone* (London, 1962).

2. H. Thornton to J. Clarkson, 14 September 1792, Ad. Mss. 41262A, f. 177.

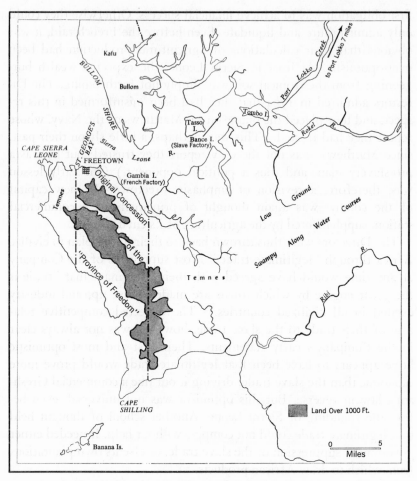

Map 7. Sierra Leone and Vicinity

they could claim that the African trade would be even larger if it were abolished. The promise of wealth through trade could still be upheld.

Meanwhile, other avenues were not abandoned. Even the plantation alternative associated with the second, or Dalrymple, phase of planning was retained. The original site on the Sierra Leone peninsula was clearly not suited to plantation agriculture, but other locations were possible on the Bullom shore, across the river from Freetown and still under African sovereignty. The Company first set up a plantation of its own, but without success. Toward the end of the century they turned it over to Major Peregrine Francis Thorne, recently retired from the Army. Thorne looked into the possibilities; but he thought the labor supply was undependable, and he feared that a plantation beyond the area of British control would not be sufficiently secure. In 1800 he gave up and went home. Governor Ludlam also tried briefly to start a plantation of his own in the higher mountains of the peninsula, but this too failed. The only European plantation with a reasonably continuous history in the whole region was on Tasso Island, worked as an appendage to the slave-trade post at Bance Island and worked by slave labor.[3]

Several different conclusions could be drawn from the failure of planting under the Company's auspices. Philip Beaver retained his old faith in plantations, but he thought that Sierra Leone was the wrong place on the right continent: "On the Bullom shore, the soil is very poor, but on the Sierra Leone side there is scarcely any soil at all; and when they make a hogshead of sugar there, I will engage to do the same at Charing Cross."[4]

He thought the Company had also been guilty of mismanagement, both in running the plantation and in their relations with the neighboring African authorities. Without the cooperation of the chiefs, there could be no steady supply of labor for hire. For Beaver, therefore, the Sierra Leone experiments were no fair test, and his dream of an African bonanza remained undefiled.[5]

Other critics of the Company's plantation effort also tended to stress the question of labor supply. J. B. L. Durand, a French observer, argued that the "natural and invincible indolence" of the Africans was too great for a successful wage labor system. Plantations could only be successful under some form of labor coercion. His suggestion was to buy the labor of slaves from nearby African chiefs, just as a West Indian planter might buy the labor of a jobbing gang from another slave owner. Once the slaves had become disciplined plantation workers, they might safely be purchased from their owners and given their freedom.[6]

3. Sierra Leone Council Minutes, 1 May 1800, CO 270/4, pp. 34–37; Report of the Directors of the Sierra Leone Company, 1802, in PP, 1803–1804, v (24), pp. 18, 27–28; Sierra Leone Company, Report (1801), pp. 27–29.

4. Philip Beaver, African Memoranda (London, 1805), p. 305 n.

5. Beaver, African Memoranda, pp. 305 and 386.

6. J. B. L. Durand, A Voyage to Senegal (London, 1806), pp. 83–88. First published, Paris, 1802.

Such a device had its appeal, even in anti-slavery circles. Both Granville Sharp and Thomas Clarkson had thought of using "redeemed" slaves to work the Company's land. Coercion was, indeed, used by the Crown administration of the colony after 1808, though not for plantations. By that time, numbers of "liberated Africans" were being landed from the slavers captured by the Royal Navy, and their forced labor was made available to the earlier settlers through a system of "apprenticeship." For itself, the Company stayed clear of forced labor, though their public statements occasionally returned to the problem of labor supply, which remained a serious concern. In 1802, Henry Thornton blamed the scarcity of labor on the local Temne people and their opposition to the Company; but in later years the matter was dropped, and Thornton finally claimed in 1807 that the "natives" had been willing to work as free laborers, and at reasonable rates.[7]

In fact, the Company quietly dropped their plantation experiments after 1800 and based their agricultural hopes on the smaller plots of the peasantry. This alternative had been dominant from 1791, even though it was not part of the original plan. The Nova Scotian settlers had been added only fortuitously and at the last moment, but the Company thought of them as a source of revenue in two different ways. They were expected to grow exportable produce, which would then pass through the Company's hands at a profit before being sold in Europe. At the same time, the Company set the prices of European goods in the settlement so as to make a net profit of 10 per cent on turnover. "Legitimate trade" of this kind was limited to their own bailiwick, and it was only partly free of competition from the slave trade. It might well have been profitable, if it were not for military and administrative expenses.[8] The second source of revenue was taxation of the settlers, principally taxes on commerce and quitrents on the land granted out to peasant proprietors.

Before either source of profit could become substantial, it was essential to produce crops for export. The Company's principal device

7. Sierra Leone Company Directors, in PP, 1803–1804, v (24), pp. 27–28; Henry Thornton, Commons, 29 July 1807, H 9, c. 1005.
8. Practical limits to the Company's selling monopoly were set by the presence of a French post at Gambia Island until 1794 and an English post at Bance Island. There were, in addition, a half dozen other merchants in the slave trade within a day's canoe travel of the settlement, and many of these would have been willing to sell European goods in return for food or other produce.

for achieving this end was a system of premiums and subsidies. In the first years, they offered competitive prizes, designed to reduce the colony's dependence on imported food. They began by offering £100 in various awards to the settlers who raised the greatest quantities of rice, yams, plantains, eddows, cabbages, maize, and cotton.

As time passed, the objectives changed. In 1794 and 1795, settlers were encouraged by prize money to build houses on their land and to cultivate land in the hills at some distance from the shore, rather than live in Freetown. The new emphasis also fell on export items, with tobacco, camwood, and ivory added to the list of encouraged products. By 1798 food crops had been dropped, and only cattle and export crops were on the list. The nature of the award was also shifted from a competitive prize to subsidies payable to any farmer who reached the production quotas set in advance by the government.[9] The system continued till the end of the Company's administration in 1808, and even afterwards it was taken over briefly by the African Institution.

While the Company's administrators clearly considered incentive payments a useful device, the practical results were far below expectations. By 1800, only about 180 of the 300 heads-of-family among the settlers seem to have been engaged in any farming at all, and land under cultivation averaged only about 3.5 acres per family. Only a third of those who did farm grew crops for export, and then only in small quantities.[10]

If the attempt to encourage export agriculture was a failure, the attempt to collect direct taxation was a disaster, and one that followed from the Company's initial errors. They believed that Sierra Leone would be infinitely productive with very little work. It followed that some of the productivity might be fairly drawn off in the form of taxes. The over-estimate of land values extended even to the Company's opponents, one of whom set a value of four to five million pounds on the undeveloped concession.[11] It was only natural that the

9. Sierra Leone Company, *Account of the Colony of Sierra Leone from its First Establishment in [sic] 1793* . . . (London, 1795), pp. 70–72. Sierra Leone Council Minutes, 7 January and 8 May 1794, CO 270/2, pp. 139 and 162; 19 May 1795, CO 270/3, p. 155; 5 February 1798 and 1 December 1799, CO 270/4, pp. 191–93 and 317; 20 January 1801, CO 270/5, p. 142.

10. Sierra Leone Council Minutes, 1 May 1800, CO 270/4; Z. Macaulay, Evidence before Select Committee on Sierra Leone, PP, 1803–1804, v (24), p. 54.

11. [Campbel], *Reasons Against Giving a Territorial Grant to a Company of Merchants to Colonize and Cultivate the Peninsula of Sierra Leone* . . . (London, 1791), pp. 8–9.

Company should sooner or later try to realize something from this asset.

The Company began, however, without a clear land policy. The Nova Scotians were promised in Nova Scotia that they would receive land in Sierra Leone "free of expense" at the rate of twenty acres for each male settler, plus an additional ten acres for a wife and five for each child. A family with two children might thus expect to receive a grant of forty acres.[12] In practice, the promise could not be kept. The Company in England thought of the grant as measuring about 250,000 acres—about twenty miles along the northern shore of the Sierra Leone peninsula and about twenty miles inland. As it turned out the actual concession measured less than ten miles along the shore of the Sierra Leone River. The Sierra Leone peninsula was not twenty miles wide, so that part of the concession was the water of the Atlantic Ocean. The area was also a parallelogram rather than a rectangle, as supposed. The southern shore of the peninsula was unsafe from European or African raids. The interior was mountainous and unfit in large part for agriculture, and much of the north coast was occupied by Temne villages. The villagers did not understand that their land had been sold, and to save quarrels, Governor Clarkson was forced to confirm their claims to the land they actually occupied.[13]

Initial allotments in 1792 and 1793 therefore averaged only about five acres per family, ranging from two acres up to eleven. The Company's failure to keep its promise became an immediate cause of discontent among the settlers, and the discontent was multiplied when the Company made the tenures conditional. They were to be withdrawn if one-third of the area were not cleared and cultivated at the end of two years, and two-thirds by the end of three years.

By the time the settlers had actually arrived in Sierra Leone, the Company emerged from its original indecision about the finer points of land policy and decided to impose a quitrent. The rate was set at one shilling an acre during the first two years, changing then to a variable assessment based on the gross annual produce of the land,

12. For the Company's policy on land and taxation see N. A. Cox-George, "Direct Taxation in the Early History of Sierra Leone," *Sierra Leone Studies*, II (n.s.), 20–35 (December, 1955) and *Finance and Development in West Africa. The Sierra Leone Experience* (London, 1961), pp. 38–52.

13. Fyfe, *Sierra Leone*, p. 47.

and rising gradually until it reached the rate of 7 per cent by 1797.[14] These rates reveal something of the Company's expectations. The initial annual quitrent was set at a figure higher than the original purchase price, only £150 in trade goods for the entire concession.[15] To ask for any payment seemed, to the settlers, to contradict the promise that land would be given them "free of expense." They took the position that a quitrent was a rent, presumably out of ignorance of the legal niceties. Their interpretation, however, was more nearly correct than that of the Company. A quitrent in English law is a permanent obligation, not subject to variation in amount at the will of either party. By tradition the quitrents in royal colonies during the eighteenth century had been set at a very low rate. They were in fact merely token payments. Both in level and variability, the quitrent demanded in Sierra Leone was not a quitrent in the ordinary sense. It was partly a property tax and partly an income tax.[16] More serious still from a practical rather than a legal point of view, the rate of 4 to 7 per cent of gross product was higher than the full economic rent on the land. Any settler seriously interested in farming could have found land much more cheaply, merely by applying to the African authorities outside of the Company's jurisdiction.

The quitrent policy caused more trouble than any other aspect of the Company's administration, in spite of the fact that quitrents were not generally collected. The first attempt was abandoned after the French attack of 1794. A second in 1797 led only to a bitter resistance on the part of the settlers and helped to cause a revolt against the Company's rule in 1800. A final effort in 1801 and 1803 failed as well, and the net result was a serious dampening of economic development. Even when quitrents were not actively collected, settlers were unwilling to take up land while the threat remained, and they might someday be asked for unpaid arrears plus interest.

In retrospect, one lesson to be drawn from the quitrent controversy is clear enough: cheap land cannot be made valuable by putting a high price on it. The Directors never admitted their original miscalculation. Only Granville Sharp, whom the others often considered a utopian dreamer, tried to get to the bottom of the land problem. In 1792, he returned to his favorite occupation of drawing up proj-

14. Sierra Leone Council Minutes, 22 August 1797, CO 270/4.
15. Fyfe, *Sierra Leone*, p. 22.
16. Cox-George, *Finance and Development*, pp. 45–48.

ects—in this case a project for making cheap land valuable by changing the economic environment. In form, the scheme was a plan for
the allocation of land and the layout of townships in a newly founded
colony. He held that after each township has been surveyed, part of
the land should be granted free of charge to settlers, while the proprietors held the rest. Once the settlers had established a thriving
community, the reserved lots would begin to take on a scarcity value,
based on their location near a bustling economic center. They might
then be sold, to the profit of the proprietors. Sharp sent an outline of
this plan to John Clarkson in Sierra Leone, but it was not accepted;
and he finally worked it out in more detail as a pamphlet project for
possible application elsewhere.[17]

A second lesson might have been drawn, and was drawn by some—
Sierra Leone, and perhaps all of West Africa, was simply not a land
of agricultural wealth. While the Sierra Leone Company admitted
its initial disappointment, Henry Thornton still argued as late as 1807
that Sierra Leone had fine soil for agriculture, though he must have
done so with less conviction than he had shown fifteen years earlier.[18]
Others were less optimistic, and the sceptics had Sierra Leone as a
living example.

It was an example of political failure as well. The political constitution of the colony was confused from the beginning, torn as it
was between the radical democracy of Granville Sharp and the Tory-
ism of William Wilberforce and Henry Thornton. Both groups,
however, counted on being able to impose whatever political forms
they chose. They made no allowance for the wishes of the settlers
themselves, assuming the Nova Scotians would be grateful to bene-
factors who had made it possible for them to settle again in the
land of their ancestors—that in their gratitude, the settlers would be
willing to accept advice and direction.

John Clarkson, who recruited the settlers in Nova Scotia and came
with them to Africa, knew they were not the pliant and unformed
human material of the British mental image. Instead, they were
men and women whose background first as slaves and then as displaced persons made them especially suspicious of "arbitrary proceed-

17. G. Sharp to J. Clarkson, 24 July 1792, Ad. Mss. 41262A, f. 153; G. Sharp,
*A General Plan for Laying out Towns and Townships, of the New-Acquired Lands
in the East Indies, America, and Elsewhere* . . . , 2nd ed. (London, 1804), esp.
pp. 5–6. First published 1794.
18. Henry Thornton, Commons, 29 July 1807, H 9, c. 1005.

ings." As he wrote in his diary, kept as a semi-public record for the use of the Directors,

The people have been deceived through life and have scarcely ever had a promise made that was performed; they have been removed from America in the hopes of bettering their condition and of improving the black character, under the protecting laws of the British Constitution. A person likely to be of benefit here must be very circumspect in his conduct to the blacks—he must bear with their ignorance, make allowances for their change of situation, and must not be hasty with them always keeping in mind, that the success of the Colony and the civilization of Africa will greatly depend upon the management of the Nova Scotians.[19]

Unfortunately, the warning was not taken to heart by Directors in London—nor by William Dawes and Zachary Macaulay, who acted as Governor in rotation between 1792 and 1799. Dawes was moderately popular at times, but the Company's administration soon lost the confidence of the settlers. There was an organized strike in 1793 against the Company's rate of wages. The land grievance appeared, and later in the same year settlers circulated a petition and sent two representatives to England to protest against the Sierra Leone authorities—specifically against the lack of full land distribution, against the prices charged for European goods, and against the general non-fulfillment of the promises made them in Nova Scotia. The strike and the deputation were followed by riots and another deputation shortly before the French attack in 1794.[20]

The raid was followed by a year of relative peace and joint rebuilding, but political relations between the government and the settlers deteriorated again in 1796. In addition to old grievances new issues appeared—racial discrimination, land distribution, quit-rents, and a sectarian quarrel between the Company's Anglican officials and the settlers, who were mainly Dissenters. Mutual confidence declined rapidly from 1797 through the year 1799.

On the government side, Zachary Macaulay tended to take an increasingly self-righteous attitude. He was given to issuing proclamations, exhorting the settlers to be grateful to himself and members of council, who had come out to "an unhealthy climate, and among a murmering people" in order to raise up "God's Temple" in Sierra

19. "Diary of Lieutenant J. Clarkson, R.N., Governor, 1792," *Sierra Leone Studies*, VIII, 31 (1927), entry for 29 August 1792.
20. CO 270/2, ff. 178–88.

Leone.[21] He kept himself aloof as a matter of policy, but the policy led to resentment instead of the intended respect for his person and office. On the matter of the quitrent, the settlers certainly had a legitimate grievance, and one on which compromise might have been possible. Macaulay, however, was intransigent. When, in 1797, the settlers presented a letter of protest, he answered in these terms: "I will be bold to say, that this letter has been sent to me not because there is anything hard, or unfair, or unreasonable in your paying a Quit Rent; but because there is in 'some' of you, a spirit of opposition, contradiction, dishonesty, and discontent, which, because there is no real ground for complaint, labours to create strife, and contention, by means however unjust and falsehoods however gross."[22]

The settlers became more suspicious than ever, and the more radical among them prepared for resistance. They seized on the embryonic representative institutions provided by the elective offices of tythingman and hundredor. In theory, the tythingmen and hundredors had very limited responsibility. They were supposed to maintain the peace within their respective tythings and hundreds and generally to help the administration as minor executive officers. They had some authority over the police in the town, executed the warrants of the Governor-in-Council, and examined grievances, reporting just grievances to the government. Their independent authority was restricted to minor regulatory functions such as setting the price of bread or conditions for the retail sale of meat.[23]

In this restricted form, representative democracy appears to have worked fairly well during the first five years of the colony. Especially in the era of good feelings around 1795, it met the approval of both Macaulay and Dawes. At that time, Macaulay praised the efforts of the tythingmen and hundredors and told them their activities promised that "a future house of Commons might arise to give Laws to Africa . . . were they to prove themselves worthy [of] the privileges that had been extended to them."[24]

21. "Proclamation of the Council to the People of Sierra Leone," 25 June 1794, Council Minutes, CO 270/2. See also speech to the tythingmen and hundredors, 4 March 1795, CO 270/3, p. 52; and CO 270/4, esp. pp. 159 ff. (1797).
22. "Address to the Settlers," 21 August 1797, CO 270/4, f. 162. See also Z. Macaulay's journal entry for 24 November 1794, printed in M. J. Holland, Vicountess Knutsford, *Life and Letters of Zachary Macaulay* (London, 1900), p. 83.
23. Sierra Leone Council Minutes, 2 March and 9 June 1795, CO 270/3, ff. 78–79 and 175.
24. Sierra Leone Council Minutes, 4 March 1795, CO 270/3, f. 62; Dawes to Court of Directors, 13 July 1795, CO 268/5, ff. 78–79.

After 1797 the more radical settlers began to see the institution not as a privilege, but a means of asserting rights. As they did so, friction increased, and government benevolence waned. In 1799, the hundredors and tythingmen tried to increase their own power by petitioning for elected justices of the peace. The request was refused but they kept up pressure by voting a tax on the white settlers the government was then trying to introduce. The government attitude hardened still more, and the Governor tried to set aside the election of undesirable representatives. Having failed, he appealed to London for greater authority. The Directors then stiffened their constitutional position by obtaining a Parliamentary "Charter of Justice," in order to regularize the judicial power of the Company's executive officers. They also sent out a small force of European soldiers. In short, the Company's reaction to assertive democracy was first to shore up its legal authority, and then to increase its physical power to enforce its will.[25]

As the government appealed for outside aid from England, the radical settlers appealed to the Temne chiefs. The showdown came in September 1800. The radical leaders called for open rebellion, and only a minority of the settlers was willing to stand by the government. Three days after the outbreak of fighting, and before the issue was decided, transports arrived in the harbor in the proverbial nick of time. They brought not only the new garrison of European soldiers but also a new group of Negro settlers, who, in the event, were willing to fight on the side of the government. The result was rapid military defeat for the rebels. Two of the leaders were executed and others deported to Gorée, though some also managed to escape to the safety of neighboring African states.[26]

The combination of rebellion and reinforcement drastically changed the position of the government. The new settlers were a body of about 550 Maroon Negroes, also from Nova Scotia. They had originally lived in the mountains of Jamaica as escaped slaves maintaining their own communities beyond the area of British administration. In the Maroon War of 1795–96, they had been defeated by the forces of the Jamaican government, and many had been deported to Nova Scotia. Now they were moved again to Sierra Leone. In spite of their earlier record of resistance to British rule, they settled down in the colony as a separate element in the population, more amenable to government influence than the earlier group of

25. See CO 270/4, *passim;* Sierra Leone Company, *Report* (1801), pp. 3–7.
26. See CO 270/5, *passim.*

Negro Americans had been. As a result, the government was internally very much stronger, and the threat of rebellion died away.

At the same time, the external relations of the colony deteriorated. The Temnes were increasingly fearful of the growing power of the colony. They had, therefore, helped the rebels of 1800 and had received dissident refugees after the defeat. The result was an emigré-Temne alliance which attacked the colony in 1801 as the first engagement in a war that was to last, off and on, until 1807. The wars further inhibited rational planning for colonial development. The Company had to meet extraordinary expenses for fortifications and military expeditions. Agriculture at a distance from Freetown and its defenses became virtually impossible. The only compensating advantages to the Company were slight. They annexed the western tip of the Sierra Leone peninsula as part of the ultimate peace settlement, and they received some financial help from the British government, begining with an annual parliamentary grant of £4,000 in 1800, later increased to £10,000 a year.

By the early years of the nineteenth century, it was clear that the Sierra Leone Company was not a financial success and would never be one. Parliamentary committees considered the problem in 1802 and again in 1804. On their recommendation, the subsidies were continued and increased, but the Directors were increasingly eager to lay down their responsibilities. On January 1, 1808, Sierra Leone passed from Company hands and became a Crown Colony.

Political and military problems overshadowed all other concerns during the last decade of the Company's administration. Foreign wars and internal rebellion could be used as a sufficient excuse for economic failure, but the Directors were merely forced back from one kind of explanation to another. In the main, they blamed the settlers and excused the errors of their own administration. As a result, they revised their earlier ideas about the nature and capabilities of the human material they had dealt with.

They had begun by saying the Nova Scotians were "superior to the generality of people of the same order in this country," even though they seemed ungrateful for favors done them. The native Africans near Sierra Leone were also relatively well thought of in the be-beginning. No Christian could, of course, approve of Temne religion, and the Company thought the Africans were "superstitious to the highest degree" and far gone in savagery. But they also seemed to be reclaimable. They were more grateful for favors than the Nova Scotians, and they were eager for Christian knowledge and improvement. The Company at first reserved complete disapproval for those Africans who lived near the slave factories. They were found to be "much given to liquor, . . . suspicious of white men, crafty, and deceitful, as well as savage and ferocious: they are said likewise to be selfish, unreasonable, and encroaching." These faults, however, were blamed on contact with slave traders and might be corrected in time.[27]

While these views were by no means completely favorable to Africans, the Company's attitude hardened still more as time passed. After 1800, the Directors accepted Zachary Macaulay's analysis of Sierra Leone politics. They blamed the troubles on the "idle, turbulent, and unreasonable" settlers, whose behavior was one of the chief obstacles to progress.[28] As for the Temnes, according to the Directors' report to the Parliamentary Committee of 1802: "The Timmaneys have the general character of being remarkably indolent, faithless, and ferocious; and their Chiefs, who were also the principals of the late attack on the Settlement, have proved to be rapacious, drunken, and deceitful; easily impressed by Artifice and Misrepresentation, and ready to promote any Design, however flagitious, which promised to gratify their Avarice or Passions."[29]

The Company, in short, needed a scapegoat: the Temnes and settlers were the most convenient ones available. The pro-slave-trade publicists had already helped to prepare the public with an image of savage Africa. The Company's new views fitted well into the existing preconceptions. At the same time, there appeared to be no danger of aiding the cause of the slave trade. The failings of the Temnes, as friends and allies of the slave dealers, and of the settlers, as ex-slaves, could both be traced back as the evil results of the South Atlantic System.[30] The intermediate African scapegoats could be made to appear as a creature of the ultimate scapegoat—the institution of slavery itself.

One conclusion that followed from the sterner appraisal of African

27. Sierra Leone Company, *Account of the Colony,* pp. 80–82, 86–87, 201–03.
28. Sierra Leone Company, *Report* (1801), p. 8; Sierra Leone Company Directors. Report (1802), PP, 1803–1804, v (24), p. 22.
29. PP, 1803–1804, v (24), pp. 22–23.
30. See arguments of Henry Thornton and William Wilberforce, Commons, 3 April 1798, *Parliamentary Register,* V (new series), 526 and 546–48.

or Creole culture was a modified constitutional policy in the colony. After the rebellion of 1800, the Company no longer talked of representative institutions leading to an African parliament. For them, the hundredors and tythingmen had been "more often ready to patronize the unjust pretentions of the settlers, and to join in their unreasonable clamours, than to enforce the authority of the laws."[31] The offices were abolished in 1800. The sin of the elected representatives was to have chosen to represent the interests of the electorate, rather than serve as prefects for the government. The lesson was applied in arrangements for the Maroons. The obligations of the new settlers were made known in advance, and nothing was said about any rights to land or other favors. Stress was laid instead on the necessity for "subordination and industry."[32]

The humanitarians had come a long way from the radical democracy of Smeathman and Sharp. In the last year of Company administration, the most glowing claim of the African Institution was merely to say "that free Negroes are capable of being governed by mild laws, and require neither whips nor chains to enforce their submission to civil authority."[33]

This assessment of political capabilities was fully in line with the new humanitarian assessment of Africans in general. There had always been an ambivalence between Christian acceptance of spiritual equality, and the obviously unchristian state of African culture. Disappointment in the Sierra Leone experiment shifted the emphasis. Humanitarians seldom defended African culture after 1800, as they had occasionally done in the 1790's. But the Company's final statement of *potential* equality was still uncompromising in 1808: "It is now proved beyond reach of controversy, and this Company have been the chief instruments in establishing the point, that the African does not labour under the intellectual inferiority, which had been so long imputed to him; that he is capable of comprehending and fulfilling every civil and social obligation; and that he can feel with the same

31. Sierra Leone Company, *Report* (1801), pp. 3–4.
32. Sierra Leone Company, *Report* (1801), especially p. 24; Governor and Council to Directors of the Sierra Leone Company, undated, enclosed with Governor and Council to Duke of Portland, 10 June 1799, CO 267/10.
33. African Institution, *Reports of the Committee of the African Institution*. 18 vols. (London, 1807–1824), I (1807), 51.

force as the Europeans, the considerations by which Christianity exalts the mind of man."[34]

This was a fine ringing statement, but it has to be read in the light of their other belief that Africans had a very long way to go before they could realize this potential. The shift in humanitarian attitude between 1788 and 1808 was from one point of view only a subtle shift in the balance of opinion, but its consequences were more serious. One of the few groups in Britain that had ever made an effort to understand and defend African culture had gone into opposition. The remaining guarantee of spiritual equality was not enough to prevent a broader swing of British opinion in non-humanitarian circles, where the promise and implication of spiritual equality was not given so much weight.

34. Sierra Leone Company, *Report* (1808), p. 13.

6

WEST AFRICA

IN THE NEW CENTURY:

A

PATTERN OF DISCOVERY

During the fifteen years in which the Sierra Leone Company unhappily carried out its experiments with colonization and legitimate trade, the British Empire was almost constantly at war, and the fortunes of war profoundly changed the British outlook on the world. Britain and the Allies were unable to hold Napoleon at bay in Europe, but the French were gradually deprived of all the most valuable parts of their tropical empire. Saint Domingue, in chronic civil war since 1791, was permanently lost when the Haitians defeated a French expeditionary force in 1802–03. Disorders in the other French West Indian colonies, combined with interruptions of maritime contact, broke the French segment of the South Atlantic System, at least for the time being. For the British West India interest, a French loss was as good as a British victory. The British sugar islands now held a sellers' monopoly in tropical staples, and there was less reason than ever to break that monopoly by opening new plantations in Africa.

Elsewhere, the change in Britain's position in the tropical world was equally impressive. Coastal Ceylon was seized from the Dutch

in 1795–96 and made a Crown Colony in 1802. On the Indian mainland during the 1780's and 1790's, the British East India Company
slowly made themselves the ruler of the sub-continent. By 1805 the
area of British India had doubled, and the Company increasingly
exerted a vague though substantial power within the Indian states
beyond their immediate sphere. As long as this remained a private
empire, protected by the Company's legal monopoly over trade between Britain and the East, private traders had to look elsewhere
for tropical markets and sources of supply. When, in 1813, the
Company lost their monopoly over the India trade, their sphere of
sovereignty and influence promised the independent British merchant
a great deal more than he was likely to find on the uncertain and
fever-ridden coast of West Africa.

 After 1808 there were also greater opportunities in South America.
With Napoleon's invasion of Spain, the Spanish-American empire
fell to pieces, never to be restored in its old form. British traders
could now exploit legally and openly the trade they had been gradually building up through encroachment, smuggling, and the gradual
relaxation of Spanish commercial controls. The situation was more
favorable still in Portuguese America. Portugal was an ally with
ancient commercial ties to Britain. In the face of the French threat
to the metropolis, the Portuguese court was carried to Brazil by a
British fleet, and it remained there during the French occupation of
Portugal. Unlike Spanish America, Brazil had no civil wars to dis-
turb trade, and the Strangford Treaty of 1810 gave British goods a
special place in Brazilian markets.

 By contrast, West Africa had little to offer for the time being.
The failure of Sierra Leone, at least in a financial sense, was fully
recognized by 1802, and this was one straw in the wind, casting
doubts on the future of "legitimate trade." The really significant
African trade was still in slaves until 1807, when Parliament made
the trans-Atlantic slave trade illegal for British subjects. From 1808,
Anglo-African commerce was permanently changed. In the first instance, it was reduced to a fraction of its earlier value, but the place
of West Africa in the pattern of British economic interests changed
too. The West Indians and their commercial associates in Britain
no longer cared about maintaining West African posts for the sake
of their labor supply. For them, West Africa was out of bounds,
and any British activity there was a threat to their own position in

British markets. British slave traders were forced into a period of difficult readjustment. For all the advertised wealth to be had from legitimate trade, Africa merchants found no immediate alternative to the slaves traditionally exchanged for British goods. Some of the ex-slave traders held on and did what business they could on the Coast, but others turned away from West Africa and found more profitable commerce elsewhere.

For all of these reasons, British interest which had begun to shift away from West Africa about 1794—initially on account of wartime pressures—never fully returned. (Even during the great "scramble for Africa" after 1880, West Africa followed well behind the Nile Valley or South Africa on the list of British priorities.) The new trend of the nineteenth century was clearly visible in its first decade, and it was reinforced after the victory over France in 1815. In a sense, the pattern of the 1780's was now reversed: as British fortunes rose, British interest in West Africa declined. The new situation was underlined by a lack of public interest in Africa or African affairs. The press, the reviews, and Parliament preferred to talk and write about other and more promising subjects. The first British scramble for Africa was finished.

Even the old generation of African enthusiasts gradually responded to new conditions and new opportunities. Granville Sharp reworked the utopian project he had designed for Sierra Leone and published it for use in India, where he hoped that properly laid out townships, with tythingmen and hundredors, would help to break down caste lines and undermine Hindu law and religion.[1] From the later 1790's the Clapham Sect, which had worked together in the Sierra Leone Company, also worked together to help found the Church Missionary Society, the British and Foreign Bible Society, and other philanthropic enterprises. For any of these organizations, West Africa was only one concern among many. Even the African Institution, founded in 1807 to keep up the humanitarian objectives of the Sierra Leone Company, soon shifted away from its first and narrowly African focus. The suppression of the non-British slave trade took priority, and the Institution moved on to help improve the lot of

1. G. Sharp, *A General Plan for Laying out Towns and Townships, of the New-Acquired Lands in the East Indies, America, and Elsewhere . . .* , 2nd ed. (London, 1804), especially pp. 17–24.

slaves in the British West Indies. West Africa in general, and even Sierra Leone, soon dropped to secondary importance, though the Institution itself continued until 1826.[2]

Along with this increasing breadth of world interest, there came a second major change in the British attitude of the early nineteenth century. This was a new note of confidence, even of arrogance. It was too gradual and pervasive to be pinpointed in time or origin. In essence, the British arrived at a different assessment of the heights to which British "civilization" had come. They saw, by contrast, a wider gap between their own achievements and those of other peoples.

Some roots of the change lay in the self-confidence of a victorious power after a long war—not merely the war beginning in 1793, though this was victory enough. In the longer run, it was victory over France in a struggle that went back a century and a half. British power had never stood higher within the European state system. Still another important factor was the rise of Evangelical religion and a new consciousness of Britain as a moral and Christian country—in certain respects *the* Christian country, in contrast with popish error across the Channel and heathen error further overseas. But most of all the new attitude rested on the facts of material achievement.

By the first decade of the new century, Britain had passed through the most critical phase on the way to full industrialization. This phase can be called the "industrial revolution" and traced back into the mid-eighteenth century, or more narrowly defined in W. W. Rostow's terms, as a period of "take-off" toward sustained economic growth. Rostow locates "take-off" for Britain in approximately the period 1783–1802. After 1802, industrialization spread more widely into new sectors of the economy, but the crucial beginning had already been made.[3] Even before the end of the Napoleonic Wars, there was a new awareness of material growth, and it continued in the face of post-war depression, increasing and changing in subtle ways. Whatever the voices of doom, Malthusian or otherwise, the new canals and the flow of cheap cotton textiles were an outward and visible sign of changes running deep within the body

2. African Institution, *Reports of the Committee of the African Institution,* 18 vols. (London, 1807–1824).

3. W. W. Rostow, *The Stages of Economic Growth* (Cambridge, 1960), pp. 38–40.

economic. Self-satisfaction was already building toward its mid-
century pinnacle of the early railway age.

The new economic base also helped to prevent an even more
thoroughgoing withdrawal of British interest in West Africa. As
economic growth continued, it came to be expected, and it was clear
that present commercial outlets would not satisfy future needs. West
Africa might be without immediate promise, but future prospects
were another matter. The Africa boom of the 1780's had collapsed
before its most grandiose claims of great wealth in the far interior
had even been investigated, and the failures of coastal colonizers
were beside the point in this context. The death of so many explorers was paradoxically a cause for continued optimism: the veil
of African mystery still hid the promise of possible wealth, as well
as knowledge to be gained for its own sake.

In spite of the difficulties of the 1790's, exploration had continued
on a modified scale. The Sierra Leone Company sent James Watt
and Matthew Winterbottom, the brother of their physician, into the
hinterland during the period of Company activity before the French
raid.[4] The explorers visited Timbo and Labe in the substantial Islamic
state of Futa Jallon, about 300 miles from Sierra Leone and 150
from the coast. This success did something to revive the promise
of still greater discoveries, but the real impetus for a thorough exploration of the interior came from another direction. In 1797
Mungo Park re-emerged on the Gambia after almost two years in
the interior between the upper Gambia and the upper Niger. He
brought back the first solid and recent information about the Western
Sudan, including an eye-witness account of the fabled River Niger
previously known only through ancient or Arabic texts. From Park's
descriptions of populous agricultural villages and commercial centers, a whole range of new possibilities opened to European speculations. With the publication of his *Travels in the Interior Districts
of Africa* in 1799, the information became available throughout
Europe.[5] It "opened" the Western Sudan to Western penetration,
and it opened the classic age of European exploration in West

4. A manuscript journal of James Watt's trip to Timbo is preserved at Rhodes
House, Oxford.

5. Mungo Park, *Travels in the Interior Districts of Africa* (London, 1799). See
also A. A. Boahen, "British Penetration of North-West Africa and the Western Sudan,
1788–1861," (Unpublished Ph.D. thesis, London, 1959), pp. 65–68, J. M. Gray,
A History of the Gambia (Cambridge, 1940), p. 283.

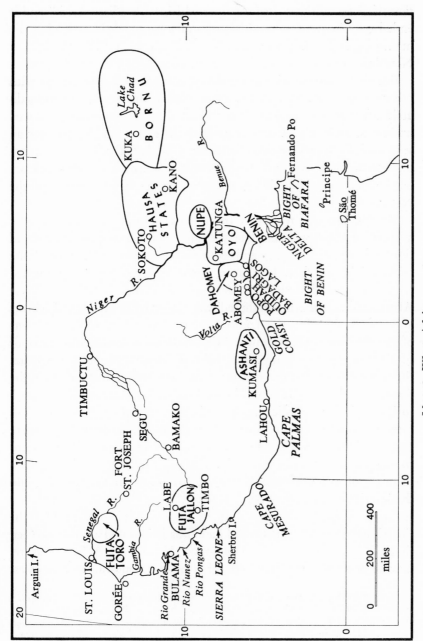

Map 8. West Africa, c. 1800

Africa. The first phase naturally centered on the course and destination of West Africa's greatest river which Park "discovered," and it ended only in 1830, when Richard and John Lander emerged at the mouth after having explored the lower course through modern Nigeria.

But the progress of exploration was fitful and interlocked with other events. Little could be done during the war years immediately after Park's return, though the African Association followed up immediately with a new effort from the east. Frederick Horneman set out from Cairo toward the Western Sudan. During 1797–1800, he was able to send back reports of his journey as far as Fezzan, but he died somewhere beyond Murzuk on the way to Bornu and the Niger.

The signature of the Peace of Amiens in 1801, however, brought a spate of new projects. The wartime rivalry between France and England was still fresh, and enthusiasts in each were afraid the other might act first. In France, three different authors published elaborate works in 1802 and 1803, calling French attention to West Africa. Pierre Labarthe gathered the reports of French naval officers and others, weaving them into two separate geographical accounts of Senegal and the Windward Coast. J. B. L. Durand, a Director of the Senegal Company before the Revolution, began to petition the government for the charter of a new company to exploit the Senegal trade, and he too published an elaborate two-volume work to help whip up public support. The most ambitious project of all came from S. M. X. de Golbéry. It called for a French protectorate over all West Africa from Cape Blanc to Cape Palmas and eastward to the upper waters of the Niger. The project included the establishment of a line of posts along the coast, and another leading into the interior by way of the Senegal River.[6]

None of these projects was likely to find much support with the French government. The Consul had already initiated another project, that of reconquering Saint Domingue. He was unlikely to risk renewing the war with England for a prize as questionable as West

6. P. Labarthe, *Voyage en Sénégal pendant les anées 1784 et 1785, d'après les mémoires de Lajaille* (Paris, 1802); P. Labarthe, *Voyage à la côte de Guinée* (Paris, 1803); J. B. L. Durand, *Voyage au Sénégal*, 2 vols. (Paris, 1802); S. M. X. Golberry [S. M. X. de Golbéry], *Travels in Africa Performed during the Years 1785, 1786, and 1787*, 2 vols. (London, 1803). See also P. Cultru, *Histoire du Sénégal du xv⁰ siècle à 1870* (Paris, 1910), pp. 295–96.

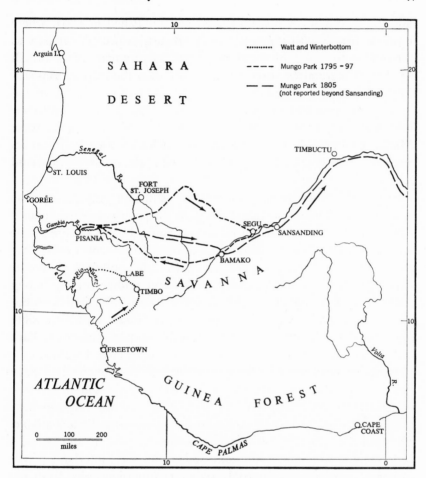

Map 9. British Exploration, 1795–1805

Africa. In addition, the French position in West Africa was extremely weak. They had lost Gorée to the English in 1800, and their only remaining post was Saint Louis, at the mouth of the Senegal. Saint Louis itself was garrisoned by less than a hundred soldiers, and they rebelled against the Governor in 1802, forcing him to take refuge with the English on Gorée. Whatever might be published in Paris, there was no new French activity on the Senegal, and no likelihood of French activity.[7]

The main weight of the French projects was felt instead in Eng-

7. Cultru, *Sénégal,* pp. 282 ff.

land. Golbéry's work was translated and published in 1803, where
it fell in neatly with the needs of the British projectors—if only as
a red flag to wave in the face of the government. The British
Africanists were already on the move. In 1799 the African Associa-
tion had passed a resolution in favor of a British occupation of the
Gambia Valley and the intervening country as far as the upper Niger.
This was, of course, a reversion to a much older concept of West
African commercial strategy, repeated by Chief Justice Morse as re-
cently as 1783. It was now merely extended to the recently discovered
Niger.

Sir Joseph Banks himself went further still in a proposal of 1799
—in effect a British equivalent of the Golbéry project—for annexation of the whole coast from Arguin to Sierra Leone, seizure of the
Senegal Valley, and formation of a chartered company to carry the
march of empire into the interior. After the outbreak of peace,
Banks was joined by Zachary Macaulay and Philip Beaver, among
others, each with his own strategic and institutional suggestions but
all with the same goal. The object was to establish a defensible
route between the coast and the navigable upper Niger that Park
had visited, aiming for a point near the modern city of Bamako.[8]

These projects raised issues of political and commercial strategy
that were to be hotly debated for a half century and more. The
object was agreed, but the route was not; and it was far from easy
to select the best point of entry with the information then available.
The choice involved a consideration of the topography and political
geography of the whole Western Sudan and the hinterland of the
western Guinea coast. The only recent information came from the
French publications, from Watt and Winterbottom's penetration to
Fera Jallon, and from Park himself. It was little to go on, but the
self-appointed authorities went to work, selecting a route over mountains none of them had seen, along rivers of speculative navigability,
and through conjectured kingdoms.

Four routes came under active consideration during the Peace of
Amiens. One was the Senegal River, temporarily out of the question because of the French base at its mouth, but still in the background. A second was the Gambia. A third was the valley of the
Rio Grande, which flows into the Atlantic opposite Bulama Island.

8. Banks to Lord Liverpool, 8 June 1799; Z. Macaulay's memorandum of 4 September 1802; Capt. Philip Beaver's memorandum of 13 August 1802, CO 2/1.

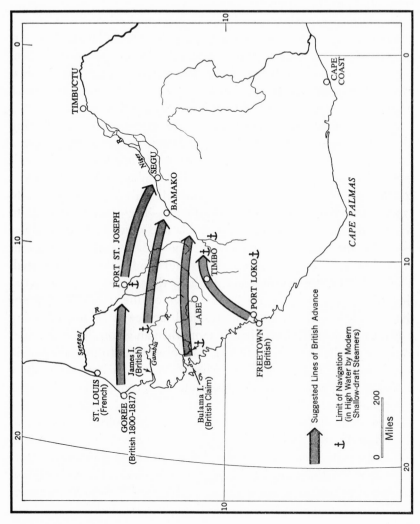

Map 10. The Strategy of Western Approaches to the Upper Niger, 1799–1805

149

A fourth led to Port Loko on the Sierra Leone River, then to Timbo and on to the upper Niger. The possibility of entry by way of the rivers Pongas, Nunez, or Mesurado was also considered, but less seriously than the others.

By curious coincidence, each of the principal advocates of a particular route favored one that began at whatever point on the coast he knew best. Sir Joseph Banks, Mungo Park, and the military commander at Gorée, all believed the best entry was up the Gambia. Philip Beaver wanted to use the Rio Grande and base the enterprise on Bulama Island. Zachary Macaulay preferred Sierra Leone.[9]

A plan was ultimately drawn up by the government, coordinating all of these suggestions. In its most elaborate version, it called for a four-pronged attack, with military expeditions moving inland simultaneously from Sierra Leone, Bulama, the Gambia, and directly across country from Gorée to the upper Senegal. This latter force was to capture Fort Saint Joseph from the French. The other three were to solidify the British hold on the Gambia and move on to the Niger, exploring the country along the way. The effort was to take place in 1803, but a series of postponements and modifications intervened. The war in Europe began again. Perhaps the government discovered that there were, in fact, no French posts on the upper Senegal for them to attack. In any case, the residual legatee of all this planning was a small military force, hardly more than an escort, led by Mungo Park along the familiar route he had pioneered from the Gambia to the Niger. The purpose was changed from an impressive show of force to a mere exploration of routes and commercial conditions along the Niger.

Even so, it was not a success. Park marched from the Gambia to the Niger in 1805, sending back a series of reports, but most of the escort died of disease on the first leg of the trip. Park's last report came from Sansanding, hardly further than his earlier penetration. He and the few survivors who were able to descend the Niger by canoe were killed near Bussa in Northern Nigeria, and the expedition ended as a spectacular failure which added very little to existing knowledge.

The Park expedition of 1805 was nevertheless a new kind of ex-

9. Z. Macaulay to Lord Hobart, printed in Macaulay, *A Letter to His Highness the Duke of Gloucester* . . . (London, 1815), appendix, pp. 23–30; Philip Beaver, *African Memoranda* (London, 1805), pp. 403–10; Gray, *Gambia*, pp. 287–89; Boahen, "British Penetration of North-West Africa," pp. 108–32; and CO 2/1, *passim*.

pedition. It marked the beginning of government sponsorship of African exploration, and it marked the beginning of a new emphasis. The enlightened travellers of an earlier generation had been confined to the coast, where they necessarily concentrated on a detailed study of peoples and plants. The new generation beginning with Park went into the far interior, where they saw more, but in less detail. They were now interested in roads, rivers, and the potential returns of trade, coupled with a growing interest in putting down the African slave trade.

The African Association still sent occasional expenditions, but they never repeated the great success of Park's first expedition. Horneman's death in 1800 was one source of discouragement. Another of the Association's explorers died in Calabar in 1805, before he had even moved from the coast. They later sent two explorers to attempt the approach from Egypt, but neither one reached West Africa. Sir Joseph Banks, the moving spirit, died in 1820 and the Association became less active. In 1831, it merged with the Royal Geographical Society.

The new phase of government-sponsored exploration nevertheless retained its links with the earlier period. The principal figure to replace Banks and the Association was John Barrow, who had himself been one of the enlightened travellers in South Africa during the 1790's. As Under-Secretary of State at the Admiralty from 1805 to 1845, he was in a position to send out expeditions to many different parts of the world and to help explorers secure sponsorship from other government departments. As a founder of the Royal Geographical Society, he was also active in the cause of geographical scholarship.[10]

In spite of Barrow's interest, the renewal of the war and the death of Mungo Park effectively ended all serious thought of further African activity for a decade after 1805, and after Waterloo the nature of British commmercial interests in West Africa had changed beyond recognition. The abolition of the British slave trade and the transfer of Sierra Leone to the Crown forced the government to reconsider the role of the Company of Merchants Trading to Africa. The Company had been created and supported specifically to control the slave-trade forts on the Gold Coast and elsewhere. Their initial

10. Boahen, "British Penetration of North-West Africa," pp. 102–6, 137–42. A. A. Boahen, "The African Association, 1788–1805," *Transactions of the Historical Society of Ghana*, V, 43–64 (1961).

reason for being disappeared with the slave trade. In the new situation, it seemed logical either to abandon the posts altogether or to take them under royal administration. To meet either threat, the African Committee made a serious effort to change with changing times. They accepted the end of the slave trade and tried to adjust to the new possibilities of "legitimate trade." George Torrane was sent out as Governor in 1805 to reform the administration and strengthen the Company against the coming transition.[11]

This assignment was difficult for reasons quite unconnected with events in Europe. The region now including Ghana, Togo, Dahomey, and Nigeria was passing through its own period of revolutionary political change in the first decades of the nineteenth century.

On the Gold Coast, the major alteration was the emergence of Ashanti. Most of the hinterland of the Gold Coast forts was Akan in language and culture, organized in a multitude of petty states. Larger confederations had been formed from time to time in the past, such as the Akwamu Empire which flourished in the hinterland of Accra in the later seventeenth century. By the eighteenth century, the most important larger confederation had come to be Ashanti, founded about 1700 and centered on Kumasi, 100 miles inland from Cape Coast. Ashanti had followed a course of aggressive expansion during a great part of the eighteenth century. The Dutch, Danish, and English authorities had watched from a distance and maintained occasional diplomatic contact with the Asantehene's court. There were, however, a number of smaller states separating the forts from direct contact with the center of Ashanti power. From the British point of view, the most important of these were the Fante states, forming a belt from a point slightly west of Cape Coast to a few miles west of Accra. The Fantes were the principal trade partners and, in a sense, the political allies of the British at most times. Their territory was by no means a British "protectorate," rather the reverse. The British were allowed *de facto* sovereignty within the forts, but they paid ground rent and minor tribute for the right to be there. The prosperity of the Fantes and the Europeans alike rested on the slave trade with the interior. Ashanti also depended both economically and politically on the slave trade, exporting slaves

11. E. C. Martin, *The British West African Settlements, 1750–1821* (London, 1927), pp. 147–51.

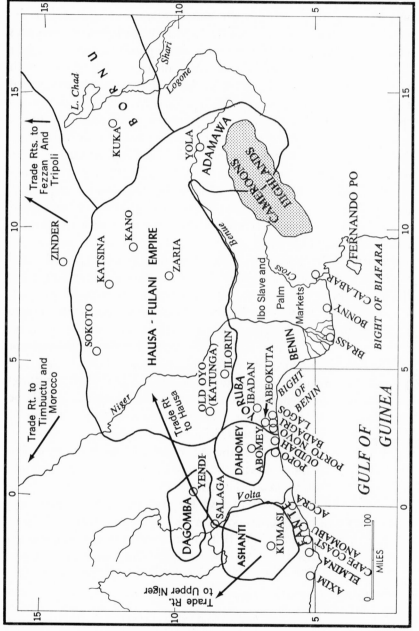

Map 11. The Fulani Empire and Its Neighbors, *c.* 1830

toward the coast in return for firearms and European manufactures.[12]

From the point of view of Ashanti, the Fante, and other coastal peoples were mere middlemen, exacting a profit that might be avoided if Ashanti could deal directly with the forts. The Fante states were turbulent toward the end of the eighteenth century. Their political disorganization was a constant cause of friction with Kumasi, and it was bad for trade. Some coastal people recognized a rather vague Ashanti claim to suzerainty, but Ashanti armies appeared on the coast itself only in the early nineteenth century. In an apparent attempt to subdue disorder on their southern frontier, the Ashanti armies drove through to the coast and appeared in the vicinity of the forts in 1806–07, 1809–11, and 1814–16, defeating a coastal alliance and breaking Fante military power in the process. It is doubtful that Ashanti intended to conquer and rule the coastal states, but in 1816 they tightened their indirect suzerainty over a corridor leading to the sea.[13]

From the British point of view, the rise of Ashanti power raised a problem that was not effectively settled on a permanent basis for almost a century. Either of two clear policies might have been chosen —providing always that the British were unwilling or unable to carry a full conquest of all that is now southern Ghana. One was to form an alliance with the Fante and other coastal peoples and attempt to build a military force strong enough to keep Ashanti at bay. The other was to maintain a genuine neutrality, coupled with a willingness to deal with whatever African power effectively occupied the hinterland of the forts. In practice, the British followed neither of these policies but practiced instead a vacillating alternation between the two. Governor Torrane, the African Committee's new broom, began by first trying to defend the remnant of a defeated Fante army at Anomabu fort in 1806. Then he surrendered a number of his Fante quasi-allies in order to save the fort itself. In 1807 he had swung over to a pro-Ashanti position and suggested using an Ashanti alliance as means of pushing British trade into the interior—first to

12. M. Priestly, "The Ashanti Question and the British: Eighteenth-Century Origins," *Journal of African History*, II (1), pp. 35–59 (1961); Ivor Wilks, "The Rise of the Akwamu Empire, 1650–1710," *Transactions of the Historical Society of Ghana*, III, 99–136 (1957).

13. For a general account of Anglo-Ashanti relations see W. E. F. Ward, *A History of the Gold Coast* (London, 1948), especially pp. 130–54.

Kumasi and then on north as far as Timbuctu and the sources of the Niger.[14] In short, for Torrane and some of the other Gold Coast officials, the rise of Ashanti opened a new possibility of penetration toward the eldorado of the Western Sudan trade.

To the east of Ashanti, there were other political changes of even greater importance, and these also contributed to the new look of African politics. Toward the end of the eighteenth century two strong African states were located, as Ashanti was, on the northern fringe of the forest. These were Dahomey, centered on Abomey, and Oyo, centered at Old Oyo or Katunga in the far north of what is now Western Nigeria. Dahomey had conquered its own road to the sea even earlier than Ashanti, though Oyo still dealt with the Europeans through coastal middlemen based on the trading cities of Lagos, Badagri, and Porto Novo. Still further north, in the Hausa-speaking part of Northern Nigeria, the relatively dense agricultural population was organized around a series of walled cities. Each of them was a political power of considerable local importance, but the group as a whole was not united as a single Hausa state. They had, therefore, less weight in international affairs than their wealth and population might indicate.

Of these three—Dahomey, Oyo, and the Hausa states—Oyo was by far the most powerful in the later eighteenth century, exacting tribute at times from Dahomey and raiding northward across the Niger into Nupe and the fringes of Hausa. But at the turn of the eighteenth century there was a revolutionary shift in the locus of political and military power. The Alafins (or kings) of Oyo were clearly over extended, with more tributary peoples than their popular following or military power could effectively control. Even in the Yoruba-speaking core area, there were elements of dissidence, and the strength of Oyo was fragile. About 1800 an internal revolt broke out against the Alafin in power. He was overthrown, and no successor could re-establish the old dominance. The Oyo state began to disintegrate. In some areas power was re-established on a more local level, but in general the former Oyo territories fell into a condition of quasi-anarchy, lasting in its most serious form throughout the first three decades of the nineteenth century.

The disintegration of Oyo was made still worse by the simul-

14. G. Torrane to African Committee, 20 July 1807, T 70/35, ff. 66–67.

taneous rise of a new power to the north. In addition to the Hausa peasants and townsmen, the Hausa kingdoms contained sizeable minorities of Fulani or Fulbe peoples.[15] These were migrants from further west, who had been drifting into Hausa over the past several centuries. Some of them were cattle-keeping people, who lived symbiotically with the Hausa farmers. Others were urban, Muslim, and partly integrated into the dominant culture of the Hausa cities. At the end of the eighteenth century the urban Fulani had begun to respond to the winds of religious change blowing through the Muslim world. Under the leadership of Usuman dan Fodio, some of them organized a military revolt in the name of religious purity and preached a *jihad* against the rulers of the Hausa states. Between 1804 and about 1810, the Fulani purists had conquered all of Hausa, and Usuman dan Fodio established his domination from a capital at Sokoto. Individual Hausa states were put in charge of Fulani Emirs, ultimately owing political and religious allegiance to the Sultan at Sokoto.

Once Hausa had been conquered, the Fulani were free to carry their conquests to the surrounding non-Hausa areas; and the disintegrating Empire of Oyo was a relatively easy target. Different Yoruba authorities could be played off against one another. Katunga itself was attacked and later deserted by the Yoruba, many of whom moved southward into the protection of the forest. Ilorin, formerly near the core area of Oyo, became the seat of a Fulani Emirate, and the center of gravity of Yoruba power shifted to new centers like Ibadan and Abeokuta. Gradually about 1830 some order emerged from Yoruba anarchy. The military drive from Ilorin was stopped, and a new series of smaller states sprang up within the Oyo empire. It was only a relative recovery, however, and the remainder of the nineteenth century was marked by frequent wars between the various Yoruba states themselves.[16]

15. The accepted English-language terminology for these people is in a state of confusion. In Nigeria they are called Fulani, as the Hausa called them. In Gambia and Sierra Leone, they are called Fula, a Bambara word. The French call them by the Wolof term, Peuls. Their own name for themselves is Fulbe (sing. Pullo). (D. J. Stenning, *Savanna Nomads* [London, 1959], p. 2.) For purposes of this book, I shall use the term, Fulbe, for the people as a whole, reserving the more familiar "Fulani" for the Fulbe of Northern Nigeria, who raised a large state in the nineteenth century.

16. The account of Yoruba history given here and below is based on J. D. Fage, *An Introduction to the History of West Africa* (Cambridge, 1955); Samuel Johnson, *The History of the Yorubas* (Lagos, 1921); S. O. Biobaku, *The Egba and their Neighbours, 1842–1872* (London, 1957).

These events were only dimly perceived in Europe before the mid-1820's, but some of their consequences were more immediately apparent. The fall of Oyo and the rise of Fulani power moved the center of the slave trade to the Bight of Benin, between the mouths of the Volta and the Niger, especially to the ports of Ouidah, Lagos, Porto Novo, and Badagri which were in a position to draw in prisoners captured during the Yoruba wars. The presence of slaves for sale brought European slave dealers, after 1807 principally Spanish, Portuguese, and Brazilian. This was not a part of Africa where British merchants were especially strongly entrenched—less so, for example, than in the Niger Delta or the Bight of Biafara further east. The only official British post was a small factory at Ouidah, and the anarchy inland rendered the area less promising for legitimate trade than it had been for the slave trade. In time, however, British attention would necessarily shift to the Bights of Benin and Biafara, led on in part by the activities of the foreign slave traders.

Meanwhile, what little attention could be spared for coastal West Africa during the later years of the Napoleonic Wars went to the Sierra Leone and the Gold Coast, where the British were already committed. The principal problem of creating a new administration suitable to a post-slave-trade era was not met head on. Instead, the government responded as it was pushed by various pressure groups. The two most important between 1808 and 1815 were the African Institution and the African Committee. The Institution, in spite of its primary concern with the suppression of the foreign slave trade, maintained a watching brief for Sierra Leone. It gathered and disseminated information, provided a little aid to African education, and a little encouragement for African exploration (though this was still the special sphere of the African Association). It was especially anxious to have the government use Sierra Leone as its principal base on the African coast, mainly for the suppression of the slave trade but also for the more general object of diffusing Western culture throughout Africa. Zachary Macaulay was by now a man of some influence, and he became the principal spokesman for the Institution. It was partly on his advice that a Vice-Admiralty Court was established at Sierra Leone, and slave ships captured by the Royal Navy were brought there for adjudication. Since there was no easy way of returning the captured slaves to their homes, they were liberated in

Sierra Leone and became in a short time the majority of the population.

The Navy also became an important factor in coastal affairs. Its long-term interest in the suppression of the foreign slave trade began almost by accident, certainly without any foreknowledge that the work would continue for the next sixty years. The Navy was automatically responsible for enforcing the British abolition act on the high seas. During the war years, it was a normal naval function to capture enemy ships, whether carrying slaves or not. Since the enemy initially included France, Holland, and Spain, suppression of a fair portion of the foreign slave trade was also a legitimate goal. Since the slave trade was also illegal for Danish and United States ships, the Royal Navy took it upon themselves (with doubtful legality) to search these ships for slaves as well. After 1810 Portuguese (including Brazilian) ships were also stopped, since the Strangford Treaty prohibited the slave trade, except that between parts of the Portuguese Empire. In effect, the Navy had a free hand in West Africa to capture slavers of all nations, except Portuguese ships sailing between Portuguese ports.

In the concluding years of the war, the Foreign Office worked through diplomatic channels to continue the Navy's wartime work. It was successful to the extent of inserting an anti-slavery declaration in the final act of the Congress of Vienna, but the declaration was valueless without enforcement; and other powers were unwilling either to enforce it themselves or to allow the British to do so freely against their ships. Further legal complications arose in 1817 when British courts held, in the case of Le Louis, that the Navy could not legally seize or search foreign slavers in peacetime.[17]

After the peace, anti-slavery sentiment was still strong in Britain; and it was reinforced by the material interests of the West Indian planters, who could hardly stand by with their own labor supply cut off and see their foreign competitors receiving a steady stream of manpower from Africa. Under both kinds of pressure, the government entered into direct negotiations with Portugal and Spain. They obtained a treaty with each in 1817, limiting the legal slave trade to the region south of the equator, giving the Royal Navy a right of search and a right of capture if slaves were actually found

17. African Institution, Reports, esp. I, 69–71.

on board. The captured slavers were to be taken for adjudication to a Court of Mixed Commission, of which three were created—one in Havana, one in Brazil, and one at Sierra Leone. When Brazil became independent, the Portuguese treaty applied to Brazil as well. The treaties were extended and modified in various ways over the years, beginning what was to become a very elaborate network of bilateral treaties, all of them to be enforced by the Royal Navy and enforced in very large part by cruisers stationed off the coast of West Africa.[18] Thus the conduct and administration of the naval blockade was added to the problem of administering the West African posts.

A decision on the future of these posts was slow in coming. There were first the unsettled wartime conditions, and later the continuing cross current of strategic interest—the African Institution and the humanitarians generally favoring more activity centered on Sierra Leone, while the African Committee wanted to develop their care-taking function over the Gold Coast forts into something more substantial. Three Commissioners—Thomas Ludlam and William Dawes, both former Governors of Sierra Leone, and Captain E. H. Columbine, the current Governor—were asked to report on conditions from the Gambia to the Gold Coast, but their report was not presented until 1811.

The four years' wait between abolition and the Commissioners' report left room for a flurry of new suggestions for an African policy. Governor George Torrane of the Gold Coast had his pet project for commercial penetration through an Ashanti alliance, and it was generally supported by the African Committee. Most of the others returned to the strategic thinking common duing the Peace of Amiens. Joseph Corry published a new variant of the basic scheme proposed by Sir Joseph Banks and by Golbéry. Like its predecessors, it called for a wholesale declaration of a protectorate, from Cape Palmas westward along the coast and northward to the desert. It was to be backed by fortified strongpoints along the coast and a chain of forts running into the interior from Sierra Leone to Timbo, beyond to the navigable Niger, and downstream to Timbuctu. As with the Banks' proposal of 1799, the whole operation was to be controlled by a chartered company operating under a parliamentary

18. For the British suppression of the foreign slave trade see C. Lloyd, *The Navy and the Slave Trade* (London, 1949) and W. L. Mathieson, *Great Britain and the Slave Trade, 1839–1865* (London, 1929).

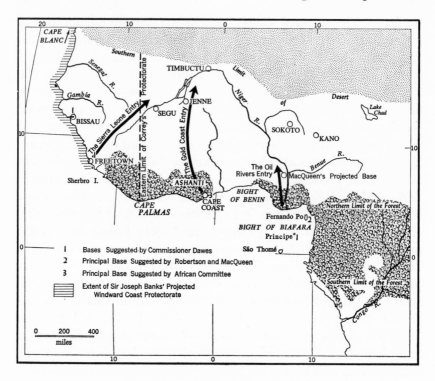

Map 12. Post-War Strategic Plans

monopoly.[19] The basic concept could be varied to taste. Governor T. Perronet Thompson of Sierra Leone suggested a similar plan of attack, with military rather than commercial control—he was a military man—and with the coastal factories omitted. He offered himself as a volunteer to lead an expedition to Timbo as the first stage of the operation.[20]

When the Commissioners finally reported, they disagreed among themselves. All were cautious about plans for inland penetration. They concentrated on the suppression of the slave trade, and the majority report, principally the work of Captain Columbine, wanted to continue the strategic emphasis on the Windward Coast. It argued that anti-slavery patrols could not police the whole coast. Therefore they should concentrate on the vicinity of Sierra Leone and let the

19. J. Corry, *Observations upon the Windward Coast of Africa . . . made in the Years 1805–1806* (London, 1807), pp. 85–89.
20. P. Thompson to C. Jenkins, 6 June 1810, CO 267/28.

rest go for the time being. Even the Gold Coast establishment should be reduced to three forts, and the African Committee should be re-organized.

Dawes disagreed with the windward emphasis and presented a minority report in which he claimed (quite correctly) that the slavers were most common in the Bight of Benin, and the cruisers ought to be there too. He followed with a more detailed proposal for the whole coast, suggesting three bases—Bissau for the far west, Sierra Leone for the center, and the island of Principe to cover the Bights. Dawes thought that Britain ought to buy out the Dutch and Danish forts on the Gold Coast, but his was otherwise an anti-Gold Coast view. He would have kept only three forts in active service. The rest could either be dismantled or sold to private British firms. Neither Dawes's nor any other plan was adopted, but Dawes's was the first official response to the new slave trade drawn from the Yoruba wars. The strategic claims of the Bights of Benin and Biafara were now given a hearing along with those of Sierra Leone, Sene-gambia, and the Gold Coast.[21]

For ten more years, from 1811 to 1821, the question of future strategy in West Africa was undecided. Public discussions in Britain drew diverse threads into a complex net, in which the obvious rivalry between the African Institution and the African Committee had an important part. The proper form of administration was another element—chartered company or royal colony, and if a company, what company? The issue of West Indian slavery was also involved. Pro-slavery writers saw the possibility of scoring a point against the emancipators if they could show free Africans in Africa to be nearly incapable of "advance" without coercion. Thus an attack on the Sierra Leone experiment was a defence for the West Indian planters.

The West African question was again before Parliament in 1816 and 1817, when Select Committees were appointed to look into it. It remained before the public until 1821, with the debate roughly divided according to two alliances of factions. The cause of African Institution was combined with the strategic claims of Sierra Leone and the Windward Coast, opposition to West Indian slavery, and administration of the West African posts by a royal government. The pro-slavery people, on the other hand, preferred company ad-

21. Report of the Commissioners, PP, 1812, x (101) and (180); William Dawes, Memorandum of 27 August 1811, CO 267/29.

ministration and a strategic emphasis on Cape Coast; and they launched a bitter public attack on the Sierra Leone experiment.[22]

Other strategic suggestions called for a principal base still further east. G. A. Robertson, a Liverpool merchant with African experience, repeated in 1819 most elements of the Dawes report of 1811, and in a way that sought to compromise with the existing interests on the Coast. The desires of the Sierra Leone group were to be met by reviving the idea of a Windward Coast protectorate, this time stretching from the Gambia to the Sherbro. The African Committee was to be protected by an effort to drive trade inland through Ashanti, but Robertson's main interest centered on the Bights. He suggested Fernando Po (in place of Dawes's choice of Principe) as the principal base, and it was to be more than a convenient coastal base near the most active slaving area. Robertson brought out evidence that the Oil Rivers were in fact the mouths of the Niger. Thus Fernando Po lay opposite a navigable entry into the heart of Africa: commerce and humanity both demanded an eastern focus and an eastern base. But Robertson's ideas on commercial organization were thoroughly traditional. He still thought in terms of the older system of the slave trade, where African middlemen alone went into the interior and British merchants stayed on the coast.[23]

James MacQueen took up where Robertson left off, adding an anti-Sierra Leone and pro-West Indian element to his case. He supported the Oil Rivers theory about the Niger mouth, and he went to the Admiralty in 1820 with a suggestion for thorough exploration up the rivers. In 1821 he published a geographical survey, reconstructing the course of the Niger from known information. He also spelled out an elaborate plan for the penetration of Africa. As a first step, Sierra Leone should be evacuated. It was useless as a stepping stone into the interior; and it was a bad center for landing captured slaves, since most slavers were captured in the Bights. His preferred coastal base was also Fernando Po, but only as an entry to a second major base in the interior. Without the aid of direct evidence, MacQueen deduced that a second river joined the main branch of the Niger near the point where the Niger turns southward toward

22. See, for example, Joseph Marryat, Commons, 19 March 1819, 1 H 34, cc. 1105–10.
23. G. A. Robertson, Notes on Africa . . . with Hints for the Melioration of the Whole African Population (London, 1819), especially pp. 12–13, 21–23, 132–45, 210–13, and 297–98.

the coast. He was, of course, correct, and the second river was the Benue. His projected inland base was to be located at the confluence, where the town of Lokoja now stands, and linked to Fernando Po by steamboat.[24] Decades later he was justified, and the principal British inland station grew up at the point he had selected sight unseen.

The difference between Robertson and MacQueen reflected a second basic division in strategic thought—the difference between a coastal strategy and one aimed mainly at the penetration of the interior. It was superimposed on the other quarrel over the best point for a coastal base; and it had hardly been raised by the eighteenth-century projectors, who took it for granted that a coastal base would lead to closer contact with the hinterland. With the 1810's, however, the lines of argument were more closely drawn, and a controversy was born which was to have an active life for a half century and more. The disappointments on the coast themselves helped to bring it on. On one hand, it could be argued that commercial failure on the coast had proved nothing, since the valuable trade of West Africa was to be found in the interior. On the other, the clear and increasing evidence of high European mortality suggested that the number of Europeans present in West Africa must be strictly limited, and this in turn implied a limitation to a very few coastal points, leaving the interior trade to African middlemen.

The medical problem influenced other details of strategic planning. Principe and Fernando Po were favored because they were offshore islands, presumably less dangerous than the mainland. Captain John Adams, formerly the master of a slaver, suggested an eastern base at the town of Malemba, now in Cabinda, just north of the Congo mouth. At this point the coast is dry during a part of the year and backed by savanna rather than the forest usual along most of Upper Guinea. The absence of dense vegetation suggested the absence of fevers.[25]

Another recurrent hope was to reach the interior by some route that avoided the Guinea coast altogether. One possibility was to use the desert route from the north. James Grey Jackson, who had been

24. James MacQueen, *Geographical and Commercial View of Northern Central Africa Containing a Particular Account of the Course and Termination of the Great River Niger in the Atlantic Ocean* (Edinburgh, 1821), pp. 169–207.

25. John Adams, *Remarks on the Country Extending from Cape Palmas to the River Congo* (London, 1823), pp. 155–59.

a resident in Morocco for several years, gathered together and published in 1809 whatever he could find out there about the trans-Sahara caravans and the trade of the Western Sudan. Later on, he used this information as the basis of an elaborate project, calling for a large chartered company to organize the trade of the Western Sudan and bring it into British hands. His chosen route avoided both the dangers of Guinea and the political problems of dealing with the Muslim powers of the Maghrib. It began with a base on the desert coast north of the Senegal and south of Morocco. From that point the British-managed caravans could move directly inland to Timbuctu on the Niger bend.[26] An even more far-fetched suggestion called for an entry from the Red Sea to Timbuctu. The base was to be at Massawa, from which point trade could be driven inland into Ethiopia, across the Nile valley, and westward through Darfur, Bornu, and Kano.[27]

Against this background of suggestion, and while the decision about coastal administration was still hanging fire, the eldorado of the Western Sudan was by no means forgotten. Exploration had stopped between the death of Mungo Park in 1805 and the end of the wars in 1815, but new information about the interior kept alive the prospect of marvels still to be found. Some came from the Maghrib, like that furnished by J. G. Jackson. The prominent pressure groups exploited every opening for publicity. In 1815, the African Institution published Mungo Park's last journals and letters along with a glowing account of the riches to be won in the interior by British commerce. In 1816, the African Committee sponsored another, and more suspect, account of the Western Sudan. Robert Adams, the author of this narrative, was a sailor wrecked on the Sahara coast near Cape Blanc. He claimed to have been taken inland to Timbuctu by his Moorish captors before making his way across the desert to Morocco. A second and similar sailor's tale appeared in 1821. Whether the shipwrecked sailors were merely mistaken about where they had been, or deliberately falsified their

26. James Grey Jackson, *Account of the Empire of Morocco* (London, 1809); Vasco de Gama [Pseud. for J. G. Jackson], *Blackwood's Magazine*, IV, 652–53 (March, 1819); J. G. Jackson, *Account of Timbuctoo and Houssa* (London, 1820), esp. pp. 247–71.

27. Poplicola [Pseud.], *Letter the Second to Lord Liverpool on the Political and Commercial Importance of Africa to Great Britain . . .* (Manchester, 1815).

narratives, the interest their stories aroused indicates the continuing fascination of Timbuctu the mysterious.[28]

With the coming of peace, the Government fell in with the enthusiasm for further exploration. Two coordinate efforts were launched to take up the unfinished work of Mungo Park. A Colonial Office expedition under Major Peddie was ordered to make an entry from the Windward Coast and strike the Niger near the scene of Park's original discovery. For the five years, 1816–21, the expedition tried successively to penetrate by way of the Senegal, the Gambia, and the Nunez, meeting the usual problem of high mortality and political difficulties with the African authorities. Peddie died. His successor, Captain Campbell, also died. The expedition was finally commanded by Major William Gray. He and Staff-Surgeon Dorchard were able to traverse a good deal of the country lying between the upper Gambia, the Upper Niger, and Sierra Leone, but only with small parties. The expedition as a whole was finally withdrawn without having accomplished its main objectives.[29]

A second expedition under Admiralty sponsorship was sent to examine the rivers around the Bight of Biafara, to see if one of them might turn out to be the mouth of the Niger. It was elaborately organized with a staff of scientists under the general command of Captain Tuckey, R.N. The first objective was the Congo, with the Rio del Rey and the Formosa also on the agenda. In fact, the Formosa was a mouth of the Niger, but the expedition never reached it. It went inland about 150 miles along the course of the Congo

28. Jackson, *Morocco;* Robert Adams, *The Narrative of R. Adams, A Sailor who was Wrecked on the West Coast of Africa in . . . 1810* (London, 1816); T. S. Traill, "Account of the Captivity of Alexander Scott among Wandering Arabs of the Great African Desert," *The Edinburgh Philosophical Journal,* IV, 38–54, 225–34 (January and April, 1821). Another, similar tale was so specious as to be not merely a hoax, but a parody on the earlier hoaxes. See "Specimens of Timbuctoo Anthology," *New Monthly Magazine,* XI, 22–28 (1824).

29. William Gray, *Travels in Western Africa in the Years 1818, 19, 20, and 21* (London, 1825). In imagining these and other European "explorations" of West Africa, it is necessary to avoid the tendency to see too close a resemblance to European explorations in North America or Australia. In contrast to those other two continents, this part of Africa was relatively densely populated and had its own commercial system with a network of trade routes stretching from the desert to the Guinea coast. African commercial travellers regularly moved about with a security roughly comparable to that of twelfth-century Europe. African exploration was difficult and dangerous for Europeans, mainly on account of disease, but, for all that, they were merely outsiders investigating an alien society—not by any means the first men to march or ride over their long routes.

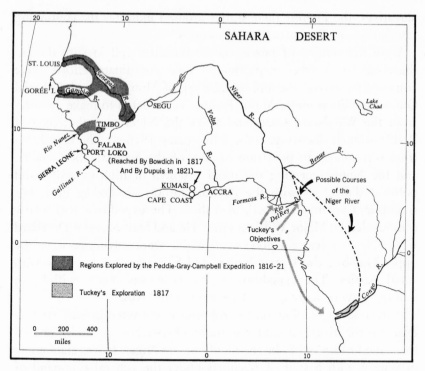

Map 13. Post-War Explorations, 1815–1821

in 1816–17, but Tuckey and all of the scientists died. The survivors were withdrawn before they could attempt any of the other rivers.[30]

A third possible approach also appeared in the post-war years. This was to enter West Africa along the caravan routes from the Maghrib. One such route was especially inviting in the later 1810's and it was called to the Government's attention by a series of widely separated events. In Tripoli, Yusuf Caramanli (1795–1830) was Pasha, theoretically under the suzerainty of Turkey but effectively an independent ruler. In the early nineteenth century he began to strengthen his control over the hinterland, subduing Fezzan by 1811. Traffic could then move safely southward from Tripoli to the oases lying on the route to Bornu and Lake Chad or further west to the Hausa states. At the southern end of the caravan route, the Hausa states had been seriously disturbed in the first decade of the century by the Fulani rising, and Bornu had had its own troubles with the

30. Boahen, "British Penetration of North-West Africa," pp. 132–50.

Fulani *jihad*. By 1814, however, Bornu had responded with a religious and political resurgence of its own, led by Mohammed el-Amin el-Kanemi, himself a religious leader like Shehu Usuman dan Fodio. He was able to contain the military threat on his western frontiers by 1814. The Mai of Bornu returned to power in his own kingdom, but with El-Kanemi as *de facto* ruler until his death in 1835. Internal peace was thus re-established at the southern terminus of the route from Tripoli, and El-Kanemi also established an entente with Tripoli as a makeweight against the Fulani Empire. Thus the caravan road was held at either end by a strong power, and these powers were on friendly terms with each other.

The possibilities thus opened were brought to British attention by the combined efforts of Col. G. H. Warrington and Captain William Henry Smyth, R.N. Warrington served as H. M. Vice-Consul in Tripoli from 1814 to 1846, and he was initially on close personal terms with the Pasha. Smyth had served with Philip Beaver in the Indian Ocean during the later phases of the Napoleonic Wars. He was infected with Beaver's enthusiasm for African colonization and later became Beaver's biographer. In 1815 he was appointed to survey the coasts of Sicily and the nearby shores of Africa and Italy, and he took this assignment as an excuse for travelling south from Tripoli. On the basis of his reconaissance, he showed that a full-scale expedition could be sent toward the Western Sudan. The suggestion was seconded by Warrington, who also obtained the Pasha's consent and support. As a result, Joseph Ritchie was appointed Vice-Consul for Fezzan and posted to Murzuk, with orders to obtain scientific and commercial information and to travel overland to Timbuctu if possible. Ritchie and his party actually reached Murzuk in 1818, but he died there and his two companions returned to England. One of them, George Francis Lyon, wrote an account of their travels, though it did little to modify the earlier reports from Murzuk by Hormeman and Lucas.[31] Thus all three of the post-war government expeditions ended in failure and the death of their leaders.

A fourth effort in these same years met with more success. The African Committee were interested in showing their competence to handle British affairs on the Gold Coast. They also wanted to dem-

31. Boahen, "British Penetration of North-West Africa," pp. 164–81; G. F. Lyon, *A Narrative of Travels in Northern Africa in the Years 1818, 19, and 20* (London, 1821); Heinrich Barth, *Travels and Discoveries in North and Central Africa*, 5 vols. (London, 1857–1858), I, xiii.

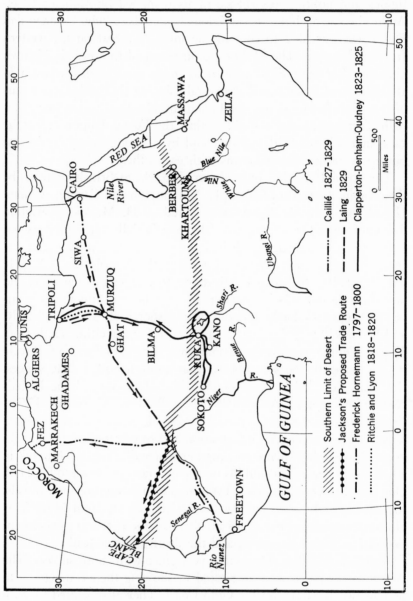

Map 14. The Northern Approaches, *c.* 1825–1830

onstrate the potential value of their forts as a base for inland trade. In 1817, they sent an expedition to Kumasi to open direct negotiations with the Asantehene. Although the original leader was Frederick James, the Company's governor of Accra fort, one of the members was Thomas Edward Bowdich, an amateur naturalist and ethnographer, and a writer in the service of the Company. Bowdich ultimately assumed command, and in 1819 he published an account that went far beyond the original orders to report on political and commercial conditions.

His glowing description of Ashanti society caught the public imagination at a time when other expeditions were ending in failure. His reports of hearsay evidence about the trade routes still further into the interior indicated, quite correctly, that Kumasi was one of the way points on a major route leading from the coast to the Fulani Empire. He therefore recommended a commercial and political alliance with Ashanti (reminiscent of Torrane's Ashanti policy a decade earlier). British trade could then be carried directly into the interior, first to the great market at Salaga and ultimately still further to Yendi, Wawa, and Hausa.[32]

The main line of Bowdich's suggestion was accepted by the Government, but not in a form the African Committee could approve.[33] Joseph Dupuis was sent to Kumasi in 1820 as a resident British representative reporting directly to the Foreign Office. He signed a new agreement with Osei Bonsu, the Asantehene. For reasons partly personal and partly political it was opposed by the Company's officials on the coast, and the treaty failed ratification in England.

The Dupuis mission took place at a time when the government was finally reaching a decision about the future administration of the West African posts. By an act of Parliament in 1821, the Company of Merchants Trading to Africa was disbanded. Their forts were turned over to the Crown to be placed, along with the new post at Bathurst on the Gambia, under a single West African government at Sierra Leone. The implications for coastal strategy were clear. It was a defeat for the advocates of more activity in the Bights of Benin and Biafara, a defeat for the African Committee, and a victory for the Sierra Leone faction. The failure of Dupuis' treaty with

32. T. E. Bowdich, *Mission from Cape Coast Castle to Ashantee* . . . (London, 1819), esp. pp. 341–43, 453–60.
33. Arbuthnot to African Committee, 3 September 1818, T 70/36.

Ashanti was also a defeat for those who hoped for diplomatic aid in pushing British trade inland. After fourteen years of uncertainty some kind of decision had finally been reached.

The decision implied only limited activity—and that centered on the Windward Coast. It was soon reinforced by further events on the Gold Coast. Sir Charles MacCarthy, whose Governorship of Sierra Leone now included command of the Gold Coast forts, was soon embroiled in a war with Ashanti, in alliance with the Fante and other coastal peoples. He himself was killed in a skirmish with the Ashanti army in 1824. The coastal alliance retrieved the defeat with a decisive victory at Dodowa in 1826, but there was no formal peace until 1831. Hence there was no possibility of penetration by way of Ashanti. MacCarthy's death, furthermore, made a strong public impression at home and went far to erase the high hopes Bowdich had aroused. The cost of the war made an even stronger impression on the Treasury, and no further schemes based on the Gold Coast would be favorably received in high places for some time to come.[34]

Meanwhile, men-on-the-spot in Sierra Leone worked unofficially for an opening toward their own hinterland, much as Bowdich had done from the Gold Coast. The home government had been thoroughly discouraged by the failure of the Peddie-Campbell-Gray expedition of 1816–21; but enthusiasts could rest their continued optimism on the successful journey of Gaspard Théodore Mollien, who travelled overland in 1818 from St. Louis to Timbo and then down to the coast in what is now Portuguese Guinea. His report was translated into English by T. E. Bowdich and published in 1820.[35] The Sierra Leone government also kept up the rather tenuous relations established with the Almami of Futa Jallon and the Bambara King of Segu by the expedition of the later twenties. Embassies went up from Sierra Leone to Timbo in 1821 and again in 1822. The second of these was led by Captain Alexander Gordon Laing, later the first European to reach Timbuctu in the nineteenth century. Laing followed his trip to Timbo with a suggestion for establishing close relations with selected African states, his own choice being Sulima in the vicinity of Falaba.[36]

In 1825 and 1826 even more ambitious plans for diplomatic ac-

34. See Ward, *Gold Coast*, pp. 169–82.
35. G. T. Mollien, *Travels in the Interior of Africa* (London, 1820).
36. A. G. Laing, *Travels in the Timanee, Kooranko, and Soolima Countries in Western Africa* (London, 1825), pp. 387–98.

tion were taken up by General Charles Turner, the Governor of
Sierra Leone. During his short governorship he bombarded the Colonial Office with projects representing an extreme version of the
Windward Coast strategy. Among other things, he wanted two small
steamers to patrol the coast from the Gambia to the Gallinas, plus
small military posts located so as to command the river mouths.
Britain could then control the trade with the interior. The power to
cut off trade would give control without the necessity of using large
forces inland. Peaceful commercial penetration could proceed with
the aid of a British resident at Timbo, pushing down the trade routes
to the Niger and on to Segu and Timbuctu.[37]

The idea itself was simply a revival of the project for a Windward Coast protectorate, but Turner followed ideas with action. He
signed treaties taking Sherbro Island and other coastal territory under
the protection of Sierra Leone. He led two small military and naval
expeditions to the south and another to Port Loko on the Sierra
Leone River. Then he died. His work was left unfinished—not only
unfinished but undone by the Colonial Office, which refused to accept most of his annexations.[38]

After so many failures and the death of so many of its officers,
the British government was less and less inclined by the mid-1820's
to look with favor on increased commitments in Guinea. The Colonial Office had a vastly increased body of commitments elsewhere.[39]
It rejected Turner's plans for expansion from Sierra Leone, but it
fell in easily enough with his suggestion that Britain should withdraw from the Gold Coast. A first decision, shortly after MacCarthy's
death, was to evacuate all but Accra and Cape Coast.[40] In 1826 it
was changed to complete withdrawal from the Gold Coast.

Not only had the Guinea coast produced one disappointment after

37. See Turner's despatches of 22 February 1825, 9 April 1825, 25 June 1825,
20 July 1825, and 20 December 1825, in CO 267/65 and 267/66.

38. Relevant despatches are in CO 267/65 and 267/66. See also J. J. Crooks, *A
History of the Colony of Sierra Leone Western Africa* (London, 1903), pp. 117–29.

39. It would, however, be a mistake to underestimate the official concern with West
Africa in the mid-1820's. In 1806 the Secretary of State had sent out only 209 despatches to all colonies. At that time in West Africa, only Gorée was directly under
Crown government, and it received only four of these communications. By 1824, the
total number of outgoing dispatches rose to 3,460, of which 324 went to Sierra Leone
and the other West African posts. By this measure, at least, West Africa now bulked
larger than all colonial business had done in 1806. The volume of West African business in 1824 was also larger than that of the Cape of Good Hope, the only other part
of sub-Saharan Africa then within the British sphere. (D. M. Young, *The Colonial
Office in the Early Nineteenth Century* [London, 1961], pp. 248–49.)

40. See Minute of 2 July 1825 on Turner to Bathurst, 9 April 1825, CO 267/65.

another, it now appeared that better routes to the Western Sudan were available. In 1825 an expedition returned to Tripoli, having made a successful round-trip crossing of the Sahara and a detailed survey of what is now Northern Nigeria. It was the first really successful British expedition to the interior of West Africa since Mungo Park's first journey, in the 1790's.

In spite of Ritchie's death, the effort to open the Tripoli-Bornu route had been continuous from 1818 onward. The expedition that ultimately succeeded had been mounted in 1821, through the co-operation of the Colonial Office and John Barrow at the Admiralty. The staff consisted of Dr. Walter Oudney, a medical man with an interest in natural history, Hugh Clapperton of the Navy, and Dixon Denham of the Army. They were ordered to penetrate to Bornu and carry out the scientific and commercial investigations originally assigned to Ritchie. After crossing the desert they moved about widely between 1822 and 1824, often in separate parties. Denham explored to the south and east of Lake Chad, while Clapperton travelled west to Hausa, visiting Kano and Sokoto, where he made contact with Sultan Bello. Even though Dr. Oudney died, the results were extremely encouraging.[41]

New efforts in the same direction began at once, attempting to exploit both the Tripoli opening and the new contact with the Fulani Empire. In a pair of simultaneous expeditions, Major Laing was sent toward Timbuctu by way of Tripoli, while Clapperton was sent to try a southern approach to the Fulani Empire from Badagri on the Bight of Benin. He travelled up from the coast, keeping just to the west of the most disturbed parts of Yoruba, and crossed the Niger at Bussa, near the point where Mungo Park had been killed. Most of the Europeans in the party died before the expedition crossed the Niger, but Clapperton continued with his personal servant, Richard Lemon Lander, going on into Hausa through Zaria and Kano, until he ultimately arrived once again at Sokoto. His luck held no further. Sultan Bello declined to sign the hoped-for treaty of commerce and friendship with Britain, and Clapperton himself died in

41. Dixon Denham and Hugh Clapperton, *Narrative of Travels and Discoveries in Northern and Central Africa in the Years 1822, 1823, and 1824*, 2 vols. (London, 1826). See also Boahen, "British Penetration of North-West Africa," pp. 190–98, 249–55.

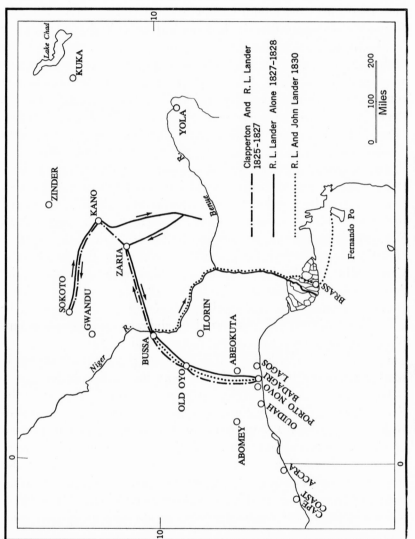

Map 15. Clapperton, Lander, and the Lower Niger

Sokoto. Lander, however, made his way back to the coast, retracing the overland route to Badagri.[42]

Meanwhile, Laing had left Tripoli and reached Timbuctu in August 1826, the same month Clapperton arrived at Sokoto. His misfortunes also began after he had reached his objective. On leaving Timbuctu, Laing was killed, and his papers disappeared, though one of his servants lived to bring word to Tripoli. The repercussions were more far reaching than the mere death of another explorer, a common enough occurrence. The difficulty came from the fact that René Caillié, a free-lance French explorer, reached Timbuctu two years later, following a route inland from the River Nunez near Sierra Leone, along the valley of the upper Niger, then home across the desert by way of Fez and Tangier. When Caillié's report was published, Consul Warrington in Tripoli believed it was a fabrication —that it was, in fact, based on Laing's journal which he presumed to have been stolen and sold to the French. Among other things, Warrington accused the Pasha of Tripoli of bad faith, and the affair of Laing's papers ended good relations between Britain and the Caramanlis. The British government withdrew its support of the dynasty. Revolts broke out in both Tripoli and Fezzan. After 1831 the Tripoli route was no longer open to British travellers. In 1834 Yusuf Caramanli was forced to abdicate. The Ottoman Empire, previously only the most distant suzerain, intervened and began to re-establish order; but it was a long process, and the roads south from Tripoli were unsafe for more than a decade.[43]

For the time being, therefore, the only useful way to reach the Fulani Empire (or solve the Niger problem) was the route from Badagri opened by Clapperton and Lander. By 1829, most geographical authorities had come to believe that the Oil Rivers were the Niger mouth, but there was still no conclusive proof. On the strength of Lander's book and experience, and in spite of his social origins, he was given a commission from the Colonial Office to return and explore the lower Niger. He set out with his brother John

42. Hugh Clapperton, *Journal of a Second Expedition into the Interior of Africa, from the Bight of Benin to Soccatoo* (London, 1829); R. L. Lander, *Records of Captain Clapperton's Last Expedition to Africa . . . with Subsequent Adventures of the Author*, 2 vols. (London, 1830).

43. René Caillié, *Travels Through Central Africa to Timbuctoo*, 2 vols. (London, 1830); Boahen, "British Penetration of North-West Africa," pp. 270–92.

in 1830 over the familiar route overland to Bussa. On reaching the Niger, they returned to the coast by canoe.[44]

This final evidence of the Niger's lower course did more than settle an academic puzzle. It showed without question that an all-water route into the interior existed. The claims of Sierra Leone as the principal focus of British interest were now decisively ended, and the Niger was to dominate British strategic thought for the next quarter century.

But the Landers' exploration was not alone in producing this result, and there was no immediate revival of interest in West Africa. The home government had been increasingly disappointed with all its operations on the Coast. The decision of 1826 to evacuate the Gold Coast was an early sign, though the evacuation never took place. It was only barely prevented by the protests of British merchants who traded there. As a compromise, the government withdrew in 1828 as the administering authority, turning the forts over to a committee of merchants sitting in London. Local control was vested in a President and Council at Cape Coast, with limited jurisdiction and a government subsidy of only £4,000 a year.

The value of Sierra Leone was again called into question in these same years. A new set of royal commissioners, James Rowan and Henry Wellington, were sent to survey the West African settlements, and their report was far from favorable. The commissioners' report was presented to Parliament, and another Select Committee of the House of Commons considered West African policy in 1830.

The Committee followed the main lines of the Commissioners' report. The Sierra Leone peninsula was to be kept, but with European staff reduced to a bare minimum. If it were not for the fact that Sierra Leone had a Westernized population, settled there through British agency, it too would have been evacuated. The main base for the anti-slavery patrols and the headquarters of the Court of Mixed Commission was to be moved to Fernando Po.[45] In preparation for the move, the island was occupied by a British naval expedition from 1827 to 1832, but there was a problem of sovereignty. Spain

44. Richard and John Lander, *Journal of an Expedition to Explore the Course and Termination of the Niger* . . . 2 vols., Rev. ed. (New York, 1858). First published in 3 vols., London, 1832.
45. Report of the Commissioners, PP, 1826–1827, vii (312) and (552).

still had a highly theoretical title to the island, and she refused to sell except at a price the British considered prohibitively expensive. In the end, therefore, Sierra Leone continued to be the seat of British government on the Coast, and the principal naval base—but only on suffrance.

In spite of a few short bursts of excitement, the trend of British thinking about West Africa was one of steadily increasing pessimism throughout the first three decades of the nineteenth century. The 1830 Committee marked the nadir, both for West Africa in general and Sierra Leone as a British colony.[46] The only hope for the future lay in the incorrigible optimism of an small group of enthusiasts, many of whom had served on the Coast—and on the still untried promise of the Niger as an all-water route into the interior.

46. Report of the Committee, PP, 1830, x (661), pp. 1–5.

7

THE

PROBLEM OF SURVIVAL

During the whole of the nineteenth century, the most important problem for Europeans in West Africa was simply that of keeping alive. Until the 1840's the essential facts about the "climate" remained what they had been in the eighteenth century. Any European activity exacted an appalling price. Every assignment of missionaries or officials, every journey of exploration, every trading voyage or anti-slavery patrol took its toll. Unlike the situation of the later eighteenth century, when men could plan in optimistic ignorance, the facts were now more broadly publicized. Lind and some others had spoken out earlier, but the coastal experiments of the 1790's brought the image of West Africa as "the white man's grave" into new focus. The initial death rate for Europeans sent to the Province of Freedom had been 46 per cent. The Sierra Leone Company lost 49 per cent of its European staff, and the Bulama Island Association lost 61 per cent in the first year.[1] These figures were not far out of line with the eighteenth-

1. See Appendix.

century expectation of a 20 per cent loss from the crew on a slaving voyage to the Coast, but they were something to ponder.

Even so, the full implications were only gradually recognized. The projectors of the 1790's were very much disturbed when the death rate was known, but their public reaction was to explain it away and hope for something better in the future. They pointed to the reduced mortality in the second and later years at any settlement (which we would now expect in the light of modern malariology) and they sensed correctly that the "seasoning sickness" was the serious hurdle to be passed. They fell back, this time incorrectly, on their own prediction that Sierra Leone could be made healthy if it was cleared and cultivated. Some of the more religious humanitarians also saw the high death rates as a form of retributive justice. Granville Sharp blamed the drunkenness of the settlers for the mortality at the Province of Freedom. A rapid death had been their punishment, but better conduct from future settlers might solve the problem. Other consolation could be sought in the continued hope of finding a healthy place on the coast or a better climate inland. An undertone of continuing optimism was therefore still possible, even after the mid-1790's.[2]

This remaining optimism was only gradually eroded away during the quarter century after 1792. Even the African enthusiasts in the first years of the nineteenth century were not quite so enthusiastic about the health prospects as their predecessors had been. Golbéry chose the ancient personification of Africa as a woman holding a cornucopia and a scorpion. The one was a "just symbol of the treasures hidden in the bowels of this auriferous country, and the riches which its inexhaustible fecundity offers to Europe," the other a symbol of "all the diseases and dangers of a burning climate."[3] The

    2. Sierra Leone Company, *Report of the Court of Directors of the Sierra Leone Company to the General Court,* 7 vols. (title varies) (London, 1791–1808), I (1791), 11; H. Thornton to J. Clarkson, 14 September 1792, Ad. Mss. 41262A, f. 179; Sierra Leone Company, *Account of the Colony of Sierra Leone from its First Establishment in* [*sic*] *1793 . . .* (London, 1795), p. 53; C. B. Wadström, *An Essay on Colonization, Particularly Applied to the Western Coast of Africa . . . ,* 2 vols. (London, 1794–1795), I, 39; Philip Beaver, *African Memoranda* (London, 1805), pp. 365–66; G. Sharp to a New York Lady, 12 January 1788, quoted in Prince Hoare, *Memoirs of Granville Sharp,* 2nd ed., 2 vols. (London, 1828), II, 84; J. Corry, *Observations upon the Windward Coast of Africa . . . Made in the Years 1805–1806* (London, 1807), pp. 100–101.
    3. S. M. X. Golberry [S. M. X. de Golbéry], *Travels in Africa Performed during the Years 1785, 1786, and 1787,* 2 vols. (London, 1803), II, 209.

price to be paid was now recognized, even though the reward might justify the cost.

By the 1820's the cost seemed to rise in the eyes of the British public. It was in this decade that Sierra Leone received its reputation as the "white man's grave" *par excellence.*[4] The high mortality among new arrivals continued. It seemed, indeed, to be worse than ever, and there were political reasons for giving the facts full publicity. The opponents of Sierra Leone could and did point out that all of the full Governors of the colony between 1810 and 1830, with the single exception of Col. C. W. Maxwell, died either in Africa or on the way home. But the full force of gubernational mortality was not felt until after 1827. The entire period, 1816-1824, was taken up with the long Governorship of Sir Charles MacCarthy, and he was finally killed by the Ashanti, not by the "climate." Between 1826 and 1830, however, precisely when the future strategy for West Africa was under discussion in the press and Parliament, MacCarthy's three successors died in three successive years—Charles Turner in 1826, Sir Neil Campbell in 1827, and Lt. Col. Dixon Denham in 1828. During these years the image of the "white man's grave" was set in the public mind.[5]

It was supported by abundant statistical evidence furnished by the investigation of Commissioners Wellington and Rowan, sent out in 1826. They looked into the mortality figures reaching back to the foundation of Sierra Leone, and they circulated a questionnaire to the medical officers then on duty. The answers were universally unfavorable, and the Commissioners' conclusions were even more damaging. They called attention for the first time to the apparent death rates for Sierra Leone Negroes. These figures had been largely ignored, even though the published data showed an initial death rate of 39 per cent for the "black poor" who settled the Province of Freedom, and at least 17 per cent for the Nova Scotian settlers at Sierra Leone a few years later. The Commissioners' new data showed that the Nova Scotians and their descendants had continued to de-

4. To my knowledge, the earliest use of the phrase in print occurs in J. C. de Figaniere e Morao, *Descripçao de Serra Leon* (Lisboa, 1822), p. 38, where he refers to the colony as the "sepulcro dos Europêos." (C. Fyfe, *A History of Sierra Leone* [London, 1962], p. 151.)

5. See, for example, *John Bull*, 22 April and 30 April 1827 and 30 August 1829; *The Times*, 17 November 1827; Joseph Hume, Commons, 15 June 1830, 2 H 25, cc. 394–99; *Quarterly Review*, XXXIX, 180–83 (January, 1829).

cline in numbers ever since, dropping from 1,131 in 1792, to 722 in 1822, and 578 in 1826. Even the Maroon population had declined for a time before it began slowly to rise again. Over the whole period from 1787 to 1826, some 22,000 non-European settlers had entered the colony, but the population in 1826 was only 13,000.

The Commissioners drew no explicit medical conclusion from these data, but a conclusion was clearly implied. Sierra Leone was not simply the white man's grave. It was everyman's grave. In fact, the high mortality of the "black poor" is explicable enough. Though Negro in race, they had been absent from regions of endemic malaria for decades or generations. Their mortality in Sierra Leone was therefore within the range that might have been expected for European settlers. Roughly the same pattern would be expected of the Nova Scotians, and even the Maroons from Jamaica had not known hyperendemic *falciparum* malaria before. By far the largest number of settlers in Sierra Leone by 1826, however, were "liberated Africans" and the sharp decrease in their numbers cannot be explained on medical grounds. In this case, the Commissioners apparently made a mistake. There is known to have been a considerable emigration from Sierra Leone into the hinterland, partly for trade and partly by the return of some "liberated Africans" to homes not far away. The Commissioners made no allowance for this.[6]

In other respects as well, they tried to undermine the props that had shored up optimism about the West African "climate." They held, as Lind had done, that mortality was not accountable to the "misconduct" of individuals. Nor was there any evidence that one part of the Coast was more healthy than another. In the long run, it was all unhealthy, though mortality varied in the short run with the appearance of epidemics. They could find no evidence that either clearing, cultivation, or sanitary regulations brought an improvement. In all these matters they were correct. It was a thoroughly damning report, and a thoroughly realistic one.[7] The only remaining cause for hope was the prospect of a better "climate" in the interior, and on this point there was still insufficient evidence. The later 1820's and early 1830's thus marked the nadir of pessimism about the Afri-

6. R. R. Kuczynski, *Demographic Survey of the British Colonial Empire, Volume I: West Africa* (London, 1948), p. 71.

7. Report of Commissioners, PP, 1826–1827, vii (312), pp. 12–13, 20, and 104–9. For answers to medical questionnaire see PP, 1830, xxi (57), pp. 63 ff.

can "climate" and the possibility of European activity on the Guinea coast.

It is not easy to explain, for this period or any other, why so many Europeans were willing to go to West Africa in the face of the known facts about the "climate." The dreams of untold wealth or the special religious zeal of the missionaries must be counted as part of the answer. And again, most Europeans who went to West Africa before 1830 did not, in fact, go voluntarily. The European soldiers of the Royal African Corps were recruited by allowing them to serve on the Coast in commutation of punishment in Britain.[8] The others, the voluntary travellers with no intention either to save souls or grow rich, seem to have been sustained by a strain of personal optimism. For the veterans, optimism was natural, once they themselves had safely passed the seasoning sickness. Those with most experience in Africa were often the most optimistic. Mungo Park, after losing more than three-quarters of his men on the overland stage of his last expedition, still wrote back that health conditions had not been so bad. He thought he could do it again with a loss of only 6 or 8 per cent, if only he had chosen the right season for the march.[9] Almost any explanation was more satisfying than the truth—that virtually everyone would come down with "fever," many would die, and there was no real hope (with the knowledge then available) of controlling the random selection of victims.

Planners in Britain had a further cause for optimism in the progress of science and technology. Faith in medical science was misplaced in the short run, as mortality rates showed, but European medicine was moving in new directions. Even though the germ theory of disease and the cellular structure of the body were still unknown, the rationalism of the Enlightenment came belatedly into medicine toward the end of the eighteenth century. The general systems of one-cause pathology decayed slowly. There was a new trend toward more accurate clinical observation and more extensive autopsy. These changes in turn were associated with the broader social and economic development of Western Europe. The Industrial Revolution brought rapid urbanization and with it the development of hospitals, where many of the uprooted came for their final medical

8. PP, 1830, xxi (57), p. 49.
9. Mungo Park, *The Journal of a Mission to the Interior of Africa in 1805,* 2nd ed. (London, 1815), II, 190.

treatment and ultimate dissection. The new era of hospital practice made possible mass clinical observation far beyond the range of doctors who merely worked at the bedside of individual patients.[10]

During the Napoleonic Wars, doctors accustomed to hospital work went to the tropics with the armies, and the new generation of military doctors took with them the new precision, the new techniques, and a knowledge of new work in the basic sciences. Priestly and Lavoisier had opened an interest in the chemistry of respiration, with obvious implications for the study of the tropical fevers "known" to be caused by the miasma in tropical air. Closer analysis and speculation about the nature and cause of miasma was one opening for further investigation. Mass clinical observation of various remedies was another.

Very little of the new work, however, was done in West Africa. Britain's medical concern went where the troops went, in this period to either India—to the West to protect the valuable remnant of an old empire, or to the East to create a new one. The only new and substantial West African medical reports came from Sierra Leone; and the best of them came during the Sierra Leone Company's early years, when the company still hoped to use their colony as a base for scientific investigation. Their physician in the 1790's was Thomas Winterbottom, whose *Account of the Native Africans in the Neighbourhood of Sierra Leone* became the pioneer work in African medical ethnography. The whole of the second volume was a study of tropical medicine based on his practice in the colony, and it included a detailed account of the medical practices of the Africans themselves. It was patterned on the work of Benjamin Rush with the North American Indians and based on the assumption that European medical men might learn something of value from the Africans. This enquiring spirit, however, was closer to that of the "enlightened travellers" of the eighteenth century than to the more self-confident attitude that followed the Napoleonic Wars.[11]

Other medical investigations were more narrowly concerned with the problem of European survival. One possible line of inquiry fol-

10. E. H. Acherknecht, *A Short History of Medicine* (New York, 1955), p. 134; R. H. Shryock, "Nineteenth Century Medicine: Scientific Aspects," *Journal of World History*, III, 881–908 (1957).

11. T. Winterbottom, *An Account of the Native Africans in the Neighborhood of Sierra Leone,* 2 vols. (London, 1803), II, esp. 1–4.

lowed the tradition of Lind's detailed assessment of West African geography and its possible medical implications, the object being to select the most healthy places for European posts or settlements. By the early nineteenth century, "medical topography" was recognized as a special department of medical science. One of the early works in their field was presented as a thesis to the Faculty of Medicine in Paris by Charles Stormont, a Scot who had been in Sierra Leone.[12] It described the general topography of West Africa, with information on meteorology, epidemiology, and estimates or statistics of the incidence of disease.

By the 1820's, medical topography was a regular feature in the official reports from the Coast, notably that of Commissioners Wellington and Rowan. If the investigators were not themselves medical men, they could still depend (as Wellington and Rowan did) on the evidence of medical practitioners already established in the settlements. But in the 1820's the West Coast of Africa was not the kind of place to attract original investigators. Most of the medical men there were merely the ordinary run of army doctors, and West African medicine tended to follow the lead of tropical medicine elsewhere.

Tropical fevers, still undifferentiated with any precision, remained the key problem of tropical medicine, and the principal medical controversy of the period involved the continuing uncertainty of classification and diagnosis. It began with the epidemic spread of yellow fever from Africa to the West Indies to North America. In 1793, a disease now recognized as yellow fever appeared as an epidemic in Grenada. Dr. Colin Chisholm, a surgeon of His Majesty's Ordnance, quickly identified it as distinct from the ordinary fevers of the country. He then developed the hypothesis that it came to Grenada from West Africa in a ship carrying refugee settlers from Bulama Island. For scientific purposes, he identified it as "malignant pestilential fever," but the popular name "Bulam fever" followed from the supposed source and became one of the common terms for yellow fever during the next half century. The epidemic was so severe and spread so rapidly that every military doctor in the West Indies had the opportunity to see hundreds of cases. The same privilege was soon visited

12. Charles Stormont, *Essai sur la topographie médicale de la côte occidentale d'Afrique et particulièrement sur celle de la colonie de Sierra Leone* (Paris, 1822).

on the medical men of the North American coast, especially in Philadelphia.[13]

The result was a burst of medical interest in fevers, with a stream
of articles and books, first from the West Indies, then from America,
and finally in Britain as well. There, it developed into a fifty-year
controversy, with ramifications far beyond the initial problem of correctly explaining a single epidemic. The original argument turned
on the correct classification of "Bulam fever"—whether it was a
separate disease or merely a more serious form of the ordinary fevers
of the tropics. This was by no means the petty question it may appear.
Chisholm claimed that "Bulam fever" was infectious, and its spread
could be prevented by proper quarantine. He thus raised questions of
public medical policy. William Pym took up the case for quarantine
and fought for decades (though mainly without success) for the
adoption of more stringent quarantine regulations in the military
services.

The assumption of infection raised further medical problems involving the nature of disease itself and the transmission of disease
from one individual to another. From this point, the quarrel could be
further extended to the attack or defense of the systems of monistic
pathology. Throughout, there were important implications for the
treatment of "fevers." Chisholm defended his position with a two-
volume study of yellow fever in 1801 and a later work in 1822, and
others came to his support, at least in part.[14] Critics attacked from
many different points of view, and initially they carried the day by
sheer weight of numbers and reputation.[15] But even the immediate
issue of classification was not settled, and the broader issues rising
from the controversy were not to be settled for many decades.

13. Colin Chisholm, *An Essay on the Malignant Pestilential Fever introduced into
the West Indian Islands from Boullam, on the Coast of Guinea* . . . (London, 1795).

14. C. Chisholm, *An Essay on Malignant Pestilential Fever* . . . , 2 vols. (London,
1801); C. Chisholm, *Manual of the Climate and Diseases of Tropical Countries*
(London, 1822); William Pym, *Observations upon Bulam Fever* . . . (London, 1815);
Nodes Dickinson, *Observations on the Inflammatory Endemic, Incidental to Strangers
in the West Indies from Temperate Climates, Commonly Called Yellow Fever* . . .
(London, 1819), pp. 1–9.

15. T. Trotter, *Medica Nautica*, 3 vols. (London, 1797–1803), I, 325–32; Henry
Clutterbuck, *An Inquiry into the Seat and Nature of Fever* (London, 1807); E. N.
Bancroft, *An Essay on the Disease called Yellow Fever* (London, 1811); E. N. Bancroft, *A Sequel to an Essay on Yellow Fever* (London, 1817); W. Ferguson, "On
the Nature and History of Marsh Poison," *Transactions of the Royal Society of Edinburgh*, IX, 273–98 (1823), esp. pp. 294–95; E. Doughty, *Observations and Inquiries
into the Nature of Yellow Fever* . . . (London, 1816), esp. pp. 1–9.

Meanwhile, medical men practicing in West Africa could follow any one of three different schools of thought about classification. They could have "Bulam Fever" as a separate and infectious disease. They could consider it as merely one of the many varieties of "endemic ardent" or "yellow fever" (in both cases meaning malaria) of the tropics. Or else, they could use a geographical classification, which named each variety of "fever" according to the part of the world where it was prevalent. By this system, neat distinctions were possible between Coimbatore Fever, Guzzerata Fever, Seringapatam Fever, and Coromandel Fever, without even leaving India.[16] In practice, West African practitioners were not so concerned about terminology as the medical writers at home. They continued to treat remittents, intermittents, and an occasional case of "yellow fever," which might or might not be the disease now called by that name.

Gradually, however, yellow fever was recognized as a separate entity, if only when it took an epidemic form, and there was some clearing of the air as medical men attempted to be more precise. The effort to achieve a new level of precision was especially marked in the new analysis of the cause of fevers. The yellow fever controversy raised new hypotheses, and Chisholm himself made a distinction between two sources of infections: Bulam fever was caused by infectious *effluvia* thrown off by persons already infected, while the *miasmata* of swamps was the cause of all other tropical fevers.

The connection between the type of miasma and the type of disease could be carried further still. Dickinson, for example, took the position that *both* human effluvia and marsh miasmata were the causes of ordinary tropical fevers (in short, malaria), while yellow fever was caused solely by *change* of climate aggravated by drunkenness and overeating.[17] Johnson also accepted human effluvia as a cause of fevers and argued further that the type of effluvia inhaled by the victim controlled the symptoms of the fever that would follow. Thus, the effluvia of a typhus victim would produce typhus, while the effluvia of a malaria victim would produce malaria.[18] In trying to establish a mode of transmission from one fever victim to the next, these men were more nearly correct than the majority of their colleagues, though

16. James Johnson, *The Influence of Tropical Climates on European Constitutions,* 2 vols. (Philadelphia, 1821), I, 67. First published London, 1813.

17. Dickinson, *Observations,* pp. 7–8.

18. Doughty, *Observations,* pp. vi–vii; Johnson, *Tropical Climates,* I, 32–38. See also Bancroft, *Essay on Yellow Fever,* pp. 156–97.

they took as their starting point the older belief that fevers must be transmitted by some quality of the air.

Most authorities never departed from the theory of gaseous transmission, nor from the association of tropical fevers with the miasmata of marshes or swamps. Popular opinion still held with the traditional connection between fevers and dampness, and especially between fever and tropical rain or dew, and it was supported by ancient folk fears and aversions. After all, reptiles and insects flourished during the rains. The rains produced mold and mildew, and a "foetid and disgusting odour" escaped from the ground during the rainy season. Thomas Winterbottom tried to defend the rains as harmless in themselves, but by the 1820's the residents in Sierra Leone blamed the rains and not the marshes for their fevers.[19]

Advanced medical opinion in Britain kept the fear of marshes and tried to work toward a more precise chemical definition of the harmful gas. The phlogiston theory was now dead, while a new theory suggested that a combination of nitrogen and oxygen might be at fault. Others suspected "azotic gases." Chisholm thought it was more likely to be "hydrogenous gas, or a combination of hydrogenous gas and carbonic acid." Thus, one tendency was to define and isolate the offending gas, but other authorities still held with a broader spectrum of gasses, merely relabeling it "vegeto-animal effluvium" for the sake of greater scientific precision.[20]

The most careful study of the empirical evidence came from William Ferguson, who reached a verdict widely accepted as authoritative. According to him, marsh poison was neither vegetable nor "aqueous putrefaction." Nor was it necessarily always to be found associated with marshes. It must therefore be connected in some way with the drying process. There was evidence for this view in the presence of fevers along the margins of swamps, or along drying water courses. Large bodies of water were not only safe; they seemed to have the capacity to absorb miasma passing over them. Ferguson's studies also showed some of the other characteristics of the dangerous gas. It

---

19. Winterbottom, *Native Africans*, I, 37–39. See also Stormont, *Topographie médicale*, pp. 38–47.

20. See C. Chisholm, *Malignant Fever* (1801), I, 270–81; Johnson, *Tropical Climates*, I, 39; John MacCulloch, *Malaria: An Essay on the Production and Propagation of this Poison . . .* (Philadelphia, 1829), pp. 21–77. First published London, 1827.

was heavier than air and tended to creep along the ground. It gathered strength during the night and was dissipated somewhat by the strength of the sun. The only real preventive was the cultivation of the land, which allows the pestilential gases to escape from the earth and thus exhausts its "morbific principle by a constant succession of crops."[21]

Ferguson's study was, in many ways, an accurate piece of pure empiricism. It took account of the behavior of many varieties of mosquitos, without being aware that mosquitos were being described. In other hands, similar views could be developed more fully. John MacCulloch carried this trend to its logical conclusion. He imported the term "malaria" from Italian—not as a name for the disease, but for the poison that causes many diseases in both tropical and temparate regions. For him, it was the danger above all others: "This is the Destroying Angel, the real pestilence which walks at noon day; and to which all the other causes of mortality are but as feeble auxiliaries in the work of destruction. This is Malaria, the neglected subject to which I am desirous of calling attention, that, by this, its powers may be diminished...."[22]

Before he finished, MacCulloch had arrived at something approaching a whole system of pathology based on his malarial gas. He was not universally followed, but he helped lead other investigators into a fruitless *cul de sac*.

By the 1820's, there was a broad measure of agreement among medical men on the Coast. They were now convinced that fevers were caused by a noxious gas, originating from the decay of animal or vegetable matter and not simply from the proximity of marshes.[23] Like Ferguson's work, the new view represented a kind of progress. It accounted for the empirical data with greater care and precision than ever before, going as far as men could go without shifting completely from a gas theory to a mosquito theory. (There were, indeed, occasional hints to suggest a mosquito theory, but they were only hints. Winterbottom, for example, coupled the fact that African villages in the bush were both mosquito-infested and unhealthy. There were other suggestions that the ova of insects found in low

---

21. Ferguson, "Marsh Poison," pp. 273–94.
22. MacCulloch, *Malaria,* p. 8.
23. See answers to the Commissioners' Questionnaire, PP, 1830, xxi (57), pp. 63 ff.

or swampy ground might be a cause of fevers.[24] Such hints were not yet enough to distract men from the apparently overwhelming evidence in favor of a miasma theory.)

Most of the suggested public health measures followed the miasma theory, combined with some of the apparent lessons of broadening experience. The Sierra Leone Company, for example, thought they had discovered a panacea in the nature of food and shelter provided for Europeans in the colony. They were struck by the fact that the death rate of their "Upper Servants" had dropped by 1802 to only about twenty to forty per thousand per annum. At the same time, that of the "lower orders" remained shockingly high. The upper servants were better fed and better housed, while the lower orders were less well cared for. They were also less often imbued with the religious zeal of the Evangelical officials in the colony. Hence they were more given to drunkenness and fornication, and these sins received increasing emphasis as "predisposing causes" of fever, in step with the growth of Evangelical piety in Britain.[25] The Company's reaction was to dispense with the services of subordinate officials, who could be neither properly controlled nor cared for. The early possibility that Europeans might be settled in the colony was quietly

24. Winterbottom, *Native Africans,* I, 79–80; Edward Griffith and others, "Supplemental History of Man," in G. Cuvier, *The Animal Kingdom,* 16 vols. (London, 1827–1835), I, 137.

25. PP, 1803–1804, v (24), 23–24. The Parliamentary Committee on Sierra Leone accepted the Company's explanation. (Report of the Committee, PP, 1803–1804, v (24), p. 6.) In fact, the Company's claim of 20 to 40 per thousand per annum as a death rate for their "Upper Servants" would have been very low and seems to indicate that they were nearly all "acclimatized" by this time, though the numbers involved were too small to have much statistical validity. Other evidence, however, indicates a more general pattern of lower death rates in West Africa for the higher officials than for those in subordinate posts or for soldiers. A statistical survey of all forces stationed in West Africa between 1819 and 1836, for example, showed a death rate of only 209 per thousand mean strength among the officers, as against 483 per thousand for other ranks. (PP, 1840, xxx [C. 228], p. 24.) The most likely explanation of this pattern is the fact that "upper servants" and officers tended to acquire an immunity, after which they could return for several tours of duty on the Coast, whereas the artisan class or the common soldiers served their time and went home. Thus William Dawes and Thomas Ludlam both served three terms as Governor of Sierra Leone under the Company, and three other Governors served twice. Later on, others, notably Sir Charles MacCarthy, served long terms under the Crown. These men probably acquired at least a limited immunity against *falciparum* malaria, while many others died within the first year. Among the very small group of European officials, there were enough of these immune long-term residents and returnees to affect the statistical mortality of the group as a whole. The very high death rate among the European soldiers may also owe something to psychological depression in the face of imminent death, to drink, and to the severity of military punishments.

dropped, and the only European settlers encouraged after the early 1790's were capitalists of means, who might establish plantations.[26]

By contrast, the Bulama Island Association placed its faith in technology and spent a good deal of time and energy thinking up ways to prevent high mortality on a possible second venture. Wadström studied the problem of a pure water supply.[27] Philip Beaver thought the principal errors of his first attempt had been lack of shelter on arrival at the beginning of the rains. The obvious remedy was better timing and the preparation of prefabricated houses that could be erected immediately on landing.[28]

The suggestion was taken up by Anders Johansen, a Swede who worked as a publicist for the Bulama Association. He invented a tropical house for pioneering conditions and an improved type to be built once the settlement was established. The latter was a new design for tropical architecture, which took full account of medical theory. It was to be raised about ten feet off the ground on stilts, to avoid the noxious vapors arising from the ground. The exterior walls were protected from direct sunlight by a broad verandah on all sides, with further protection in the form of venetian blinds or awnings around the verandah. The house was further insulated by a double roof, with free circulation of air between the inner and outer shell. The interior was also air conditioned. A water-driven air pump maintained a constant circulation of air, which could be cooled by water, warmed by a fire, and kept insect free by smoke treatment, before it was led into the house through a system of ducts. Although the house was never built, it was a most ingenious attempt to bring technology to bear on the problems of tropical life. In both conception and detail it foreshadowed a great deal of modern tropical architecture.[29]

Later suggestions for public action to improve tropical health followed the rising concern about sanitation in Britain itself. Dr. Chisholm and his successors in the yellow fever controversy went beyond their key recommendation of quarantine. Chisholm proposed a whole sanitary code for West Indian towns, including compulsory building in brick and stone rather than wood, widening the streets, control of

26. Sierra Leone Company, *Report* (1791), 11; Sierra Leone Company, *Account of the Colony,* pp. 49–53; Statement of the Directors, PP, 1803–1804, v (24), pp. 23–24.

27. Wadström, *Colonization,* I, 28–31.

28. P. Beaver to Bulama Island Association, 24 June 1794, CO 267/10.

29. Andrew Johansen, *Description of Bulama Island* (London, 1794), p. 20; Wadström, *Colonization,* I, 49 and II, diagram, plate I.

privies and stables, butchershops and slaughterhouses. Dr. Sweeney, the Surgeon of the Forces at Cape Coast, recommended similar measures for West Africa and added some new ones. He wanted, among other things, to move the African town to a new site at some distance from the European fort— in short, the "sanitary segragation" that was to become a popular panacea in the early twentieth century. His other suggestions were to drain the surrounding country, improve the water supply to the forts, and clear the brush for some distance around the area where Europeans lived. Clearing the brush was, indeed, the most popular anti-fever measure of all.[30]

Little enough was done along any of the lines suggested, and the results were far from promising. Some authorities came to the conclusion that West Africa was hopeless and nothing could be done. Dr. William Barry, the principal medical officer in West Africa at the time of the 1826 investigation, held that no sanitary regulations or any other improvements could make an appreciable difference to the health of the troops, his principal concern.[31] The facts were on his side, but many authorities continued to hope, and they put their faith, where public measures either failed or were not attempted, in personal precautions to avoid the "predisposing causes" of fevers.

There was plenty of room here for personal action to forestall the influence of malarial poison. The very concept of "predisposing" causes left an opening for older ideas to live on in the face of the new developments in medical science. Humoral pathology in slightly changed forms reappeared in the work of James Johnson, perhaps the standard author on tropical medicine in this period. He held that persipiration was especially dangerous because of a sympathetic relation between certain organs of the body, or the "consent of parts." Thus, if the skin perspires, there will be a sympathetic reaction from the liver, which then increases the quantity of bilious secretion. In hot climates, this "cutaneo-hepatic sympathy" will bring on a chain of responses: heat leads to perspiration, leading to a degree of liver malfunction, weakening the body, and thus preparing the way for the

30. Charles Dunne to African Committee, 16 November 1811, T 70/35; G. A. Robertson, *Notes on Africa . . . with Hints for the Melioration of the Whole African Population* (London, 1819), p. 24; Sir N. Campbell, Memorandum on the Gold Coast, November 1826, SLA, Gold Coast Misc., 1826–1827; Chisholm, *Malignant Fever* (1795), pp. 204–10; M. Sweeney to James Rowan, 20 September 1826, PP, 1830, xxi (57), p. 88. See also Stormont, *Topographie médicale,* p. 68 for an anti-clearing opinion.

31. PP, 1826–1827, vii (312), p. 108.

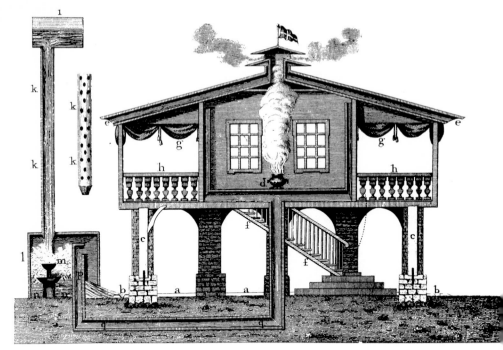

Figure 1. Johansen's design for an air conditioned
tropical house, as modified by C. B. Wadström.

Explanation

a. The ground on which the House is to be erected & which ought to be covered with a Coat of cement or mortar, to prevent the ascent of Vapours from the Earth.

b. A small trench which may be made all round the House through which water should be constantly running if the Situation admit of it, to prevent Ants & other Insects from entering the House.

c. Pillars on which the dwelling House should be raised to a proper elevation above the ground in order to give a free circulation of Air underneath, to carry off the Vapours. These pillars may be covered with bricks & plastered if found necessary.

d. A Fire Urn or grate from which the Smoke rises through the opening in the top of the Roof.

e. The Roof also double, like the floor, in order to give a free circulation to the Air & render the roof, & consequently the room, cool.

f. The stairs to be wound up in order to render the house a place of defence, in case of necessity, particularly at night time.

g. Curtains to let down on the side the Sun enters, but moveable Venetian blinds are preferable.

h. A Gallery covered by the projecting roof of the House all round in order to keep off the Sunshine.

To Mr. Johansen's Invention I have added an apparatus which I have seen frequently used in Germany for blowing their furnaces in Situations where they have water-falls. But where that advantage is wanting, a sufficient quantity of water for cooling a House may be easily raised by a pump.

i. Is a Cistern from which the water falls through the pipe *k* full of holes by which the Air enters & is forced downwards by the violent discent [*sic*] of the water into the close barrel *l*. The water dashing on the basons *m* is broken into froth & falls into the lower part of the barrel *n*, whence it runs off by the hole *o* and may then supply the above mentioned trench *b*. The Air being disengaged from the broken Water & confined on all sides is driven into the pipe *p*, by which Mr. Johansen's pipe *q* under the earth is furnished with a constant stream of Air, which ascending through this pipe spreads itself into the air reservoir under the floor of the house & continues the ascent through the side pipes. The cool and purified Air thus delivered by these pipes, being specifically heavier than the Air in the room, descends toward the floor & takes the place of the rarefied Air which constantly ascends till it escapes by the opening in the top of the Roof.

onset of fever. But excessive perspiration was not alone among the predisposing causes. Johnson listed "plethora—inanition from excessive evacuations—depressing passions—excess, whether in eating, drinking, or gratification of the sensual passions—mental or corporeal exertions—extremes of atmospheric heat and cold, especially alternations of these or of heat and moisture—sollunal influences," and a few more.[32]

The recommended personal regimen therefore remained as diverse and as broad as it had been in the eighteenth century. The key was still "moderation, regularity, and temperance," and above all not living as the "natives" did. In detail, this normally meant the avoidance of alcoholic drink, sexual intercourse, and eating meat. These were, of course, nothing but the proscriptions of traditional Christian asceticism, and they underscore the continued half-conscious belief in a connection between morality and disease. The principal change was a gradual shift of emphasis. Joy and sorrow—and indeed all mental activity—were more frowned upon than they had been a few decades earlier. Light exercise tended to fall into disfavor, while bathing was now more often permissible. At the same time, the recommended clothing increased in quantity and weight. Cotton was less popular, while linen and especially flannel next to the skin was increasingly recommended. The popularity of flannel came partly from its ability to absorb dangerous perspiration, and partly from the belief that change of temperature rather than uncomfortable heat was the most serious danger.[33]

Other advice was more specific. The gauze net or *canopeum* now made its apperance, though not merely as a protection against mosquitos. The cloth was supposed to filter the dangerous effluvia, and it was recommended as a head net for naval crews sent ashore on the West African coast. Other prophylactic measures were connected with the old belief in artificial "acclimatization," to protect against the inevitable "seasoning sickness." Chisholm, for example, was convinced that tropical air contains more oxygen than temperate air—an old belief set in terms of the new chemistry—but the preventive measures were traditional. The newcomer, according to Chisholm, should have himself bled and purged when the ship crossed the Tropic of

32. Johnson, *Tropical Climates,* I, 32–33. See also I, 8–27.
33. For some representative advice, see Henry Meredith, *An Account of the Gold Coast of Africa* . . . (London, 1812), pp. 42–50; Johnson, *Tropical Climates,* II, 228–93; MacCulloch, *Malaria,* pp. 132–64.

Cancer, and again on arrival at his tropical destination. This prophylactic treatment could be topped off by a course of calomel,
tartarized antimony, and doses of sea water.[34]

The more valuable prophylactic use of chinchona bark retained
some popularity during the 1790's and then began to decline, though
it continued in the official practice of the Navy. The printed Instructions for Surgeons for 1814 and 1825 ordered ship's surgeons to give
chinchona to all men going ashore in the tropics, at the rate of "a
drachm of bark in half a gill of sound wine" both morning and
evening. They were, furthermore, to report the results to the Commissioners for Transports and Sick and Wounded Seamen.[35] Depending on the quality of the bark used, this treatment would have been
beneficial, but the instructions were not often followed in practice.
The men disliked the taste, and surgeons followed the medical
fashions which, after the 1790's, had gradually moved into an anti-
chinchona phase.[36]

The unpopularity of chinchona came from several sources. The best
of the barks, and after the 1790's this meant *Chinchona succirubra*
or "Red Bark" from Ecuador, might contain up to 4 per cent by
weight of the anti-malarial alkaloids. But other barks that looked
very much the same also found their way into the British market in
the early nineteenth century, and they sometimes contained no alkaloids at all. Even an occasional shipment of *C. succirubra* which had
been poorly preserved might be free of anti-malarial qualities.[37] There
was thus room for pharmaceutical error, and there was room for
error in diagnosis. Dr. Wade in Bengal had tried bark extensively on
his patients, and he published the finding that it was not only useless
for the treatment of fevers but could in some cases be an active
poison. Chisholm in the West Indies and others in North America
during the yellow fever epidemics of 1793–94 also reported that the
drug was useless—as it surely was for the treatment of yellow fever.[38]

Chinchona thus became involved in the yellow fever controversy.
Chisholm, who distinguished yellow fever from other fevers, recom-

34. MacCulloch, *Malaria*, p. 138; Chisholm, *Malignant Fever* (1801), II, 56–57;
Trotter, *Medica Nautica*, I, 339–40.

35. *Instructions for Surgeons of the Royal Navy* ([London], 1814), pp. 13–14.

36. A. Bryson, "Prophylactic Influence of Quinine," *Medical Times and Gazette*,
VII (n.s.), 6–7 (7 January 1854).

37. J. E. Howard, *Illustrations of the Nueva Quinologia of Pavon* (London,
1862), esp. p. 15 on *Chinchona succirubra*.

38. Chisholm, *Malignant Fever* (1801), I, 364–68.

mended mercury treatments with calomel as far preferable to chinchona. Those who made no such distinction took up mercury for all
tropical fevers, and calomel gradually came into more common use
—and in larger doses.[39] The authority of James Johnson was soon
added to the anti-chinchona school, with a special emphasis on bleeding as the best alternative. As he put it, "In these scrutinising days
of investigation and experiment, the lancet has dispelled the mists
of prejudice, the phantoms of debility and putrescency, with the de-
lusions of the Brunonian school; and bleeding is justly regarded as
the paramount remedy. . . ."[40]

As it happened, the two treatments combined in a new phase of
popularity for heroic doses of calomel, heroic bleeding, and a combination of other minor remedies which might include blisters, and
perhaps chinchona bark at the later stages of the disease as a "tonic."
Some carried the new fashion to extremes. Doughty recommended
taking as much as two pounds (or about thirty-two ounces) of blood
the minute a patient appeared to suffer from fever, following this
with mercury treatments. Others took from twenty to fifty ounces of
blood at the first sign of disease, and still more later on. Blisters were
applied to the head, the nape of the neck, and the stomach, theoretically in order to relieve the pressure of blood on the internal organs.
Blue ointment, a mercurial preparation, was occasionally rubbed into
the skin of the arms and legs and applied to the blistered sores in
order to increase the intake of mercury. In the last stages of illness,
blisters were sometimes applied to the extremities in order to arouse
the patient to life. Most painful of all was the night-cap blister, which
covered the whole head.[41]

There is every reason to believe that these new forms of treatment
were positively harmful, aside from the unnecessary pain caused by
the blisters. Sixteen to twenty ounces of blood is the amount normally
taken from the donor for a blood transfusion. It would certainly
cause no harm to a healthy individual. To take 100 ounces, as was
often done, meant taking half of the blood in the body, and it would
certainly have caused some harm, even to a healthy individual. As
little as twenty to fifty ounces, taken from a patient with malaria,

39. Chisholm, *Malignant Fever* (1801), I, 418–519; Clutterbuck, *Inquiry*, 404–5,
40. Johnson, *Tropical Climates*, I, 53.
41. Doughty, *Observations*, pp. 11–12; Dickinson, *Observations*, pp. 121–68;
A. Bryson, *Report on the Climate and Principal Diseases of the African Station* (London, 1847), pp. 243–44 and 246–47.

could be very serious. Anemia normally accompanies malaria, and any victim needs all the blood he has.

The mercury treatments would have had a similar result. Malaria is seriously dehydrating. Calomel is a strong purgative, causing still more dehydration. But the dosage of the early nineteenth century was not merely enough to purge the intestinal tract. The intention was to produce a profuse salivation, since it was observed that a patient who salivated after mercury treatment usually lived. In this case, the doctors mistook the sign of recovery for the cause of recovery. They tended to load the patient with more and more calomel until he either died or recovered. At times the dosage went as high as fifty to sixty grains a day for four or five days, in some instances exceeding a total of 500 grains.[42]

These two treatments in combination, or either one of them in its more extreme form, would certainly have been enough to kill a malaria victim already on the borderline between life and death. It can be assumed, therefore, that they had some influence, and probably a significant influence, on the high death rates of the 1820's. The inference is further strengthened by the fact that the mercury-bleeding combination reached a peak of acceptance in the 1820's, precisely the decade when the qualitative impression of West Africa as the "white man's grave" reached its peak. In spite of the progress of European medicine generally, the trend in tropical medicine, as it was practiced on the West Coast of Africa, was clearly one of declining efficiency.

But even in its worst decade there were some signs of change. Chinchona began to come slowly back into favor, especially in the later 1820's, building up its reputation from its continued use as tonic in the latter stages of a fever. As early as 1822, Chisholm himself was advising chinchona bark as a prophylactic, but only against further attacks of fever once recovery had begun.[43] More important still, in 1820 Pelletier and Caventou in France isolated two alkaloids of the chinchona bark, and the sulfate of one of these, quinine, gradually came into pharmaceutical use. During the 1820's the price was still prohibitive for ordinary use as a superior substitute for raw bark, but the Clapperton-Oudney-Denham expedition of 1821–25 and Clapperton's later expedition with Lander were both supplied with quinine, though in quantities too small to be used

42. Bryson, *Principal Diseases,* pp. 240–44.
43. Chisholm, *Manual,* p. 52.

prophylactically. By 1826 a few of the doctors in West Africa were experimenting with the new drug and reporting excellent results, even though they were still using it in conjunction with bleeding, blisters, calomel, and even ordinary chinchona bark.[44] The way was at last prepared, though the reformed treatment of fever would not be the standard procedure for another quarter century.

Compared with their overwhelming interest in tropical fevers, medical men had relatively little time for writing or research about other tropical diseases. Dysentery was simply the "fluxes" and was treated in the same way it was treated in temperate climates. Medical men on the Coast were not concerned in most cases with the treatment of Africans. They therefore paid little attention to Guinea worm, leprosy, elephantiasis, yaws, and the other diseases that seemed more serious for the African population than for the intrusive Europeans. Investigation of these diseases was more often left to the plantation surgeons of the West Indies.

Only Thomas Winterbottom reported extensively on the treatment of Africans in West Africa. He was particularly interested in yaws, which he correctly believed to be infectious and transmitted by contact. He was also correct in stating that Guinea worm is not caused (as many then believed) by impure water, but by "animalcules" which enter the body through the skin. In other respects as well, his work on minor tropical diseases was far ahead of his time. He pointed out, for example, that there was no such thing as sun stroke in Sierra Leone, either among Africans or Europeans. Europeans in the tropics, however, continued to have "sun stroke" for the next century and a half, and as recently as 1958 the British Medical Council was still trying to abolish the term from the classification of heat illness.[45]

44. E. H. Acherknecht, *Malaria in the Upper Mississippi Valley, 1760–1900* (Baltimore, 1945), pp. 101–4; A. A. Boahen, "British Penetration of North-West Africa and the Western Sudan, 1788–1861" (Unpublished Ph.D. thesis, London, 1959), p. 252; R. L. Lander, *Records of Captain Clapperton's Last Expedition to Africa . . . With Subsequent Adventures of the Author,* 2 vols. (London, 1830), II, 333–37; Dr. Sweeney to James Rowan, 20 September 1826, PP, 1830, xxi (57), pp. 87–88; Dr. Alexander Stewart to Commissioners, 4 November 1826, PP, 1830, xxi (57), p. 58.

45. Winterbottom, *Native Africans,* II, esp. 38–40; *The Times,* 5 September 1958. Most of the reported cases of "sun stroke" were in fact cerebral malaria. See S. F. Dudley, "Yellow Fever as seen by the Medical Officers of the Royal Navy in the Nineteenth Century," *Proceedings of the Royal Society of Medicine,* XXVI, 443–56 (1932), p. 443.

Whether or not medical practice was successful in solving the problem of survival, the evidence of medical men impinged on policy decisions at many points around the periphery of medical thought. One point of constant interaction between tropical medicine and tropical policy was the old rivalry between West Africa and the West Indies. Whatever the facts of European mortality in West Africa— and they were bad enough—the West India interest was anxious to show the West African "climate" in the worst possible light. They felt threatened by the possibility of West African production of tropical staples. The humanitarians, their chief political opponents in Britain, were identified with the settlement at Sierra Leone, and therefore that colony became a prime target.

From the 1790's onward, almost any medical writing about West Africa had some political overtones. Chisholm was not merely a scientist. He used his work on "Bulam fever" to damn the African coast as its source, and along with it the humanitarians and all of their works. Both the lay defenders of the "Saints" and some medical journals took up the other side of the case. Dr. Elihu Hubbard Smith of New York attacked Chisholm in a scientific journal, claiming that he had invented "Bulam fever" in order to cast aspersions on West African colonization. Thus the yellow fever controversy was a trans-Atlantic political issue from the beginning.[46]

Much of the later publicity given to European mortality in Sierra Leone was politically inspired, though the facts themselves were mainly true. The many articles and pamphlets of James MacQueen, the newspaper *John Bull*,[47] and other anti-humanitarian organs carried a running campaign during the 1820's, which linked the bad "climate" of Sierra Leone and the defense of West Indian slavery. *The Times* joined in and roundly condemned Bathurst for yielding to "the mixture of quackery and hypocracy which has instigated a certain class of people in this country to press upon the Government the retention of a costly grave for British subjects, by nicknaming it a school for the civilization of negroes." Their solution was to give up all West African settlements and concentrate on more hopeful areas.[48]

In the face of this kind of attack, even before the Wellington and

46. See Chisholm, *Malignant Fever* (1801), I, xv–xvi and 98–102.
47. See, for example, leaders of 15 August 1824 and 30 August 1829.
48. *The Times,* 17 and 21 November 1827.

Rowan report, the humanitarians and the pro-West African faction were thrown on the defensive. It was impossible to deny the facts of European mortality, and it was difficult to advocate further African activity in the face of these facts. But there was one possible way out. It was an ancient and universally accepted belief that Negroes were immune to the "climate," even though white men died. Medical opinion of the 1820's still sustained this conclusion in spite of Wellington and Rowan's suggestion to the contrary.[49] The obvious solution had been advocated long ago by Lind—that is, to staff the West African posts with Westernized Africans. As early as 1823 the possibility of using Africans as missionaries was seriously considered by the Church Missionary Society. After 1825, the idea of using African personnel in government posts was widely discussed.[50]

The line of government strategic decisions from 1826 to 1830 was mainly a surrender in the face of the African "climate." Sierra Leone's reputation was given a final turn downward in 1829 by the appearance of a disastrous yellow fever epidemic, which came just in time to influence the Parliamentary Committee of 1830. There would be no extension of the British sphere of interest in West Africa. It would, indeed, contract within the limits of irreducible commitments to the anti-slavery blockade and to those people already settled in Sierra Leone through British agency. But as it withdrew, the government accepted the outlines of a policy of Africanization. Sir George Murray announced that in future all official posts would (as far as possible) be filled by people of color, either native Africans or men born in the West Indies, and this policy was to be followed until all positions were filled by men of African descent.[51] The decision grew mainly from the medical failure, but it also drew its detail from several decades of stategic thought and exploration; and it rested on some further basic assumptions about culture, race, and the process of culture change.

---

49. Chisholm, *Malignant Fever* (1801), I, 141–42; Winterbottom, *Native Africans,* I, 65 and II, 13, 22–23; Johnson, *Tropical Climates,* I, 2–4; Doughty, *Observations,* p. 50; Dickinson, *Observations,* pp. 12–13. Ferguson, "Marsh Poison," pp. 297–98.
50. E. Stock, *A History of the Church Missionary Society,* 4 vols. (London, 1899–1917), I, 244.
51. Report of the Select Committee on Sierra Leone and Fernando Po, PP, 1830, x (661), p. 3; Sir George Murray, Commons, 15 June 1830, 2 H 25, cc. 402–5.

8

TOWNS

AND ELEPHANTS

... Geographers in Afric-Maps
With Savage-Pictures fill their Gaps,
And o'er inhabitable Downs
Place Elephants for want of Towns.
—Swift, *On Poetry*

It is almost an accepted convention that no book shall deal with African exploration without some reference to Swift's famous lines on cartography. Geographers of the early nineteenth century began the wholesale replacement of elephants with towns, at least in West Africa. The increase in geographical knowledge between 1790 and 1830 was greater than that of any comparable period. Explorers followed virtually the whole course of the Niger. They crossed West Africa from the Guinea Coast to the Maghrib. The major cities were either visited or known by hearsay, and their positions were plotted with tolerable accuracy. Chains of mountains, the important drainage, the principal political units—all these were located and described in outline. New maps had every right to the towns, but geographers might well have left a liberal sprinkling of elephants, symbolically representing certain remaining areas of ignorance and misunderstanding, especially in the field of ethnography. In cartography and political geography, the work of scholars in Britain was closely integrated with that of travellers on the spot. Many of the explorers were tough, practical men without a broad general education; but they were well briefed in the existing state of geographical knowledge, and they knew precisely what data was needed to fill out the picture. The educated public also followed the course of geographical scholarship. The unknown heart of the African continent captured the imagination, and works of geographical synthesis were widely read along with the accounts of the explorers. In scholarly circles, new information was rapidly rechecked and fitted into the existing pattern of knowledge.

This geographical tradition was organized and reinforced after 1788 by the work of the African Association and the scholarship of James Rennell, who followed his initial reports for the Association with *Elucidations of African Geography* in 1793. Using this work as a base, Rennell continued with a series of commentaries on the new explorations. By the end of the century his scholarly prestige stood so high that Mungo Park deferred to Rennell's view on the Niger problem, even though it differed from his own.[1]

Paul Jacob Bruns in Germany meanwhile published an even more detailed and systematic treatment of the whole continent in six volumes, of which one and one-half were devoted to West Africa.[2] Bruns's synthesis in time replaced Rennell's as the most authoritative work on African geography; but it reached British readers at second hand, and Rennell remained the geographer with the greatest popular reputation.

The scholarly syntheses were, in any case, received as mere hypotheses to be checked and amplified on the basis of new information, and new data was by no means limited to the work of the more spectacular exploring expeditions. It was now more frequently sought from people already in Africa. Rennell's map, for example, was checked with the cooperation of the Secretary of State for Colonies, who passed a dozen copies to the African Committee for distribution to officials of the African posts. They were asked both for their criticisms of the map and for answers to a geographical questionnaire.[3]

1. J. Rennell, "Geographical Illustrations of Mr. Park's Journey," in M. Park, *Travels in the Interior Districts of Africa,* 2nd ed., 2 vols. (London, 1799), II, iii-xcii; "Account of the Life of Mungo Park," in M. Park, *The Journal of a Mission to the Interior of Africa in 1805,* 2nd ed. (London, 1815), pp. 46-51.

2. P. J. Bruns, *Neue systematische Erdbeschreibung von Africa,* 6 vols. (Nuremberg, 1793-1799).

3. Minutes of the African Committee, 12 November 1802, in J. J. Crooks (ed.), *Records Relating to the Gold Coast Settlements from 1750 to 1874* (Dublin, 1923), p. 99.

Information about coastal waters increased constantly, in spite of
a decline of trade after 1807. The technology of seafaring was itself
improving, and the Navy had its own need of charts for the anti-
slavery patrols. A new *African Pilot* with a set of 24 sheets of charts
and a book of sailing directions appeared in 1807 to replace the
standard *English Pilot* which had served throughout the eighteenth
century. In 1819 it was supplemented by Lt. Edward Bold's *Merchants' and Mariners' African Guide,* which dealt with both navigation and commerce. The commercial side was carried further still by
Captain Adams's *Remarks on the Country Extending from Cape
Palmas to the River Congo,* containing a manual of mercantile practice with full information on systems of currency, prices, and the
goods in greatest demand on each section of the coast.[4]

During the 1820's the Admiralty began to sponsor coastal surveys
to correct the charts of certain regions, such as the Windward Coast
and the navigable course of the Gambia. The French, however, were
first in the field with an official pilot guide, covering the whole coast
from Cape Bojador to the vicinity of the modern city of Conakry. It
was immediately translated into English; but British publications of
this kind were left to private enterprise until 1856, when the Hydrographic Office published the first volume of the official *African Pilot,*
from the Straits of Gibraltar to the Cameroons.[5]

Hearsay information about the interior was also gathered and col-
lated with increasing care. Rennell received and used reports from
British Consuls in the Maghrib. Travellers in Morocco, like J. G.
Jackson, were increasingly careful to record what they might hear of
the far side of the desert.[6] From time to time, a North African traveller to the Sudan might even appear in England. One such, known to
the English as "El Hage Abd Shabeeny" of Tetuan, had spent twelve

4. *Laurie and Whittle's New Sailing Directions for the Coasts of Africa, from
Cape Spartel to the Cape of Good-Hope . . .* (London, 1807), published to accompany
the charts of the *African Pilot;* E. Bold, *The Merchant's and Mariners' African Guide*
(London, 1819); John Adams, *Remarks on the Country Extending from Cape Palmas
to the River Congo* (London, 1823), pp. 223–65.

5. Great Britain, Hydrographic Office, *The African Pilot, or Sailing Directions for
the Western Coast of Africa. Part I Cape Spartel to the River Cameroons* (London,
1856); W. F. Owen, *Narrative of Voyages to Explore the Shores of Africa, Arabia,
and Madagascar . . . ,* 2 vols.(London, 1833): T. Boteler, *The West Coast of Africa,
from the Isles de Los to Sierra Leone* (London, n. d. [c. 1831]); A. Roussin, *Memoir
on the Navigation of the Western Coast of Africa from Cape Bojador to Mount
Souzos* (London, 1827), translated from French by Lt. James Badgley, R. N.

6. James Grey Jackson, *Account of the Empire of Morocco* (London, 1809),
pp. 237–66.

years in Timbuctu and Hausa before his visit to Britain. His account was published in England in 1820 and later used extensively by Jackson.[7]

Still other notices came from northeastern Africa. J. L. Burckhardt, who was sent by the African Association in 1808 to penetrate the Western Sudan by way of Egypt, wandered in the Levant for almost a decade. He travelled south to Nubia and along the Red Sea but was unable to move west of the Nile valley. He was, however, able to collect hearsay information, bringing news, for example, of the rise of the Sokoto Fulani.[8]

Captain G. F. Lyon had even better opportunity to gather information during his long residence in Fezzan. At his base in Murzuk he interrogated men from the caravans trading to Bornu and Hausa and slaves passing northward toward Libya and Egypt. The itineraries he collected gave stages and travel times to the opposite side of the desert and on to Nupe, Dagomba, Gonja, and Ashanti. They also showed the route westward to Timbuctu, Jenne, and back across the desert to Tafilelt.

All of this North African information, whether itineraries or geographical speculations, had the defects of earlier Maghribi accounts. The detail and accuracy dropped off sharply south of Adamawa, Zaria, or Nupe—that is, in the "middle belt" of modern Nigeria. Reporters from a distance, like Lyon, were thus unable to follow the course of the Niger after it flowed south of Nupe. The dominant North African hypothesis about the Niger was still set in the classical Islamic mold, and men like Lyon and Jackson followed it, concluding that the great river must ultimately flow into the Nile.[9]

Among scholars in Europe, the most careful collation of North African information was the work of Baron Walckenaer, who collected and published itineraries leading into the desert and beyond, trying to fix the position of towns and oases by cross-reference.[10] T. E. Bowdich planned to translate this work into English but the intention was cut off by his death. His interest, however, is evidence of the link between Maghribi and Guinean sources of information,

7. It first appeared in *The Literary Gazette,* No. 171 (1820).

8. J. L. Burckhardt, *Travels in Nubia* (London, 1819).

9. G. F. Lyon, *A Narrative of Travels in Northern Africa in the Years 1818, 19, and 20* (London, 1821), pp. 121–63.

10. C. A. Walckenaer, *Recherches géographique sur l'interieur de l'Afrique septentorionale . . .* (Paris, 1821).

since Bowdich himself was the most important collector and collator of information gathered on the southern approaches to the Sudan. A long chapter in his *Mission to Ashantee* took up where Rennell left off and attempted a new statement of the outlines of Sudanese geography.[11]

Others collected geographical data—on the Coast, in Kumasi, or even further afield in America. Dupuis, Bowdich's successor in Ashanti, attempted to correct what he considered to be Bowdich's errors. G. A. Robertson published information from Lagos, Bonny, and Lahou (on the Ivory Coast), showing, among other things, the trade route from the Gold Coast to the Niger.[12] In Brazil, a careful interrogation of Hausa slaves led to a correct solution of the Niger problem—the conclusion that it did indeed flow into the Gulf of Guinea.[13] Even *The Times* fed the public interest by publishing an account of the route from Lagos to Hausa, gathered from Hausa merchants in the port.[14]

The flow of new hearsay data was a striking change from the previous century. Information of this kind must have been available in earlier decades, but Europeans now began to collect and publish whatever they could find out. The hiatus in successful exploration between Park and Clapperton was, therefore, no hiatus in the growth of geographical knowledge. By the 1820's the way was open to a solution of the Niger problem, first by scholarship then confirmed by exploration.

After Mungo Park had shown that a large river (identified as the Niger of the ancients) flowed from west to east, five general theories emerged to explain its course beyond Sansanding, where Park's reporting ended. Rennell thought it ran into Lake Chad or some equivalent inland lake and disappeared there through evaporation. Park himself thought it probably emerged as the Congo or Zaire of lower Guinea, though he never bothered to argue the point in public.[15] The theory of an outlet into the Nile had been familiar for centuries.

11. T. E. Bowdich, *Mission from Cape Coast Castle to Ashantee* . . . (London, 1819), pp. 161–227.

12. J. Dupuis, *Journal of Residence in Ashantee* (London, 1824); G. A. Robertson, *Notes on Africa* . . . *With Hints for the Melioration of the Whole African Population* (London, 1819), especially pp. 179–80, 185–88, and 206–7.

13. Menèzes de Drumond, "Lettres sur l'Afrique ancienne et moderne," *Journal des voyages*, XXXII, 190–224 (December, 1826).

14. *The Times*, 18 May 1815.

15. Park, *Journal of a Mission*, II, 46–51.

In 1829, Lt.-Gen. Sir Rufane Donkin published an even more outlandish Mediterranean hypothesis. He suggested that the Niger
flowed into Lake Chad, then out of Lake Chad toward the north,
disappearing under the desert in an underground stream that finally
emerged in the Gulf of Sidra.[16]

The correct identification of the Oil Rivers as the mouths of the
Niger was first made by the German geographer, Christian Gottlieb
Reichard in 1802. In the following year, he worked out the theory in
more detail and published again, this time with his own map of
northern Africa. His argument rested on the rate of flow of the
known portions of the Niger. Both Park and al-Idrīsi long before had
described a river much too large to be evaporated from the surface of
a lake the size of any known to exist in Africa. Furthermore, the flow
of water from the system of rivers extending from the Formosa on
the west to the Rio del Rey on the east was enough to account for the
Niger's flow—and was far too great for a smaller watershed, limited
to the immediate hinterland.[17]

In other respects Reichard followed Rennell, and one particular
was to have important geographical consequences. Reichard's Niger,
like Rennell's, flowed from the foothills of the Futa Jallon Mountains
northward to the latitude of Timbuctu and then directly eastward
through the heart of Hausa to the vicinity of Lake Chad (or about
15° East). There it picked up tributaries flowing from points still
further east. Other tributaries were assumed to flow down from the
north, through an apparently well watered region lying between Lake
Chad and Tibesti, where in fact there is nothing but desert. By accepting Rennell's concept of a Niger basin stretching out to the east
and north of Lake Chad, Reichard vastly magnified the Niger Valley.
By the time the river reached its destination in the Bights it drained
an imaginary river basin twice the size of the actual Niger basin, and
one that included most of northern central Africa.

Reichard's theory found its way into English geographical thought

16. R. Donkin, *A Dissertation on the Course and Probable Termination of the
Niger* (London, 1829).

17. C. G. Reichard, "Ueber die Vermuthung des Dr. Seetzen zu Jever, dass sich
der Niger in Afrika viellicht mit dem Zaire vereinigen könne," *Monatliche Corre-
spondenz zur Beförderung der Erd-und-Himmels Kunde*, V, 402–15 (Gotha, May 1802);
Reichard, "Ueber den angekündigten, nun bald erscheinenden, Atlas des ganzen
Erdkreises," *Allegemeine Geographische Ephemeriden*, XII, 129–70 and map opposite
p. 265 (August 1803), esp. pp. 157–67.

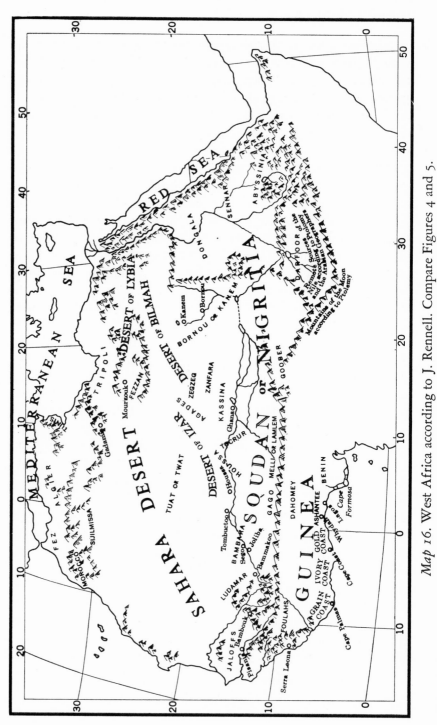

Map 16. West Africa according to J. Rennell. Compare Figures 4 and 5.

through the work of the French geographer, Malte-Brun, and it appears to have been first published in England in 1816.[18] From that time onward a number of English theorists took up some variant of the Oil Rivers thesis. G. A. Robertson, for example, believed that three parallel branches flowed out of a large lake near Gao directly toward the Bights. Thus for him the Niger basin lay entirely to the west of the Niger delta.[19]

The most important and best publicized of the British theories, however, was that of James MacQueen. It was so well publicized, indeed, that MacQueen has often been given credit for Reichard's discovery. MacQueen was more a publicist than a scholar, and his geographical work was accompanied by a detailed plan for British West African strategy. From a geographical point of view, his construction of the West African map was very much that of Reichard, even though he claimed not to have seen Reichard's work until after his own was published. His vision of an eastern as well as a western Niger basin was even more extensive than Reichard's had been. For MacQueen, Niger drainage began at about 28° East, or almost the longitude of Alexandria. His eastern Sahara was even narrower than Reichard's, confined to the north of the Tropic of Cancer and thus only half its actual width. If this projection had been true, the well watered region to the north and east of Lake Chad would have had an area equivalent to all of the actual agricultural land in West Africa south of the desert. No wonder, then, that MacQueen worked so hard to direct British strategic entry toward the Bights rather than Sierra Leone.[20]

MacQueen also made a serious error about the political geography of the interior. Perhaps because he knew that many of the peoples of the Western Sudan were Muslim, he assumed that they must be under "Arab domination" and ruled by white North Africans. The belief fitted well with his racial views. Since he held that Negroes were congenitally inferior, he believed they could never have created or maintained elaborate political structures like the Empire of Bornu or the Hausa city-states.[21] In fact, there had been cultural diffusion

18. C. Malte-Brun, *Précis de la géographie universelle* . . . 8 vols. (Paris, 1810–1829), IV, 635; "Appendix No. IV," in M. Park, *Journal of a Mission*, II, 364–66.
19. Robertson, *Notes on Africa*, frontispiece map.
20. J. MacQueen, *Geographical and Commercial View of Northern Central Africa, Containing a Particular Account of the Course and Termination of the Great River Niger in the Atlantic Ocean* (Edinburgh, 1821).
21. MacQueen, *Northern Central Africa*, pp. 185–87.

across the Sahara for centuries, but conquest from the north had been a rare occurrence. The nineteenth-century states in the Western Sudan were ruled by sub-Saharan Africans and based on an indigenous political and cultural tradition, in spite of their considerable cultural debt to Islam. "Arab domination" in countless variants, however, became a commonplace of ill-informed thought about Africa for a century to come.

In its broader pattern, MacQueen's synthesis dominated British geographical thought for a generation, even though he himself revised it drastically in 1840, and explorers modified many points of detail. But acceptance was not immediate. Throughout the 1820's the Niger question was still open, and hotly debated in the reviews. The reports of Denham and Clapperton were greeted by the *Quarterly* in 1826 as further proof that the Niger really flowed eastward to the Nile. *Blackwood's* answered with an article (probably written by MacQueen himself) in further defense of the Oil Rivers hypothesis. As an indication of public interest, the *Edinburgh* gave its reviewer twice the usual space to deal with Denham's and Clapperton's book, and it followed up with another long reconstruction of African geography based on the Clapperton-Lander expedition.[22] The Niger question was finally closed only when the Oil Rivers theory was confirmed by the emergence of Richard and John Lander in 1830. With that, the principal mystery was solved, and public interest in West African geography began to decline. The classic age of West African exploration was finished.

The reporting of the explorers during this classic age had a special place in forming the British image of Africa. It was the first solid information about the recent Western Sudan. It came from Europeans, who wrote vividly in a way that appealed to their contemporaries. It caught the wide public interest generated by the Niger problem and the romance of the unknown. But the data of the explorers was very uneven in quality. It was very good within the narrow range of geographical problems that were their special concern. Otherwise it was often less complete and less accurate than the accounts of the eighteenth-century "enlightened travellers." The earlier generation of European visitors to West Africa had come out with a broad educational background and a universal curiosity, even though their spe-

22. *Blackwood's Edinburgh Magazine,* XIX, 687–709 (June 1826); *Edinburgh Review,* XLIV, 173–209 (June 1826) and XLIX, 127–49 (March 1829).

Figure 2. A slave-trade fort on the coast of Ghana.
Fort St. George, Elmina, formerly the principal Dutch post
on the Gold Coast. (Photograph by the author.)

Figure 3. The Accra waterfront. The former English Fort James
(*upper right*) and the Dutch Fort Crèvcoeur (*center,* now Ussher Fort)
stood side by side in the era of the slave trade. (Photograph by the author.)

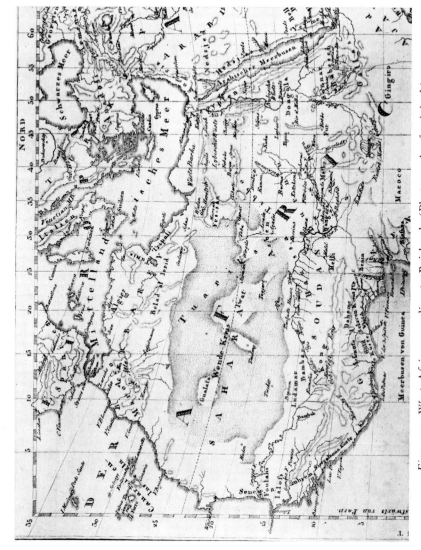

Figure 4. West Africa according to Reichard. (Photograph of original.)

Figure 5. West Africa according to MacQueen. (Photograph of original.)

Figure 6. "The Oil Rivers." A creek in the Niger Delta in 1832.
(From Allen, *Picturesque Views on the River Niger.*)

Figure 7. A scene on the Niger. This illustration
from Captain Allen's *Picturesque Views* combines an appeal
to the English taste of the period with a certain didacticism.
A romantic aspect comes out in the exaggeration of the hills
on the far side of the river, helping to spur the lure of the Niger
as a scene for British enterprise. The decapitation scene
in the foreground appeals to the "Gothick" aspect of the romantic movement,
while it also underlines the alleged "savagery" of the African people.

Figure 8. The Attah of Igala holding court.
(From Allen, *Picturesque Views.*)

Figure 9. The rooftops of Timbuctu, Sankoré Mosque in the distance.
(From Barth, *Travels in North and Central Africa.*)

Figure 10. The entrance of a caravan into Timbuctu.
(From Barth, *Travels in North and Central Africa.*)

Figure 11. A man and woman of Gaman. (From Dupuis.)
The decapitated head is still another way of showing
the alleged character of the people in illustrative form.

Figure 12. Street scenes in Kumasi. (From Bowdich.)

Figure 13. Dixcove Fort, an English trading fort on the Gold Coast.

Figure 14. Moslems from Dagomba and Salaga
in the costumes of their countries. (From Dupuis.)

cific mission might be the collection of botanical specimens in one spot. The new generation were men of a different stamp. They were selected for their ability to make a difficult journey and still survive. Many of them were military officers. Others had made their reputation by hard travel in the past.

Mungo Park as an individual and the emissaries of the African Association as a group represent a transitional phase between the enlightened travellers and the nineteenth-century explorers. They were often selected for their background and interest in Africa. The best, like Park himself, were very good indeed. Park was surprisingly successful in stepping over the culture barrier that entangled so many of his predecessors. His basic attitude was one of neutrality toward the African way of life. He simply told with he had seen, without arrogance, without special pleading, and (since he was not a scholar) without interpretation. His work has rightly become one of the classics of European travel literature, but the amount of space he could devote to ethnographic description was relatively small in comparison with the enlightened travellers who saw one society at leisure.

Park's successors tended to be less well educated for the task at hand, though a lack of formal education was not necessarily a bar to good reporting or careful research. Clapperton was mainly self-educated, yet he located Kano within 50 miles of its actual position, calculating the longitude by dead-reckoning. More important (and unfortunately more rare among his colleagues) he portrayed the culture of the Western Sudan with sympathy and an unusual degree of modesty.

When ignorance was combined with cultural arrogance, the result was quite different. Richard Lander also lacked a formal education, but he saw Africa through a haze of cross-cultural misunderstanding. Where his report touched on African culture, it was usually to poke fun and provide a little comic relief for his readers. The queer superstitions and peculiar doings of the Africans were made to look as ridiculous as possible in contrast to the "achievements" of Western civilization. This was probably Lander's own attitude, but it was also a way to tickle the prejudices of his audience and play on their sense of superiority. As a result his errors were more serious and more frequent than those of other travellers. In his view, for example, all African states were complete despotisms, and the enforcement of Muslim law in Hausa was nothing but the whim of the judge. He stated bluntly that none of the *mallams,* the educated class in Hausa, could actually read Arabic. Clapperton, in contrast, was candid enough to admit that he was not sufficiently educated in Christian theology to discuss the subject on the same level as Sultan Bello. It is hard to avoid the conclusion that Lander was not merely ignorant but intentionally disparaging in order to increase the popular appeal of his books.[23] He was by no means the last traveller to Africa to write in this vein.

All of the travellers over the long routes in the interior faced a special problem in their many-sided role as the only source of information about Africa. They had an adventure story to tell, and they knew they would be read mainly for the sake of their adventures. They also travelled fast, often under conditions of difficulty and danger. They spent long periods down with malaria, which is psychologically depressing in the best of circumstances. They were therefore in no position to check facts or work to a critical standard, even if they wanted to do so. It was the easiest course to stop short with a personal narrative combined with geographical detail. Very often little of Africa emerged, beyond a rather flat backdrop to set the scene.

What was not actually culture-bound tended to be naive and superficial. Denham included a good deal of information about Bornu, but his description of the Bornu "character" shows how little he got below the surface to Sudanese life: "The Bornu people, or Kanowry, as they are called, have large unmeaning faces, with flat Negro noses, and mouths of great dimensions, with good teeth and high foreheads. They are peaceable, quiet, and civil; they salute each other with courteousness and warmth; and there is a remarkable good-natured heaviness about them which is interesting. They are no warriors, but revengeful; and the best of them given to commit petty larcenies, on every opportunity that offers."[24]

The passage reads like the opinion of a badly educated tourist after his first brief trip abroad. Yet it was taken seriously: it was almost the only information available.

The reporting from the Coast was different, in quality, quantity,

23. R. L. Lander, *Records of Captain Clapperton's Last Expedition to Africa . . . with Subsequent Adventures of the Author,* 2 vols. (London, 1830), esp. I, 270–85.

24. D. Denham and H. Clapperton, *Narrative of Travels and Discoveries in Northern and Central Africa in the Years 1822, 1823, and 1824,* 2 vols. (London, 1826), I, 316.

and methods of gathering information. There was a persistent tradition of enlightened travel, and the Sierra Leone Company in their earlier and more hopeful years recruited scientists as members of their African staff. They were able to draw especially on the African interest of the Swedenborgians. Augustus Nordenskiold, one of the more eccentric of Wadström's group, went out to Sierra Leone as the official mineralogist. He considered himself something of an alchemist, and he had dreams of discovering the pure people in the heart of Africa. He died, however, in 1792, shortly after his arrival. Adam Afzelius, on the other hand, became the Company's botanist and did valuable work. In spite of the loss of his initial collections in the French raid of 1794, he stayed on and lived to return to Sweden with his specimens.[25]

Still other visitors to Guinea had strong scholarly interests. Bowdich, Golbéry, Mollien, and Dupuis all belong to the tradition of the Enlightenment. Thomas Winterbottom was the culminating field investigator of that school, by far the most competent and careful field ethnographer to visit West Africa before the second half of the nineteenth century. His *Account of the Native Africans in the Neighbourhood of Sierra Leone* was partly the result of his own field work and partly a work of ethnographic synthesis. Aside from his contribution to medical ethnography, which was unique for Africa at this period, his general ethnography was the first publication of its kind based on fieldwork by an English scholar. It was so far in advance of the general development of ethnographic fieldwork that Winterbottom has nearly become a forgotten figure in the history of anthropology.

Even though many of his substantive findings have long since been superceded by newer work, he made on the first serious efforts to apply critical standards to field investigations; and his warning to other ethnographers is as valid today as it was a century and a half ago:

The difficulty of procuring satisfactory intelligence from the natives of Africa, respecting themselves or their country, is known only to those who have made the experiment; they frequently lead Europeans into error by answering questions in the affirmative, merely to avoid trouble and escape importunity.

25. R. L. Tafel, *Documents Concerning the Life and Character of Emanuel Swedenborg,* 2 vols. (London, 1875–1877), I, 640–42. The Afzelius papers, including his journals from Sierra Leone, are preserved in the University Library, Upsala.

The questions themselves sometimes awaken jealousy of those to whom they are addressed; feeling that the curiosity of Europeans has some sinister end in view. It requires also much time, and a fund of patience, to propose the necessary queries; to vary them in such a manner as to enable the natives to comprehend their precise import; and to compare testimonies of different individuals in order to avoid the risk of misconception. Even interpreters are not to be implicitly relied on, as they are apt to give to answers that colour which they perceive will be most agreeable to their employer.[26]

He put this critical spirit to work in his own investigations. Among other things, he tried to overturn the widespread myth about the prevalence of cannibalism in West Africa. After checking the earlier European reports, he came to the conclusion that, aside from occasional ritual cannibalism, there was not a single authentic account by a reliable witness. The prevalence of the myth arose instead from the fact that most Africans "appear struck with horror when questioned individually on the subject; though at the same time they make no scruple of accusing other nations at a distance, and whom they barely know by name, of cannibalism."[27]

Other visitors to the coast, who were by no means scholars, occasionally tried to investigate and report in the light of existing culture theory. Philip Beaver, whose physical problems were at least as great as those of the explorers in the interior, still took time to investigate the culture of the Africans near Bulama Island. He even tried to assign them a place on the traditional scheme according to their "stage of civilization." Since they practiced hunting, fishing, pastoralism, and agriculture all at the same time, the task was beyond him. He thought that African culture was "debased," but he also saw a common humanity behind the differences in custom. As he put it in one instance: "Powdering the hair is only painting it white, and I see no rational difference between that, and the Bijugas filling theirs with red ocre, except, that red ocre best becomes a black countenance."[28]

G. A. Robertson continued the relatively unbiased tradition of the eighteenth-century merchants. His manual of mercantile affairs was designed for practical men of business, rather than scholars, but it included a good deal of ethnographic information, especially on the commercial customs and the nature and distribution of political

26. T. Winterbottom, *An Account of the Native Africans in the Neighbourhood of Sierra Leone,* 2 vols. (London, 1803), I, v.

27. Winterbottom, *Native Africans,* I, 166–67.

28. Philip Beaver, *African Memoranda* (London, 1805), pp. 318–36, quotation on p. 326.

power in each African state. He was no reformer. Perhaps for this reason, he was less culture-bound than many of the humanitarians, who were committed to the goal of civilizing and Christianizing Africa.[29]

Thomas Edward Bowdich was both an official and something of a scholar, though with less critical sense than Winterbottom. His report on Ashanti included a record of the traditional history back to the beginning of the eighteenth century, and it extended to aspects of African culture that were often neglected. In addition to the more usual description of customs and "superstitutions," he noted down bits of Ashanti music and gave a chapter to Ashanti law and constitution. As a result, readers at home had a much better picture of Ashanti as a functioning society than they had of the Fante states after almost three centuries of contact.[30]

But the tradition of enlightened travel to West Africa was slowly dying in the early decades of the nineteenth cenury. Neither the government nor the Sierra Leone Company sponsored professional scientists after Winterbottom and Afzelius, except on the exploring expeditions. The African Institution, however, tried to keep up the tradition of research by the questionnaire method. In 1810, they published one of the most elaborate questionnaires so far, with 114 questions to serve as a guide to the investigations of any traveller who happened to be in Africa. The questions were somewhat slanted toward geographical and statistical information, but about half were broadly concerned with the history, laws, politics, and culture of the people. In this sense, it was the forerunner of a whole succession of later ethnographic questionnaires.[31]

The Institution itself published two brief articles based on the questionnaire. One was the work of Henry Meredith, governor at Winnebah on the Gold Coast, who dealt with Angona, the small Akan state in his immediate hinterland. The second, by Thomas Ludlam, discussed the Kru people of Liberia, who were already in the habit of coming to Sierra Leone as transient laborers.[32] Later writers

29. Robertson, *Notes on Africa, passim.* A part of Robertson's work was reprinted in Germany for its ethnographic contribution as "Die Republik der Fantees an der Westküste von Afrika," *Ethnographisches Archiv,* X, 142–92 (Jena, 1820). For traders' ethnography see also J. Adams, *Remarks,* pp. 8–43.

30. Bowdich, *Mission to Ashantee, passim.*

31. "Queries Relative to Africa," African Institution, *Reports of the Committee of the African Institution,* 18 vols. (London, 1807–1824), Fourth Report, pp. 75–82.

32. African Institution, *Reports,* Fourth Report, pp. 82–93; Sixth Report, pp. 87–102.

also occasionally used the questionnaire more loosely as a guide to general orientation.[33]

Other questionnaires, for administrative rather than scholarly purposes, came into use at about the same time. Both sets of Commissioners, Ludlam and Dawes in 1810 and Wellington and Rowan in 1827, circulated questionnaires to the commanders of the forts and other European residents. The questions of 1810 were mainly concerned with political and economic prospects, or the state of the slave trade. The Commissioners were not interested in African society as a functioning whole, but only in selected aspects that might affect the future British position. Both the questions and the answers were much less sophisticated than those of the amateur scholars. The flavor of ethnocentric suggestion is clear from the question on the African character:

9. What is the general character of the people; more particularly, can Europeans confide in them with safety? Are they remarkable for fidelity to one another in times of danger? Do they repose confidence in Europeans, or in one another, where their pecuniary interests are concerned? Are they revengeful; or are quarrels, especially between families, easily made up? If shipwrecked or distressed Europeans fall into their hands, how do they treat them? Are they fond of war? Are they much bigotted to ancient customs? Do they readily change part of those customs (their mode of building or dress for instance) in imitation of Europeans? What customs do they most rigidly adhere to? What means have been tried (by persuasion, instruction, example, &c.) to wean them from their most prejudicial customs?[34]

Answers from the eight commanders of Gold Coast forts were more culture-bound than the usual attitudes expressed by eighteenth-century slave traders. George Richardson of Anomabu struck a note that was representative of the group. "The natives in general are addicted to many vices, but particularly stealing, lying, deceit, imposition, &c. &c. Europeans cannot confide in them with safety, . . . they are much bigotted to ancient customs; some of them do attempt improvements in their houses in the European manner, but their dress is always the same. Europeans have tried, in vain, to convince them of the folly of their more absurd customs; but they do not wish to enter much on the subject."[35]

33. As may have been the case with Peter McLachlan's *Travels into the Baga and Soosoo Countries* (Freetown, 1821), a brief ethnographic report prepared by the Assistant Staff Surgeon of Sierra Leone, first incorporated in his official half-yearly report, and then separately published.

34. PP, 1816, vii (506), p. 156.

35. Answer dated 16 August 1810, PP, 1816, vii (506), p. 161.

The answers give some insight into the "official mind" on the Gold Coast, showing among other things how rare the attitude of a Winterbottom or a Bowdich was among the administrative class. A similar arrogance was echoed by the press at home. High adventure was one thing, and Mungo Park was avidly read. Ethnography was another, and Winterbottom's book was generally neglected. The *Edinburgh Review* completely missed Winterbottom's point. The reviewer devoted his space to an essay against the slave trade, brushing off the Africans themselves as a people "divided by different shades of barbarism, and disputed limited of territory, plunged in the darkest ignorance and superstition.[36] The *Anti-Jacobin* openly attacked Winterbottom, especially for his failure to recognize the "fact" of African inferiority."[37]

Bowdich fared little better, though his mission to Kumasi was a "discovery," and his work was more widely read than Winterbottom's had been. *Blackwood's* thought it might improve the racial reputation of Africans by showing that they were "capable of improvement."[38] The reviewer in the *Quarterly,* however, used it as an occasion for poking fun at African customs and took Bowdich to task for attempting to write seriously about African language or music. As for history, "The 'history' of the Ashantees, to which Mr. Bowdich has dedicated a whole chapter, is, like that of all other savages who can neither read nor write, the history of a day, and little worthy of notice."[39]

Even though writing about African ethnography was unpopular in some quarters, it was still widely published and read, smuggled in, as it were, under the guise of travel literature. The edition and publication of collected travellers' tales was continuous, while ephemeral literary fads rose and fell. Some collections placed a new emphasis on personal narrative and reduced the space given to "manners and customs," but the tradition of Astley's *Voyages* and the *Universal History* also persisted. It was especially important in the editions of John Leyden and Hugh Murray. Leyden began the series with his *Historical and Philosophical Sketch of the Discoveries and Settlements of the Europeans in Northern and Western Africa at the Close of the Eighteenth Century,* first published in Edinburgh in 1799. Its

36. *Edinburgh Review,* III, 355 (January 1804).
37. *Anti-Jacobin Review,* XVIII, 47 (May 1804).
38. *Blackwood's,* V, 175–83 and 302–10 (May–June 1819).
39. *Quarterly Review,* XXII, 286 (January 1820).

title notwithstanding, the work was mainly concerned with the society and culture of the Africans themselves. The achievements of the
explorers fell into second place. Taking his point of departure from
moral philosophy, Leyden believed that, "By contemplating their
manners and customs, we may discover the simple and unmixed operation of those principles which, in civilized society, are always combined with extraneous circumstances."[40]

He thus reaffirmed the eighteenth-century search for man-in-general, and his work passed through several editions in both English
and French to become a summary and text for a new generation of
colonial theorists and planners. Hugh Murray, the Scottish geographer, joined in the preparation of later revisions, and Murray too had
an interest in ethnological theory. The size, scope, and title of the
publication changed gradually through the early nineteenth century.
The history of colonization dropped out, and the discoveries of the
most recent explorers were added. In all, the enterprise lasted more
than half a century, with a final edition in 1853, after Murray's
death.[41]

The most ambitious and complete publication of African information, however, come from France. Between 1826 and 1831, Baron
Walckenaer edited a series of twenty-one volumes, designed as the
first stage of a world-wide collection of voyages. In fact, he never
got beyond Africa. Five and one-half volumes devoted to West Africa brought back into print very nearly the whole canon of earlier
African travels, plus the recent explorations in the Western Sudan.
The format was similar to Astley's *Voyages,* with authorities edited
and interlaced to form a running account of each geographical region. It made easier reading, but it often obscured the original
source.[42] Some other French publications were equally elaborate.
Grasset de Saint-Saveur's *Encyclopédie des voyages,* for example, depicted West African costume in twenty-eight hand-colored plates.[43]

Periodical publication of travellers' accounts was also a Continental

40. Leyden, *Historical and Philosophical Sketch,* p. ix.

41. J. Leyden and H. Murray, *Historical Account of Discoveries and Voyages in
Africa,* 2 vols. (Edinburgh, 1817); R. Jameson, J. Wilson, and H. Murray, *Narrative
of Discovery and Adventure in Africa from the Earliest Ages to the Present Time*
(Edinburgh and London, 1830); Hugh Murray, *The African Continent* (Edinburgh,
1853).

42. C. A. Walckenaer (ed.), *Histoire générale des voyages,* 21 vols. (Paris,
1826–1831).

43. J. Grasset de Saint-Saveur, *Encyclopédie des Voyages,* 5 vols. (Paris, 1795), IV.

phenomenon. Malte-Brun's *Annales des Voyages* ran through 24 volumes between 1809 and 1814. It was succeeded by the *Nouvelles Annales des Voyages et de la Géographie et de l'Histoire* and by the *Journal des Voyages, Découvertes et Navigations Modernes,* which published 44 volumes between 1813 and 1826. The German equivalent was the *Journal für die neuesten Land- und Seereisen,* published in Berlin. None of these was chiefly concerned with Africa, but the French journals kept track of French accounts from Senegal. All of them lifted and republished translations of the major British explorations and occasionally printed a review of recent British activities.[44]

As English interests pushed out to many parts of the overseas world, the major English travel collections came to be less concerned with Africa. Less than 3 per cent of Kerr's voyages was devoted to African material, and Pinkerton's gave Africa no more space than North America, and less than Asia.[45] This tendency was redressed to some extent by the publication of smaller compendia, specifically designed to catch the public interest in African exploration. Some of these synthesized and popularized the new information at a high level of competence. Catherine Hutton's *Tour of Africa* is an example of the better work of this kind. She selected from the work of the travellers so as to produce an account of a single tour of Africa told in the first person. In spite of this eccentric presentation, she told her story without the usual single-minded concentration on the slave trade, and with less cultural bias than most.

In a more limited sphere, Frederick Shoberl's account of Mauritania and Senegambia for children was equally well done. He simplified and explained, as is characteristic of this type of literature but the result was a well balanced description of Wolof culture and political structure, with some information on surrounding peoples.[46]

Most popularization came nowhere near the quality of these two,

44. See, for example, N. V., "Coup-d'oeil sur la guerre des Ashantis et sur l'état des possessions anglaises de la Côte-d'or," *Journal des Voyages,* XXV, 169–89 (February, 1825).

45. Robert Kerr (ed.), *A General History and Collection of Voyages and Travels . . . ,* 18 vols. (Edinburgh, 1811–1824); John Pinkerton, *A General Collection of the Best and Most Interesting Voyages and Travels in All Parts of the World,* 17 vols. (London, 1808–1814).

46. Catherine Hutton, *The Tour of Africa . . . with the Manners and Customs of the Inhabitants,* 3 vols. (London, 1819–1821); F. Shoberl, *The World in Miniature. Africa. A Description of the Manners and Customs of the Moors of the Zahara, and of the Negro Nations between the Rivers Senegal and Gambia,* 4 vols. (London, n. d. [c. 1821]).

and many editors used the medium of travel literature for their own didactic purposes. An imitation of Catherine Hutton's format, for example, taught cultural chauvinism by concentrating on the evil of "heathen" customs.[47] Charles Hulbert's two scissors-and-paste compilations of Africana were designed to attract British emigrants to South Africa.[48]

Travel books compiled for the young were especially inclined to moral preaching. At best, they merely boiled down selected passages from the explorers,[49] but many editors combined exhortation with an easy disregard for the facts. One, for example, presented authentic travel narratives interlarded with fanciful accounts, endowing the Western Sudan with "mountains covered with impenetrable forests, and barren solitudes parched by the raging heat of the torrid climate."[50] Another used the travellers for a juvenile anti-slavery tract, concentrating on the horrors of the slave trade and the virtue of the English for abolishing their share of it. As for the Africans, they were dismissed with such statements as: "Bornou is a very considerable tract of country, north west of Darfur; and may be described as resembling the other tribes, in ignorance, ferocity, and power." Or, in regard to Timbuctu: "The people being negro, and so much separated from other nations, are very ignorant and of course superstitious."[51]

The ignorance was certainly mutual, since this was published before Clapperton had reached Bornu or Caillié, Timbuctu. While the intention was to encourage morality and support of Christian missions, the obvious by-product was racial and cultural arrogance.

Little of the writing about Africa was, in any case, politically neutral—nor could it be in an era when first the slave trade and then West Indian slavery were debated in Parliament. Both the humanitarians and their opponents needed data to support their efforts in Britain. Wilberforce frequently appealed to the Sierra Leone officials of the 1790's for evidence to support the case he was about to make in the House. In 1804, he wrote to Lord Muncaster with a list of eight propositions about Africa and the Africans, asking Muncaster

47. *Travels in Africa* (Dublin, C. Bentham, 1821).
48. C. Hulbert, *The African Traveller* . . . (Shrewsbury, 1817) and *Museum Africanum* (Shrewsbury, 1822).
49. Mrs. Barbara Hofland [née Houle], *Africa Described* (London, 1828).
50. William Bingley, *Travels in Africa, from Modern Writers* (London, 1819), p. 202.
51. Isaac Taylor, *Scenes in Africa* (London, 1820), pp. 31 and 33

to check through his library of African travellers and furnish proof that these points were correct.[52] Defenders of slavery and the trade did the same kind of thing, and old "evidence" like the horrors of Dahomey depicted by Dalzel in the 1790's cropped up for thirty years and more, with a drumming repetition that must have carried conviction to the casual reader.

There was not yet an established professional or scholarly group whose business it was to receive, check, and assimilate new cultural data from overseas for the sake of knowledge itself. To some extent this function was performed by the publishers of travel collections and their editors, but it was rarely done in a way that measured up to the best standards of scholarship as then understood. So far, only geographers posed an effective series of concrete questions suggesting the data they needed.

Anthropology had only reached its barest beginning as a body of systematic knowledge. The discipline, as it is now understood, was still divided between biology on one hand and moral philosophy on the other. While moral philosophers were anxious to use ethnographic data, they did not see it as a part of their work to collect these data or to assimilate them in a systematic way.

Leadership in organized ethnography came from other sources. One of these was an extension from the biological study of man, and the key figure was James Cowles Prichard. Originally trained as a physician, his first interest was physical anthropology, which formed the bulk of the first edition of his *Researches into the Physical History of Man* (1813). As times passed, however, the new editions took on a new emphasis. By 1826, the two-volume second edition already contained an ethnographic survey of Africa based on the reports of the travellers.[53] The final five-volume version (and with it Prichard's greatest reputation) came only later, but the base was laid in the 1820's. Guidance for travellers began even earlier with such efforts as the African Institution's ethnographic questionnaire of 1810. By the 1820's the word "ethnography" was coming into use.[54]

52. Wilberforce to Z. Macaulay, 23 August 1793 and Wilberforce to Muncaster, 18 December 1804, in Wilberforce, R. I. and S. (eds.), *Correspondence of William Wilberforce*, 5 vols. (London, 1838), II, 409–13 and III, 203.

53. J. C. Prichard, *Researches into the Physical History of Man*, 2nd ed., 2 vols. (London, 1826), I, 250–81.

54. As in the title of the *Ethnographisches Archiv* published in Jena, but the precise meaning was still uncertain. Adriano Balbi's *Atlas ethnographique du globe* (Paris, 1826) was in fact a set of tables of language classification, rather than a broader study of human culture.

The new science was then new enough, yet familiar enough, to be worthy of a playful lampoon in the *New Monthly Magazine*.[55] The way was prepared for the more extensive developments to follow.

Meanwhile, travellers reported selectively—even though their criteria for selection were rarely conscious or based on a desire for systematic knowledge. The pattern was, indeed, little changed from that of the later eighteenth century. The interest in commerce remained, but with a new bias, as the need for new openings to replace the slave trade became evident. From 1805, government-sponsored expeditions carried orders to report on trade and markets. Partly for the same reason, political structures and military capabilities of inland states attracted a new interest. Outward signs of political authority, however, were still reported more accurately than the constitutional base on which they rested. In religion, "superstitious practices" still held little interest, unless they took the form of spectacular festivals or rites particularly abhorrent to Europeans.

Even in the area of their special concern, travellers often made curious mistakes. African agriculture was still widely misunderstood, though it necessarily formed the base for economic development. The principal error was the continuing assumption of tropical exuberance. If African soils were endlessly rich, the usual West African practice of shifting cultivation could only be understood as an irrational and ignorant use of the land—but West African soils were not rich. Travellers also missed the relationship between shifting cultivation and the systems of land tenure—and the influence of both on African concepts of real and personal property. Leyden, for example, reported at one stage that all African agriculture was communal, that all contributed their labor and received a share of the crop. This, in his view, discouraged individual enterprise and hence economic development. He was, of course, wrong on both counts, and the error was partly corrected in later editions. Still, the belief persisted that each African town or village was surrounded by large tracts of unused land, which would be granted freely to anyone who cared to undertake the labor of cultivating it.[56] This land was often considered ripe for the skill and direction of the European entrepreneur.

New interests also appeared. One was a concern for African

55. W. E., "Anthropology," *New Monthly Magazine*, XXII, 505–09 (1828).
56. Leyden, *Historical and Philosophical Sketch*, pp. 99–101; Leyden and Murray, *Discoveries and Voyages in Africa*, II, 491.

women and the place of women in African society. It echoed John
Millar's emphasis on the position of women as the touchstone for
judging social development (and the final edition of Millar's *Distinction of Ranks* did not appear until 1806). Winterbottom, for example, accepted Millar's distinction in preference to Montesquieu's view
that money was the true mark of civilization.[57] Polygyny was also a
repulsive institution to most European travellers, who saw it as male
oppression of the weaker sex. In part, this new sympathy reflected the
rising status of women in Europe—not yet, to be sure, to positions of
equality with men, but deserving of chivalrous protection. Mungo
Park's report of kindness shown him by some African women caught
the public imagination more than anything else in his narrative. The
incident was set to music and became a popular song, inspired in part
by its political usefulness as an attack on the slave trade. In this case,
the association of womanhood, motherhood, and a common humanity
appears to have been a convenient way to by-pass the unsympathetic
image of African men. Then, too, the new concern for African
women was fully supported by the romantic movement: one aspect of
Lovejoy's "diversificationism" was the admiration of exotic beauty.
Golbéry caught this spirit in his praise of the *Sénégalaises:* "Those
who imagine that black, or shades of black, are sufficient to designate
in painting a young and handsome negress, have no correct idea of
her charms; the roses likewise combine with the carnations, and as
we say in Europe, when speaking of a beautiful complexion of an
African beauty, that it is an union of ebony and roses."[58]

African arts and crafts were also favored by romanticism. As classical standards declined, exotic designs were more acceptable. Even
Richard Lander, who otherwise had little admiration for things African, admired African skill in painting, sculpture, leather and iron
works, dyes, and textiles.[59]

African languages received new attention as well, though for more
practical reasons. At the turn of the eighteenth century, the science of
linguistics had reached a stage of development roughly equivalent to
that of biology a century earlier. European philologists were taking
inventory of the languages of the world. Enormous surveys of several

57. Winterbottom, *Native Africans,* I, 144 and 188.

58. S. M. X. Golberry [S. M. X. de Golbéry], *Travels in Africa Performed during
the Years 1785, 1786, and 1787,* 2 vols. (London, 1803), II, 310. See also F. B. Spilsbury, *A Voyage to the Western Coast of Africa* (London, 1807), pp. 22–23.

59. Lander, *Clapperton's Last Expedition,* I, 305–7.

hundred languages were published by P. S. Pallas in 1786–87 and
Lorenzo Hervas y Panduro in 1800–05. Pallas took notice of some
thirty African languages, and Hervas was the first to identify Am-
haric as a Semitic language.[60]

By the 1790's, West African languages had entered the picture.
Even before Europeans had direct access to the West African interior, comparative vocabularies were collected from Africans in other
parts of the world, as Oldendorp had done earlier in the Danish
West Indies. Ulrich Jasper Seetzen took down vocabularies supplied
by Negro Africans in Cairo, and his information was ultimately published by J. S. Vater of Königsberg.[61] Later on, in 1816–17, J. L.
Burkhardt again used Cairo as a listening post for linguistic data
from West Africa, tapping the information of pilgrims passing
through on the way to Mecca.[62] Other travellers in the Maghrib, and
especially Lyon, recorded brief vocabularies of sub-Saharan languages, as they met informants from south of the desert; and the
explorers continued the work of vocabulary collection as they began
to move into the interior.

Meanwhile, the practical need for a knowledge of African languages was increasing along the West African coast, as travellers
began to penetrate beyond the range of accepted European *linguae
francae*. Adanson had learned Wolof for his ethnographic studies in
Senegal. Mungo Park used Mandingo as the most convenient *lingua
franca* for the Senegambian interior. For similar practical reasons the
French Senegal Company compiled a dictionary in the 1790's, giving
about 2000 words in French and their equivalents in 11 languages of
the Senegambia.[63]

The most serious linguistic studies, indeed, came from the Guinea
Coast. Sierra Leone was a natural base. The pioneer linguist there
was Henry Brunton of the Edinburgh Missionary Society, who
worked on the Rio Pongas in the later 1790's and reduced the Susu
language to writing in Roman characters. Among other works, he
published a Susu grammar and vocabulary, an abridgement of the

60. Holgar Pedersen, *Linguistic Science in the Nineteenth Century* (Cambridge,
Mass., 1931), pp. 9–10. R. N. Cust, *A Sketch of the Modern Languages of Africa*,
2 vols. (London, 1883), I, 25–26.

61. J. C. Prichard, "Abstract of a Comparative Review of Philological and Physical
Researches as applied to the History of the Human Species," *Reports of the British
Association for the Advancement of Science*, II, 529–44 (1832), p. 531.

62. Burckhardt, *Travels in Nubia*, pp. 477–83.

63. *Mémories de la Société Ethnologique*, II (2), 205–67 (1845).

Bible, and some devotional works of his own composition. These included three dialogues on the advantages of literacy, the absurdity of the Susu religion, and the superiority of Christianity over Islam.[64]

Other visitors took a hand in linguistic research, at least in an amateur way. Winterbottom worked with Bullom, Temne, and Susu, publishing a brief grammatical study, the usual vocabularies, and a suggested system of orthography for African languages.[65] At this stage, however, most orthography was so careless and unstandardized, and most travellers were so lacking in broad linguistic background, that the pioneer work had little or no permanent value to scholarship.

Even so, a few of the early travellers approached the theoretical problems of linguistic science, if only in a very unsophisticated manner. Bowdich in Ashanti tried to assess the relationships between Akan languages, concluding that Ashanti was the "Attic" of the group, others, such as Fante, being derived from it. He was on weaker ground in his discussion of the origin of language, claiming both that language was revealed to man by God and that languages develop in an evolutionary manner from "primitive simplicity."[66] At the very least, people interested in such questions were now actually carrying on research in Africa.

The most systematic investigations of this period were those of Mrs. Hannah Kilham, who spent most of the period 1820–1832 on linguistic research for the sake of more effective missionary work. She made three separate trips to Sierra Leone or the Gambia, sponsored by the Society of Friends; and she produced an exercise book for teaching Wolof to English-speakers, some translations into Wolof, and a substantial comparative vocabulary of English words with their equivalents in some thirty African languages. She was also interested in technical problems and prepared a brief guide for discovering the grammar of an unknown language and reducing it to writing with a phonetic orthography.[67]

As the new linguistic data flowed in from Africa, it was studied by

64. Winterbottom, *Native Africans*, I, 218 *n*.
65. Winterbottom, *Native Africans*, I, 337–62.
66. Bowdich, *Mission to Ashantee*, pp. 344–50 and 503–12.
67. Peter Bedford and others, "Address to Friends," 22 May 1820, Thomas Hodgkin Papers; Hannah Kilham, *African Lessons. Wolof and English* (London, 1823) and *Specimens of African Language Spoken in the Colony of Sierra Leone* (London, 1828). See also C. P. Groves, *The Planting of Christianity in Africa*, 4 vols. (London, 1948–1958), I, 286–88.

European linguists. In the first decades of the nineteenth century Johann Christoph Adelung was compiling the last of the great inventories of world languages. The final version, completed after Adelung's death by Johan Severin Vater, contained the first detailed and systematic discussion of African languages.[68] As such, it served as the point of departure both for Prichard's treatment of West African languages in his *Researches into the Physical History of Man* and for Balbi's *Atlas ethnographique du globe.*

The classification of African languages was barely beginning, though the group now known as the Bantu languages was understood to be a single family. The Portuguese had recognized the similarity between Kikongo on the west coast and the "kaffir" languages of southeast Africa as early as the seventeenth century. This affinity and its extensions throughout southern Africa was rediscovered and publicized in Britain in the later eighteenth century by William Marsden, the Orientalist.[69] In West Africa, the only commonly recognized affinities were in the Mande and Akan families, and in the more obvious unity of the various Fulbe dialects spread across West Africa from the Atlantic to the Cameroons. Otherwise, the languages were only arranged in rather uncertain regional groupings.

In spite of these beginnings of serious scholarly study, the British stereotype of "the African character" drew far more from the reports of the travellers, than it did from the synthesis of the scholars. But scholars and travellers alike were virtually unanimous about one point—there was such a thing as an "African character," different in significant ways from the character of man in Europe. There was, of course, disagreement about the exact ingredients of this character, but the range of opinion was somewhat narrower than it had been in the later eighteenth century. There were now more (and more varied) sources of information, and a common image of "the African" was well publicized. Individual writers could hardly do more than adjust the focus or alter the detail.

It was generally believed that African emotions tended toward extremes: "The understanding is much less cultivated among the Negroes than among Europeans; but their passions, whether benevo-

68. J. C. Adelung and J. S. Vater, *Mithridates oder allgemeine Sprachenkunde,* 4 vols. (Berlin, 1806–1817), III, 1–305.

69. H. H. Johnston, *A Comparative Study of the Bantu and Semi-Bantu Languages,* 2 vols. (Oxford, 1919–1922), I, 1–5; C. M. Doke, "Bantu Language Pioneers of the Nineteenth Century," *African Studies,* XVIII, 1–27 (1959).

lent or malevolent, are proportionately more violent. . . . Though addicted to hatred and revenge, they are equally susceptible to love, affection, and gratitude."[70]

This belief, with various modifications, was extremely common. It was based more on the general theories of the eighteenth-century environmentalists than on observation. A hot temper and violent passions were the prime characteristics of southerners. The travellers, of course, knew this before they left England, and their reports were influenced accordingly.

Further discussions of the "African character" tended to list virtues and vices as a kind of balance of good and evil, following a tradition borrowed from moral philosophy. Different lists were surprisingly uniform. The chief African vices were held to be indolence, ferocity, cowardice, and superstitution. The virtues were mild manners, a peaceful disposition, politeness, charity, respect for the aged, and sometimes gratitude and nobility of character.[71] Different opinions merely shifted the balance of these traits, adding here and subtracting there. A poet still writing in the mood of noble savagery with anti-slavery overtones, for example, might idealize the virtue side of the ledger. James Montgomery's "The West Indies" hinted at a highly Christian paradise in Africa:

> There, as with nature's warmest filial fire,
> He soothes his blind, and feeds his helpless sire;
> His children sporting round his hut behold
> How they shall cherish him when he is old,
> Train'd by example from their tenderest youth
> To deeds of charity, and words of truth.[72]

Or the balance might be struck on the negative side, with reservations, as with Durand: "The character of the blacks is nearly the same everywhere: they are indolent, except when animated by the desire for vengeance; implacable, perfidious, and dissimulating when they have received an injury, in order that they may find an opportunity of avenging it with impunity: on the other hand, they are

---

70. Leyden, *Historical and Philosophical Sketch*, p. 98.

71. A convenient summary, based on a wide variety of sources, is found in Abbé Henri Baptiste Grégoire, *De la littérature des nègres, ou recherches sur leur facultés intellectuelles, leur qualités morales, et leur littérature* (Paris, 1808), translated by D. B. Warden as *An Enquiry Concerning the Intellectual and Moral Faculties, and Literature of Negroes* . . . (Brooklyn, N.Y., 1810), pp. 89–106.

72. J. Montgomery, *Poetical Works*, 4 vols. (London, 1828), I, 36. "The West Indies" was first published in 1807.

gentle and hospitable to every one, but inclined to larceny, and re-markable for an extreme inconstancy of taste and conduct."[73]

In extreme cases, the positive qualities might drop out altogether. Nollan, the commander of Secondi fort reported in 1810: "Like the inhabitants of all barbarous countries, the natives here are addicted to many vices, and their characters as liars, thieves, and cheats are noto-riously known. If they posses any virtues, I must confess they have entirely escaped my observation. . . ."[74]

The derivation of the lists is curious, both on the side of virtue and the side of vice. The vices of cowardice and sloth were standard "southern" vices, recognized as such in a centuries-old European tra-dition having nothing to do with empirical data from tropical Africa. The vice of "superstition" represented little more than a reaction to religious difference between Europe and Africa. Cowardice, on the other hand, was not so frequently reported as idleness, and many writers maintained a contradictory listing of both ferocity and cow-ardice. The explanation appears to be that all "savages" were nat-urally ferocious, and southern savages were expected to be cowards as well.

Laziness was the vice most frequently reported, and the emphasis was repeated from several sides. It was believed to be characteristic of Negro slaves in the West Indies. It was reinforced by mistaken ob-servation in West Africa, where the myth of tropical exuberance encouraged the Europeans to think that Africans had no need to work. In addition, agricultural work in West Africa was often sea-sonal, on account of alternation of dry and wet periods. The usual dry-season under-employment became a wet-season labor shortage. The dry-season pattern might look like simple laziness. Lethargy pro-duced by certain intestinal parasites and other African diseases may also have reinforced the impression.

On the side of virtue, reflections of environmentalism combined with other data drawn from actual observation. A formal politeness

73. J. B. L. Durand, *A Voyage to Senegal,* (London, 1806), p. 99.
74. PP, 1816, vii (506), p. 176. For other summary views of the "Negro character" see M. Park, *Travels in the Interior Districts of Africa,* 2nd ed. (London, 1799), pp. 261–64; Golbéry, *Travels in Africa,* I, 70 and II, 310; J. Corry, *Observations upon the Windward Coast of Africa . . . made in the Years 1805–1806* (London, 1807), esp. p. 60; PP, 1816, vii (506), pp. 156–97; J. MacLoed, *A Voyage to Africa, with Some Account of the Manners and Customs of the Dahomean People* (London, 1820), p. 129; John Adams, *Sketches Taken During Ten Voyages to Africa, Between the Years 1786 and 1800 . . .* (London, 1822), p. 72; Balbi, *Atlas ethnographique,* table 19.

is still common in many West African cultures. It must have been all the more striking to travellers who expected to find savages. Respect for the aged is equally characteristic—partly for theological reasons, connected with the veneration of ancestral spirits. The code of African hospitality is often rigorous, and so important to travellers that it could hardly escape notice.

The most significant aspect of the virtue column, however, was the attribution of Christian virtues to the Africans. Faith, hope, and charity had appeared occasionally in the literary image of the noble savage, whether African or not. They appeared again in the Christianized noble African of the anti-slavery writers. The result was not so favorable to Africans as it might appear to be. Europeans always paid lip service to the Sermon on the Mount, but they also admired aggressive self-assertion. The sin of pride was the cardinal sin for theologians, but rarely in the moral attitude of the ordinary person. This moral ambivalence in European thought, however, was not mere hypocrisy. Europeans still retained a genuine respect for child-like simplicity and submissiveness—lost long ago by themselves, according to their own mythology, in the Garden of Eden.

During the European Middle Ages, men hoped and expected that somewhere beyond the seas there might still be a terrestrial paradise. The belief had, indeed, contributed to the early travellers' accounts, which had been, in turn, one foundation for the motif of the noble savage.

In another direction, the medieval tradition influenced the missionary image of the potential convert. As early as the sixteenth century, Spanish missionaries in Mexico had laid special emphasis on the meekness and humility of the Indians, qualities which allegedly made them especially susceptible to Christian influence.[75] The description they gave of the Indians was strikingly similar to the virtue side of the nineteenth-century balance sheet of African character, and the picture of the Africans as natural Christians was to grow in strength as time passed.

In contrast to the standardized picture of "the African character," new data about African cultures led those with a more specialized knowledge to emphasize the diversity of peoples and civilizations. According to Prichard: "we find in general that the whole country is

75. J. L. Phelan, *The Millenial Kingdom of the Franciscans in the New World* (Berkeley, Cal., 1956), pp. 56–57.

divided between a great number of small and distinct tribes, who have no connexion with each other than can be discovered by resemblance of language or by any other trait. On passing over a river, or a ridge of mountains, the traveller finds the race of men completely changed, as far as the race can be distinguished by customs and peculiar language."[76]

Others agreed, and the most common practice was to draw a sharp distinction between the "superior" peoples of the interior and the "degraded" nations of the coast. The old belief in the good interior was reinforced by Mungo Park's early reports of dense population, brisk commerce, and relatively stable political order beyond the headwaters of the Gambia.

Particular peoples also came in for special praise or blame. The French writers tended to think highly of the Wolof in the hinterland of Gorée.[77] The Mandinka,[78] Hausa,[79] and Ashanti[80] were also singled out as islands of barbarism in a sea of savagery. The British preference for Ashanti over their Fante allies was a curious choice, since Ashanti was a constant threat, if it was not actively hostile. The cultures of Ashanti and the Fante states were remarkably similar. Yet Ashanti was the only non-Muslim state to be consistently praised, and the Fante were usually roundly condemned. In this case, it appears that the myth of the interior plus Bowdich's glowing account combined with the existing dislike of partly-Westernized Africans. In Sierra Leone, and for similar reasons, the British approved of the Maroons and disapproved of the Nova Scotians. As the liberated Africans began to come ashore from the slavers, the British also thought better of the Yoruba than of the Ibo or Bakongo.[81] Though they neglected formal ethnography, they had firm opinions about the qualities of distinct African cultures.

76. Prichard, *Researches* (1826), I, 250.

77. Durand, *Voyage to Senegal*, pp. 98–99; Golbéry, *Travels in Africa*, I, 70–74.

78. Golbéry, *Travels in Africa*, I, 73; Report of the Commissioners on African Settlements, PP, 1812, x (101), p. 5.

79. Jackson, *Morocco*, p. 247; Leyden and Murray, *Discoveries and Voyages in Africa*, II, 486–87.

80. Torrane to African Committee, 20 July 1807, T 70/35, f. 66; Dupuis, *Residence in Ashantee*, lxiv; *Edinburgh Review*, XLI, 341–43 (January 1825); [J. MacQueen], "British Settlements in Western Africa," *Blackwood's Edinburgh Magazine*, XXVI, 342 (September 1829).

81. See, for example, R. C. Dallas, *The History of the Maroons from their Origin to the Establishment of their Chief Tribe in Sierra Leone*, 2 vols. (London, 1803), I, 87–88; Spilsbury, *Western Coast of Africa*, p. 38; H. I. Ricketts, *Narrative of the Ashantee War with a view of the Present State of Sierra Leone* (London, 1831), pp. 191–93 and 209.

9

BARBARISM:

ITS PHYSICAL CAUSES

Faced, as they were, with the necessary adjustment to the era of "legitimate trade," the British began to look more closely at African society. Any rationally conceived policy required some understanding of what Africa would become if left to herself, and what she might become under British influence. This understanding, in turn, called on the theoretical knowledge of scholars and scientists—on their beliefs about the nature of race, environment, and culture.

British discussions of Africa in the early nineteenth century necessarily took their departure from the eighteenth-century image of Africa. They began with the accepted "fact" that Negro Africans were, at best, barbarians who had never known civilization. They were also Negro in race. Were these two factors related? If so, what was the precise nature of the relationship? Would the racial heritage of the Negroes prevent the rise of civilization in Africa, or would their racial characteristics themselves change with the "improvement" of the African way of life? In the priority of logic, the first answer was necessarily that of the physical anthropologists. If they made a convincing argument that African man was biologically incapable of change, there was no need to consult moral philosophers or other social theorists.

The starting point for biological science in the early nineteenth century was the knowledge and theory built up in the great age of biological classification. Physical anthropology was still largely undifferentiated from the amorphous body of biology in general. Biological knowledge was itself constantly changing, but it was still firmly pre-Darwinian. New evidence was brought forward, and new theories were propounded. The new theories were often no more accurate, by modern standards, than the ones they replaced, but they were more important: in an age where the prestige of science was steadily increasing, the dicta of the scientists began to carry a new kind of weight. The biological view of race could no longer be ignored as Granville Sharp had ignored it in the 1770's, and it could no longer be put off by a mere citation of scripture as the humanitarians had tended to do since the 1780's.

At the same time, much of the new prestige of the biologists came from their work in fields with little immediate application to questions of race. Paralleling the development of clinical medicine, the first decades of the nineteenth century saw the true foundation of comparative anatomy and paleontology. This work was centered in France and especially associated with the name of the Swiss scientist, Baron George Cuvier (1769–1832). Like the earlier problem of classification, it was concerned with the whole animal kingdom, and the varieties of man were not given serious or concentrated attention. Data on the physical structure of the African race were still drawn from Soemmering, and the even more suspect evidence of Edward Long was sometimes cited by reputable biologists.

The only important attempt to correct some of these errors by actually investigating African anatomy was that of Thomas Winterbottom in Sierra Leone during the 1790's. Winterbottom had an opportunity to examine large numbers of Africans, which was not possible in Europe. He was also concerned for religious reasons to undermine the polygenist position summed up by Charles White at the end of the century. With more data, it was easy enough to show that Soemmering had generalized about African skull capacity by measuring only a few skulls. In fact, skull capacity varied greatly from one individual to another irrespective of race. Winterbottom showed that Soemmering had simply mistaken the anatomical features of a few individuals for the characteristics of the Negro race as a whole.[1]

The old libels of popular belief were still more serious than Soemmering's scientific errors, and Winterbottom set out systematically to refute these on the basis of his African experience. One of the basic supports of polygenesis, for example, had been the assumed difference between African and European nervous systems—the belief that African women could give birth without pain, that the Negro nervous system was generally less sensitive in matters of touch and taste, though not in eyesight. The Negro brain, bile, and blood had also been held to be of a different color from those of other races. It was a common belief that Negro sexual organs were larger, that Negro women menstruated in greater quantity and with less disturbance than Europeans, that Negro women had long and pendulous breasts as an inherited physical trait. All these points were corrected easily enough on the basis of a few years of medical practice among Negroes.[2]

Another support for polygenesis was the claim that Africans mature faster than Europeans and have a shorter life span, thus approaching the pattern of animals. The idea originated from the uncritical and mistaken observation by West Indian planters and travellers to Africa. Winterbottom made a careful investigation of the age of sexual maturity among the "Nova Scotians" at Sierra Leone and found it was not significantly different from that of Europeans. The question of longevity, however, was more difficult for lack of statistical data. Winterbottom was a careful scientist. He left the question open, rather than come out with a snap judgement which might have strengthened his case.[3] In this work, as in other aspects of his many-sided investigations, Winterbottom had no immediate successors, but it stood for half a century as a mine of evidence. The defenders of African equality and African membership in a common mankind could and did draw on it freely.

The theory of polygenesis was declining in British anthropological circles after the turn of the century, and for several reasons. The unfettered rationalism of Long, Kames, and White now met with an increasing current of theological opposition. The Evangelical movement, the religious revival, the disappointment with the French Revo-

1. T. Winterbottom, *An Account of the Native Africans in the Neighbourhood of Sierra Leone,* 2 vols. (London, 1803), II, 255–56.
2. Winterbottom, *Native Africans,* I, 190–91; II, 214–15 and 270–71.
3. Winterbottom, *Native Africans,* II, 263.

lution after its early promise—all of these turned some men back to the Bible, and the Bible seemed perfectly clear. God had "made of one blood all nations of men for to dwell on the face of the earth, and hath determined the times appointed, and bounds of their habitation" (Acts 17:26). Influential biologists were also more inclined than before to support monogenesis. Blumenbach in his later work used Winterbottom's evidence and arrived at a new and authoritative statement, which was accepted with variations by the other eminent biologists of the period—by Cuvier in France and by Lawrence and Prichard in England.[4] While several of the lesser authorities remained convinced polygenists and kept the belief alive, the center of that school was now in France, represented principally by Bory de Saint-Vincent and Geoffroy de Saint-Hilaire.[5]

This temporary resurgence of monogenesis countered the polygenetic insistence on Negro inferiority, but it did not necessarily imply a belief in human equality regardless of race. Even monogenists used the hierarchical forms of race classification, though the idea of the "Great Chain of Being" was gradually losing ground. Blumenbach restated his older five-fold classification in 1795. Even though he was now a conscious publicist in defense of Negro abilities, he continued to believe that the non-European races were "degenerations" from the white race.[6] Other views, and especially those on the Continent, were still less favorable. In 1809 Lamarck classified all mankind as *Bimania,* sub-divided into six races arranged in order from Caucasian at the top to Negro at the bottom. Cuvier followed a similar order in 1817, but returned to a three-fold division into Caucasian, Mongolian, and Negro. This system had the advantage of simplicity, and it reflected the Biblical division according to the descendents of Ham, Shem, and Japhet. With Cuvier's immense prestige behind it, the three-fold classification gradually displaced Blumenbach's system and became the most common schema from that time onward.[7]

4. J. F. Blumenbach, "Contributions to Natural History," in T. Bendyshe, Ed., *Anthropological Treatises of Johann Friedrich Blumenbach* (London, 1865). First published in 1806; G. Cuvier, *The Animal Kingdom,* 16 vols. (London, 1827–1835), I, 80; Sir William Lawrence, *Lectures on Physiology, Zoology, and the Natural History of Man* (London, 1819), p. 493; J. C. Prichard, *Researches into the Physical History of Man,* 2nd ed., 2 vols. (London, 1826), II, 586–87.

5. A. C. Haddon, *History of Anthropology,* 2nd. ed. (London, 1934), p. 40; J. Barzun, *Race: a Study in Modern Superstition* (New York, 1937), pp. 64-65.

6. J. F. Blumenbach, "On the Natural Varieties of Mankind," in T. Bendyshe, Ed., *Anthropological Treatises of Johann Friedrich Blumenbach,* pp. 264 ff.

7. E. W. Count (Ed.), *This is Race* (New York, 1950), pp. 40 and 706.

Cuvier's view epitomized the beliefs of Continental scientists, with results that were unfortunate for the racial reputation of the Africans. His system was not only openly hierarchical, it also made the implicit assumption that race and culture are intimately connected. His summary description is worth quoting in full, if only for its tone of racial and cultural chauvinism.

The Caucasian, to which we ourselves belong, is chiefly distinguished by the beautiful form of the head, which approximates to a perfect oval. It is also remarkable for variations in the shade of the complexion, and colour of the hair. From this variety have sprung the most civilized nations, and such as have most generally exercised dominion over the rest of mankind.

The Mongolian variety is recognized by prominent cheek-bones, flat visage, narrow and oblique eyes, hair straight and black, scanty beard, and olive complexion. This race has formed mighty empires in China and Japan, and occasionally extended its conquests on this side of the Great Desert, but its civilization has long appeared stationary.

The negro race is confined to the south of Mount Atlas. Its characters are, black complexion, woolly hair, compressed cranium, and flattish nose. In the prominence of the lower part of the face, and the thickness of the lips, it manifestly approaches to the monkey tribe. The hordes of which this variety is composed have always remained in a state of complete barbarism.[8]

English writers on physical anthropology were more moderate in their anti-Negro strictures and increasingly suspicious of such clear divisions into neat categories. Both Sir William Lawrence and James Cowles Prichard, the most influential British authorities of their time, abandoned the "Great Chain of Being." Both were impressed with the range of individual difference within any of the major racial groupings. Lawrence followed Blumenbach's five-fold system, but only for the sake of convenience, holding that lines of classification were merely conventional and arbitrary. At the same time, he believed firmly in white superiority—not as the highest term in a series but as the single superior race standing above all of the "dark races" grouped together at a lower level. The conception followed Blumenbach, but, where Blumenbach saw only a small degree of separation between the races, Lawrence emphasized the gulf he believed to exist between the superior Europeans and their degenerate off-shoots.[9]

Like the earlier biological writers, Lawrence had to find grounds for his belief in qualities that were not scientifically measurable. He

8. Cuvier, *Animal Kingdom*, I, 97.
9. Lawrence, *Lectures*, pp. 327–29 and 549–72.

found one criterion in esthetics—that is, in self-admiration of his own physical type. He also called in ethnographic evidence in order to "prove" an inborn racial difference of intellect, and (a new emphasis as the nineteenth century progressed) in natural moral character as well.

The distinction of colour between the white and black races is not more striking than the pre-eminence of the former in moral feelings and in mental endowments. The latter, it is true, exhibit generally a great acuteness of the external senses, which in some instances is heightened by exercise to a degree nearly incredible. Yet they indulge, almost universally, in disgusting debauchery and sensuality, and display gross selfishness, indifference to the pains and pleasures of others, insensibility to beauty of form, order, and harmony, and an almost entire want of what we comprehend altogether under the expression of elevated sentiments, manly virtues, and moral feelings.[10]

On the face of it, this opinion is hardly more favorable than that of Cuvier, but it was qualified in a number of ways. In discussing Africans in particular, Lawrence accepted the usual stereotype of the African character, and with it the accepted list of African virtues. From these, it could be deduced that Negroes were not so inferior in morality as he believed them to be in mental ability. Furthermore, he thought of racial endowments as a kind of average for the whole group: individual Africans might well excel beyond the usual standard of the white race. In addition, Lawrence's racial views, like those of Charles White before him, were no bar to humanitarian sentiments, and he included an attack on slavery and the slave trade in his scientific lectures.[11]

James Cowles Prichard was even more closely associated with the humanitarian movement, and his major contribution to British thought about Africa was to continue Blumenbach's work as a defender of Negro ability. He despised the African way of life but insisted there was no physical limitation to the *potential* achievement of any people, no matter what their racial type. He also followed Blumenbach in minimizing the differences between the major racial groups—so much so that he preferred not to use an overall classification. While there were roughly recognizable differences between Africans, Asians, and Europeans, there were innumerable transitions as well. "The swarthy nations of Africa do not appear to form that dis-

10. Lawrence, *Lectures,* p. 476.
11. Lawrence, *Lectures,* pp. 364, 478–79, 491, and 493–94.

tinct kind of people, separated from all other races of men by a broad line, and uniform among themselves, which we ideally represent under the term *Negro*. There is perhaps not one single nation in which all the characters ascribed to the negro are found in the highest degree, and in general they are distributed to different nations in all manner of ways, and combined in each instance with more or fewer of the characters belonging to the European and the Asiatic."[12]

It was partly on account of this belief that Prichard moved gradually away from purely physical anthropology. In his later years he came to believe that language was the only valid criterion for classifying the peoples of the world. As early as the 1826 edition of the *Physical History of Mankind,* he laid out a mixed linguistic-physical classification of African races. He found three great divisions: the northern Africans who resemble Europeans in physical appearance; the "red or copper-colored" peoples stretching in a belt across Africa from Ethiopia to Cape Verde and including the Fulbe of West Africa; and finally the "woolly-haired" peoples. This group was in turn subdivided into the Negroes of the Guinea coast and western savannas, the Bantu-speaking peoples of central and southern Africa, and the Hottentots of the far southwest.[13]

One observation that bothered many of the early nineteenth-century classifiers of race was the fact that physical characteristics—skin color, form of hair, skull shape, and facial features—seemed to vary independently of one another. In addition to Prichard's solution of loose physical classification modified by language, it was possible to search for a single, rationally valid criterion, which could then serve as the sole basis of classification. If this were successful, it might also be possible to rank the races of man in an order of merit on physical grounds alone.

Scientists approached the problem by looking for some definite link between physical traits and mental ability. The effort began in the eighteenth century. Soemmering believed the form of the skull showed the psychological make-up of its former owner, and he tried to prove that Negro skulls were intermediate between those of Europeans and those of monkeys. Camper's facial angle was a further step. From the 1790's onward the supposed link between psychology and physiology was a special concern of the French school of *Idéalogues,*

12. Prichard, *Researches* (1826), I, 356.
13. Prichard, *Researches* (1826), I, 241–42.

among whom Cabanis, Vicq d'Azyr, and Destutt de Tracy were
perhaps the most important.[14]

The most influential step in this direction in the first decade of the
nineteenth century came from the new science of phrenology. The
principles were first laid down by Franz Joseph Gall (1757–1828)
of Vienna and further developed with the collaboration of Johann
Gaspar Spurzheim (1774–1832) of Trier. The essence of the phrenological system was the belief that the human mind could be divided
into thirty-seven different "faculties," each of which was to be found
in a different part of the cortex. For any individual, the strength or
weakness of each of these faculties could be discovered by carefully
measuring the shape of the skull. Thus character could be analyzed
merely by external examination of the head.[15]

Phrenology was, of course, mistaken on almost every point. Even
the correct guess that different "faculties" were located in discrete
portions of the brain was covered over by the incorrect assumption
that these qualities would, in turn, influence the external shape of
the head. Nevertheless, its original claims were limited: it was not
conceived as a key to physical anthropology, only to the psychological
make-up of individual men. But it soon began to spread beyond these
early claims. If it seemed to work for individuals, why not for nations
and races as well? The desire to overgeneralize about races, social
classes, and nations was, in any case, a common intellectual failing
of the early nineteenth century. Gall himself warned against any such
misuse of his invention, but it was all too convenient. New devotees,
particularly outside of the Germanys, were anxious to broaden the
system to its fullest social implications. It was taken up in England by
George Combe, who had himself been converted by Spurzheim in
1816. Through Combe's efforts, the system acquired a popular following first in the British Isles and later in North America; in time
Combe himself was to use the system for the analysis of race.[16]

Meanwhile, some influences from phrenology made their way into
the thought of established biologists. Lawrence used phrenological evidence as early as 1819 to prove that race and culture were inter-

14. Barzun, *Race*, pp. 58–60.

15. For a convenient summary of the system see J. C. Flügel, *A Hundred Years of
Psychology, 1833–1933*, 2nd ed. (London, 1951), pp. 36–44.

16. George Combe, *A System of Phrenology* (New York, 1845), p. 423. The first
edition was published in 1819 under the title *Essays on Phrenology*. Later editions were
much enlarged. The fourth London edition of 1836 served as the basis for the American edition of 1845.

connected as part of the permanent order of things. He stopped short of using it as the basis for race classification, but the implications were clear—if head shape was the key to character and mental ability, then headshape was an outward physical sign of the greatest importance. The head was the outer covering of the brain. Hence it should be the prime criterion for race classification. But there were serious problems. The phrenological system consisted of thirty-seven independent variables, and these were not quantitatively measurable. Furthermore, skin color was too obvious a trait to be ignored.

By the 1820's the importance of headshape was emphasized by a new kind of problem. W. F. Edwards, an English scientist living in Paris, was inspired by the writings of Amadée and Augustin Thierry, who had seen racial rather than individual character as the key to historical change. He set out to bring anthropology to the aid of history and arrive at a large-scale, scientifically established, racial history of Europe. With his work confined to Europe, skin color was no longer in question. Racial sub-types had to be distinguished in some other way. Edwards made his bow to phrenology and chose "the form and proportion of the head and face" as the crucial trait for distinguishing one race from another.[17] His theories had nothing directly to do with Africa, but their indirect influence was to be of the greatest importance. If racial interpretations of European history could be made to look "scientific," racial explanations of African culture seemed all the more plausible.

The full impact of these developments was to come only in the 1830's and 1840's. English thought during the first three decades of the century was more generally favorable to Africans than it had been in the recent past or would be in the decades that followed. With polygenesis out of fashion, Lawrence preaching humanitarianism, and Prichard consciously working to use science for humanitarian ends, the contrast with Continental opinion was apparent. In 1827, the English editors of Cuvier's *Animal Kingdom* found it necessary to explain and modify his strictures on African capabilities.[18] The views

17. W. F. Edwards, "Des caractères physiologiques des races humaines, considérés dans leurs rapports avec l'histoire . . . ," *Mémoires de la Société Ethnologique*, I (1), 1–108 (1841). First published as a separate book in 1829. See also Edwards, "Esquisse de l'état actuel de l'Anthropologie ou de l'historie naturelle de l'homme," *Mémoires de la Société Ethnologique*, I (1), 123-25 for the author's retrospective appreciation of his own earlier achievement.

18. Edward Griffith and others, "Supplemental History of Man," in G. Cuvier, *The Animal Kingdom*, 16 vols. (London, 1827–1835), esp. I, 172–74.

they expressed were essentially those of Lawrence. While accepting race difference as a fact, they added: "Man as we see him around us, morally speaking, is a creature of art and education. . . . Knowledge, then, is not indigenous to his mind: it is an exotic, acquired by art, and approaches more or less to perfection, in proportion to the care and industry employed in its cultivation."[19]

Thus, while many—perhaps most—English authorities believed in the inferiority of other races, they also left room for the operation of "moral causes," which might drastically modify or even eliminate the "barbarity" of African culture. Even within the narrow range of race theory, there remained an opening for the "lower races." With polygenesis disposed of, it was necessary to assume that these "inferior races" had become inferior at some finite point in time—and not long ago, since the creation itself was thought to be only a few millennia away. If their "inferiority" had been acquired so quickly, it might disappear with equal speed.

Meanwhile, some of the more naive eighteenth-century suppositions about the origins of race were gradually swept away. The older view that dark skin color might represent the inheritance of an acquired suntan over several generations had some obvious faults. Travellers pointed out that the darkest people in Africa were the Wolof living near Cape Verde, not the people living nearest the equator.[20] Nor were the white creoles of the West Indies turning darker in successive generations of tropical life.[21] Newer explanations arose, such as the belief that African skin color came from the habitual breathing of "phlogistonated" air,[22] but this too fell before the test of empiricism. By the early nineteenth century, the most prominent of the British anthropologists had come to believe that acquired characteristics could not be inherited. New varieties must therefore occur in a manner that appeared to be accidental and could not be explained.[23]

19. Griffiths and others, "Supplemental History," I, 113.
20. S. M. X. Golberry [S. M. X. de Golbéry], *Travels in Africa Performed during the Years 1785, 1786, 1787*, 2 vols. (London, 1803), I, 75; J. Corry, *Observations upon the Windward Coast of Africa . . . made in the years 1805–1806* (London, 1807), p. 96.
21. Prichard, *Researches* (1826), II, 532–36.
22. Richard Shannon, *Practical Observations on the Operation and Effects of Certain Medicines in the Prevention and Cure of Diseases to which Europeans are Subject in Hot Climates and in these Kingdoms* (London, 1794), p. 395.
23. Prichard, *Researches* (1826), II, 548–49; Lawrence, *Lectures*, 508–10; William

William Wells, an American physician settled in London, seized on the element of uncertainty, and on the recent developments in tropical medicine, to produce a theory of racial origins through natural selection. (It was, incidentally, more nearly precursory of Darwin's later discovery than any other theory of the early nineteenth century.) Wells began with the proposition that Europeans and Africans differed most markedly in their resistance to disease, not in external traits like skin color. He cited the recent data from Africa, showing that Europeans could not create a self-reproductive society in tropical Africa. Nor, he claimed, could Africans permanently reproduce their own kind in the north. Furthermore, among men as among animals, individual variations are constantly produced by nature. Of these accidental varieties born in Africa, some would be, "better fitted than others to bear the diseases of the country. This race would consequently multiply, while the others would decrease, not only from their inability to sustain the attacks of disease, but from their incapacity of contending with their more vigorous neighbours. The colour of this vigorous race I take for granted, from what has been already said, would be dark."[24]

By the same process, a superior race would emerge in the north, and here the color would be light—not because skin color gave immunity to disease, but because this particular skin color accidentally accompanied climatic adaptation.

It goes without saying that the evidence on which this theory was based was erroneous. African immunity to the "tropical climate" was not racial but environmental in origin, and Africans could survive perfectly well in the north. Nevertheless, the only important point separating Wells's theory from Darwin's was the fact that Wells dealt only with human races, while Darwin dealt with all animals. Wells's statement also lacked the full justification that Darwin was to supply, and it was put forward so diffidently that it seems to have

---

C. Wells, *An Account of a Female of the White Race of Mankind, Part of Whose Skin Resembles that of a Negro; with some Observations on the Causes of the Differences in Color and Form Between the White and Negro Races of Men Appended to Two Essays: One Upon Single Vision with Two Eyes and the Other on Dew . . .* (London, 1818), pp. 435–46.

24. Wells, *Account*, pp. 435–36. A degree of relative immunity is found with the "sickle-cell" trait and perhaps with certain other hemoglobin characteristics. While these are clearly genetic, they are not "racial" in the sense that they invariably accompany certain physical types.

had little direct influence on the formation of Darwin's ideas. It was only called to his attention after the publication of *The Origin of Species.*[25]

The indirect influence of Wells's idea was much greater. The essence of the theory was restated by Prichard in 1826, and from that point it went on to become one of the common hypotheses about the origins of race differences.[26] It explained in ostensibly scientific and evolutionary terms why, to all appearances, the Europeans were not able to survive on the Coast. It also suggested that, whatever Europeans might think of their own racial superiority, in the conditions of tropical Africa, the Africans themselves were the more "vigorous" race. When, in the 1830's and '40's, culture contact and race contact were discussed in increasingly evolutionary terms, Wells's hypothesis would be developed and expanded in a variety of ways.

Wells's hypothesis was important in still another direction, and one more closely connected with the Africans. He accepted the common view that the supposed cultural inferiority of the Africans was somehow related to their physical type. But he remained uncertain as to which was cause and which effect. The possibility remained that "Negro features" were the result of a "low state of civilization" and would "improve" as the Africans became more civilized. After all, as he pointed out, ancient Egyptian art showed people who were clearly negroid in appearance. Yet modern Egyptians were not Negroes. Could this change be one that somehow accompanies the rise of civilization? He left the question unanswered.[27] Others, however, did not, and the possibility remained that, even though race and culture were linked, an "improving" culture could "improve" racial characteristics as well.[28] Thus even the most binding assumptions of racial inferiority and an iron-clad link between race and culture failed to prove that inferiority was necessarily permanent. Scope remained

25. R. H. Shryock, "The Strange Case of Wells' Theory of Natural Selection," in M. F. Ashley (Ed.), *Studies and Essays in the History of Science and Learning in Honor of George Sarton* (New York, 1944).

26. Prichard, *Researches* (1826), II, 575–82. Darwin was, of course, familiar with Prichard's work, as he was with Robert Knox's *The Races of Man* (London, 1850), where the theme of natural selection among human races was given even greater emphasis.

27. Wells, *Account,* pp. 438 ff.

28. This view was put forward by J. C. Prichard in many of his writings. For his final argument on the subject see Prichard, *Researches into the Physical History of Man,* 4th ed., 5 vols. (London, 1851), II, 388 and 340–46 or his *Natural History of Man,* 4th ed., 2 vols. (London, 1855), I, 97–101.

for the operation of moral causes—even to the extent of removing "physical inferiority."

These racial theories might seem, at first glance, to have an important bearing on British policy toward Africans in the Old World or the New. The theory of polygenesis had, indeed, been used in the 1790's as a defense of the slave trade, but "scientific" racism played only a minor role in the debates about slavery after the Napoleonic Wars. In part, the decline of racist arguments is explained by the anti-slavery position taken by the humanitarians themselves. They did not claim full equality for all races of men, only the minimum condition of monogenesis. As the argument usually ran, the Negroes' right to freedom derived from the Christian charity that was owing to any of God's creatures, regardless of racial character. It appeared in the motto of the Anti-Slavery Society, inscribed under the picture of a Negro in chains: "Am I not a Man and a brother?" Any monogenist—and at this period any orthodox Christian—necessarily had to answer in the affirmative. With this point safely accepted, humanitarian pamphleteers could concede the inferiority of African culture and character. As one of them put it: "The Negro may indeed have rather more of that volatile sensibility, or irritability, which seems to make all human character as it approaches the sun,—warmer, yet weaker;—their sentiments more ardent, seem to be more transient than ours; and their faculties may be somewhat different, but certainly not beyond the power of habit and education to model and assimilate."[29]

The argument could be given a further turn, and the claims of the Africans made to appear the more pressing *because* of their assumed inferiority. Sir William Lawrence himself put the case for racist paternalism in a way that strongly suggested a "white man's burden."

In the warm and long disputes on this subject [of Negro slavery], both parties have contrived to be in the wrong regarding Negro faculties. The abolitionists have erred in denying a natural inferiority so clearly evinced by the concurring evidence of anatomical structures and experience. But it was only an error of fact, and may be the more readily excused as it was on the side of humanity.

Their opponents have committed the more serious moral mistake of perverting what should constitute a claim to kindness and indulgence into justification or palliation of the revolting and antichristian practice of traffic in human flesh. . . . Superior endowments, higher intellect, greater capacity for knowledge, arts, and science, should be employed to extend the blessings of civiliza-

29. *West African Sketches* . . . (London, 1824), p. 22.

tion, and multiply the enjoyments of social life; not as a means of oppressing the weak and ignorant, of plunging those who are naturally low in the intellectual scale still more deeply into the abyss of barbarism.[30]

In the atmosphere of religious revival, any argument that could be made to appear immoral was hardly useful in political debate. Pro-slavery writers therefore dwelt on the political and economic expediency of continuing slavery. When they took up the question of race they placed the emphasis on emotional xenophobia and cultural chauvinism, rather than pseudo-scientific racial theories. Cobbett had the touch. In a single paragraph he could ring the changes on nationalism, sexual competition, and economic self-interest, jumping from the enlistment of Negro soldiers as a disgrace to the King's uniform, to the "disgusting spectacle" of miscegenation and mixed marriage in England, to the taxpayer's burden in supporting the colony of Sierra Leone—where, unaccountably, the Africans were condemned as "sable intruders."[31]

And there was a fund of racial xenophobia to play on. In a period before Negroes were a common sight in English cities, even the missionaries going out to Africa were caught short by the unfamiliar appearance of the people they had come to "save." As William Singleton, a Quaker missionary agent, reported of his own arrival in Bathurst in 1821: "The first object that engaged my attention as I passed along the beach was the great variety in the countenances and forms of the natives. Some appeared to possess so little of the human face, so little indication of intellect, that, at the first glance, I was rather painfully affected . . ."[32]

Some humanitarian publicists were fully aware of the need to combat prejudice, both scientific and emotional. Building on the body of pro-Negro arguments gathered together by Blumenbach and James Ramsay, a literary tradition grew up in defense of the Negroes. Blumenbach continued his earlier work with a new publication in 1806. In this, he drew on the new biological researches of Winterbot-

30. Lawrence, *Lectures*, p. 364.

31. *Cobbett's Annual Register*, I, 701–2 (June 1802).

32. [William Singleton and others], *Report of the Committee Managing a Fund Raised by Some Friends for the Purpose of Promoting African Instruction; with an Account of a Visit to the Gambia and Sierra Leone* (London, 1822), p. 25. See also John Morgan, *Reminiscences of the Founding of a Christian Mission on the Gambia* (London, 1864), p. 45, for a similar reaction on the author's first arrival in Bathurst in 1827.

tom and leaned even more heavily on literary authority to extend and amplify his list of eminent Negroes. He concluded that, "there is no so-called savage nation known under the sun which has so distinguished itself by such examples of perfectibility and original capacity for scientific culture, and thereby attached itself so closely to the most civilized nations of the earth, *as the Negro.*"[33]

Another important work dating from the period of slave-trade abolition was Abbé Grégoire's *De la literature des nègres,* which drew heavily from Blumenbach and the earlier works and came to stand for the next forty years as the principal thesaurus of pro-Negro debate. The work is therefore especially useful as a touchstone for understanding some of the cultural and racial attitudes of the time, even though the only English translation was published in America.[34] Grégoire was clearly not a scientist. He had only a slight understanding of recent biological developments, but he felt it necessary to begin with a defense of monogenesis, built largely on the work of Winterbottom and Blumenbach. He was obviously much more at home within the range of moral philosophy, and his study of the "African character" was a classic compilation. "The African" that emerged was very much the noble savage with Christian overtones. His only real vice was laziness, and this could be corrected by Christianity and civilization. Grégoire had a mild admiration for what he took to be the African political achievement in erecting limited monarchies and republics, but otherwise he had little respect for African culture.

His final argument was Blumenbach's point about cultural assimilation: if individual Africans could succeed in Western society, then African society as a whole could become "civilized." But Blumenbach and Grégoire both passed over African achievements within African culture, and the weight of Grégoire's evidence merely extended and amplified Blumenbach's list of Negro worthies. It was now lengthened to more than eighty pages of biographical detail, replete with Latin odes of Negro composition.[35]

One Negro writer used the work of the anthropologists for his

33. Blumenbach, "Contributions to Natural History," p. 312.

34. Abbé Henri Baptiste Grégoire, *De la littérature des nègres, ou recherches sur leur facultés intellectuelles, leur qualités morales, et leur littérature* (Paris, 1808), translated by D. B. Warden as *An Enquiry Concerning the Intellectual and Moral Facilities and Literature of Negroes* . . . (Brooklyn, 1810).

35. Grégoire, *Enquiry,* pp. 155–241. See also *Anecdotes of Africans* (London, 1827) for a later derivative English work in the same vein.

own ends. The Baron de Vastey of Haiti argued the case for monogenesis in the orthodox way, but he admitted that there were different racial endowments which worked to the advantage of people
of African descent living in the tropics. He cited Montesquieu's opinion that southerners were cowards and agreed that this was the case
of all Europeans who came to live in hot countries. Men of African
descent, however, were not subject to the same climatic determinism,
and if Europeans wanted to prove their superiority they would have
to do so by showing they could survive in the tropics as successfully
as the blacks.[36]

The main line of English pro-African argument, however, was
epitomized in a sermon by the Reverend Richard Watson, delivered
in 1824, when he was Secretary of the Wesleyan-Methodist Missionary Society. Although Watson had absorbed the Blumenbach-
Grégoire data about the achievement of individual Negroes, his principal defense remained the Biblical authority for monogenesis, which
was still more convincing than science. Watson was also perceptive
in picking out the two principal enemies of racial equality—the
planters and the scientists:

[T]he first is composed of those who have had to contend with the passions and vices of the negro in his purely pagan state, and have applied no
other instrument to elicit the virtues they have demanded than the stimulus
of the whip, and the stern voice of authority. . . . The second class are our
minute philosophers, who take the gauge of intellectual capacity from the
disposition of the bones of the head, and link mortality and the contour of
the countenance; men who measure mind by the rule and compasses; and estimate capacity for knowledge and salvation by a scale of inches and the acuteness
of angles.[37]

Watson spoke for religious orthodoxy, and religious orthodoxy
had a strong appeal. On the other hand, Thomas Fowell Buxton was
probably correct in gauging the opinion of the British ruling class in
1830, when he admitted in the House of Commons that his belief
in racial equality was a minority position. Not many would agree,
he said, "that there is no difference between the Black and the White,

36. Baron J. L. de Vastey, *Reflexions sur une lettre de Mazères, ex-colon français,
adressée à M. J. C. L. Sismonde de Sismondi, sur les noires et blancs, le civilisation de
l'Afrique, le Royaume d'Hayti, etc.* (Paris, 1816).

37. Richard Watson, "The Religious Instruction of Slaves in the West India Colonies
Advocated and Defended," *Works of the Rev. Richard Watson* (London, 1834), II, 94.
The sermon was first preached in April 1824.

except that which is produced by superior opportunities of receiving information."[38]

The crucial question was the kind and quality of this racism. In 1830 the belief was still rare than the African race was inevitably condemned to a permanent state of "barbarism." Both science and religion, each in its own way, held the door open to improvement through "moral influences."

38. Thomas Fowell Buxton, Commons, 15 June 1830, 2 H 25, c. 399.

10

BARBARISM:

ITS MORAL CAUSES

While most Britons assumed that African culture and African race were somehow interdependent, the accepted social theories still gave priority to man's moral, rather than his physical nature. In spite of the growing prestige of the new biology, most educated men were still trained in the classical tradition of humane letters. They were neither accustomed to the scientific outlook nor imbued with the fullest faith in the conclusions science might reach. They believed, to be sure, what science had to say in new areas of knowledge, but belief stopped short when it came into conflict with older preconceptions. Not only the authority of the Bible, but the more general attitude of seeking truth by reference to literary authority retained much of its old strength, even after a century of rationalism.

The tradition of humane letters was principally an ethnocentric tradition. It was concerned with European society, and with its roots in Mediterranean civilization. Western civilization was thought of as the only true civilization, the only one epitomizing mankind's path of progress. Non-Western societies were, at best, exotic variants from the main stream of history. They were, in present-day jargon, "control groups" against which Europeans could measure their own achievements.

The nature of human progress was, indeed, the principal concern of social theory in the early nineteenth century. The idea of progress had infiltrated many aspects of Western thought since the middle of the seventeenth century. Eighteenth-century rationalists had helped it along in the variant readings of Condorcet in France or the Scottish moral philosophers, and most versions were still optimistic: it was still far too early for the later nineteenth-century belief that the "less fit" must go to the wall to make room for the "fittest." With the French Revolution, the optimistic strain was sometimes continued, as it was with utopians like William Godwin, but disillusionment also set in. As the early promise of the French Revolution degenerated into the long wars for European hegemony, this attitude was sometimes expressed as a revived Christian pessimism, sometimes in secular forms. In 1789 Thomas Malthus published his *Essay on Population* as explicit ammunition against the more naive hopes, but the idea of progress itself was barely shaken. In decades following the Napoleonic Wars, it went on to new heights, carried there by a generation of publicists who saw around them the material fruits of the Industrial Revolution and the "moral" fruits of the Evangelical revival. English society seemed not only richer but better—more devout, wiser, more just than any the world had seen before.

With progress so notable, writers in many fields became more conscious of change as a factor to be explained. Dynamic forms of analysis gradually replaced the static analysis so common a century earlier, and the new tendency of thought was clear in moral philosophy, as it was in the physical sciences. The static world of mercantilist economics was disappearing in favor of a new school with Adam Smith at its head, and the bare beginnings of development economics were already visible. John Millar, Adam Ferguson, and the rest had laid the groundwork for a dynamic theory of history and society, and they were widely read.

Their work impinged on the British image of Africa at several points, but principally in discussing the "early stages of society," assumed to be that of existing African societies. Most of the Scottish school had something to say about early society, but few made special studies of the subject. Hugh Murray, however, tried to lay down a general and systematic theory of early social development based on ethnographic data. His *Enquiries Historical and Moral Respecting the Character of Nations and the Progress of Society* was largely derived from the older members of the Scottish school, but it remains an important and neglected work in the history of anthropological thought.

His point of departure was the idea of progress: "the aspect of human society is continually changing: it is continually becoming more numerous, more splendid, more civilized. Particular nations may have remained a long time stationary; nay, same have even experienced a temporary retrogradation; still, however, the general progress made by the species is certainly as above described."[1]

He believed that, by understanding the laws of progress, men could influence the course of history, since historical change took place according to the action of observable laws or principles. These laws, however, were not all-determining. Individual action and legislative interference were still possible, within limits. The study of "moral history" was necessary precisely in order to enable the legislator to "strike the medium between a superstitious attachment to what is ancient, and a tendency to rash innovations."[2]

This much was a common attitude of the Enlightenment, but Murray went beyond most of the eighteenth-century philosophers in considering the possible relations between race, climate, and culture, He began with the significant and rare assumption that race and culture are separate facts of the human condition; and furthermore, "that between any two great portions of the human species, (whatever be the age or country to which they belong,) there exists no radical distinction; that the total amount of moral and intellectual endowments originally conferred by nature is altogether or very nearly, the same; and that the wide differences which we observe, arise from the influence of external circumstances."[3]

He regarded racial characteristics as mere adaptations to environment. Though they might survive for some time after an individual

1. Hugh Murray, *Enquiries Historical and Moral Respecting the Character of Nations and the Progress of Society* (Edinburgh, 1808), p. 2.
2. Murray, *Enquiries,* pp. 1–4.
3. Murray, *Enquiries,* pp. 12–13.

had left his ancestral home, they were, for all that, only differences
of external form having nothing whatever to do with the "dispositions of the mind."[4]

The direct influence of climate was also dismissed, in explicit disagreement with Kames, Hume, Volney, and Montesquieu, and with
the support of new ethnographic data from Africa. He showed that
Montesquieu's evidence for the prevalence of despotism in southern
countries rested entirely on the despotisms of South Asia. West
Africa, well to the south of India, had a whole range of different
political systems—"republican" in the case of the Akan states, in
other regions a form of chieftancy controlled by intricate checks and
balances, in still others an irregular kind of feudalism. The West
Africans, furthermore, far from being timid and sluggish, were fierce
and tenacious of their independence. Any direct operation of the
climate on the individual, then, had to be disallowed, but Murray
still left room for the "moral" influence of climate, meaning in this
case the role of climate in setting underlying conditions of human
ecology.[5]

Murray's own theory of human progress was an intricate system,
based in essence on a form of challenge and response. He held that
history ultimately moves according to the operation of four progressive principles and two repressive principles. Each of the progressive
principles operates in society so that its first influence, when present
in a small degree, is negative, but its continued operation brings a
reversal, and ultimately progress itself. In the same way, the repressive principles were held to work first toward progress and then
against it.

The four progressive principles were a diverse lot. The first was
called "numbers collected into one place," by which he meant the
formation of social groups. Small groups and small societies were
held to be less prone to vice than large ones, but also unable to
achieve progress because they could not pool their resources and
knowledge. As larger groups were formed, the first result was an
increase in vice, but as time passed the value of intercommunication
would outweigh the detrimental effects of vice. One conclusion for
Africa was that large and complex societies can attain progress (at a

4. Murray, *Enquiries,* pp. 148–49.
5. Murray, *Enquiries,* pp. 140–47.

price), while small and segmented societies cannot; and Africa had many small societies.

The second principle was free communication, within societies and between societies. Murray used the example of culture contact. An individual first encountering other ways of life would initially lose his faith in any real or permanent standard of behavior, but in the longer run he would learn from the experience. The result would be cross-cultural borrowing, hence progress. As examples he cited the European demoralization of the Tahitians, or the corruption of the Spanish *conquistadores* in their contact with Mexican and Peruvian civilizations. In contact between "advanced" and "backward" cultures, both would be corrupted in the first instance, though both might gain in the long run.

The third progressive principle was simply wealth. For individuals and societies alike, the first increase in wealth brings indulgence and sensuality, but as time passes the newness wears off. Refinement and civilization follow.

Finally, there was the category of "Great Public Events," by which Murray meant such instances of social disorganization as war or revolution. These might appear to be completely destructive of progress, since they break down the normal social restraints. But a disorganized society also allows unusual social mobility and makes possible the rise of new and able men to positions of importance.[6]

The two repressive principles were more reminiscent of earlier social theories. The first principle was the necessity for labor. A little labor is progressive, since it makes for a sedate and sober character; but too much work leaves no leisure to cultivate the arts or the intellect. Applied to society as a whole, the optimum conditions for progress were to be found where the environment is neither too hard nor too easy. A moderate environmental challenge might even serve to keep the operation of this principle in its progressive phase. The obvious retort was the Malthusian argument that population pressure would, in the long run prevent progress—in Murray's terminology, by driving this principle into its repressive phase. But Murray answered that population pressure was not necessarily inimical to progress. In easy environments, it might even provide a necessary challenge to be met by the right amount of labor.

The second repressive principle was "coercion," meaning any and

6. Murray, *Enquiries*, pp. 21–63.

all forms of social subordination. A little coercion was necessary for people to organize a society, but increased coercion would diminish the liberty of the individual and thus stifle invention, initiative, and further progress.[7]

For Murray, the repressive and progressive principles were intimately related. The untrammelled action of a progressive principle would call forth one of the repressive principles as a balance. Following this theory, he outlined the schematic history of mankind. The basic pattern was the familiar four stages, called by Murray primitive society, savagery, barbarism, and civilization. The first steps toward civilization required a warm climate, where agriculture was easy—in short, the exuberant growth of the tropics. The progressive principles of wealth and "numbers collected in one place" could soon make themselves felt. But progress was self-limiting in this setting: it was soon brought to an end by the repressive principle of coercion. Coercion would be especially severe, since the other repressive principle, the necessity for labor, could not operate fully in such a soft environment. Progress would therefore cease, as, according to Murray, it had already ceased in the original cradle of civilization—the belt of despotisms stretching from Egypt through South Asia to China. Further progress could only take place where the need for labor made possible a relaxation of coercion. "Thus, there has been, for the arts and sciences, a continual progress northward from happier climates to those less favoured by nature."[8]

One aspect of Murray's thesis—the concept of a moving focus of "civilization"—was both ancient and persistent. Virgil had traced the westward course of empire from Troy to Rome. Medieval German theorists justified its further transfer from Rome to Germany. Geoffrey of Monmouth in twelfth-century England carried it on to his own country, and Berkeley projected the couse of empire forward to America.[9]

The idea of moving empire contained two threads, one of westward movement and one of movement to the north. Where Berkeley chose to emphasize the westerly drift, Murray took the northward movement and set it in the terms of eighteenth-century rationalism. The focus of civilization was no longer conceived to move by the

7. Murray, *Enquiries*, pp. 64–95.
8. Murray, *Enquiries*, pp. 147–48.
9. See Loren Baritz, "The Idea of the West," *American Historical Review*, LXVI, 618–40 (April, 1961) for a history of this idea.

will of God, but for purely natural causes resting essentially on the relationship between environment, technology, and political institutions.

Although not solely concerned with West Africa, Murray's theory could serve to explain the "backwardness" of African culture, drawing in many partial explanations made in the past. The connection between labor and civilization, so often assumed, was explained as part of a broader and more elaborate theory. The failings of "despotism" found in some African societies, and the fragmentation of political institutions found in others, were equally taken into account as part of a grand sweep of history. Even the mutual corruption of Africans and Europeans in the course of the slave trade could be seen as a natural result of culture contact in its early stages.

Murray's views were not widely influential, but they represent one version of a series of ideas very widely held by British intellectuals of the period, and in particular by those trained in the Scottish tradition. They were especially compatible to the early Utilitarians, and we find James Mill, in 1817, tracing the stages of human society in India through much the same course of development as that outlined by Murray. With Mill, as with Murray, the key to movement upward through the stages of progress was population growth pressing on subsistence and thus forcing people to organize into a civil society—and into a society which in India stopped with the achievement of despotism. Mill too used African data, especially that provided by travellers like Mungo Park: he believed that Africa illustrated the earlier stages through which India had passed. He borrowed a great deal of his general social theory from John Millar, laying special emphasis on the social position of women as a gauge of the level of development.

While Murray lacked a broad following, Mill did not. Where Murray, for his time and place, was relatively friendly to African culture, Mill was extremely unfriendly to the culture of India. His discussion of Indian society was also drawn for a purpose—specifically to tear down the appreciative view of Indian civilization put forward by Sir William Jones. His attitude, and that of the Utilitarians he influenced, had a new note of cultural arrogance in regard to any and all non-Western peoples. In this respect Murray was closer to the eighteenth-century tradition on which both drew so heavily.

Mill was closer to the dominant attitude of the decades to come, which he himself was helping to create.[10]

Travellers to Africa and publicists writing about Africa sometimes relied on Murray's general theory, or on Mill's. More frequently, they drew on the Scottish intellectual tradition on which both were based. But a common background and the occasional use of the same theoretical principles could lead to a variety of different conclusions. Among the travellers, for example, Golbéry and Winterbottom visited adjacent parts of West African and published in the same year, but their analyses were poles apart. For Golbéry the Africans were vastly inferior to Europeans, but they were the happiest of men:

> Gifted with a carelessness which is totally unique, with an extreme agility, indolence, sloth, and great sobriety; the negro exists on his native soil, in the sweetest apathy, unconscious of want, or pain of privation, tormented neither with the cares of ambition, nor with the devouring ardour of desire.
>
> To him the necessary and indispensable articles of life are reduced to a very small number; and those endless wants, which torment Europeans are not known amongst the negroes of Africa.[11]

If not quite the noble savage, here at least was the happy savage. Golbéry supposed that Africans had come to achieve this state of bliss through a combination of race, climate, and religion. Race provided the natural bias toward "sloth," which kept the Africans from seeking the unattainable. Climate provided against the need for clothing or shelter, and tropical exuberance supplied plentiful food. African religion gave the necessary fatalism, protection both against fear of the future and the "fatal venom" of *ennui*. Together these conditions made for a society with an extremely high birth rate, where happy and healthy savages could father children until the age of sixty-five or seventy. Hence Africa was densely populated, and the slave trade was to some extent justified as a way of carrying off the excess people.[12]

Winterbottom, on the other hand, contradicted Golbéry's analysis on almost every point. He denied all direct influence of race or climate on human ability and thought of African culture as merely an

10. James Mill, *The History of British India,* 3 vols. (London, 1817). The discussion of culture theory and Indian-culture history occupies I, 91–480. See especially I, 102–7, 180–81, 293–94 and 429 ff.

11. S. M. X. Golberry [S. M. X. de Golbéry], *Travels in Africa Performed in the Years 1785, 1786, and 1787,* 2 vols. (London, 1803), II, 240.

12. Golbéry, *Travels,* II, 231–52.

earlier stage of civilization. Nor was civilization the exclusive property of any single people: "The annals of history prove to us, that
genius and empire have been constantly changing their seats, and that
no people or country have been favoured hitherto with the exclusive
enjoyment of them."[13]

Whatever this might promise for the future of Africa, the African
present was a far cry from Golbéry's Elysium. It was, for Winterbottom, a land of misery based on ignorance, poverty, polygyny, and
slavery. Polygyny stood out as a special evil, epitomizing the low
condition of women and hence the low state of society. It also caused
a low birth rate, slow population growth, and, by implication, slow
progress toward civilization.[14]

The influence of eighteenth-century social thought is as evident
here as it is in the work of Hugh Murray. Still other aspects of that
thought were selected and re-expressed by humanitarian publicists.
Wilberforce, in many ways the intellectual as well as the political
leader of the group, accepted the customary low esteem in which
African culture was then held, but he saw hope for the future in the
rule of law and the process of cultural diffusion:

How is it that civilization and the arts grow up in any country? The reign
of law and of civil order must be first established. From law, says a writer
of acute discernment and great historical research, from law arises security;
from security curiosity; from curiosity, knowledge. As property is accumulated,
industry is excited, a taste for new gratification is formed, comforts of all
kinds multiply, and the arts and sciences naturally spring and flourish in a soil
and climate thus prepared for their reception. Yet, even under these circumstances, the progress of the arts and sciences would be extremely slow, if a
nation were not to import the improvements of former times and other countries. And we are well warranted, by the experience of all ages, in laying it
down as an incontrovertible position—that the arts and sciences, knowledge,
and civilization, have never yet been found to be a native growth of any
country; but that they have ever been communicated from one nation to
another, from the more to the less civilized.[15]

13. Thomas Winterbottom, *An Account of the Native Africans in the Neighbourhood of Sierra Leone,* 2 vols. (London, 1803), I, 145–51, 176–77, and 215–18.
14. Winterbottom, *Native Africans,* I, 145–51, 176-77, 215–18.
15. W. Wilberforce, *A Letter on the Abolition of the Slave Trade, Addressed to the
Freeholders and other Inhabitants of Yorkshire* (London, 1807), pp. 73–74. The author
to whom Wilberforce refers might possible be Adam Ferguson. See *An Essay on the
History of Civil Society* (Edinburgh, 1767), Pt. II, Sec. 2. In other respects, however,
the passage suggests derivation from Adam Smith.

This diffusionist position was, of course, intimately connected with hope for African progress through legitimate trade, so often expressed by Wilberforce and his group in the past. It now found support in general social theory, and came to be buttressed with ethnographic evidence as well. The African Institution, for example, backed its plans for carrying European culture into Africa by pointing to the frequent appearance of a semi-divine culture bearer in the myths of many lands.[16]

In Wilberforce's own explanation of African "barbarism," the belief in cultural diffusion was linked with the equally prevalent idea of a moving focus of civilization. His reconstruction of history found the "original seat of the human race" in Mesopotamia. After the flood, men moved from this original cradle in many directions, but "civilization" moved to the north and west, developing as it went— first to the Egyptians, then Phoenicians, then Greeks, Romans, and ultimately northwest Europe. The root cause of African backwardness came from the fact that the Africans had hived off from the rest of mankind before the rise of Egyptian civilization. They were, therefore, unable to rise with the others. Thus deprived of diffused innovations, they had nevertheless, in Wilberforce's opinion, done very well: "it may be even affirmed, that the Africans, without the advantages to be derived from an intercourse with polished nations, have made greater advancements toward civilization than perhaps any other uncivilized people on earth."[17]

While such dynamic forms of analysis were the new fashion and widely used, they still competed with the older static analysis. Three standard explanations of African "barbarism" recurred constantly. These were race, climate (either through indolence or tropical exuberance, or both), and the evil influence of the slave trade. Most writers either rang the changes on these three, or used them in combination with a favorite bugaboo—the economic evils of insufficient division of labor, or the social evils of polygyny. Even so, the climatic explanation dominated. It found its way into the standard reference works, into Grégoire's defense of the Africans, into MacQueen's

16. African Institution, *Reports of the Committee of the African Institution,* 18 vols. (London, 1807–1824), I, 12–13.
17. Wilberforce, *Letter to Yorkshire,* p. 80. For his historical theory in general see pp. 72–76.

attack on them, into the journals and reviews, and into the supposedly empirical accounts of the travellers.[18]

The direct influence of climate through tropical exuberance was peculiarly ambivalent in its political uses. On one hand it could be used to magnify the sin of the slave traders by showing the African paradise from which the slave was torn:

> ——Is the Negro blest? His generous soil
> With harvest-plenty crowns his simple toil;
> More than his wants his flocks and fields afford: . . .[19]

But much the same picture was used by Golbéry as an apology for the slave trade, and it was used by the British and the West Indian defenders of slavery. After all, if the tropical lands produced food in such abundance, no man would ever work for mere wages.[20]

This use of the myth of tropical exuberance as an ecological cause of barbarism was not weakened in the slightest by the adverse evidence from Sierra Leone, where agriculture had failed so miserably. Other parts of the tropical world still seemed to confirm the older view, and agricultural abundance might yet be found in some part of Africa. At best, a theorist might try to explain why Sierra Leone was a special case, or the exception proving the rule. Charles Stormont, a Scottish physician who spent some time in the colony, came to the conclusion that the African climate enormously increased the fecundity of all nature. But, just as "civilized" man died in that "climate," so also domesticated animals and plants either died before maturity, were imperfect, or failed to bear fruit.[21] Thus the colony could still bring the evils of abundance to the Africans, while withholding its riches from the Europeans.

The slave trade was the most hotly debated of the possible causes

18. [J. Leyden], *A Historical and Philosophical Sketch of the Discoveries and Settlements of the Europeans in Northern and Western Africa at the Close of the Eighteenth Century* (Edinburgh, 1799), pp. 78–79; H. B. Gregoire, *An Enquiry Concerning the Intellectual and Moral Faculties, and Literature of Negroes* . . . (Brooklyn, 1810), pp. 47–48; C. Malte-Brun, *Universal Geography*, 6 vols. (Philadelphia, 1827), II, 519 and III, 20–21; James MacQueen, "Geography of Central Africa," *Blackwood's Magazine*, XIX, 707 (June, 1826); John Adams, *Sketches Taken during Ten Voyages to Africa, Between the Years 1786 and 1800* . . . (London, 1822), pp. 70–71.

19. James Montgomery, "The West Indies," *Poetical Works*, 4 vols. (London, 1828), I, 36. First published 1807.

20. See my *Two Jamaicas* (Cambridge, Mass., 1955), pp. 68–69, and works there cited.

21. Charles Stormont, *Essai sur la topographie médicale de la côte occidentale d'Afrique et particulièrement sur celle de la colonie de Sierra Leone* (Paris, 1822), pp. 24–26.

of African barbarism, and along lines already laid down as far back as the 1780's. Up until 1807, pro-slavery writers reiterated their claim that the trade was a civilizing force: it brought savage Africans into contact with civilized people. At first, the humanitarians had sometimes countered by claiming that Africans were not really savage, but this argument was less heard after the 1790's. The new line was to admit that *coastal* Africa was savage, made so by the evil influence of the slave trade itself. Now both the humanitarians and their opponents could be found roundly condemning African culture, with results that were most unfortunate for the Africans' reputation.

In the realm of theory, the shift in debate posed problems of a different kind. The diffusionists, with Wilberforce at their head, had insisted that trade carried civilization with it. Hence, the seacoasts and river valleys were always the first regions to move upward in the scale. Yet in West Africa, Wilberforce believed the non-maritime interior was the center of civilization and the commercial coast was "degraded." Clearly, in his view, only "legitimate trade" carried civilization, while the slave trade carried savagery.[22] A very few commentators, however, carried on and tried to show that even the slave trade could be a civilizing influence. Captain John Adams went further still as a minority voice and maintained that the slave trade had already begun to act as a culture-bearer—that in time coastal West Africa would emerge as the most westernized part of tropical Africa.[23]

Several commentators on the humanitarian side began to realize as early as 1807 that false hopes might be created by blaming all the "barbarism" of Africa on the slave trade. Governor Thomas Ludlam, for example, wrote to Zachary Macaulay from Sierra Leone, saying, "In the first place, the Abolition of itself will not prevent the Africans from remaining a savage and uncivilized people. To abolish the Slave Trade is not to abolish the violent passions which now find vent in that particular direction. Were it to cease, the misery of Africa would arise from other causes; but it does not follow that Africa would be less miserable: she might even be less miserable, and yet be savage and uncivilized."[24]

22. Wilberforce, *Letter to Yorkshire,* p. 86; William Wilberforce, Commons, 1 March 1799, *Parliamentary Register,* VIII (new series), 139–40.

23. John Adams, *Ten Voyages,* p. 73; *Remarks on the Country Extending from Cape Palmas to the River Congo* (London, 1823), pp. 208–13.

24. Thomas Ludlam to Zachary Macaulay, Sierra Leone, 14 April 1807, printed in Z. Macaulay, *A Letter to His Royal Highness the Duke of Gloucester . . .* (London, 1815), p. 49.

Although it is always hard in retrospect to assess the genuine conviction that might or might not lie behind the aging phrases of
polemic, it appears that humanitarians gradually lost their belief in
the slave trade as the sole cause of African barbarism. The old
phrases were still repeated, and the foreign slave trade remained to
be destroyed, but extensive reading of debate and discussion carries
the impression that most observers came round gradually after 1807
to the belief that, evil as the slave trade had been, it was only one
evil among many.

Attempts to account for the cultural level of the West African
interior followed a slightly different course. The old belief in a better
interior lost nothing during the first two decades of the nineteenth
century, even though explorers were unable for the time being to
penetrate to the fabled walls of Timbuctu, Jenne, or Kano. The
dominant impression was fortified by Mungo Park, recalled by humanitarians,[25] and supported by commercial enthusiasts, who wanted
to push trade routes toward the cities of the Western Sudan.[26]

The natural and immediate explanation on all sides was to consider
the civilization of the Western Sudan as a product of cultural diffusion
across the Sahara, or possibly westward from the Nilotic Sudan.[27] It
was usually assumed, incorrectly as it turned out, that such large and
well organized states as the medieval Arab travellers or Mungo Park
reported could not have been developed by Negro Africans. They
must therefore have been brought to Africa by Islamic influence, but
European opinion regarded Islam itself as a mixed blessing. Muslim
North Africa was itself thought of as a barbarous country possessing
a powerful but totally false religion. Nevertheless, the influence of
Islam in sub-Saharan Africa was generally looked on with approval,
even in Evangelical circles. The Sierra Leone Company, for example,
made a special effort to encourage Muslim visitors to their colony
and to establish friendly relations with the Muslim states of the interior. In the light of traditional British opposition to Catholicism,
the uncompromising monotheism of Islam had a certain attraction

25. Wilberforce, *Letter to Yorkshire*, p. 86.
26. See, for example, G. Torrane to African Committee, 20 July 1807, T 70/35,
f. 66; J. MacQueen, *Geographical and Commercial View of Northern Central Africa*
... (Edinburgh, 1821), p. 185.
27. G. T. Mollien, *Travels in the Interior of Africa* (London, 1820), p. vii; John
McCormack, Evidence before Sierra Leone Committee, 1 July 1830, PP 1830, x (661),
p. 7; Winterbottom, *Native Africans*, I, 85–86.

for extreme Protestants.[28] Furthermore, Muslim states appeared to have moved at least one step upward from savagery, though it was a step with its own special dangers. As Prichard put it, Islam might well awaken the faculties from the "brutal sloth of savage life," but at the same time render the morals "more depraved rather than improved."[29]

Some writers looked further afield for the ultimate source of Sudanese civilization. Whether diffusionists or not, most European travellers had a classical education. They tended to compare what they saw with what they knew, and they frequently saw African customs as the "degraded" off-shoots of imperial Rome. Mollien, indeed, set out for Africa in the hope of finding "civilized nations, the relics of Egyptian or Carthaginian colonies."[30] The precise origins and routes of cultural diffusion soon came to be an object of scholarly research. In 1821, T. E. Bowdich, the traveller to Ashanti, published the first full-length study of West African culture-history. Picking up an earlier suggestion by Golbéry, he traced the origin of the Ashanti aristocracy back to the highlands of Ethiopia—and their cultural heritage still further back to ancient Egypt. Bowdich's thesis is by no means unknown in present-day historiography, and it was carefully worked out from the archaeological and ethnographic literature then available, as well as his own field work in Ashanti.[31]

During the 1820's the nature of the problem shifted slightly. The new explorations brought new evidence. They also reduced the wilder dreams of a glorious civilization in the interior. Timbuctu, Sokoto, and Kano could hardly rise in reality to the heights of imagined grandeur sometimes portrayed in earlier decades. Some writers looked at the other side of the coin and set out to explain why the interior was so barbarous. An *Edinburgh* reviewer returned to the diffusionist hypothesis and explained that the Western Sudan was stagnant because it had no seacoast, hence no contact with the outside world. He also claimed the topography of the region was such that no large

28. C. Fyfe, *A History of Sierra Leone* (London, 1962), p. 67.

29. Wilberforce, *Letter to Yorkshire*, pp. 79–80; MacQueen, "Geography of Central Africa," *Blackwood's Magazine*, XIX, 707; J. C. Prichard, *Researches into the Physical History of Man*, 2nd ed., 2 vols. (London, 1826), I, 278.

30. Mollien, *Travels*, pp. 1–2.

31. T. E. Bowdich, *An Essay on the Superstitions, Customs, and Arts Common to the Ancient Egyptians, Abyssinians, and Ashantees* (Paris, 1821); Golbéry, *Travels*, I, 79.

political units could ever be formed there.[32] He was, of course, wrong on all counts. It was precisely the far interior of the Western Sudan that had had the most intense commercial contact with the outside world through the caravan trade with North Africa. Not only were there no natural barriers to prevent the growth of large states: large states actually existed, as they had for some centuries. Far from being stagnant, several of these states were just then passing through the violent readjustment of religious revolution.

It was, in fact, too early for scholars to attempt a general view of African history with the evidence then at hand. Prichard refused even to try, but others were more courageous in groping for an outline of past events. Hugh Murray sketched a broad pattern that was probably the most common view, even to the point of its vagueness. He thought of Africa as peopled by two waves of migrants out of Asia. The first wave, the Negro Africans, had come at such an early date as to have deviated from the Asian pattern toward "aspect, manners, and institutions" which could be considered indigenous. South of a line extending across Africa from the mouth of the Senegal, along the Niger, and eastward to the Mountains of the Moon, "native Africa" lived its life with relatively little change. North of that line it was subject to recent modification by newer migrations, principally of Arabs and Berbers, and by the influence of these alien cultures.[33] Murray's error was to believe that change in Africa could come only from the outside, and this particular fallacy was to be repeated by several later generations much better informed than Murray's had been.

In any case, the Africanists of the early nineteenth century were not primarily interested in the problems of history and ethnology for their own sake. They wanted to know how Africa had come to be as it was, but mainly for the sake of changing it in the direction of their own desires. Thus knowledge of the moral causes of "African barbarism" was useful knowledge—essential background for the grand problem of deciding how it might be cured.

32. "Interior of Africa," *Edinburgh Review,* XLIV, 127–28 (March, 1829).
33. Prichard, *Researches* (1826), I, 355; J. Leyden and H. Murray, *Historical Account of Discoveries and Voyages in Africa,* 2 vols. (Edinburgh, 1817), II, 475–76.

TECHNIQUES

FOR

CULTURE CHANGE

Among British enthusiasts for a more active West African policy, the theme of induced culture change was a constant feature. Many civilizations—perhaps most—have overvalued their own way of life and undervalued that of their neighbors. This attitude was one of long standing in the Western tradition, and it increased in force throughout the nineteenth century; but it was accompanied by another, less common belief. Most Europeans thought their own way of life represented values of universal application. Barbarians might therefore acquire "civilization." Even more, for some Europeans, to carry civilization to the barbarians was not only possible, it was desirable. It might even become a moral duty.[1]

The intensity of this belief and the justifications that sustained it differed from time to time, but its roots seem to lie in the theoretical universality of the Christian religion and the injunction to preach the gospel among the heathen. Western missionary efforts had been at a low ebb during the seventeenth and eighteenth centuries, but the

---

1. See, for example: Alfred, "On the Most Rational Means of Promoting Civilization in Barbarous States," *The Philanthropist*, I, 8–21 (1811).

religious revival in Europe as a whole and the Evangelical revival in Great Britain toward the end of the eighteenth century pointed toward a new and greater burst of missionary enthusiasm. Britain was not alone in catching the spirit of proselytizing Christianity; but Britain was one of the earliest and strongest centers of the missionary revival, and this fact colored much of the British attitude toward West Africa.

The new interest in reforming the barbarians also had foundations in secular thought. During the eighteenth century, Europeans had come increasingly to realize that human misery was not only an evil: to some degree it was a preventable evil. The new humanitarianism drew something from a secularized belief in Christian charity. It also drew from the idea of progress and the new hope for improvement of the human condition. Egalitarian social and political thought, setting forth the rights of man as the rights of all men, encouraged the belief that human progress should be shared by all. This sentiment merged with the new pride in Western civilization and led to the easy assumption that the good life was possible only within the framework of Western culture. Belief in the moral value of spreading Western civilization was not limited to the "Saints" or to those with a narrowly religious concept of civilization. Secular reformers, even enlightened unbelievers, could share some aspects of the missionary zeal to carry the light of "civilization" to the "dark places."

There was also an economic motive. It was widely believed that British economic growth moved forward with the increase in British commerce. If Britain were to trade with West Africa, West Africa would have to produce goods for export. Production for export was not possible without culture change. In 1807, the Committee of the African Institution held that, "Indolence, it must be admitted is a common characteristic of all un-civilized people. . . . But indolence is a disease which it is the business of civilization to cure. The motives and means of industry must be supplied before men can begin to be industrious."[2]

This being the case, the satisfaction of a moral obligation, economic growth for Great Britain, and commercial profits for those engaged in the African trade would all follow from the "civilization" of Africa. There is no use in this context worrying the old question

2. African Institution, *Reports of the Committee of the African Institution,* 18 vols. (London, 1807–1824), I (1807), 27–28.

whether economic profits or moral proscriptions were more important. Certainly both were important, and they were thought to be nearly identical. Where profit and morality seemed, at the time, to demand the same action, the two motives can hardly be separated by retrospective analysis.

This is not to say that all Europeans (or all Britons) believed the "civilization" of Africa was desirable or even possible. Most people were either uninterested or apathetic, and a minority were actively hostile to the idea. It was possible to admit the essential goodness of the good works planned by the enthusiasts, and yet oppose them in detail. The greatest fund of hostility was found in a widespread isolationist sentiment, though it took many different and even contradictory forms. Popular xenophobia of the type represented by Cobbett was one ingredient. Other social reformers went beyond a simple dislike of strangers and argued that the English poor had first claim to whatever charity the English nation could supply. From the right wing of English politics, the West India interest could be counted on to oppose any activity in Africa other than the suppression of the foreign slave trade, and West Indian propaganda could draw on deep-seated Tory sentiments—distrust of religious fanatics, like the Quakers and Evangelicals with their "Methodistical nostrums," and an even more profound dislike of paying taxes. "We are expending our thousands and tens of thousands a year: to do what, Sir? To wash the Blackamoor white;—monstrous absurdity!"[3]

Some few believed the "civilization" of Africa was not even desirable for the Africans, since Africans were racially incapable of attaining the "heights" of Western civilization. If they also accepted an image of Africa set in terms such as Golbéry's picture of savage contentment, then it would indeed be a disservice to increase contact between Africa and the West. William Mudford, Golbéry's translator, took this line: "Rather let them remain forever in a state of contented barbarism, than by civilizing their minds, only awaken them to a bitter consciousness of their fate; or by polishing their manners render them susceptible of desires which you never mean them to gratify."[4]

This sentiment was dying out slowly in the first decades of the

3. "Senegal" to the Editor, *John Bull*, 8 June 1823.
4. Translator's note in S. M. X. Golberry [S. M. X. de Golbéry], *Travels in Africa Performed During the Years 1785, 1786, and 1787*, 2 vols. (London, 1803), II, 262.

nineteenth century (step by step with the decline of the idea of the noble savage) but it was still heard. The more common position was to stop short with a warning of the problems to be surmounted. Lawrence, the biologist, urged missionaries not to expect too much. In his view, the Africans were people of limited capacities: thus only limited "improvement" was possible. Or, in another variant, the problems of climate could be stressed. Edward William White, the Governor of Cape Coast Castle, argued, in terms reminiscent of Hugh Murray's theory of history, that successful acculturation of the Gold Coast Africans could take place only with a degree of coercion to counteract the easy life of the tropics. He therefore pleaded for British annexation and administration to reduce the Africans to civilization and agricultural labor. From the perspective of Downing Street, White's warning meant that real acculturation was so difficult and expensive, it was better to do nothing.[5]

Views like these, simple inertia, government reluctance to spend money on African projects, and the European mortality on the Coast, all tended to keep the political classes in Britain vaguely opposed to any effort to change African culture, even though they might agree in principle that the effort was laudable. A convinced minority of conversionists, however, kept up a steady pressure through the press and Parliament. They could accomplish very little in the way of public action, though their influence helped prevent the complete abandonment of government posts on the Guinea coast.

The way to private action was more open. Western education and Christian missions could operate with little or no government support. The attempt to convert the Africans by teaching and example was continuous from the foundation of Sierra Leone, though the Europeans began with very naive ideas about education and culture change. Only gradually, they formulated more careful and explicit plans for achieving their objectives. The projects of the 1780's had tended to assume that African culture was a texture of wickedness, which the Africans themselves would abandon once a "better way" was shown them. Thus the Sierra Leone Company began with hardly any thought about the possible uses of either education or missionary work. Their original clientele, the Nova Scotians, were both Western

5. Sir William Lawrence, *Lectures on Physiology, Zoology, and the Natural History of Man* (London, 1819), pp. 500–1; Edward William White to African Committee, Cape Coast, 30 April 1814, T 70/36 (also printed version in PP, 1817, vi [431], p. 46).

and Christian, and many of them were literate as well. The Company therefore began by merely sending a Chaplain for the colony and some schoolmasters for the children. There seemed little need to raise the general educational level, and the principal religious problem was the fact that the settlers had "imbibed very inadequate or enthusiastic notions of Christianity," which is to say, they were Dissenters.[6]

The education policy of Sierra Leone under the Company and under the Crown continued as it had begun. There was no special consideration of the proper education for non-Western children, and any native Africans who were attracted to schools were educated along with the settlers. It was difficult enough in the first decades to keep any schools going. Schoolmasters died and were hard to replace. Still other problems arose during the political struggles of the later 1790's, and the Company's appropriation for all religious and educational purposes in 1802 was only £770 for a community of 1600 people.[7] In spite of these practical limitations, the intention was to give as much education as possible, following contemporary English forms. A few of the brighter students were selected in 1794 and again in 1799 and sent to England for advanced training, paid for by private subscription. Some of these young men advanced rapidly. One of them, a son of the chief of Kafu Bullom, renamed John Macaulay Wilson, returned to the colony with a medical education and rose by 1822 to be Assistant Colonial Surgeon.[8]

The mortality problem in the early decades of the new century underlined the need for still more Western-trained Africans to relieve Europeans in the subordinate posts of government, in the missions, and in education itself. The early Governors under the Crown were especially active. T. Perronet Thompson tried, unsuccessfully, to introduce more advanced education. Governor Charles MacCarthy, however, was the true founder of what was to be one of the most extensive systems of public education in the early nineteenth century. From the beginning of his governorship in 1816, he was impressed

6. Sierra Leone Company, *Account of the Colony of Sierra Leone from Its First Establishment in* [sic] *1793* . . . (London, 1795), p. 80.

7. PP, 1803–4, v (24), p. 38.

8. Sierra Leone Company, *Substance of the Report of the Court of Directors of the Sierra Leone Company to the General Court* . . . , 7 vols. (London, 1791–1808), V, 49–54, (report for 1801); Evidence of William Greaves, Parliamentary Committee on Sierra Leone (1802), PP, 1803–1804, v (24), p. 37; M. C. P. Easmon, "Sierra Leone Doctors," *Sierra Leone Studies,* II (n. s.), 81–82 (June, 1956).

by the possibilities and the needs presented by the stream of liberated Africans coming ashore from the captured slave ships. He worked closely with the missions, particularly with the Church Missionary Society, and set the precedent of moderately large government subsidies to the mission schools. In doing so, he moved ahead of the English practice of the day, which was to leave education to private enterprise or private philanthropy. In this as in other matters, MacCarthy's long tenure in office, until 1824, enabled him to lay down a form of post-war settlement for the administration of Sierra Leone. In time, the Sierra Leoneans were to look back on his governorship as a kind of golden age.[9]

The new subsidies for schools came at a significant moment for the future of African education. Andrew Bell had recently developed in Madras a system of instruction which economized on staff by using the more advanced students to teach the rest. Bell's system was taken up in England by some of the Evangelicals, and especially by Zachary Macaulay, who helped to found the National Society for the Education of the Poor in the Principles of the Church of England, with Dr. Bell as its director. It was only natural that the "National system" should be adopted in Sierra Leone by the schools of the Church Missionary Society. In the same way, the Methodist missions took up the similar but competing Lancastrian or "British" system.[10] In either case, the missions transferred to Africa a curriculum and method designed specifically to meet the needs of the British working class. Since the goal of both systems was to teach the virtue of hard work and the principles of evangelical Christianity, the choice was natural.

But it implied a decision to present a Western, literary education in Africa, and it was not made without opposition. Many believed that Africans had neither the capacity nor the need for a taste of the Western heritage. Wilberforce himself would have limited the education of native Africans to "our language & religion, habits of industry, the mode of cultivating lands, & mechanical arts," arguing that, "It would be vain to expect to prevail on the people of the sort we have to do with to submit to the drudgery of formal instruction; but in this mode [of learning by imitation] they will insensibly grow familiarized with all we wish them to know."[11]

9. C. Fyfe, *A History of Sierra Leone* (London, 1962), pp. 127–47.
10. C. P. Groves, *The Planting of Christianity in Africa,* 4 vols. (London, 1948–1958), I, 278–79.
11. Wm. Wilberforce to John Clarkson, 27 April 1792, Ad. Mss. 41262A, p. 82.

Other men with experience on the Coast strongly resented partly Westernized Africans. Philip Beaver blamed the political troubles of Sierra Leone on the fact that the colonists were Westernized, Negro Americans. As for any future colony of his own: "I would not take with me a single African who had ever been in London. I would rather carry thither a rattlesnake."[12] In line with this distrust, several commentators wished to limit Western education. One idea was to stop literary education after the most elementary level, continuing only with "useful trades" likely to establish habits of industry. Robert Thorpe, sometime Chief Justice of Sierra Leone, had a grandiose scheme of this kind. He wanted to dot the coast of Africa with British trading posts, each of them with a labor-recruiting center and a school. The quality of the education he had in mind is indicated by his further suggestion that schoolmasters might well be found among artisans condemned to death for their crimes in England.[13]

Still another line of opposition came from certain missionaries, who saw their proper role as that of saving souls, not training black Englishmen. Among these critics was Edward Bickersteth, a Secretary of the Church Missionary Society, who, though a minority voice in his own society, opposed secular education as "fixing the minds of the Natives on worldly advantages," and distracting the attention of the missionaries.[14]

Other problems centered on the *how* rather than the *what* of African education. The rise from "barbarism" to "civilization" was often thought of as a process similar to recovery from a disease. The patient had not only to be cured, but afterwards protected from a relapse which might seize him if he returned to his own people. At the same time, a few observers realized how difficult it was for young students to move sharply across the barriers between their own culture and that of England.

A group of Quakers with an interest in ethnology and linguistics developed a plan for phased acculturation. Rather than begin at once with primary education in English, they preferred to begin with elementary instruction in African languages alone. Once the student had learned about the nature of language and could read and write

12. Philip Beaver, *African Memoranda* (London, 1805), p. 396 n.
13. Robert Thorpe, *A View of the Present Increase of the Slave Trade* (London, 1818), p. 96.
14. The quotation is from Bickersteth's missionary questionnaire in CMSA, CA 1/E5. See also "Private Instructions to E. Bickersteth," n.d., CA 1/E5 and E. Bickersteth to Josiah Pratt, 20 April 1816, CMSA, CA 1/E4.

his own, he could then move on to more advanced education in English. But the full measure of Westernization required a break from Africa itself. Thomas Hodgkin, later to be founder of the Aborigines Protection Society, hoped to set up competitive examinations in each colony, by which students could be selected, brought to England for a complete Western education, and then sent back to Africa to fill the higher posts in colonial government.[15]

A less expensive way of achieving this enforced break between the student and his home environment was to set up boarding schools in Africa. For this reason, two commanders of Gold Coast forts suggested that students should be educated, boarded, and clothed at the public expense.[16] The more sophisticated approach to African education, represented by these ideas, appeared only in the later 1820's, when it could rest on the experience of forty years.

Religious missions also passed from naive beginnings toward a gradual improvement in methods. The Sierra Leone Directors had hoped to convey both Christianity and civilization to Africa, but they began at a time when the English missionary movement was still in its infancy. The older Society for the Propagation of the Gospel was no longer active in West Africa, and the Church Missionary Society was not organized until 1799. In the first decade of the settlement, the Company's chaplain could make little headway even with the Nova Scotians, who preferred their own lay preachers. A few other missionaries came to Sierra Leone during the Company regime, but most of them died within a short time. The only bright spot during the whole period was the work of Henry Brunton in reducing the Susu language to writing, and that was faulty by the standard of later linguistic science.[17]

The early failures are explicable enough. Christian zeal was the only qualification expected of a missionary. In 1796, for example, Dr. Thomas Coke recruited a small group of missionaries from

15. H. Kilham, *African Lessons* (London, 1823), ii; T. Hodgkin, *A Letter from Dr. Hodgkin to Hannah Kilham, On the State of the Colony of Sierra Leone* (Lindfield, 1827), pp. 6–7; Adolphus Back to Thomas Hodgkin, 19 July 1831, ASP, C 112/2; W. Singleton and others, *Report of the Committee Managing a Fund Raised by Some Friends for the Purpose of Promoting African Instruction; with an Account of a Visit to the Gambia and Sierra Leone* (London, 1822).

16. See testimony of W. J. Purchase, Sierra Leone Committee, 24 June 1830, PP, 1830, x (661), p. 31; Smith and Mollan to African Committee, Cape Coast, 23 February 1818, T 70/36.

17. Groves, *Planting of Christianity*, I, 209–17.

among the mechanics and lay preachers of the Methodist connection and sent them off to Sierra Leone, bound for the theocratically organized Muslim state of Futa Jallon. In his letter of introduction to its ruler, Dr. Coke promised that his missionaries would be able to set "an example of all the virtues and all the graces" and were qualified to instruct the people in "all the important arts of Europe."[18] It was probably just as well that the missionaries refused to leave Freetown, where they concerned themselves in sectarian controversy with the Company's chaplain.

Even such an enlightened and well informed man as Sir Joseph Banks seriously underrated the strength of Islam in the Western Sudan, as he also misunderstood the nature of religious conversion. On the strength of Mungo Park's account, he wrote to Lord Liverpool in 1799:

It uniformly appears [that] the small superiority in useful Acquirements which the Moors possess is sufficient to induce the negroes ardently to embrace the tenets of the Alcoran, not because these Tenets appear in themselves wise, but because those people who teach them, are supposed to have gained from them their superiority in the use of the Art they teach, which is the knowledge of writing. How much more then would the more intelligible Doctrine of the Scriptures if made part of an Education contrived to teach the more useful Branches of Mechanics be followed—and how much [more] completely would those who are taught be civilized.[19]

More concerted missionary work began in 1804 when the CMS began sending missionaries to Sierra Leone, followed by the Wesleyan-Methodist Missionary Society in 1811, but the organization was still haphazard and the death rate was extremely high. It was not until 1816, when Edward Bickersteth made a tour of inspection and reorganization, that the CMS mission became an established institution.

Among other things, Bickersteth circulated a questionnaire on missionary methods and problems. The questions asked reveal some of the basic policy decisions still to be reached. There were such matters as the relative emphasis to be given to educational work and preaching the gospel, the proper language for preaching, whether to

18. Dr. Thomas Coke to the King of the Foulahs, quoted in M. J. Holland, Viscountess Knutsford, *Life and Letters of Zachary Macaulay* (London, 1900), pp. 116–17.
19. J. Banks to Lord Liverpool, 8 June 1799, CO 2/1.

work hard with a few individuals or to instruct the masses more superficially, the proper level of missionaries' salaries, and the best way to choose a site for a mission station. The key problem was to organize the mission as a functioning institution, rather than a disorganized group of individuals each separately carrying the Word to the heathen. Mission work, in short, was just beginning to move into a new phase of group effort, based on a body of accumulated experience and a body of theoretical suppositions.[20]

In this situation, missionary methods could hardly escape outside criticism, including the demand that missions should be subject to government inspection and control.[21] Some of the non-missionary critics and observers pointed out serious problems of cross-cultural misunderstanding and tension that might result from missionary work. Philip Beaver lampooned the naive attitude of the early missionaries:

> The absurdity of very well meaning persons in thinking that they can overcome vices, customs, or prejudices, immemorially rooted in an unenlightened people, by shocking, instead of gradually enlightening their understandings, has done a great deal of mischief already. To begin by telling a chief, the instant you have got into his country, that of his six wives he must put away five, because it is a great sin, and forbidden by the laws of God, to have more than one will certainly astonish the chief, but will not induce him to part with his wives. . . . When his European instructor goes on from one dogma to another, all alike unintelligible to the present intellectual state of the chief, till he finishes with the doctrine of the Trinity, the belief in which, he tells the chief, is essential to his salvation; the latter, who thought him unreasonable at first, now thinks him outrageously so; and that he is either a mad man, a fool, or an imposter; and to get rid of people professing such doctrines, will be his constant endeavour.[22]

Hugh Murray, on the basis of his broader theory, warned of the special dangers of missionary enterprise, since "intercourse . . . between Europeans and Savages, has a tendency injurious to the character of both." Culture contact was one of his progressive principles,

20. For Bickersteth's report on Sierra Leone see African Institution, *Reports of the Committee, Eleventh Report* (1817), p. 126–52.

21. See G. A. Robertson, *Notes on Africa . . . with Hints for the Melioration of the Whole African Population* (London, 1819), p. 18; A. G. Laing, *Travels in the Timanee, Kooranko, and Soolima Countries in Western Africa* (London, 1825), pp. 391–98.

22. Beaver, *African Memoranda*, pp. 392–93.

and he believed it should be countered by conscious application of a regressive principle, in this case "coercion" in the form of very strict discipline over any missionaries sent into the field. Murray's warning was underscored by one of the early CMS missionaries to Sierra Leone, who pointed out the psychological disturbance likely to result from working in the context of another culture, and the need for Christian perseverance to overcome the hearty dislike of Africans that was bound to result.[23]

According to Murray, damage to the African character should be met with the same prescription—coercion, though not in the sense of physical force. Instead, he believed that missionaries could and should establish themselves as the leaders over their flocks in secular as well as religious matters. Like Banks, he thought such leadership would not be hard to establish, since it would follow naturally from the recognized technological superiority of Europe.

In spite of a minority insistence on the Gospel before all else, technological superiority was the missionaries' trump card. The ends might be spiritual, but, especially among the lay supporters of the missions, the means were material. The dominant attitude of the nineteenth century was a reversal of Samuel Purchas' famous call for English colonization in seventeenth-century Virginia. According to Purchas, "God in his wisdome having enriched the Savage Countries, that those riches might be attractive for Christian suters," the English should go there with the Christian message in order to "sowe spirituals and reape temporals."[24] The new proposal was to sow temporals in the form of economic development and to reap spirituals in the form of conversion for the heathen and a spiritual reward for the Europeans who did God's work.

There would also be an economic reward for the Europeans, and the balance of emphasis varied considerably with different commentators. Some, indeed, would have relegated the spiritual reward to a minor place as the long-run product of missionary work. The missionaries they wanted were technical missionaries, carrying European

23. H. Murray, *Enquiries Historical and Moral Respecting the Character of Nations and the Progress of Society* (Edinburgh, 1808), pp. 422–23; M. Renner to E. Bickersteth, Bashia, 1 May 1816, CMSA, CA 1/E5.

24. Samuel Purchas, *Hakluytus Postumus, or Purchas His Pilgrimes* (Glasgow, 1906), XIX, 232. See R. H. Pearce, *The Savages of America: A Study of the Indian and the Idea of Civilization* (Baltimore, 1953).

material culture to the "savages" rather than Christianity to the "heathen." The preaching of religion was an ultimate aim, but it would come later, after the process of acculturation had already begun.[25]

Those who desired a secular emphasis in the missionary movement were fully in line with the dominant attitudes of their period. In spite of the missionary revival and the hope of changing African culture by direct persuasion, most publicists put their faith in the roundabout influence of "legitimate trade." Just as tropical exuberance was considered to be the sovereign cause of African "barbarism," this was to be the sovereign remedy. But the demand for "legitimate trade" had many shades of meaning. As a least-common-assumption, most commentators understood that trade would create a demand for European goods. This in turn would encourage Africans to perform agricultural work. For many, a flourishing agriculture was civilization enough for Africa.

Occasional explicit and detailed analysis could go further, however, and explain that the wealth of nations depends on division of labor and hence on the exchange of goods. Increasing wealth in Africa would bring leisure, schools, and a developed intellectual culture. Or, in a version published by the *Quarterly Review* in 1823, this theory of economic development could be combined with a sociology of slavery to show that legitimate trade would ultimately put an end to slavery in Africa. In this view, slavery was an institution typical of the middle phases of social development. Primitive hunters had only a rudimentary division of labor. The men hunted and protected the community, while the women did the menial work. There was no need for slavery. But with the invention of agriculture, war prisoners could be put to work. They were therefore enslaved rather than killed. Their labor could also be bought and sold; but, in the absence of an exchange economy, payment was difficult—so difficult that it was most easily arranged by a single payment giving command over an individual's labor for life. Africa was held to have reached this stage of economic development. Further development would bring further specialization, further division of labor, an ex-

25. Murray, *Enquiries,* pp. 421–24; Robertson, *Notes on Africa,* pp. 15–16; *Edinburgh Review,* VIII, 442–50 (July, 1806); T. E. Bowdich, *The British and French Expeditions to Teembo, with Remarks on Civilization in Africa* (Paris, 1821), pp. 7–9; Sir Neil Campbell, "Memorandum on the Gold Coast," November 1826, SLA, Gold Coast Misc., 1826–1827; Alfred, "Means of Promoting Civilization," pp. 16–17.

change economy, and a fluid labor market. At this higher stage slavery would again be unnecessary.[26]

While all of this might be projected as the automatic working of economic law, most authorities no longer believed that natural economic law would destroy the overseas slave trade. Both the Sierra Leone Company in the 1790's and the Company of Merchants after 1807 had found their legitimate trade at a disadvantage in competition with foreign slave traders.[27] It was not gratifying to discover that commercial and moral advantage did not go together as they were supposed to do, and various explanations were brought forward. Some blamed the cupidity of the African slave dealers. Others attacked the criminal behavior of the Americans, Portuguese, French, or Spanish, who, as citizens of civilized countries, should have been enlightened enough to give up the trade at the same time Britain did. Economic explanations were also possible. John Adams, formerly captain of a slaver, believed that, given the existing level of technology, slaves were in fact a superior product. The cost of their production was borne by the society in which they grew up. They were captured in wars that might well have taken place even if there had been no slave trade. The price in the interior was therefore very low, and transportation to the coast was cheap. Slaves were locomotive and needed only a little food to keep them going.[28]

Whatever the cause, it was agreed that legitimate trade could enter Africa only under the cover of military or political intervention. The question at issue was—what kind of intervention? Even before the issue could be discussed in the light of peacetime conditions, one kind of intervention was already present in the form of anti-slavery patrols by the Royal Navy. Most commentators accepted this much as an essential beginning. Methods and strategy might be questioned, but the usefulness of the blockade itself was not seriously doubted until the 1840's. The issue discussed in the early decades of the century was thus—what *more* should be done?

If Britain were to make a serious national effort to eliminate African "barbarism," the obvious way to do it was by outright annexation,

26. "The Condition of the Negroes in Our Colonies," *Quarterly Review*, XXIX, 497–99 (July, 1823).

27. African Institution, *Reports of the Committee*, I (1807), 44; African Committee to the Lords of Treasury, 29 April 1812, T 70/32.

28. John Adams, *Sketches Taken During Ten Voyages to Africa, Between the Years 1786 and 1800* ... (London, 1822), p. 73.

as Edward William White and others occasionally suggested. There was talk of annexing the Fante states on the Gold Coast, or of taking over the Dutch and Danish forts. The African Committee proposed a general forward move in 1812 as a wartime measure,[29] but nothing came of it then; and it was even more difficult to convince the home government once peace had returned in Europe. The possibility of annexation was nevertheless open during the first fifteen years of the century, and projectors were free during this period to make their plans for enforced acculturation on the assumption of a British administration.

When they did so, it was clear that they often had little faith in the civilizing nature of legitimate trade operating by itself, even if the foreign slave trade were suppressed. In the common view, either the innate racial indolence of the Africans or the bountiful climate would prevent Africans from responding to purely commercial incentives. Managerial cadres of white colonists would therefore be necessary in order to speed up the process of culture change. A projector writing for the African Institution argued that European example, not merely European trade, would be the first necessity: "Example works more rapidly than precept on all who are quick to perceive, but slow to reason; and such are children of uncultivated nations. An African will discern characters as acutely as an Englishman, while much labour is required to make him comprehend a logical proposition."[30]

Furthermore, according to this projector, civilization would not come simply through the production of goods for the European market. It could come only through the consumption of goods produced in Europe, and not only luxury goods but the whole range of European material culture. The shift to European habits of consumption would be crucial: "[If the Africans] . . . can be taught to desire decent apparel, and comfortable habitations, innumerable blessings will spring up from these humble shoots. Habits of domestic virtue, order, and happiness, habits of self-estimation, sense of character and propriety, a desire for knowledge, prospective industry, and all the lovely family and social charities which peace and contentment engender, will gradually be diffused."[31]

29. African Committee to Lords of Treasury, 29 April 1812, T 70/73.
30. African Institution, *Reports of the Committee*, II (1808), 37, This anonymous project was published by the African Institution, but not necessarily with the full support of the committee.
31. African Institution, *Reports of the Committee*, II (1808), 37.

This was a lot to expect from a change in material culture, and most projectors were less sanguine. They thought European managerial cadres would be necessary—but to give orders, not merely as an example. Virtually all of those who demanded annexation or colonization did so *because* they believed Africans would not respond without some form of coercion. Especially during the 1810's, when the future West African strategy was still in question, several projects appeared, designed to produce enforced acculturation from a limited territorial base.

In Joseph Corry's elaboration of the current scheme for an inland trading-post empire, the nuclear colony on the coast was planned with a managerial force of white settlers to direct a combined system of forced labor and forced education. Slaves would be purchased in the interior. The adults would then go to work on plantations, learning the mechanical and agricultural arts of Europe in the time-honored West Indian way. Children between the ages of five and seven would be trained briefly in "letters, religion, and science" and then pass on to advanced work in "domestic economy, agriculture, and mechanics." At maturity they were to be examined under controlled conditions. Those with high marks would be sent back to their country of origin, there to form small centers for the spread of civilization and Christianity. Those who failed presumably remained slaves and continued their training in the cane fields. Corry had high hopes for this system: "Thus may the long seclusion of the African from the light of truth and revealed religion be annihilated, his inveterate jealousies allayed, his nature regenerated, and his barbarism fall before the emanations of enlightened existence."[32]

Another suggestion came from Henry Meredith, who had served on the Gold Coast. He believed plantations could be established near the European forts, with firm control over the labor force but without slavery, by adopting the Akan institution of the pawn (*Awowa* in Ashanti). In the law of most Akan states, it was possible to borrow money, leaving a member of one's family or household with the creditor as a pledge. During the period of the debt, the pawn's labor took the place of interest. At an earlier period, this institution had operated only within closely related families, but by the early nineteenth century it had already changed, and the position of the pawn was intermediate between that of a domestic slave and that of a free

32. J. Corry, *Observations upon the Windward Coast of Africa . . . made in the Years 1805–1806* (London, 1807), pp. 81–84.

man.[33] According to Meredith's plan, it could be extended still further to become the basis for enforced plantation labor.[34] The difficulty with this scheme or any other scheme for establishing plantations on the Gold Coast was the political disturbance of the Ashanti Wars. The English, Danes, and Dutch all attempted small plantations, but production never reached significant levels and could not do so without effective European occupation.

As time passed it became increasingly clear that the home government was unwilling to annex and administer any part of West Africa. Experimental acculturation by government agency was therefore limited to the existing establishment at Sierra Leone, and human material began to pour in after 1808 as the Navy unloaded liberated Africans from the captured slave ships. The Evangelical promoters of Sierra Leone had had no objection to forced labor under legal control and limited in time. It had, indeed, been a part of Granville Sharp's original utopian project. One of the first devices for the acculturation of the new arrivals was to place them with the European officials or with the settlers as "apprentices." The practice was begun in the last days of the Company, and it was justified as a means of initial training under discipline before the emancipated Africans were allowed to fend for themselves in the fluid society of the colony.

But the use of forced labor as a training device touched off a prolonged storm of protest. It began with the Governorship of T. Perronet Thompson in 1808–10. Thompson himself raised the question in a protest to London. Although he was a Methodist and close to Evangelical circles, the apprenticeship question brought him into direct conflict with the African Institution and ended in his recall. The quarrel was then taken up in Britain and argued with widening ramifications. One issue was that of agriculture vs. trade, and part of Thompson's objection was his belief that the future of the colony lay in its trade with the hinterland.[35] The West India interest was also involved, since they feared that tropical agriculture in Africa, equipped with endless supplies of forced labor, might threaten their monopoly in the British market for tropical staples. The issue was

33. See R. S. Rattray, *Ashanti Law and Constitution* (London, 1929), pp. 47–55 for the Ashanti variant of these practices.

34. Henry Meredith, *An Account of the Gold Coast of Africa* . . . (London, 1812), p. 212.

35. P. Thompson to C. Jenkinson, 6 June 1810, CO 267/28. See L. G. Johnson, *General T. Perronet Thompson, 1783–1869* (London, 1957), pp. 38 ff.

taken up by the defenders of colonial slavery, who used it to show the humanitarians as hypocrites, who practiced slavery in Africa while trying to deny it to the West Indian planters.[36] The controversy ran through the whole decade of the 1810's before it finally died away. It did nothing to stop the practice of apprenticeship in Sierra Leone, but it did serve as a warning that schemes for the "civilization" of Africa through forced labor would be sure to meet a powerful and diverse opposition in Britain.

Both the government authorities in Sierra Leone and those who tried to influence policy from London still hoped to develop the agricultural potentialities of the colony, and in ways that were frequently coupled with the effort to introduce European civilization. The practice of granting land to the settlers was resumed in the early years of Crown administration—this time to the full extent of the initial promises—but quitrents were revived as well. Few of the Nova Scotians or Maroons took up additional land. Instead, Governor Charles W. Maxwell bought some of the land forfeited for non-payment of quitrents and began cultivating it himself with the labor of liberated African "apprentices." Kenneth and George Macaulay, government servants who were second cousins of the earlier governor, also took up land for plantations. By 1814, Maxwell and the Macaulays held more than half of the cultivated land in the colony.[37]

The tendency toward a plantation form of enterprise, however, was reversed after 1814. Maxwell himself had begun settling some of the liberated Africans in villages of their own. Governor Mac-Carthy widely extended this practice, reforming the pattern of settlement of the Sierra Leone peninsula. It now came to be dotted with

36. The following tracts are a sample of the controversy: Robert Thorpe, *A Letter to William Wilberforce Containing Remarks on the Reports of the Sierra Leone Company* (London, 1815); Z. Macaulay, *A Letter to His Highness the Duke of Glouces-ter* . . . (London, 1815); African Institution, *Special Report of the Directors of the African Institution, Made at the Annual General Meeting, on 12th of April, 1815, Respecting the Allegations . . . by R. Thorpe* (London, 1815); Robert Thorpe, *A Reply "Point by Point" to the Special Report of the Directors of the African Institution, and of the Controversy with Dr. Thorpe, with some Reasons against the Registry of Slaves in the British Colonies* (London, 1816); "African Institution and the Slave Trade," *Anti-Jacobin Review*, L, 139–45 (January, 1816); J. Marryat, *Thoughts on the Aboli-tion of the Slave Trade, and Civilization of Africa, with Remarks on the African Insti-tution, and an Examination of the Report of their Committee, recommending a General Registry of Slaves in the British West-India Islands* (London, 1816). The sequence of titles shows the way in which the controversy jumped the Atlantic and ended as a part of the literature pro and contra slavery in the West Indies.

37. Fyfe, *Sierra Leone*, pp. 117–18.

agricultural villages bearing names like Wilberforce, Regent, Glouces-
ter, and Bathurst, each in theory the seat of a Christian parish
with a minister subsidized by the government to superintend and
civilize the new arrivals.[38] Many forms of administration and malad-
ministration were to follow, but the pattern of peasant villages
persisted.

Both the actual settlers on the land and the idea of agricultural
villages found a particular friend and supporter in Britain. William
Allen, a Quaker businessman in London and publisher of *The Philanthropist,* seriously took up their cause in 1810 and followed it for
more than twenty years. Among other activities, he defended the
settlers from the misrepresentations of the Sierra Leone Company
and the African Institution, both of which had often blamed the
Sierra Leoneans for the colony's shortcomings. He also enlisted the
help of Paul Cuffee, a Quaker and a Negro American, to form the
Friendly Society of Sierra Leone. This society was actually a cooperative trading firm, designed to help settlers combine their produce
for sale abroad and to order European goods directly from London.
The English side of the transaction was handled by a non-profit
concern set up for the purpose by Allen and his friends. The Friendly
Society disappeared after Cuffee's death in 1817, but Allen was again
active a decade later trying to establish a model village copied after
the Mennonite communities of southern Russia.[39]

In spite of occasional temporary achievements, the peasant villages
were not the kind of success many had hoped for. Even William
Allen was tempted by the plantation alternative and urged it on
Major-General Turner before the latter became Governor in 1825.[40]
Turner himself was a firm believer in agricultural work as the most
effective agent of civilization: "until it is encouraged and understood
no progress will have been made in Civilization, no foundation laid
for Morals, Religion, or the Decencies of life."[41] Turner's solution
was to use the power of the government to create favorable conditions for European capital investment in plantations. His plan, based
on nonsensical economic reasoning, was to use the government's
control over immigration, and its position as the largest employer of
labor, to depress the rate of wages.

38. Fyfe, *Sierra Leone,* pp. 128–30.
39. Fyfe, *Sierra Leone,* pp. 112–13, 122–23, 132 and 167.
40. Fyfe, *Sierra Leone,* p. 155.
41. Gen. Charles Turner to Bathurst, 22 February 1825, CO 267/65.

Turner died before his plan could be put into operation, but in 1827 Commissioners Wellington and Rowan returned to the necessity for control over labor to speed acculturation. They produced two alternative plans. The preferred recommendation was to send all newly emancipated Africans to a government plantation for several years of forced labor producing crops for export. At the end of the term, they would be given a share of the profits and a small grant of land, subject to quitrent. Presumably they would continue to produce the cash crops they had learned to grow in government service, and the necessity of paying quitrents would be an added incentive. Since the Commissioners realized that this plan was not likely to be accepted in London, they included an alternative: liberated Africans might be given allotments of land immediately, but on condition that they practice European rather than African forms of agriculture. Shifting cultivation in particular was to be discouraged so that peasants would "improve their plots in order to be able to farm them season after season."[42] The Commissioners assumed without question that European methods must be better than African. In the case of shifting cultivation, they could hardly have been more mistaken; and its abolition at that time would have destroyed what little fertility the soils of Sierra Leone may have had.

It was only natural to concentrate on problems of economic development. The projectors of the 1780's had thought little about it, and their unplanned hopes had not been realized. They had, on the other hand, devoted much time and study to political development, but the subject was hardly mentioned by the commentators of the early nineteenth century. The new concern was administration. The question was automatically raised when the Sierra Leone Company decided to pass its burden over to the Crown. Even after the transfer of 1808 and the Crown's resumption of the Gold Coast forts from the Company of Merchants in 1821, colonial government through a chartered company still had its advocates.[43] The establishment of a general West African government based on Sierra Leone was not an adequate solution. Numerous complaints of inefficiency, dishonesty, and muddle continued through the 1820's. Apparently royal government was not even good for trade: in 1829, more than half of the total

42. Report of the Commissioners, PP, 1826–1827, vii (312), pp. 55–56.
43. See, for example, J. MacQueen, *Geographical and Commercial View of Northern Central Africa . . .* , (Edinburgh, 1821), pp. 264–84; J. G. Jackson, *Account of Timbuctu and Houssa* (London, 1820), pp. 251–54.

British trade with West Africa went to the region east of the Volta, where there were no British posts of any kind.[44] Administrative problems filled the bulk of the Commissioners' report in 1827,[45] but the Government's reaction was not to administer better—it preferred to stop administering altogether, if that were possible. The attempted withdrawal of 1826–30 was, therefore, a kind of solution to a much-discussed problem.

Even the withdrawal, however, raised some political questions, at least for Sierra Leone. Throughout the 1820's, the Africanization of the public service (to use the modern phrase) had been suggested as a way of saving European lives. A more thoroughgoing scheme was brought by John McCormack before the Sierra Leone Committee in 1830. McCormack was a merchant, resident in Sierra Leone since 1808. He argued that European officials were not only subject to disease, they were also less competent than the more able Negro settlers. In his opinion, the government of Sierra Leone required no more than four European officials. The other civilian officials, the officers of the militia, and a partly elected Legislative Council could all be supplied by Sierra Leoneans of color.[46]

McCormack's position was supported by the *Westminster Review,* then under the editorship of T. Peronnet Thompson, the former governor. The *Westminster* went further still, and claimed the relative failure of the colony had come about because the "wise views" of Granville Sharp had been set aside in favor of a repressive political regime. The Government had no intention of giving wider representation to Africans, but they accepted in principle the Africanization of the civil service. In both Sierra Leone and the Gold Coast, the militia was to be commanded by African officers. As part of the withdrawal policy, Sir George Murray spoke in Parliament of the Government's ultimate intent to transform Sierra Leone into a "free African colony."[47]

He mentioned no date at which this goal might be realized. Those who discussed African affairs, indeed, had little to say about the dis-

44. PP, 1830, x (661), pp. 110–11.

45. Report of Commissioners Wellington and Rowan, PP, 1826–1827, vii (312), pp. 47 ff.

46. John McCormack, Evidence before Sierra Leone Committee, 1 July 1830, PP, 1830, x (661), pp. 57–72.

47. Hutchinson and Williams to Sir Neil Campbell, Cape Coast, 5 November 1826, SLA, Gold Coast Misc. 1826–1827, f. 32; *Westminster Review,* XV, 506–22 (1831); Sir George Murray, Commons, 15 June 1830, 2 H 25, c. 404.

tant future, and even less about what the Africans might choose to do on their own initiative. The dominant assumption was that Africans could be expected to imitate the West, but little more.

A single projection of the future, made in 1807 by James Montgomery, suggested something quite different. Montgomery ended his long anti-slavery poem, "The West Indies," on a note that rings curiously of modern Pan-Africanism. In the epic poem, African salvation came not through the agency of Western civilization alone, but through that of an African hero, the son of a slave returned from the West Indies. After youthful training combining his father's lore of the West with native sources of savage nobility, he stood forth as a Pan-African messiah:

> He spreads his banner; crowding from afar
> Innumerable armies rush to war;
> Resistless as the pillar'd whirlwinds fly
> O'er Libyan sands, revolving to the sky,
> In fire and wrath through every realm they run,
> Where the noon-shadow shrinks beneath the sun;
> Till at the Conqueror's feet, from sea to sea,
> A hundred nations bow the servile knee,
> And throned in nature's unreveal'd domains,
> The Jenghis Khan of Africa he reigns.
>
> Dim though the night of these tempestuous years
> A Sabbath dawn o'er Africa appears;
> Then shall her neck from Europe's yoke be freed,
> And healing arts to hideous arms succeed;
> At home fraternal bonds her tribes shall bind,
> Commerce abroad espouse them with mankind,
> While truth shall build, and pure Religion bless
> The Church of God amidst the wilderness.[48]

It is fair to say that few in Britain at the end of the slave trade thought in terms even vaguely resembling these.

The formal relations between European and African states were still conducted on the basis of theoretical equality. African heads of state had not yet been downgraded from Kings to Chiefs. The rights of African states in international law were perfectly clear. According to the most respected writers, whatever paramount political authority existed in the non-Western world constituted a sovereign state. Its

48. J. Montgomery, "The West Indies," *Poetical Works,* 4 vols. (London, 1828), I, 63–64. First published 1807.

territory could be legally taken away only by conquest or by treaty of voluntary surrender. Some parts of the overseas world were subject to legal annexation by European powers, but they were very few. According to Blackstone, such *territoria nullius* was limited to unpopulated regions. Vattel, whose opinion was also much respected in England, made additional exceptions. Predatory peoples, hunting and gathering tribes, and nomadic herdsmen were a danger to their neighbors, or else they pursued an "Idle mode of life" occupying "more land than they would have need of under a system of honest labor." Such people might be legally displaced by a more industrious nation in search of land.[49] Even so, virtually all of West Africa would have been exempt. Being sedentary and agricultural, the West African states were legal states. No one suggested at this point that shifting cultivation was a form of nomadism and thus an illicit use of land, though the idea would come with time.

Legal sovereignty, however, was no guarantee of equal treatment. African states were clearly not considered members of the family of nations. They sent no accredited ambassadors to Europe and received none in return. Their dealings with the Europeans were more often conducted through naval officers and colonial governors, and even consuls were rare. Nevertheless, their legal rights were recognized in a series of treaties on which the Europeans based their own rights to their footholds along the Coast.

African states, however, were conceded a stronger position in law than in morality, and the distinction between international law and international morality was of some consequence. In law, for example, right of conquest was considered a valid claim to territory, without regard to the morality of the war that led to it. In West Africa, Britain claimed a moral right to intervene for the suppression of the slave trade, valid against both African and European slave dealers. But there was no legal right to intervene, and legality was guarded by British courts as well as foreign opinion. The Foreign Office therefore sought to broaden the area of legality by international agreement and through bilateral anti-slave-trade treaties.

By extension from the moral right to intervene in the slave trade,

49. M. F. Lindley, *The Acquistion and Government of Backward Territories in International Law* (London, 1926), pp. 11–18; William Blackstone, *Commentaries on the Law* (Washington, 1941), p. 53 (Introduction, Sec. 4). First published 1765–1769; Emer de Vattel, *Le droit de gens,* 3 vols. (Washington, 1916), III, 37–38 (Bk. I, Ch. 7).

it was possible to claim a moral right to intervene in Africa for the sake of carrying civilization to the barbarians. Arguments to this effect, later summarized in Lord Lugard's phrase, "the dual mandate," were already present: intervention would be for the mutual benefit of Africans and Europeans alike. It might be a question merely of opening new trade routes, as with Mungo Park's second expedition, sent out to see whether "commercial intercourse can be opened . . . for the mutual benefit of the natives and of His Majesty's subjects."[50] Or, the same arguments might justify British domination. James MacQueen used them in this sense. He recognized that Britain had no legal right to any part of Africa beyond what might be purchased and certified by treaty.[51] But morality might provide a claim where law gave none. He argued that Britain had a moral right to intervene because "constant coercion by the arm of civilized man can alone reclaim the savage." Therefore:

> If we really wish to do good in Africa, we must teach her savage sons that white men are their superiors. By this charm alone can we insure their obedience. Without they remain obedient, we never will succeed in rendering them industrious, or in instructing them in any useful branch of knowledge. White men cannot labour in that climate; black men only can labour there. But unless we can command the labour of the latter, so as to direct it to some purpose beneficial alike to themselves and to us, we never can reclaim Africans from their present state of barbarity and ignorance, nor succeed in raising that quarter of the world from its present extremely debased and demoralized state."[52]

While other justifications might not be set precisely in these terms, there existed a broad concensus that Britain had the right, in morality if not in law, to exert informal pressure beyond the walls of the forts or the boundaries of Sierra Leone. The problem was to find the means to exercise this pressure cheaply and efficiently. Military power was available, but its use in West Africa was out of the question except in an emergency. British influence, if it were to carry beyond the reach of ships' guns, would have to be carried in some other way.

The time-honored method on the Coast was economic. All the European trading companies had made payments to African authorities, in customary duties, for ground rent, for favors done, or simply

50. Camden to Park, 2 January 1805, quoted in M. Park, *The Journal of a Mission to the Interior of Africa in 1805*, 2nd ed. (London, 1815), p. 53.
51. MacQueen, *Northern Cenertal Africa*, pp. 202–3.
52. MacQueen, *Northern Central Africa*, p. 328.

to secure good will.[53] The Sierra Leone Company had used a similar system of bounties and prizes to direct the settlers, and even missionaries tended to protect their position by regular payments to the ruler when they worked beyond the European colony. Similar subsidies were granted by the royal governors in both Sierra Leone and the Gold Coast, and some kind of monetary payment was the usual inducement offered by the government in return for an anti-slave-trade treaty—both in Europe and in Africa. It was only natural to consider the possibility of extending the subsidies and using them for new purposes,[54] but large concessions would have required large payments. A cheaper and wider form of economic control would be to enforce penalties rather than grant rewards. The possibility of dominating African states by controlling coastal trade was constantly inviting. One obvious place for such a policy was the Gold Coast, where the purchase of the Dutch and Danish forts would have given control over a 300-mile stretch of coast. Similar plans were applied to the region around Sierra Leone, notably by Governor Turner, but the Navy's difficulties in trying to suppress the foreign slave trade showed the practical limitations of the idea.

Client-states in the interior might also be secured by other means. Alexander Laing hoped to use government-sponsored missionary work, applied with real concentration. He argued that, if a single nation in the interior could be converted to Christianity, it would serve as a center for the spread of the Gospel and British manufactures as well. T. E. Bowdich had a more hard-headed scheme for creating a client-state by supplying one country with arms and denying them to its rivals. His choice for this policy was Ashanti, and he claimed Ashanti could be made to cooperate by the threat to by-pass Kumasi with a new trade route up the Volta valley to the market at Salaga. With this threat in the background, the Asantehene could be offered the exclusive right to buy firearms, in return for commer-

53. The African Committee on the Gold Coast spent something more than one hundred pounds a year at the larger forts and as little as thirty or forty at the smaller ones. About half the total went to ground rent, the rest being distributed according to need—for keeping paths open to the interior, to important men in the town outside the fort, or in small sums to the headmen of neighboring fishing villages in return for flying the British flag and maintaining a friendly posture. (S. Cock to Lords of the Treasury, 22 September 1820, printed in J. J. Crooks, *Records Relating to the Gold Coast Settlements from 1750 to 1874* (Dublin, 1923), p. 128.

54. African Institution, *Reports of the Committee*, I (1807), 56–60; Robertson, *Notes on Africa*, pp. 21–22; Gen. Charles Turner to Bathurst, 20 December 1825, CO 267/66.

cial concessions in whatever empire he might then conquer. If Ashanti rejected the offer it could still be made to Dagomba or some other state.[55] These schemes were quite unacceptable in the British political setting of the time, but Bowdich was correct in sensing that modern firearms were the key to political power. Outlandish as his suggestion may sound in retrospect, he was merely proposing that Ashanti follow the course of Egypt would soon follow in the Nilotic Sudan, or that Zanzibar would follow in East Africa later in the century.

Other projects for spreading British influence called for a measure of more formal political control. The anonymous project published by the African Institution in 1808 included the usual monopoly over coastal trade, the settlement of European managerial cadres at selected centers of plantation agriculture, and, beyond this, an informal protectorate to be established in cooperation with the chiefs. They were to be grouped politically into councils and groups of councils, all ultimately under British protection and control but without the necessity of extensive British administration. British officials would be needed, but only to arbitrate quarrels, keep the peace, and see that justice would be done.[56]

Such ideas might be considered distant relatives of the theory and practice of "indirect rule" as it developed in the twentieth century. If so, the line of descent was long and devious, since the practice of ruling through the indigenous authorities had been used in Spanish America three centuries earlier. In the setting of nineteenth-century Africa, where the combined threats of the Treasury and the "climate" barred the way to most government activity, it was natural to think of economizing on European staff. The existing chiefs were the natural alternative. J. G. Jackson, for example, made much of the possible uses of chiefly self-interest in his project of 1819, calling for a chartered company to exploit the all-desert route from the Atlantic Sahara to Timbuctu.[57]

Jackson's project and the similar suggestion of the African Institution in 1808 were far too extreme to be acceptable in their own time, but they led indirectly to the Niger Expedition of 1841–42 through

55. A. G. Laing, *Travels in the Timanee, Kooranko, and Soolima Countries in Western Africa* (London, 1825), pp. 387–98; T. E. Bowdich, *Mission from Cape Coast Castle to Ashantee* . . . (London, 1819), pp. 341–43.

56. African Institution, *Reports of the Committee*, II (1808), appendix, pp. 33–41.

57. Vasco da Gama [Pseud. for J. G. Jackson], *Blackwood's Magazine*, IV, 652–53 (March 1819); Jackson, *Account of Timbuctoo and Houssa*, pp. 247–71.

the mediation of James MacQueen. MacQueen was not an original thinker, but he had read widely in the earlier literature about West Africa. He also had a knack for picking up diverse strands of theory and suggestion and incorporating them in a comprehensive project. The talent was not unlike that displayed by Edward Gibbon Wakefield, the theorist of British settlement in Australasia. The two careers were similar in other ways as well. Both men were able to influence the Establishment, though neither was fully accepted by it, and the practice that followed from their theories was something less than the full-strength dose they prescribed.

We have already seen MacQueen as a strategist and a geographical synthesizer. His suggestions for political and economic penetration of Africa were closely integrated with the Oil Rivers theory of the Niger mouth, and they were equally unoriginal. His theory of culture was racist, but he believed that a limited "improvement" was possible through the agency of "legitimate trade." He followed the line of the African Institution in proposing to deal with the chiefs in the interior by appealing to their economic interests, and he believed that African workers would not work for the mere lure of wages, at least in a land as bountiful as West Africa was assumed to be. All of this was the common coin of the time.

He believed, however, that all problems could be met through a single elaborate scheme, based on a strong post at Fernando Po and another at the confluence of the Niger and the Benue. With these two, Britain would have a competitive advantage on the Niger so strong that her control would amount to monopoly. Hence she could exert the kind of economic pressure chronically suggested, but practically impossible, from coastal bases alone. The key to the project, however, was the position of the chiefs. MacQueen assumed, correctly, that the slave trade continued in part because it served the interest of important groups of Africans with political power. If they would use their power to produce goods for export, rather than exporting manpower, the slave trade would end. They had command over the land. They had slaves who could be coerced to work it. "Only teach them and shew them that we will give them more for their produce than for the hand that rears it, and the work is done. All other methods and means will prove ineffectual."[58]

58. MacQueen, *Northern Central Africa*, p. 189. The plan as a whole is presented on pp. 169–207. The passage quoted makes an interesting comparison with J. G.

Very few Europeans would be needed, since the motive force was African self-interest. What troops were required could come from India. "By these means we should make India the means of preparing for us an Empire of equal importance to replace her strength, when that, in the course of political change, is withdrawn from our allegiance."[59]

Even the assumed racial inferiority of the Africans would rebound to British advantage, since this "weakness" combined with the tropical environment would assure the permanence of the British hold on West Africa. Such people in such a country, MacQueen believed, could never build an industrial machine able to compete with British manufactures. His list of the potential wealth of the Western Sudan reads like a prospectus of the 1780's. An immediate trade worth three millions would fall into British hands, with more to come with development.[60]

For all its plausibility, MacQueen's project was not immediately influential. It came to an audience that had already heard about the promised eldorado in West Africa—had, in fact, been hearing about it for forty years, and there was still nothing to show from the promises. Such cynics as Joseph Hume could point to a level of Anglo-African trade barely recovered to the monetary values of 1787, and these values were now relatively insignificant, compared to British trade as a whole.[61] Aside even from the discouraging mortality figures, MacQueen's project was offensive to important groups which might otherwise have been interested. Many humanitarians were less than pleased with MacQueen's attacks on Sierra Leone, and his substitution of African plantation slavery for the intercontinental slave trade was not quite what they had in mind when they talked about the beneficent consequences to follow from "legitimate trade." The West Indian interest, whom MacQueen sometimes defended, were also violently opposed to the competitive development of tropical agriculture in Africa.

Like the other projects of the early nineteenth century, MacQueen's

---

Jackson's statement that the African continent could not be explored or its wealth exploited, except "by calling to our aid the cooperation of the native chiefs, by holding out to them the benefits which they will derive from commercial intercourse as a reward for their assistance and exertions in promoting this desirable object." (Jackson, *Timbuctu and Houssa*, p. 251.)

59. MacQueen, *Northern Central Africa*, p. 192.
60. MacQueen, *Northern Central Africa*, 212–57.
61. J. Hume, Commons, 15 June 1830, 2 H 25, c. 398.

plan lay dormant in a climate of opinion where even the humanitarian champions of Sierra Leone were nearing the nadir of discouragement. In 1830, Fowell Buxton, who had now replaced Wilberforce as parliamentary leader of the group, admitted in the House of Commons that Sierra Leone had failed. His only saving qualification was to claim that it had not failed quite so miserably as some of its critics had said.[62] Yet, in the longer run, it was to be Buxton and his followers who breathed life into MacQueen's project and with it a renewed activity in West Africa on a scale not seen since the 1790's.

62. Fowell Buxton, Commons, 15 June 1830, 2 H 25, c. 399.

PART III

The Age of Humanitarianism

1830–1852

THE ERA

OF

THE NIGER EXPEDITION

Eighteen hundred and thirty seems to mark the end of an era in Anglo-West African relations. To the well-informed contemporary observer, it must have appeared that even the unsubstantial British effort of past decades was to be written off. From the side of government, the 1830 Parliamentary Committee and the decision to reduce commitments seemed final. In exploration, the Landers had settled the Niger problem, but the route from Tripoli was now closed. Private missionary efforts went on, but only on a very small scale, and the well-publicized mortality figures were a strengthened deterrent to any kind of activity. Yet other events of 1830 were to lead, indirectly and only after a decade of gestation, to a reversal of the apparent trend.

These events took place in Europe, not Africa. The July Revolution in France, the death of George IV, the election of a new Parliament, and the growing threat of revolution in England itself all conspired to bring about the Reform Act of 1832—though the importance of Parliamentary reform can easily be exaggerated. The act of 1832 was no revolution, but it brought a shift in the balance, and in the method and spirit, of English political life. The Whigs and their allies who came into office in the 1830's were mainly old-line politicians operating in old-line ways, but they could sometimes be made to respond to the opinions of the new electorate. The effective voice of Evangelicals, Non-Conformists, and Radicals was stronger than it had been.

This new balance of Parliamentary opinion first made itself felt on colonial issues with the act of 1833, emancipating the slaves in the British colonies. Even if the anti-slavery movement had gone no further, emancipation in itself changed the basic alignment of British interests on either side of the South Atlantic. Some of the consequences were not apparent for a decade or more, but some were immediate. The victory over colonial slavery proved that a well-organized political agitation could influence national policy. The impetus of the victory carried the humanitarians further into colonial affairs. Their parliamentary leaders kept a watching brief over the transition from slavery to freedom in tropical America, and they looked with renewed concern to the continuing slave trade from tropical Africa.

During most of the 1830's and 1840's, humanitarian opinion had more effective access to the Colonial Office than ever before, or ever again. In part, this was mere chance—the fact that James Stephen became Assistant Under-Secretary for Colonies in 1834 and Permanent Under-Secretary in 1836. As the son of an anti-slavery leader, he had been active in the anti-slavery cause. He had left his private law practice in 1825 to become Permanent Counsel of the Colonial Office, partly in order to work against slavery from within the administration. Once in the higher posts of the permanent staff, he was able to dominate many routine decisions of the Office. Parliamentary Secretaries of State came and went, but Stephen stayed on; and his influence on colonial affairs remained important even after he was succeeded in office by Herman Merivale in 1847.

Humanitarian influence reached the Colonial Office in other ways as well. Stephen served under a succession of Secretaries of State who were responsive to humanitarian suggestion. Lord Glenelg in 1835–39 was a convinced humanitarian, as zealous as Stephen himself. The succession of Lord Normanby in 1839 and Lord John Russell in 1839–41 was also favorable, and the six years 1835 to 1841 can be taken as the high-water mark of humanitarian dominance in British colonial affairs. The wave receded in the administrations of Lord Stanley and William Gladstone under the Tory Government of

1841–46, but it rose again when the Government of Lord John Russell in 1846–52 put the third Earl Grey into the Colonial Office. Grey was far too much the aristocrat to be dominated by "Exeter Hall," (the collective name for the missionary and philanthropic societies, many of which held their annual meetings at Exeter Hall in the Strand). The third Earl, however, was a son of the second Earl Grey, whose Government had passed the Reform Bill. As Lord Howick, he had served in the Colonial Office during the 1830's. When he returned as head of the Office in 1846, his administration continued in the spirit of the humanitarian era. When he left it in 1852, that era came to an end.

If the winds from Exeter Hall blew strongly through the Colonial Office in the years between 1833 and 1852, they were also in competition with new breezes from other directions. Two distinct, and sometimes contradictory, tendencies became stronger after 1830. One of these was the vaguely Benthamite belief that legislation could correct some of the evils of society. It was not a belief in "planning" in a modern sense—not intervention in economic and social processes by regular and continuous administration. It called, rather, for the creation of legislative guide lines, setting limits, so that self-interested individuals would act in socially desirable ways. Most of the Benthamite Radicals had little interest in the colonies, but an off-shoot group, commonly called the "Colonial Reformers," wished to apply the same principles overseas. The best known publicist of this group was E. Gibbon Wakefield. Their principal interest was the land policies of Australasia and Canada. Their efforts to manipulate land policies in order to create a "good society" in the settlement colonies could, however, be extended to other matters. In time, some of their suggestions for colonial reform were applied in the tropical dependencies as well. Both the spirit of their suggestions and the means they proposed could be used in West Africa, though rarely by the Colonial Reformers themselves.

The second tendency was the economic doctrine of laissez faire, the belief that maximum economic productivity and social benefit will be achieved through the least possible government interference in the economic process. By any rigorous use of logic, laissez faire was incompatible with Benthamite tinkering with society, but individual politicians and publicists could create their own mixture of Ricardian and Benthamite doctrine. In the political debate of the 1830's and

1840's, the issue was not laissez faire as a general policy, but free trade—more specifically the abolition of the Corn Laws. The demand for cheap food was perfectly compatible with any degree of Benthamite Radicalism. Free trade could even become a moral issue, and the Anti-Corn-Law League brought to bear the same moral fervor shown by the anti-slavery agitation. It was not initially a colonial issue, much less an African issue, but the abolition of the Corn Laws in 1846 was immediately followed by the Sugar Act; and the Sugar Act did affect West Africa. By providing for the gradual removal of the duties which had formerly protected British West Indian sugar in the British domestic market, it destroyed the traditional British economic policy toward the tropical Atlantic. The economic relations of tropical America with tropical Africa, and of both with Britain, had to be reconsidered from the roots upward.

None of these major tendencies of British thought—none of the major issues of colonial policy—were concerned principally with Africa. Humanitarians took some interest in Africa, but this interest was secondary to their broader, world-wide missionary effort, or to their special concern with West Indian slavery. Colonial Reformers and the Anti-Corn-Law League hardly thought about West Africa at all. Thought and writing about West Africa remained what it had been—a field of great interest for a small group of enthusiasts, supported by the occasional excursions of major theorists or major statesmen.

There was reason enough for this relative neglect. British North America, Australia, and New Zealand after 1840 were much more promising centers for overseas Britons. India was by now a great empire, under British control, and a much more promising scene for missionary activity, or the investment of British capital. On the African continent itself, Britain had acquired new interests and responsibilities. The Cape had been in British hands since 1806, though its importance was merely strategic until the 1820's, when frontier wars pointed to the fact that South Africa also had a hinterland. Missionary work and missionary publicity in Britain, the attempt to reform Boer society, and finally the Great Trek carried British interests further and further north during the 1830's and 1840's. By 1850 the Boers had spread far into the interior, and the missionaries even further. Livingstone had set out on his greatest missionary journey, and West Africa had to share the limelight with the rest of the continent.

In this respect a dividing line occurs in the mid-forties: before that time, West Africa dominated British thought about Africa; it never did so again, except in moments of particular crisis.

Because of West Africa's continued position in the shadow of greater issues, the greater issues set the physical and intellectual environment in which West African policy was formed. This was the "Age of Reform," the "Age of Improvement," and also the age of the greatest relative economic success for the British Isles. During the two decades from 1830 to 1850, Great Britain became the first nation to build a general railway network. Industrial production was still increasing at the annual rate established during economic "take-off" at the end of the eighteenth century. Other countries were now industrializing; but they were only entering take-off, and they were not to catch up for some decades to come.

One of the concomitants of British industrial power and security in that power, was a free hand in international affairs. With no major war between 1815 and the Crimean War, the 1830's and '40's were the apogee of *pax britannica*. They were also a period of relatively slack tensions within the European state system. Though there might be alarms in the eastern Mediterranean, neither France nor Russia was a serious threat to British security. The unifications of Italy and Germany had not yet raised the need for delicate adjustment to change. The absence of serious diplomatic concerns freed the Foreign Office for its endless negotiations to end the Atlantic slave trade— and freed the Navy for blockade duty off the African coast. These activities, both naval and diplomatic, were, indeed, the only source of sustained interest keeping West Africa before the British public and Parliament.

Still another result of economic development was a continuous increase in national self-confidence, beginning shortly after the victory of 1815 and continuing to a peak of self-satisfaction in the 1850's. Doubts and difficulties were, of course, present even in the first half of the nineteenth century. The working classes complained. The Irish complained. But the Chartist agitation passed without breaking the accustomed order of society. Eighteen-forty-eight was hardly more than a ripple, at least compared with the Continent. No wonder, then, that the Great Exhibition of 1851 marked such a pinnacle of pride. No wonder, also, that the pride of achievement should carry with it pride of race, pride in British religion and British culture and British morality, and, in the face of African "barbarism," a rise in arrogance and cultural chauvinism even surpassing the clear beginnings already visible during the first three decades of the century.

In West Africa itself, the scale of British activity was indeed small in the 1830's. Fewer British subjects of European extraction were resident on shore than in any recent decade—and fewer than would ever be there again. In the early decades of the century, a military force of one to three hundred soldiers had been the usual thing. After 1830 it was reduced to a few officers, usually less than ten, in command of African troops. In Sierra Leone there were about eighty to a hundred white merchants and officials, about two dozen in the Gambia, and the same on the Gold Coast. Making allowance for those beyond the sphere of direct British control, the total number of British Europeans on the Coast could seldom have exceeded two hundred.[1] By contrast, the mean annual strength of the anti-slavery squadron off West Africa was at least five hundred and sometimes as high as a thousand men, but the squadron stayed at sea as much as possible to escape the "climate" on shore.

British trade was another matter—though not one for precise discussion. There were too few customs houses and too many creeks and inlets where unofficial trade could go on. Masters of ships clearing from Britain were not always accurate in stating their destinations, and they sometimes gave intentionally misleading information. To all appearance, however, the 1830's and 1840's were a period of increasing British trade. The annual average declared value of British exports to the Western Coast of Africa rose from £270,000 in 1829–33 to £591,000 in 1847–52. Some of the optimistic sheen is taken off these figures, however, if they are compared with British exports as a whole. West Africa took only .72 per cent of British exports in 1829–33 and only .89 per cent in 1847–52. West Africa, in short, kept its place in the pattern of British trade, but that place was small indeed compared with 1783–87, when the equivalent figure had been 4.4 per cent of the whole. In the eighteen century, furthermore, West Africa had been the most important region for British trade on the African continent. By 1847–52, West Africa took only about a quarter of British exports to Africa. A trans-Atlantic comparison is also indicative: in these same years, Brazil took more British exports than

1. R. R. Kuczynski, *Demographic Survey of the British Colonial Empire, Volume I: West Africa* (London, 1948), pp. 187 and 318.

all of Africa. Brazil, the British West Indies, and the Foreign West
Indies together took ten times as much as West Africa—and this at
a period when the British West Indies were in the depths of a prolonged depression. In 1829–33, at the height of the pre-emancipation
prosperity, the British West Indies had imported from Britain 100
times more than West Africa.[2]

But the economic importance of West Africa was increasing
sharply in certain commodities, principally palm oil from the tropical
forest belt. Demand in Britain, both for lubricating oil and for soap,
had risen sharply with the rise of British industry. British imports of
palm oil doubled between 1827 and 1830, then trebled again during
the course of the 1830's. Almost the whole of this supply came from
West Africa, and mainly from the Niger Delta. By the mid-thirties,
half the value of West African exports to Britain was in this single
commodity.[3]

The rise of the palm oil trade shifted the economic center of gravity in West Africa markedly to the east—away from the Windward
Coast and the Gold Coast and toward the Bights. But this shift implied no absolute decline in the far west. The Gambia found its own
staple of legitimate trade, and the first groundnuts were shipped in
1835. Gambian groundnuts, however, went mainly to France, and the
trade was dominated by French merchants. The region was therefore
not recognized in London as one of increasing British economic activity. In Sierra Leone, the recaptives were moving out into the
coastal trade and into the interior, but the total trade of the colony
was relatively stable. It hardly increased during the 1830's, and by
1850 the level of combined imports and exports was barely 25 per
cent higher than it had been in 1830.[4]

While the trends of West African trade were mildly encouraging,
they were not encouraging enough to prompt the government to further action. During the 1830's indeed, the discouragement of the
1820's lived on, and the series of government exploring expeditions
came to an end. The Admiralty limited itself to coastal surveys,

2. J. R. McCulloch, *A Descriptive and Statistical Account of the British Empire,*
2 vols. (London, 1837 and subsequent editions), edition of 1839, II, 19; edition of
1854, II, 20.

3. K. O. Dike, *Trade and Politics in the Niger Delta, 1830–1885* (London, 1956),
pp. 50, 57, and 63; M. Laird and R. A. K. Oldfield, *Narrative of an Expedition into
the Interior of Africa by the River Niger in 1832–4,* 2 vols. (London, 1837), II, 356.

4. N. A. Cox-George, *Finance and Development in West Africa. The Sierra Leone
Experience* (London, 1961), p. 142.

linked to the needs of the anti-slavery squadron. Only minor private expeditions tried to reach the far interior—such as the Davidson expedition, which set out from southern Morocco for Timbuctu and disappeared in the desert in 1836.

In the Niger valley, the only substantial new explorations of the 1830's were those sponsored by merchants. Of these, the most important was an expedition mounted by the African Inland Commercial Company in 1832–33, with the leadership and principal financial support of Macgregor Laird. Up to 1832, Laird had been connected with his family's firm of shipbuilders in Birkenhead. He now shifted his interest to African trade, and especially to river navigation on the Niger. For the next thirty years, he was the prime mover in a whole series of efforts to develop the Niger route to the interior, and he became one of the principal publicists for the cause of African commerce.

Two iron steamers were especially designed and built for the expedition of 1832–33. Richard Lander was hired as a guide to the river, and Lt. William Allen, R.N., went along as a representative of the Admiralty. The principal aim was to establish a trading post at the confluence of the Niger and Benue, where a supercargo would remain on shore to collect produce between the projected regular visits of the steamers. Laird's steamers sailed up the Niger in two successive seasons of high water, proving that the river was open to steam navigation. The expedition also brought back the first detailed European knowledge of African trade on the Niger, but it was not a commercial success. Forty of the forty-nine Europeans who took part died, including Richard Lander, and Laird himself returned to England after the first season.[5]

Laird was ruined financially by this first attempt, but the Niger effort was continued by other merchants. When the African Inland Commercial Company dissolved in 1834, it sold one of the ships, the *Quorra,* to Robert Jamieson of Glasgow. The *Quorra* had been left in Fernando Po, where the British had established a small post in the expectation of being able to buy the island from Spain. One of the commercial agents attracted to the island during the brief British

---

5. Laird and Oldfield, *Narrative of an Expedition.* The most authoritative recent account of this and the subsequent Niger expeditions is C. C. Ifemesia, "British Enterprise on the Niger, 1830–1869," (Unpublished Ph.D. thesis, London, 1959). Lt. (later Rear-Admiral) William Allen (1793–1864) should not be confused with William Allen, the Quaker philanthropist (1770–1843).

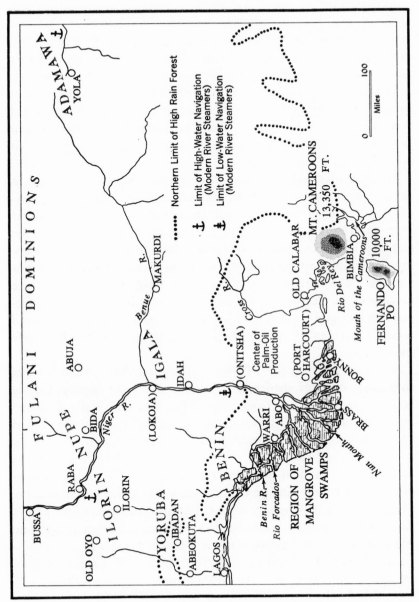

Map 17. The Lower Niger, c. 1840

occupation was Captain John Beecroft. When the government post was evacuated in 1834, Beecroft stayed on as a merchant with a small trading post on the island and another at Bimbia in the Cameroons. Jamieson now secured Beecroft's services as Captain of the *Quorra*. With a crew of six Europeans, including two survivors of Laird's expedition, and some thirty Africans, Beecroft took her up the Niger again in 1835. In 1836 he moved east to the Cross River, hoping (incorrectly, as it turned out) that the Cross might prove a more useful entrance into the Niger than the Nun mouth, which steamers had been using up to this time.[6] *Quorra* was subsequently wrecked, but Jamieson sent out another small steamer, *Ethiope,* which first began operating on the Niger in 1840.

These smaller Niger expeditions of the 1830's showed what might be done with steam navigation, but they were only indirectly a precedent for the great government-sponsored Niger Expedition of 1841–42. That effort was no mere exploring expedition. It was the first step toward a general "forward policy" in West Africa, reversing the established doctrine of minimum commitments. Its origins went back to the stream of projects put forward during the first three decades of the century; and it was carried out in the face of Jamieson's violent and vocal opposition, since Jamieson believed it would ruin the commercial opening he had developed at so much trouble and expense.

Although the plan for a forward policy was drawn from African enthusiasts of many shades of political opinion, the impetus for the Niger Expedition came from Exeter Hall, and specifically from the leadership of T. Fowell Buxton. The victory over colonial slavery had been only one part of a much broader humanitarian program: at its most radical and far-reaching it was nothing less than the intention to use British national power in the cause of world-wide Christian morality—the same kind of Christian morality which had moved the Clapham Sect a half century earlier. The humanitarians of the 1780's may not have seen the road ahead as a Fabian campaign against one evil at a time, but each achievement opened new worlds to be conquered, first the British slave trade, then the foreign slave trade, then colonial slavery. Even after the Emancipation Act of 1833 the job was not finished. The foreign slave trade continued; so did slavery in the United States and much of tropical America. There was also a new

6. Ifemesia, "British Enterprise," pp. 56–67.

concern with the plight of the aborigines in British settlements, and finally the broadest missionary objective of carrying Christianity and civilization to the whole world.[7]

Buxton, as Parliamentary leader of the humanitarian faction moved on to the aborigines question in 1835–37, when he became chairman of a Select Committee of the House of Commons during successive sessions. The Committee's responsibility was to investigate government policy in regard to "Native Inhabitants of Countries where British Settlements are made, and to the neighbouring Tribes, in order to secure to them the due observation of Justice, and the protection of Rights; to promote the spread of Civilization among them; and to lead them to the peaceful and voluntary reception of the Christian religion."[8] West Africa was not directly concerned in these terms of reference; but the Committee's investigation led to a general discussion of the moral position of non-Western peoples in the face of expanding Europe.

After the end of 1837, Buxton was again free to move on to other topics, and he turned his attention to the foreign slave trade. Inevitably, this led him to a further concern with West Africa. By August, 1838, he had completed a detailed plan, which was submitted to the government. After further elaboration it was published in two fat volumes.[9] The point of departure was clear enough. In spite of thirty years of British effort, the African slave trade had not ended. Instead, it appeared to be increasing. According to Buxton's estimate, it was then running at about 150,000 slaves exported by Europeans each year. The figure may have been slightly exaggerated, but in certain years the trade certainly came close to this order of magnitude.

Buxton's crucial point, however, was not the number of slaves exported. It was the failure of the Navy to render the trade unprofitable. In its best year, 1837, the Navy had been able to capture and liberate only 8,652 slaves in transit—surely no more than 10 per cent of those shipped, and probably a good deal less.[10] The Navy's problem was formidable. The commanders of the squadron had to work with reference to an intricate set of regulations, based on treaties the

7. For the political background of the Niger expedition see J. Gallagher, "Fowell Buxton and the New African Policy," *Cambridge Historical Journal*, X, 36–58 (1950).

8. PP, 1837, vii (425), p. 3.

9. T. Fowell Buxton, *The African Slave Trade* (London, 1839) and *The Remedy: Being a Sequel to the African Slave Trade* (London, 1840).

10. Christopher Lloyd, *The Navy and the Slave Trade* (London, 1949). pp. 275–77.

Foreign Office had been able to sign with individual foreign powers. These treaties gave varying rights of search, capture, and condemnation, and the slavers could switch from one flag to another according to the diplomatic situation of the moment. Up to 1835, when the so-called equipment clause was inserted into the treaty with Spain, slave ships could be condemned only when found with slaves actually on board. Furthermore, Brazil and the Spanish government of Cuba were unwilling at most times to enforce their own anti-slave-trade legislation. Naval forces at sea could impede the slave trade, but Buxton was correct in believing that naval force alone could not stop it, at least without a radical change in the size of the force or its mode of operation. Others agreed that some change to policy was called for—either to make the blockade effective, to give it up altogether, or to supplement it with other kinds of action—but there was far less agreement about which course to follow.

Buxton said his own proposed solution came to him suddenly in the summer of 1837. Perhaps so, but it was modified so much during the next two years that no part of the final published version was really new. All the elements were present in the West African literature of the earlier nineteenth century, and Buxton enlisted the help of James MacQueen, whose knowledge of that literature was second to none. Buxton's real contribution was to draw up a coherent plan, based on many sources in fact and theory, and to present it to the public with the organized weight of Exeter Hall behind it.[11]

The substance of Buxton's plan was a four-point program. Its first item was an intensified campaign against the slave trade at sea and along the coasts, based on a strengthened naval blockade and the co-operation of the African authorities, to be obtained through a series of anti-slave-trade treaties. The treaties were to bind African states to help put down the slave trade, to open their frontiers to European commerce, and to permit agricultural settlement. The net of treaties was to stretch into the interior, until it had created a "confederacy with the chiefs from the Gambia in the West to Begharmi [Bagirmi, now in the Chad Republic] in the East; and from the Desert on the North to the Gulf of Guinea on the South."[12]

This first point had diverse origins. The blockading squadron was

11. Charles Buxton (Ed.), *Memoirs of Sir Thomas Fowell Buxton, Baronet* (London, 1848), pp. 429–34; T. F. Buxton, *The Remedy*, pp. 236–37.

12. Buxton, *The Remedy*, p. 17.

now an old policy, pursued in practice since 1808, and even older in Wadström's suggestion. The treaty policy was also old. Treaties had been signed in the past, if less systematically. T. Perronet Thompson, Sir Charles MacCarthy, and Charles Turner, among the Governors of Sierra Leone, had all wanted to create a more systematic network of treaties. Both the practice of granting subsidies in return for favors, and the assumption that Africans would willingly sign such treaties were an ancient aspect of European action and thought in West Africa. The Buxtonian strategy for penetration inland was equally old. It was his suggestion to establish a series of posts in the interior, which would serve as centers of trade and influence. The British would not directly administer the territory around the posts. Instead, they would sign a series of treaties binding African authorities to each other and to the British government. In essence it was precisely the kind of overland trading-post establishment used by the Hudson's Bay Company or by the Russian fur traders in seventeenth-century Siberia. With variations, it had already been suggested for West Africa by Banks, Golbéry, Corry, MacQueen, and the anonymous project presented by the African Institution—among others.

Buxton's second point was even more familiar. It was to use the power of the government to encourage legitimate commerce as a key to the "civilization" of Africa, and it incorporated the assumption of the early nineteenth century, that legitimate commerce could not thrive without some form of intervention to hold the ring free of slavers.

The third point called for the development of African agriculture. By this, Buxton meant agricultural production managed by Africans, but modeled on European plantations to be established as an example. He thus took the side of agriculture in the old controversy of trade vs. agriculture. He argued that commerce alone could not "civilize" Africa, since commerce could only call forth the "spontaneous productions of nature." Real civilization demanded "habits of settled industry," which could only be formed by regular agricultural labor.[13] Buxton's thought on this point closely followed the project put forward by the African Institution in 1808, and repeated with variations by MacQueen, but the base lay even further back in the ideas of Wadström, Beaver, or, less precisely, in the hopes of Malachy Postlethwayt.

13. Buxton, *The Slave Trade*, pp. 55–56.

Finally, and primarily, Buxton counted on direct exhortation through moral and religious instruction. The primacy he gave to this factor may have been a bow to the missionary movement, since Buxton's principal discussion focused on the other three points. In any event, the missionary movement was too strong to be set aside, even if Buxton himself had not been closely associated with Christian humanitarianism.

In short, Buxton's plan was little more than a pulling together of certain strands, and often the dominant strands, from the mass of older suggestion. It could hardly have struck the permanent officials at the Colonial Office as a revelation of new insights. James Stephen, in spite of his humanitarian connections, was opposed to it, as he was opposed to all increased British intervention in West Africa. Lord Melbourne, the Prime Minister, was not favourably impressed. Nor was Palmerston, who believed in diplomatic negotiation with the European slaving powers as the best weapon against the slave trade. The Parliamentary position of the Government, however, was very weak in 1838 and continued so until it finally fell in 1841. It was so weak that Melbourne had been forced to resign briefly in May, 1839, when a block of Radicals deserted. A similar revolt of the humanitarians would have brought down the Government.

Buxton's plan was therefore accepted in principle in the autumn of 1838, but not without elaborate modification. James MacQueen gave further advice directly to the government. Several other authorities were consulted, among them Governor Rendall of the Gambia. James Bandinel, the Foreign Office specialist on anti-slave-trade treaties, prepared a new draft plan, and the higher officials of the Colonial Office, both permanent and Parliamentary, took a hand in whittling down the grandiose all-West-Africa concept until it became a modest trial expedition bound for the Niger. Finally, with more pressure from Buxton, the project grew again—but not to its original size, even though it gained the crucial support of Lord John Russell, who had meanwhile become Secretary of State for Colonies.[14]

While the Government were investigating, Buxton organized a major public agitation to mobilize opinion in support of the project. For the future British image of Africa, this publicity was almost as important as the expedition itself. West African affairs were more

14. Gallagher, "Fowell Buxton," pp. 44–45.

widely discussed between 1839 and 1842 than at any previous time—and not entirely in a pro-Buxton vein. The original suggestion led to many differing projects, objections, and counter-proposals, though these were drowned in the first instance by the voice of the humanitarians. The Buxton supporters organized a series of mass meetings, one of them with the Prince Consort himself in the chair. They formed the African Civilization Society, under Buxton's chairmanship, to carry out certain parts of the plan. The missionary societies joined in with their own projects for West Africa. Even when they were not directed to the Niger, they were able to ride the crest of enthusiasm and raise funds where no funds had been available.

The government expedition sailed in April 1841 in a mood of high hope. Every care was taken. The steamers were especially constructed and placed under the command of experienced naval officers. They were ordered to explore the Niger, making the fullest possible report of political and commercial conditions. They were also to sign anti-slave-trade treaties with the African authorities and establish one or more trading posts, plus a "model farm" on land purchased from the Africans at the juncture of the Niger and Benue. The government supplied the ships. The African Civilization Society supplied the scientific staff. The Church Missionary Society sent representatives to make a missionary reconnaissance. A separate Agricultural Association, organized as a private firm, took responsibility for the model farm.[15]

To a point, it all worked according to plan. The ships sailed up the river. The Commissioners signed treaties in the recommended form. The scientists and observers gathered a great deal of new information. Everything else failed in the face of high mortality. Forty-eight of the Europeans died during the first two months in the river, and 55 of the 159 who went along died before the expedition returned to England in 1842.[16] In fact, this mortality was no higher than should have been expected; but it was higher than the planners had anticipated, and the disaster was magnified in the public mind by the false hopes of the enthusiasts.

The initial withdrawal from the Niger to Fernando Po in 1841 was ordered by the commanders of the expedition, but the final decision not to repeat the effort came from England. Melbourne had

15. Buxton, *Memoirs*, pp. 514–16.
16. PP, 1843, xxxi (83), p. 1.

resigned while the expedition was still in Africa, and in 1841 the Peel Government brought Lord Stanley to the Colonial Office. The new Government was less responsive to humanitarian pressure than its predecessor had been. During the dry season of 1841–42, while the ships and survivors waited at Fernando Po for the next season of high water, they were ordered to evacuate the inland post and abandon the effort.[17] One ship re-entered the river in 1842, but that was the end. The normal Colonial Office disenchantment with West Africa returned, and the upsurge of public zeal ebbed away during the course of 1842, exposing the mud flats of apathy and disappointment.

But it would be a mistake to write off the expedition as just another failure of the Europeans to survive in Africa. The government and the broader public were disillusioned, but apathy about West Africa was their usual state of mind. However temporary, the unusual enthusiasm of 1840 and 1841 provided the impetus for a new round of African activity, and the activity remained even after the general enthusiasm died away. In time, it was to alter the whole of British relations with West Africa.

Even from the side of the government, there were by-products that could not be wiped out. Further exploration on the Niger was out of the question, but the Niger expedition in a narrow sense had been only one part of a broader policy. In response to the Niger agitation, Parliament passed the "Equipment Act" in 1839, legalizing the capture (without Portuguese consent) of Portuguese vessels equipped for the slave trade, even when there were no slaves on board. Expenditure for the blockading squadron rose by 50 per cent between 1829 and 1841, and the tactics were changed. Ships now began to cruise close inshore. In 1840 they began raiding the baracoons where slaves were kept waiting shipment. Anti-slave-trade treaties with African states, legalizing such raids, were signed as part of the Niger effort, and they remained in force. As a result, the annual average numbers of slavers captured rose from thirty-one in the quinquennium 1834–38 to sixty-five in 1839–43,[18] and still higher in the later 1840's. Even though the right of search and seizure was never legally perfect, and even though the policy of raiding baracoons was abandoned between

17. Ifemesia, "British Enterprise," pp. 326–27.
18. Gallagher, "Fowell Buxton," pp. 54–55; Lloyd, *Navy and the Slave Trade,* p. 275.

1842 and 1848 on account of legal qualms, the commitment of the Navy remained at its new, post-Niger level.

As another facet of the new policy, the Government began to reconsider the status of the older posts and settlements. Dr. R. R. Madden was sent out as a commissioner to visit the Gambia, Sierra Leone, and the Gold Coast—with orders drafted in November 1839, one month before those of the Niger Expedition. Madden was a medical man who had served in post-emancipation Jamaica as a Special Magistrate, had written on slavery in Cuba, and had the confidence of the humanitarians. It was a natural choice. His orders called for special attention to rumors that British merchants on the Coast were selling supplies to foreign slavers, to the operations of the merchants' government on the Gold Coast, to European mortality, and to the possibilities either of expanding the exsiting settlements or of creating a system of organized labor emigration to the West Indies.[19]

His report, when presented toward the end of 1841, was full of humanitarian zeal and harsh strictures. It was unfavorable to the merchants' government on the Gold Coast and to the administration of the Gambia, though Madden was rather better pleased than most with the recent progress of Sierra Leone. Like the Niger Expedition itself, the report fell in badly with the timing of English political change. It was well received by Lord John Russell, but Russell immediately left the Colonial Office, to be replaced by Lord Stanley. Stanley disliked humanitarian meddling; he was also deluged with the angered protests of the merchants and others who had borne the brunt of the Commissioner's zeal. In spite of James Stephen's efforts on his behalf, Madden was quietly dropped from the public service, and in 1842 a Parliamentary Select Committee reconsidered his report.[20]

The Committee's recommendations were framed to suit the new, and less humanitarian, political climate—if not the post-Niger apathy of the public. The Committee's attitude, however, was far different than that of its predecessor in 1830. It played down the pessimism of the recent Niger failure and the pseudo-scandals that Madden had unearthed. Instead, it called for a more active British role in West

19. Lord John Russell to R. R. Madden, 26 November 1840, PP, 1842, xii (551), p. 1.
20. See Russell's minute of 26 August 1841, Stanley's minute of 25 September 1841, and James Stephen's minute of 5 October 1841 in CO 267/170.

Africa to exploit existing commercial openings. Without explicit credit to Buxton, it intended to keep some aspects of his plan, shifting the focus away from the Niger and back to the Windward Coast. The new strategy called for new coastal strongpoints. Among others, the Committee recommended the reoccupation of Bulama, the erection of small blockhouses along the Gambia and the coasts near Sierra Leone, and the reoccupation of several Gold Coast forts abandoned in 1828, including Ouidah in Dahomey. British interest in the Bights was to be protected by buying one of the Portuguese islands, either Principe or São Thomé.[21]

The administration of the Gold Coast was a matter of special concern. Under the merchants' government from 1828 onward, Gold Coast affairs had largely dropped from public sight in Britain, except for extraneous matters like the romantic and mysterious death of Letitia Landon ("L.E.L."), the popular poetess and wife of George Maclean, President of the Council at Cape Coast. Serious interest had revived with the case of *Dos Amigos,* a slaver whose capture and condemnation at Freetown in 1839 revealed that she had bought supplies from British merchants on the Gold Coast. The scandal was one of the special subjects for Madden's investigation and it was soon apparent that British merchants on the Gold Coast made a regular practice of outfitting foreign slavers who called there. It was equally apparent that, in their anomalous legal position, the merchants' government had no clear power to prevent this.[22] Partly because James Stephen was suspicious of merchants, partly because of Madden's damning report, and largely in order to clear the legal ground for stronger measures against the slave trade, the government accepted the Committee's recommendation. The Gold Coast forts were returned to the direct control of the Crown, but as a separate colony and no longer as a mere dependency of Sierra Leone.

The investigations of Madden and the 1842 Committee also publicized other, and positive, achievements on the Gold Coast. Because of its peculiar legal position, the merchants' government under George Maclean had been able to carry out practical innovations in

21. PP, 1842, xi (551), pp. iv–x.
22. Gold Coast Council Minutes, 12 November 1839, AG, Acc. 68/1954. The authoritative study of the Gold Coast under the merchants' government is G. E. Metcalfe, *Maclean of the Gold Coast* (London, 1962). For Gold Coast administration after the return of royal government, see Freda Wolfson, "British Relations with the Gold Coast, 1843–1880" (Unpublished Ph.D. thesis, London, 1952).

the process of "civilizing" Africa. Maclean, as effective ruler for the merchants between 1830 and 1844, had used his personal prestige to create an *ad hoc* judicial protectorate extending well beyond the forts themselves. With the informal consent of the African authorities, he began by arbitrating disputes, especially those between the tiny Fante states. After this initial opening, he began to sit on certain African courts administering African law, while at the same time urging the Africans to modify their law. By 1840, he had gone far toward illegalizing human sacrifice, and he had secured a wide, if informal, sphere of British judicial influence.

When the forts were taken over in 1843 by the royal government, the judicial protectorate was preserved. The new office of Judicial Assessor was created to continue Maclean's informal jurisdiction, with Maclean himself holding the post until his death in 1847. The informal jurisdiction was formalized by treaty. In 1844 the first of the series of "Bonds" was signed by the Gold Coast government and the African authorities. The Bonds empowered the Gold Coast government to put down human sacrifice and the practice of "panyarring" (kidnapping an individual in order to force his family to pay a debt or redress a grievance), and to try certain other cases. These treaties were the first extension of British legal authority beyond the walls of the forts, the first significant move forward in two hundred years, and they established the Gold Coast "protectorate"—though it was a protectorate for judicial purposes only in the first instance. Dutch and Danish forts were still interspersed with the British, but the new quality of the British presence after 1844 fostered a new habit of thought: the Gold Coast began to be talked of as British "territory," and not simply a series of British posts. In 1850, the British purchased the Danish forts, thus extending their influence eastward from Accra to the Volta. On the Gold Coast at least, the Niger failure and the 1842 Committee marked the beginning of a new British advance, however slow.

South Atlantic migration was another interest of Madden's mission, and of the 1842 Committee. Here again the impetus for change came from events in Europe and America. The legal emancipation of the West Indian slaves in 1834 was followed by a period of "apprenticeship," ending with complete freedom in 1838. After that date, the ex-slaves in many colonies were unwilling to work the sugar and coffee estates—not, at least, on terms the planters offered.

One obvious and early suggestion was to establish a paid-labor equivalent of the slave trade and bring contract workers from the African coast. The 1842 Committee accepted the idea in principle, and justified its morality as a benefit to Africa. Emigrants would return to Africa with some of the "civilization" they had acquired working in the cane fields of the Caribbean.[23] In this sense too, the Committee paid lip service to the goal of Buxton's plan, while radically altering the method.

Meanwhile, the impetus of the Niger Expedition was felt in other ways as well. One was the increased pace of African exploration—not, of course, in government hands, since the Government had sworn off any such effort, but with the support of private commercial, scientific, or humanitarian interests. On the Niger itself, the commercial explorers, who had been there before the government, were still exploring after the government ships left. Jamieson's *Ethiope* under Beecroft's command explored three new mouths of the Niger in the season of 1840 and ascended the main river as far as Raba, which turned out to be the practical limit of navigation. During part of the next season, *Ethiope* helped the government steamers. Later in the year Beecroft moved east again to the Cross River where he had earlier explored with *Quorra*. Again in 1842, he took *Ethiope* to the limit of navigation on the Cross, and in 1845 he was back on the Niger. *Ethiope* later met with an accident, and Niger exploration was given up for almost a decade; but the hiatus had little connection with the spectacular government failure of 1841.[24]

Other new exploration was more closely associated with the Buxton plan. William Cooper Thomson, a CMS missionary, was sent by the government of Sierra Leone in 1841 to try again along the old route to Timbo, first used by Watt and Winterbottom a half century earlier. The object was to keep Sierra Leone in the Niger game by opening a land route from Freetown to the headwaters of the river. An uncertain royal succession in Timbo delayed the party, and finally Thomson died there after a residence of almost two years. His twelve-year-old son brought his journal back to the coast.[25]

The same strategy of reaching toward the upper Niger had its repercussions in the Senegambia. A French expedition under Huard-

23. PP, 1842, xi (551), pp. x–xv.

24. *Journal of the Royal Geographical Society*, XI, 184–92 (April, 1841) and XIV, 260–63 (1844).

25. *Journal of the Royal Geographical Society*, XVII, 106–138 (1846).

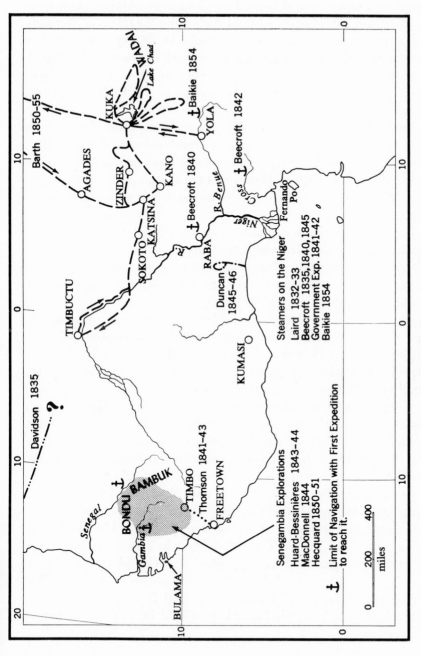

Map 18. Explorations, 1830–1855

Bessinières moved inland to the Falémé River in 1843–44, principally to investigate the prospect of gold trade from the mines of Bambuk, but also (in the aspiration of its members) to prepare for further French expansion eastward from the Senegal. A simultaneous British expedition under the Governor of Gambia, Richard Graves MacDonnell, travelled overland from the Gambia to the Falémé to sign a commercial treaty with Bondu. This time the object was not British expansion, but the security of the caravan routes from the Niger to the Gambia. In 1850–51 still another French expedition, under L. H. Hecquard explored the region from the upper Gambia to Timbo in Futa Jallon, and north to Bondu and the French posts on the upper Senegal.[26] The western approaches to the Niger were certainly not neglected.

Another short-range exploration of the mid-1840's was based on Dahomey. The traveller was John Duncan, who had served in the Life Guards and resigned in 1839 to become master-at-arms of the Niger Expedition. He now returned to Africa with the support of the Royal Geographical Society to try an overland route from Ouidah north to the "Kong Mountains." His travels in 1845–46 took him into the central part of the modern Republic of Dahomey, but no further. Like the journeys of Thomson and MacDonnell, Duncan's expedition added something to geographical knowledge, but provided small encouragement for further efforts in these particular regions.[27]

More consequential new explorations started at the Mediterranean coast. Even here, the impulse of the Niger agitation had an influence. Buxton had emphasized the slave trade from coastal Guinea, but he had also attacked the Muslim-dominated trans-Sahara slave trade. The British government responded by sending Vice-Consuls to a number of posts in the Sahara, and the Anti-Slavery Society sent James Richardson to the Maghrib as an observer, where he occasionally functioned as a government representative as well. He was in Morocco in 1843–44, then in Tunis, and finally in Tripoli in 1845. There he met Warrington and was appointed Vice-Consul for Ghadames. The Turkish conquest of Libya was now secure enough to allow travel to the south, and Richardson visited Ghat, Ghadames, and Murzuk in 1845–46. His journal, published in 1848, in turn pro-

26. A. Raffenel, *Noveau voyage dans le pays des Nègres* (Paris, 1847); MacDonnell to Grey, 16 June 1849, PP, 1849, xxxvi [C. 1126], pp. 325–27; L. H. Hecquard, *Voyage sur la côte et dans l'intérieur de l'Afrique occidentale* (Paris, 1853).

27. J. Duncan, *Travels in Western Africa,* 2 vols. (London, 1847).

voked a further British interest in the suppression of the trans-Sahara slave trade.[28]

The Government accepted Richardson's proposal for a major expedition to the Western Sudan. Richardson was put in command, accompanied by two German scholars, Heinrich Barth and Adolf Overweg. The three set out from Tripoli early in 1850, but disease followed its usual course: Richardson died in Bornu in 1851; Overweg died in 1852, and Barth was left to continue alone. Richardson's journal was recovered and published, and Barth was joined from 1853 to 1856 by Edouard Vogel; but the real accomplishment of the expedition was Barth's. His investigations were those of an experienced scholar, based on five years of travel from Wadai on the east to Timbuctu on the west. His five published volumes still remain the greatest single contribution to European knowledge of West Africa.[29]

It was the Richardson-Barth-Overweg expedition that reawakened the Government's interest in the Niger. Barth reached the upper course of the Benue in 1851 and reported that it was navigable for steamers as far as Adamawa. His message reached London early in 1853, where it coincided with the renewed interest of Macgregor Laird. Partly in the hope of finding Barth, Laird was able to persuade the Admiralty to furnish a subsidy for a private venture up the Niger and Benue. He had the *Pleiad* especially designed and built in his brother's yard at Birkenhead. John Beecroft was selected for command, and the Admiralty sent along three naval officers as observers. Beecroft died before the expedition could actually sail, but Dr. W. B. Baikie of the Navy took his place and the expedition steamed up the Niger and Benue in the summer of 1854. It was not a commercial success, but for the first time in Niger exploration no lives were lost. This achievement was possible for a variety of reasons, among others the use of prophylactic quinine, but its crucial importance was to demonstrate, on the very scene of widely publicized death from the "climate," that the Niger was now open.[30] The success of the *Pleiad*

28. J. Richardson, *Travels in the Great Desert of Sahara*, 2 vols. (London, 1848). See A. A. Boahen, "British Penetration of North-West Africa and the Western Sudan, 1788–1861" (Uupublished Ph.D. thesis, London, 1959), pp. 506–8.

29. J. Richardson, *Narrative of a Mission to Central Africa*, 2 vols. (London, 1853); H. Barth, *Travels and Discoveries in North and Central Africa*, 5 vols. (London, 1857–1858).

30. For accounts of the expedition see W. B. Baikie, *Narrative of an Exploring Voyage up the Rivers Kwora and Binue (Commonly Known as the Niger and Tsadda) in 1854* (London, 1856); T. J. Hutchinson, *Narrative of the Niger, Tshadda, &*

marked the end of the experimental era for steam navigation on the Niger, just as Barth's work opened the Western Sudan to a new depth of scientific investigation.

Missionary activity during the 1830's and 1840's followed much the same pattern as exploration. The missionary awakening was now moving at full speed in Europe, though work in West Africa was halting and uncertain during the 1830's. Missionaries died at the usual rate, and the effort suffered from the past reputation of the Coast. Some projects, however, foreshadowed the kind of broad effort the Niger Expedition was to represent. An "Institution for Benefitting the Foulah Tribe" worked in the Gambia from 1831 onward, in close cooperation with the Wesleyan mission. The object was to settle pastoral Fulbe on MacCarthy's Island (the same island which had seemed attractive for the convict project of the 1780's). The missionaries were to teach both agriculture and Christianity in a way suggestive of Buxton's plan for a "model farm." The project failed. Missionaries and agents died, and the Fulbe showed little interest in the sedentary life.

Once the Niger agitation began in Britain, however, the missionary societies used the glare of publicity to highlight missionary opportunities throughout West Africa. Since only the CMS was allowed to send its agents up the river with the government steamers, the other societies chose other regions. The Wesleyans picked Ashanti, and the Rev. T. B. Freeman from their Gold Coast mission made a tour of reconnaissance to Kumasi in 1839, returning again in 1842 to establish the first Christian mission. The Basel Mission, which had been working in the hinterland of Accra since 1828, had only one missionary still alive in 1840; but they launched a new effort in 1843, built around a nucleus of Christian West Indian settlers. This time the foundation was permanent. The Baptist Missionary Society of England followed a similar policy of staffing their missions from the West Indies. The first, established on Fernando Po in 1841, was based on a small group of Jamaican Baptists. In 1846 they moved to the Cameroons mainland. In the same year the Scottish Missionary Society began work in Calabar, again with a missionary transferred

---

Binuë Exploration (London, 1855); S. Crowther, *Journal of an Expedition up the Niger and Tshada in 1854* (London, 1855). See also Ifemesia, "British Enterprise," esp. pp. 342–47 and 402–3.

from Jamaica. The Catholic missions were also re-established in 1842, leading to the creation of a lasting Vicarate-Apostolic in 1847, with initial efforts directed toward Liberia and the French posts.[31]

In point of future British involvement, however, the most important missionary departure of the 1840's was in Yoruba. As early as the 1830's, some degree of order began to return out of the anarchy which followed the collapse of Oyo and the Fulani incursions from the north. The cities of southern Yoruba, some of them newly founded, began to function as nuclei of a returning stability. A new Egba state centered on Abeokuta and the new city of Ibadan began to attract and assimilate refugees from the north. The return of moderate stability presented an unusual opportunity for missionary work. During the period of anarchy the Yoruba had been the largest single group sold into slavery, hence the largest single group to be captured from the slave ships and landed in Sierra Leone. By 1838, a few of them had made their way back to Badagri as coastal traders. In 1839, with an impetus quite separate from that of the Niger Expedition, three liberated Africans in Sierra Leone bought a ship and sailed with trade goods and sixty-seven passengers for Badagri. By 1844, several hundred returnees from Sierra Leone had moved inland and settled in Abeokuta. Since they were already Christian and partly Western in culture, they found ready-made congregations and centers for further proselytizing; and those in Badagri appealed on their own initiative for British protection and missionary assistance. The Methodists answered with a mission station at Badagri in 1842. The CMS established one at Abeokuta in 1846, hoping to extend this mission field overland to the Niger in the vicinity of Raba. The Southern Baptist Convention in the United States followed in 1851 with their own Yoruba Mission.[32]

31. Ifemesia, "British Enterprise," p. 357; T. B. Freeman, *Journal of Various Visits to the Kingdoms of Ashanti, Aku, and Dahomi*, 2nd ed. (London, 1844); J. Beecham, *Ashantee and the Gold Coast* (London, 1841); Basler Evangelische Missions Gesellshaft, *The Basel Mission on the Gold Coast, Western Africa* (Basel, 1879); R. M. Wiltgen, *Gold Coast Missionary History* (Techny, Illinois, 1956), pp. 109–26. The most authoritative recent study of the missionary follow-up of the Niger expedition is J. F. Ade Ajayi, "Christian Missions and the Making of Nigeria, 1841–1891" (Unpublished Ph.D. thesis, London, 1958).

32. This account of missions and British intervention in Yoruba is based on Ajayi, "Christian Missions"; S. O. Biobaku, *The Egba and their Neighbours 1842–1872* (Oxford, 1957); Dike, *Trade and Politics;* A. N. Cook, *British Enterprise in Nigeria* (Philadelphia, 1943); C. W. Newbury, *The Western Slave Coast and its Rulers* (London, 1961); and C. Fyfe, *A History of Sierra Leone* (London, 1962), esp. pp. 212–13.

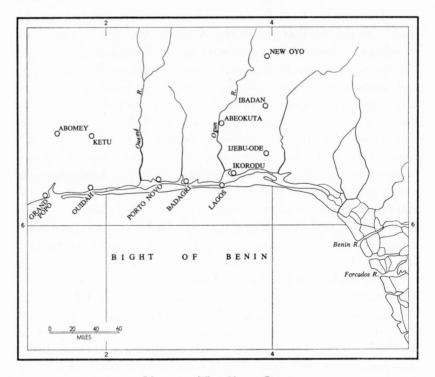

Map 19. The Slave Coast

The spread of British mission stations inevitably involved the British government. The Navy was always present off shore, and officers of the squadron were accustomed to political dealings with African authorities in connection with the anti-slave-trade treaties. By 1849 John Beecroft was appointed Consul for the Bights, with his residence on the still-Spanish island of Fernando Po. In spite of the official policy of no further commitments, the presence of British interests on shore, British power at sea, and the continued intention to suppress the slave trade easily led to more forceful intervention. The decisive action occurred in 1851, and it grew out of the missionary interest in the Yoruba hinterland of Lagos and Badagri. The principal rivals in this region were the new Abeokuta, with its contingent of British missionaries, and the older power of Dahomey. Dahomey controlled its own exit to the sea through Ouidah, while Abeokuta had to deal through one of the independent city-states, either Lagos, Porto-Novo, or Badagri. When Dahomey invaded Abeokuta, the pol-

icy of no commitment broke down. How could the British government withstand the appeal made (for public consumption) by the
Reverend Henry Townsend to the Church Missionary Society? "Can
England stand by, and look on and see Christians who have become
so through England's love of the Gospel, filling the baracoons of the
slave merchant first, and then suffering and dying under the cruel
usage of the taskmaster?"[33]

Consul Beecroft decided for action, first by sending military supplies inland to Abeokuta, then by ordering a blockade of all ports
except Badagri (at that time Abeokuta's principal avenue to the sea),
finally by landing a naval force to reduce Lagos. It was believed at
the time that a single intervention could install a more cooperative
ruler in Lagos. "Legitimate trade" could then flow freely to Abeokuta, and British power would no longer be needed. In fact, this
belief was mistaken. A fresh landing at Lagos was necessary in 1853,
and, in 1861, intervention was followed by outright British annexation of the port; but the annexation merely confirmed the *de facto*
relations established in 1851. Once the British had thrown their
weight on the balance of African rivalries, they could not withdraw
without accepting the defeat of their allies, and the defeat of their
allies would have meant victory for those who were now the enemies
of Britain as well. However firmly the Government may have decided
in 1842 to withdraw from the Niger, within a decade they were
firmly established on the Bight of Benin. Only a decision to abandon
the effort to suppress the slave trade by naval force could have loos-
ened that commitment.

A final ripple from the foundering of the Niger Expedition almost
brought about such a change. The necessity of maintaining the blockade had hardly been questioned before 1840. More than once the
needs of the squadron had saved the West African posts from evacuation. Buxton, however, exposed the fact that blockading the African
coast had not, in fact, stopped or even seriously discouraged the foreign slave trade. His own recommendation to reinforce the squadron
was not the only possibility. A movement to remove it altogether
grew in strength during the 1840's.

One source of opposition was humanitarian. It was alleged that the
blockade increased the suffering of the slaves in transit, by forcing

33. Townsend to Secretary of the Church Missionary Society, 17 October 1849,
PP, 1852, liv [C. 1455], p. 33.

the shippers to pack them even more tightly and treat them less humanely than they had done in the days of the legal slave trade. Many Quakers also objected to the use of force by the Navy, even in a good cause. A pacifist wing led by Joseph Sturge broke more or less openly with the Buxton group in 1839 and formed the British and Foreign Anti-Slavery Society to work for emancipation everywhere—but only by peaceful means.

Another and stronger objection came from those who disliked the cost in money and lives of a naval operation that seemed to accomplish nothing. In 1848, William Hutt, a free-trader formerly associated with the Colonial Reformers in the settlement of New Zealand, mustered a Parliamentary following and moved for a Select Committee of the House of Commons to investigate the foreign slave trade and its prevention. The Hutt Committee took evidence during two sessions and recommended in 1849 that the squadron should be withdrawn. Supporters of the squadron in turn organized their own following and moved for a similar Committee of the House of Lords. The Lord's Committee heard evidence under the chairmanship of Samuel Wilberforce, Bishop of Oxford and son of the great anti-slavery leader. It recommended that the squadron should be maintained and strengthened.

The issue drawn between the two Committees had broader implications than appear on the surface. The evidence they took represented a broad spectrum of British attitudes. In matters far beyond the issue at stake, it revealed a fundamental revision since 1830 of British thought about African problems. Some of the old fire was gone from the supporters of humanitarian action. A new faith in the efficacy of the "unseen hand" of economic interest was replacing the earlier faith in British morality and British gunboats as twin arbiters of the South Atlantic. But the humanitarians were not yet defeated. They rallied their friends, and conducted a new political agitation in Parliament and in the country. In March 1850 they once more won a decisive victory in the House of Commons—and in the face of the adverse report of the Hutt Committee.[34]

It was not, perhaps, their last victory, but it was the last victory they needed on this particular issue. Not quite by coincidence, the

34. The evidence and reports of the two Committees are found in PP, 1847–1848, xxii (272) (336) (536) (623); PP, 1849, xix (308) (410); PP (Lords), 1849, xviii (32); PP (Lords), 1850, xxiv (35).

Brazilian government accepted the inevitable later in 1850. Under anti-slavery pressure from the British and the Brazilians alike, Brazil began enforcing her own anti-slave-trade legislation. The estimated numbers of slaves imported into the country dropped from 54,000 in 1849, to just over 3,000 in 1851, to a mere trickle of smuggled slaves after 1852.[35] This change broke the back of the Atlantic slave trade. It continued for another fifteen years, but in vastly diminished quantity, and with cargoes drawn mainly from Lower Guinea.

For most of West Africa the era of the slave trade had come to an end. The era of the Niger expedition was thus the last era of humanitarian dominance in British policy, the last era of important slave trade, and the last era in which British investigators stood off from West Africa as a continent they hardly dared to enter.

35. Lloyd, *Navy and the Slave Trade*, pp. 139–48, 176.

REPORTING WEST AFRICA:

SOURCES

AND USES OF INFORMATION

Even during the disinterested decade of the 1830's, some new data continued to flow from West Africa to Britain, but the quality and quantity were both altered. Exploration no longer had its old appeal. With the Niger problem solved and "Timbuctu the mysterious" visited by two expeditions, the quarterlies turned to other matters. Travellers' accounts were limited to the now-familiar regions of the Guinea coast.

Buxton's *Slave Trade,* however, awakened a new kind of interest, beginning in 1839. A new stream of literature began to appear, growing into a small flood during the course of the 1840's, but publishers of that decade had nothing equivalent to the earlier classics of Mungo Park or Clapperton. Instead, they seemed to make up the deficiency in sheer quantity, turning out books, pamphlets, and secondary surveys designed to summarize what was known or to plead the case for a specific policy.

The boom in West Africana lasted through the 1840's, declining slowly as the decade progressed. After a short revival timed with the meeting of the Hutt Committee, it died away in the course of the

1850's to the level of popular disinterest shown in the 1820's or early 1830's. The decline was apparent as early as 1851.[1] The reviews carried less and less African material. *Blackwood's,* which had published so many of MacQueen's essays in the great era of exploration, published nothing at all about West Africa in the whole decade of the 1850's.

Richard Burton himself wrote in 1848 that readers were becoming bored with "the montonous recital of rapine, treachery, and murder; of ugly savages . . . of bleared misery by day, and animated filth by night, of hunting adventures and hairbreadth escapes, lacking the interest of catastrophe."[2] He was, perhaps, a little pessimistic, since he was to have a large audience for his accounts of East Africa and the Arab lands. Still, he was correct, contrasting this period with the 1820's.

David Livingstone's report of 1857 on his first great missionary journey, however, struck the right mixture of "hunting adventures and hairbreadth escapes" combined with moral purpose, and Livingstone himself helped to draw public attention from the Niger to the Zambezi. By contrast, Barth's masterpiece of West African scholarship and exploration, published in the same year as Livingstone's, was a commercial failure. The first three volumes sold so poorly that the modest print order of 2,250 copies was reduced to 1,000 for the later volumes.[3]

In part, Barth's lesser popularity was to be expected. He was a scholar writing for a scholarly as well as a popular audience, and his work was translated from German in a way that made it stylistically unattractive. In addition, Livingstone visited totally new country. He could report its marvels and horrors to an astonished public, even as Park or Bowdich had once done in West Africa. By contrast, Barth was going over old ground, although he went over it far more thoroughly than any of his predecessors had done. Park, Clapperton, and Denham had, nevertheless, set the initial image of the Western Sudan —and at a time when such reports were widely read and commented on. Barth's work might alter the knowledge of the specialists, but it could not change the superficial image of the broader public.

1. *Westminster Review,* XLV, 1 (1851).
2. R. Burton, "Zanzibar; and Two Months in East Africa," *Blackwood's Magazine,* LXXXIII, 282 (1858).
3. A. H. M. Kirk-Greene, "Barth: A Centenary Memoir," *West Africa,* XLII, 1231 (27 December 1958).

The new generation of explorers also began to write to a new
pattern. They were, in part, reduced to retelling an old story. Buxton's agitation, for example, created a public demand for books about
the Niger, and publishers appeared willing to meet this demand over
and over again. Twelve of the seventeen book-length accounts by
British explorers in West Africa in this period were concerned with
the lower course of the Niger.[4] With so many narratives in the field,
the most apparent excuse for still another was a new story of adventure. The Niger travellers of the 1840's were thus more personal
and less inclined than their predecessors to describe people and
places.

Exploration on the Niger posed still another problem. Travel by
steamer necessarily followed a pattern of rapid penetration and withdrawal, before the river could fall at the onset of the dry season.
Only Laird and Oldfield in the early 1830's enjoyed a relatively
leisurely trip followed by detailed publication. Beecroft saw more of
the river than anyone else, but very little of his information was published. Many of the scientists of the government expedition of 1841–

4. William Allen and T. R. H. Thomson, *A Narrative of the Expedition to the
River Niger in 1841*, 2 vols. (London, 1848); W. Allen, *Picturesque Views on the
River Niger* (London, 1840); W. B. Baikie, *Narrative of an Exploring Voyage up
the Rivers Kwora and Binue (Commonly Known as the Niger and Tsadda) in 1854*
(London, 1856); H. Barth, *Travels and Discoveries in North and Central Africa,* 5
vols. (London, 1857–1858); Samuel Crowther, *Journal of an Expedition up the Niger
and Tshada in 1854* (London, 1855); John Duncan, *Travels in Western Africa,* 2 vols.
(London, 1847); F. E. Forbes, *Dahomey and the Dahomans,* 2 vols. (London, 1851);
T. B. Freeman, *Journal of Various Visits to the Kingdoms of Ashanti, Aku, and
Dahomi,* 2nd ed. (London, 1844); T. J. Hutchinson, *Narrative of the Niger, Tshadda
& Binuë Exploration* (London, 1855); S. W. Koelle, *Narrative of an Expedition into
the Vy Country of West Africa* (London, 1849); R. and J. Lander, *Journal of an
Expedition to Explore the Course and Termination of the Niger . . . ,* 3 vols. (London,
1832); M. Laird and R. A. K. Oldfield, *Narrative of an Expedition into the Interior
of Africa by the River Niger in 1832–4,* 2 vols. (London, 1837); J. O. M'William,
Medical History of the Expedition to the Niger during the years 1841–42 . . . (London, 1843); James Richardson, *Narrative of a Mission to Central Africa,* 2 vols. (London, 1853); J. F. Schön and S. Crowther, *Journals of the Rev. James Frederick Schön
and Mr. Samuel Crowther, who with the Sanction of Her Majesty's Government Accompanied the Expedition up the Niger in 1841* (London, 1842); William Simpson,
Private Journal Kept During the Niger Expedition (London, 1843). The Niger cover-
age represented here includes one report from Lander's successful descent of the river
in 1830, two from the 1832–1834 expedition, five from the government Niger Expedition of 1841–1842, and three from the *Pleiad* expedition of 1854. In addition to the
final reports of Barth and Richardson, the Richardson-Barth-Overweg-Vogel expedition
was covered in an interim report by A. Peterman, *An Account of the Progress of the
Expedition to Central Africa . . .* (London, 1854), and Dr. Vogel's journals were
edited in Germany by Hermann Wagner as *Schilderung der Reisen und Entdeckungen
des Dr. Eduard Vogel in Central-Afrika* (Leipzig, 1860).

42 died before they could finish their work. Although Allen and Thomson tried to pull together the threads in a brief report on botany, zoology, and ethnography for their semi-official account, they too were hampered by the shortness of their visit. Thus the Niger narratives bulked large, but they fell far below the intentions of the promoters—or the hopes of the scholars.

The professional background of the explorers continued to be non-scholarly and non-scientific. Only the three Germans, Schön, Koelle, and Barth, had scholarly training, all three in linguistics or philology. Of these, both Schön and Koelle were professional linguists employed by the Church Missionary Society, and their reports were often narrowly confined to their professional specialties. Two other inland explorers of the period were missionaries, Samuel Crowther of CMS and T. B. Freeman of the Wesleyan-Methodist Missionary Society. Both were Western in culture but African in descent. Freeman was born in Britain of a British mother and an African father. Crowther was born in Yoruba, emancipated from a slave ship, and educated in Sierra Leone. Perhaps because of their race, both Freeman and Crowther were less culture-bound than most Western explorers. They depicted real people with a comprehensible way of life, in place of the cardboard savages in the accounts of most of their colleagues; but they too measured Africa by Western standards and found it wanting. They were less successful than Barth in really penetrating the culture barrier.

Most of the explorers were either military or medical men. Duncan, Forbes, and Allen were officers in the forces. Baikie, M'William, Oldfield, Hutchinson, and Thomson were doctors, often with a military background as well. Both the medical and military travellers had a professional tradition of accurate reporting, but neither were well equipped to understand an alien society. The value of their data was therefore highly variable. The best of them, such as Allen, Baikie, and Forbes, simply reported what they saw, from a slightly ethnocentric point of view, but avoiding both theory and value judgements. Thomson and M'William tended to confine their reports to medical matters in which they specialized. At the other end of the scale, Hutchinson and Duncan were culture bound in the extreme and followed Lander's device of poking fun at African culture.

This particular technique for keeping the readers' interest was increasingly characteristic of travel writing as the government exploring missions gave way to a less official kind of visit. The naval blockade came, by the 1830's, to provide a special reservoir of leisured would-be literary talent, and military or naval reminiscences began to appear with greater frequency.[5] The authors rarely had any real interest in Africa as such. They wrote to give their fellow countrymen a vicarious enjoyment of their adventures—laced with occasional political recommendations about the blockade or other timely topics. Vignettes of life on shore were introduced for light amusement or sensationalism. Human sacrifice in Ashanti, the female army in Dahomey, the "humorous" attempts of the emancipated Africans in Sierra Leone to re-educate themselves in the ways of the Western world—all this was standard fare.

The memoirs of civilian visitors or residents formed another and allied class of literature,[6] but it was more diverse than the military memoirs. The worst were very bad indeed, and the worst of all was J. Smith's *Trade and Travel in the Gulph of Guinea,* where sensationalism reached a peak. The sub-heads under the chapter on Human Sacrifice give the flavor: "Nailing prisoners—Jack Ketch—Decapitation—Cooking and eating human flesh—Priests—King Pepple eats

5. The following are a representative selection of this class of literature: J. E. Alexander, *Narrative of a Voyage of Observation among the Colonies of Western Africa,* 2 vols. (London, 1837); [Horatio Bridge], Nathaniel Hawthorne (Ed.), *Journal of an African Cruiser by an Officer of the U.S. Navy* (London, 1845); F. E. Forbes, *Six Months' Service in the African Blockade* (London, 1849); Pascoe G. Hill, *A Voyage to the Slave Coasts of West and East Africa* (London, 1849); H. V. Huntley, *Seven Years' Service on the Slave Coast of Western Africa,* 2 vols. (London, 1850); Peter Leonard, *Records of a Voyage to the Western Coast of Africa . . . in the Years 1830, 1831, and 1832* (Edinburgh, 1833); T. E. Poole, *Life, Scenery, and Customs in Sierra Leone and the Gambia,* 2 vols. (London, 1850); "Reminiscences of the Gold Coast Being Extracts from Notes taken during a Tour of Service in 1847-8," *Colburn's United Service Magazine,* 1850 (III), (III), 67–18, 573–88, 1851 (I), 93–103; H. I. Ricketts, *Narrative of the Ashantee War with a View of the Present State of Sierra Leone* (London, 1831).

6. See, for example, Robert Clarke, *Sierra Leone: Description of the Manners and Customs of the Liberated Africans . . .* (London, 1843); Hugh Crow, *Memoirs* (London, 1830); Brodie Cruickshank, *Eighteen Years on the Gold Coast of Africa, Including an Account of the Native Tribes, and Their Intercourse with Europeans,* 2 vols. (London, 1853); J. Fawckner, *Narrative of Captain James Fawckner's Travels on the Coast of Benin, West Africa* (London, 1837); James Holman, *A Voyage Round the World . . . ,* 4 vols. (London, 1834–1835); [Elizabeth Melville], *A Residence in Sierra Leone* (London, 1849); "Private Journal of a Voyage to the Western Coast of Africa," *Edinburgh New Philosophical Journal* (October, 1830); F. Harrison Rankin, *The White Man's Grave: A Visit to Sierra Leona in 1834,* 2 vols. (London, 1836); A. R. Ridgeway, "Journal of a Visit to Dahomey; or the Snake Country," *New Monthly Magazine,* LXXXI, 187–98, 299–309, 406–14 (1847); W. W. Shreeve, *Sierra Leone: The Principal British Colony on the Western Coast of Africa* (London, 1847); J. Smith, *Trade and Travel in the Gulph of Guinea* (London, 1851).

King Amacree's heart—Sacrifice human beings to the god of the Bar —Shipwrecks." In other respects as well, Smith's attitude toward Africans was uncordial. According to his recommendation, "the best way to treat a black man, is to hold out one hand to shake hands with him, while the other is doubled ready to knock him down."[7] Yet the work seems to carry no overt propaganda message: it was simply written to amuse.

A few of the civilian accounts, however, were minor classics of nineteenth-century travel literature. Brodie Cruickshank's *Eighteen Years on the Gold Coast* was one of these. Unlike most visitors, Cruickshank stayed long enough to gain real understanding and attachment for one part of Africa. The common attitude of the time, for example, was to interpret the tropical environment as both alien and forbidding. A romantic antithesis was often drawn between the beauty of nature and the sinister shadow of tropical death: "But with all that it is pleasing to the eye, it is but a painted sepulcre. It is painful to the imagination to conceive that this very exuberance of vegetation is the remote cause of that great destruction of European life, for which the place [Sierra Leone] is so distinguished—contaminating the surrounding atmosphere with mephitic exalations by its annual death and putrefaction."[8]

For Cruickshank, by contrast, the spell of the tropics was what it had been for Smeathman, attractive in its exoticism, yet friendly:

The Gold Coast of Africa, extending from Asinee to the River Volta, presents a wide field for curious and varied speculation. Its sunny skies, but seldom disfigured by gloom or tempest; its modulating sweep of hill and dale; its deep impenetrable thickets; its magnificent forest trees, the ever-verdant freshness of its luxurious vegetation; the richness of its mineral wealth, still shrouded in the mysterious recesses of its mountains, or in the depths of its dark and muddy streams; its luscious fruits; the gorgeous plumage of its birds; and the endless variety of animal and insect life, which inhabit its wild jungle tracts; invest it with an indescribable charm of vague and wandering curiosity.[9]

Cruickshank was also able to discuss African culture from a base of extensive experience. Though he was no scholar, his treatment of Fante customs and religion was one of the best of the nineteenth century. His judgments were often as unfavorable as those of his contemporaries, but real understanding came first, and the judgment

7. Smith, *Trade and Travel*, p. 197.
8. Leonard, *Voyage to the Western Coast of Africa*, pp. 38–39.
9. Cruickshank, *Eighteen Years*, I, 1–2.

followed. Cruickshank also paid a price for staying in one place: he had few "adventures"—and few readers—and the image dominant in Britain came from other sources.

Rankin's *White Man's Grave* was of great importance as an unusually full account of Sierra Leone, widely read in the 1830's. The title became a famous catch phrase, though Rankin himself meant it ironically. He was, in fact, one of the very few advocates of European colonization. In other respects, his work was very nearly typical of the reports that well intentioned travellers produced over and over again. He defended the Sierra Leone experiment and opposed the slave trade and slavery. His attitude toward the Africans was kindly, without trace of racial fear or real dislike, but the two volumes are full of sly digs and small jokes at the Africans' expense. The total impression he gave was that of an amusing, pleasant, and childlike people, but a people whose ultimate capacity was very much in doubt.

The missionary image of Africa was again different from that of secular humanitarians like Rankin—and far more important in the sheer quantity of print that began to deluge the English public. Publication was essential to the missions. Unlike the government or the traders, they lived on voluntary contributions. If the missions in the field were to continue their day to day operations, the missionary societies at home had to maintain a regular flow of contributions: sole dependence on spectacular events, like the Niger Expedition, was not enough. The link between publicity and fund raising was established early in the century. Article VIII of the Wesleyan-Methodist "Instructions to Missionaries" read: "It is *preemptorily required* of every Missionary in our Connexion to keep a Journal, and to send home frequently such copious extracts of it as may give full and particular account of his labours, success, and prospects. He is also required to give such details of a religious kind, as may be generally interesting to the friends of the Missions at home; particularly accounts of conversions. . . ."[10] The Church Missionary Society had a similar requirement, and these two were the most important British societies on the West Coast.

By the 1830's, both had developed a systematic range of publications designed to carry their message to all groups and classes of their supporters. For the leaders of the movement there were annual reports, outlining administrative dispositions, the state of missionary affairs in all parts of the world, and the financial condition of the

10. Wesleyan-Methodist Missionary Society, *Annual Report*, 1827, pp. xiii–xiv.

organization.[11] Educated laymen and the clergy were given further information in religious journals like the *Methodist Magazine,* or, after 1849, the *Church Missionary Intelligencer.* The *Intelligencer* published reviews, articles on missionary work and methods, and the scholarly contributions of field missionaries. It was, in short, a medium of inter-communication among the elite of the movement.

A second type of publication was designed for the general public. Here the journals and letters from field missionaries came into their own, printed either as verbatim extracts or rewritten in a more popular style. In this way, each contributor could have a sense of vicarious participation in the righting of wrongs and the eradication of paganism. These periodicals were scaled to reach as many different levels of British society as possible. The monthlies, such as the *Church Missionary Record* or the *Wesleyan Missionary Notices,* were designed for the educated middle class. In the CMS series, the *Juvenile Instructor* carried the message to young people, while the CMS *Quarterly Paper* was designed for circulation "amongst our friends in the humbler ranks of life."[12]

The same range and type of material also appeared in the missionary book trade. One common form of publication was an edition of the letters and journals of a single missionary, either worked up by the missionary himself,[13] put together by a pious relative, or compiled by the missionary society as part of its public relations work.[14] These accounts were sometimes rewritten with embellishments for the more popular audience. Miss Tucker's *Abbeokuta: or Sunrise within the Tropics* was so successful as a secondary account of the CMS Yoruba mission, it was immediately copied by a similar popularization of W. A. B. Johnson's memoir of his work in Sierra Leone.[15] With a broader sweep, popular ethnography could be combined with exhorta-

11. Wesleyan-Methodist Missionary Society, *Annual Reports; Proceedings of the Church Missionary Society* (annual).

12. *Church Missionary Intelligencer,* I, 2 (1849). See J. F. Ade Ajayi, "Christian Missions and the Making of Nigeria 1841–1891" (Unpublished Ph.D. thesis, London, 1958), pp. 649ff. for a discussion of the missionary literature of the period.

13. See, for example, R. M. Macbrair, *Sketches of a Missionary's Travels in Egypt, Syria, Western Africa, &c., &c.* (London, 1839); J. L. Wilson, *Western Africa: its History, Condition, and Prospects* (New York, 1856); William Fox, *A Brief History of the Wesleyan Missions on the Western Coast of Africa* (London, 1851).

14. See Sarah Biller (Ed.), *Memoir of the Late Hannah Kilham . . .* (London, 1837); *A Memoir of the Rev. W. A. B. Johnson* (London, 1852); George Townsend (Ed.), *Memoir of the Rev. Henry Townsend* (London, 1887).

15. Sarah Tucker, *Abbeokuta, or Sunrise within the Tropics . . .* (London, 1853); [Maria Louisa Charlesworth], *Africa's Mountain Valley; or, the Church in Regent's Town, West Africa* (London, 1856).

tion to support missions;[16] or a narrower focus, appropriate to the children's trade, could be given through the life of a single convert. Samuel Crowther, the former Yoruba slave boy who became a CMS missionary, and later a bishop, was most useful for this purpose.[17] The message of racial equality was combined with moral exhortation and a brief sermon on "self help," exemplified by Crowther's rise from lowly origins. The sins of Portuguese slave traders were even associated with the fact that many were Catholic, thus teaching the superiority of Protestant Christianity.

The burden of the argument in all the popular missionary publications, however, was to demonstrate the overwhelming need for missionary work. They insisted on the ultimate racial equality of all men, but they also embodied the worst aspects of cultural chauvinism. It was not enough to show that the unconverted Africans were doomed hereafter as worshippers of idols and followers of false gods. They were doomed on this earth as well to a nasty and barbarous way of life from which only Christianity could save them. The darker the picture of African barbarism, the more necessary the work of the missionaries. While the cultural chauvinism of private missionary letters or the more scholarly missionary journals was no greater than that of other Western writers on African affairs, the popular missionary publications were selective. They consciously chose to report on those aspects of African culture most likely to be shocking to their readers, and they often omitted sections of journals and letters that stressed elements common to all human cultures.

The force of the argument was heightened by setting present misery against possible achievement. The contrast commonly drawn between West Africa as a land of beauty and a land of death became, in missionary hands, a contrast between natural beauty and the evil of man. In the version of the Reverend D. J. East it was given a further twist to set material riches against moral poverty: "Africa itself is one of the finest and most beautiful as well as the most fruitful portions of the globe. No other country surpasses it in native riches. Its fertile plains will raise almost every production peculiar to a tropical climate. . . . Its mineral wealth is immense. Some dis-

16. As in D. J. East, *Western Africa; Its Condition, and Christianity the Means of Its Recovery* (London, 1844).

17. See *The African Slave Boy, A Memoir of the Rev. Samuel Crowther, Church Missionary, at Abbeokuta, Western Africa* (London, [1852?]).

tricts are literally impregnated with precious metals, and their stores of gold, in particular are inexhaustible."

But he held that man had failed to develop what God gave him, because: "Africa is a moral wilderness, and her inhabitants, as they have been too correctly described, are wolves to each other."[18]

An even more common theme showed the Africans before and after their conversion, often in a way that drew on the older balance of virtue and vice in the "African character." The "before" image featured slave raiding, human sacrifice, lascivious dances, highly sexual religious ceremonies, and the wicked excesses of polygyny— incidentally providing a mild titilation to keep up the readers' interest. By contrast, the "after" image showed the mild and gentle disposition of the converted Africans, their respect for the white missionaries, their childlike innocence.[19]

The combined impression was ideal for missionary purposes and it repeated familiar elements. It recalled the old legend of Negro sexuality. It supported the possibility of rapid conversion by reference to the Christianized version of the noble savage—the belief that Africans were, in some sense, natural Christians. Fowell Buxton accepted this view, saying: "I have no hesitation in stating my belief that there is in the negro race a capacity for receiving the truths of the Gospel beyond most other heathen nations; . . . ."[20]

W. R. Greg explained it in greater detail: "The European is vehement, energetic, proud, tenacious, and revengeful: the African is docile, gentle, humble, grateful, and commonly forgiving. The one is ambitious, and easily aroused; the other meek, easily contented, and easily subdued. The one is to the other as the willow to the oak. The European character appears to be the soil best fitted for the growth of the hardy and active virtues hallowed by Pagan morality; the African character to be more especially adapted for developing the mild and passive excellencies which the gentle spirit of Christianity delights to honour."[21] Greg's statement was so apposite for missionary purposes, it was quoted in full (without credit to Greg) in the Reverend D. J. East's general work on missionary theory.

The greatest diffusion of the idea, however, came only with the

18. East, *Western Africa,* pp. 5–6.
19. See Ajayi, "Christian Missions," pp. 598–99.
20. T. Fowell Buxton, *The African Slave Trade* (London, 1839), p. xi.
21. *Westminster Review,* XXXIX, 5 (January 1843).

1850's, when Harriet Beecher Stowe gave it dramatic form in *Uncle Tom's Cabin*. *Uncle Tom* became the most widely read book ever produced on the subject of race relations, and many more copies were sold in England than in America.[22]

While the missionary literature preserved and extended the Christianized image of the noble savage, missionary ethnography killed once and for all the secular, eighteenth-century literary motif—so much so that a missionary commentator could even boast of the deed: "The universal degredation and misery of unreclaimed man, even of that boast of a false philosophy, the North American Indian—has chiefly, by the circulation of Missionary information, become a fact as fully accredited as that of his existence. In vain would it be for a certain class of Europeans to paint in glowing colours as they once did, the virtue of Asiatic pagans. . . ."[23]

The missionaries were not alone to blame for the increasing cultural arrogance of the British public, but they bear a special responsibility. The views presented in their popular press were unequivocal, and they were very widely circulated. By contrast, their more sophisticated reports and works of scholarship were circulated to a narrower public in journals like the *Church Missionary Intelligencer*—or else remained in the files. The broader public, furthermore, could easily miss the point that the sins of African culture were not caused by the race of those who practiced them. It is hard to escape the conclusion that the systematic misrepresentation of African culture in the missionary press contributed unintentionally to the rise of racial as well as cultural arrogance.

The missionary image was all the more important, because it reached its real flowering in the 1830's and '40's when the possible antidote of critical scholarly investigation based on first-hand information was lacking. From the death of Bowdich to the expedition which took Barth to Africa in 1849, the ethnography of Africa depended almost entirely on data supplied by men who happened to be in Africa for some other purpose. Dr. W. F. Daniell gave a report

22. East, *Western Africa,* pp. 102–4; J. C. Furnas, *Goodbye to Uncle Tom* (New York, 1956).

23. John Harris, *The Great Commission* (London, 1842), p. 233. See also *Eclectic Review,* XII (n.s.), 79–80 (1847). The missionary movement had even earlier opposed the image of the noble savage outside of Africa. (See Bernard Smith, *European Vision and the South Pacific 1768–1850. A Study in the History of Art and Ideas* [London, 1960], pp. 107–9 and 243–47.)

on the ethnography of Old Calabar to the British Association in 1845, and another scholarly paper on the Ga-Adangme peoples in 1842, which was followed by still another on Ga ethnography in 1849.[24] Otherwise, ethnographers were armchair scholars. Modern field research was still many decades away, and the kind of work done by a generation of enlightened travellers had died out. The single exception was the research of linguists who came to West Africa in the service of the missionary societies. Perhaps Guinea's growing reputation as a land of death was enough to discourage scholars who lacked the special drive of missionary zeal. In any event, general ethnographers stayed at home.

Meanwhile, the social sciences in Europe were passing through a period of development and reorganization. New lines of investigation gradually became formalized into separate disciplines. One of the first steps was the formation of a scholarly society, such as the Royal Geographical Society, founded in 1831. The Society with its journal set out to improve the quantity and quality of reporting from all parts of the world, prepared special instructions for travellers, and acted as a clearing house for the new data.

Other disciplines were less fortunate, lacking the traditional recognition geography already enjoyed. Scholars came to an interest in African culture and history from many and diverse backgrounds— from medicine, from moral philosophy, from botany, from linguistics, or from a Christian humanitarian concern about government policy. As these interests coalesced into a new and separate discipline, the strongest pull came from the biological sciences. J. C. Prichard had already established a precedent by annexing ethnography to his study of man's physical nature. The first anthropological societies came from a further merger of Prichard's biological orientation with the political concerns of the humanitarians.

The occasion arose in 1837, at the time of Buxton's Parliamentary Committee on the Aborigines. Dr. Thomas Hodgkin, a Quaker humanitarian, a friend of Prichard, and Professor of Anatomy at Guy's Hospital, began to work informally, supplying the Committee

24. *Reports of the British Association for the Advancement of Science*, XV, 79–80 (1845); W. F. Daniell, "On the Natives of Old Callebar, West Coast of Africa," *Journal of the Ethnological Society*, I, 210–27 (1848), W. F. Daniell, "On the Ethnography of Akkrah and Adampe, Gold Coast, Western Africa," *Journal of the Ethnological Society*, IV, 1–32 (1856); *Reports of the British Association*, 1849 (II), 85.

with ethnological data. He then formed a permanent organization with a dual purpose: one objective was to save the aborigines in the British settlement colonies from possible extinction as a result of European immigration; the other was to study those peoples who seemed to be on the point of disappearance. The new society, called the Aborigines Protection Society (APS), was thus partly a political pressure group and partly an ethnological society. Buxton himself became the first chairman, though Thomas Hodgkin dominated its affairs until 1847.[25]

The first purely scientific ethnological society was founded in France rather than England, but it too was a direct outgrowth of Hodgkin's efforts. In 1838, Hodgkin wrote to W. F. Edwards in Paris, suggesting that he organize a French companion society to the APS. Edwards agreed, but the French scholars were more interested in scientific than humanitarian objectives. They therefore reversed the order of priority and formed the Société Ethnologique, with the preservation of the aborigines as a secondary objective.

Being first in the field, the French ethnologists set the earliest definition of its subject matter. Ethnology on either side of the Channel was already the study of human races. The crucial point was the precise definition of race. On the basis of Edwards' assumption that culture and history were largely determined by physical race, the Société Ethnologique held that races were to be distinguished by "physical organisation, intellectual and moral character, and historical traditions." Only the first of these items would be recognized today as a racial characteristic: the rest are cultural or historical. The mistaken identity of race and culture was thus incorporated in the very beginnings of the science, and physical and cultural anthropology were brought together in the unhappy marriage that has not yet dissolved.

British ethnologists would have agreed in linking race and culture, without assuming that one or the other was the dominant factor. They therefore accepted the essence of the French definition, but they added some assumptions of their own. The founders of the APS were convinced monogenists, and the motto of the Society was "Ab Uno Sanguine."[26]

25. Aborigines Protection Society, *Extracts from the Papers and Proceedings . . .* , I, 99–100 (August–September, 1839); *The Aborigines Protection Society, Chapters in its History* (London, 1899), pp. 3–14.

26. *Mémoires de la Société Ethnologique*, I (1), i–v (1841). The definition of

The English Society's curious double function as political pressure group combined with a scientific body was not to last. In its early years, the humanitarian side was dominant, so much so that the scientific members began to meet separately. In 1843 they formed a separate Ethnological Society—apparently in order to have a more efficient organization, not because of disagreement within the group. Early meetings of the Ethnological Society were held at Thomas Hodgkin's house, and Prichard still lent his scientific prestige to the humanitarian cause.[27]

Even the formation of a separate society could not rescue British ethnology from a special kind of limbo in the shadow of traditional humanities and the natural sciences. The Ethnological Society claimed an interest in linguistic studies, but so did the Philological Society of London, founded in 1842 and principally concerned with the languages of the Mediterranean basin. Until 1847, ethnological papers were presented to the British Association for the Advancement of Science under the heading of Physiology. Even after 1847, when an Ethnological sub-section was created, it fell under the general heading of Zoology and Botany. Ethnology was recognized, but not yet as an entity separate from its biological origins.

Ethnologists also had a problem of data. Few were able to make a full-time professional commitment to the new science. They began, therefore, by expanding and refining the technique of the questionnaire, following the practice of the Geographers. In 1834, Colonel John R. Jackson, a correspondent of the Royal Geographical Society living in St. Petersburg, had prepared a mammoth 500-page questionnaire for geography.[28] The ubiquitous Thomas Hodgkin presented a plan to the Philological Society for a similar language questionnaire as part of a large effort to record dying and out of the way languages.[29] In ethnology itself, Prichard presented a similar project to

---

ethnology and of culture developed in the same decade by Gustav Klemm in *Allegemeine Cultur-Geschicte der Menschheit*, 10 parts (Leipzig, 1843–1852) was considerably closer to modern anthropological usage, but it was not influential in England.

27. Richard King, "Anniversary Address, May 1844," *Journal of the Ethnological Society*, II, 14–16 (1854).

28. [J. R. Jackson], *Aide-mémoire du voyageur, ou questions relatives à la géographie physique et politique . . .* (Paris, 1834). See *Journal of the Royal Geographical Society*, IV, 229–339 (1834).

29. Thomas Hodgkin, "On the Importance of Studying and Preserving the Languages Spoken by Uncivilized Nations, with the View of Elucidating the Physical History of Man," *London and Edinburgh Philosophical Magazine and Journal of Science*, VII, 27–36, 94–106 (July–August, 1835).

the British Association in 1839, pleading the evidence of Buxton's Aborigines Committee that many peoples were moving rapidly toward extinction.

The result was a new ethnological questionnaire, published in 1841 by a committee of the Association working under the chairmanship of Thomas Hodgkin. It drew heavily on a similar questionnaire published in the same year by Edwards and the Société Ethnologique in Paris. Both questionnaires assumed a close connection between race and language. Both asked especially for descriptions and measurements of the head—following Edwards' predilection and the tenets of phrenology. Both requested detailed descriptions of individual and family life, including the life-cycle, which was to become standard fare in later ethnographic reports. On other points, they diverged in emphasis. Hodgkin was more interested in political institutions, while Edwards had a special concern about material culture, a greater variety of physical measurements, and his favorite hypothesis that most nations would be found to contain several different races whose identity might not be immediately obvious. Neither made a special point of kinship structure, but otherwise the future course of ethnographic investigation was laid out.[30]

It was also laid out in a way that suggested answers. The emphasis on physical measurement suggested racial interpretations—which were, indeed, explicit in Edwards' own work. His questions on language suggested that language was related to physical type and urged investigators to look for these connections. In Hodgkin's version, the policy concerns of the APS were also apparent. His question of "psychological character" asked not merely for information, but for suggestions which might "contribute to an estimation of the probable result of an effort to develop and improve the character."[31]

In later years British ethnology moved still more in the direction of Edward's interest in physical man. The Hodgkin questionnaire was revised and reprinted in 1852, with considerably enlarged sections on physical measurements, particularly of the shape of the skull. The language sections also grew, and both changes reflected the most recent tendencies of ethnological research: physical anthro-

30. *Mémoires de la Société Ethnologique,* I (1), vi–xv (1841); [Thomas Hodgkin and others], "Queries Respecting the Human Race, to be addressed to Travellers and others," *Reports of the British Association,* XI, 332–39 (1841).
31. Hodgkin and others, "Queries Respecting the Human Race," p. 339.

pology and linguistics shot ahead, while general ethnography languished.[32]

Questionnaires were more widely used for governmental than for scientific purposes. Preparations for the Niger Expedition included the circulation of a questionnaire to officials and travellers, but its main concern was the physical problem of travel in Africa—navigability of rivers, availability of fuel for steamers, climatic dangers, and the military capabilities of the African states. Cultural questions were limited to language, belief in a supreme being, and the probable reception of European missionaries. Even these were naive, for example: "Do they ever attempt to poison strangers? What species of poison do they use?"[33]

The Expedition itself was designed to produce practical knowledge, not to conduct basic research. In spite of James MacQueen's warning that planned culture change required a careful study of the existing way of life, the choice of scientific personnel sent by the African Civilization Society clearly implied its intention to investigate the country and not the people of Africa. The complement included a botanist, mineralogist, geologist, gardener, zoologist, and draftsman—but no ethnographer. The Government's orders to the Niger Commissioners were in the same vein. Commercial and political matters were given highest priority. The Commissioners were asked to report on the "state of civilization," but the emphasis was still on useful knowledge—the habits and customs of the people and "any striking virtues, vices, talents, or capabilities of which they are possessed."[34]

By comparison, the fact-finding aspect of R. R. Madden's simultaneous Commission to the Windward Coast was much more elaborately organized. In addition to his own enquiries, Madden circulated five printed questionnaires to officials and to some private citizens. One dealt with the state of the forts and settlements, a second with commerce, a third with the slave trade, and a fourth with climate, soil, and health conditions. Only the fifth and final questionnaire on

32. Thomas Hodgkin and Richard Cull, "A Manual of Ethnological Inquiry; being a Series of Questions Concerning the Human Race," *Reports of the British Association*, XXII, 243–52 (1852).

33. *Queries Relating to the Coast of Africa*, 2 parts (London, 1840).

34. James MacQueen, Memorandum of 12 January 1839, CO 2/22; Lord John Russell to Commissioners of the Niger Expedition, 30 January 1841, PP, 1843 xlviii [C. 472], pp. 11–12.

schools and missions asked about African culture.[35] Madden's effort nevertheless reflects an understanding that both theory and policy required data not then available. His aim was more practical than scholarly, and the answers left much to be desired, but it was a comprehensive plan of investigation.

The systematic attempt to gather information from overseas was more common in the 1840's. The Admiralty followed up the earlier private questionnaires with its own guide to scientific enquiry, published in 1849. Individual chapters on the different branches of science were prepared by outstanding specialists—Geology by Charles Darwin, Ethnology by James Cowles Prichard, Medicine by Alexander Bryson.[36]

Thus, when the *Pleiad* expedition entered the Niger in 1854, it did so with much more exact preparation than was possible in 1841. A full set of particular instructions was prepared for each of the fields of geology, geography and meteorology, terrestrial magnetism, zoology and botany, and (for the first time) ethnography and philology. The ethnographic requests were now specific—not a general outline of useful subjects of enquiry, but a list of desiderata to fill in the existing knowledge.[37] Given the speed with which the expedition ascended the rivers and returned before the end of the high water, however, the results could hardly have been anything but disappointing.

Still another substitute for field investigation was to interrogate Africans who happened to be in Europe. The most thoroughgoing effort in this direction was that of d'Avezac-Macaya, who worked through Edwards' ethnological questionnaire with a Yoruba informant from Ijebu, then in Paris after a period of slavery in Brazil. The result was the most comprehensive account we now have of Yoruba culture in the early nineteenth century.[38] Other African accounts also found their way into print, either as narrated to a Western amanuensis or written by the African author himself.[39] The quality varied

35. The questionnaires and original answers are found in CO 267/171 and 173. They were printed for Parliament in PP, 1842, xii (551).

36. Sir John F. W. Herschel, (Ed.), *A Manual of Scientific Enquiry Prepared for the Use of Her Majesty's Navy and Adapted for Travellers in General* (London, 1849).

37. IA, Calprof 1/10.

38. M. A. d'Avezac-Macaya, "Notice sur le pays et le peuple des Yébous en Afrique," *Mémoires de la Société Ethnologique*, II (2) 1–196 (1845).

39. See, for example; "Narrative of Joseph Wright," in J. Beecham, *Ashantee and the Gold Coast* (London, 1841), pp. 349–58; "Narrative of Lamen Kebe," in T. Dwight, "On the Sereculeh Nation, in Nigritia," *American Annals of Education and*

considerably, since many of these narratives were the work of ex-slaves who wrote down their experiences after many years of absence from their homeland.

John Beecham of the Wesleyan-Methodist Missionary Society, however, used the information of more recent arrivals from Africa. His study of *Ashantee and the Gold Coast* sought to draw together all that was known about Ashanti culture and history—from printed accounts, from the missionary reports of T. B. Freeman—but corrected and supplemented with the aid of Joseph Smith and William de Graft, African Methodist leaders who happened to be in London. The result was not completely satisfactory by standards of modern ethnography, and it was rarely pro-Akan in its judgment of African culture, but it did portray one African society as a working whole.[40]

European penetration in North Africa also added to British knowledge about the Western Sudan. With the French occupation of Algiers in 1830 and the conquest of Algeria in the following decades, French Islamic scholarship extended from its earlier interest in Egypt to take in the Maghrib as well.

In the process, the three great medieval Arabic authorities, whose works had been only partly known, came to light and were given Western translations. The first short section of al-Bakri's geography appeared in French in 1825 and another in 1831; but the most complete Arabic text was not known in Europe until 1851, when it was found among other manuscripts captured by the French in Constantine.[41] In much the same way, ibn-Khaldūn's *History of the Berbers and the Muslim Dynasties of North Africa* came to the attention of European scholars only in 1825; and even then it was not available in full until after 1851, when Baron MacGurckin de

Instruction, V, 451–56 (1835); "Narrative of Sali-bul-Ali," in W. B. Hodgson, *Notes on Northern Africa, the Sahara, and the Soudan* (New York, 1844), pp. 68–76; "Narrative of Ali Eisami Gazir," in S. W. Koelle, *African Native Literature* (London, 1854), pp. 248–56; G. C. Renouard, "Routes in North Africa, by Abu Bekr es siddik," *Journal of the Royal Geographical Society*, VI, 100–113 (1836); "Narrative of Samuel Crowther's Capture," in Schön and Crowther, *Journals*, pp. 371–85; Captain Washington, "Some Account of Mohammedu Seisei," A Mandingo of Nyani-Maru on the Gambia," *Journal of the Royal Geographical Society*, VIII, 448–54 (1838).

40. J. Beecham, *Ashantee and the Gold Coast* (London, 1841).

41. The first fragment of al-Bakri's work appeared in Société de Géographie, Paris, *Receuil des voyages et mémoires*, 8 vols. (1825–1866), II, issued in 1825. Another appeared in M. Quatremère, "Notice d'un manuscrit arabe contennant la description de l'Afrique," *Notices et extraits des mss. de la bibliotheque du roi*, XII, 437–664 (Paris, 1831). Baron de Slane's translation based in part on the Constantine text appeared as *Description de l'Afrique septentrionale par Abou-Obeid-el-Bekri* (Algiers, 1857). See *Revue Africaine*, II, 73 (1857).

Slane's translation began to appear.[42] Ibn-Battūta emerged in similar sequence—first a brief English translation in 1829, followed by the discovery of the full text in the Maghrib, and complete translation into French in 1858.[43] Arabic sources were also discovered south of the Sahara. Barth was shown a copy of Ahmad Baba's history of Songhai and had it in his possession long enough to copy extensive passages. These too were ultimately translated and published in Europe.[44]

Even before all these sources were fully translated, some of them were used by William Desborough Cooley for a new synthesis outlining the state of knowledge about the Western Sudan. Cooley was an Arabist with geographical interests. He worked with the known texts of al-Bakri, ibn-Khaldūn, and ibn-Battūta to produce *The Negroland of the Arabs* in 1841. This work both corrected and amplified the earlier geographical reconstructions of Rennell and MacQueen and presented a concise history of the Western Sudan. The vaguely rumored empires of Ghana, Mali, and Songhai were now seen to have a consecutive history; and those who read Cooley's work might have had cause to doubt the prevalent belief that African society was a changeless barbarism.[45]

British ethnology produced nothing to match the work of either Beecham or Cooley. Prichard still dominated the field. His *Researches into the Physical History of Man* reached five volumes in its third edition of 1836–47. His newer *Natural History of Man* passed through four editions between 1843 and 1852; but Prichard followed the fashion and concentrated on race and language, rather than giving a broader view of human culture. R. G. Latham, who came out with his own major ethnological survey in 1850, was even more narrowly concerned with the classification of human varieties,

42. Attention was first called to the work of ibn-Khaldūn by a note published in the *Journal Asiatique* in 1825. The French Ministry of War commissioned a translation by Baron de Slane in 1840, which began to appear in Paris in 1851. MacGurckin de Slane, "Introduction," ibn-Khaldūn, *Histoire des berbères et des dynasties musulmanes de l'Afrique septentrionelle,* 2nd ed., 4 vols. [Paris, 1925–1934], I, lxiv.

43. Sir Hamilton Gibb, "Forward," in Gibb (Ed.), *The Travels of Ibn Battuta,* 4 vols. (Cambridge, 1958), I, xiii–xiv.

44. Ahmad Baba, "Beiträge zur Geschiche und Geographie des Sudan. Nach dem Arabischen bearbeitet von C. Ralfs," *Zeitschrift der Deutschen Morgenländischen Gesellschaft,* IX, 518–94 (Leipzig, 1855).

45. W. D. Cooley, *The Negroland of the Arabs Examined and Explained* (London, 1841).

and the standard of his scholarship in discussing West African culture was a step downward from Prichard's work of more than twenty years earlier.[46]

Latham was nevertheless a respected scholar in his own time, and the deterioration of cultural anthropology is illustrated by his attempt to popularize the subject. In a series of six lectures on the "Ethnology of the British Colonies and Dependencies," delivered in Manchester in 1851, he devoted one to West Africa. In fact, his material was taken almost entirely from the Gold Coast, and it was anything but scholarly. Most of it was lifted bodily from the memoirs of a military officer, published the previous year in one of the service journals, and the borrowing was selective. Where the original had dealt generally with Akan culture, and even had an occasional word of praise, Latham picked out and quoted from those sections dealing with ordeals, human sacrifices, and "obscene" dances. He also forgot to say, as his source had done, that the human sacrifice he described had long since been abolished within the judicial protectorate on the Gold Coast.[47]

The lack of protest against distortion of this kind is a striking feature of the period. Only a very few commentators complained that the image they received at home was seriously wrong in the light of their experience in Africa itself.[48] Some Africans, however, tried to protest: Joseph Smith, an African merchant from Cape Coast and one of Beecham's informants, found his opportunity in giving evidence before the Hutt Committee.[49] Another protest was made, unexpectedly, in Africa itself. In 1848, when Governor Winniett went up to Kumasi as the first European of his rank to pay a formal visit, he found the Asantehene incensed at the false reports about Ashanti recently published in Britain. The Governor was reminded that good relations between his country and Ashanti could only be built on truthful information, and the Asantehene further pointed out that Africans had once thought Europeans were canibals. Now

46. R. G. Latham, *Natural History of the Varieties of Man* (London, 1850).

47. Compare R. G. Latham, *The Ethnology of the British Colonies and Dependencies* (London, 1851), pp. 34–68 with "Reminiscences of the Gold Coast," *Colburn's United Service Magazine* (1850–51).

48. Curiously enough, Latham's source for his popular ethnology was one of these. See "Reminiscences of the Gold Coast," p. 410.

49. Evidence of 4 April 1848, PP, 1847–1848, xii (272), p. 150.

they had learned better, while Africans were still maligned in Europe.[50]

The lack of protest against error was merely one symptom of a deeper misunderstanding, and one associated with the general self-confidence of the age. Neither the scholars nor the publicists understood the limitations of their data. Only scholarly field work or careful observation by long-term residence could have given the kind of understanding needed to replace the false confidence that Europe had really come to understand something about Africa. The telling criticism was made by J. Leighton Wilson, an American missionary with almost twenty years' experience on the Coast: "little is known, even at the present day, of the actual state of the country. The interior life of the people, their moral, social, civil, and religious condition, as well as their peculiar notions and customs, have always been a sealed book to the rest of the world. There have been no lack of books on Africa, but most of them have been confined, in the information they give, to single and isolated districts, or been written by transient visitors, who could see nothing but the surface of things."[51]

The self-confidence of the observers, however, was passed on to the general public—and with lowered standards of care and accuracy, as the reading habits of the British public changed. More people were educated, and more people could afford to buy books. The book trade responded to the needs of middle-class readers with books consciously aimed at the lowest common denominator of the largest possible audience. The immense spread and diversity in the missionary publications was one symptom of the change.

Another was the decline of the great collections of travel literature which had appeared with such regularity in the past and had made available the first-hand accounts. Shorter collections and anthologies were now more popular, and specialized West African works were less common. With more of Africa to know about, the old area of contact was necessarily treated more briefly. Hugh Murray's editions had long since ceased to deal with West Africa alone. When James MacQueen revised his *Northern Central Africa*

---

50. W. Winniett, "Journal of a Visit to Kumasi," entry for 26 October 1848, PP, 1849, xviii (32), p. 179.
51. J. L. Wilson, *Western Africa*, p. iii.

in 1840 to catch the Niger enthusiasm, he also shifted ground to take in all of Africa, reducing the West African sections by half.

A similar change of emphasis came with the newer French editions of travel literature. *L'Univers,* published in 70 volumes between 1835 and 1863 claimed to be the history and description of the whole world, but it was a world seen in the eyes of mid-nineteenth-century France. Africa as a whole received only seven volumes, and West Africa only one.[52]

At the same time, West Africa began to find a small but significant place in a whole range of new British periodicals, designed mainly for middle-class readers, and often to promote a special cause or policy. On the side of the humanitarians, the *Anti-Slavery Reporter* had been published since 1823 as the organ of the Anti-Slavery Society, but the victory over West Indian slavery ended the real unity of the anti-slavery movement. With the split between Sturge and Buxton in 1839, Sturge led the pacifists into a new British and Foreign Anti-Slavery Society, which kept the *Reporter.* Buxton's Society for the Suppression of the Slave Trade and the Civilization of Africa (more commonly called the African Civilization Society) launched its own journal, *The Friend of Africa,* with the special purpose of supporting the Niger Expedition.

Buxton was also concerned with the Aborigines Protection Society, which had similar humanitarian interests, but the APS at first left West African affairs to the African Civilization Society, just as it left Indian affairs to the specialized British India Association. As long as the other societies flourished, APS could devote its principal attention to the Australian aborigines and the American Indians of Upper Canada. As the African Civilization Society weakened and died in the mid-forties, APS took over its concerns. Especially after 1847, when it began publishing its own journal, *The Aborigines Friend,* it took an increasing interest in West Africa.

Enthusiasm for converting the barbarians to Western civilization spread from the Niger effort and led to the formation of still another society. The Society for the Advancement of Civilization was, like the APS, world-wide in scope, but it was less concerned with specific

52. Hugh Murray, *The African Continent* (Edinburgh, 1853); James MacQueen, *A Geographical Survey of Africa* (London, 1840); *L'Univers. Histoire et description de tous les peuples,* 70 vols. (Paris, 1835–1863).

policies and projects and more concerned with broader problems of culture change. *The Journal of Civilization,* which it published during 1841, was more elaborate than the usual run of humanitarian journals. It offered a series of articles on popular ethnography, building on the fascination with the exotic and ostensibly designed to acquaint the British public with the barbarism still flourishing overseas.

Another group of periodicals served the interests of colonial enthusiasts. They were not specifically humanitarian, but they might express humanitarian attitudes along with their special interests in Colonial Reform, free trade, or some particular region of the world. The principal organ of the Colonial Reformers was the *Colonial Gazette,* the weekly publication of the Colonial Society from 1838 onward. Its first object was to promote overseas settlement, but it took at least a negative interest in West Africa, opposing the whole Sierra Leone experiment and favoring government-sponsored emigration of Africans to the West Indies. For the African continent, the semi-weekly *African Colonizer,* modeled on the *Gazette,* was published briefly in 1840–41. Its main concern was European settlement in South Africa, and editorial policy followed the Colonial Reformers' opposition to the Colonial Office in general and to James Stephen in particular. But the editors also believed in the protection of the aborigines, the equality of all races of men, and the future of a multi-racial Empire. To this end, they supported the Niger Expedition.

Still other colonial journals were mainly commercial in emphasis. *The Colonial Magazine and Commercial Maritime Journal* was founded by R. M. Martin, who was also one of the founders of the British India Association. Under his editorship between 1840 and 1843, it followed a line that was generally humanitarian and mildly favorable to further government activity in West Africa. The competing *Colonial Magazine,* edited by P. L. Simmonds between 1844 and 1848, was less humanitarian and less interested in West Africa, though it too provided a forum for the discussion of West African affairs.

In addition to the specialized periodical press, political pamphlets and books followed in the wake of each important debate on public policy. The appearance of these pamphlets was almost continuous during the 1840's; since the Niger Expedition was followed in 1842 by the West Africa Committee and the debate on emigration to the West Indies, and this by a prolific literature for and against the anti-slavery blockade.[53]

These periodicals and pamphlets were not published to convey information, but to argue questions of policy. They had little influence on the British image of Africa. The image was already formed by the travellers and the missionary press, which did convey information. But the secular press was important. It summarized and popularized and transmitted a stereotype to a wider public. In the process, the detail available from the new flow of data was lost. The understanding available in the best of the new scholarship was also lost, and the image became more uniform. The range of journalistic opinion had been narrowing gradually since the eigtheenth century, when only a few people knew much or cared to know much about Africa. By the middle of the nineteenth, few cared, but almost everyone knew a little. The little they knew was epitomized by a reviewer in *Blackwood's,* describing Negro Africa in general.

Thus is Central Africa; distinguished from all the earth by the unspeakable mixture of squalidness and magnificence, simplicity of life yet fury of passion, the savage ignorance of its religious notions yet fearful worship of evil powers, its homage to magic, and desperate beliefs in spells, incantations, and the *fetish.* The configuration of the country, so far as it can be conjectured, assists this primeval barbarism. . . . The very fertility of the soil, at once rendering

53. The controversy over the anti-slavery blockade was an especially rich source of pamphlets and books. See William Allen, *A Plan for the Immediate Extinction of the Slave Trade, for the Relief of the West India Colonies, and for the Diffusion of Civilization and Christianity in Africa, by the co-operation of Mammon with Philanthropy* (London, 1849); J. Bandinel, *Some Account of the Trade in Slaves from Africa* (London, 1842); Buxton, *The African Slave Trade;* Thomas, Lord Denman, *A Letter from Lord Denman to Lord Brougham, on the Final Extinction of the Slave Trade,* 2nd ed. (London, 1848), *A Second Letter . . . to Lord Brougham . . .* (London, 1849), and *Uncle Tom's Cabin, Bleak House, Slavery and the Slave Trade* (London, 1853); W. R. Greg, *Past and Present Efforts for the Extinction of the African Slave Trade* (London, 1840); Robert Jamieson, *Commerce with Africa: the Inefficiency of Treaties,* 2nd ed. (London, 1859); T. Kehoe, *Some Considerations in Favour of Forming a Settlement at the Confluence of the Niger and Tchadda* (Waterford, 1847); Macgregor Laird, *Remedies for the Slave Trade* (London, 1844); J. S. Mansfield, *Remarks on the African Squadron* (London, 1851); H. Matson, *Remarks on the Slave Trade and the African Squadron,* 2nd ed. (London, 1848); P. Read, *Lord John Russell, Sir Thomas Fowell Buxton, and the Niger Expedition* (London, 1840); J. Richardson, *The Cruisers* (London, 1849); Sir George Stephen, *The Niger Trade Considered in Connexion with the African Blockade* (London, 1849); Robert Stokes, *Regulated Slave Trade* (London, 1851); H. Townsend, *Letter to Capt. Trotter, R. N. on the African Coast Blockade* (London, 1849); J. L. Wilson, *The British Squadron on the Coast of Africa* (London, 1851); Sir Henry Yule, *The African Squadron Vindicated* (London, 1850).

them indolent and luxurious, excites their passions, and the land is a scene alike of profligacy and profusion.[54]

In this popular form, the image of Africa was less favorable and no more accurate than that of the later eighteenth century. A half century of exploration and investigation—and simply of British presence on the West African coast—had greatly increased British knowledge of Africa, but the best of the new knowledge was locked in the low-circulation works of Barth, Cruickshank, Beecham, and Cooley. The rarity of these work was, of course, no evidence of their lack of influence among men who specialized in West African affairs. To a degree, these men were better informed than other people, even among the educated classes. On the other hand, the well informed had also picked up some beliefs of the popular image, which they cherished in spite of their later and more specialized knowledge. Among the most important of these was undoubtedly the general attitude of cultural chauvinism, and it was fortified by new tendencies in British thought about the meaning of race. In general, the political classes in Britain were no better informed than ever, but they were more confident of their information. The errors once confined to a few specialized works had now become "common knowledge."

54. *Blackwood's Magazine,* LV, 291 (1844).

TROPICAL MEDICINE

AND

THE VICTORY OF EMPIRICISM

I hinted that the climate—
"The finest climate in the world!" said Mrs.
Jellyby.
"Indeed, ma'am?"
"Certainly. With precaution," said Mrs. Jellyby.
"You may go into Holborn, without precaution,
and be run over. You may go into Holborn, with
precaution, and never be run over. Just so with
Africa."
I said, "No Doubt."—I meant as to Holborn.
Charles Dickens—*Bleak House*

When *Bleak House* was published,
ten years after the sailing of the Niger Expedition, the memory of
the famous failure was still fresh enough to serve Dickens' purpose.
He chose it as the favorite philanthropy of Mrs. Jellyby, his parody
of all that was narrow, impractical, and unhumane in the humanitarianism of Exeter Hall. It was a useful target. First of all, it was
philanthropy at a distance, a convenient point for his attack on the
"telescopic philanthropists," who righted wrongs only in the far
corners of the world and ignored the evils on their own doorstep.
Furthermore, it proved how impractical Exeter Hall could be, and
in this case the impracticality was dominated by their apparent unconcern for the known facts of the African "climate." The high
mortality, which had served as the excuse for recall, raised still
higher West Africa's reputation as the most dangerous climate in
the world. In 1848, *The Times* merely echoed the popular impression when it called the Bights, "the most deadly sea," and Fernando
Po, "the most pestiferous land which the universe is known to con-

tain."[1] When Dickens, the most popular writer of his day, chose the African climate for a further round of abuse, he helped to keep alive for later generations the image of the white man's grave.

The emphasis on high mortality was unfair to the Niger Expedition, which suffered no worse than the usual European experience in West Africa. Dickens' attack was also badly timed for another reason. During the decade between the Niger Expedition and the publication of *Bleak House,* tropical medicine passed through the most important series of practical reforms of the entire nineteenth century. Europeans would still die on the Guinea Coast at a higher rate than in England, but the death rate for newcomers was cut in half.

The Niger Expedition itself contributed greatly to these reforms, but the concentrated effort to solve the problem of survival went back to the earlier impact of European mortality in the 1820's. Before that time, medical practice in West Africa took its lead from other parts of the tropical world. From then on, empirical data was gathered in West Africa itself, and gathered far more systematically than ever before. The new trend appeared as early as 1826, when Commissioners Wellington and Rowan brought a new emphasis on health and survival to their investigation. The Navy also played a crucial role. Naval surgeons were ordered to report on the "medical topography" of foreign stations, the prevalent diseases, the mode of treatment, medicinal plants, and other information that might be of value to science.[2] As these reports accumulated they formed a mass of data about disease off the West African coast. They were further supplemented by Major Alexander Tulloch's detailed statistical surveys of military mortality in the Atlantic tropics, published in 1838 and 1840. Individual medical men with experience on the Coast also published more often than before. In 1831, James Boyle, a naval surgeon acting as Colonial Surgeon of Sierra Leone, brought out the *Practical Medico-Historical Account of the Western Coast of Africa,* the first full-length study actually based on African conditions since Winterbottom's work in the 1790's.[3]

1. *The Times,* 13 September 1848, p. 4.
2. *Regulations and Instructions for the Medical Officers of His Majesty's Fleet* (London, 1835), p. 40.
3. James Boyle, *A Practical Medico-Historical Account of the Western Coast of Africa* (London, 1831); A. Tulloch, "Statistical Reports on the Sickness, Mortality, and Invaliding among Troops," PP, 1837–1838, xl (138) and PP, 1840, xxx [C. 228].

With the preparations for the Niger Expedition, the effort was intensified. The government circulated questionnaires to recent African travellers, consulted medical authorities in England, and sent out Dr. R. R. Madden to the western portion of the Guinea coast with a commission that was both medical and political. The Niger Expedition itself spent more of its scientific effort on medical problems than on any other type of investigation. When the expedition was proclaimed a failure, and on medical grounds, the ships themselves were withdrawn, but the effort to solve the problem of survival in West Africa went on. The Navy in particular still had to protect the health of the anti-slavery squadron. Following a similar report already published by the French Navy, Dr. Alexander Bryson studied all of the data available on the health of the squadron and published a far-reaching series of recommendations in 1847.[4]

Meanwhile, in the later 1840's the half-century-old yellow fever controversy broke out again among British medical men. A special committee of the staff of the Army Medical Department held an inquiry on the disease in 1849–50. The Royal College of Physicians followed with its own investigation, and a third report was published by the General Board of Health in 1852. These discussions were especially marked by personal bitterness and factional rivalries. In the end, they may have done more to raise the temperatures of the British medical profession than to lower those of yellow fever victims in Africa, but they kept alive a general concern about tropical medicine. By the early 1850's, a very large body of empirical data, of a kind and quantity previously unknown, was available on disease in West Africa.

But the analytical tools for dealing with these data had not changed very greatly in fifty years. The principal cause of death was still "fevers," and the effort to classify fevers led relentlessly back to the yellow fever problem—in much the same form that Chisholm had raised it in 1795. The main questions were two: first, is yellow fever a disease *sui generis,* or is it a special form of the disease now called malaria? Second, is it contagious? The reason these questions touched off so much controversy was not simply the problem of survival in the tropics. These relatively simple problems in a single

4. J. P. F. Thévenot, *Traité des maladies des européens dans les pays chauds, et spécialement au Sénégal* (Paris, 1840); A. Bryson, *Report on the Climate and Principal Diseases of the African Station* (London, 1847).

disease led to other, more important questions about infection, contagion, and the nature of disease itself—as, indeed, they had done since the 1790's.

Two facts were universally recognized as empirically true. Some diseases seemed to have the power to spread from one person to another, as in the case of smallpox. Other diseases, such as tropical fevers, were confined to particular areas of the world, where they seemed to be endemic, affecting large numbers but without clearly established transmission from one individual to the next. From these observations, a distinction could be made between contagion and infection. Contagion was sometimes defined as the power of communicating a disease from one individual to another. Infection, on the other hand, was defined as the "principle which produces the disease, depending altogether upon *local* causes, and having no relation to emanations from persons labouring under the disease, or from bodies of those who have died of it."[5] Thus an epidemic outbreak might be started by the appearance of a diseased person, or it might be started by some subtle change in the state of the atmosphere.

To draw further conclusions from the empirical evidence, it was necessary to identify individual diseases. If a doctor distinguished between yellow fever and other tropical fevers, he produced one kind of data. Those who lumped all fevers, together produced another kind, that was in fact a description of at least two separate diseases—yellow fever and malaria—with dengue fever, typhus, and typhoid often thrown in for good measure. The case for a separate yellow fever was still unproved; and it remained so until after 1866–67, when J. J. L. Donnet in Jamaica developed the diagnoses based on quantitative albumin records.[6] Meanwhile, it was forcefully sustained by William Pym, already a thirty-year veteran of the controversy and now Inspector General of Naval Hospitals. He was supported by the Army Medical Service and contradicted by both the Royal Society of Physicians and the General Board of Health. After some initial uncertainties, however, Alexander Bryson established the distinction in the practice of the Navy off the African

5. Dr. Gilkrest, in Board of Health Report, PP, 1852, xx [C. 1473], p. 157.
6. S. F. Dudley, "Yellow Fever as seen by the Medical Officers of the Royal Navy in the Nineteenth Century," *Proceedings of the Royal Society of Medicine*, XXVI, 443–56 (1932), p. 447.

coast, and yellow fever entered the official naval terminology alongside remittent and intermittent fevers.[7]

Even the common distinction between remittent and intermittent
fevers beclouded the issue in its own way. The fever which doctors
saw most often in West Africa was *Plasmodium falciparum,* a form
of malaria which produces apparently different symptoms at different
phases of infestation. Remittent fever, as the name suggests, was
a very high fever marked by regular intervals of remission, and it
was descriptive of the symptoms of an initial attack of *P. falciparum.*
Intermittent fever, on the other hand, was the term used to describe
the later appearance of clinical symptoms, in a milder form among
those who had already survived the "seasoning sickness." Thus most
medical men failed to distinguish yellow fever from malaria, but
made a false distinction between different phases of malaria.[8]

Some, however, were trying to break out of the old framework
of fever classifications. One escape was to argue that fever was not
a disease at all, but a symptom of some more specific pathological
condition. Perhaps it was caused by inflammation of the brain, or,
according to Broussais and his followers, by infection of the mucous
membrane and the alimentary canal. Bascombe took the position that
fever was even more generally a symptom of some "condition inimical
to vitality" and "nothing more than Nature's effort to attempt the
curative process."[9] Even though these views led to no immediate
changes in medical practice, they marked the path that modern
medicine was to follow.

On the West African coast, James Boyle initiated a new classification of fevers, which did nothing to improve clinical description or
understanding of disease but did lead to changes in medical practice.
Boyle was influenced by the earlier habit of classifying tropical fevers

7. W. Pym, *Observations upon Bulam, Vomito Negro or Yellow Fever* (London,
1848); PP, 1852, xx [C. 1473]; Bryson, *Principal Diseases,* p. 250; A. Bryson, *Account
of the Origin, Spread, and Decline of the Epidemic Fevers of Sierra Leone* (London,
1849), pp. 173–74.

8. Report of Commissioner R. R. Madden, PP, 1842, xii (551), p. 423; E. J. Burton, "Observations on the Climate, Topography, and Diseases of the British Colonies
in Africa," *Provincial Medical and Surgical Journal,* 1841-1842 (I), pp. 219 ff., 265
ff., 287 ff., 306 ff., 323 ff., 346 ff., 365 ff., 392 ff. (25 December 1841 to 12 February
1842), p. 309; Bryson, *Principal Diseases,* p. 250.

9. Burton, "Observations," pp. 323–24; E. Bascombe, *On the Nature and Causes of
Fever, Especially that Termed Yellow Fever* (London, 1852), pp. 8–9.

according to their geographical homes. He held, therefore, that two different fevers occurred near Sierra Leone, though the symptoms were identical. One of these, the "climatorial bilious remittent fever," occurred only at sea. The other, the "African local bilious remittent" occurred only on land and only in Africa. Subsequent attacks, again with identical symptoms, were called "irregular bilious fever" on the first return of symptoms, and "intermittent fever" on still later occurrences. By giving African fevers new names, Boyle was able to break with the authority of British medicine and its recommended treatment with large doses of calomel and copious bloodletting. This reaction against dangerous treatments and the return to those which seemed empirically more sound was the beginning of a major medical reform.[10]

In spite of the bitter quarrels at home, new evidence about yellow fever emerged from West Africa. Doctors in Sierra Leone were especially well placed to study the epidemiology of the disease. Serious epidemics broke out in Freetown in 1823, 1829, in 1836 to 1839, and again in 1847. There were others on the Gambia and the Gold Coast and aboard the ships of the anti-slavery squadron. In spite of the uncertainty about diagnoses, careful study established a new base of empirical knowledge. It was recognized that epidemics tended to come in the dry season, rather than during the rains when malaria was most prevalent. It was established that the disease spread rapidly among Europeans, but in a way that was difficult to explain. Its course could be traced through a town, with relatively short jumps from one victim to the next. Yet it might skip several houses, and those in daily contact with a victim might escape altogether. When, in 1829, Lt. MacKinnial of H.M.S. *Sybille* drank a glass of black vomit from a yellow fever victim, it was proven that, at the very least, the disease was not contagious in the same way smallpox was. At the same time, it was known that whole ships' companies could come down with it at once. It was therefore clearly epidemic, if not contagious.[11]

This description of a yellow fever epidemic was empirically accurate, and it can be explained in the light of modern knowledge. *Aedes aegypti,* the carrier of yellow fever, breeds in small containers

    10. Boyle, *Medico-Historical Account,* pp. 84–137 and 188.
    11. R. R. Madden, Commissioner's Report, PP, 1842, xii (551), pp. 427–30; Bryson, *Epidemic Fevers,* pp. 173–74; Boyle, *Medico-Historical Account,* pp. 201–7; PP, 1842, xx [C. 1473]; Dudley, "Yellow Fever," p. 444.

and is found in large numbers around human habitation. Unlike *Anopheles gambiae* and *A. funestus,* the principal West African carriers of malaria, *A. aegypti,* could breed aboard ship. Epidemics in the dry season are possible because this mosquito does not depend on rain water alone. The pattern of transmission through a town came about because *Aedes aegypti* has both a short life and a short range. A single infected mosquito might not carry the disease more than a few yards, but the parasite is then left to develop in the human host, only to be picked up again by another mosquito of a later generation.

When these facts were fully understood, yellow fever turned out to be one of the easiest to control of all mosquito-borne diseases, but the bitterness of the yellow fever controversy limited the use that could be made of the knowledge already available. The Army Board of Inquiry, for example, recognized that all yellow fever victims were immune to further attack, but the information was obscured by many incorrect opinions to the contrary. More important, the isolation of yellow fever victims might well have saved a number of lives and stopped the spread of the disease, but the violently anti-quarantine report of the General Board of Health in 1852 tended to cut off action in this direction. One important reform was made in naval practice. On Bryson's recommendation, orders were issued that any ship in the tropics with a case of fever marked by early yellowness of the skin and black vomit was to proceed immediately to a cold climate. In some instances, this measure was enough to stop the epidemic which might otherwise have carried off most of the crew.[12]

The search for the causes of fevers followed the pattern set earlier in the century. Although some authorities still placed their faith in such factors as the angle of the sun's rays or the influence of the moon, the search for the "exciting cause" focused more and more narrowly on the dangerous "miasma." Hypotheses about chemical poisons in the air enjoyed a general vogue in Europe, and the authority of Liebig was added to MacCulloch's earlier theory that most disease was caused by the chemical products of putrefaction.[13]

The miasma causing tropical fevers might originate, according

12. Henry R. Carter, *Yellow Fever, An Epidemiological and Historical Study of its Place of Origin* (Baltimore, 1931), p. 67; Bryson, *Principal Diseases,* p. 228.

13. J. Liebig, *Chemistry and Physics in Relation to Physiology and Pathology* (Philadelphia, [1852]), pp. 17–26.

to differing opinions, from uncultivated land, from swamps, from green wood, from rotting ships, timbers, from bilge water, or from a variety of other sources. The common element, however, was an association with decay (especially of vegetable matter), with heat, and with dampness. The new empirical data, however, made it possible to narrow the field somewhat. Swamps had always been associated with fevers, but Major Tulloch concluded from his statistics on military mortality that no such correlation applied in West Africa. Commissioner Madden came to the same conclusion, and both were right.[14] The plans of the Niger Expedition were nevertheless based on an inordinate fear of the swamps of the delta and an unwarranted confidence in the healthiness of the drier interior.

The search for the chemical properties of the fatal gas represented another line of effort. Excessive oxygen and excessive carbon dioxide in the air were both investigated. Just as the Niger Expedition was about to sail, attention turned to hydrogen sulfide as a third alternative. This possibility was brought to light by Sir William Burnett's effort to prevent corrosion of copper sheathing on ship's bottoms. He collected samples of water from the African coast and found they contained an unusual proportion of hydrogen sulfide. Professor J. F. Daniel of Kings' College, London, then advanced the hypothesis that this gas, known to be poisonous, was in fact the cause of African fevers. The suggestion was preposterous, and its failings were soon pointed out. Hydrogen sulfide smells like rotten eggs, and its symptoms as a poison are nothing like those of malaria.[15] Further investigation showed that the waters off the African coast were chemically identical with other sea water.

The flurry of chemical interest nevertheless led to an elaborate effort to prevent fever on the Niger Expedition. The steamers were equipped with mechanical ventilators and chemical air-purifiers capable of drying the air, passing it over charcoal, and filtering any small particles that might be in it.[16] In practice the apparatus turned out to be a bulky nuisance. The medical staff of the expedition conducted extensive chemical tests of both air and water, and they con-

14. PP, 1840, xxx [C. 228], p. 26; PP, 1842, xii (551), p. 416.

15. J. F. Daniel, "On the Waters of the African Coast," Friend of Africa, I, 18–23 (January, 1841), first published as a series of letters in The Nautical Magazine of January 1841. For the refutation see Friend of Africa, I, 213–14 (December 1841).

16. D. B. Reid, Friend of Africa, I, 44–47 and 65–73 (February, 1841).

cluded that the fever was caused by "a certain peculiarity of atmosphere . . . inappreciable by chemical agency."[17]

Other authorities, however, thought they knew enough about the
nature of the gas to devise preventive measures. In 1831, James
Boyle had proposed an elaborate scheme to protect Freetown from
the swamps on the opposite side of the Sierra Leone River. This
scheme included the formation on the Bullom shore of a kind of
anti-malarial colony, densely settled by Africans. The settlers were
to drain the land, plant paw-paw trees, keep the brush clear, and,
in the wet season, maintain continuous fires in a range of clay kilns.
The carbon dioxide of the fires would then purify the atmosphere
before it crossed the water to Freetown.[18]

Still other preventive possibilities were implicit in the theory that
the miasma was heavier than air, a belief already old but still
strongly held. One of the more exotic projects was the suggestion
of F. H. Rankin. Like Boyle, his object was to protect Freetown from
the Bullom swamps, this time by building a wall along the Bullom
shore, thirty feet high and about eighteen miles long. This measure
would save the city from the "travelling miasma; creeping, as it
does, assassin-like, close to the earth."[19]

Buxton also shared the belief that the miasma would not be found
at any great distance above sea level. He based his planning for the
Niger Expedition on the assumption that safe altitudes would be
reached at about 400 feet. He was not only wrong, but better evidence was already available through careful work in medical topography. Even at the time the expedition was preparing to sail, T. Sterling, who had been financially involved in Laird's earlier effort, protested to the Colonial Office that real safety could only be found at
altitudes higher than 4,000 feet. This figure was an accurate estimate
of the upper range of *Anopheles gambiae* or *A. funestus* in West
African conditions. Macgregor Laird himself had set the lower limit
of safety at 3,000 feet in 1837 but raised it to 5,000 feet in 1842. Inso-
far as a solution to the problem of survival could be found through

17. William Allen and T. R. H. Thomson, *A Narrative of the Expedition to the
River Niger in 1841*, 2 vols. (London, 1848), II, 165. See also J. O. M'William, *Medical
History of the Expedition to the Niger during the Years 1841–42* . . . (London, 1843),
pp. 157–162.

18. Boyle, *Medico-Historical Account*, pp. 60–64.

19. F. H. Rankin, *The White Man's Grave: A Visit to Sierra Leone in 1834*, 2
vols. (London, 1836), pp. 147–48.

medical topography, Laird had found it. He suggested the formation of British settlements high on the slopes of Mount Cameroons and on the high mountains of Fernando Po, but his vision of dominating the mouths of the Niger from these two healthy hill stations was not acted upon.[20]

Broad studies of medical topography became an even more popular form of investigation after 1830 than they had been in the early decades of the century.[21] The published reports led off in many directions, some less useful than others. The very idea of medical topography contained strong undertones of the earlier belief that different diseases were peculiar to distinct geographical environments. The idea had no future in the history of medicine, but it led to the first investigations of climatology in West Africa. Investigators looked into the pattern of the rains, which apparently moved northward during the summer months and then receded to the south. The appearance of severe electrical storms just before the onset of the rainy season raised questions about possible relationships of electrical discharges and disease. The dry and dusty harmattan winds that blew down from the Sahara for a few weeks during the winter raised still further questions about the causes of climate, as well as the relation of climate to disease.[22] Incidentally and without notice, most of the writers on medical topography abandoned the glib environmental generalizations of the eighteenth century. Assumptions about the possible influence of heat or humidity on the human psyche were not so much forgotten as left out of the field of investigation. The new attitude was more narrowly empirical and more narrowly centered on the problem of disease.

The goal was still to find a healthy spot and to define the healthiest possible environment in general terms. The results were not par-

20. T. F. Buxton, *The Remedy: Being a Sequel to the African Slave Trade* (London, 1840), p. 67; T. Sterling, Memorandum of 3 March 1846. CO 2/22; M. Laird and R. A. K. Oldfield, *Narrative of an Expedition into the Interior of Africa by the River Niger in 1832–4*, 2 vols. (London, 1837), I, 299; M. Laird, Memorandum for the West Africa Committee, PP, 1842, xi (551), pp. 350–51.

21. The principal studies in this field were: Charles Stormont, *Essai sur la topographie médicale de la côte occidentale d'Afrique . . .* (Paris, 1822); Boyle, *Medico-Historical Account;* Thévenot, *Traité des maladies des européens;* Burton, "Observations"; W. F. Daniell, *Sketches of the Medical Topography and Native Diseases of the Gulf of Guinea* (London, 1849); Bryson, *Principal Diseases,* especially pp. 1–31.

22. For meteorology and climatology, see, in addition to the standard works on medical topography: R. R. Madden, Commissioner's Report, PP, 1842, xii (551), p. 412; A. Tulloch, PP, 1840, xxx [C. 228], p. 26; T. H. Hutchinson, *Narrative of the Niger, Tshadda, and Binuë Exploration* (London, 1855), pp. 31 and 81.

ticularly heartening. The very best of the investigations found that there was very little difference between one part of West Africa and another. Laird's solution of taking to the high mountains was all very well, but most of West Africa was not high enough. Real safety near the coast was in fact limited to the heights of Mount Cameroons and Fernando Po. Even the belief in a healthy interior was shown to be wrong by R. R. Madden's study of the mortality statistics of inland exploration, and the warning was repeated again after the experience of the Niger expedition.[23]

In such matters as these, however, the best of the empirical investigations had to compete with popular belief that not only survived but remained the dominant opinion. The myth of the healthy interior lived on into the twentieth century. Certain points on the coast also retained their good reputation, one decade after another. Gorée was one of these. Another was the Banana Islands, Smeathman's "tropical paradise" and the original goal for the Province of Freedom. The Bananas fitted exactly into the established picture of healthfulness—a heavily cultivated island, free of swamps, with some elevation, and enjoying the sea breeze.[24] Other coastal points enjoyed rapidly changing reputations, depending on the incidence of yellow fever epidemics or unusual publicity, and these changes had an important influence on strategic planning. Fernando Po, whose special reputation for lack of disease in the 1820's had been one source of the government's intention to make it their principal base, lost its good reputation during the early 1830's. Sierra Leone lost its bad one. By the mid-1840's, Sierra Leone and the Gold Coast were considered among the safest places on the whole coast, while the Oil Rivers were most widely feared.[25]

The familiar rules for personal conduct and personal hygiene also survived from earlier decades—often without empirical support.

23. R. R. Madden, Commissioner's Report, PP, 1842, xii (551), p. 415; T. R. H. Thomson, Evidence before the Hutt Committee, 23 May 1848, PP, 1847–1848, xxii (366), p. 129; Hutchinson, Narrative of the Niger, p. 192.

24. H. I. Ricketts, Narrative of the Ashantee War with a View of the Present State of Sierra Leone (London, 1831), pp. 212–13; Boyle, Medico-Historical Account, pp. 64–70; J. Rendall to Glenelg, 3 January 1839, CO 2/22.

25. See especially: R. M. Martin, History of the British Possessions in the Indian and Atlantic Oceans (London, 1837), p. 533; Rankin, White Man's Grave, pp. 164–79; Daniell, Sketches of Medical Topography, pp. 58–59; W. F. Daniell, "Some Observations on the Medical Topography, Climate, and Diseases of the Bights of Benin and Biafara, West Coast of Africa," Friend of the African, III, 105–8, 111–13, 138–40 (December 1845–February 1846), p. 106.

There was still a stress on moderation, with special beliefs about the proper hours for meals and the best place to sleep, avoidance of fatigue, damp, and the night air. The recommended quantity of clothing continued to increase. Flannel waist-belts were added to the older recommendation of flannel next to the skin. The hat formerly worn for protection against the sun now took on insulated padding.[26] But some of the new rules brought real improvements. After malaria and yellow fever, dysentery was the most serious threat. By 1841, the Niger Expedition ordered the men to boil all drinking water. The expedition of 1854 drank only water that had passed through the ship's boilers before being filtered. Mosquito nets also came into more common use, becoming standard equipment on the Niger, both in 1841 and 1854. While they certainly made the travellers more comfortable, in conditions of hyperendemic malaria, the most as-siduous use of nets and protective clothing was only likely to delay infection. Those who travelled into the interior or lived on shore were certain to receive an infective mosquito bite within a few weeks or months. But rules of conduct, whether sensible or not, were psy-chologically necessary. Where death was both common and mysteri-ous, it was essential to lay out an area of personal responsibility, so that each could consider "all men mortal but himself."[27]

The sailors of the anti-slavery squadron were in a much better position to protect themselves from infestation with malarial para-sites. Alexander Bryson's detailed study of naval health records led to a new understanding of the empirical behavior of the disease and to a number of preventive reforms. He was able to establish the incuba-tion period for malaria, so that the incidence of fever could be re-lated systematically to the place it was contracted. It was found that the men came down with fever about two weeks after contact with the shore, gathering wood and water or chasing slavers up rivers and creeks in open boats. Thereafter, detached service was carefully con-trolled, and any commander who sent boats away overnight had to justify his action in writing to the Commander-in-Chief of the Station.

26. For the rules of conduct given in the General Orders of the Niger Expedition, see: M'William, *Medical History of the Expedition*, pp. 16–24. For a semi-official set of French rules for West Africa at the same period, see: Thévenot, *Traité des maladies des européens*, pp. 256–83.

27. The psychological function of these rules was remarked at the time. See: Madden, Commissioner's Report, PP, 1842, xii (551), pp. 533–34; "Reminiscences of the Gold Coast, Being Extracts from Notes Taken during a Tour of Service in 1847–8," *Colburn's United Service Magazine*, III, 587 (1850).

Bryson also found that malaria was rarely contracted more than a mile from shore, a correct estimate of the maximum range of the more common West African vectors. These discoveries were all passed on as orders and advice to individual commanders and ships' surgeons. Taken along with Bryson's orders for the control of epidemic yellow fever aboard ship, they clearly had an important influence on the improving health of the squadron.[28]

The development of regular quinine prophylaxis against malaria was still more important in reducing the mortality from malaria. The standard dosage of chinchona bark and wine continued in the *Instructions for Surgeons* reissued by the navy in 1835 and 1844, and the drug appears to have been more frequently used for prophylaxis as it came to be more popular for the cure of malaria. Really effective chinchona prophylaxis, however, had to wait for the development of more palatable and reliable chinchona derivatives, cheaply produced, and backed by medical authority. Quinine, isolated in 1820, was produced commercially in Britain from 1827 onward. By the early 1830's, the price was low enough to make general use possible.[29] By the later 1830's, quinine was gradually coming into popularity on the Coast as a superior substitute for bark, but the significant change came only with the Niger Expedition.

The medical officers of the Expedition were ordered to give the men bark and wine daily in the usual way and were allowed to substitute quinine if they thought necessary.[30] Some of them followed this advice, at least part of the time, and two of them were very favorably impressed with the results.[31] Dr. T. R. H. Thomson continued his experiments after the Expedition withdrew from the river. He found, among other things, that the quinine had not been used with sufficient regularity or in sufficient quantities. In place of the recommended dose of two or three grains, he switched to a routine daily intake of six to ten grains. He experimented on himself on this new basis and had no clinical symptoms of fever while he was in West Africa, even though he was ashore a great deal. When he re-

28. Bryson, *Principal Diseases,* 178; Frederick E. Forbes, *Six Months' Service in the African Blockade* (London, 1849), pp. 123–24.
29. P. F. Russell, *Man's Mastery of Malaria* (London, 1955), pp. 105–6 and 132–33.
30. General order, signed by H. D. Trotter, 16 June 1841, PP, 1842, xlviii [C. 472], p. 114.
31. M'William, *Medical History,* p. 188.

turned to England and stopped taking quinine, however, he came down with malaria.[32]

The train of thought which led Thomson to this discovery is an instructive example of the way in which deduction from false premises might lead to discoveries that were empirically effective. Thomson began by accepting the common practice of labeling the two different phases of malaria as intermittent and remittent fevers. The later phase, or intermittent, was already commonly treated with quinine. He further observed that people with intermittent fever never came down with remittent at the same time. He therefore concluded that intermittent fever had the power of controlling remittent fever, and quinine had the power of controlling intermittent. Might not quinine then have the power of controlling remittent as well?

Though Thomson was the first to publish his results in a prominent journal, other observers were reporting similar evidence. Dr. Madden showed in 1841 that boat companies on detached service, which were actually forced to take the prescribed bark and wine, emerged with significantly lower rates of morbidity and mortality.[33] Alexander Bryson's collection and collation of the reports from naval surgeons proved even more conclusively in 1847 that both bark and quinine, taken regularly, could provide moderately effective protection against fever, and he confirmed this finding in 1854.[34]

As a result, the Navy changed over to quinine as the usual prophylactic, and the new orders were issued extending its use by shore parties. At the end of 1848, the Director-General of the Medical Department of the Army sent a circular to West African Governors, ad-

32. T. R. H. Thomson, "On the Value of Quinine in African Remittent Fever," *The Lancet,* 1846 (I), 244–45 (28 February 1846).

33. A problem arises in trying to assess the statistics of sickness and death during the period when bark and wine was the official naval prophylaxis against fever. In spite of standing orders, the men disliked the taste of the medicine and many surgeons were lax in enforcing the treatment (C. Lloyd, *The Navy and the Slave Trade* [London, 1949], p. 137; A. Bryson, "Prophylactic Influence of Quinine," *Medical Times and Gazette,* VII [n.s.,] 6–7 [7 January 1854]). Madden's case in point was a raid against the slave baracoons in the Gallinas River east of Sierra Leone in November 1840. On this occasion, the treatment was enforced among a group of 130 officers and men who spent seven days in the river. Of those attacked by fever on the Gallinas raid, only 15 per cent died, as against a corresponding figure of 31 per cent on the Niger Expedition the following year. In spite of many unknown circumstances, the contrast between these rates of mortality suggests that the bark used on the Niger Expedition may have been of poor quality, that its use was not fully enforced, or that the treatment of the disease was in some other respect less effective than the measures taken at the Gallinas. (Madden, Commissioner's Report, PP, 1842, xii (551), p. 226).

34. Bryson, "Prophylactic Influence of Quinine," pp. 6–7.

vising the general use of quinine prophylaxis. The quinine habit was already spreading among Europeans on the Coast, even before this official notification. Early in 1848 it had already become common practice for Europeans on the Gold Coast to keep a bottle of quinine on the side table, to be taken at the slightest feeling of danger.[35]

But even yet the knowledge was fragile. No one understoood what quinine actually did to the human body. Some feared that it might have harmful side effects, and in the long run they were proved correct when quinine was found to be a contributing factor in blackwater fever. The final mark of success for quinine came only with the *Pleiad* expedition of 1854. With medical orders drafted by Bryson himself, and commanded by a medical man, Dr. W. B. Baikie, the expedition returned without a single fatality, and it was hailed as a medical triumph. Its startling contrast to the medical failure of 1841 helped to set the reputation of quinine in the public mind, both in Britain and on the African coast. Curiously enough, Baikie himself was not at first convinced. His early reports played down the role of quinine and gave special credit to his own care in selecting the proper season for entering the river.[36] The general and overwhelming impression, however, was that quinine prophylaxis had made the Niger usable as it had never been before, and many authorities were so struck by the burst of publicity, they gave Dr. Baikie credit for inventing the treatment.

The triumph of quinine was one part of the triumph of empiricism, but it was not alone among the important medical reforms of the 1840's. The abolition of dangerous forms of treatment was perhaps of equal importance, and it too drew on the experience of medical men in Africa itself. While copious bloodletting and strong doses of mercurial preparations remained the standard recommendation of the British medical world into the 1850's and beyond, medical practice on the Coast began to change as early as the 1830's. Following Boyle's attack in 1831 on the general bleeding of fever victims, the practice began to decline. By 1841, R. R. Madden found that only one out of eight doctors on the Coast was still making free use of

35. Bryson, *Principal Diseases,* pp. 218–19; Bryson, "Prophylactic Influence of Quinine"; Acting Lt.-Gov. Fitzpatrick to Earl Grey, 10 March 1850, PP, 1850, xxxvi [C. 1232], p. 95; "Reminiscences of the Gold Coast," p. 584.
36. A. Bryson, undated memorandum for the Chadda Expedition [c. 1853], IA, Calprof 1/9; W. B. Baikie, in *Reports of the British Association for the Advancement of Science,* XXVI, 106–7 (1856).

the lancet. Leeches and cupping were still in style, but local bleeding of this kind was more unpleasant than dangerous to the patient.[37]

Overdosage with mercury declined more slowly. Only one of eight medical men in West Africa had abandoned it by 1841, though the investigations of Dr. William Stevens in the Danish West Indies suggested it was dangerous. Dr. Madden's report reflected the state of affairs at the beginning of the 1840's. He was forthright in his condemnation of heavy bleeding but still deferential to the mercurial school in his condemnation of calomel. The Niger Expedition sailed with the needed reforms half accomplished. Only local bleeding was used on the expedition, but calomel to the point of salavation was still practiced. One can only guess that this treatment may have offset some of the benefits of quinine prophylaxis and helped to produce a higher death rate than might have been necessary.[38] During the 1840's the remaining popularity of mercury treatments gradually waned. Bryson condemned both mercury and excessive bleeding, and his authority helped to change the practice not only of the navy but of civilian doctors as well.[39] He was opposed, indeed, to all painful forms of treatment. Seamen would still die of fever, but at least they would be spared the additional agony of a "night-cap blister" covering the whole scalp.

The treatment of fever improved in positive ways as well. Quinine, which was adopted for treatment before it was popular for prophylaxis, came into general use during the 1830's. Five of Madden's eight medical informants recommended it as early as 1841, but only for "intermittents" or to replace the chinchona bark as a "tonic" at the stage of recuperation. It would have been more effective in larger quantities and at earlier stages of the disease. Further improvements came gradually between Boyle's hesitant acceptance in 1831 and Bryson's authoritative recommendation in 1847, and there were many byways of experimentation. Madden thought quinine might be most effective, if applied externally to the raw surface of a blister. Favorite remedies survived long after the 1840's, though often in conjunction with quinine. Hot sand, steam baths, and hot water might be tried experimentally, and Bryson himself allowed small doses of

37. R. R. Madden, Commission's Report, PP, 1842, xii (551), pp. 424–25.
38. Burton, "Observations," p. 346; Allen and Thomson, *A Narrative of the Expedition*, II, 162–63; M'William, *Medical History*, pp. 194–98.
39. Bryson, *Principal Diseases*, pp. xi–xii, 232–34.

strychnine or arsenic in cases that did not yield to quinine.[40] Experimentation went on, and empirical discoveries remained fragile knowledge, but the success of quinine as a prophylactic confirmed its reputation for treating fevers as well. It remained the principal anti-malarial drug for nearly a century.

Both the new evidence and the greater care in its interpretation led Europeans to reconsider some old beliefs about the tropics as a human environment. The basic assumption behind all colonial thought and policy was the belief that black men could live and work in hot countries, while white men could not. This belief also lay at the heart of Western thought about the African race—the one unquestioned "fact" about race difference. It was to remain dominant in the popular mind and even in official British thought, but the best of the new investigations raised doubts.

The demography of Sierra Leone posed a special problem and increased these doubts. Commissioners Wellington and Rowan had shown in 1826 that the population was far too low, given the constant immigration of liberated Africans. Whatever the errors in their calculations, they had raised the problem of African mortality in Africa; and the Sierra Leone population continued to puzzle later investigators. It grew from about 13,000 in 1826 to 45,000 by the mid-1840's and then levelled off at about that figure for the next quarter century. Meanwhile, more than 75,000 liberated Africans had been emancipated in Sierra Leone by 1845, and various commentators tried to explain what had become of them.[41]

The problem of African mortality was taken up from another angle by Commissioner Madden's investigation of 1841. His questionnaire addressed to officials and medical men asked about the general health of the Africans. The answers were mixed. Half thought that Africans were healthy, and half thought they were unhealthy. Nine

---

40. Bryson, *Principal Diseases*, pp. 244–46; Bryson, "Memorandum for the Chadda Expedition," IA, Calprof 1/9; Daniell, *Sketches of Medical Topography*, pp. 120–21; Boyle, *Medico-Historical Account*, pp. 114–15, 127–37, 188.

41. For demographic discussions at the time see: Chief Justice J. W. Jeffcott, PP, 1831–1832, xlvii (364), p. 5; R. R. Madden, Commissioner's Report, PP, 1842, xii (551), pp. 248–49; Macgregor Laird, Memorandum for the West Africa Committee, presented 11 July 1842, PP, 1842, xi (551), p. 570. For recent discussions of the same problem see: R. R. Kuczynski, *Demographic Survey of the British Colonial Empire, Volume I: West Africa* (London, 1948), pp. 95–150; N. A. Cox-George, *Finance and Development in West Africa. The Sierra Leone Experience* (London, 1961), pp. 112–21; and C. Fyfe, *A History of Sierra Leone* (London, 1962), pp. 182–84.

out of twelve answers gave the opinion that the African life span was shorter than that of Europeans.[42]

Other evidence took the form of mortality figures for African troops. A decade after the Government's 1829 decision to use only colored troops in West Africa, Major Tulloch's statistical survey of military mortality led to some unexpected conclusions. African soldiers, mainly recruited liberated Africans, had a low mortality from "fevers" as long as they served in Africa—only 2.4 per thousand per annum. But when men of the same origin were assigned to Jamaica, the corresponding figure rose to 8.2 per thousand per annum.[43] The facts were especially striking, because Jamaica was almost universally thought to have a much better "climate" than West Africa.

Negro Americans coming to Africa fared even worse. Those who settled in Liberia died at a frightening rate, especially if they had come from northern states. West Indians of African descent were also attacked by the African "climate." One group of West Indian missionary agents for the Baptist Missionary Society died even more rapidly than the Society's European agents. Some Africans were recruited for the Niger Expedition in Britain, and those who had been absent from Africa for some time appeared to have lost their allegedly racial immunity.[44] Still other investigations and impressions seemed to show that certain people of European descent had a degree of protection against the most serious forms of fever. Italians, Spaniards, Brazilians, Portuguese, and those from the south of France were all noted at various times as especially favored in the West African "climate."[45] (These people all came from areas that were malarial in the nineteenth century.)

If these reports had been put together systematically, they could have revealed something very close to the modern conception of tropical disease and tropical immunities. They were not put together, however, and they were not brought forward with sufficient publicity to shake the older beliefs in racial immunity; but they were enough to

42. PP, 1842, xii (551), passim.
43. Tulloch, PP, 1840, xxx [C. 288], pp. 16–17.
44. "Civilization of Africa," Westminster Review, XV, 518 (1831); J. Angus, Evidence to Lords' Committee on the Slave Trade, 14 May 1849, PP, (Lords) 1849, xxviii (32), p. 134; William Allen to Lord Stanley, 5 February 1843, PP, 1843, xlviii [C. 472], p. 138.
45. Boyle, Medico-Historical Account, pp. 121–22; Burton, "Observations," p. 307; Thévenot, Traité des maladies des européens, pp. 157–68.

shift the dominant opinion among those who had a special concern about West African health conditions. Major Tulloch argued, in his official army report, that continuous residence in Africa, and not race *per se*, was the factor most closely correlated with immunity to fevers. This conclusion could be associated with the older European understanding that a newcomer would be relatively safe after he had passed through the "seasoning sickness." The medical officials of the Niger Expedition agreed with this general line of analysis.[46]

But other conclusions were also possible, and some of them kept to the racial explanations of African disease. Prichard, for example, used some of these data to refine his theory about the origins of race. He was concerned to prove that racial differences came from adaptations to different climates, and he thought racial change could take place in only a few generations. Rather than accept the apparent immunity of Negroes as non-racial, he argued that even a relatively short absence from Africa had the power to change their race.[47] Prichard's voice was the authoritative voice of British anthropology, and his analysis fitted both the old preconceptions and a new emphasis on racial explanations. The anti-racist implications of the new data fell on barren ground.

Instead, the real triumph of empiricism was in solving the problem of survival. The most important breakthrough of all was not to come until the first decade of the twentieth century, but the combination of quinine therapy, better precautionary measures, and the abolition of dangerous treatments was enough to make a real difference. The best statistics for West African mortality are those of the African squadron of the Royal Navy. Mortality per thousand mean strength dropped from 65 per annum during the period 1825–45 to 22 per annum in the period 1858–67, and the sharpest decline centered in the mid-1840's.[48]

Death rates on shore were much higher than these in any period, but such statistical information as we have indicates a similar improvement with a similar timing. As to timing, officials and other ob-

46. Tulloch, PP, 1840, xxx [C. 288], pp. 16–17; William Allen to Lord Stanley, 5 February 1843, PP, 1843, xlviii [C. 472], p. 138; M'William, *Medical History,* pp. 179–80.

47. J. C. Prichard, *Natural History of Man,* 4th ed., 2 vols. (London, 1855), II, 650.

48. The average annual mortality from all causes was still 58 per thousand during the period 1840–1842. By 1846–1848, it had already dropped to 27 per thousand (Bryson, *Principal Diseases,* pp. 177–78; PP, 1850, xxiv (35), appendix, p. 211; PP, 1867–1868, lxiv (158), p. 7).

servers in all three of the British coastal holdings reported a very
marked "improvement of the climate" in the later 1840's and early
1850's, and this in spite of the yellow fever epidemic at Sierra Leone
in 1847.[49] Some suggestion of the probable magnitude of the change
between the early and late nineteenth century is found in the two
surveys most nearly covering statistically viable groups of Europeans.
Between 1819 and 1836, the annual average death rate per thousand
mean strength of European troops on the West African coast was 483
for enlisted men and 209 for officers. Between 1881 and 1897, the
annual average death rate for officials was 76 on the Gold Coast and
53 in Lagos.[50] Since further medical reforms after 1850 and before
the 1880's were not comparable in importance to those of the 1840's,
it is fair to assume that quinine prophylaxis and the abolition of dangerous treatments reduced European mortality in West Africa by at
least half—possibly much more.

These medical reforms helped to close an epoch. The image of
Africa as the "white man's grave" lived on in the British popular
mind, but the improvement over the recent past was understood well
enough in official and missionary circles to reduce sharply the most
serious impedient to any African activity. Europeans could not yet go
to West Africa with the same confidence they might feel in embark-
ing for the West Indies or India, but the price in human life was
much lower. They could go there, as Mrs. Jellyby put it, "with precaution."

49. [Elizabeth Melville], *A Residence in Sierra Leone* (London, 1849), p. 77;
Benjamin Pine, Annual Report for Sierra Leone, 1847, PP, 1847–1848, xlvi [C. 1005],
p. 196; N. W. Macdonald, Evidence before Lords' Slave Trade Committee, 14 May
1849, PP, 1849 (Lords), xxxviii (32), p. 123; J. Bannerman to Earl Grey, 7 April
1851, PP, 1851, xxxiv [C. 1421], p. 198; S. J. Hill, Annual Report for the Gold
Coast, 1851, PP, 1852, xxxi [C. 1539], p. 186; J. L. Wilson, *Western Africa: its
History, Condition, and Prospects* (New York, 1856), pp. 511–14; three opinions from
the Gambia quoted in Kuczynski, *Demographic Survey*, I, 386. The impact of these
reports was felt in high government circles, and their importance was mentioned in
Parliament, see: Earl of Aberdeen, Lords, 22 February 1848, 3 H 96, c. 1039.

50. PP, 1840, xxx [C. 228], pp. 7 and 24; Kuczynski, *Demographic Survey*, I,
535–36.

15

THE RACISTS

AND

THEIR OPPONENTS

The three decades ending in 1859 with the publication of Darwin's *Origin of Species,* were a period of basic reorientation in British biology. Evolution was already in the air and in the works of some scientists. Only Darwin's general hypothesis was missing; but, lacking the Darwinian revolution, many older forms of biological thought flourished alongside the new. Physical anthropology (more commonly called ethnology in this period) was caught up in the general ferment of the biological sciences, but in ways that were to be disastrous for its future development. Edwards' *Caractères physiologique des races humaines* (1829) marked the beginning of a new flowering for pseudo-scientific racism. Between Edwards' publication and Darwin's, the groundwork was laid for the racial doctrines which were to dominate Western thought about non-Western peoples for a half century or more.

The Darwinian revolution was to cut off many of the meanderings of early nineteenth-century biology, but it allowed the racist error to stand. While it neither confirmed nor denied the pre-Darwinian racial theories, its consequences were to be far more disastrous to the supporters of Christian and anti-racist monogenesis than to their opponents. For Darwinians, both polygenesis and monogenesis were beside the point, but racists could use the theory of natural selection to "prove" that human varieties must be vastly different from one another. For monogenists, not only was the scientific basis for their position swept away; its other support in the authority of Christian revelation was no more valid for Darwinians than other aspects of the Christian tradition—when that tradition was confronted by scientific truth.

Meanwhile, in the last pre-Darwinian decades, as the racist position grew progressively stronger, the change was mainly one of degree: where earlier writers had held that race was *an* important influence on human culture, the new generation saw race as *the* crucial determinant, not only of culture but of human character and of all history. Hundreds of variant theories were to appear in the mood of this new emphasis. Some would claim the rigor of historical law, conceived in detail and projected into the future. Others were content to use the fact of race as a key to understanding the present condition of man. In either case, the basic theories were followed in turn by countless specific applications, special formulations, calls to action, warnings of danger, and racio-political policies adopted by governments.

In time, the new racism was to become the most important cluster of ideas in British imperial theory, but that time was not yet. Prichard still dominated British anthropological thought into the 1850's, just as humanitarianism still dominated at the seat of political power. In addition, Negroes dropped from their old central place in the scientific literature of race. Racial differences, seen in black and white, were the natural place to begin, but more minute racial variations now claimed the attention of scientists. Even so, the new emphasis on race inevitably came to affect European attitudes toward the Africans.

The rising public interest in biology extended to the study of race. The new ethnological societies helped to promote that interest, and the recognition of ethnology by the British Association in 1847 was a sign of success. In the 1840's and 1850's, the major literary quarterlies gave the same kind of attention to racial questions they had once given to geographical exploration.

The intellectual atmosphere of ethnology was nevertheless pre-Darwinian, still working on the old hypotheses, still pushing along lines of investigation set earlier in the century. One of these earlier directions of racial theory had been the association of race and language, already followed by some anthropologists to the point of using language as one basis for racial classifications. It was a point of some importance, since it increased the tendency to confuse race and culture. If language could become a racial trait, then other aspects of culture might be added, even though they had nothing whatever to do with the physical nature of man. The tendency was logical enough in its pre-Darwinian setting. Orthodox Christians still thought in terms of a world only some six thousand years old. All human diversity, therefore—both racial and cultural—must have arisen in that relatively short period since Adam and Eve left the garden. The anthropologists had some data on the speed of linguistic change, say from Latin to Italian, and the pace of change had not been very great over two thousand years. Given the existing differences in physical race, it was possible to assume (for lack of better data) that the pace of physical change might be much greater. Thus Prichard himself suggested that purely physical traits might be merely transitory, while language differences were "perhaps much more ancient distinctions than the varieties of form and colour."[1]

The primacy of linguistic traits could be justified in other ways as well. According to one ethnologist, "Language distinguishes man from the inferior animals. The communication of his inward feelings, the expression of his thoughts by means of words, is common to man, in all the different stages of physical, mental, and social development. From his language we can perceive the structure and disposition of his mind, his prevailing passions and tendencies: in language the changes and revolutions which the mind of the nation has undergone have left indelible traces. . . ."[2]

Linguistic differences were taken up still more readily by the polygenists. Holding, as they did, that God had created each race separately, they could also believe that he had endowed each with an appropriate language. Hence, Edwards and his school used linguistic evidence as the key to migrations and subsequent racial mixture. Since Edwards was principally interested in Europe, he had to depend

1. J. C. Prichard, "Abstract of a Comparative Review of Philological and Physical Researches as Applied to the History of the Human Species," *Reports of the British Association for the Advancement of Science*, II, 529–44 (1832), p. 544.
2. E. Diffenbach, "The Study of Ethnology," *Journal of the Ethnological Society*, I, 15–26 (1848), pp. 20–21.

largely on linguistic evidence: physical differences among Europeans were relatively small, and data about physical race in the distant past were hard to come by.

Along with the shift toward language as a criterion of race classification, there was a further shift toward head shape and away from skin color. Continental ethnologists led this tendency. They had done so since the beginning—from Camper's now-discredited "facial angle," through the early development of phrenology, and more recently in Edwards' insistence on the primacy of head shape. Phrenology, with its hope of discerning the inner nature of the human mind by examining its outer covering, was the crucial mediating influence, even though most ethnologists rejected the specific dicta of phrenological theory. They turned instead to other forms of craniometry. The most influential of these was the cephalic index, first announced in 1840 by Anders Retzius of Stockholm. By measuring the relation between the length and width of the skull, Retzius established the familiar classification into brachycephalic and dolichocephalic, but his full craniometric system was still more complex. He combined the cephalic index with measurements of the face, the height, and the jugular breadth of the head to produce a four-fold system of numerical classification. This system gradually came into general use on the Continent during the 1840's, and somewhat later in England. Retzius was thus the effective founder of craniometry, but he had no wish to distinguish race by physical criteria alone. Like other ethnologists of his time, he too accepted language as a racial trait.[3]

Meanwhile, phrenology went its own way as an influential but separate study. As it spread to England and America it moved beyond its original purpose as a guide to individual psychology. George Combe violated Gall's warning against applying the system to groups of people and tried to analyze the character of entire races. According to his analysis of African skulls, they showed a higher stage of development than those of American Indians or Australian aborigines, but lower than those of Europeans. Specifically, African skulls showed that, "The organs of Philoprogenitiveness and Concentrativeness are largely developed; the former of which produces love of

3. A. C. Haddon, *History of Anthropology*, 2nd ed. (London, 1934), pp. 20–21; E. W. Count (Ed.), *This is Race* (New York, 1950), p. 707; E. W. Count, "The Evolution of the Race Idea in Modern Western Culture during the period of the Pre-Darwinian Nineteenth Century," *Transactions of the New York Academy of Sciences*, VIII (2nd series), 139–65 (February, 1946), p. 151.

Figure 15. An Ashanti war captain.
(From Bowdich, *Mission from Cape Coast to Ashantee.*)

Figure 16. "A Caboceer of Ashantee equipt for War."
(From Dupuis, *Journal of Residence in Ashantee.*)

The image of Africa was presented to English readers of the early nineteenth century in a literal as well as a figurative sense. The illustrations of travel books, in particular, could carry the sense of the romantic beauty of African scenery and people, or else they could carry the message of African savagery.

The different treatment of illustrative material was especially striking in the first two reports from Ashanti by Bowdich and Dupuis. Both, for example, published illustrations of Ashanti soldiers. Bowdich's soldier showed a rather picturesque barbarism (*Fig. 15*), while Dupuis leaned much further toward the image of a savage Africa (*Fig. 16*). Bowdich's illustrations of Ashanti architecture were exotic, but remarkably close to the canons of British taste at a period when Georgian was giving way to the first stirrings of the Gothic revival (*Fig. 17*). Dupuis' illustrations of Ashanti priests were equally clear in their intent to show graphically the bloodthirsty character of African "paganism" (*Fig. 18*). Neither author, however, was absolutely consistent in the point of view of his illustrations. Both Bowdich and Dupuis showed Ashanti festivals that were more "barbarous" than "savage" (*Figs. 19 and 20*).

With the growth of pseudo-scientific racism, much the same kind of bias could be introduced in the portrayal of facial features. In this respect there were three alternatives. One was to show a more or less accurate rendition of negroid features, without exaggeration and without modification to make them appear more European (*Fig. 21*). But even an anthropologist such as Prichard chose his illustrations with care, so as to emphasize the inter-relations of race and culture. He published a pair of portraits, showing the less civilized man of Mandara with exaggerated negroid traits, while the more "civilized" type of Bornu could have been a European who merely happened to have a black skin (*Fig. 22*). Nor was this point left to the reader's imagination. After describing the Hausa people as "acute, intelligent, and industrious," Prichard included a portrait of a single individual (*Fig. 23*), taken in London, and pointed out that, "the countenance, if the complexion were white instead of black, would have nothing unlike the European." (J. C. Prichard, *The Natural History of Man,* I, 296.)

Figure 17. A Courtyard in Kumasi. The seated figures
are playing Warri, the traditional West African board game. (From Bowdich.)

Figure 18. "Priests or Magicians of Ashantee
invoking the National deities." (From Dupuis.)

Figure 19. "The First Day of the Yam Custom" (detail
showing three British visitors with the Asantehene). (From Bowdich.)

Figure 20. "The Close of the Adai Custom." (From Dupuis.)

Figure 21. King Gezo of Dahomey in 1850.
(From Forbes, *Dahomey and the Dahomans.*)

Figure 22. African racial types from Mandara (*left*)
and Bornu (*right*). (From Prichard, *The Natural History of Man.*)

Figure 23. "A Native of Hausa."
(From Prichard, *The Natural History of Man.*)

children, and the latter that concentration of mind which is favorable to settled and sedentary employments. The organs of Veneration and Hope are also considerable in size. The greatest deficiencies lie in Conscientiousness, Cautiousness, Ideality, and Reflection."[4]

We need hardly be surprised that this description fitted the traditional concept of the "Negro character," since Combe backed his phrenological conclusions by citing the appropriate passages from Leyden and Murray's *Historical Account of Dicovery and Travels in Africa*. It might appear to Combe that "science" could now "confirm" the findings of the travellers to Africa, but it is equally clear in retrospect that Combe started with the data of the travellers and caused phrenology to say the same. Furthermore, new generations of travellers would now be doubly prepared. They would know in advance the findings of science and those of past travellers. The circular flow of repetitive error was thus reinforced.

Phrenology was still more important indirectly, through its influence on prominent American anthropologists. Partly through Combe's influence, Samuel George Morton, a Philadelphia physician and professor of anatomy, became interested in collecting and measuring skulls. In 1839 he published *Crania Americana,* which compared American Indian, "Caucasian," "Malay," Negro, and "Mongolian" skulls. The study was supplemented with the help of George Robins Gliddon, a former United States Vice-Consul in Cairo, and *Crania Aegyptiaca* appeared in 1844 with still more measurements of African skulls.[5]

Morton was more interested in the size, than in the shape of the skull. He measured cranial capacity in cubic inches by filling each skull with white pepper seeds and then measuring the volume of the seeds. His published findings showed a range of mean capacity from 87 cubic inches for "Caucasians" to 78 cubic inches for Negroes. In fact, his measurements had no statistical valadity (even if the capacity of the skull were a genuine measure of intellect): his sample of Negro skulls consisted of only 20 from Negro Americans and 9 from Liberia.[6]

4. George Combe, *A System of Phrenology* (New York, 1845), p. 433. This edition was based on the fourth English edition, London, 1836.

5. S. G. Morton *Crania Americana* (Philadelphia, 1839) and *Crania Aegyptiaca* (Philadelphia, 1844); William Stanton, *The Leopard's Spots: Scientific Attitudes Toward Race in America, 1815–1859* (Chicago, 1960), pp. 24–32 and 45–54.

6. Morton, *Crania Americana,* pp. 253 and 260–61.

Morton's measurement of human intelligence by pepper seeds was, nevertheless, enormously influential. It seemed to give mathematical precision to the old belief in a scale of human races. It was, therefore, taken up in the American South and widely publicized as a pro-slavery argument. British anthropologists received it as a serious contribution to their science, and it seemed to have the support of anatomical studies in England itself. A Dr. Caldwell reported to the British Association in 1841 that the African race "bore anatomically a nearer resemblance to the higher Quadrumana than to the highest varieties of his own species."[7]

Caldwell's anatomy was simply mistaken, but comparative anatomy was not yet sufficiently developed to bring an immediate correction. In spite of real progress on the frontiers of science, there was still no adequate way to prevent empirical error from creeping in —and, once published, from enjoying the generally higher prestige of science as a whole. As late as 1831, for example, it was possible to publish respectably a multi-volume work in which orang-outangs and chimpanzees were classified as human and set in a regular hierarchy along with the other races of man.[8] Thus old errors could survive, while new ones were sometimes being added.

At times, old errors, once exposed, were revitalized. Polygenesis enjoyed a brief revival on this account during the 1850's. The incontrovertible argument for monogenesis had been the fact that all human races can breed together and produce fertile offspring: by definition, they belonged to one species.[9] The data supporting this position were absolutely correct; but data were not yet carefully checked, and pseudo-data could still be invented to prove the opposite. In this case, Robert Knox advanced the "fact" that mulattoes might be fertile for a generation or so, but, after that, one or the other of the original, "pure" races would predominate: a cross-bred race could not survive in competition with "pure" races. (He revived, in short, the century-old pseudo-data of Long.) The claim was plainly contrary to centuries of experience in the West Indies and elsewhere, but it was widely believed. Edwin Norris accepted Knox's data on this point and "corrected" the fourth and posthumous edition

8. Thomas Hope, *An Essay on the Origin and Prospects of Man,* 3 vols. (London, 1831), II, 391–97.

7. *Reports of the British Association,* XI, 75 (1841).

9. J. C. Prichard, *Natural History of Man,* 3rd ed., 2 vols. London, 1848), I, 7–24.

of Prichard's *Natural History*. Paul Broca in France took the same data from Knox and used it to restate the case for polygenesis.[10]

An argument for polygenesis as late as the 1850's was not so much mistaken as beside the point. Evolutionary ideas had made the old quarrel irrelevant and raised new issues in its place. Robert Knox, for example, chose not to use his newly invented data about human hybridity in a polygenist sense: he was already an evolutionist. According to his view, there had been one creation, in which all existing species were implicit, but not present. They evolved later according to a great original plan. First came "animals lowest on the scale, acquatic chiefly; then the mollusca and shellfish; then fishes; next birds, then quadrupeds, and, lastly, man." What Knox lacked and Darwin supplied was a notion of how this might have taken place. For Knox it was simply caused by "continuous generation." His data came mainly from embryology, where he recognized the principle later represented by the phrase, "phylogeny recapitulates ontogeny."[11] As for the origins of human races, Knox held that, however they may have evolved, they could be considered permanent, "for at least a term of years which history does not yet enable us to determine."[12]

Most British anthropologists, however, accepted monogenesis for the reasons Prichard had earlier laid down. They then went on to other problems. Race classification was one of these, since the new criteria suggested new possibilities in place of the familiar divisions by skin color. Prichard had, indeed, pointed out that skin color would yield no clear divisions but only imperceptible gradations from one race to the next. R. G. Latham tried to straighten out matters by depending still more heavily on the factor of language. As a starting point, he accepted Cuvier's three-fold system, rechristening the races as Mongolidae, Atlantidae (African), and Lapetidae (European), but the result only multiplied the confusion between cultural and physical characteristics. His Atlantidae, for example, included not only Negro Africans but all people who spoke Semitic languages. Thus Arabs, Jews, Berbers, and Egyptians—clearly non-Negro in physical type—

10. Robert Knox, *Races of Man: a Fragment*, 2nd ed. (London, 1862), pp. 64–66 and 89–90; Edwin Norris in J. C. Prichard, *Natural History of Man*, 4th ed., 2 vols. (London, 1855), I, xviii; P. Broca, *On the Phenomena of Hybridity in Genus Homo* (London, 1864), pp. 61–71.

11. Knox, *Races of Man*, pp. 171–76.

12. Knox, *Races of Man*, p. 448.

were removed from the racial group of the other light-skinned peoples. Latham was also inconsistent. Though he knew the Malgache spoke a language related to Malay, he classified them as Atlantidae on grounds of physical appearance.[13]

In the hands of non-scholarly writers, the confusion between physical and cultural criteria reached the point of absurdity. Combe, the phrenologist, claimed that the Negro people of the Western Sudan were not really Negroes at all. They were physically like other Negro peoples, but their "state of comparative civilization," as reported by Clapperton, showed they had reached heights impossible for the "inferior" Negro race. In this case, the stereotype of Negro inferiority was strong enough to counteract the custom of dividing mankind according to physical appearance.[14] For other writers, the image of the ugly Negro had a similar result. A military officer who served on the Gold Coast argued that the Fante could not be "pure Ethiopian" in race because they were a strong and handsome people.[15] A missionary to the Gambia claimed the Mandinka must be a mixed race because they lacked the "flat nose and thick lips" of the stereotype.[16]

With some scholars, the concept of race as a physical fact dwindled to the point of disappearance. Carl Gustav Carus in Germany used a classification that was largely cultural, though he tried to support his conclusions by reference to Morton's tables of cranial measurement. He divided mankind into four groups. First there were the "day people" of Europe, North Africa, Arabia, and India, who had achieved the highest civilizations. At a lower level were the "eastern twilight people" of East Asia and the "western twilight people" of the Americas, whose progress was more limited. Last of all were the "night people" of Africa, Australia, and New Guinea, who were held to be the natural slaves of the others.[17]

These new classifications implied a basic shift in the concept of race, but the shift was not seriously questioned or even discussed. Scholarly debate centered instead on racial theories with clear politi-

13. R. G. Latham, *Natural History of the Varieties of Man* (London, 1850), esp. p. 14. For still another new system of classification see P. A. Browne, *The Classification of Mankind, by the Hair and Wool of their Heads* (Philadelphia, 1852).

14. Combe, *System of Phrenology*, p. 421. See also Hope, *Origin and Prospects of Man*, II, 400–401 for a similar re-classification.

15. "Reminiscences of the Gold Coast, Being Extracts from Notes taken during a Tour of Service in 1847–8," *Colburn's United Service Magazine*, 1850 (III), 72.

16. R. M. Macbriar, *Sketches of a Missionary's Travels in Egypt, Syria, Western Africa, &c., &c.* (London, 1839), p. 246.

17. C. G. Carus, *Ueber ungleiche Befähigung der verschiedenen Menschheitsstämme für höhere geistige Entwicklung* (Leipzig, 1849), esp. pp. 17–25 and 32–35.

cal implications, and the focal issue of the 1840's and 1850's was American Negro slavery. This controversy made a curious contrast to the earlier British discussion of slave emancipation in the colonies. Racial theory had hardly entered the British decision of 1833. The pro-slavery forces at that time argued their case as one of economic necessity, dropping the claim that slavery was good for the Negroes themselves; but the racial justification for slavery reappeared in America during the 1830's.

It was precisely at this time that American abolitionists imported the whole paraphernalia of the British anti-slavery movement. With its "peculiar institution" thus called to account, the American South looked to its defenses. Most southerners had believed all along that their slaves were an inferior race, but they now felt called upon to prove that slavery was the natural and proper condition for Negroes. As Christians, they preferred the Biblical curse on the sons of Ham to scientific racial arguments which seemed to contradict the Bible; but the possibility of buttressing the case for Negro inferiority had its attractions, if only for a minority. In the 1830's, there was still a dearth of recent works in the tradition of pseudo-scientific racism. The first move was therefore to revive the racists of the later eighteenth century. J. H. Guenebault of South Carolina, for example, went to Julien Joseph Virey's *Histoire naturelle du genre humaine,* first published in 1800 and incorporating all of the polygenetic anti-African arguments of the previous decades—back to Edward Long and the others whose theories had been worked over in the French and English debates about slavery in the 1790's. Guenebault translated and selected the anti-African sections from Virey's work and published the result as *The Natural History of the Negro Race.* The book was read in England as well as America, and the older group of racist pro-slavery arguments took a new lease on life.[18]

But these arguments were no longer in tune with the recent findings of science. During the 1840's, some of the American supporters of slavery began to look for newer scientific arguments. George Combe's effort to popularize phrenology in America provided one source which merged with S. G. Morton's work on cranial capacities.

18. J. J. Virey, *Histoire naturelle du genre humaine,* 2 vols. (Paris, 1800); J. H. Guenebault, *The Natural History of the Negro Race* (Charleston, S.C., 1837). For the American controversy over race and slavery see: Stanton, *The Leopard's Spots;* W. S. Jenkins, *Pro-Slavery Thought in the Old South* (Chapel Hill, 1935); E. Lurie, "Louis Agassiz and the Races of Man," *Isis,* XLV, 227–42 (September, 1954); J. C. Furnas, *The Road to Harpers Ferry* (New York, 1959).

A new group of American polygenists received the scientific benediction of Louis Agassiz, who had immigrated from Switzerland in 1846. From Britain they drew in the new pseudo-scientific racism of Robert Knox, whose *Races of Man* (1850) was immediately given an American edition. It was soon joined by newer and equally "scientific" racist publications of the Americans themselves. The culminating production was that of Dr. Josiah Clark Nott, one of the most respected physicians in the South, and G. R. Gliddon, who had helped Morton collect skulls from Egypt. Their principal publications were two: *Types of Mankind* in 1854 and *The Indigenous Races of the Earth* in 1857. Both were thoroughly scientific in tone, drawing widely on the recent work of European anthropologists. For the popular audience and those who preferred literary evidence, John Campbell collected all the anti-African authorities he could find—from Herodotus to Robert Knox and Thomas Carlyle—and put together *Negro-Mania* to prove that Africans had never produced a civilization, nor a single individual of outstanding ability.[19]

American polygenetic ethnology never became the most popular defense of slavery, even in the United States. Its denial of revealed religion was too much of a handicap. Nor was it generally accepted in the dominant circles of British ethnology.[20] But Nott and Gliddon's *Types of Mankind* was published in England in 1854, where it was seriously reviewed and sometimes favorably received. Its principal role in England was to add one more voice to the growing chorus of pseudo-scientific racists, which included by 1855 Carus of Germany, Gobineau of France, and Robert Knox in Britain itself. In the trans-Atlantic exchange of ideas, Britain gave the anti-slavery crusade to America in the 1830's and received back the American racism of the 1850's.

Even earlier, American experience had added another and different aspect to British racial thought. From the first settlement of the Americas, European immigrants and travellers noticed that the Indians appeared to die out. The demographic pattern—clear enough in retrospect—was one of differential mortality similar to the "white man's grave" on the Guinea Coast. Only now the non-Europeans

19. J. Campbell, *"Negro-Mania" Being an Examination of the Falsely Assumed Equality Between the Various Races of Men; Demonstrated by the Investigations of Champollion, Wilkinson and Others, together with a Concluding Chapter, Presenting a Comparative Statement of the Condition of the Negroes in the West Indies Before and Since Emancipation* (Philadelphia, 1851).

20. See Richard Cull, "On Recent Progress in Ethnology," *Journal of the Ethnological Society,* IV, 297–316 (1856).

rather than the Europeans were the victims. It can be easily explained in the light of modern knowledge. The Indians of the Americas, the Australians, the Polynesians, and, indeed, any of the various peoples who were cut off from the major Eurasian-African land mass for centuries, had lost contact with the diseases or strains of disease common to the rest of the world. In some cases, they developed new diseases of their own, such as syphilis, but the exchange of disease on the re-establishment of contact was unequal. The Europeans were able to survive in the new environment, but isolated non-Europeans were less well prepared to combat the new diseases brought from Europe and Africa. Within a century after 1492, the Caribbean lowlands of tropical America were depopulated. In the tropical highlands and temperate North America the Indians survived, but only after a prolonged decline of population before demographic recovery could begin.

From the first, the Europeans sought to explain the death of the Indians. For Las Casas, it was caused by the cruelty and immorality of the Spanish settlers. Seventeenth-century British commentators also blamed Spanish cruelty for the death of the Arawaks, but they preferred other explanations for the decline of the North American Indians. The most common theories followed a line of thought advanced by Daniel Denton as early as 1670. The extinction of the aborigines was the work of Providence, acting in the interests of the English nation: "where the English come to settle, a Divine Hand makes way for them by removing or cutting off the *Indians,* either by Wars one with the other, or by some raging mortal Disease."[21]

During the course of the eighteenth century, British settlers in North America took up variations on this theme, shifting away from the initial emphasis on God's favor to the English nation toward an allied theory of Divine intervention in the cause of civilization. The aborigines were seen as "savages," whose death made room for the "civilization" of the westward-moving settlers and confirmed the law of human progress.[22]

Neither the problem nor its explanation attracted much British attention in the eighteenth century, but new waves of emigration to the settlement colonies in the early nineteenth century raised the issue more forcefully, especially in regard to Canada and Australia. The new settlement colonies were administered more tightly from

21. D. Denton, *A Brief Description of New York* . . . (London, 1670), p. 7.
22. R. H. Pearce, *The Savages of America: A Study of the Indian and the Idea of Civilization* (Baltimore, 1953), pp. 42–49.

London than the lost thirteen of North America. The disappearance of the aborigines was now seen as a metropolitan problem, and reports of the missionaries brought it to the attention of British humanitarians. Thomas Fowell Buxton took it up in Parliament. Under his chairmanship, a Select Committee on the Aborigines sat through three sessions, from 1835 to 1837. The hearings were accompanied by a flood of books and pamphlets and abundant notice in the press (with an incidental result in the foundation of the Aborigines Protection Society and later of the Ethnological Society). British scientists were attracted to the problem of aboriginal mortality. Prichard stated an ecological variant of the eighteenth-century American theory—when contact occurred between agricultural and pastoral peoples, the pastoralists died out, as though by divine law from "the time when the first shepherd fell by the hand of the first tiller of the soil."[23] Racial explanations, however, were much more popular. The importance of race was already widely discussed. The exterminated people were all of "the colored races," while the exterminators always appeared to be European. It seemed obvious that some natural law of race relations was at work, that the extinction of the non-Europeans was part of the natural evolution of the world.[24] William C. Wells had long before published an evolutionary theory of the origin of race. The new theories of racial evolution were now much more widely publicized.

The publicity, both of the Committee's hearings and the theorizing that followed, profoundly influenced British colonial theory and practice during the middle decades of the nineteenth century. At one extreme it was argued that the death of the aborigines proved the inferiority of the "colored races." Let them therefore die as the laws of progress command! As a middle course, humanitarian settlers sometimes urged that the "natives" be removed to distant reserves for their own protection—incidentally leaving good agricultural land open for white settlement. At the other extreme, some missionaries wished to restrict settlement by Europeans. If missionaries, and only missionaries, were allowed to visit the aborigines, they argued, "demoralization" at the hands of the settlers could be stopped.

23. J. C. Prichard, *Ethnological Extracts* (London, Spottiswoode, n.d.), p. 3.

24. For a sample of these discussions see: PP, 1836, vii (538); PP, 1837, vii (425); Saxe Bannister, *Humane Policy; or Justice to the Aborigines of New Settlements . . .* (London, 1830); H. Merivale, *Lectures on Colonisation and Colonies,* 2 vols. (London, 1841–1842), esp. II, 202–217; William MacCann, *Two Thousand Mile Ride through the Argentine Provinces,* 2 vols. (London, 1853), esp. I, 253–70; and the publications of the Aborigines Protection Society.

West Africa was largely absolved from the direct influence of
these discussions, but some elements filtered in to become suggestions
for African policy. Most observers realized that differential mortality
in West Africa ran against the Europeans, not against the Africans.
A few, however, were so impressed by the world-wide disappearance
of the aborigines, they were unable to conceive of West Africa as an
exception to so universal a "law." The exact nature of the law, however, was in dispute. Some saw it as a cultural law, in which the
savages fell away before the civilized. In this sense, it was predicted
as early as 1822 that the newly acquired civilization of the Sierra
Leoneans would make them the inevitable conquerors of Africa.[25]
But if the law were understood to be a racial law, then it was possible
to argue that contact with the Europeans was already demoralizing
the people of Sierra Leone and preparing for their extinction—that
all Africans, indeed, were destined for inevitable disappearance.[26]
The only practical result of such misapplied theory was the beginning
of a long series of suggestions that Africans must be kept from drinking spirits on account of their "racial weakness." For the time being,
it was only suggestion, though in the later nineteenth century it became the official policy of the British government.[27]

The more immediate and far more important consequence for
West Africa was indirect. It lay in the realm of ideas, where the
aborigines debate strengthened evolutionary racism and led it in new
directions. A few Continental historians had already looked to racial
determinism as the key to history—as, indeed, had the eighteenth-
century American theorists who saw their triumph over "savagery"
as the triumph of progress. During the 1840's and 1850's, British
theorists whose background lay in moral, rather than natural, philosophy began to borrow the racial thought of the scientists. Under
a strong impression from the "facts" of aboriginal extinction, they
too began to set up racial theories of history.

Thomas Arnold put forward one of the earliest of these, and one
of the most influential, if only because of the prominence of its author. At his inaugural lecture as Regius Professor of History at
Oxford in December 1841, he resurrected the ancient idea of a mov-

25. *Quarterly Review*, XXVIII, 175–77 (October, 1822).

26. J. Howison, *European Colonies in Various Parts of the World, Viewed in
Their Social, Moral, and Physical Condition*, 2 vols. (London, 1834), I, 99; *Westminster Review*, XXV, 185 (July 1836); MacCann, *Argentine Provinces*, I, 257.

27. See, for example: Paul Read, *Lord John Russell, Sir Thomas Fowell Buxton,
and the Niger Expedition* (London, 1840), p. 40; *Blackwood's Magazine*, XLIX,
112 (1840); F. E. Forbes, *Dahomey and the Dahomans*, 2 vols. (London, 1851), I, 38.

ing focus of civilization—now set in terms of race. In Arnold's view, the force of world history came from a series of creative races, each of which made its maximum contribution and then sank into oblivion, leaving the heritage of civilization to a greater successor. What the Greeks gave to the Romans, the Romans passed in turn to the Germanic race; and of that race the greatest nation was England. For Bishop Berkeley, a century earlier, the process had been similar—if non-racial—and it would continue at least one more step.

> Westward the course of empire takes its way;
> The first four Acts already past,
> A fifth shall close the Drama with the Day;
> Time's noblest offspring is the last.

Not so for Arnold—England's achievement was not merely the latest stage in history, it was the last. No great race remained to carry on. The alternative for other peoples was clear: "they either receive the impression of foreign elements so completely that their own individual character is absorbed, and they take their whole being from without; or being incapable of taking in higher elements, they dwindle away when brought into the presence of a more powerful life, and become at last extinct altogether."[28]

After Arnold's death, W. R. Greg took up the speculation in the *Westminster Review,* and with more direct application to the future of Africa. He admitted that some races were indeed becoming extinct, but the Negro race appeared to be a striking exception. North American census figures showed that Negroes could survive and multiply, not only away from their tropical home but in contact with Europeans. Greg held a low opinion of African intellectual ability; but he thought Negroes were racially endowed with an imitative quality. They could therefore assimilate what the West had to offer. Europeans also had their racial faults, and it was in this context that Greg laid down his famous contrast between their "vehement, energetic, proud, tenacious, and revengeful" character set against the natural Christian submissiveness of the Africans. Human progress would still be possible, once European achievements were grafted onto African stock. Greg believed that, "the future progress of mankind will present an aspect rather moral than intellectual; that, to the advance in the material and mental civilisation which the world

28. T. Arnold, *Introductory Lectures on Modern History* (New York, 1842), pp. 46–47.

owes to the classic and Teutonic races, will now be added improvement in those mild and happier virtues which Christianity has so
long and so fruitlessly enjoined; that the seed, which eighteen centuries ago was sown by the way side, or on the rock or amid thorns,
may now bear an ample harvest in more kindly and congenial soil."[29]

Continental theorists of the 1840's also took up the theme of
racially determined history, and often with more elaboration than the
English essays. Gustav Klemm's *Allegemeine Cultur-Geschichte der
Menschheit* began to appear in 1843 and ran to ten volumes in the
decade that followed. Klemm distinguished between "active" and
"passive" races. Each type had characteristics suitable to a particular
phase of human progress. The passive races made the first steps toward civilization, but they soon lost creativity. More active races then
took up the burden of achievement. Persians, Arabs, Greeks, and
Romans each made their contribution, until the pinnacle was finally
reached by the German race of northern Europe.[30]

The theme of achievement by a lineal succession of great races
might also be modified into a form of counterpoint. Baron Christian
de Bunsen, the Prussian Ambassador to Britain, took the view that
civilization was the joint achievement of two "great races," the
Japhetic (that is, the speakers of Indo-European languages) and the
Semitic, each of which had influenced the other throughout history.[31]
Neither Klemm nor De Bunsen, however, were thoroughgoing racists. Klemm was mainly interested in culture, and in very nearly the
modern sense of the term.[32] De Bunsen was mainly interested in
language. The use of racial interpretations was, for them, merely a
fashionable supplement to an argument that was essentially non-
racist.

A thoroughly racial theory of history, however, was not far behind. The first important proponent in Great Britain was Dr. Robert
Knox, the real founder of British racism and one of the key figures
in the general Western movement toward a dogmatic pseudo-scientific racism. Knox's importance has often been underrated, perhaps

29. [W. R. Greg], "Dr. Arnold," *Westminster Review*, XXX, 7 (January 1843).

30. G. Klemm, *Allegemeine Cultur-Geschichte der Menschheit*, 10 parts (Leipzig,
1843–1852), esp. I, 195–205.

31. C. C. J. Bunsen, "On the Results of Recent Egyptian Researches in Reference
to Asiatic and African Ethnology, and the Classification of Languages," *Reports of the
British Association*, XVII, 254–99 (1847).

32. R. H. Lowie, *The History of Ethnological Theory* (New York, 1937), pp. 11–
14.

on account of his professional career. In his youth he had shown great promise as an anatomist. After military service in Europe during the Napoleonic Wars, he kept his commission as an army surgeon and served in South Africa from 1817 to 1820. While there, he became interested in the anatomy of the various South African races and began thinking about the role of race in history. On his return he studied briefly in Paris with Cuvier and was further impressed by the racial theories of French writers such as Geoffroy de Saint-Hilaire.

On his return to Edinburgh, he established a school of anatomy and was soon recognized as one of the outstanding British authorities. Then, in 1828, his chance of continuing an orthodox scientific career was destroyed. At that time there were no regular legal channels for obtaining anatomical specimens, and it was the usual practice of anatomists to purchase them from grave robbers. William Burke and William Hare who supplied Knox, however, were discovered to have used more direct methods. Knox was not personally implicated in the murders, but the scandal ruined both his school and his reputation. Barred from professional work, he became a popular lecturer on scientific subjects and was forced to live by his pen rather than his practice.[33]

The nature of his new audience had an important influence on the style and content of Knox's later writing. His *Races of Man* was first presented in lecture form in 1846, and the published version retained the oratorical style of the lecture platform. Knox also leaned slightly toward charlatanism, ready and able to serve the ordinary man's desire to know the full implications of the new biology. He called his system "transcendental anatomy," implying a rather nebulous extension beyond the range of empirical data. His conclusions were presented without qualification, without question, and without solid evidence. In this way he reached a wider audience than most scientists could hope to reach, and his work was also accepted by some other scientists. Darwin, for example, was to cite from it with approval.

Knox left no doubt about the key to understanding human affairs: "Race is everything: literature, science, art—in a word, civilization depends on it."[34] On account of his rambling style, it was not always precisely clear how the influence of race made itself felt, but the

33. H. Lonsdale, *A Sketch of the Life and Writings of Robert Knox, the Anatomist* (London, 1870) is the only biography, written partly to clear Knox's name of the continuing scandal.

34. Knox, *Races of Man*, v.

history of the world was seen as an evolutionary struggle between races—especially between the light and the dark races. The dark-skinned peoples were supposed to have developed first in the course of human evolution, but having reached their maximum achievement they had become stagnant. The later, light-skinned peoples were destined to achieve much more, and in the course of their achievement they would wage a war to the death against the rest, until the dark races became extinct.

According to Knox, the factor of race was crucial within Europe as well. The people of the great race were, for him the "Saxons." The Semites were not even considered to be members of the white race, and the Greeks and Italians were "weak races" whose achievements in the classical world must have come from race mixture with the "Celtic, Gothic, and Saxon." The *Pax Romana* had, furthermore, brought peace to Europe at the price of stultifying the struggle of the races, which alone was the source of human creativity. It was only after Rome fell that the Europeans were able to resume their antagonisms and advance on the road to progress.[35]

These ideas in milder form were already common, but Knox's treatment of race and empire was more original. He conceded a very important role to climatic environment. Europeans could flourish only in Europe. Overseas, the power of Europe could only be sustained by constant immigration or by the kind of military dominance Britain maintained in India. "A *real native* permanent American, or Australian race of pure Saxon blood, is a dream which can never be realized."[36] The future of the Europeans in the tropical world was still more in doubt. Knox was fully aware that the aborigines might well die out in America and Australia, but the Europeans died in Africa. The natural enemy was therefore the race that could survive. "Look at the Negro, so well known to you, and say, need I describe him? Is he shaped like any white person? Is the anatomy of his frame, of his muscles, or organs like ours? Does he walk like us, think like us, act like us? Not in the least. What an innate hatred the Saxon has for him and how I have laughed at the mock philanthropy of England! . . . and yet this despised race drove the warlike French from St. Domingo, and the issue of the struggle with them in Jamaica might be doubtful."[37]

35. Knox, *Races of Man*. The theory as a whole is summarized on pp. 588–600.
36. Knox, *Races of Man*, p. 51.
37. Knox, *Races of Man*, pp. 243–44.

Here was a new note in British racial thought. Earlier generations had sometimes despised the Africans, sometimes pitied them, but never feared them. Yet, for Knox: "If there be a dark race destined to contend with the fair races of man for a portion of the earth, given to man as an inheritance, it is the Negro. The tropical regions of the earth seem peculiarly to belong to him; his energy is considerable: aided by the tropical sun, he repels the white invader. From St. Domingo he drove out the Celt; from Jamaica he will expel the Saxon; and the expulsion of the Lusitanian from Brazil, by the Negro, is merely a matter of time."[38]

Nor was the African threat merely the Negro ability to survive in the tropics. Knox had served in South Africa at a period when a European victory in the frontier wars was not quite a foregone conclusion. Perhaps for this reason, he stressed the military power of the African race, a threat that was the more serious because the Africans were, in his opinion, innately incapable of attaining "civilization." His policy for the West Indies—suggested in hyperbole—was to expel the fierce Negroes and bring in more docile and feeble Chinese and Indians: "Over these the Saxon and Celt might lord it, as we do in India, with a few European bayonets, levying taxes and land-rent; holding a monopoly of trade; furnishing them with salt at fifty times its value; but we cannot do this with the true Negro."[39]

As for the future of Africa itself, Knox left the question open— but with the suggestion that the Africans might well be able to defend themselves indefinitely on their home ground.

Knox's voice was clearly that of a minority, and he carried the idea of race struggle further even than his fellow racists; but he was not alone. The older, non-evolutionary variant of the racial myth was also gaining strength during the 1840's. Only a year before *The Races of Man,* Thomas Carlyle had published his "Occasional Discourse on the Nigger Question" in *Fraser's Magazine.* Carlyle's special concern was the West Indies, and his racism was teleological rather than evolutionary. For him, Africans were not inferior merely by chance or for the time being. They had been created inferior *in order* to serve their European masters: "That, you may depend on it, my obscure Black friends, is and was always the Law of the World, for you and for all men: To *be* servants, the more foolish of us to

38. Knox, *Races of Man,* p. 456.
39. Knox, *Races of Man,* p. 268. See also p. 246.

the more wise; and only sorrow, futility and disappointment will betide both, till both in some approximate degree get to conform to the same."[40]

Carlyle's point of view represented the heart of the pro-slavery racism found in the American South and other slave-holding societies, but Knox's evolutionary racism gained popularity through the 1850's. When Disraeli argued in 1852 against the wisdom of having emancipated the West Indian slaves, he did so in Knoxian terms: "In the structure, the decay, and the development of the various families of man, the vicissitudes of history find their main solution. All is race."[41]

Eighteen fifty-four was the great year for racist publications. Nott and Gliddon accepted Knox and proclaimed that human progress came from a "war of races." Bulwer Lytton, later to become Secretary of State for Colonies, presented his own racial interpretation of history. In France, Count de Gobineau began publication of his *Essai sur l'inégalité des races humaines,* the most famous and perhaps the most influential of all racist works in the nineteenth century, and de Gobineau based his theory solidly on the groundwork laid during the previous decade—on Knox, Morton, and Carus.[42]

The impact of these theorists was already felt outside the scientific circle immediately concerned with raciology. The change was especially marked in the prominent literary reviews. The *Edinburgh Review,* with a long liberal and anti-slavery record, attacked Earl Grey's colonial policy in 1853 on grounds that Grey had disregarded innate racial differences. The reviewer rested his case on Knox's ideas and on an extreme belief in the inevitability of aboriginal extinction. A year later another reviewer repeated Knox's special fear that the Africans, alone of the "dark races," would avoid their "natural fate" and defy European power. The *Westminster* praised the work of Nott and Gliddon and hailed Knox's *Races of Man* as a "singular work" which "explains much heretofore most obscure." By the later 1850's, Heinrich Barth, the least prejudiced, least culture bound of all the travellers to Africa accepted the teachings of European "sci-

40. [T. Carlyle], "Occasional Discourse on the Nigger Question," *Fraser's Magazine,* XL, 670–79 (December, 1849), p. 677.
41. B. Disraeli, *Lord George Bentinck: A Political Biography,* 10th ed. (London, 1881), p. 239. See also p. 234.
42. J. C. Nott and G. R. Gliddon, *Types of Mankind* (London, 1854), p. 53; E. Bulwer Lytton, Speech to the Leeds Mechanics Institute, 25 January 1854, in *Speeches of Edward Lord Lytton,* 2 vols. (London, 1874), I, 172–89; Arthur, Comte de Gobineau, *Essai sur l'inégalité des races humaines,* 4 vols. (Paris, 1853–55).

ence"—that language was a racial trait, and race was an important determinant of African culture. Even so, the acceptance of racism was not universal. The Ethnological Society still held out for potential equality and condemned the religious unorthodoxy of Nott and Gliddon. An important shift in scientific opinion had nevertheless begun.[43]

Much of this shift was in the realm of general theory rather than specific attitudes toward Africans. It is much more difficult to gauge the opinions of the small and often tacit group of Europeans who either served in West Africa or had an important role in forming West African policy. It is, however, clear that the most ferocious racist opinion came either from white West Indians, whose experience was formed in a slave-holding society, or else from theorists whose actual contact with Africans was very small. The general pattern of racist opinion was, in short, very nearly what it had been since the later eighteenth century. Just as the slave dealers of the earlier period had inclined to think of Africans as men like themselves, the new generation of legitimate traders and colonial officials were more liberal than the English at home. Sir George Stephen noticed this fact in 1849. While he recognized that there was a good deal of anti-Negro sentiment among "good society" in Britain, "yet men whom business or colonial connection has brought into familiar intercourse with the black or coloured races, know well that the educated among them are not inferior to whites in any of those qualities which acquire esteem for the gentleman or confidence for the merchant."[44]

Dr. Madden's investigation of 1841 provides a modicum of quantitative evidence in support of this generalization. Among the questions addressed to medical and administrative officers, one read: "Is there any peculiarity in . . . [the Africans'] . . . physical structure that would justify the opinion of their being a distinct, or of their mental capacity that would justify their being considered an inferior race?"

Of the nine clear answers, only two held the Africans to be inherently inferior. Two, including George Maclean, the President of the Gold Coast Council, gave the opinion of present inferiority, but

43. *Edinburgh Review,* XCVIII, 79–80 and 95 (July 1853), and C, 199 (July 1854); *Westminster Review,* LXV, 199–204, 209 (1856); H. Barth, "A General Historical Description of the State of Human Society in Northern Central Africa," *Journal of the Royal Geographical Society,* XXX, 112–28 (1860); Cull, "On Recent Progress in Ethnology."

44. Sir George Stephen, *The Niger Trade Considered in Connexion with the African Blockade* (London, 1849), pp. 63–64.

potential equality. The other five answered in favor of equality.[45] A second series of questions on the learning ability of African children was put to a group of nine, mainly missionaries and teachers. Of those answering, only Maclean held that Africans had less learning capacity than white children would have done in similar circumstances.[46]

While Madden's survey cannot be taken seriously as an opinion questionnaire of unquestioned reliability, its results are generally consonant with the impression given by other West African reports. There was plenty of cultural arrogance on the Coast, plenty of plain xenophobia about Africa and the Africans, but relatively little serious racism of the kind expressed by a theorist like Knox. The balance of opinion on the Coast appears to have become gradually less sanguine about the racial status of the Africans, but the change in attitude came very slowly in comparison with the more rapid rise of racism at home. It was only in the 1850's and later that a new generation of officials began to arrive, already imbued with the new fashion of theoretical racism.

In Britain itself, the vast majority of the educated public appears to have accepted at least some aspects of the new racial doctrine, if only as a vague feeling that science supported the common xenophobic prejudice. The range of European opinion, however, was very much wider than the range of opinion among Europeans in Africa. Coastal opinion was kept more uniform by the fact that all observers had a common experience in dealing with Africans. By contrast, few Europeans in Europe had intimate contact with African visitors. There was plenty of room for imagination or theoretical belief to distort whatever empirical information they might have. A single individual might combine several diverse images of "the African." De Gobineau, for example, described the general character of the Africa race in terms more malevolent than the most vitriolic of the reports from Africa. Yet at other times he recognized that individual Africans deviated widely from his own stereotype. "A good number

45. PP, 1842, xii (551), pp. 99, 101, 104, 106, 111, 118, 223, 354, 356, and 359.
46. PP, 1842, xii (551), pp. 88–89, 90–96, 219–20, 342, 345–46, and 348–50. Neither group of answers is large enough to be a statistically valid sample, but the first set seems to have included most of the medical men on the Coast, while the second included the leading missionaries of all denominations. Thus the results have more validity than the small size of the sample would indicate. On the other hand, Madden was far from being an impartial investigator, and the published results of his questionnaire may reflect his own anti-racist point of view. The original questionnaires and answers are to be found in CO 267/171, 172, and 173.

of black chiefs surpass, in the force and abundance of their ideas, in the power of their minds, and in the intensity of their active faculties, the common level which our peasants, or even our bourgeois of ordinary education and endowment, can attain."[47]

One tendency of British thought was especially marked. As scholars began to use racial explanations for all sorts of social phenomena, less sophisticated commentators also introduced the factor of race. In the days of the Sierra Leone Company, the Africans or the Nova Scotians had served as a useful scapegoat when things went wrong in Africa. Later on, the alleged racial traits of the "natives" made it even easier to blame them for European failures. This tendency often carried commonplace British attitudes through curious and irrational channels. By the 1840's or 1850's, for example, all rational assessments of the British failures on the Coast picked the "climate" as the single factor most seriously limiting any and all European activity. At another and less conscious level of analysis, a subtle shift took place. The missionary image of African savagery was set in the public mind, and the opposition of a fierce people was added to that of a fierce "climate."[48] This tendency appeared especially in the retrospective assessment of the Niger failure. After a decade, the public had forgotten the details and remembered only that something had gone wrong. If, after such expense and sacrifice, the Africans were not civilized, it was easy to assume they were uncivilizable.[49]

A similar tendency to implicate the Africans ran as a minor strand through the British debate about the failure of the anti-slave-trade blockade. In the later 1840's it occurred again to explain the "failure" of West Indian slave emancipation. The ruin of the West Indian plantations was loudly proclaimed after 1846, partly because of a change in the British sugar duties and partly because of a general financial panic in 1847. The true cause of the crisis was not well understood at the time, and it was too complex for easy popular explanation; but everyone "knew" that Negroes were inherently lazy, and it was simple enough to blame the ex-slaves. In this atmosphere,

47. Arthur, Comte de Gobineau, *Essai sur l'inégalité des races humaines*, 2nd ed., 2 vols. (Paris, 1884), I, 214–15, 185–86.

48. See, for example: A. B. B., "Introduction," to R. and J. Lander, *Journal of an Expedition to Explore the Course and Termination of the Niger . . .* , 2 vols. (New York, 1858).

49. For a contemporaneous discussion of the psychology of this transfer from climate to people, see B. Cruickshank, *Eighteen Years on the Gold Coast of Africa, Including an Account of the Native Tribes, and Their Intercourse with Europeans*, 2 vols. (London, 1853), I, 8.

Disraeli suggested that slavery might well be reimposed, and Carlyle's "Nigger Question" gave a plausible racist solution to the whole problem.[50]

The Africans nevertheless had their champions after the 1830's, but the defense was gradually weakening. The old magic of the anti-slavery cause no longer brought an automatic emotional response. For one thing, the humanitarians had promised too much, too soon: as 1850 approached, the West Indies were not prosperous, and West Africa was not "civilized." Newer causes were more exciting. A generation whose parents had been roused to erase the evil of the slave trade, was stirred in its turn by the new hope for perpetual peace through free trade. The immense effort required in 1850 to muster a Parliamentary majority merely to preserve the anti-slavery squadron was symptomatic of the general trend of opinion.[51]

The case presented by the pro-African writers was also intellectually weak—no weaker, perhaps, than it had been in the past, but less convincing in the new intellectual atmosphere of the 1840's or 1850's. The strongest argument, for the humanitarians themselves, was that of religion, and Richard Watson's classic statement of 1824 was reprinted and paraphrased for decades afterward. But Watson was explicitly opposed to science and its teachings. As the prestige of science increased—as the old Evangelical fervor dwindled away into mere Victorian respectability—a strict interpretation of the Bible no longer carried the weight it once had done.

Humanitarian writers were also trapped by their own dislike of African culture as it was, and by their prejudice in favor of their own physical type. An occasional humanitarian traveller might admit that Africans could be, in their own way, as handsome as Europeans, but the view was rare.[52] Many works, overtly in defense of the Africans, gave way to cultural or racial prejudice on almost every point short of the minimum claims of "spiritual equality."[53] Edward Binns, for example, attacked African culture in terms as violent as those of the

50. B. Disraeli, Commons, 28 July 1846, 3 H 88, cc. 165–66.
51. See Thomas, Lord Denman, *Uncle Tom's Cabin, Bleak House, Slavery and Slave Trade* (London, 1853), p. 8.
52. See, for example, F. H. Rankin, *The White Man's Grave: A Visit to Sierra Leone in 1834*, 2 vols. (London, 1836), II, 50–52.
53. See, for example, B. L., "Sierra Leone," *Westminster Review*, XXV, 176–77 (July 1836); W. B. K., "On the Varieties of the Human Race," *The Colonial Magazine*, IV, 83–87, 179–88, 360–69, 484–91 and V, 37 (January–May, 1841), p. 86; W. and R. Chambers (Eds.), "Intelligent Negroes," *Chambers's Miscellany of Useful and Entertaining Tracts*, Vol. VII (Edinburgh, 1845), p. 32; C. P. W., *The Natives of Africa* (London, [1853]), p. 7.

racists. He believed that most Africans were cannibals, and he characterized "the African" as "suspicious, fickle, fierce, libidinous, cruel,
cunning, treacherous, blood-thirsty, in his uncivilized state."[54] Binns
gave away another argument to the pseudo-scientists by adopting
phrenology and trying to prove by its techniques that Africans were
fully equal to whites in their natural abilities.[55]

The defenders of the Africans were, in fact, almost always inept
in discussing the "scientific" aspects of race. They used literary authority much more effectively. Blumenbach's list of "noble Negroes,"
as extended by Abbé Grégoire, continued to grow until it reached
its apogee in Wilson Armistead's *Tribute to the Negro* (1848).
Armistead's proofs of Negro equality ran to more than five hundred
close-packed pages, and he soon replaced Grégoire as the standard
mine for pro-Negro arguments. By 1856, Edward Blyden of Liberia
was using the list of "noble Negroes" to answer the racists of Europe.[56] But even here there was a weakness, which Carus and then
Gobineau were quick to point out. The list of "noble Negroes" was
made up almost entirely of Africans who had made good in the West
or under a very strong influence from Western culture. It was, indeed,
originally drawn up to prove that Africans could attain "civilization."
Now the racists pointed out that it merely proved Africans were inferior, since it showed they had the ability to imitate but not the creative drive to make a civilization of their own.[57] On this point, as on
many others, the cultural chauvinism of the pro-Negro group rebounded to the aid of racism.

The crucial weakness of the anti-racist case in the early nineteenth
century was the failure to distinguish between race and culture. It not
only weakened the public arguments of those who wished to stem the
rising tide of racism; it also led serious scholars of good will into an
acceptance of racial doctrines. Prichard's attempt (and ultimate failure) to defend the racial equality of mankind through the theory

54. Edward Binns, "Prodromus Toward a Philosophical Inquiry into the Intellectual
Powers of the Negro," *Simmonds's Colonial Magazine*, I, 464–70 and II, 48–59, 154–
84 (April–July, 1844), I, 467.
55. Binns, "Intellectual Powers of the Negro," II, 159–60, 183–84.
56. For lists or biographies of eminent Negroes, published in this period, see:
Binns, "Intellectual Powers of the Negro," II, 48–59; Chambers, "Intelligent Negroes;"
W. Armistead, *A Tribute to the Negro* (Manchester, 1848), p. 120–43 and 191–564;
H. G. Adams, *God's Image in Ebony* (London, 1854); E. W. Blyden, *A Voice from
Bleeding Africa* (Liberia, 1856).
57. Gobineau, *L'inégalité des races* (1884), I, 74.

of monogenesis illustrates the way this crucial error led nineteenth-century science into the racist myth. Prichard admitted, to begin with, that African culture was a barbarism to be deplored. He also accepted the supposition of other ethnologists that race and culture were intimately connected. On the basis of these two assumptions, the Africans were necessarily regarded as an inferior race—at present. Prichard tried to save the Christian tradition of racial equality by adding a time element. The equality of all races existed, but it was potential, not actual. That was enough, if one accepted Prichard's assumption that physical characteristics would change rapidly with a change in culture.[58] On this specific point, he was not only wrong in the light of modern anthropology; the error could be demonstrated before his own death. Morton showed in 1844 that the Egyptian skeletons associated with the earliest phases of Egyptian civilization were physically like those of modern men. Hence: "The physical or organic characters which distinguish the several races of man, are as old as the oldest records of our species."[59] Morton's data were, of course, correct, though neither he nor Prichard understood that the "oldest records of our species" were very new indeed measured against the scale of time usually needed to produce a radical change of racial type. Nevertheless, any scientist who accepted Prichard's assumptions and Morton's data would have to conclude that the African peoples were not only inferior at present. They were permanently so. The intellectual foundation of racial egalitarianism was thus destroyed, and it was not to be recovered until scientists could start over again with new assumptions.

In spite of this erosion of its basic ideology, humanitarianism was still the philosophy in office throughout the 1840's. Both the ideology and the political influence of the humanitarians were secure at least until the end of the Russell Government in 1852. The rise of the new pseudo-scientific racism, however, pointed to a new frame of thought that was to dominate the second half of the century. Meanwhile, there was merely a crack in the pre-Darwinian world view. The forms and meanings of African life were still investigated, and the British plans for the future of Africa were still laid, in the light of the older tradition.

58. J. C. Prichard, *Researches into the Physical History of Man,* 4th ed., 5 vols. (London, 1851), II, 340–46; Prichard, *Natural History of Man* (1855), I, 97–101.
59. Morton, *Crania Aegyptiaca,* p. 66.

16

LANGUAGE, CULTURE,

AND

HISTORY

The literary tradition in African studies altered slowly as the mid-century approached, with nothing in the offing comparable to the Darwinian revolution which hung over biological sciences. If any revolutionary change had taken place, it was the eighteenth-century shift from an emphasis on static analysis of society to the nineteenth-century emphasis on historical or evolutionary analysis.[1] This new attitude, however, was firmly in office by the 1830's, when the great works of Von Ranke, Michelet, and Macaulay began to appear. It gained some further impetus from the romantic movement of the early nineteenth century, but that was all.

Genuine innovation in the social studies, however, continued at another point, where historical knowledge and analysis could be linked with data not commonly taken into account by historians. The racists from Edwards through Knox and Gobineau brought physical anthropology into historical explanations. Karl Marx joined history and classical economics. Gustav Klemm combined history and eth-

1. A. O. Lovejoy, *The Great Chain of Being* (Cambridge, Mass., 1936), pp. 242–87.

nography in a more thorough and detailed presentation than had
been common in the past, but, for all his talk of the need to create a
"culture history" and study mankind's changing way of life, rather
than the deeds of kings, his basic assumptions were those of the eighteenth-century moral philosophers. Klemm looked, as they had done,
for the earliest stages of man, frozen, as it were, in the present-day
life of the Eskimos or South American Indians.

Klemm's work and that of other historical ethnographers nevertheless brought about a slightly different attitude toward the data
about African culture. The examples from Africa were more detailed
than ever before, and Klemm used Ashanti for a case study of the
"second stage" of human development. The general assessment of
cultural stages also began to change in small ways. Where the common belief of the early nineteenth century had set pastoralism at a
second stage, above mere hunting and below sedentary agriculture,
Klemm and some of his contemporaries tended to promote it to a
place one stage higher than agriculture. The exact reason for the
change was rarely explicit, but it was clearly associated with admiration for the military strength of mounted warriors, and seems to have
gained something from the social superiority of European cavalry. In
any event, it raised the status of certain African cultures, such as the
pastoral southern Bantu or the Fulbe of West Africa. Even the sedentary African cultures were now more clearly marked out at a level
superior to the American Indians or Polynesians, the most admired of
the eighteenth-century "noble savages."[2] But these small alterations
in assigned status were a minor matter. For most Europeans, all "barbarous" societies were seen across a widening gap from the civilization of Europe, even though Europeans were more willing than before to extend the scope of their studies to the far side of the cultural gulf and take greater account of the "primitive" condition of
man.

The new histories and discussions of early man raised some new
problems and exposed old problems which had been passed over. One
point of increasing interest was an implicit conflict with the Christian
tradition: even non-scientific histories of culture could have some
dangerous implications. According to the usual understanding of

2. G. Klemm, *Allegemeine Cultur-Geschichte der Menschheit,* 10 parts (Leipzig,
1843–1852), esp. I, 20–23. See also H. Merivale, *Lectures on Colonisation and
Colonies,* 2 vols. (London, 1841–1842), II, 155–57; *The Colonial Intelligencer,* II,
132–33 (1848).

Genesis, Adam and Eve had not been savages. They were thought of as endowed from the beginning with a reasonably "advanced" culture. The new picture of mankind advancing only very slowly during centuries of cultural evolution could not be squared with the common opinion. The usual impression was, indeed, based on conjecture rather than scripture—the Bible has very little ethnographic information about the Garden of Eden—but it was firmly believed.

Another point of difficulty was the question of cultural diffusion or independent invention. The assumption that human society advances toward civilization through a fixed progression of stages might be taken to imply that all stages were necessary—even that each society must invent by itself all the techniques required for advance from one stage to the next. Traditional Christian historiography had rarely dealt explicitly with the problem—had not even been especially conscious that it was a problem—but Christian writers took for granted the fact that "religious truth" was one cultural trait which had diffused from a single center. By implication, they had often assumed that all cultural change was the product of similar diffusion.

These problems and their implications for Africa were taken up in 1844 by the Reverend D. J. East. He accepted the idea of stages in human progress. This idea was, in fact, implicit in the Biblical story and in most of the Christian historical tradition. The creation, the fall of Adam, the coming of Christ, and the Last Judgment are all marks along a road of spiritual progress. But East was also an uncompromising diffusionist. For him, the first stage of progress was merely that period when religious truth had been the sole possession of the family of Abraham. In a second stage, the Greek philosophers gained some elements of truth through natural reason. The third stage began when "the Everlasting Word was made flesh" through the coming of Christ. At this point the completed message was available for general diffusion to all mankind, and mankind could not pass on to the fourth stage until all had heard it. When this had happened, history would enter a higher stage. Christian conduct would be perfected on earth, and the agents of this perfection would be the Africans, who, as natural Christians, would teach Christian humility to the Asians and Europeans, until at last the world would know peace and Christian unity.[3]

3. D. J. East, *Western Africa; Its Condition, and Christianity the Means of its Recovery* (London, 1844), pp. 107–8.

Other Christian writers chose to meet the threat of new and unorthodox theories of society and history in other ways. One of the most elaborate defenses was William Cooke Taylor's *Natural History of Society,* published in 1841. He denied that man could have evolved, either physically from the apes, as Lamarck had suggested, or culturally from savagery, as the moral philosophers claimed. He denied, furthermore, that man in the savage state was innocent and good, and had later become evil—a view he attributed to Rousseau. He denied the whole of the racist doctrine and concluded, "that the capacity of becoming civilized belongs to the whole human race—that civilization is natural to man—that barbarism is not 'a state of nature,' and that there is no *prima facie* evidence for assuming it to be the original condition of man."[4]

For Taylor, man had originally been endowed by God with a knowledge of both agriculture and mineralogy. But the world had changed since then. Some men had slipped downward into barbarism (and here Taylor reintroduced the strain of pessimism so common in early Christian historiography), while others had known progress. Thus the idea of progress could be retained, and Taylor went further and proclaimed progress in social life as the dominant mark of "civilization." It was an ingenious theory, since it retained the nineteenth-century feeling of cultural superiority over the "degraded" part of mankind, while denying both racism and the usual view of historical evolution. The condition he assigned to savages and barbarians, moreover, was no better than that ascribed to them by the racist writers. They were considered physically weak, unable to visualize mentally what was not physically present, unable to think in terms of means and ends, unable to count beyond a very few numbers—often no further than three.[5]

Other Christian commentators held similar opinions, but made a distinction between savages and barbarians. Rufus Anderson, an American missionary theorist, held that barbarians, like the East Indians, suffered mainly from "plenitude of error—the unrestrained accumulations and perversions of depraved intellect for three thousand years." Savages, on the other hand, had the opposite failing, "For, the savage has few ideas, sees only the objects just about him,

4. W. Cooke Taylor, *The Natural History of Society in the Barbarous and Civilized State: an Essay Towards Discovering the Origin and Course of Human Improvement,* 2 vols. (New York, 1841), I, 17–30. First edition London, 1840.
5. Taylor, *Natural History,* esp. I, 17–46 and 210–300.

perceives nothing of the relations of things, and occupies his thoughts only about his physical experiences and wants."[6]

Meanwhile, new data were accumulating, which might provide the basis for accepting or rejecting these broader theories. While the contribution of general ethnography was slight, linguistic research pushed rapidly forward from the 1830's onward, supported by the dual need of ethnologists, with their emphasis on linguistic traits, and missionaries, with their need to know African languages in order to reach the Africans. So many vocabularies were available by 1840 that Edwin Norris was able to compile a small multilingual dictionary for the use of the Niger Expedition. In it, he gave more than fifteen hundred English words, with their equivalents in Hausa, Ibo, Yoruba, Fulfulde (the language of the Fulani), Mandinka, Bambara, Fante, and Wolof.[7] It was not complete in all these languages, but it represented a continuation of the Senegal Company's earlier effort to prepare a multilingual dictionary of African languages.[8] By 1847, R. G. Latham had available some fourteen vocabularies of Akan languages, eleven of various Ibo dialects, and eight of Yoruba, among others.[9]

While these vocabularies were used with confidence—and often with too much confidence—by the linguists in Europe, they were nearly useless for missionary purposes. Comparative word lists, made hurriedly and without a uniform orthography, were far from a usable knowledge of a language. By 1840, the Church Missionary Society had come to realize that much of its earlier linguistic work would have to be scrapped and a new start made. Missionary societies now had enough field staff to allow specialized linguistic research, and European linguists were beginning to develop a distinct discipline and method. When Baron C. C. J. de Bunsen, himself a linguist, became Prussian Ambassador to London in 1841, he played a mediating role

6. Rufus Anderson, *The Theory of Missions to the Heathen* (Boston, 1845), p. 13.

7. E. Norris, *Outline of a Vocabulary of a Few of the Principal Languages of Western and Central Africa: Compiled for the use of the Niger Expedition* (London, 1841).

8. This work contained about two thousand words in the seven most important languages of the Senegambia. It was published in: *Mémoires de la Société Ethnologique*, II (2), 205–67 (1845).

9. R. G. Latham, "On the Present State and Recent Progress of Ethnographical Philology," *Reports of the British Association for the Advancement of Science*, XVII, 154–229 (1847). As a guide to linguistic material available at this time, see: J. S. Vater, *Litteratur der Grammatiken, Lexika und Wörtersammlungen aller Sprachen der Erde*, 2nd ed. (Berlin, 1847); revised and enlarged by B. Jülg. See also R. N. Cust, *A Sketch of the Modern Languages of Africa*, 2 vols. (London, 1883), I, 23–38.

between the new school of scientific linguistics in Germany and the practical needs of the English missionary societies. It was through his efforts that the CMS introduced a uniform orthography in 1848, and they changed it again in 1854 to conform to the more modern system of K. R. Lepsius from Berlin.

Anglo-German missionary cooperation in Africa was already an established tradition, and the CMS in particular employed German trained linguists. The Reverend J. F. Schön accompanied the Niger Expedition and worked with Ibo and Hausa. His successor, S. W. Koelle, became a full-time linguist attached to the CMS staff in Sierra Leone, where he studied Vai and Kanuri. Other missionaries in Sierra Leone worked with Bullom, Susu, Sherbro, and Temne; and the studies of Yoruba published by the Reverend Samuel Crowther were the first in English by an African scholar studying an African language. Other missionary societies took up the languages appropriate to their own work, such as Efik studies by the Presbyterians in Calabar, and Akan studies by Basel missionaries and Wesleyans on the Gold Coast.[10]

The high point of these missionary linguistic studies was Koelle's *Polyglotta Africana,* the first really trustworthy comparative vocabulary of African languages. From his base in Sierra Leone, Koelle collected the equivalents of about 300 words and phrases in 160 different African languages. His informants were mainly liberated Africans, but he carefully recorded the length of their absence from their home country and thus established a standard of reliability. Koelle feared that the work would suffer from the fact that it was purely lexical, but it was an important step forward. With all languages in the collection recorded by a single trained observer, using a single system of orthography, vocabulary comparisons could be made on a sound basis.[11]

West African languages posed a special problem for linguists in Europe, who tried to depend on data gathered by other people. Most of these languages are tonal, a fact which Europeans were slow both to recognize and to record. Even those who recognized the importance

10. J. F. Ade Ajayi, "Christian Missions and the Making of Nigeria 1841–1891," (Unpublished Ph.D. thesis, London, 1958), pp. 302ff.; H. Halleur, *A.B.C. darium der Ashanti-Sprache* (Basel, 1845); R. Brookings, *Nucleus of a Grammar of the Fanti Language: With a Vocabulary* (London, 1843).

11. S. W. Koelle, *Polyglotta Africana, or a Comparative Vocabulary of Nearly 300 Words and Phrases in more than 100 Distinct African Languages* (London, 1854).

of tonal variations had no easy way of describing them to a European audience. The Reverend J. Raban could only note in his Yoruba vocabulary of 1831 that certain words were "uttered with a depressed voice," though Samuel Crowther distinguished the three Yoruba tones in his vocabulary of 1843. The discovery of tonality in other languages was much slower. Riis devoted more than one hundred pages to a grammatical analysis of Twi without any obvious recognition of tone; and Koelle made no attempt to indicate tone in the *Polyglotta Africana,* though he was conscious that some of the languages included were tonal.[12]

It is clear that many of the pejorative judgments of African languages throughout the nineteenth century were based on an ignorance of tonal differences. Where the grammatical context or even the meaning of a word depended on tone, the Europeans were quick to assume that the language was "primitive," because it seemed to them to lack grammatical regularity.

However weak their empirical base in African languages, linguistic studies in Europe were developing along the lines already taken by anthropology. One effort was to arrange languages on an absolute scale of value, not unlike the Great Chain of Being. In another direction, linguists were trying to arrive at an evolutionary theory of language. A third effort was to discover the familial relations between similar languages, showing, for example, whether related languages were parent and offspring or collateral descendants from a common ancestor language.

The influence of biological thought is obvious. Even a humanitarian like Thomas Hodgkin believed that a "natural history of language" would be found to parallel the "natural history of man." Hodgkin accepted language as a genuine racial trait—believing that men of one race were physically unable to pronounce correctly the words used by another. Some of the pseudo-scientific racists went much further. Guenebault tried a kind of phonetic phrenology, arguing that people who could not pronounce the sound of the letter "R" were "pusillanimous," while those who used this sound frequently were brave. For Gobineau, linguistic theory and racial theory were identi-

12. J. Raban, *Vocabulary of Eyo, or Aku, a Dialect of Western Africa,* 2 parts (London, 1831); S. Crowther, *Vocabulary of the Yoruba Language* (London, 1843), pp. 1–5; H. N. Riis, *Grammatical Outlines of the Oji Language, with Special Reference to the Akwapim Dialect together with a Collection of Proverbs* (Basel, 1854).

cal: "The hierarchy of language corresponds rigorously to the hierarchy of races."[13]

Even the theorists who opposed the new racism pictured an evolution of language following the same course as cultural evolution. Cooke Taylor, for example, sketched a theory of linguistic development parallel to his Christian view of culture history. In this view, God gave language to man in the Garden of Eden. After the fall of Adam, some languages had advanced, while others became degenerate. The degraded languages were thought to "err both in excess and defect." They had too many suffixes and affixes, too many synonyms, and yet too few objects or concepts for which there were any words at all. Baron de Bunsen took a similar view, presenting the linguistic aspect in much greater detail. For him, the original language was monosyllabic, like Chinese. It might degenerate, but, if it progressed, it passed through a series of stages. At a second and higher level, it would develop suffixes, affixes, and compound words. At the third and highest level, words would be inflected to show additional meanings and grammatical relations.[14]

It was against this background of developing theory that authorities on African languages passed their judgments. Since African languages were neither monosyllabic, nor yet so inflectional as Latin, they might be placed half-way up the ascending scale—and this would agree with the usual African place on the "scale of civilization." Latham and the most respected English authorities tended toward this view, but others disagreed. It was equally possible to place African languages on the descending scale. Guenebault, for example, believed African languages were "degenerate" and described them as they should have been in his theory—monosyllabic and, of course, without the "R" sound.[15]

13. T. Hodgkin, "On the Importance of Studying and Preserving the Languages Spoken by uncivilized Nations, with the View of Elucidating the Physical History of Man," *London and Edinburgh Philosophical Magazine*, VII, 27–36, 94–106 (July–August 1835) ; J. H. Guenebault, *The Natural History of the Negro Race* (Charleston, S.C., 1837); Arthur, Comte de Gobineau, *Essai sur l'inégalité des races humaines*, 2nd ed., 2 vols. (Paris, 1884), I, 187–214. Quotation from p. 213.

14. Cooke Taylor, *Natural History*, I, 37; C. C. J. de Bunsen, "On the Results of Recent Egyptian Researches in Reference to Asiatic and African Ethnology, and the Classification of Languages," *Reports of the British Association*, XVII, 254–99 (1847), pp. 265–90.

15. Latham, "Recent Progress of Ethnographical Philology," p. 217; Guenebault, *Natural History*, p. 34.

Still other authorities (often unconsciously) adopted Latin as the standard of linguistic perfection. The strongly tonal languages, which were also the most difficult for Europeans to learn, were thus placed lowest on the scale of value. Bantu languages were generally preferred, partly because they were less tonal and easier to learn, and partly because they were highly inflected. Hausa was also esteemed, for similar reasons. Schön, the first Hausa scholar, became the founder of a pro-Hausa tradition which was to have a long history.[16] Given these attitudes, it was only natural that some of the missionary linguists who prepared the first grammars should try to "improve" the African languages, bringing them closer to the "laws of construction," meaning the rules of Latin grammar.[17]

In other respects, however, the linguistic reputation of the West Africans improved as a result of better knowledge. The belief that all African societies were non-literate was shaken in 1849 by the rediscovery of the Vai syllabary, which was well publicized by the discoverer, Lt. Forbes of the Navy. Koelle immediately set out from Sierra Leone to the Vai country (in present-day Liberia) to make a further study, and CMS had a set of Vai syllables cast in type for printing the language.[18]

Linguistic studies also led to a new appreciation of African literature. It was a common European myth that Africans had no memory of the past, no tradition, and no literature. As early as 1828, Baron Roger had published a selection of Wolof fables from Senegal, but oral literature was more frequently taken down and translated after 1840. Riis recorded 268 Twi proverbs and published them with a translation and commentary. Koelle prepared a book of Kanuri material, including proverbs, fables, stories, and historical accounts, mainly to serve as an introductory reader for missionary students

16. J. F. Schön in *Journals of the Rev. James Frederick Schön and Mr. Samuel Crowther, who with the Sanction of Her Majesty's Government Accompanied the Expedition up the Niger in 1841* (London, 1842), pp. 119–20; J. L. Wilson, "Comparative Vocabularies of Some of the Principal Negro Dialects of Africa," *Journal of the American Oriental Society*, I, 317–82 (New York, 1851); J. L. Wilson, *Western Africa: Its History, Condition, and Prospects* (New York, 1856), pp. 455 and 457–61.

17. R. M. Macbriar, *Mandingo Grammar* (London, 1837), p. vi.

18. F. E. Forbes, *Dahomey and the Dahomans*, 2 vols. (London, 1851), I, 196; S. W. Koelle, *Outlines of a Grammar of the Vei Language* (London, 1854), pp. 1–8; S. W. Koelle, *Narrative of an Expedition into the Vy Country of West Africa* (London, 1849). In fact, the Mum language of the Cameroons also had a system of notation, and it was common to write several African languages in Arabic script. The independent invention of a system of notation was therefore as unnecessary in much of Africa as it was for Europe itself.

of the language. O. E. Vidal studied Yoruba proverbs, both as a form of literature to be appreciated for its esthetic merit and for the sake of understanding the Yoruba system of values. French researchers in Algeria also began to throw some light on the Arabic literature of the Western Sudan. Cherbonneau published a brief account of Ahmad Baba and sixteen other literary figures from Timbuctu. These authors who appreciated African literature also tried to counteract the dominant cultural arrogance of their time by showing that Africa had a cultural tradition of its own, and one worthy of notice. In this they failed. Their works were obscurely published, and the unfavorable image of African letters was already too firmly set in the public mind to be easily changed.[19]

The study of African language could also be used as one possible key to early African history, hence to an understanding of the way in which African culture came to be as it was. Relationships between different African languages were accepted as evidence about earlier contact between different African peoples, and linguistic relations between African and non-African languages were used to provide clues to historic relations between Africa and the outside world. Linguistic evidence had already been used for historical purposes in Europe, notably by ethnological historians like W. F. Edwards. Any attempt to reach similar conclusions about Africa, however, necessarily had to wait for an accurate classification of African languages.

A new attempt was possible wih the new data of the 1840's; but linquistic classification, like race classification, required accepted criteria, and no such criteria existed. The earliest classifications depended mainly on a superficial comparison of vocabularies, but the new scientific school of Grimm, Humboldt, Bopp, and de Bunsen, among others, demanded something more. They demanded systematic structural comparisons, being suspicious of chance analogy and the intrusion of loan-words. Even the new West African data were not sufficient to meet this standard. Classifiers therefore continued to rely on lexical affinities, even when, as in Koelle's case, the author realized

---

19. See J. Howison, *European Colonies in Various Parts of the World, Viewed in their Social, Moral, and Physical Conditions*, 2 vols. (London, 1834), I, 91–97 for the usual negative opinion. See also: Riis, *Grammatical Outlines*, pp. 110–36; S. W. Koelle, *African Native Literature* (London, 1854); O. E. Vidal, "Introductory Remarks," in S. Crowther, *Vocabulary of the Yòruba Language*, 2nd ed. (London, 1852), pp. 17–38; Baron Roger, *Fables sénégalaises, recueilliés de l'ouolof et mises en vers français* (Paris, 1828); A. Cherbonneau, "Essai sur la litterature arabe du Soudan," *Annuaire de la Société Archaeologique de Constantine*, II, 1–48 (1854–1855).

that this classification would be criticized.[20] Others were less careful. Prichard combined linguistic and racial characteristics, while Latham used analogies of grammatical structure at one point, and vocabulary at another.

Latham was, indeed, the most industrious of the English classifiers of West African languages. He published his original classification in 1844 and modified it later in 1846, 1847, 1850, and 1858. His underlying scheme consisted of a five-fold division, placing a large central African language group alongside Coptic, Hottentot, Berber, and "Kaffrarian" (meaning the group now called Bantu). In fact, his large central African group extended as far east as the Nile and beyond, and took in languages as diverse as Somali, Nubian, Hausa, and Dinka, grouping them with languages of the Guinea Coast and the Western Sudan. His sub-divisions within this larger division were more nearly accurate. He identified the large Mandingo group, the Akan languages, and picked out an Ibo-Ashanti sub-family, which approximately parallels the present-day Kwa sub-family, stretching from southern Sierra Leone along the coast through Western Nigeria.[21]

In later revisions, Latham altered this classification, sometimes toward greater accuracy and sometimes not. By 1846, he had come (quite correctly) to suspect an affinity between Coptic, Berber, and the Semitic languages. By 1847 he began to believe that all African languages might well be related to one another, and related to Semitic as well. He may someday be proven correct, but it was only a guess. Finally, in 1858, he become so confused between the lexical and structural forms of classification that he stopped classifying altogether. Instead, he insisted that African languages could not be put into language families. They stretched out as an indefinite series, each related to its neighbors, but in several different ways.

Both Koelle and Wilhelm Bleek drew up classifications of African languages based on a single criterion. For Bleek, it was grammatical

20. Bunsen, "Recent Egyptian Researches," p. 255; Koelle, *Polyglotta Africana,* p. iv.

21. R. G. Latham, "On the Ethnography of Africa as Determined by its Languages," *Reports of the British Association,* XIV, 79–80 (1844); "Contributions to the study of the Languages of Africa," *Proceedings of the Philological Society,* II, 218–22 (2 February 1846); "Recent Progress of Ethnographical Philology," pp. 222-29; *Natural History of the Varieties of Man* (London, 1850), pp. 471–86; "On Certain Classes in African Philology; Especially the Mandingo, Kouri, Nufi, and Fula Groups," *Transactions of the Philological Society for 1885,* pp. 107–22. Cf. J. H. Greenberg, *Studies in African Linguistic Classification* (New Haven, 1955).

structure; but his general scheme was no more accurate than Latham's had been, and he had little to say in detail about West African languages.[22] Koelle had the advantage of using lexical comparisons, for which there were more published data, and for which he could gather large quantities of data himself. Koelle, therefore, became the pioneer classifier of West African languages, laying the base on which others were to build, even though they were to modify much of his work.[23]

Koelle himself stayed clear of broad historical conclusions based on his linguistic data, but others were less cautious. As early as 1839, R. M. Macbriar, a Wesleyan missionary in the Gambia, believed he had discovered a linguistic relationship between Fulfulde and the Bantu languages. He concluded that neither the Fulbe nor the Bantu-speaking peoples were "true Negroes." They must therefore be related peoples who had entered Africa together and then separated, as the Fulbe moved off toward Cape Verde and the Bantu toward the Cape of Good Hope.[24] This suggestion was an early version of the "Hamite myth," by which later racist historians transformed the Bantu language group into a racial group with "Hamite blood" and thus distinct from the "true Negroes" of West Africa.

Somewhat later, the Rev. D. H. Schmid, working for CMS in Sierra Leone, believed he had found a similar connection between the neighboring and related languages of the Temne, Bullom, and Sherbro, and the Bantu family.[25] In 1855, Bleek, who had by then

22. W. H. I. Bleek, *De Nominum Generibus Linguarum Africae Australis, Copticae, Semiticarum Aliarumque Sexualium* (Bonn, 1851), esp. p. 59.

23. His work may be compared with the recent and authoritative classification of J. H. Greenberg. Koelle's "North-West Atlantic" language family is substantially the same as Greenberg's "West Atlantic" without Fulfulde and Wolof, which Koelle left unclassified. Greenberg's "Mandingo" compares with Koelle's "North-Western High-Sudan." Greenberg's "Kwa" is nearly the same as Koelle's "Upper-Guinea Languages," though Koelle left Ashanti unclassified and made the Nupe group and the Edo-Ibo group separate language families. Greenberg's "Gur" approximates Koelle's "North-Eastern High Sudan." Koelle left Hausa unclassified, with proper caution, since it is a distant relative of the Semitic languages. Kanuri and related languages, which Koelle called "Central African," became Greenberg's "Central Saharan."

Koelle placed all of the above language families in a larger West African group, separate from another major grouping of "South African" languages, recognized by initial inflection. He included in this grouping both the Bantu language family and the languages later called Semi-Bantu. It corresponds closely, therefore, to the group Greenberg calls the "Central Group" of the "Niger-Congo Language Family." (Koelle, *Polyglotta Africana*, pp. 1-13; Greenberg, *African Linguistic Classification*.)

24. R. M. Macbriar, *Sketches of a Missionary's Travels in Egypt, Syria, Western Africa, &c., &c.* (London, 1839), pp. 242-43.

25. *Church Missionary Intelligencer*, III, 115-20 (May, 1852).

conducted linguistic research on Fernando Po, combined the Schmid and Macbriar hypotheses and added Wolof and the Akan languages to the group supposed to have Bantu affinities. He concluded on linguistic grounds that all of these West African peoples must have migrated northward from the Cape and, indeed, that the cradle of African life must be in the country of the Xhosa and the Hottentots of the far south.[26] His underlying data contained a germ of truth. Most West African languages are now recognized as members of the same Niger-Congo language family to which the Bantu languages also belong. The probable direction of the migration, however, was from north to south, and not the reverse.

The broad historical theories of the professional linguists merged with those of non-professional commentators, who were still concerned with the problem of explaining the causes of African "barbarism." The older static forms of analysis were still important, but the balance was shifting toward historical explanations on one hand and racial explanations on the other. Humanitarians continued to prefer historical and diffusionist theories. If they could show that African culture had been formed by diffusion from centers in southwestern Asia, they could also show the possibility of more cultural diffusion from Europe. The elementary principle was expressed in the couplet:

> "Let *us* not the Negro Slave despise,
> *Just such our sires* appeared in Caesar's eyes."[27]

Travellers to West Africa continued to turn up evidence, both spurious and genuine, indicating an earlier contact with the east. In the light of culture theories suggesting possible "degeneration" from an earlier, higher stage of development, it was natural to interpret West African religion as a "corrupted" version of Zoroastrianism or a "degraded" form of the religion of ancient Egypt.[28]

The most elaborate new exposition of this kind came from Brodie

26. W. H. Bleek, "On the Languages of Western and Southern Africa," *Transactions of the Philological Society of London* (1855), pp. 40–50.

27. W. Armistead, *A Tribute to the Negro* (Manchester, 1848), p. 31. See also: T. Fowell Buxton, *The African Slave Trade,* 2nd ed. (Lodon, 1839), p. xiv; "On the Practicality of Civilizing Aboriginal Populations," *Ethnological Abstracts* (London, Spottiswoode, [1840?]).

28. W. Allen and T. R. H. Thomson, *A Narrative of the Expedition to the River Niger in 1841,* 2 vols. (London, 1848), II, 378–401; W. F. Daniell, *Sketches of the Medical Topography and Native Diseases of the Gulf of Guinea* (London, 1849), pp. 26–36, 90–91, and 99.

Cruickshank. He began with the basic assumption that all races of men are roughly equal in their abilities, but the human endowment includes original sin—"the corrupt tendency of the human heart, . . . to which white men and black are equally subject."[29] Therefore, all human societies contained both the seeds of progress and the seeds of degeneration. Cruickshank also held that acquired characteristics were heritable.[30] Therefore, progress would beget further progress, but the movement either upwards or downwards would be relatively slow and society at any stage would be relatively stable.

Cruickshank accepted the usual stages of progress—for those societies which had made progress. That is, they began as isolated hunting and gathering families, then moved to organized hunting in larger groups, then to agriculture, and so on. West African society had reached the agricultural stage, and it was not a pleasant state of society. At that stage the strong were able to subordinate the weak: "Physical strength we take to be the foundation of all power in a barbarous state, and injustice the foundation of all property."[31] But there were, for Cruickshank, limits set by a limited productivity. He held that inequalities of status, wealth, and power, are necessarily small in poor societies, since the whole society is too close to subsistence to support a real aristocracy.

But, for Cruickshank, a further question was crucial: had this stage been reached in Africa by independent development or by degeneration from a higher state of progress elsewhere? He found some evidence for either view. Degeneration was suggested by certain parallels between Gold Coast customs and those of ancient Egypt, though the Egyptian traits appeared to be "corrupted by the uncertain light of tradition." On the other hand, he recognized the possibility that the human mind might be nearly the same everywhere. In that case, even isolated societies might be expected to invent such traits independently as they entered the agricultural stage.[32] Cruickshank leaned toward the diffusionist position, but he left room for the other possibility.

He believed, in any event, that the agricultural stage in West

29. B. Cruickshank, *Eighteen Years on the Gold Coast of Africa, Including an Account of the Native Tribes, and Their Intercourse with Europeans*, 2 vols. (London, 1853), II, 2.

30. Cruickshank, *Eighteen Years*, II, 57–58.

31. Cruickshank, *Eighteen Years*, I, 291.

32. Cruickshank, *Eighteen Years*, I, 6–7; II, 256.

Africa had been reached at least some centuries before the birth of
Christ. From that time till the coming of the European slave trade in
the later fifteenth century, West African society had neither advanced toward a higher stage, nor had it regressed. The only significant historical change had been the introduction of the trans-
Sahara slave trade, and its principal influence south of the forest
had been to drive refugees down from the northern savannas and
force them to league together in stronger states like Ashanti.[33]

Maritime contact with the Europeans, however, had brought progressive debasement, caused by the slave trade. Cruickshank recognized that the Africans themselves lived in a slave-holding society,
but he also saw important differences between the African institution
and the plantation slavery of tropical America. He believed that
the nature of slavery changed with the different stages of human
progress. At the earliest stages, it was a natural labor system, but it
was also relatively mild. The lot of the slave was not very different
from that of his master. As society progressed, however, the position
of the slave became increasingly miserable. It reached its nadir with
the commercial stage. West Africa's misfortune was that Europeans,
having reached this stage, introduced the worst possible form of
slavery through the slave trade. With it came greed. It destroyed
the precarious hold of morality in African society, turning each man
and each tribe against his neighbor.[34] In the future, however, Cruickshank believed African society could turn upward again. With the
guidance of Christianity and new influences from Europe, it would
ultimately reach the same degree of civilization attainable by mankind anywhere.

Cruickshank's sketch of African history was a long step forward.
By discarding racial factors and crude environmentalism, he achieved
a point of departure essentially similar to that used by historians of
Africa a century later. His conclusions were based more on speculation than on evidence, but many of his hypotheses, dressed in the language of modern social science, would be tenable today. His basic social theory was the common coin of his time, but eighteen years of
experience in Africa allowed him to cut through the worst of the
cultural chauvinism. This combination of direct observation and a
thorough grounding in European social theory was very rare. Few of

33. Cruickshank, *Eighteen Years*, II, 298–99.
34. Cruickshank, *Eighteen Years*, II, 300–310.

Cruickshank's fellow merchants or government officials had either the education or inclination for scholarship, and scholars who stayed in Europe had to depend on data of uncertain validity.

Most commentators rested their explanations of Africa on the older forms of static analysis—when, indeed, they did not adopt a thoroughgoing racism. African "barbarism" was attributed to some combination of race, climate, and the slave trade. The commander of the Niger Expedition, for example, allowed for all three of these causes, with emphasis on the pernicious consequences of tropical exuberance. In spite of fifty-years' worth of new information about Africa, his contrast between the challenge of a hard climate and ease of life in Africa reads as though nothing had been learned since the 1770's.

With the negro . . . his climate superinduces a repugnance to exertion; he places his whole happiness in the idea of repose:—His necessities are few, and nature hardly requires solicitation to supply them, but heaps her treasures around in abundance, like trees in the Mahomedan Paradise, that require not the trouble of stretching forth the hand to pluck fruit from the bending branches. . . . The negro may therefore be characterized as having means of gratification exceeding his wants, and the white man as having wants exceeding such means of gratification as are supplied to him by nature.[35]

Even older forms of analysis were present on the fringes of European thought and comment. The ancient belief in a divine curse occasionally made an appearance. The standard version held that Africans had been cursed as the sons of Ham: this could be used to argue for permanent subordination to the Europeans. A missionary version held the curse to be only temporary: this could be used as a call for greater effort to spread the "reign of Christ" and cancel the ancient dispensation.[36] According to still another version, the Africans themselves believed they had been cursed by God, and they explained their own "inferiority" in this way.[37]

A newer line of suggestion followed from the high mortality of Europeans in Africa. One hypothesis explained the slave trade itself as the result of differential mortality. Europeans could not live as plantation managers in West Africa, but they could survive more successfully in the West Indies. Therefore they took African slaves to the West Indies, and Africa was barbarized while tropical America

35. Allen and Thomson, *A Narrative of the Expedition,* II, 420.
36. East, *Western Africa,* p. 2.
37. Howison, *European Colonies,* I, 152–53.

became rich.[38] According to another version, the principal influence of high mortality was to discourage trade and hence cultural diffusion. Thus African society had been forced to develop in isolation.[39]

The direct influence of the tropical climate still attracted some share of the blame, and in ways still derived from Montesquieu. Commissioner Madden endowed the Africans with all the usual "southern vices," and he pointed out an unnoticed implication. Sexuality was a southern trait, and sexuality led to polygyny. Polygyny, in turn, kept women in a low status, and (since Millar's time) a low status for women was known to mark a lower stage of social progress. Therefore, by implication, climatically induced sexuality somehow retarded progress.[40]

Other new factors began to attract some attention. One of these was diet. An authority on the matter claimed that: "No race of man, it might be safely asserted, ever acquired a respectable amount of civilization that had not some cereal for a portion of its food."[41]

Another was ecology. John Howison contrasted the personality type of the Moors of Mauritania and the Wolof of Senegal. The first were "tall, athletic, and active, and ferocious in temper and inclined to warfare." These characteristics were supposed to come from their life of plunder and hunting on desert and steppe. The Wolof, on the other hand, were sedentary farmers. In personality they were therefore: "mild in temper, and of a serene and placid disposition: not being harassed by any particular idea connected with their mode of life, they deliver themselves up without reserve to the impressions of the moment, and are lovers of society, hospitable, inclined to pleasure, and averse to mental exertion, but withal timid, indolent, deficient in steadiness, and destitute of foresight."[42]

Howison's theory smacks more of the standard stereotypes than empirical observation, and other theories were even more fantastic. Edward Phillips set forth a rainfall theory to explain the savagery of Africans in the forest zone: "The inhabitants of these central districts are perpetually driven about as the rains shift their geographical position, and, in consequence, a roaming and predatory

---

38. Variants of this reasoning were very common. As an example, see: William Howitt, *Colonization and Christianity* (London, 1838), pp. 501–2.

39. R. R. Madden, Commissioner's Report, PP, 1842, xii (551), p. 432.

40. PP, 1842, xii (551), pp. 430–32.

41. J. Crawfurd, *Reports of the British Association*, XXVIII, 149 (1858).

42. Howison, *European Colonies*, I, 53.

life is the inevitable birthright of those nations which occupy the central regions of Africa."[43] This completely imaginary forest nomadism was held to breed war, raids, and counter-raids, so that the Africans of the rain-forest were natural slave hunters.

With a more accurate empirical base, the same could be said of the desert. As W. D. Cooley put it:

The Desert, if it is not absolutely the root of the evil, has, at least, been from the earliest times the great nursery of slave hunters. The demoralization of the towns on the southern borders of the desert has been pointed out; and if the vast extent be considered of the region in which man has no riches but slaves, no enjoyment but slaves, no article of trade but slaves, and where the hearts of the wandering thousands are closed against pity by the galling misery of life, it will be difficult to resist the conviction that the solid buttress on which slavery rests in Africa, is—The Desert.[44]

But the desert had its defenders. James Richardson, the desert explorer, attacked Cooley's opinion and took up the cause of the Tuaregs in particular: "In deserts and mountains we find always freemen. . . ." The Tuaregs were such free men. They worked at any commerce that happened to cross their territory, but the roots of slavery were found in the luxurious and soft life of the Maghrib. Desert people were merely its agents.[45]

The desert was also the route of Islamic penetration, and the role of Islam in West African history could be variously interpreted. After Clapperton, no well read European any longer believed the Western Sudan was ruled by North Africans. A fuller understanding of Sudanese history came with Cooley's pioneer history in 1841 and especially with the publication of Barth's travels in 1857–58. European attitudes also changed. The humanitarians, whose intellectual ancestors had generally approved of Islamic influence, now went into opposition. The government in Sierra Leone, which had once welcomed Muslim visitors, began in the 1830's to distrust them, and there was occasional panic fear of a Muslim rebellion.[46] Other officials suspected that Islam was merely a religion of "outward ob-

---

43. Edward Phillips, *Simmonds's Colonial Magazine*, X, 3 (January, 1847).

44. W. D. Cooley, *The Negroland of the Arabs Examined and Explained* (London, 1841), p. 139.

45. J. Richardson, *Travels in the Great Desert of the Sahara*, 2 vols. (London, 1848), pp. xxvi–xxviii.

46. PP, 1842, xii (551), pp. 247, 370–71; Christopher Fyfe, *A History of Sierra Leone* (London, 1962), pp. 186–87 and 215.

servances" requiring no "exertion of the mind."[47] Missionaries hinted that a kind of Gresham's Law of religion was at work, and conversion to Islam might be a bar to the influence of Christianity.

The "civilizing force" once attributed to Islam was also called into question, and some claimed that Islam was the real cause of African backwardness. The point could be argued on historical grounds—that the spread of Islam into North Africa in the eighth century had cut off contact between Europe and Africa. Thus it had excluded the civilizing force of Christianity. Other writers admitted that the trans-Sahara trade should have been a progressive influence, but it was rendered ineffective by the sins of the "Arab" slave traders. As one put it: "Moreover, the religion they bring, though superior to the Paganism they find, is not a *civilizing* religion; it is very good for conquering, but very bad for improving the conquered."[48]

Many of the travellers, and especially those who used the northern approaches, countered with pro-Islamic arguments. They were better informed than earlier writers of this opinion, and they put their case more forcefully. James Richardson in particular believed that Islam had brought more civilization to Africa than Europe had done. He pointed to the degree of literacy in the desert towns of Ghat and Ghadames, which was higher than that of England. His further warning was almost unique in its time: "Let us then take care how we arrogate to ourselves the right and fact of civilizing the world."[49]

Traditional African polytheism was blamed even more often than Islam for the failings of West African society. All travellers, and especially the missionaries, were opposed to "paganism," but few understood it. Some claimed that West Africa had no religion at all— "no regular system of mythology, and no received and defined mode of belief."[50] Others believed that Africans worshipped the devil— quite literally, the same devil known to Western belief—and they were seemingly unable to conceive of a theological system distinct from the religions of southwestern Asia.[51] The "fetish," a material

47. William Allen to Lord Stanley, 5 February 1843, PP, 1843, xlviii [C. 472], p. 3.
48. "Expedition to the Niger," *Edinburgh Review*, LXXII, 460 (January, 1841). See also Saxe Bannister, *Humane Policy; or Justice to the Aborigines of New Settlements* . . . (London, 1830), pp. 2–3.
49. J. Richardson, *Travels in the Sahara*, I, xxxvi.
50. Howison, *European Colonies*, I, 75.
51. See, as a particular example: W. Fox, *A Brief History of the Wesleyan Missions on the Western Coast of Africa* (London, 1851), p. 250.

object endowed with certain spiritual powers, was almost universally misconstrued. It was generally believed that the "worship" of such objects was the beginning and end of African "superstition," and some missionaries thought the "fetish" was simply any object chosen at random.[52] A few missionaries, however, recognized that African polytheism was a genuine religion, and a very few tried to acquire a systematic understanding of the beliefs they sought to replace.[53]

All missionaries and lay commentators, however, had a general concept of African religion, whether based on study or on mere supposition. For some, probably in the minority, it appeared as a neutral force—merely the absence of religious truth. For most, it was something more, a positive evil depressing society below the moral level attainable by unaided natural reason. Cruickshank stated this position in theological terms. For him, the idols of the Fante represented the "worst passions of our nature" in deified form, and thus aggravated the natural depravity of man.[54] Most of the missionaries were less precise, but no less firm, in the belief that somehow "paganism" caused "barbarism."

African political systems were also occasionally given some share of the blame. They were understood to be "despotisms" and despotism was understood to be inimical to progress. A deeper understanding of African political systems was apparently less common that it had been in the past, though occasional travellers paid some attention. J. L. Wilson, an American missionary, put Dahomey and Ashanti on a par in size and power with the second-rate kingdoms of Europe—perhaps on account of republican prejudice. He reported, quite accurately, that: "The form of government every where is nominal monarchy, but, when closely scrutinized, it shows much more of the popular or patriarchal element than the monarchic."[55]

Most African rulers were stigmatized as "blood-thirsty tyrants," yet the most accurate reporting showed a different picture. Cruickshank's report on his government mission to Abomey in 1848 portrayed Gezo of Dahomey in terms unusually free of cultural bias:

52. See, in particular: William Allen to Lord Stanley, 5 February 1843, PP, 1843, xlviii [C. 472], p. 136; *Journal of Civilization*, 3 July 1841, p. 133. Cf. Geoffrey Parrinder, *West African Religion*, 2nd ed. (London, 1961).

53. For example: J. Beecham, *Ashantee and the Gold Coast* (London, 1841), pp. 170–256.

54. Cruickshank, *Eighteen Years*, II, 257. See also Beecham, *Ashantee*, pp. 250 ff.

55. Wilson, *Western Africa*, p. 31.

I left him with the conviction on my mind, that he is a man of superior intellect, and endowed with an extraordinary capacity for government. Surrounded by the adulation of his people, which amounts to adoration, he nevertheless maintains a degree of modesty and equanimity in his deportment which is truly astonishing. His police, fiscal and judicial arrangements, excited my admiration, and are worthy of a people much further advanced in the scale of civilization. The nature of his government renders him dependent upon the efficiency and fidelity of his troops, and the manner in which he maintains them bespeaks the skillful commander. With power in his hands the most despotic, he is yet served with love rather than fear, and no aspersion has ever been cast upon appeals made to his justice. To strangers he is hospitable and kind; to his subjects, equitable and generous. Impressed with the dignity of his station, he maintains great frugality and temperance in his personal habits, and rarely gives way to sudden ebullitions of anger. His mind is active and inquiring, and he betrays a laudable anxiety to be made acquainted with the laws, manners, and customs of foreign nations. Like all uneducated Africans, he is strongly attached to the customs of his fathers, and regards with much suspicion any attempted innovation. . . .[56]

Aside from Cruickshank and a few others, there were remarkably few who made an effort to understand the internal workings of African politics or to deal with the recent history of the various African states. Barth contributed greatly to an understanding to the political life of the Fulani emirates and of Bornu, and J. L. Wilson tried to analyze the decline of the three great kingdoms of the forest and forest edge—Dahomey, Oyo, and Benin.[57] Otherwise, investigation of the rapidly changing African scene seems to have been overshadowed by the assumption that Africa was stagnant and devoid of change.

Most discussion of African internal affairs turned instead to the distinctions between differing African peoples—distinctions which were normally viewed as a permanent and static part of the nature of things. The superiority of the interior was now an article of faith and the point of departure for further discussion. Prichard lent his scientific authority and gave the idea certain racial overtones:

We may further remark, and perhaps this observation is fully as important as that of any other connected fact or coincidence, that physical qualities of particular races of Africans are evidently related to their moral or social condition, and to the degrees of barbarism or civilization under which they

56. Cruickshank, Report of 9 November 1848, PP, 1849 (Lords), xxviii (32), Appendix, p. 187.
57. Wilson, *Western Africa,* pp. 189–91.

exist. The tribes in whose prevalent conformation the Negro type is discernible in an exaggerated degree, are, uniformly in the lowest stage of human society; they are either ferocious savages, or stupid, sensual, and indolent—such as the Papels, Bulloms, and other rude hordes on the coast of Western Guinea, and many tribes near the Slave Coast, and in the Bight of Benin, countries where the slave-trade has been carried on to the greatest extent, and has exercised its usual baneful influence. On the other hand, whenever we hear of a Negro state, the inhabitants of which have attained any considerable degree of improvement in their social condition, we constantly find that their physical characters deviate considerably from the strongly-marked or exaggerated type of the Negro. The Ashanti, Sulima, the Dahomans, are exemplifications of this remark. The Negroes of Guber [Gobir] and Hausa, where a considerable degree of civilization has long existed, are perhaps the finest race of genuine Negroes in the whole continent, unless the Iolofs [Wolofs] are to be excepted.[58]

Latham concurred in principle and drew a division between interior and coastal peoples. His "Western Negro Atlantidae" included all coastal peoples from the Wolof of the lower Senegal to the Ibo of eastern Nigeria, including some of the peoples Prichard had admired. His "Central Negro Atlantidae," on the other hand, ran from Yoruba on the west, through Nupe and Hausa to Bagirmi on the east. With the exception of the Yoruba, all these people lived well inland.[59] The classification makes no sense in either linguistic or physical terms, but it does make sense in geographical terms. The people of the interior became a separate race, ostensibly because of their location.

The Europeans engaged in Niger exploration had a more concrete reason for preferring inland peoples. The Niger expeditions usually met a hostile reception from the trading towns of the delta, which were fearful of losing their monopoly over the commerce of the interior. Once beyond the delta, however, the Africans were more friendly, and especially so near the confluence of the Niger and Benue, where the danger of Fulani raids made the Europeans welcome as possible allies. In these circumstances, it is hardly surprising that coastal traders were put down as "viscious" and the inland Africans praised for their politeness.[60] The new reports merged easily with presuppositions dating back to the time of Swedenborg.

58. J. C. Prichard, *Researches into the Physical History of Man*, 4th ed., 5 vols. (London, 1851), II, 338.

59. Latham, *Natural History*, pp. 471–86.

60. See C. C. Ifemesia, "British Enterprise on the Niger, 1830–1869," (Unpublished Ph.D. thesis, London, 1959).

Individual rating scales for West African "tribes" usually followed the coastal-interior dichotomy, placing either the Mandinka or the Fulbe at the top and one of the coastal peoples at the bottom, but there was endless room for individual opinion. One might have the Ashanti at the bottom, on grounds that they were "uncivilized, conceited, bloodthirsty, insolent, superstitious, and untrustworthy," while another would place the Ashanti quite high and save the bottom slot for either Dahomey or the Ibo.[61] Ashanti gradually lost ground, however, to the Fante, who were more closely associated with the British posts after Maclean's administration. The Yoruba reputation rose markedly, while that of Dahomey remained low. The Kru people of Liberia kept a good reputation, since they served as sailors on British ships; while other peoples in the vicinity of Sierra Leone gradually lost out in favor of the liberated Africans, whose rapid acculturation brought them into a new era of good repute from the mid-1830's onward into the 1850's. Among the various groups represented in Sierra Leone, the Ibo began to lose their old reputation for savagery and to gain a new one for commercial enterprise. As one official put it: "the Eboes of Freetown are the most intelligent and the most parsimonious race in the whole country; they will go anywhere and everywhere for money."[62]

An occasional author tried to account for these "racial" differences within West Africa. Daniell thought that climate and soil might explain the differences between the Ijaw people of Bonny in the Niger delta and the Efik of the more elevated sandstone region around the mouth of the Cross River.[63] Rankin tried to distinguish between West Indians of African descent and West Africans by claiming the slave trade had been racially selective: "The slaves who find their way from the West India plantations to England are totally unlike the free natives of Africa: they are, with few exceptions, specimens of the lowest grade of mankind, and are taken from certain tribes despised by their black neighbours. Amongst the more intellectual and

61. [Jane Marcet], *History of Africa* (London, 1830), pp. 168–74; W. B. K., "On the Varieties of the Human Race," *Colonial Magazine*, V, 37–40 (January–May, 1841); R. G. Latham, *The Ethnology of the British Colonies and Dependencies* (London, 1851), pp. 34 and 62.
62. Logan Hook, Evidence before the West Africa Committee, 8 July 1842, PP, 1842, xi (451), p. 535.
63. W. F. Daniell, "On the Natives of Old Callebar, West Coast of Africa," *Journal of the Ethnological Society*, I, 210–27 (1848), pp. 212–13.

more cultivated [in Africa], as noble features, as lofty an expression, as fine a countenance is discovered as Europe could offer."[64]

Rankin's impression was simply mistaken, but the slightly non-Negroid appearance of the Fulbe people posed a problem for anthropologists and historians alike. Europeans had been in occasional contact with some of the Fulbe in the Senegambia from the earliest voyages to West Africa. In the eighteenth and nineteenth centuries a new interest was roused by the foundation of a series of Fulbe-dominated states from Futa Toro and Futa Jallon in the west to the Sokoto Fulani in the east. By the 1830's, the reputed Fulbe superiority rested on three different grounds. Some of them were pastoral in an era when pastoralism was valued above sedentary agriculture. As the founders of new states, they appeared to be a conquering people. Their Europeanoid features suggested, in an era of incipient racism, that they might be racially superior as well.

The question of Fulbe origins and their role in West African history therefore came to be the historical question which aroused the most general interest, especially in France. A variety of different theories were advanced. Fulbe origins were traced to a group of Persians who were supposed to have come to Morocco with Hercules. Another fanciful hypothesis identified them with the Carthaginians and suggested possible contacts with the ancient Britons. Still others traced Fulbe migrations from Bornu, Arabia, or even made them the original inhabitants of West Africa. The most elaborate theory was published in France by Gustave d'Eichthal, who traced hypothetical Fulbe migrations from Malaya to Madagascar to Merowe to Darfur and finally to West Africa. It was not universally accepted, but it has a certain importance as another precursor of the "Hamite" myth, similar to the hypothesis already suggested by Macbriar. By assigning the Fulbe a very long migration route, they could be given the role of cultural bearers for all of Africa. Racists with a very low opinion of Negro capabilities could explain any "higher" trait in Africa by introducing the Fulbe, or later the "Hamites." D'Eichthal himself used his theory in this sense, claiming the "noble negroes" of pro-African literature were not Negroes at all, but Fulbe.[65]

64. F. H. Rankin, *The White Man's Grave: A Visit to Sierra Leone in 1834,* 2 vols. (London, 1836), II, 10–11.

65. G. d'Eichthal, "Histoire de origine des Foulahs ou Fellans," *Mémoires de la Société Ethnologique,* I (2), 1–296 (1841), esp. p. 118. For other speculations on

Barth tried to bring studies of the Fulbe problem into closer touch with reality. Among other things, he pointed to three pieces of evidence still recognized as valid. Fulfulde is a West Atlantic language, related to Wolof and other languages spoken in the immediate hinterland of Cape Verde. Secondly, Fulbe social structure has certain similarities to Wolof social structure, again indicating a cradle near the lower Senegal. Third, traditional history throughout the Western Sudan clearly indicated Fulbe emigrants coming from the west, not the east. But this evidence raised a further problem. It was the general assumption that race, language, and culture were closely related. The Fulbe were related in language and culture to the Wolof but were racially distinct. Barth explained these facts, and the peopling of West Africa generally, by a two-stream theory. One stream of intrusive population was held to be of Berber origin and to come from the region of Libya: these people would be light in color. Another stream was black in color and originated in southern Arabia. Once the two reached the Western Sudan they met and mingled for centuries, but the race mixture was never quite complete. One remnant was the Fulbe as a stabilized mixed race. Others were to be found here and there throughout the western Sudan, where some social classes and other groupings were lighter in color than their neighbors.[66]

Scholars have not yet reached full agreement on the question of Fulbe origins, but some aspects of Barth's hypothesis are still tenable. His important contribution, however, was not the precise hypotheses he laid down. It was his method of working with a combination of ethnographic, linguistic, and documentary evidence to solve the problems of early African history. Some of Barth's views, such as his racist preconceptions, would no longer be considered valid, but the questions he posed and the way he went about answering them were closer to the methods of the 1960's than to those of the 1830's.

Fulbe origins see: Marcet, *History of Africa*, pp. 167–68; T. J. Hutchinson, *Narrative of the Niger, Tshadda, & Binuë Exploration* (London, 1855), pp. 66–67 and 75–76; *Journal of Civilization*, 3 July 1841, p. 133; Macbriar, *Missionary Travels*, pp. 239–41; A. Raffenel, *Voyage dans l'Afrique occidentale exécuté en 1843 et 1844* (Paris, 1846), esp. pp. 106 and 262–66; P. D. Boilat, *Esquisses sénégalaises* (Paris, 1853), pp. 384–413; L. H. Hecquard, *Voyage sur la côte et dans l'Intérieur de l'Afrique occidentale* (Paris, 1853).

66. H. Barth, *Travels and Discoveries in North and Central Africa*, 5 vols. (London, 1857–1858), IV, 146–56; Barth, "A General Historical Description of the State of Human Society in Northern Central Africa," *Journal of the Royal Geographical Society*, XXX, 112–28 (1860), pp. 115–19.

Alongside the scholarly interest in establishing the racial status of various West African peoples, there was a further interest in assessing the place of West Africans as a whole—especially in relation to other African peoples. Bunsen arranged all African peoples in a hierarchy, according to linguistic criteria. As a result of Bantu inflections, he placed the Bantu-speakers high on the list. The Bantu languages were even identified as "Japhetic" (that is, European); but they were a much degraded form of Japhetic, and they had been subject to still further degeneration until certain branches had become Hottentot and finally the language of the Bushmen.[67] Morton in 1839 had made a similar distinction, dividing the Negro race within Africa into three sub-groups—Negro (which would include West Africans), "Caffrarian" (meaning the Bantu-speakers), and Hottentots—and he placed them in that order, West Africans at the top and southern Africans at the bottom.[68] He was followed by Nott and Gliddon, who placed the West Africans lower on the scale than the Nubians, Ethiopians, and Fulbe, but higher than the Bantu-speakers, Hottentots, and Bushmen.[69] The consensus thus placed the West Africans quite high on the scale of African life—though for reasons that were quite mistaken—while maintaining a wider gap than ever between Africans and Europeans.

In all, British thought about African culture and history in these decades raised more new questions than it answered. The best of the new scholarship marked a new beginning, perhaps *the* beginning, of scholarly knowledge about West Africa. But the availability of relatively good analysis was not enough to override the mass of incorrect information and conjecture. The missionary press, the pamphlets, or the polemics of debate about African questions were read by far more people than read the works of the scholars. Nor could the careful attention to the many influences forming African society—the kind of attention given by a scholar like Barth—have the popular appeal of the simple explanation of the world given by a pseudo-scientist like Knox. The understanding of African culture, even in educated circles, therefore, continued very much as it had been in the early decades of the century, but it was now much less accurate than the best understanding available.

67. Bunsen, "Recent Egyptian Research," pp. 297–99.
68. S. G. Morton, *Crania Americana* (Philadelphia, 1839), pp. 6–7.
69. J. C. Nott and R. G. Gliddon, *Types of Mankind* (London, 1854), pp. 182–90 and 209.

17

CULTURE CONTACT

AND

CONVERSION

> I lay great stress upon African com-
> merce, *more* upon the cultivation of
> the soil, but *most* of all upon the
> elevation of the native mind.
> T. F. Buxton, *The Remedy*

Τ he Niger Expedition was mainly based on a body of ideas which grew up during the early part of the century. Further experience in Africa, however, brought new ideas and modified old ones. New trends in Western thought brought new emphases. The idea that civilization meant Westernization enjoyed a special vogue in the mid-nineteenth century—and not only in regard to Africa. E. G. Wakefield was incensed at the neo-barbarism of the North American frontiersmen, and his projects for Australia and New Zealand were contrived to avoid a similar decline of standards. Thomas Babington Macaulay's famous "Minute" on Indian education in 1835 was a clear call to Anglicize and snuff out the "barbarous" traditions of the East. D. F. Sarmiento's classic, *Facundo—civilización y barbarie,* was a similar call to wipe out the barbarism of the Argentine *gauchos.* Elsewhere in Latin America, the remnants of Indian culture were meeting opposition. The Mexican *reforma* in the time of Benito Juárez attacked a dual enemy: the corporate powers of the church and the corporate forms of Indian village life.

In both cases, the cause was that of "civilization," meaning the industrial civilization of contemporary Europe and North America.

The dominant British attitude toward Africa became more conversionist than ever. The Niger Expedition itself was a large-scale public effort to convert barbarians to Western ways. The middle decades of the century represent, indeed, the height of conversionist sentiment. The dominant tone of the early century had been insular, almost isolationist, concerned at most with the British position in Western Europe. After the great cost of the wars against Napoleon, the British were inclined to be parsimonious about expensive charities at a distance. The missionary movement was growing, but, before 1830, it was a faint shadow of what it would become. After 1870, on the other hand, the idea of conversion declined. Humanitarian motives found new manifestations. In that great age of imperialism racism became dominant in European thought. Few believed that any "lower race" could actually reach the heights of Western achievement. Their salvation would have to be achieved in some other way; but meanwhile they were entitled, in their inferiority, to the paternal protection of a Western power. The idea of trusteeship gradually replaced that of conversion.

The conversionist sentiment of the mid-century and trusteeship at the end were two ways of assessing the proper goals for non-Western peoples. They were, in turn, associated with distinct political aims in British imperial theory at these two periods. To become, in any full sense, the trustee of the "lower races" required the annexation of their territory. To convert them to the Western way of life implied informal influence, but it avoided the burden of direct administration.[1] Both policies demanded more intense overseas activity than was called for early in the century, and the new call for action after 1830 was reinforced by a growing net of British trade and investment in the tropical world. Between 1816–20 and 1838–42, the increased value of British exports to tropical and sub-tropical lands exceeded the total increase in British exports.[2]

West Africa was still peripheral to Britain's commercial interests, but the potential commerce of West Africa could hardly be ignored;

1. For the mid-century British tendency to keep the African empire informal, see R. Robinson and J. Gallagher, *Africa and the Victorians* (London, 1961), pp. 1–52.
2. A. Imlah, *Economic Elements in the Pax Britannica* (Cambridge, Mass., 1958), p. 130.

and West Africa had a special claim to the British conscience on account of the slave trade. Even among the opponents of the Niger Expedition only a minority believed that Britain should avoid all forms of activity in West Africa. The rest favored British action, but they wanted some other kind of action. The failure and withdrawal of 1842 was not, therefore, a withdrawal from West Africa, but merely the withdrawal of one particular scheme. The continued missionary effort and the Parliamentary Committee of 1842 confirm, in different ways, the continued private and public intention to convert West Africa from barbarism to civilization and commerce with the world.

Problems arising from the contact of two cultures were widely discussed, but seldom with great depth of understanding. The increasing emphasis on racial factors tended to turn the discussion aside. The Aborigines Committee, for example, were deeply concerned with the impact of European settlers on societies technically less proficient. The public and the scholars, however, saw mainly the racial aspect and ignored the cultural, social, and psychological implications of the evidence.

Increasing cultural chauvinism had a similar effect. Contact between the West and the aborigines was consistently set in terms of relations between superiors and inferiors. Assuming their own superiority, the Europeans believed that Africans must have a strong sense of inferiority. (If anything, West African rulers tended to underestimate the technical prowess and resources of their alien visitors.)

Commentators could, nevertheless, draw two opposite conclusions from the superior-inferior relationship. According to John Howison, it was a bar to culture change: "The general adherence of the negroes to their own customs is, in my opinion, to be chiefly attributed to the conviction that prevails amongst them that they are a peculiar and distinct race of beings, and that they have nothing in common with white men, and are unfitted to partake of their interests, avocations, and pleasures."[3]

In the more authoritative opinion of Herman Merivale, the reverse might well be the case: "the strong impression of the superiority of the whites as a different race, which leads the savage to despair of

---

3. J. Howison, *European Colonies in Various Parts of the World, Viewed in their Social, Moral and Physical Condition*, 2 vols. (London, 1834), I, 152–53.

raising himself out of his abject condition in respect to material or intellectual advancement, seems, if his sentiments be properly studied and directed, rather to have the tendency of disposing him to welcome instruction in those doctrines which point out that the diversity of gifts in this world is consistent with the equality of all under one common Father."[4]

Brodie Cruickshank, on the other hand, had actual experience of Afro-European relations on the Gold Coast and probed deeper into their psychological complexity:

The native, keenly alive to his interests, supple and fawning, readily acknowledged the superiority of the white man in words, and hailed him, without any scruples of pride, as his master. But he had, and ever has had, a reservation in his mind which limits the signification of the term to his own construction of it, and has no more intention of giving implicit obedience, if he can help himself, when his pleasure and profit appear to him to be compromised, than if he had never entered into any undertaking upon the subject. Neither would he wish to shake himself free from the necessity of obedience. His object is to endeavour, on all occasions, to magnify the sacrifice which he is making to gratify your wishes, not so much from a determination not to obey them, as to obtain some bribe or concession for his obedience.

A service of this description, appears to have been the nature of the dependence of the African upon the European on the Gold Coast from their earliest intercourse. It had certainly given rise to an incessant struggle, productive of every species of artifice on both sides, in the attempt of one party to extend their power and influence, and of the other to obtain new privileges. The relation in which they stood to each other never, in fact, appears to have been clearly defined or understood. Indeed, it is possible neither party wished it to be so, as any certainty upon the point would lessen the probability of advantages which might possibly turn up in the chapter of accidents.[5]

Still another kind of conclusion about culture contact followed from the evidence before the Aborigines Committee. It was clear that aborigines in the settlement colonies had not profited from the presence and example of the Europeans. Standish Motte was commissioned by the Aborigines Protection Society to prepare an outline of protective legislation that might be introduced in these colonies.

4. H. Merivale, *Lectures on Colonisation and Colonies,* 2 vols. (London, 1841–1842), II, 184. See also *Colonial Intelligencer,* II, 68 (1848); Sir George Stephen, *The Niger Trade Considered in Connexion with the African Blockade* (London, 1849), pp. 57–58.

5. Brodie Cruickshank, *Eighteen Years on the Gold Coast of Africa, Including an Account of the Native Tribes, and Their Intercourse with Europeans,* 2 vols. (London, 1853), I, 28–29.

He seized on the theoretical proposition that human societies might follow either the path of progress or the path of retrogression. It seemed to him that contact across a wide gap of cultural difference might carry the "untutored savage" downward rather than upward toward civilization: "Can it be wondered at that such a being becomes contaminated—that he becomes physically diseased, morally debased, and losing the simple and noble attributes of his native character, forgets the virtues of his race and clothes himself in the vices of civilized society?"[6]

He concluded that the problem could be met only after detailed study of each individual case. Correct action could only follow a, "consideration of, the moral, physical, and political condition of each nation and class of aborigines, the locality and nature of the soil they inhabit, its climate, productions, and capabilities; in fact, all the circumstances making a physiological, or political distinction, between the various aboriginal races of man now existing and a geographical and political difference between the countries they inhabit."[7]

In spite of occasional suggestions that civilization would drive the West Africans down the path toward extinction,[8] British commentators were not seriously worried about demoralization in that region. They were much more impressed by the fact that West African cultures had shown a peculiar staying power in the face of long contact with "civilization." Neither "legitimate trade" nor missionary teaching had produced much result by the 1840's. The failing could be explained in various ways—high European mortality, continued slave trade, incorrect methods—but it was clear that acculturation would be more difficult and more complex than earlier generations had thought.[9]

Yet the liberated Africans of Sierra Leone had taken to Christianity and civilization readily enough. So too had the ex-slaves of the West Indies. Perhaps people needed to pass through some form of cultural shock or uprooting from their own society. It was suggested that,

6. S. Motte, *Outline of a System of Legislation for Securing the Protection of the Aboriginal Inhabitants of all Countries Colonized by Great Britain* (London, 1840), pp. 7–8.

7. Motte, *System of Legislation*, pp. 11–12.

8. Howison, *European Colonies*, I, 99.

9. See, for example, H. V. Huntley, *Seven Years' Service on the Slave Coast of Western Africa*, 2 vols. (London, 1850), esp. I, 88; "Western Africa," *Westminster Review*, LVI, 6–12 (October, 1851).

"demoralization is one of the processes through which barbarism has to pass before it becomes susceptible to improvement as revolutions are considered the ordeals through which anarchy is brought into civil order."[10] Variations on this theme were used to justify large-scale African emigration to the West Indies. Workers sent to America on long-term contracts would ultimately return to Africa bringing civilization with them.[11] Lord John Russell laid down the official Government position in 1840: "It appears to H. M.'s Govt that on the one hand, men of African birth who have been trained in civilization and instructed in Christianity in Jamaica, or Barbados would be the best teachers of the Negro race in Africa itself:—on the other hand the miserable subjects of an African chief might acquire in Jamaica, Trinidad, or Guiana, competent means, the knowledge of true Religion and the arts of Social Life."[12]

The more common reaction of the conversionists was to concede that African "barbarism" was a "natural" condition. It could be changed only with "artificial" stimulation from the outside. For the actual program of stimulation, they usually fell back on a broad spectrum of action drawn from the older theories of acculturation. The civilizing effect of direct discipline was more often mentioned,[13] but the usual program called for a combination of British law, trade and economic development, religious and secular education.[14] Under each of these headings, there was a further elaboration of theory and suggestion.

Within the missionary movement, a special set of problems centered on the relationship of religious conversion to cultural change. Some of these were old questions—could people take on the Christian

10. R. R. Madden to Lord Edward Howard (Private), 1 August 1841, CO 267/170, f. 94. This is not Madden's view, but one he cited as opposed to his own.

11. Macgregor Laird, Evidence before West Africa Committee, 15 June 1842, PP, 1842, xi (551), p. 331; *Colonial Gazette,* 2 February 1842, p. 65; G. W. Hope, Commons, 25 February 1845, 3 H 77, c. 1192; J. L. Wilson, *Western Africa: its History, Condition, and Prospects* (New York, 1856), pp. 420–21.

12. Lord John Russell to R. R. Madden, 26 November 1840, CO 267/170. This position was accepted by the next Government as well. See Lord Stanley to Macdonald, 6 February 1843, PP, 1843, xxxiv [C. 438], p. 3.

13. See Grey to Winniett, 20 January 1849, CO 402/2; S. J. Hill to Newcastle, 15 April 1853, PP, 1852–1853, lxii [C. 1693], p. 198.

14. For some specific programs see: Saxe Bannister, *Humane Policy; or Justice to the Aborigines of New Settlements* . . . (London, 1830); Report of the Aborigines Committee, PP, 1837, vii (425), esp. pp. 82–84; T. F. Buxton, *The Remedy: Being a Sequel to the African Slave Trade* (London, 1840); *Ethnological Extracts* (London, Spottiswoode, [1840?]), pp. 4–10; Cruickshank, *Eighteen Years,* I, 7–11.

religion before they had become civilized? If Christianity required a change of culture, which should come first, conversion or civilization? These questions obviously affected missionary methods, and to provide answers required reference to broader theories of culture. If, for example, the aborigines inevitably became extinct on contact with "civilization," then missionaries bearing the Gospel also bore the cup of hemlock.

The missionary leadership caught this implication and took special pains to deny it in their evidence to the Aborigines Committee. Their general position was to hold that contact with lay settlers was almost always demoralizing, while missionary work alone could save the aborigines from their fate. Only a previous indoctrination with Christianity and the ways of Western civilization could prepare them for the impact of European settlement.[15] Furthermore, in their view, Christianity and civilization were inseparable. This position could be supported by reference to a special Christian culture theory. If the savage state were thought to grow from the untrammeled operation of original sin, the fault could only be corrected by the "doctrines of man's fallen state through sin, redemption by Christ, renovation by the power of the Holy Ghost, and the great and awful sanction of an eternal judgment." Christian theology combined with Christian moral teachings would make men "honest, sober, industrious, orderly, humble, self-denying, philanthropic, and beneficent." These, indeed, were held to be the qualities of civilized men.[16]

While the missionary leadership stressed the efficacy of spiritual means, the Parliamentary Committee emphasized the secular benefits that would follow conversion. It recommended religious instruction, pointing out that "savages are dangerous neighbours and unprofitable customers."[17] By giving the argument a further twist, the civilizing and Christianizing mission could become an economic mission as well. In the words of one publicist, it would produce: "a tide of wealth poured into Europe, such as the strongest imagination can scarcely grasp; and that, too, purchased, not with the blood and tears of the

15. See evidence of Messrs. Ellis, Coates, and Beecham, representing the three principal missionary societies, PP, 1836, vii (538).

16. Evidence of Dandeson Coates, Secretary of CMS, PP, 1836, vii (538), p. 516. See also D. J. East, *Western Africa; Its Condition, and Christianity the Means of Its Recovery* (London, 1844), pp. 219–308.

17. Report of the Aborigines Committee, PP, 1837, vii (425), p. 45 ff.

miserable, but by the moral elevation and happiness of countless tribes."[18]

The dominant attitude among the supporters of the missions was especially well illustrated by the outpouring of works on missionary theory in 1842. The immediate occasion was an inter-denominational competition offering a prize for the best work "On the Duty, Privilege, and Encouragement of Christians to Send the Gospel to the Heathen." Forty-eight essays were submitted, and five were published.[19] The winning essay by The Reverend Dr. John Harris recognized that spiritual benefits were to be expected, both for the missionary and the convert, but it too laid special emphasis on the material results. Missions could erase "habitual idleness, one of the most prolific evils of savage life."[20] For Harris, and for many others, the equation was not merely, Christianity equals civilization. It was: Christianity equals civilization, which equals production for the world market.[21]

This attitude, however, was not universal among missionary theorists. In 1845, Rufus Anderson in America published a volume on mission theory, which became one of the most influential works of its kind. Anderson (being a New Englander) insisted that New England enjoyed the most perfect form of society the world had ever known and had, in Christianity, the most perfect religion; but the two were separable. They must, indeed, be kept quite separate in missionary work. Religion was, for Anderson, only one aspect of culture. It was the missionary's job to teach this, and this alone, to the heathen. In the longer run, Christianity would inevitably lead to civilization, but the missionaries had only to do with the spiritual goals. Anderson also insisted on a sharp distinction between the proper functions of a missionary and those of a pastor. It was the missionary's task to make converts and establish a congregation. Once this much had been accomplished, he must move on to new fields,

18. W. Howitt, *Colonization and Christianity* (London, 1838), pp. 504–5.
19. John Harris, *The Great Commission* (London, 1842); R. W. Hamilton, *Missions: their Authority, Scope, and Encouragement* (London, 1842); John Macfarlane, *The Jubilee of the World: An Essay on Christian Missions* (Glasgow, 1842); J. B. Melson, *'Who is my Neighbour?' An Essay on Christian Missions* (London, 1842); B. W. Noel, *Christian Missions to Heathen Nations* (London, 1842).
20. Harris, *The Great Commission,* p. 208.
21. See Harris, *The Great Commission,* pp. 187–241.

leaving the pastor to guide and improve the moral and spiritual state of the flock.[22]

A similar distinction between religion and general culture was occasionally made in other contexts, and its implications in the mid-century intellectual setting could be very far-reaching indeed. The racists could use it as an argument for denying racial equality without denying the universality of Christianity. Gobineau, for example, argued that Christian civilization could never be transmitted to a racially inferior people, but Christianity could be—its universality came from the spiritual equality of another world, not of this. Thus: "The savage Galla may remain a Galla and yet become a believer as perfect, one of the elect as pure, as the most holy prelate of Europe. That is the striking superiority of Christianity, which derives from its principal characteristic of Grace."[23]

Here was a new twist to the old belief that Africans were natural Christians. Gobineau went on to say that Africans were inferior, and Christianity was a religion naturally suited to inferior peoples, just as it was especially suited to the poor and humble of Europe.

Christian paternalism, which was to flourish later in the century, was already implied by Gobineau's proposition. If it were assumed that Africans were racially inferior, and yet spiritually equal and capable of receiving the Christian message, the moral duty of the superior race was clear. It was to take up the "white man's burden" and exercise a trust over the spiritual and material welfare of people whose racial status was equivalent to that of minors. Such people could never attain the heights of Western civilization: it was better for them not to try. They might receive all the spiritual blessings of Christianity and still remain within their own culture. Charles Dickens suggested as much. He opposed the conversionist aims of the Niger Expedition, but he favored missionary work. He merely believed that it was better to reach "the black man through the black man" than to use European missionaries, since the black man "can only be successfully approached by a studied reference to the current of his own opinions and customs instead of ours."[24] This sentiment

22. Rufus Anderson, *The Theory of Missions to the Heathen* (Boston, 1845). See also J. F. A. Ajayi, "Henry Venn and the Policy of Development," *Journal of the Historical Society of Nigeria*, I, 311–42 (December, 1959).

23. Arthur, comte de Gobineau, *Essai sur l'inégalité des races humaines,* 2nd ed., 2 vols. (Paris, 1884), I, 66–67.

24. C. Dickens, "The Niger Expedition," in *Miscellaneous Papers* (London, 1908), esp. p. 124. First published in *Household Words,* 19 August 1848.

might seem to suggest cultural relativism, but Dickens and his generation measured culture by Western values. The implication is that of Christian paternalism or trusteeship.

As a matter of practical mission policy, the role of African missionaries and the future possibility of an African church had been pressing questions since the 1820's. The handling of the problem was intimately related to the incipient conflict between Christian paternalism and full cultural conversion. The CMS began toying with the idea of converting Africa by "native agency" as soon as the full toll of European mortality was apparent. The Fourah Bay Institution was founded in 1827 near Freetown in order to train teachers and missionaries for an African church. Other missionary societies also employed educated Africans and West Indians in positions of equality or near equality with their European co-workers. The ultimate aim was not clearly stated, but the implication was clear enough: African Christendom would sooner or later become a part of the Church, whether institutionally independent or linked with the mother church in Britain.

The idea of using "native agency" persisted throughout the period of high missionary mortality,[25] but the status of African missionaries was always a matter of uncertainty. Many field missionaries doubted the ability of their African subordinates. The Rev. J. F. Schön, for example, thought that West Indians had too high notions of their own importance. His attitude toward African missionary agents was both paternalistic and suspicious.[26] For Schön and other field missionaries, "native agency" was not expected to produce an independent native clergy—not, at least, for a very long time to come.

Meanwhile, the Church Missionary Society in England considered the question of "native agency" and an African church during the 1840's and ultimately arrived at a firm policy. The key figure in the Society was Henry Venn, son of one of the Clapham group and a secretary of CMS from 1841 onwards. Venn occasionally vacillated in his attitude toward an African clergy. His instructions for the Yoruba mission in 1844 set lower pay for African than for European

25. Charles Buxton, (Ed.), *Memoirs of Sir Thomas Fowell Buxton, Baronet* (London, 1848), p. 554; CMS Committee, "Preface" to *Journals of the Rev. James Frederick Schon and Mr. Samuel Crowther, who with the Sanction of Her Majesty's Government Accompanied the Expedition up the Niger in 1841* (London, 1842), pp. vi ff.; J. M. Trew, *Africa Wasted by Britain and Restored by Native Agency* (London, 1843).

26. J. F. Schön, in *Journals of Schon and Crowther*, pp. 62–63 and 95–97.

missionaries—partly to keep them near the material level of their fellow countrymen, and partly from fear of promoting "self-indulgence." Again in 1851 he had some doubts about the wisdom of providing equal education for African pastors.[27] His final opinion, however, was firm. It was to aim for the goal of a self-supporting, self-governing, and self-propagating African church. In these aims, Venn was directly influenced by Rufus Anderson. He urged the missionaries to control their natural desire to stay on as pastors, and he tried to keep them moving to new fields once a congregation had been founded.[28] Venn held the CMS to the goal of full conversion during his secretaryship, but they too turned toward paternalism later in the century.[29]

Even with a firm goal, many questions remained. How soon, and how nearly, could an African church be created with full African control and full equality? What was the transitional role of the missionary? In particular, what were his responsibilities for temporal leadership over his flock? Individual missionaries answered these questions for themselves in many different ways, and some passed over from the mere preaching of the gospel to other activities: as long as the goal was complete conversion to Western civilization, something more than the gospel seemed to be required. The Rev. T. B. Freeman ran an experimental plantation for a time on the Gold Coast.[30] The Wesleyan-sponsored "Institution for Benefitting the Foulah Tribe," with its agricultural settlement at MacCarthy's Island in the Gambia, was created for material as well as spiritual ends, even though its explicit policy was Christianity first and civilization second, and control rested with the missionaries rather than the lay technicians of civilization.[31]

More extreme projects called for genuine theocracy. The Rev. R. W. Macbriar, for example, had a scheme for forming liberated

27. William Knight, *The Missionary Secretariat of Henry Venn, B.D.* (London, 1880), p. 306; Venn to Townsend, Gollmer and Crowther, 22 October and 25 October 1844, CMSA, CA 2/L1.

28. *Proceedings of the Church Missionary Society,* 1849–1850, p. lxiii; *Church Missionary Intelligencer,* I, 147–50 (November 1849); Henry Venn, CMS Committee Minutes on the Native Pastorate, printed in Knight, *Missionary Secretariat,* pp. 305–7.

29. See J. F. Ade Ajayi, "Christian Missions and the Making of Nigeria, 1841–1891" (Unpublished Ph.D. thesis, University of London, 1958).

30. PP, 1852–1853, lxii [C. 1693], pp. 200 ff.

31. William Fox, *A Brief History of the Wesleyan Missions on the Western Coast of Africa* (London, 1851), pp. 345, 444–45, 497–99, 506, 599.

Africans into a Christian community. Each family was to receive a plot of land to be farmed under strict regulation. Labor would be compulsory. Church-going would be compulsory. "Industrial education" for the children would be compulsory. Morality legislation would regulate the forms of dress and even the distribution of tasks between the sexes. Liquor, tobacco, sport, and Sunday work would all be prohibited. The ideal of a puritan theocracy, long dead as a possibility in England, could still be revived as a plan for Africa.[32]

Education, however, was the non-spiritual task which occupied the greatest part of the missionary effort. During the 1840's educational policy was also caught between the opposing tendencies of full conversion and trusteeship. Earlier education had been a near monopoly of the missionary societies, and it was strictly assimilationist. In spite of occasional protests against a literary education for Africans, there had been no easy way to avoid it. Missionary societies needed native agents and, if possible, African ministers with the full training of a European missionary. Business and government needed clerks, agents, and officials: Europeans were both expensive and short-lived. On this question the merchants and the missionaries saw eye to eye, and merchant houses occasionally asked the government to help with more and better education for Africans.[33]

At the same time, opinion on the Coast had often disapproved of educated Africans. They were supposed to be uppity, aggressive, undisciplined, and dishonest, lacking the good qualities of the Europeans and "bush Africans" alike. For many visitors, they were objects of fun—humorous caricatures of "civilized" men. This unfavorable image undoubtedly reflected certain aspects of reality. The educated Africans had been shaken loose from their social moorings in traditional society, without gaining a secure acceptance or a complete conversion to the Western way of life. They valued Western education very highly—their critics said too highly—but this was only natural when education was the road to advancement and prestige on the Coast. The fragment of Western society in Sierra Leone and the smaller posts was one of extreme social mobility, both for Africans and Europeans. For Europeans, service on the Coast in government or trade often brought high prestige or pay in return for brav-

---

32. R. M. Macbrair, *Sketches of a Missionary's Travels in Egypt, Syria, Western Africa, &c., &c.* (London, 1839), pp. 328 ff.
33. Hutton and Nicholls to J. Stephen, 23 March 1843, CO 96/2.

ing the dangers of the "climate." Men who had themselves recently moved upward in society tended to be all the more resentful of the pushiness of Africans trying to do the same. Those who looked on Africans as their inferior dependents especially disliked the kind of education that was calculated to give them feelings of equality.

Literary education was increasingly criticized, with a persistent demand for instruction in the agricultural and mechanical arts. In fact, both the criticism and the demand might shelter distinctly different points of view. Some men believed that, as education spread more broadly, it would produce an over supply of potential clerks and officials; and most children would find themselves ill prepared for other occupations. This group, therefore, called for the addition of technical education to the existing literary system. Other reformers, however, wanted to do away with the existing system for all African children, and substitute labor indoctrination. This second kind of demand rose not from a desire to make education useful, but from a xenophobic resentment of the educated Africans; and it was often justified on grounds that were frankly racist—that Africans were innately incapable of undertaking an education fitted for Europeans.[34]

Projects for educational reform could thus be turned to many purposes. One kind of plan was presented by Edward Nicholls in 1842. He called for a system of elementary schools in each British post, with selection of the best students to continue at a Normal School on Ascension Island, and a second selection of the very best to continue their higher education in England. The industrial aspect would be satisfied by apprenticing certain students in trades, and every school was to have an experimental farm. But even industrial training was to be limited. Africans were to be taught how to repair, but now how to manufacture the industrial products of England. Nicholls added: "I am clearly of the opinion that confining the Natives of Africa to the production of the raw materials of their native land with which it so richly abounds, is the most advantageous employ-

34. See, for example: R. R. Madden, Commissioner's Report, PP, 1842, xii (551), pp. 17, 430; J. Miller, Memorandum on Sierra Leone Schools, 1 February 1841, PP, 1842, xii (551), pp. 383–90; J. F. Schön, Evidence before West Africa Committee, 29 June 1842, PP, 1842, xi (551), p. 461; J. Duncan, Travels in Western Africa, 2 vols. (London, 1847), I, 36–37 and 42–43; [E. Melville], A Residence in Sierra Leone (London, 1849), p. 253; N. W. Macdonald, Evidence before Lords' Slave Trade Committee, 14 May 1849, PP (Lords), 1849, xxviii (32), p. 117; T. E. Poole, Life, Scenery, and Customs in Sierra Leone and the Gambia, 2 vols. (London, 1850), II, 8–11.

ment both for that and this country (at least) for a very long time to come."[35]

Other complaints against educational assimilation came from the West Indies especially during the 1840's. As a result, Earl Grey launched a general investigation of educational policy for the tropical colonies. The Committee of Council on Education were asked to report on "the mode in which . . . Industrial Schools for the coloured races may be conducted in the colonies, so as to combine intellectual and industrial education, and to render the labour of the children available towards meeting some part of the expense of their education." The terms of reference thus set industrial education as the desired goal. The Committee made three further assumptions on its own. It assumed that Negroes, as a race, had different mental capacities from Europeans. It assumed that tropical exuberance necessitated special training in order to free the people from "habits of listless contentment with the almost spontaneous gifts of a tropical climate." It assumed that people of African descent would only aspire to posts in "the humbler machinery of local affairs."

These assumptions led naturally to a plan of education designed for social and racial inferiors. It was to consist first of religious instruction, then of agriculture for boys and domestic science for girls, and the whole scheme was to be governed by the need to provide a docile and uncomplaining working class. The children were to be taught "habits of self-control and moral discipline." They were to be instructed in "the mutual interests of the mother-country and her dependencies; the rational basis of their connection, and the domestic and social duties of the coloured races." Their education in economics and politics was to include "the relation of wages, capital, and labour, and the influence of local and general government on personal security, independence, and order."[36]

This report was prepared with first consideration for the West Indian colonies, but it was circulated to the Governors of the West African dependencies. In 1847 and the following years, there was a spate of government correspondence on education policy. Governor Norman Macdonald of Sierra Leone took up the full doctrine. He centered his attack on Freetown Grammar School and the Fourah

35. Memorandum of 20 July 1842, enclosed with Nicholls to Canning, 28 June 1845, FO 82/616, f. 277.
36. Schuttleworth to Hawes, 9 January 1847. Printed version to be found in Miscellaneous Pamphlets, Vol. I, Colonial Office Library.

Bay Institution, demanding a change to a kind of education "more adapted to the mental energies and capabilities of the native population of the colony."[37] In this he failed. Men of African descent were too well established in the West African posts to tolerate an attack on their most advanced educational institutions. (Three of them, John Carr and William Fergusson in Sierra Leone, and James Bannerman in the Gold Coast, had acted as governor before the time of Macdonald's complaint.) For that matter, Earl Grey and most of the influential men in African affairs had never intended "industrial education" to be more than a supplement to the literary education of the elite.[38]

Of all the earlier devices for acculturation, "legitimate trade" was the only continuous rival to the plans for direct training. By the 1840's, it had become so much a catch phrase with an assumed meaning, commentators no longer took the trouble to explain precisely how it was to work. This was deceptive, since the meaning of the term was actually changing slowly through time. Five quite different values were now attached to "legitimate trade," though they were often confused with one another.[39] One was the value of trade for its own sake, the stimulation of the mental powers supposed to come from commercial dealings. A second was the old belief in trade as the necessary basis for an efficient division of labor. A third was its function as an avenue of cultural diffusion, promoting "civilization" by showing the barbarians the advanced technology of the West. Fourth, trade (and especially free trade of the Cobdenite variety) was supposed to promote international peace and friendly relations between peoples. Finally, there was MacQueen's more specific claim that African rulers could be weaned away from the slave trade, if only they would put their slaves to work at agricultural production for export. With the publicity of the Buxton campaign, this

37. N. Macdonald, Annual Report for 1850, PP, 1851, xxxiv [C. 1421], p. 192.

38. H. S. Scott, "The Development of the Education of the African in Relation to Western Contact," *The Year Book of Education,* 1938 (London, 1938), p. 711; N. Macdonald, Annual Report for 1851, PP, 1852, xxxi [C. 1539], p. 183; Grey to Winniett, 6 August 1849, CO 96/9; M. Laird and R. A. K. Oldfield, *Narrative of an Expedition into the Interior of Africa by the River Niger in 1832–4,* 2 vols. (London, 1837), II, 394–95; Aborigines Protection Society, *Second Annual Report* (London, 1839), pp. 22–24; T. B. Freeman to S. J. Hill, Cape Coast, 23 February 1852, PP, 1852, xxxi [C. 1539], p. 189.

39. See, for example: C. Johnston, "The Friends of the African," *Simmonds's Colonial Magazine,* XIII, 292–96, 435–39 (March–April, 1848), p. 295.

rather narrower usage came into prominence, often replacing the earlier meanings.

This ambiguity merged in turn with a change in the importance attached to "legitimate trade" as a factor promoting African civilization. As we have seen, legitimate trade had appeared in the eighteenth century as a champion capable of defeating the slave trade; but in the first decades of the nineteenth it appeared as a weaker tool, effective only if the slave trade were first destroyed. During the 1830's, and with the new connotations given by MacQueen, its reputation again rose—and especially among those interested in African commerce. Men like Macgregor Laird and Robert Jamieson began to claim that legitimate trade could defeat the slave trade after all.[40]

The new opponents of the anti-slavery squadron carried the argument a step further in the 1840's and 1850's. If, as some claimed, "legitimate trade" could do its work without assistance, the squadron was a useless expense.[41] A still more extreme position could be taken—that any commerce, including the slave trade, helped to spread civilization. From this point of view, the squadron was a positive evil, since, as one spokesman put it, "every obstacle to commerce in slaves even becomes a drawback, in my opinion, to the civilization of the African people."[42]

Humanitarians, on the other hand, began to doubt the civilizing virtues of commerce, whether "legitimate" or not. Missionaries still pictured the "degraded" coastal peoples, even after the slave trade had ceased to operate. Commissioner Madden suspected the influence of European traders, whose personal character was "not calculated to leave many germs of civilization in any barbarous soil."[43] The supposedly "higher" culture of the interior also suggested that "legitimate trade" could not be the only cause of cultural progress. (The

40. Laird and Oldfield, *Narrative of an Expedition,* I, 3; Jamieson's strongest argument is in R. Jamieson, *Commerce with Africa: The Inefficacy of Treaties,* 2nd ed. (London, 1859), but the idea occurs here and there in his earlier works. Laird later changed his mind. See [M. Laird], "Remedies for the Slave Trade," *Westminster Review,* XXXIV, 147, (June, 1840).

41. W. B. Baikie, *Narrative of an Exploring Voyage up the Rivers Kwora and Binue (Commonly Known as the Niger and Tsadda) in 1854* (London, 1856), pp. 388–89; F. E. Forbes, *Six Months' Service in the African Blockade* (London, 1849), p. viii.

42. J. King, Evidence before the Hutt Committee, 9 May 1848, PP, 1847–1848, xxii (366), p. 34, q. 4061.

43. R. R. Madden, Commissioner's Report, 31 July 1841, PP, 1842, xii (551), p. 34.

trans-Sahara trade, being largely in slaves, was not "legitimate" in European eyes.)

Various explanations began to appear, trying to account for the failure of "legitimate trade." A writer in *Blackwood's* explained that commerce brings civilization only at the higher stages of society: savages desire commerce only for the sake of trade gin and guns. The step from savagery to barbarism must come first—then commerce, and progress toward still higher stages.[44] The Wesleyan missionary, T. B. Freeman, suggested another explanation. Aside from the evil of rum as a commercial article, there was also an "unhealthy excitement of petty trading," and commerce developed a "spirit of chicanery." More important still, he held that Africans were spoiled by growing rich and independent too fast, and with only a smattering of education.[45]

For those who began to fear the dangers of commercial intercourse, there were two major alternatives. One was to call for more active government intervention. Commissioner Madden, for example, wanted government regulation to reform the abusive practices, as he saw them, of the British merchants on the Coast. Others called for still more education, more missionaries. As a last resource, there remained the possibility of even more direct intervention. Macgregor Laird came to this in 1842, saying: "The Gambia is in our possession; we put down the slave trade at the Gambia not by commerce, because commerce created the slave trade; we put it down by the moral force of our fort establishment. . . . Moral power on the coast of Africa means a 24-pounder, with British seamen behind it."[46]

The second alternative was to fall back from "legitimate" commerce to agriculture. This was, indeed, the essence of MacQueen's plan: "Commerce must follow agriculture in every country. It is by her agriculture alone, the cultivation of her soil, that Africa can be regenerated. . . ."[47] Buxton's acceptance of this view helped to convince the humanitarians,[48] and it revived many of the older arguments about the superiority of agricultural to commercial development. Even

44. "Africa," *Blackwood's Magazine*, XLIX, 109–13 (January, 1841). See also Huntley, *Seven Years' Service*, I, 400; Ajayi, "Christian Missions," pp. 202–3.

45. T. B. Freeman, 23 February 1852, PP, 1852, xxxi [C. 1539], p. 191.

46. Macgregor Laird, Evidence before West Africa Committee, 15 June 1842, PP, 1842, xi (551), p. 348.

47. J. MacQueen, *A Geographical Survey of Africa* (London, 1840), p. xlvii.

48. See T. Fowell Buxton, *The African Slave Trade*, 2nd ed. (London, 1839), pp. 55–56.

officials, like Governor MacDonnell of the Gambia, began to point out the positive values of agricultural life. He found the roving habits of the ivory hunters and palm-oil gatherers harmful: these occupations required neither foresight nor steady labor, and they were fostered by commerce. Farmers who produced peanuts, on the other hand, had to supply "steady labour and deliberate purpose," thus producing a taste for peaceful pursuits, for European goods, and hence for civilization.[49]

The common ground of all these theories of acculturation was the belief that culture change and economic development went hand in hand. The rival claims of agriculture and commerce as agents of civilization merged with a broader problem of promoting economic development, not only for Africa, but for the whole tropical world, and for Britain herself.

49. Macdonnell to Pakington, 12 July 1852, PP, 1852, xxi [C. 1539], p. 197.

18

WEST AFRICA

IN

THE SOUTH ATLANTIC ECONOMY

B ritish statesmen and publicists at most times thought of West Africa as a special region with its own individual problems. When they considered British economic interests and intentions, however, they thought in broader terms. The tropical Atlantic was still conceived as an inter-related economic entity, and with some justice. The flourishing South Atlantic System of the eighteenth century was no longer fully operating, but it was not yet completely dismantled either. Between the 1780's and the 1830's, each of the national sectors had undergone its own kind of evolution without destroying the essence of the system—the combination of forced African labor producing tropical staples in America for consumption in Europe. British legislation had cut off the labor supply to the British sector in 1807, emancipated the slaves as of 1838, and tried to impede the flow of labor to the other national sectors through the anti-slavery blockade. Nevertheless, the greater part of the tropical staples entering world trade was still produced in tropical America, still produced with the labor of slaves, still maintained and expanded by the slave trade from Africa.

There had, of course, been important changes. The supply of slave labor to the southern United States no longer came from the slave trade, but from the normal population growth of the slave caste. With Saint Domingue out of the system—now the Republic of Haiti and relatively unproductive for world markets—the French sector was very much reduced in size. Whether because of abolition and emancipation, or for other reasons, economic growth in the British sector lagged behind the pace set in Cuba and Brazil.

Britain was not, by this token, any the less involved. Two vital changes, which affected her relations to the international system as a whole, had taken place since the 1780's. First, even before the real beginning of the free-trade era, trade barriers between the national sectors of the South Atlantic System had broken down. Each European power tried to protect its national economic interests, but none of them made a serious attempt after 1815 to recreate a complete and self-sufficient empire of trade and plantations. As a result, trade and investment flowed in broader channels. North American and British capitalists invested in Cuba and Brazil. Only a fraction of Cuban and Brazilian agricultural production was sold in the Iberian peninsula. The very illegality of the slave trade opened it to international participation. Typically, a Baltimore-built ship, manned by a polyglot crew, might carry British-made textiles and iron ware to the coast of Africa in return for slaves destined for Havana.

In addition, Great Britain was by far the world leader in economic growth during this half century. It produced the cheapest manufactured goods, consumed an increasing share of the raw materials entering trade, and served as the world's principal money market. Wherever political control might rest, the economic metropolis was London. This was especially true for the fastest growing portion of the whole system—the cotton kingdom of the American South. The southern United States had been peripheral to the eighteenth-century South Atlantic System with its emphasis on sugar, but the southern states were central to the modified and industrialized version of the early nineteenth century. Still, there remained genuine and important British interests south of the Straits of Florida. The British West Indies supplied most of the British demand for sugar and coffee until the 1850's, and British exports went everywhere in the South Atlantic. During the six years, 1847-52, when West Africa took .89 per cent of British exports and the British West Indies took 3.14 per cent, Brazil took 4.16 per cent—more than both the others combined. In addition, Cuba and the other foreign West Indies took 2.18 per cent.[1] In short, the truly tropical sections of the old South Atlantic System still took about 10 per cent of all British exports.

The British had been forced since the 1780's to reconsider the South Atlantic System and their relations to it, with a peculiarly important line of decisions from the Emancipation Act of 1833 to the 1850 decision to keep the blockade on the African coast.

West Africa was implicated both directly and indirectly. The dream of an African eldorado was still alive. For some at least, West Africa was still a place where, "nature seems everywhere bountiful and prolific, and the animal and vegetable worlds develop a countless variety of forms; and even the processes of their decay and reproduction go on more rapidly than in almost any other country. The soil is so fertile that grain is sowed and reaped in the space of three months . . . ."[2]

The economic faith underlying Buxton's plan was the same dream of plenty which had tempted the projectors of the 1780's. Only the promised commodities changed in pace with changing British needs. The tropical woods, nuts, gums, coffee, and sugar of the earlier aspiration were now joined by gold, iron ore, and cotton—especially cotton.[3] British manufacturers were more and more concerned about their dependence on the United States for this key raw material. Though Africa was not alone among possible alternate sources of supply, the promise of cotton gave West Africa another claim to attention—something beyond its claims on British charity or its pitifully small share of British trade—and enthusiasts for African empire were eager to exploit the opening. In 1849, James MacQueen told the Lords' Committee on the slave trade: "there is no country in the world which can produce such an immense quantity of cotton of a quality so fine; it is finer cotton than any description of cotton we know in the world: common cotton in Africa I have seen and had in

1. J. R. McCulloch, *A Descriptive and Statistical Account of the British Empire,* 4th ed., 2 vols. (London, 1854), II, 20.

2. J. Howison, *European Colonies in Various Parts of the World, Viewed in their Social, Moral and Physical Condition,* 2 vols. (London, 1834), I, 34.

3. T. Fowell Buxton, *The African Slave Trade,* 2nd ed. (London, 1839), pp. 200–220; *The Remedy: Being a Sequel to the African Slave Trade* (London, 1840), pp. 19–61.

my possession which was equal to the finest quality of American cotton."[4]

Still another West African possibility was perennially attractive. The enforced labor-mobility of the slave trade appeared to be uneconomic. If, as the enthusiasts claimed, African soils were unused and as rich as those of tropical America, tropical crops could be grown more cheaply in Africa itself. This economic concept underlay a whole succession of projects for African development, from the seventeenth century down to the period of MacQueen and the Buxton plan. Earlier opposition to these projects had justified the slave trade as a nursery for seamen, and mercantilist doctrine had favored production within the existing British colonies. In the light of free-trade economics, both arguments fell to the ground. If the lowest costs of production for tropical raw materials were to be found in Africa, then African production should be encouraged. There was still no empirical evidence that African products *were* cheaper, but the economic reasoning was persuasive. In theory, at least, the old South Atlantic System was inefficient.

Great Britain had, indeed, been trying since 1807 to stop the trans-Atlantic slave trade (though not entirely for economic reasons). The economic results by the 1830's, were not very promising. To the extent that the anti-slave-trade policy was successful—and it was successfully enforced only in the British sector of the System—it seemed merely to impede the economic growth of the British West Indies. African development was still retarded by the continued illegal slave trade. Brazil and Cuba received the slaves and expanded their production of sugar and coffee at the expense of the British colonies. It appeared by 1840 that the foreign slave trade was not only morally wrong but economically disastrous to British interests. Furthermore the slave trade was economically viable in at least one sense. Cuban and Brazilian planters could afford to pay the high cost of smuggled labor and

---

4. PP, 1849 (Lords), xxviii (32), p. 341. For the special promise of cotton see also MacQueen, Memorandum of 12 January 1839, CO 2/22; C. Johnston, "The Friends of the African," *Simmonds's Colonial Magazine*, XIII, 292–96, 435–39 (March–April, 1848), p. 293; Macdonald to Grey, 18 August 1851, PP, 1851, xxxiv [C. 1421], p. 173; Sir George Stephen, *The Niger Trade Considered in Connexion with the African Blockade* (London, 1849), p. 66; W. B. Baikie, *Narrative of an Exploring Voyage up the Rivers Kwora and Binue (Commonly Known as the Niger and Tsadda) in 1854* (London, 1856), pp. 385–86.

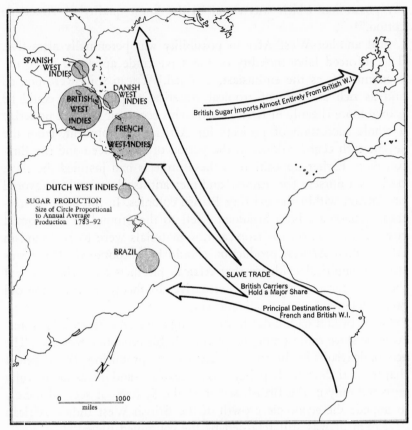

Map 20. Britain in the South Atlantic, 1780's

still compete in world markets. Clearly, then, there was a marked difference between what ought to have happened and what had happened.

Those who thought of the slave trade in economic terms saw it as
a matter of supply and demand. As long ago as 1792, Edmund Burke
had warned that demand for slaves was a natural economic demand,
which would be filled (whether legally or illegally) as long as it continued.[5] After three decades of trying to impede the slave trade by
force and diplomatic pressure, Burke's warning seemed all the more
valid: it went on because it was profitable.

Buxton's adaptation of MacQueen's economic reasoning was designed to render it unprofitable. Britain had failed to stop the eco-

5. E. Burke, "Letter to the Right Honourable Henry Dundas . . ." in *Works,* 16
vols. (London, 1803–1827), IX, 278–79.

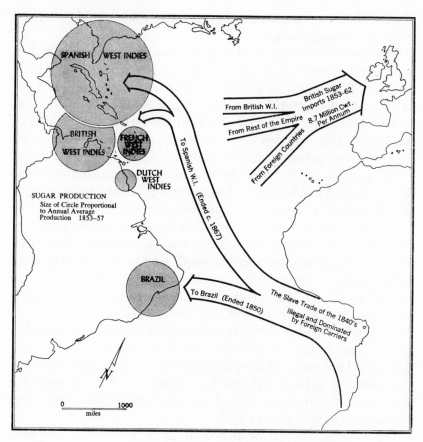

Map 21. Britain in the South Atlantic, 1850's

nomic demand for slaves, but it might be possible to change the cost conditions on the supply side, in Africa itself. Buxton showed that a slave sold in Brazil was worth £100, while the same slave in the interior of Africa brought only £3. The spread between these two prices was the economic force that drove the slave trade. It existed because there was no effective demand for labor in Africa itself. It could be cured when the African authorities had learned "the superior value of man as a labourer on the soil, to man as an object of merchandise."[6] Economic development in Africa would raise the price of slaves, make it unprofitable for the Brazilians to buy them, and thus bring the slave trade to an end. The blockade would still be necessary as an interim

6. Buxton, *The African Slave Trade*, p. 195.

measure, but the permanent end of the slave trade would have to be found in economic change.[7]

This line of reasoning could attract a broad following. Humanitarians would support it because of the ultimate goal of slave-trade abolition. Enthusiasts for African development would support it for its own sake. Some British economic nationalists would support it, because it promised a greater sphere of British interests and the ruin of the American slave-holders—a popular prospect, as much because they were American as because they were slave-holders.

The position of the West India interest was a mixed one. The British planters had been forced to accept legal emancipation in 1834 and the end of a transitional "apprenticeship system" in 1838. The change to a system of wage labor had been peaceful but unhappy. Neither the planters nor the ex-slaves were accustomed to wage payments. The problem was further complicated by the fact that West Indian planters were under-capitalized and saddled with an outmoded scale of production. Their costs of production were high in comparison with those elsewhere, and the British West Indian sugar and coffee industries kept going as well as they did only because they sold their products in the protected British market. On the one hand, they feared the potential competition of the more modern, slave-run plantations of Cuba and Puerto Rico. They, therefore, opposed the slave trade. But they also feared new production from Africa and opposed the Buxton plan as well.

The favorite solution of the West India interest was to lower British West Indian costs. The planters were naturally conscious of the regular payroll as a new item in their accounts. Their own assessment of their plight therefore stressed a wage bill that was "too high." Many British analysts agreed. The money wages commonly paid in the West Indies after 1838 were higher than those paid to English agricultural laborers, but this evidence was misleading. Price levels were also normally much higher in the West Indies than in England so that comparisons of money wages had no meaning in real terms.[8] British economic thought nevertheless followed West Indian,

7. Buxton, *The Remedy*, esp. pp. 155–56.
8. The error of comparing money wages was occasionally pointed out at the time. See, for example, *African Colonizer*, 6 March 1841, p. 158. Wages also differed very markedly from one West Indian colony to another. See P. D. Curtin, "The British Sugar Duties and West Indian Prosperity," *Journal of Economic History*, XIV, 157–64 (Spring, 1954), p. 163.

and concentrated on the problem of lowering the cost of West Indian labor.

Regarding labor costs, the most common affirmation of the classical economists had been that free labor would be cheaper than slave—at equilibrium. The equilibrium wage rate would, indeed, be the bare cost of subsistence. Any lower rate would bring about a decline of population, thus a shortage of labor and a return to equilibrium. Any higher rate would bring about population growth and new hands to compete on the labor market.

The known demographic trends in the West Indies seemed to confirm the belief in a labor shortage. When the immigration of slaves was cut off in 1808, the population of many islands declined slightly before it began to rise again in about the 1830's. Even then, the rate of increase was low at first.[9] The apparent scarcity of labor was also influenced by the fact that many colonies—almost all except Barbados—contained tracts of land unused by the plantation economy but perfectly suitable for cultivation. On emancipation, many of the ex-slaves preferred to farm on their own rather than accept wage labor on the plantations. The existence of this alternative to plantation labor made it difficult to depress wages by tacit agreement among the planters. As long as the planters were forced to accept a free market for labor, and as long as they believed the wages they had to pay were far above the equilibrium rate, the logical alternative was to encourage immigration in order to force the wage rate back to its "natural" level.[10]

The idea of induced immigration was especially attractive in the two West Indian colonies acquired during the Napoleonic Wars— Trinidad and British Guiana. Neither had been intensively developed in the heyday of the South Atlantic System. Both had large areas of new land where modern sugar plantations could be laid out. Their superior prospects for development were reflected in the value of their slaves at the time of emancipation. Field slaves were worth £170 each in Guiana, £110 in Trinidad, but only £75 in Barbados and £67 in Jamaica.[11] In effect, both British Guinana and Trinidad con-

9. G. W. Roberts, *The Population of Jamaica* (Cambridge, 1957), pp. 40–45.

10. See H. Merivale, *Lectures on Colonisation and Colonies,* 2nd ed. (London, 1861), pp. 300–332, for an authoritative summary of these views. See P. D. Curtin, *Two Jamaicas* (Cambridge, Mass., 1955), pp. 133–41 for the local application of these ideas in Jamaica.

11. Merivale, *Colonisation and Colonies,* p. 333.

tained a potential planters' frontier at the time of emancipation, but it could only move forward with a large supply of imported labor.

The economic fortunes of the West Indies and West Africa were thus related, and in three different ways. West Africa was the ancient source of labor supply, and might some day again furnish immigrants to fill up the land and make development possible. Meanwhile, it provided the labor on which the prosperity of Cuba and Brazil was based. In the more distant future, West Africa itself might be an economic competitor with its own plantations.

For a British theorist wishing to maximize the value of the South Atlantic economy for the Empire as a whole, Buxton's scheme had certain disadvantages. Even if it worked, it would have beggared the British West Indies along with the rest of tropical America. Other schemes had therefore already made their appearance, beginning shortly after the emancipation of the slaves. Macgregor Laird thought he had discovered a way to ruin the slave trade and the competitive position of Latin American producers, and yet preserve the prosperity of both the West Indies and West Africa. His project was first sketched in 1837 and then developed more fully in 1840. He took the economic viability of the slave trade as his point of departure. If the slave trade were profitable, aiding labor mobility across the South Atlantic could be considered a natural and proper economic activity, though not in its current form. For Laird, the way to ruin the slave trade was to introduce even greater mobility for free labor. His plan called for a government-operated shipping service, offering free passage for contract laborers from West Africa to the British West Indies and subsidized by the West Indian colonies. He tried to forestall humanitarian opposition by insisting on careful controls over contracts, limited in any case to one year and further guarded by the provision that each group of migrants must contain both men and women in equal numbers. After a year, they would have a right to free return passage to Africa.[12]

Where the MacQueen-Buxton plan sought to raise costs on the supply side of the slave trade, Laird's scheme sought to alter the demand side by subsidizing British, wage-labor migration at the expense of Latin, slave-labor migration. In the longer run the Brazilian and Cuban demand for slaves would dry up at the source through failure

12. M. Laird and R. A. K. Oldfield, *Narrative of an Expedition into the Interior of Africa by the River Niger in 1832–4*, 2 vols. (London, 1837), II, 357–76; [M. Laird], "Remedies for the Slave Trade," *Westminster Review*, XXXIV, 155–59 (June, 1840).

of their slave plantations to compete successfully with British, wage-labor sugar and coffee. The two plans also differed in another important respect. Laird would have abandoned the expensive naval blockade. The Spanish and Brazilians would be left free to carry on the slave trade, though forbidden to buy slaves within defined spheres of British interest. In these spheres, a scheme of economic development similar to the Buxton plan would be undertaken. Laird looked to the Niger Delta-Cameroons region, supported from a base on Fernando Po. His plan included an agricultural school to provide instruction and a series of treaties with the riverine states of the Niger and Benue to secure British interests in the hinterland. This sphere was expected to grow, partly through the influence of returned laborers from America and partly through a series of small expeditions to explore the further interior.[13]

Laird's plan had an obvious appeal for all those who opposed the Buxton plan—either because of its threat to West Indian prosperity, its threat to established African trade, or its Evangelical base. W. R. Greg brought out a pamphlet presenting Laird's arguments in terms of classical economics and Benthamite legal theory.[14] The Government itself tacitly accepted many of Laird's ideas along with Buxton's, and the full West African project of 1840 was a modified combination of the two. The blockade was to be strengthened, the Niger Expedition itself was to commence African economic development, and the preliminary investigation for a labor-migration scheme was assigned to Dr. Madden.[15] In this way the Niger effort was coupled with a broader intent to reform the whole South Atlantic economy.

In the initial stages of 1840 and 1841, the emphasis lay with African development. After the Niger failure, however, the Parliamentary Committee of 1842 altered the balance in favor of the West Indies. Government assistance for inter-continental migration might appear to be contrary to the ideals of laissez faire economics, but a decade of agitation by the Colonial Reformers had already had its effect. The Australian colonies had begun to subsidize emigration out of money received for the sale of land. The idea of "systematic colonization" was given metropolitan approval in 1840 with the creation of a Board of Colonial Land and Emigration Commissioners,

13. Laird, "Remedies for the Slave Trade," pp. 139–162.

14. W. R. Greg, *Past and Present Efforts for the Extinction of the African Slave Trade* (London, 1840).

15. Lord John Russell to R. R. Madden, 26 November 1840, CO 267/170.

empowered to supervise assisted emigration from Britain to Australia.

It was an easy transfer to shift the basic scheme from temperate to tropical colonies. Sir John Jeremie wanted to remake the Buxton plan into a close copy of Wakefield's schemes for the settlement of Australia, but substituting colored West Indians for European immigrants.[16] Where Jeremie wanted an eastward migration, the *Colonial Gazette,* principal organ of the Colonial Reformers, described the more common project for a westward migration as "systematic African colonization," thus emphasizing its similarity to the accepted scheme for colonizing Australia.[17]

Some problems remained including Dr. Madden's objection that genuinely free emigration from Africa to America was not possible, but the Parliamentary Committee listened more sympathetically to Macgregor Laird. He now appeared before them with quantitative estimates: two steamers could transport 12,000 Africans a year in either direction at a one-way cost of £6 each. The Committee's report followed Laird's recommendations and called for African labor to redress the competitive balance in tropical America.[18]

The scheme was launched in 1843 with ships in charge of government officials and the cost of migration borne by the West Indian colonies. Three ships were initially placed in this service, mainly to carry recaptives who would otherwise have been settled at Sierra Leone. The migrants signed a five-year contract with a promise of free repatriation at the end of the term.[19] In all, some 14,000 free emigrants were taken to the West Indies under this and successive schemes during the 1840's, but the plan was not a success. The free emigrants of a whole decade were only a fraction of the number making a similar trip each year as slaves. They were not enough either to outdo the Cubans in economic growth, or to depress the wage levels of the British islands.

By the mid-1840's, the promise of Laird's first plan, which might have attracted broad support for the joint development of both sides of the South Atlantic, had come to nothing. The West India interest were dissatisfied with the government controls on immigration, which

16. Sir John Jeremie, *A Letter to T. F. Buxton on Negro Emancipation and African Civilization* (London, 1840), pp. 20–23.

17. *Colonial Gazette,* 2 February 1822, p. 65.

18. R. R. Madden, Commissioner's Report, PP, 1842, xii (551), pp. 255–57 and 265–67; M. Laird, Evidence before West Africa Committee, 11 July 1842, PP, 1842, xi (551), p. 572; Report of the West Africa Committee, PP, 1842, xi (551), p. x.

19. Stanley to Macdonald, 6 February 1843, PP, 1843, xxxiv [C. 438], pp. 3–5; PP, 1841, xxxiv [C. 1421], p. 189.

they regarded as onerous restrictions on their labor supply. Humanitarians tended to oppose emigration from Africa, even with controls, since it could easily turn into a disguised slave trade. They objected to the methods of recruitment in Sierra Leone, and the missionaries in particular resented the removal of liberated Africans from their own chosen training ground for the civilization of Africa through "native agency." British opinion gradually hardened into two camps —a humanitarian, pro-African group and an anti-humanitarian, West Indian group.[20] Meanwhile, the hope for tropical development under British aegis on either side of the Atlantic was unfulfilled.

A third possibility appeared during the 1840's, with the rise of the economic doctrine of free trade. Instead of promoting economic growth in either the British West Indies or a British sphere in Africa, the free-traders urged Britain to buy in the cheapest market. For sugar, the cheapest market was the slave economy of Latin America. Both the humanitarians and the West India interest were unhappy at the prospect. Both argued that moral considerations made it necessary to protect the British sugar colonies with their new systems of wage labor. They were answered by the cry for cheap sugar and claims for the ultimate morality of the "unseen hand" of economic law.[21] As for the West Indian plantations, it was argued that free trade might be painful in the short run, but open competition would be to their long-run advantage.

When the Corn Laws fell in 1846, the sugar duties followed, being scaled down gradually to reach equality for all imported sugar in 1854. The price of sugar in London dropped by 44 per cent, and the British consumption per capita doubled between 1845 and 1854. Part of the new demand was met by the planters of the British West Indies, but much more of it came from foreign colonies or other parts of the British Empire.[22]

Free trade in sugar radically altered the British view of West Africa in the South Atlantic economy. It was especially important in changing the British attitude toward the anti-slavery blockade. Objections to the blockade had been heard from the time of the Buxton

20. For representative opinions on either side of this controversy see: W. R. Greg, "The Slave Trade and the Sugar Duties," *Westminster Review,* XLI, 243–58 (June, 1844) and Dandeson Coates to Lord Stanley, 26 November 1844, PP, 1845, xxxi (158), pp. 3–8. See also the House of Commons debates of 25 February 1845, 3 H 77, cc. 1173–1203.

21. For a summary of the argument see H. Merivale, *Lectures on Colonisation and Colonies,* 2 vols. (London, 1841–1842), I, 201–2.

22. Curtin, "The British Sugar Duties," p. 160.

plan, and Laird's first scheme would have abolished it. After 1846 the older arguments that it was expensive, useless, and inhumane were joined by new considerations. The general philosophy of the free trade movement was unfriendly to government expenditure, to the use of force, and to "artificial" adjustments of the society or the economy. Its rising popularity eroded away some support for anti-slavery patrols. More directly, the end of the sugar duties ended the attempt of British tariff policy to favor the British West Indies over Latin America. It was generally conceded that non-discriminatory sugar duties would lead to an increase of Cuban and Brazilian sugar production. Higher production would necessarily call for still more slaves. To impede the slave trade with the squadron, while favoring it in tariff policy, seemed a contradiction, and one that sacrificed a profitable form of control while keeping an expensive form. Not only the free-traders took this line. Many protectionists used the same argument, with a slightly different conclusion. If the public had to pay in some form or other for the anti-slavery cause, let them buy the expensive, free-labor sugars from the British West Indies. In return, let them give up the expensive anti-slavery blockade. Finally, merchants in the Latin American trade argued that Britain's best interest lay in the growth of the Latin American market, which would develop more rapidly and humanely with a properly organized and regulated slave trade.[23]

All these tendencies of thought merged with the decline of humanitarian fervor, the rise of a tougher minded kind of racist sentiment, and the continued fact that the anti-slavery blockade did not prevent the slave trade. In 1845, William Hutt launched the Parliamentary campaign to abolish the blockade, beginning the six-year effort that was only barely defeated in 1850. The campaign has often been written off as a manifestation of economy-minded isolationist sentiment. It did, indeed, appeal to those who wanted lower taxes, but the ultimate intention was more complex. Hutt himself was no isolationist. He had served on the West Africa Committee of 1842, and he was both a free trader and a Colonial Reformer. This combination of interests made him especially conscious of labor immobility, and his attack on the blockade was part of a broad program—often in-

23. These trends of thought and sentiment are found widely scattered through the indexed debates of Parliament on the subject of the blockade and the sugar duties between 1845 and 1851 and in the hearings of the two Parliamentary Committees on the Blockade, 1848–1850. The subject was also widely discussed in the press, especially in *The Times*.

tentionally imprecise in detail—covering the whole of Britain's South Atlantic policy. Its initial objective was the removal of the squadron, for the usual variety of reasons. More positively, Hutt proposed a broad encouragement of African trade (but not agriculture) through the establishment of a series of small posts all along both coasts of Africa. This much was in line with the proposals of the 1842 Committee. Even more important, he wanted to allow the British West Indian governments to import "free" workers without interference from the imperial government, and in greater numbers than the rival slave trade.[24]

Hutt and his followers were rarely specific, but it was already clearly understood that really large numbers of Africans could be recruited only by purchase through the usual channels of the slave trade. The workers' freedom would therefore have been somewhat illusory, though they would have received wages from the time of arrival in America; and sooner or later they would have been allowed some freedom of choice in renewing their contracts.

Other plans, however, took a different line. Some were more genuinely liberal. Macgregor Laird, for example, modified his earlier scheme. In 1848, he came up with a project for absolute trans-Atlantic mobility of African labor. In place of contracts or repatriation guarantees, he wanted a system of free transportation. The British government would establish a steamship service between West Africa and the West Indies. Any individual of African descent could then obtain passage without cost in either direction at any time, and the whole operation would simply be written off as a British subsidy to tropical development.[25]

At the other extreme, some of the plans presented at the time of the Hutt Committee were openly designed to revive the British slave trade. William Allen, one-time commander of the Niger Expedition, was among the more forthright. He believed that the blockade could never stop the slave trade in tropical Africa, and that tropical exuberance would prevent a successful system of pure wage labor in tropical America. In his opinion, Britain should give up opposition to the slave trade and create an international, regulated slave trade under her own control. According to this scheme, Britain would supply

24. W. Hutt, Commons, 24 June 1845, 3 H 81, cc. 1156–1172.
25. M. Laird, Evidence before the Hutt Committee, 11 April 1848, PP, 1847–1848, xxii (272), pp. 203–4.

slaves to the remaining slave-holding territories in America, but with a limitation on the length of service. Each slave would be tattooed with his date of arrival in America. After a period of slavery in Brazil or Cuba he would be transferred to one of the wage-labor territories, such as the British West Indies, there to serve another period as an "apprentice." After this double servitude in tropical America, he would be returned to the African coast.[26]

A similar scheme was outlined to the Hutt Committee by Jose E. Cliffe, a North American turned Brazilian citizen, and a former slave trader. Cliffe explained to the Committee that Africans were natural slaves, created as such by God, who had placed them in the one region where white men could not live. It seemed part of the divine plan that they should serve as a reservoir of tropical labor. The British effort to stop the slave trade was, therefore, contrary to God's will, and the British had already been punished by the ruin of their West Indian colonies. According to Cliffe, the remedy was a system of "free immigration"—that is, the purchase of slaves in Africa for service in America. Like Allen, Cliffe would have tattooed the date of purchase on each slave, granting emancipation in America at the end of eight to ten years of slavery.[27]

Whether the justification came from a theory of tropical exuberance or teleological racism, the result would have been much the same; and both proposals had another weakness. Neither system would have given British planters an advantage over their Latin American competitors. Other suggestions, however, took this problem into account. J. L. Hook, formerly of the Sierra Leone emigration office, thought that "free" emigration could be monopolized. According to his scheme, the government should enter into contracts with African chiefs, providing an annual subsidy equal to their former profits from the slave trade, in return for the exclusive right to purchase slaves as "free immigrants."[28] Another variant suggestion was to withhold "free immigrants" from Brazil and Cuba unless they emancipated their slaves and thus put themselves on the same footing

26. William Allen, *A Plan for the Immediate Extinction of the Slave Trade, for the Relief of the West India Colonies, and for the Diffusion of Civilization and Christianity in Africa, by the co-operation of Mammon and Philanthropy* (London, 1849).

27. Jose E. Cliffe, Evidence before the Hutt Committee, 16 May 1848, PP, 1847–1848, xxii (366), pp. 72–74.

28. J. L. Hook, Evidence before the Hutt Committee, 9 May 1848, PP, 1847–1848, xxii (366), p. 27.

as the British West Indies.[29]

The strongest opposition to any of these proposals for a disguised slave trade came from predictable sources. The humanitarians; some naval officers, who took the attack on the blockade to be an attack on their profession; Lord Palmerston, who was committed to a diplomatic solution—all these united to stop the Hutt group in Parliament. There was, however, another current of opposition from a less expected source. The West Indian planters were angered by the repeal of the sugar duties, and their initial reaction was to seek a new supply of cheap African labor. But then there were second thoughts. Barbardos already had plenty of labor, and some highly placed Barbadians were even thinking of settling part of their redundant population in Africa. Jamaica had little unused land that was really suitable for sugar. The older West Indian sugar colonies as a group soon recognized that they could be ruined just as effectively by the competition of Trinidad and British Guiana as by that of Cuba and Brazil. In the summer of 1849, an organized campaign in favor of the blockade swept Jamaica. It was partly an effort to help the humanitarians on the blockade issue in return for humanitarian help with the sugar duties, but the fact remained that West Indian sugar producers would not stand together and demand large-scale immigration from Africa.[30]

The school of Africa developers were still more adamant. For them, it was clear that more intensive slave raiding in Africa would ruin any hope of realizing their dream of African agricultural bounty. They opposed the Hutt plan for a disguised slave trade as they had opposed the foreign and undisguised slave trade. If forced to choose, many would have favored the British West Indies over other parts of tropical or sub-tropical America. To this end, they occasionally suggested leaving sugar to the West Indies, while West Africa concentrated on cotton.[31] It was a useful tactic to soften West Indian opposition. It was also a claim to British support for their plans, if African development could promise to ruin the Latin American sugar planters and the North American cotton planters at one blow,

29. J. King, Evidence before the Hutt Committee, 9 May 1848, PP, 1847–1848, xxii (366), pp. 30 ff.

30. [D. Turnbull], (Ed.), *The Jamaica Movement for Promoting the Enforcement of the Slave-Trade Treaties and for the Suppression of the Slave Trade.* (London, 1850); PP, 1849, xix (308), pp. 152–55; James MacQueen, Evidence before Lords' Slave Trade Committee, 5 July 1849, PP, 1849 (Lords), xxviii (32), p. 347.

31. Edward Nicholls, Memorandum of 20 July 1842, enclosed in Nicholls to Canning, 28 July 1845, FO 84/616.

and yet preserve the West Indies' prosperity. MacQueen told the Lords' Committee on the slave trade that the slave plantations of America would be finished the minute West Africa exported a half million bales of cotton and two or three thousand tons of sugar.[32]

From the point of view of the African school, the final outcome was a stalemate. The Niger Expedition failed. The repeal of the sugar duties was allowed to stand. The projects for African labor emigration failed, and the Hutt proposals were defeated by Parliament.

But, on the whole, the decade of the 1840's ended more hopefully than it began, and the decade was marked by a whole series of new projects or alternatives to the Niger Expedition. In all these plans, the Niger project was the point of departure, drawing in, as it did, many threads of past suggestion. The Niger project had, indeed, been something of a catch-all. It included a primary emphasis on trade, but it also had a European-managed plantation in the form of the "model-farm." The model farm itself might have been a form of technical assistance—a genuine model for African entrepreneurs to copy —or it might have been the model for future European-run plantations. The only missing element was the suggestion that Africans might develop economically by producing and trading more efficiently among themselves.

When the projectors of the 1840's began to re-write the Niger plan, they could emphasize any aspect they chose. In so doing, they raised anew all the problems of economic development—trade vs. agriculture, open trade vs. monopolized trade, peasant proprietorship vs. European-managed plantations.

The most popular kind of project was to emphasize trade and let African production rise to meet the effective demand. Most projectors also preferred an open trade to monopoly. Buxton himself had a certain bias toward free trade. (He had hoped to make Fernando Po a free port, on the model of Singapore, without duties or discrimination of any kind.)[33] The more extreme supporters of laissez faire, however, disapproved of all government assistance, even that given to the Niger Expedition. The most consistent pamphleteer in this cause was Robert Jamieson, who was willing to compete with the slave traders but not with government expeditions. His economic case against the Niger Expedition was based on the superiority of free

32. J. MacQueen, Evidence before Lords' Slave Trade Committee, PP, 1849 (Lords), xxviii (32), p. 342.
33. Buxton, The Remedy, pp. 161–62.

enterprise. With government aid, his argument ran, Europeans would engage in agriculture. Once engaged in agriculture, they would want a chartered company. If they formed a chartered company, they would want monopoly powers. If they were given a monopoly, they would drive down the prices offered to the African producers. If the Africans were not paid fair prices, they would return to subsistence farming. When that happened, all development would end.[34]

Non-commercial observers were also concerned about the level of prices offered the Africans. Henry Venn took up the kind of watch-dog activity the Quaker, William Allen, had once sponsored in Sierra Leone, keeping a check on the prices paid in Africa in relation to prices on the London market. From time to time he laid out a little of his own capital in arrowroot or ginger as a way of keeping the African prices as high as possible.[35]

Most projectors thought economic development would require some government assistance. MacQueen had always wanted a char-tered company with a legal monopoly, on the order of the later Royal Niger Company. Dr. Thomas Kehoe, who had served with the army on Fernando Po, would have settled for something like the Niger Expedition restricted to its commercial aspects. That is, government subsidy to steamers on the Niger and a government entrepôt at the confluence of the Niger and Benue, but no missionaries, no model farm, and no agriculture managed by Europeans.[36]

By contrast, Sir George Stephen, brother of the Permanent Under-Secretary, wanted government commercial enterprise on a much more elaborate scale. Stephen believed in free trade for dveloped countries, but he held that, "Whatever is done for Africa, must for many years to come, be done upon the responsibility of Government; we dare not entrust the responsibility elsewhere."[37] If trade were to appear where none had flowed in the past, the producer had to be assured a firm price, a fair price, and a regular market. This automatically called for monopoly, since a free market was a fluctuating market. It also called

34. R. Jamieson, *An Appeal to the Government and People of Great Britain against the Proposed Niger Expedition* (London, 1840); *A Further Appeal against the Proposed Niger Expedition* (London, 1841); and especially *Sequel to Appeals made to the Government and People of Great Britain, against the Niger Expedition before its Departure from England* (London, 1843), pp. 10–12.

35. Henry Venn, Jr., "Notice on African Commerce," in William Knight, *The Missionary Secretariat of Henry Venn, B.D.* (London, 1880), pp. 540–41.

36. T. Kehoe, *Some Considerations in Favour of Forming a Settlement at the Confluence of the Niger and Tchadda* (Waterford, 1847).

37. Stephen, *The Niger Trade*, p. 57.

for government monopoly, since only the government could guarantee regularity of demand at a firm and fair price, willingly sustaining losses if necessary. On the basis of these considerations, Stephen arrived at a plan nearly foreshadowing the Marketing Boards of the twentieth century. The government would monopolize the Niger trade, offering a steady demand to the African producer. The goods purchased would be stored in government warehouses on Fernando Po and Annobon, where private merchants would always be sure to find a cargo.[38]

This was all very well, but the Colonial Office (and even more, the Treasury) took a narrower view. When Earl Grey was Secretary of State from 1846 to 1852, however, the Colonial Office offered at least a form of technical assistance. Grey tried to abolish shifting cultivation in Sierra Leone, and he favored peasants over plantations for the development of Gold Coast cotton. He thought that African peasants might well respond to economic demand. They were more likely to produce for export (alongside subsistence farming) than to give up subsistence agriculture and transform themselves into wage workers. Grey therefore encouraged European capitalists to set up cotton gins and buy uncleaned cotton at a firm price, rather than grow it themselves.[39]

Other projectors combined technical assistance with ideas for government investment. Governor MacDonnell of the Gambia wanted to attract migratory peanut farmers from neighboring territories by preparing plots in advance and letting them in return for a quitrent.[40] This idea of settling peasants in planned villages was persistent, and it recalled some of the early experiments at Sierra Leone. Edward Nicholls wanted to lay out villages on Fernando Po and elsewhere, letting the land on perpetual lease for 6 per cent of the gross production.[41]

Far more grandiose projects for government investment also turned up from time to time. The same Edward Phillips who thought African barbarism was caused by the alternation of wet and dry seasons sought a remedy and an impetus to economic growth in the provision

38. Stephen, *The Niger Trade, passim.*
39. Grey to Officer Administering Sierra Leone, 24 January 1849, CO 268/43; Winniett to Grey, 22 May 1850 (minuted by Grey), CO 96/18; Grey to Winniett, 14 August 1840, CO 402/2.
40. Macdonnell to Pakington, 12 July 1852, PP, 1852, xxxi [C. 1539], pp. 193–208.
41. Nicholls, Memorandum of 20 July 1842, enclosed with Nicholls to Canning, 28 June 1845, FO 84/616.

of irrigation works. In spite of his general ignorance of African conditions, he chose the interior delta of the Niger as the most promising site—exactly where the dams and cotton scheme of the *Office du Niger* were to rise a century later.[42]

Other projects emphasized technical assistance to African states beyond the range of British control. Brodie Cruickshank advanced a plan for persuading Dahomey to give up the slave trade: Britain should open a consulate in Ouidah, staffed by a diplomatic representative and a professional planter. The planter's salary would come from the British treasury as a subsidy to Dahomean economic development.[43] The King of Dahomey would provide land and labor for an experimental plantation, and retain title to the crop. In time, he would recognize his true advantage and transform himself from a slave merchant into a princely planter.

Most projects conceived in terms of large plantations, however, assumed that Europeans would be managers and owners, not mere technical advisors. But European ownership and management was difficult without European political sovereignty, and the government was set against territorial expansion. Occasional projects were nevertheless brought forward. The most elaborate was promoted in 1842 by R. Dillon Tennent, who issued a prospectus calling for a capital of £40,000 to develop part of Fernando Po and the nearby Amboizes Islands. Some of the land was to be in large plantations, "as if they were West India Estates." The rest could be let out to African, rent-paying peasants. Tennent planned, in addition, to have his own shipping line to Europe.

The project of the Barbados African Colonization Society of 1848 was similar, if more vague. They hoped to found a settlement on the coast of Africa, where members of the Barbadian planting class could take up estates. The nucleus of a labor force would be imported from Barbados and settled as peasants on labor tenures—that is, owing three days of free labor each week in return for the use of their plots. In time, it was thought that local Africans might also be brought into the colony.[44]

Plantation projects raised a further problem of the greatest importance in any plans for the development of tropical agriculture.

42. *Simmonds's Colonial Magazine,* X, 4–8 (January, 1847).
43. B. Cruickshank, Report of 9 November 1848, PP, 1849 (Lords), xxviii (32), p. 189.
44. African Agricultural Association, *Prospectus* (London, 1842); PP, 1849, xix (308), pp. 152–55.

African societies were almost all slave-holding societies, in the sense that some individuals were in a special status of peronal subordination to others. African slavery was never the same as the chattel slavery of the Americas, and the better informed Europeans recognized this fact; but they also saw the lack of a regular system of wage labor as a bar to economic development following Western capitalist norms. The Europeans themselves had not used capitalism exclusively in their earlier ventures in tropical agriculture. From the sixteenth century through to the early nineteenth, they had depended on some form of forced deliveries, forced labor, or slavery. In theory, they justified the practice as an accommodation to the social forms of non-Western society, or as the only possible way of making people work under conditions of tropical exuberance.

From the 1830's onward, however, wage labor was the official policy for the British colonies. Slavery was still tolerated in India and a few other places, but the dominant ideology of those who wished to civilize the world called for the export of British norms—including the British labor system. Yet the transition from slavery to wage labor had raised many problems in the West Indies and South Africa. European managers in the tropics remained convinced that some kind of forced labor was still a necessity. They might not want an outright return to slavery, but they were as inclined as ever to think in terms of tropical labor systems involving something more than the mere payment of wages.

James MacQueen, and virtually all the others who hoped for agricultural development beyond the area of direct British control, assumed that African authorities would simply put their slaves to work, rather than selling them. The result would have been slave production in Africa, but an end of the inter-continental slave trade.

The question of slavery in Africa was deftly handled in the preliminaries to the Niger Expedition. Buxton himself was intentionally imprecise. While it is clear that he accepted MacQueen's view—that African chiefs would use slave labor—he neither drew attention to this aspect of the plan, nor defended its morality. He insisted, indeed, that slavery should be forbidden in any territory Britain might acquire in Africa, but British territory, even in the original project, would merely have been a series of enclaves. Shortly before the expedition sailed, Buxton asked the Government to create one enclave of about one hundred square miles in which wage labor might be used as a demonstration. Otherwise, he was willing to accept slavery in Africa as a better alternative to a continued slave trade. In the end, the Niger Commissioners were only ordered to investigate the possibility of a British sovereign enclave. The Niger Expedition therefore sailed with the expectation that African economic development would rest on slavery.[45]

Protests from anti-slavery circles were surprisingly few, and most humanitarians seem to have accepted Buxton's compromise. The *Eclectic Review,* however, took the line of high principle: "In taking away from the marauder the musket with which he has been making slaves of other tribes, this scheme will put into his hands the lash by which he will aggravate the slavery of his own. He will be transformed from the slave-hunter to the slave-driver."[46]

Buxton was not alone in his compromise with forced labor in Africa. Other men who were normally humanitarian and liberal accepted its alleged necessity. George Maclean, Brodie Cruickshank, William Allen of the Niger Expedition, and Sir George Stephen all did so explicitly.[47] By the later 1840's, disappointment with the economic success of West Indian emancipation (and disappointment with the speed of African acculturation) made the compromise easier. By 1850, the *Westminster Review* felt free to justify slavery as a proper transitional measure—a "stepping stone from barbarism to civilization."[48]

At this juncture, James MacQueen, radical as ever, stepped into the position deserted by the humanitarians. He reversed himself and told the Lords' Committee on the blockade that any form of slavery in Africa would be disastrous for economic development. Slave hunting for the internal slave trade would increase in order to supply labor for the regions of greatest economic growth.[49]

Even within the British colonies and posts, officials often saw the labor problem as one requiring coercion, though outright slavery was

45. Buxton, *The Remedy,* p. 165; Lord John Russell to Treasury, 26 December 1839; Buxton and Lushington to Russell, 7 August 1840; Russell to Niger Commissioners, 30 January 1841; PP, 1842, xlviii [C. 472], pp. 1–2, 15–18.

46. "The Niger Expedition," *The Eclectic Review,* VIII (n.s.), 467–68 (1840).

47. R. R. Madden, Commissioner's Report, PP, 1842, xii (551), pp. 81–87; W. Allen and T. R. H. Thomson, *A Narrative of the Expedition to the River Niger in 1841,* 2 vols. (London, 1848), II, 432; Stephen, *Niger Trade,* p. 68.

48. "African Coast Blockade," *Westminster Review,* LII, 258 (January, 1850).

49. James MacQueen, Evidence before Lords' Slave Trade Committee, 5 July 1849, PP, 1849 (Lords), xxviii (32), pp. 351–52.

illegal. In Sierra Leone, recurrent suggestions called for forced labor from the liberated Africans.[50] An alternative was government plantations worked by African "soldiers" under military discipline.[51] Governor Winniett of the Gold Coast was anxious to introduce cotton cultivation, but he believed continuous and voluntary labor for wages would not be offered: "the Gold Coast Native desires no greater happiness than to eat the bread of idleness, which the extreme fertility of the soil enables him to do in rich abundance, without sacrificing more of his ease than is necessary for healthy recreation."[52]

Governor Winniett seems to state the usual opinion of the time— that the supply curve would quickly become non-linear, since tropical men would prefer leisure to wages once they had achieved the minimum of subsistence. But he made another point as well. He believed the free African might well offer his labor at a "rate of wages that would permanently ameliorate his condition," but not for "such fair and equitable wages, as business with moderate profits would allow."

In order to pay wages at a rate that might be effective in that labor market, in short, the employers would have needed a higher world price. Since the world price could not be altered, the alternatives remained: either no cotton for export, or cotton produced by some kind of forced labor.

Winniett decided in favor of forced labor and thought it might be obtained by using the coercive power of the chiefs within the British quasi-protectorate. If the chiefs would agree to a Labor Act, he considered that it might provide for three different kinds of forced labor. First, chiefs should hire out their slaves to British capitalists, to the advantage of both, since the slaves were only "idle profligates" in any case. Second, planters should "redeem" pawns, a plan analogous to the "redemption" of slaves, after which the ex-slaves repaid the purchase price by a period of forced labor. Finally, Winniett thought that African merchants who cheat Europeans might well be set to work at forced labor in place of a jail sentence.[53]

Earl Grey at the Colonial Office was suspicious of this scheme, fearing that it would merely make the local slave-holders rich. But he was not opposed in principle to forced labor. He believed that some special "command of labour" was necessary to permit "the

50. T. Whitfield, Evidence before West Africa Committee, 18 July 1842, PP, 1842, xi (551), pp. 629–30.

51. J. Duncan, *Travels in Western Africa*, 2 vols. (London, 1847), I, 40.

52. Winniett to Grey, 22 May 1850, CO 96/18.

53. Winniett to Grey, 22 May 1850, CO 96/18.

systematic cultivation of Cotton and other articles of Tropical produce on a large scale." As an alternative to Winniett's project, he
suggested that British capitalists might be allowed to hire slaves from
their masters under government supervision, giving half the wages
to the master and half to the slave.[54]

The plan was never tried, and Earl Grey had long since developed
an indirect form of coercion, which he thought would be preferable.
At the time of the Emancipation Act, Grey, then Lord Howick, had
been Parliamentary Under-Secretary at the Colonial Office. He had
then unsuccessfully advocated a system of stiff direct taxation to force
disciplined labor from the ex-slaves.[55] When he returned as Secretary
of State in 1846, he revived his old idea and made it into a comprehensive system of tropical development. Its theoretical principles
were given in his famous dispatch to Lord Torrington in Ceylon. It
began with the familiar belief that people in temperate regions had
made progress because of the challenge of a difficult climate. There,
necessity was the mother of invention, while in tropical countries
man's physical wants were abundantly supplied by nature. Progress
in the tropics, however, might be encouraged by providing an artificial challenge, and Grey found that challenge in direct taxation. In
fact, opposite fiscal policies were appropriate to the two climatic
zones. In temperate climates, taxation should bear on the poor as
little as possible:

> But the case is very different in tropical climates, where the population is
> very scanty in proportion to the extent of territory; where the soil, as I have
> already observed, readily yields a subsistence in return for very little labour;
> and where clothing, fuel, and lodging, such as are required, are obtained very
> easily. In such circumstances there can be but little motive to exertion, to men
> satisfied with an abundant supply of their mere physical wants; and accord-
> ingly experience proves that it is the disposition of the races of men by which
> these countries are generally inhabited, to sink into an easy and listless mode
> of life, quite incompatible with the attainment of any high degree of civiliza-
> tion.[56]

Taxation in tropical countries should, therefore, bear on the poor,
forcing them to work for wages in order to meet the tax bill. The
revenue would incidentally provide for education, roads, health services, and other essential aids to development.

54. Grey to Winniett, 14 August 1850, CO 402/2.
55. Henry George, third Earl Grey, *The Colonial Policy of Lord John Russell's Administration*, 2 vols. (London, 1853), II, 284.
56. Grey to Torrington, 24 October 1848, printed in George, Earl Grey, *Colonial
Policy*, I, 81–82.

This policy, based on West Indian experience and first suggested for Ceylon, was applied with local variations in Natal, Sierra Leone, and the Gold Coast. For the Gold Coast, Grey suggested a moderate house tax, the proceeds to be used for the support of a local military force, for roads, and for schools of the industrial as well as the intellectual variety. Since the Gold Coast was still only an informal British sphere of influence, any taxation required the consent of the chiefs. A general meeting was held in 1852. The chiefs agreed, and collection actually began late that year; but the plan failed. The tax was an annual poll tax of only one shilling—hardly enough to force anyone to work for wages—and the tax collections immediately began to decline. Nothing at all was received after 1862, and the attempt was abandoned.[57]

For Sierra Leone, Grey proposed a tax on both houses and land, and it was approved with official alacrity. Even before Grey's proposal, some officials had hoped to use direct taxation to encourage the recruitment of labor emigrants to America. Governor Benjamin Pine also shared Earl Grey's belief that shifting cultivation was an evil system, and the tax on both land and houses would force peasants to improve a "limited and fixed spot of ground."[58] Here too there were unforeseen problems. A suitable ordinance was not passed until 1852, and the tax proved so difficult to collect that it was abandoned in 1872.[59]

In either case, Earl Grey was gone from the Colonial Office before the failures were apparent. Regressive taxation nevertheless remained one of the favored devices of British policy in Africa, and the object was that of Earl Grey's proposals—the coercion of labor under conditions where the workers would not respond voluntarily to the wages offered. In West Africa, however, the failure of these first attempts was political rather than economic, and it was so interpreted. The lesson, especially on the Gold Coast, was that Britain could act efficiently only where it was sovereign. It thus led back to the troubled problem of exerting British influence without sovereign control.

57. Grey to Winniett, 20 January 1849, CO 402/2; Grey to Winniett, 18 December 1850, CO 96/19; D. Kimble, *A Political History of Ghana* (London, 1963), pp. 168–79.

58. Grey to Officer Administering Sierra Leone, 24 January 1849, CO 267/43; Benjamin Pine, Annual Report for 1848, 2 November 1849, PP, 1849, xxxvi [C. 1126], p. 298.

59. N. A. Cox-George, *Finance and Development in West Africa. The Sierra Leone Experience* (London, 1961), pp. 65–67.

19

THE THEORY AND PRACTICE

OF

INFORMAL EMPIRE

Political objectives were conspicuously missing from the British discussion of African affairs. Not only was government policy firmly opposed to annexation; few of the publicists for African activity even stressed the desirability of empire for the sake of empire. Few suggested that the power to command was worth having as a primary value, or that British dominion over Africa might be sought as a sign of British national glory and greatness. The desired ends of British policy were either wealth or the civilizing mission, or a combination of both. Only the means were political.

Yet it was clear that British power had to be exerted, as it was certainly exerted against the foreign slave-traders at sea and occasionally against recalcitrant African rulers on shore. But the British rarely discussed their relations with West Africa as relations based on physical force. At bottom, they most often assumed that African interests and British interests were congruent. The key to a successful policy was persuasion, though behind persuasion there always lay the "moral power," as Macgregor Laird so aptly put it, of the "24-

457

pounder with British seamen behind it." Potentially, this moral force
might have to become physical force, but Laird's statement reflected
the genuine sentiment of his generation. Military power was thought
to be moral in both senses—it was effective by its presence rather
than by its use, and it enforced morality as understood in Britain.

Britain's moral right to intervene in Africa was never doubted,
and it was justified in stronger language than ever before. It might
be set in the time-honored terms of mutual material advantage—"to
benefit Africa and the world," in MacQueen's phrase.[1] It might be
set in terms of a right, or even a duty, to develop a "vast, neglected
estate."[2] Alternatively, the duty might be that of carrying civilization
to the uncivilized, and the material rewards could be seen as the due
recompense of those who did their duty.[3] In the view of the Parliamentary Committee on Aborigines in 1837, however, England's material greatness came first, the God-given means for carrying out the
work of civilization:

The British Empire has been signally blessed by Providence, and her emi-
nence, her strength, her wealth, her prosperity, her intellectual, her moral and
her religious advantages, are so many reasons for peculiar obedience to the
laws of Him who guides the destiny of nations. These were given for some
higher purpose than commercial prosperity and military renown. . . . 'Can
we suppose otherwise than that it is our office to carry civilization and humanity, peace and good government, and, above all the knowledge of the
true God, to the uttermost ends of the earth.'[4]

But the call to intervene was limited, especially in the eyes of those
who saw Britain's power linked to a moral duty. That duty could
also demand a respect for the rights of others. Standish Motte took
these rights of non-Western peoples to include:

1. Their rights as an independent nation. That no country or people has
a right by force or fraud to assume the sovereignty over any other nation.
2. That such sovereignty can only be justly obtained by fair treaty, and
with their consent.
3. That every individual of a nation whether independent or owing

1. J. MacQueen, Memorandum of 12 January 1839, CO 2/22.
2. "Expedition to the Niger," *Edinburgh Review*, LXXII, 457 (January 1841).
3. Report of the Committee on Aborigines, PP, 1837, vii (425), p. 5; J. Harris,
The Great Commission (London, 1842), p. 238; W. Howitt, *Colonization and Christianity* (London, 1838), pp. 504–5; R. M. Martin, *History of the British Possessions
in the Indian and Atlantic Oceans* (London, 1837), p. 338.
4. Report of the Committee on Aborigines, PP, 1837, vii (425) p. 76. See also
H. Merivale, *Lectures on Colonisation and Colonies,* 2 vols. (London, 1841–1842), II,
212–13.

allegiance to any other power has a right to personal liberty, and protection of property and life.[5]

Motte's list was more extensive than most commentators would have allowed. The majority recognized rights, but tempered in varying degrees by the "facts" of barbarism or racial inferiority.

A second kind of limitation, and one of greater practical importance, was the fact that Britain simply lacked the means for unlimited intervention simultaneously in all parts of the world. In spite of his humanitarianism, James Stephen opposed the Niger Expedition, as he opposed any extension of Britain's sphere of activity in West Africa. The core of the argument was presented in a famous sentence, addressed to Lord Stanley in 1842 after Stanley had decided to do otherwise.

> But to what end to trouble you with a discussion to prove that the value of these African Settlements to our Commerce, or that their utility as preventives of the Slave Trade is enormously exaggerated—that in fact they are nothing else than Factories kept up at the expense of the Nation at large for the profit of half a Dozen inconsiderable Merchants who avail themselves of our national sensibility on every subject in which the Commercial wealth or National importance of Great Britain is concerned—that the Trade of all of them put together is of less value to us, present or perspective, than the Trade with the Isle of Skye—that we are recklessly increasing and dispersing our Colonial Empire in all directions and creating a demand for Naval and Military force which there are no means of meeting, except by weakening the Force where its presence is most needed—that in short neither the Gambia nor the Gold Coast are worth retaining—or that if retained they should be placed exclusively in the hands of Mulattoes or Negroes from the West Indies, and left to maintain themselves like the American Settlement of Liberia?[6]

Stephen's fears were shared by others,[7] but it was still possible to steer a course between the moral demand for intervention and the moral and physical limitations on that demand. That course has been called "informal empire," located in theory somewhere in the twilight zone between influence and sovereignty. To achieve it in practice raised a further series of strategic, legal, and administrative problems.

West Africa enjoyed a very narrow place indeed in the world picture of British strategic interests. Whatever effort the government

5. S. Motte, *Outline of a System of Legislation for Securing the Protection of the Aboriginal Inhabitants of all Countries Colonized by Great Britain* (London, 1840), p. 14.

6. James Stephen, Memorandum of 26 December 1842, CO 96/2.

7. Lord Ingestre, Commons, 16 February 1841, 3 H 55, cc. 693–95; Richard Cobden, Commons, 19 July 1850, 3 H 113, c. 42.

made in Africa would have to be limited in economic cost, and hence in geographical focus. The earlier concern about the strategy of entry into the Western Sudan, therefore, continued long after the routes were known and the interior partially explored. Strategic discussion after 1830, however, was different from that of the earlier century. The Niger entry was the undoubted favorite, and the importance of the palm-oil trade of the delta kept a British concentration on the Bights, even when Niger exploration itself was inactive.

Each apparent failure on the Niger, however, opened up at least a tentative suggestion of alternatives. Perhaps the most common reaction was simply to get out and leave West Africa alone with its deadly "climate." Better conditions in South Africa opened dreams of civilization advancing northwards. The highlands of Ethiopia were also more attractive from the point of view of safety, and even Lower Guinea between Mount Cameroons and the Congo had its appeal.[8] But the presumed riches of Africa were still located in the savanna belt of West Africa, and there too was the region of "highest civilization" and greatest potential for further development.

Of the three alternative routes of entry from British-held points on the Guinea coast, Sierra Leone and its neighborhood dropped from sight after 1830. The rivers were only navigable a short distance, and the overland routes were often closed to trade. The Gold Coast possibility was obscured from British view during the merchant's government of the 1830's; though it recovered some of its promise in the mid-1840's, when the Madden scandals died down and more was known of Maclean's judicial protectorate.[9] Meanwhile, the Gambia rose somewhat from its customary neglect. Like the Niger, it was navigable for some distance inland, and its far hinterland was relatively "civilized." Buxton's original plan called for steamships on the Gambia as well as the Niger, and for the establishment of the seat of government at MacCarthy's Island well upstream. The Gambia effort was one of the aspects cut from Buxton's plan by the Government, but Lord Glenelg had intended to follow up the Niger Expedition with one to the Gambia. That particular project died when he left the Colonial Office, but the Parliamentary Committee of 1842

8. *Quarterly Review*, LXXXVIII, 40 (December, 1850); "Ethiopia," *Blackwood's Magazine*, LV, 269–91 (1844); Commander H. J. Matson to Aberdeen, 28 March 1844, PP, 1847–1848, xxii (272), pp. 90–91.

9. T. F. Buxton, *The Remedy: Being a Sequel to the African Slave Trade* (London, 1840), pp. 80–98 and 108; Grey to Winniett, 20 January 1849, CO 402/2.

still thought the Gambia settlements were the most valuable of all British possessions on the Coast.[10]

The Niger nevertheless retained its pre-eminence, and new knowledge about conditions along the river opened new stratgic questions on the Niger itself. One of these was the problem of commercial strategy. There were three possibilities in the Niger trade, to some extent competitive, though not mutually exclusive. The first of these was to maintain and increase the existing flow of trade through the city-states of the Niger Delta, where merchants from towns like Brass and Bonny picked up European goods and went inland to the principal markets in the palm-oil belt, delivering the oil to European merchants at the coastal entrepôts. At any time after 1830, this trade was an established interest, which the African merchants and their British associates were anxious to defend. The Africans might try to defend it by force in the creeks of the delta, and Matthew Forster, M.P., of the firm of Forster and Smith, defended it consistently in the halls of Parliament.

The other two possibilities depended on breaking through the delta monopoly and entering the Niger by steamer. One was to enter into more direct contact with the palm-producing country, which began where the mangroves of the delta left off and extended inland for about a hundred miles. It might be possible to redirect the trade so that palm products flowed to European entrepôts on either side of the Niger, rather than southward through the maze of creeks to the coast. Macgregor Laird recognized this possibility in 1832, and he remained its principal advocate until his death in 1861. The economic advantage in this case was not the technological superiority of the river steamers, but the breach of the African monopoly.

Upstream from the modern city of Onitsha, however, palm production dropped off gradually on account of increasing seasonal aridity. From there to the confluence with the Benue, and beyond, the trade of immediate importance was in ivory, but the ultimate hope was cotton growing for export. To develop this trade would not be merely to shift the profits of existing trade from African to European hands; it would be a genuine economic innovation. It was this third

10. Buxton, *The Remedy*, p. 99; Glenelg, Memorandum of 18 February 1839, CO 2/22; Report of the West Africa Committee, PP, 1842, xi (551), p. vii. See also Captain Belcher, R. N., "Extracts from Observations on Various Points of the West Coast of Africa, Surveyed by His Majesty's Ship Aetna in 1830–32," *Journal of the Royal Geographical Society*, II, 278–304 (1832), p. 296.

possibility that appealed especially to Buxton and served as the basic strategy of the Niger Expedition.[11]

Special problems of political strategy ran parallel to those of commercial planning. The several African economic interests on the Niger were represented in the political goals of African states or groups of states. In the south, the delta states had an obvious interest in preventing steamers on the Niger at any cost, but those further inland might have a different attitude. The key position here was held by Abo, at the apex of the delta. Abo was strategically placed to control the passage of goods up and down the river, and it was also in a position to exert pressure on the non-food-producing delta towns by cutting off their food imports from the north. An alliance with Abo was both natural and essential in any effort to short-circuit the coastal monopoly.

Further north, just below the confluence, Igala was reckoned the most important local power. The Attah of Igala was also in a difficult political position. In addition to internal problems, he was threatened by the power of the Fulani Empire, which reached down through Zaria to the Benue and through Nupe to the Niger. Fulani raiders even appeared from time to time in Igala territory. In this situation, any of the British expeditions stood a good chance of forming an entente with Igala. Friendship with Igala, however, might also alienate the Fulani and cut off the ultimate extension of trade into the wider northern hinterland. If, on the other hand, the British were to advance beyond Igala and establish friendly relations with Nupe, they would leave an unfriendly Igala in their rear to threaten peaceful passage up and down the river, to say nothing of reducing the profits of trade in the Igala markets.[12]

The full complexity of the choice implicit in these facts of political power and interest was not immediately clear, but it emerged during the course of the 1830's and gave rise to an interlocked strategic controversy. An initial choice had to be made between Brass, Bonny, and the other delta states on one hand and the riverine powers between Abo and Igala on the other. This choice was, in fact, made implicitly at the sailing of the Niger Expedition. By the nature of its mission it favored the middle group against the delta traders.

11. This discussion of the Niger strategy is based on K.O. Dike, *Trade and Politics in the Niger Delta, 1830–1885* (London, 1956) and C. C. Ifemesia, "British Enterprise on the Niger, 1830–1869," (Unpublished Ph.D. thesis, London, 1959).

12. Ifemesia, "British Enterprise," esp. pp. 217–68 and 305–41.

Further upstream, however, there remained the choice between Igala and a possible entente with Nupe which would open the whole Fulani Empire to British trade. The earliest strategy for the Niger had been invented before the British even knew about Igala. MacQueen picked the confluence for its physical, not its political position. Buxton, however, was concerned with political goals. On the basis of Clapperton's reports, he chose the two great powers of the interior as the major objectives, hoping to sign treaties with the Fulani Sultan of Sokoto and the Mai of Bornu.[13] But any hope of coming to terms simultaneously with Igala, Bornu, and the Fulani was nearly impossible at the outset.

When the expedition arrived in 1841, they found Ocheji, the Attah of Igala, pleased to offer hospitality to such well armed strangers and perfectly willing to settle them at the confluence—on the marches of his own territory where they were bound to come into conflict with the Fulani. The Commissioners then selected a tract of land on the west bank of the Niger, stretching some sixteen miles downstream and five miles inland from the present town of Lokoja. It is doubtful that the Commissioners realized how thoroughly they were committing themselves to an Igala policy. Even after the treaty with Igala, they hoped to proceed to Nupe and sign another with the Etsu, but the sickness came first and they withdrew from the river.[14] A fully conscious decision to support Igala against the Fulani was therefore postponed; but Commander William Allen emerged with a strong anti-Fulani bias, and his actions suggested a pro-Igala policy.[15]

Meanwhile, the British Fulani policy was discussed in Europe and drew in still broader questions of policy toward Islam in Africa. Gustav d'Eichthal in France gave some detailed advice. Since he believed the Fulani were racially superior, culturally superior, and had in Islam a religion superior to African polytheism, he urged the British to work closely with the Fulani Empire. A show of force might be necessary, in the initial stages, to make the Europeans "feared and respected," but, after that, the British could build their informal empire around the existing power of Sokoto. Such a policy would, of course, force them to abandon Christian proselytization, but, in d'Eichthal's view, Islam was a civilizing religion, and it could be "purified." In

13. Buxton, *The Remedy,* pp. 5–7, 10–15, and 65–67.
14. Ifemesia, "British Enterprise," pp. 317–18.
15. William Allen to Lord Stanley, 9 February 1843, PP, 1843, xlviii [C. 472], p. 136.

any case, accommodation to Islam was preferable to a long religious war. D'Eichthal's general line of argument soon gained a British following.[16] In the early twentieth century, indeed, a variant was put into practice in Northern Nigeria; but there was no immediate possibility, once the Niger Expedition had failed, of moving further in that direction.

The principle of working through an African client state, however, was applicable elsewhere, and it was applied. Maclean's regime on the Gold Coast led to a de facto alliance with the Fante states and other coastal peoples. The missionary concentration on Abeokuta was a less official, religious equivalent, though the government was ultimately involved there as well. In both, the choice of a client state limited other possibilities of action. The Gold Coast "protectorate" made it difficult to remain friendly with Ashanti. British support for Abeokuta cut short the effort to cooperate with Dahomey in schemes for technical assistance. The end result was further commitment—in one case the series of Ashanti wars, and in the other the seizure of Lagos.[17]

The alternative political strategy was to seek a much broader network of alliances, and particularly to seek alliances with the strong states—not merely with those like Abeokuta and the Fante, who were anxious for support. Sir George Stephen advocated a grand design of this kind. He saw the African state system in the hinterland of the Bights as one dominated by six major powers—Abo, Igala, Benin, and the Fulani Empire controlling the Niger basin, while Dahomey and Ashanti dominated the forest zone and southern savanna to the west. If these six would fall into line, the smaller states would automatically come under British influence as well.[18] Diplomatic activity on this scale, however, would have required an over-

16. G. d'Eichthal, "Histoire de origine des Foulahs ou Fellans," *Mémoires de la Société Ethnologique,* I (2), 1-296 (1841), pp. 148-53, 164-65; R. Mouat, "A Narrative of the Niger Expedition," *Simmonds's Colonial Magazine,* II, 138-53, 311-24, 446-65; III, 117-26 (May–October 1844), III, 120; W. B. Baikie, *Narrative of an Exploring Voyage up the Rivers Kwora and Binue (Commonly known as the Niger and Tsadda) in 1854* (London, 1856), p. 393.

17. See J. F. Ade Ajayi, "Christian Missions and the Making of Nigeria, 1841–1891" (Unpublished Ph.D. thesis, London, 1958); S. O. Biobaku, *The Egba and Their Neighbours 1842–1872* (Oxford, 1957); G. E. Metcalfe, *Maclean of the Gold Coast* (London, 1962); C. W. Newbury, *The Western Slave Coast and its Rulers* (Oxford, 1961).

18. Sir George Stephen, *The Niger Trade Considered in Connexion with the African Blockade* (London, 1849), pp. 41-55.

whelming show of British military power. It was inconceivable in the circumstances of the time.

Even the more limited effort to create by treaty an area of British influence raised some serious theoretical and practical problems. Europeans still made international agreements with African states, but the old principle of international equality for all sovereign states, no matter how "barbarous" their culture, began to weaken toward mid-century. British international lawyers kept the principle in the text books until after the 1870's, but British opinion was already beginning to change. The Parliamentary Committee on Aborigines recommend that no treaties should be signed with the aborigines in British colonies, on grounds that genuine agreement was not possible between such unequal parties. The Committee also held that treaties were certain to be misunderstood in societies where formal and written international agreements were not customary.

William Cook, one of the four Commissioners of the Niger Expedition, used a similar argument against the validity of treaties the Commissioners had signed with Abo and Igala. He doubted that the rulers of Abo and Igala had the constitutional right to sign treaties, or the power to enforce them once signed. But Cook and other British officials on the coast recognized that treaties were useful. Even if they had to be enforced by a continuing display of British power, they gave Britain certain rights against other European powers, and they helped to avoid inconvenient legal difficulties in the British courts.[19]

Treaties were, therefore, signed in great numbers, and often in circumstances of doubtful legality. Many of the documents called treaties were really only private contracts. Merchants sometimes signed treaties with African authorities, and these agreements often contained the same provisions found in agreements between sovereign states; but they were neither signed with the Crown's authority nor ratified by the Foreign Office. Oldfield, acting as agent of the African Inland Commercial Company, for example, signed a treaty of commerce and friendship with the Attah of Igala. It may even have contained a clause promising military assistance.[20]

Other treaties lay in a half-light of semi-legality, where they might

19. Report of the Aborigines Committee, PP, 1837, vii (425), p. 80; W. Cook to Lord Stanley, 11 March 1843, PP, 1843, xlviii [C. 472], p. 158; Commander H. J. Matson to Lord Aberdeen, 28 March 1844, PP, 1847–1848, xxii (272), p. 90; MacDonnell to Grey, 16 June 1849, PP, 1849, xxxvi [C. 1126], p. 324.

20. Ifemesia, "British Enterprise," p. 230.

be picked up by the British government for later recognition and enforcement. Each of the three colonial governments at the Gambia,
Sierra Leone, and the Gold Coast signed treaties and in effect conducted their own foreign relations. Some of their agreements were
reached after consultation with the Foreign Office and were formally
ratified. Others were strictly local in character and do not appear on
the official lists of British treaties. In the Gambia, for example, the
governors of the 1840's maintained regular diplomatic relations with
some twenty-five separate African states, and occasional relations
with about twenty others. Twenty treaties were considered to be in
force in 1849.[21]

A similar web of international relations stretched out from Freetown and Cape Coast—into the hinterland where Britain would one
day rule. The principal emphasis at Sierra Leone was the payment of
subsidies to African authorities in return for keeping the trade routes
open. The agreements on the Gold Coast were more various, ranging
from major peace settlements, like the Ashanti Treaty of 1831, to
confirmation of small subsidy payments, of which the original purpose had long since been forgotten.[22] The more important development of the judicial protectorate during the 1830's was carried out
without benefit of treaties of any kind. It was only in 1844 that the
Bonds were signed to confirm in law what existed in fact.

Above and beyond the accretions of local treaties and agreements,
anti-slave-trade treaties came into fashion from the time of the Niger
Expedition. These were signed on metropolitan initiative, mainly
through the diplomatic agency of naval officers from the blockading
squadron, and they followed a number of set forms prepared in London.

This system of treaties originated partly from the precedent of ancient custom on the Guinea coast, and partly from Buxton's elaborate
plan for a great confederacy of chiefs covering all of West Africa
south of the desert. The essence of Buxton's plan, in its political aspect, was, indeed, an especially extensive informal empire. The
cement for the whole edifice was to be a series of bilateral treaties
between Great Britain and the African rulers. Buxton assumed that
treaties could be signed without the use of forceful persuasion—
partly in return for a small financial consideration, partly because

21. MacDonnell to Grey, 10 June 1849, PP, xxxvi [C. 1126], p. 324.
22. Minutes of the Gold Coast Council, 10 August 1835, copy in AG, Acc. 68/1954.

the Africans would recognize "their own forlorn and disastrous condition" and wish to improve it, and partly because they would distinguish between the good, anti-slave-trade British and the other
Europeans. Only the debased slave-trading chiefs near the coast were
expected to be uncooperative. In spite of his confidence that Africans
would willingly sign, Buxton had no intention of offering them an
agreement between equal partners, with an equivalence of consideration. His treaties were conceived as bonds between superiors and inferiors who recognized themselves as such.[23]

The Niger Expedition sailed with instructions incorporating Buxton's optimism about African subservience, but James MacQueen
had already submitted a long memorandum to the Colonial Office,
suggesting a more hard-headed appeal to self-interest. His model was
the treaty with China which gave Britain special rights in Canton.
The African ruler would be asked to abolish the slave trade, to grant
British subjects free access to his territory, freedom for economic
transactions, the right to purchase land, and a promise of security for
their property. The ruler would also have to limit customs duties
chargeable on imports from Britain, and British subjects would en-
joy extra-territorial jurisdiction under British law. Taken together,
these concessions amounted to a real infringement of African sovereignty, and MacQueen was realist enough to understand that they
would not be granted merely out of deference to a white skin. He
therefore proposed a substantial *quid pro quo,* consisting first of all
of a defensive alliance (or even an offensive and defensive alliance).
In addition, the Africans would receive most-favored-nation treatment for their exports to Britain and an annual subsidy equivalent to
their profits from the slave trade. MacQueen expected this subsidy
to run at the handsome figure of about £100,000 a year for West
Africa as a whole.[24]

The treaty forms actually sent out with the Niger Expedition contained half of MacQueen's suggestions—the half that granted privileges to Britain—and two additional concessions were demanded. The
African signatories were asked to promise toleration for the preaching of Christianity and to allow Britain to place a resident agent in
their countries. The financial consideration was reduced from a real
subsidy to a gift—the customary small change of African diplomacy,

23. Buxton, *The Remedy,* pp. 5–7, 17.
24. James MacQueen, Memorandum of 12 January 1839, CO 2/22.

worth about £50 for Abo and £100 for Igala. These two states signed, but they signed in the presence of the armed ships, and ceased to honor the treaties as soon as the ships withdrew.[25]

At the withdrawal of 1842, the treaty net of informal empire in the interior was given up, but the treaty policy was continued on the coast. The form of the coastal treaties, however, was much less rigorous than that offered on the Niger. Six were signed in 1841: none of them set a limit on import duties. Only one granted extra-territorial jurisdiction. The coastal treaties of the later 1840's fell into this milder pattern. The crucial clause was the promise to give up the slave trade, usually buttressed with promises to notify the British cruisers on the arrival of a slaver and permission for the British armed forces to land in suppression of the slave trade. Commercial provisions were limited to most-favored-nation treatment for British goods.[26]

Forty-two anti-slave-trade treaties of this kind were in effect by 1850, but their only real consequence was to legalize the actions of the cruisers. None of the major African powers were represented— no Dahomey, no Ashanti, no Benin. The result was thus a far cry from Buxton's dream of informal dominion, but it probably represents approximately the limit of the "moral force" of the squadron. Further concessions required either real subsidies or the application of physical force.

Toward the end of the 1840's, both methods were attempted. Brodie Cruickshank, was sent to Dahomey in 1848 with authorization to offer $2,000 a year in return for an anti-slave-trade treaty. He decided not to press the offer when he found out that the slave-trade revenues of the Dahomean state were in the neighborhood of $300,000 a year.[27] More forceful and less expensive diplomacy was possible nearer to the coast and the naval squadron. After 1849, John Beecroft, as Her Majesty's Consul for the Bights of Benin and Biafara, was able to intervene more extensively in the affairs of the Niger delta city-states.

The naval attack on Lagos in 1851 was followed by a stiffer kind

25. Lord John Russell to Niger Commissioners, 30 January 1841, and H. D. Trotter to G. W. Hope, 1 April 1842, PP, 1843, xlviii [C. 472], pp. 5 ff. and 57–58.

26. Admiralty, "Instructions to Senior Officers of the African Station" (1844), PP, 1844, 1 [C. 577]; PP, 1849, xxviii (32), appendix pp. 43–62; PP, 1852–1853, xxxix (920), p. 214.

27. B. Cruickshank, Report of 9 November 1848, PP, 1849 (Lords), xxviii (32), appendix, pp. 183, 186.

of treaty than that of recent years. The Lagos treaty of 1852 contained the usual articles for the suppression of the slave trade, but it also provided for the abolition of human sacrifice and the protection of both missionaries and Christian converts. A separate commercial engagement limited Lagosian import duties to 2 per cent and export duties to 3 per cent ad valorem, and it established a mixed court of African and European merchants to settle commercial disputes.[28]

Informal control short of genuine territorial empire might be sought in other ways as well. One of the favorite suggestions of past decades had been to extend the existing pattern of trading-post enclaves into the interior. MacQueen, the Buxton plan, and the Niger Expedition all combined trading posts with the treaty policy, but in some projects the trading-post empire stood alone. A Gloucestershire gentleman named Paul Read sent a plan of this kind to the Colonial Office in 1832. He was even less well informed than most of the other projectors and conceived of West Africa as a stateless area, where political institutions could only be created by the establishment of British centers of "steady and permanent power" on islands or on the banks of the Niger and its tributaries. Each post was to have an armed steamer to police the river, a garrison to protect the fort, and a complement of British convicts to grow food for the garrison.[29]

The trading-post enclave also played a role in the later projects of Thomas Kehoe, Macgregor Laird, Sir George Stephen, and Edward Nicholls. These different plans visualized the trading post in varying terms. It might or might not be colonized by British settlers. It might or might not imply the extension of British sovereignty over the surrounding country. In spite of the health problem, the idea of limited settlement was still brought forward. Read would have confined the sacrifice to convicts, but Governor Rendall of the Gambia, F. Harrison Rankin, and Governor Winniett of the Gold Coast all believed that a managerial force of capitalist colonists would be necessary.[30]

28. Treaty of 1 January 1852, engagement of 28 February 1852, PP, 1862, lxi [C. 2982], pp. 1–4. For the change to a policy of intervention see Dike, *Trade and Politics,* pp. 128–52; Newbury, *The Western Slave Coast,* pp. 49–76.

29. Both the original plan of 1832 and a later version of 1840 are found in CO 2/22. The second version was published as P. Read, *Lord John Russell, Sir Thomas Fowell Buxton, and the Niger Expedition* (London, 1840).

30. J. Rendall to Glenelg, 3 January 1839, CO 2/22; F. H. Rankin, *The White Man's Grave: A Visit to Sierra Leone in 1834,* 2 vols. (London, 1836), II, 24–29; Winniet to Grey, 22 May 1850, CO 96/18.

At an early stage in the formation of his project, Sir George Stephen could still picture really large scale white settlement: "If we found settlements in Africa, colonization must follow; wherever the British flag is raised, thousands, and tens of thousands will seek protection under it; it is sheer hypocrisy to pretend that this is not the consequence of our civilization plans, if fairly carried out. . . ."[31]

Nothing of the kind was at all likely; but the speculation remained alive, and Dickens' caricature of the Niger Expedition changed the trading post at the confluence into "Boriaboola-Ga," a colony for white settlers.[32]

By whatever devices informal empire was to be furthered, it posed special problems of administration. A variety of administrative forms had been tried in the past, from the full monopoly for trade and the power to govern, granted to the Royal Africa Company in the seventeenth century, through the device of a regulatory company such as the Company of Merchants Trading to Africa, down to the system of Crown Colony government tried experimentally in Senegambia before 1783, in Sierra Leone after 1808, and in the other posts after 1821. But Crown Colony government was designed to rule sovereign British territory, not to exercise influence beyond it. The Foreign Office was the usual institution for dealing with British interests beyond the sphere of British sovereignty, but it was equipped to negotiate and report, not to exercise continuous informal influence. No existing British institution quite met the need, and it was partly for this reason that British influence on the Coast was exercised through so many channels in the 1830's—the merchants' government on the Gold Coast from 1828 to 1843, royal colonies at Sierra Leone and Gambia, naval officers as de facto diplomats in a variety of different circumstances. The shifts and turns of administrative organization may be explained in large part as an effort to solve the problem of informal empire.

Various publicists pushed for their own favorite forms of government or influence. The merchants of the coastal school would have preferred a broad expansion of merchants' control on the Gold Coast model,[33] but the Gold Coast itself was returned to royal control

31. G. Stephen, *Letters to the Right Honourable Lord John Russell, on the Plans of the Society for the Civilization of Africa* (London, 1840), first letter, p. 28.

32. C. Dickens, *Bleak House* (London, 1853), Ch. IV.

33. Martin, *History of British Possessions*, p. 337; Stanley to Hill, 30 December 1844, CO 402/2; Petition of "Native Merchants" of the Gold Coast, 14 August 1850, CO 96/19.

on the grounds that merchants' government was too informal. James MacQueen had begun with the ideal of a single great Chartered Company, and he kept up his pressure for this form even after the Niger Expedition.[34]

Some planners drew up complex administrative projects, designed specifically to meet the problems of informal empire. One such plan was the work of Governor Rendall of the Gambia, who proposed to unify all British government agencies on the African coast under a single command located in the Banana Islands. The supreme government would then have control over four lieutenant-governors in Bathurst, Freetown, Cape Coast, and Fernando Po as well as the naval forces of the anti-slavery blockade.[35]

An even more elaborate plan was submitted to the Parliamentary Committee of 1842 by Edward Nicholls. He proposed that full powers over British African affairs from the Sahara to the Namib Desert should be given to a Governor based on St. Helena. The whole coast could then be divided into five superintendencies, with a sixth on Ascension to administer a normal school and health station. Each superintendent would have authority to acquire sovereignty over any territory or persons that might freely offer themselves. The problem of governing widely separate colonies and spheres of influence would be met by keeping either the Governor or Lieutenant-Governor constantly on the move by steamship. Nicholls estimated that a round trip to all the superintendencies would take about 81 days. The two chief officials could thus make about four circuits each in the course of a year.[36]

The mere fact that Nicholl's own estimates put the cost of his plan at £400,000 a year was enough to keep it from serious consideration. Instead, the government drifted along with the older forms, even though they were not quite appropriate. The three Crown Colonies that emerged as independent entities in 1843 continued as such, and the Foreign Office took over the informal sphere in the Bights with the establishment of the Consulate in 1849.

The internal government of the Crown Colonies posed another kind of political problem, and one with less immediate, but more

34. MacQueen, Memorandum of 12 January 1839, CO 2/22; MacQueen to Aberdeen, 6 September 1844, FO 84/555.

35. J. Rendall to Lord Glenelg, 3 January 1839, CO 2/22.

36. E. Nicholls, Memorandum of 20 July 1842, enclosed in Nicholls to Canning, 28 June 1845, FO 84/616.

long-range importance. As rulers of alien societies, however small, the British believed they had certain obligations. These were not necessarily the political obligations they felt toward the colonies populated by English settlers, who were entitled to English law and to English representative self-government at the local level. In Sierra Leone, the principal obligation was already conceived as a trusteeship over the welfare of the liberated Africans. Elsewhere the obligations were barely defined, but the ultimate question was already present— what political and legal institutions are appropriate to an African society?

Various answers were implied by some of the new ideas about race and culture, trusteeship and conversion, but the dominant position in government circles, however vaguely stated, remained the expectation that somehow and sometime Sierra Leone would become a "free African colony," as Sir George Murray had promised in 1830. The idea that African settlements should move toward independence under British influence came from other directions as well. A British African Colonization Society was formed in 1833 to establish a settlement for colored British subjects, similar to Liberia. It had patronage of the Duke of Sussex and the active support of Thomas Hodgkin, but it failed in its own aims and ultimately merged with its American counterpart.[37]

The idea of exerting British political authority in Africa through the agency of Westernized Africans, however, recurred in many different contexts. It was, indeed, the ultimate political implication of the idea of conversion. As T. Perronet Thompson told the House of Commons in 1850, "for a European nation desiring to exert itself in Africa . . . there is an instrument ready made, God's tropical man." The ultimate goal for Thompson was a multi-racial British Empire, based on the "English principle" of uniting "all races and bloods under the name of Englishmen."[38] More specific projects for an all-black colony followed the failure of the Niger Expedition, and Sir George Stephen's scheme for government-controlled trade assumed that all posts, including the highest, would be filled by Africans.[39]

37. *African Colonizer,* 20 February 1851, p. 151.
38. T. P. Thompson, Commons, 19 July 1850, 3 H 113, c. 53.
39. Allen and Thompson, *Narrative of the Expedition,* II, 435; W. Allen, Evidence before the Hutt Committee, 28 March 1848, PP, 1847–48, xxii (272), pp. 71–73; Stephen, *The Niger Trade,* p. 58.

In spite of the ordinary xenophobic tension on the Coast, the government recognized officially only one kind of racial difference—that of immunity to disease. At the Colonial Office, both James Stephen and Herman Merivale, who succeeded him as Permanent Under-Secretary from 1847 to 1859, held the line against overt racial discrimination.[40] Merivale, indeed, believed in both racial equality and racial mixture: "Diversity of races is an evil only when the law has recognized a difference in privileges; where the white is taught from infancy to regard himself as superior to the negro or the Indian, the Englishman to the Irishman, the British colonists to the Canadian *habitant*. Let all be placed on a footing of equality—let intermixture be encouraged, instead of reprobated—and all prejudice will cease to exist."[41]

The practice of the 1830's and 1840's was generally that of appointing Africans to the government service, with some local variation according to the recent death rate of Europeans and the racial opinions of the governors. Governor Alexander Findlay, for example, kept the settlers out of all important posts in Sierra Leone between 1830 and 1833. Between 1836 and 1839, however, an important group of Afro-West Indians were given key positions when the yellow fever epidemic began to kill even the older European residents.[42]

With the 1850's a shift in attitude took place all along the coast. The declining European mortality brought stiffer competition for the better government posts. Theoretical racism of British origin began to be imported to Africa with a new generation of officials. Resentment against the "educated Africans" increased markedly, and even the normally liberal Herman Merivale was to stigmatize them in a biting minute as "half-caste and half-educated."[43] Merivale's attitude was not so much racial as cultural prejudice, but cultural prejudice alone could raise doubts about the wisdom or possibility of European-style political development for Africa.

These doubts were symptomatic of a shift from ideas of conversion

40. See, for example, J. Stephen, Minute of 27 July 1848 on Doherty to Glenelg, 10 December 1837, CO 267/141. In 1851, Earl Grey stopped Governor Macdonald of Sierra Leone from instituting racial segregation in the colonial hospital. (Grey, Minute on Macdonald to Grey, 10 September 1841; Grey to Macdonald, 20 November 1851, CO 267/22.)

41. Merivale, *Colonisation and Colonies,* II, 315–16.

42. C. Fyfe, *A History of Sierra Leone* (London, 1962), pp. 188–189, 211.

43. H. Merivale, Minute of 29 February 1855, CO 96/31.

to ideas of trusteeship. The change was rarely explicit, but it was clearly present when the British turned their attention to legal and political institutions. British Gambia and Sierra Leone had begun with English law, but without British forms of representative government. By the 1830's, some authorities began to doubt that English law was appropriate in all cases.

One suggestion was to preserve the forms of English law, but to set non-Europeans in a special position under that law. Even in the fully conversionist era, the fate of the aborigines in the settlement colonies suggested that they needed special protection. The status of legal minority seemed appropriate. Herman Merivale thought it should be imposed on the aborigines of Canada and Australia. In place of full freedom of contract, for example, they would receive special protection (and special disabilities) appropriate to their minority.[44]

Merivale's idea thus approached concepts of trusteeship, but with some differences. His long-run intention was to suppress native law by allowing freedom of appeal to English law, and the status of minority was a temporary measure, to be enforced only until such time as the aborigines were fully conversant with English legal norms and able to protect themselves. The full-blown doctrine of trusteeship that was to emerge later in the century laid much less stress on the shift to English norms, and the period of minority was seen to stretch off into the indefinite future.

Another solution to the problem of legal conversion worked somewhat differently. Rather than shifting immediately to English law, the non-Europeans were to be left with their own law; and that law itself was to be changed gradually until it fell into line with Western legal norms. Standish Motte's study of the problem concluded that each different society required its own appropriate legislation, based on its own peculiarities.[45] Commander Allen of the Niger Expedition hoped to begin with African law in any colony he might plant on the Niger, letting legal reforms come through the spread of British influence.[46]

George Maclean had already done something similar on the Gold

---

44. Merivale, *Colonisation and Colonies,* II, 161–69.
45. Motte, *System of Legislation,* pp. 11–12.
46. W. Allen and T. R. H. Thomson, *A Narrative of the Expedition,* II, 424–25.

Coast. His area of jurisdiction outside the British forts was informal, by the consent of the Africans themselves, and the law he enforced was African law with certain amendments.[47] Maclean produced no theoretical defense of his methods, but Matthew Forster, the Africa merchant and Member of Parliament produced one for him before the Committee of 1842:

> Experience has shown us that political reforms, even in civilized states, should always be based upon their original institutions, and that the new should retain as many features as possible of the old customs and principles. Our own constitution contains abundant evidence of the rudeness of our original institutions in the semi-barbarous forms and maxims it preserves. On the coast of Africa, then, we should bend the state of society we find into better forms, not plant foreign institutions, as unfit to resist the climate as the officers who are to manage them. Let us modify the native customs so as to render the natives themselves not incapable hereafter of administering them in their amended state. The success of our administration on the Gold Coast may fairly be ascribed to this, that the officers in command at the different forts had the wisdom to take the native laws and customs as their rules, extracting from them, and bringing forward, that basis of justice which will always be found in the laws of the most debased tribes, and throwing into the background the cruelties and absurdities which, in a negro, as in an European code of laws, are corruptions only. In such judicious administration and combination of their own, with more enlightened principles, you will have the sympathy and assistance of the natives.[48]

Forster's argument was clearly based on a Burkean conservatism, with the belief that effective conversion must be gradual, but it was still conversionist. Here as with Merivale, however, a further shift to the late-century doctrine of trusteeship was easy. In the hands of racists, the complete transition was not expected to take place: the Africans would continue with a partially Westernized law, appropriate to their partial ability to become "civilized." Or, in still another version, the goal could be changed from Westernization to development under Western trusteeship, but development "along their own lines" and not toward "civilization," as the West understood it.

However the legal transition was to take place, it raised certain practical problems so long as British influence was only informal; and some of these problems could be very disturbing to a trained lawyer

47. See Metcalfe, *Maclean,* pp. 145–78.
48. M. Forster, Evidence before the West Africa Committee, 27 July 1842, PP, 1842, xi (551), p. 713.

like James Stephen at the Colonial Office. It was normal for a British official to enforce British law in British territory, and even outside British territory in special cases authorized by the legislature. But for a British official to decide questions according to alien law in alien territory seemed to stretch a point beyond the legitimate authority of the British Crown.[49] The issue was met for Maclean's jurisdiction by removing it altogether from the British sphere. Judicial Assessors after 1844 were Crown officials, but the authority they exercised outside the forts was not derived from the British Crown. It was held to depend solely on the consent of the "Sovereign Power of the state within which it is exercised.[50] Thus, while the goal was still conversion to Western culture, it was to be achieved by changing African culture slowly, under African authority, and not by substituting British authority and British institutions.

Meanwhile, a similar discussion was taking place on the theory and practice of representative government. Perronet Thompson and the *Westminster Review* had already raised the issue for Sierra Leone before 1830, and they kept up the demand, calling for a constitutional transition toward self government.[51] Colonial self government was no longer a contradiction in terms. The Canadians were moving toward an executive responsible to the local legislature for all local affairs. A similar transition might be possible for Sierra Leone, especially if the electoral franchise were limited to Africans of wealth or education. The demand was occasionally made; but the government could always plead the necessity of special controls to guard their special responsibility for the early training of the liberated Africans, and no significant changes were made.

The situation on the Gold Coast was different, but there the problem was to extend British influence into an informal sphere, rather than over sovereign territory. Various possibilities were considered after Earl Grey's accession to the Colonial Office. The Gold Coast was given a Legislative Council in 1850, but it was wholly appointed by the Governor and had jurisdiction only over the forts themselves. Grey was concerned to expand the informal British sphere in order to

49. J. Stephen, Memorandum of 26 December 1842, CO 96/2. See Metcalfe, *Maclean*, pp. 288–93.

50. Stanley to Hill, 22 November 1844, CO 402/2.

51. *Westminster Review*, XVI, 246 (1832). See also G. Stephen, *Letters to Russell*, first letter, pp. 24–28.

establish direct taxation within the judicial protectorate. To collect the tax required the consent, and hence the representation of the chiefs. As with the judicial sphere, there was a choice between British and African political institutions. Grey chose the African, hoping "to preserve whatever is capable of being rendered useful in the existing customs and institutions of the people." He suggested that the chiefs be formed into a Council of Chiefs, initially to authorize the direct tax but in time to meet more frequently and ultimately to become "responsible Public Officers."[52] This was an important departure from the earlier idea of ruling through the chiefs: the chiefs were to be formed into a new political unit, amalgamating the small, pre-existing units.

The idea was taken up on the Gold Coast by Brodie Cruickshank and James Bannerman, an African merchant who was also a government official. Together they drafted a memorandum of their own proposals for a Gold Coast constitution. For the forts themselves, they asked for a representative element in the Legislative Council to express the opinions of the merchant community. As for the protectorate, they wanted the Council of Chiefs made into a regular Assembly of Native Chiefs, empowered to pass laws subject to the confirmation of the Governor. Bannerman and Cruickshank also wanted the chiefs brought into the administration, with regular salary from the government, serving under a code of administrative regulations. Their justification stressed the necessity of communication between the people and the government, so that government could respond to the needs of a changing society.[53]

The Cruickshank-Bannerman proposals were a high-water mark of projected representative institutions. Grey gave only limited approval, and in a way that would have reduced chiefly functions from legislative responsibility to mere administrative work for the Cape Coast government.[54] By 1851, Bannerman and Cruickshank had themselves changed their minds and decided that representation was premature. S. J. Hill, the new Governor, disapproved, and Grey accepted this opinion.[55]

52. Grey to Winniett, 6 August 1849, CO 96/19; Grey to Winniett, 14 August 1850, CO 402/2.
53. B. Cruickshank and J. Bannerman to Winniett, 22 August 1850, CO 96/19.
54. Grey to Winniett, 18 December 1850, CO 96/19.
55. Hill to Grey (Confidential) 27 October 1851, CO 96/23. Minutes of the Gold Coast Legislative Council, 1 April 1851, copy in AG, ADM 14/1.

Incipient efforts to foster political development therefore came to an end. Grey's successors were no longer interested in the kind of informal political extension represented by the Bannerman-Cruickshank proposals. Similar efforts to join African and British political institutions, however, were to emerge during the 1860's and 1870's in both the Egba state of Abeokuta and a revived effort to unite the Fante chiefs. In both cases the initiative came from Westernized Africans rather than the metropolitan, or even the colonial, government. The Gold Coast constitutional discussions of the early 1850's were nevertheless something more than a futile exchange of correspondence. They were an attempt to grapple with the problem of Westernizing or modernizing African polities, so as to help meet the West on something like equal terms. In this sense, they were in line with the era of humanitarianism, with its insistence on cultural conversion and a limitation to informal empire.

These political trends and political suggestions were among the most fragile parts of the early-nineteenth-century image of Africa, since they were to be cut off during the 1880's and 1890's by the formation of territorial empires throughout West Africa. Nevertheless, they did not simply disappear: some aspects were taken up later on in connection with administrative devices like indirect rule. Echoes from still others were to reappear during the 1940's and 1950's, when Britain was again concerned with "political development" in West Africa. Indeed, the British theory of African empire, as it first emerged in the era of humanitarianism, showed a remarkable tenacity in the face of new conditions. As Africa entered the colonial period, the image of Africa was to be modified and developed in many new directions; but it set the base lines and became the point of departure for the British colonial regime.

POSTSCRIPT

Perhaps the most striking aspect of the British image of Africa in the early nineteenth century was its variance from the African reality, as we now understand it. There was also a marked lack of the kind of "progress" one might expect to find in a body of ideas that was constantly enlarged by accretions of new data. This is especially hard to explain, given the fact that nineteenth-century social scientists were trying to be methodical, working to a standard that was conceived as rational investigation.

One source of error has already been suggested: reporters went to Africa knowing the reports of their predecessors and the theoretical conclusions already drawn from them. They were therefore sensitive to data that seemed to confirm their European preconceptions, and they were insensitive to contradictory data. Their reports were thus passed through a double set of positive and negative filters, and filtered once more as they were assimilated in Britain. Data that did not fit the existing image were most often simply ignored. As a result, British thought about Africa responded very weakly to new data of any kind.

It responded much more strongly to changes in British thought. The travellers (and, even more, the analysts at home) took the European *weltanschauung* as their point of departure. They did not ask, "What is Africa like, and what manner of men live there" but, "How does Africa, and how do the Africans, fit into what we already know about the world" In this sense, the image of Africa was far more European than African.

479

In considering the nature of racial differences, for example, the scientists studied African races in order to answer questions posed for them by the existing state of biological theory and knowledge. Some African data were of immense importance, especially the data about differential mortality between blacks and whites on the African coast, but these data were selected because they seemed to answer problems set in their European context. In much the same way, the interdependence of race and culture was assumed because that assumption helped explain something in which the Europeans were very interested—their own leadership in the world of the nineteenth century. It was not built up by careful examination of data from Africa, or any other part of the world overseas.

At a more personal level, many affirmations about Africa were made for political, religious, or personal reasons. Prichard's belief in monogenesis came, first of all, from his desire to prove that science was congruent with Scripture. Nott and Gliddon's polygenesis came from their desire to prove that Negro slavery was licit. It is hard to avoid the conclusion that some of the wilder ravings of Knox's "transcendental anatomy" came from a blighted career, not merely from the currents of evolutionary thought.

In this way, the British image of Africa was intimately related to other strands of Western thought and life, and all the particular facets of that image were more closely related to one another than can be briefly stated. All these bodies of thought—about medicine, race, history, or political and economic development—were equally integrated with the world of events, both as cause and effect. They helped to form the plans for Sierra Leone or the Niger Expedition. They responded, in turn, to the lessons of experience, though these lessons were filtered in the same manner as other data.

The image of Africa, in short, was largely created in Europe to suit European needs—sometimes material needs, more often intellectual needs. When these needs allowed, it might touch on reality; as it did in the empirical victory of tropical medicine. Otherwise the European *Afrikaanschauung* was part of a European *weltanschauung,* and it was warped as necessary to make it fit into the larger whole. To say this, however, implies neither a moral nor an intellectual judgment of the nineteenth-century Europeans. They sought knowledge for their guidance, and the very magnitude of the effort remains as a kind of monument. Their errors, nevertheless, did as much to mold the course of history as their discoveries.

REFERENCE

MATTER

MORTALITY IN WEST AFRICA

Mortality statistics for West Africa are, at best, approximate. The groups for which they are available were generally speaking too small to have statistical validity. Very few calculations differentiate between the new arrivals and the old residents—an important distinction since old residents would be expected to have acquired a degree of immunity.

The initial attempts at colonization	*Death Rate*
Province of Freedom (within the first year)[1]	
European settlers	46%
Negro settlers	39%
Bulama (April 1792 to April 1793)[2]	
Europeans	61%
Sierra Leone Company (first year, 1792–1793)[3]	
Europeans as a whole	49%

1. Includes mortality on the outward voyage from England. R. R. Kuczynski, *Demographic Survey of the British Colonial Empire, Volume I: West Africa* (London, 1948), 43–45.
2. Philip Beaver, *African Memoranda* (London, 1805), p. 89; A. Johansen, *Description of Bulama Island* (London, 1794), p. 8. Figures include both the outward voyage from England and the homeward voyage of those who left Bulama before the end of the first year.
3. Sierra Leone Company, *Account of the Colony of Sierra Leone From Its First Establishment in [sic] 1793 . . .* (London, 1795), pp. 47–49.

Upper servants	17%
Lower servants	49%
European settlers	72%
European soldiers	69%
Nova Scotian Negro settlers	at least 17%

Sierra Leone Company (second year 1793–1794)
Remaining Europeans   10%

European personnel on exploring expeditions, 1805–1830[4]

Park's Second Expedition (May–November 1805)
Mortality on overland trip from Gambia to the Niger   87%
Ultimate mortality   100%

Tuckey's Expedition to the Congo   37%

Clapperton—Lander penetration from Badagri to the Niger   83%

Coastal posts in the early nineteenth century

Colonial Office estimate of deaths per year among "the better
class of society" (*c.* 1825)[5]
Gold Coast   12.5 %
Sierra Leone   8.3 %

Church Misssionary Society, total European personnel
(1804–1825)[6]
89 sent out; 54 died   60.5 %

Officials of the Company of Merchants Trading to Africa
(1812–1823)[7]
95 officials sent out; 44 died of disease   46.0 %

Gold Coast Government Officials (1822–1825)
111 officials (including military officers) sent out; 55 died
of disease   45.0 %

European personnel arriving in Sierra Leone over the five
years 1821–1826[8]
Civilians: 44 sent out; 20 died   44.5 %
Military and Civilians together: 1,612 sent out; 926 died   56.5 %

4. See M. Laird to Clarendon, 5 March 1855, printed in S. Crowther, *Journal of
an Expedition up the Niger and Tshada in 1854* (London, 1855), pp. viii–x.
5. Unsigned memorandum, 2 July 1825, CO 267/65. These estimates probably reflect the death rate of "acclimatized" Europeans with reasonable accuracy.
6. William Fox, *A Brief History of the Wesleyan Missions on the Western Coast
of Africa* (London, 1851), p. 617.
7. Kuczynski, *Demographic Survey,* I, 532.
8. PP, 1826–1827, xv (7), p. 209.

Total European troops sent out to all West Africa (1810–1825)[9]

    5,823 sent out; 1,912 died   33.0 %

African troops stationed in West Africa (total for 1810–1825)[10]

    Of 6,769, 254 died   3.75%

Major Tulloch's Investigation of Military Mortality[11]

    European other ranks, annual average mortality from disease only

        Sierra Leone Command, strength 1,843 men (1819–1836)   48.3 %

        West Indian Command, strength 4,333 men (1817–1836)   7.9 %

        Troops stationed in Britain (1819–1836)   1.5 %

    European officers, annual average mortality from disease only

        Sierra Leone Command (1819–1836)   20.9 %

    African troops, annual average mortality from "fevers" (1819–1836)

        Sierra Leone Command   .24%

        Windward and Leeward Command (West Indies)   .46%

        Jamaica   .82%

        British Honduras   .44%

        Bahamas   .56%

Exploring expeditions and small groups of newcomers, 1830–1850

Laird's Niger Expedition (1832–1833): 49 Europeans, of whom 40 died[12]   83%

Quorra Expedition to the Niger (1835): 6 Europeans; 1 died[13]   16%

9. Report of Commissioners Wellington and Rowan, PP, 1826–1827, vii (312), pp. 106–8. As the commissioners themselves noted, these reflect both the mortality of newcomers, which ran at about 50 per cent per annum, and that of older residents, which was much lower.

10. PP, 1826–1827, vii (312), pp. 106–8.

11. PP, 1837–1838, xl (138), pp. 5–7; PP, 1840, xxx [C. 228], pp. 16–17 and 24. Major Tulloch's survey may be considered the most careful and reliable of those conducted during the first half of the nineteenth century.

12. M. Laird and R. A. K. Oldfield, *Narrative of an Expedition into the Interior of Africa by the River Niger in 1832–4*, 2 vols. (London, 1837), II, 410–11.

13. C. C. Ifemesia, "British Enterprise on the Niger, 1830–1869," (Unpublished Ph.D. thesis, London, 1959), p. 165. The Europeans in this case were apparently recruited in Africa and hence "acclimatized."

Government Niger Expedition (1841–1842): 159 Europeans;
55 died[14]   35%

Wesleyan Missionary Society, new European personnel sent
out to Sierra Leone (1838–1850): 21 sent out; 7 died   33%

Wesleyan Missionary Society, new European personnel sent
out to all of West Africa (1838–1850); 67 sent out; 25 died.[15] 37%

Mortality of the anti-slavery blockade

Annual average mortality (1825–1845)[16]

From all causes	6.49%
From disease	5.44%
From "epidemic fevers"	3.00%

Comparative mortality from disease at other naval stations
(1825–1845)[17]

South American Stations	.77%
Mediterranean Station	.93%
Home Station	.98%
East Indian Station	1.51%
West Indian Station	1.81%

Mortality of officers and men of the blockade, percentage of
total mean strength[18]

1840	4.1 %
1841	7.9 %
1842	5.5 %
1843	2.1 %
1844	2.8 %
1845	5.0 %
1846	3.3 %
1847	2.5 %
1848	2.2 %

Annual average, 1840–1842   5.8 %

Annual average, 1846–1848   2.7 %

14. PP, 1843, xxxi (83), p. 1.
15. Fox, *Brief History,* p. 617. These figures for the period of improving mortality
make an interesting contrast with the CMS mortality of 1804–1825 (above).
16. A. Bryson, *Report on the Climate and Principal Diseases of the African Station*
(London, 1847), pp. 177–78. These figures differ slightly from some other published
figures on blockade mortality, since Bryson constructed them from the pay books rather
than the medical reports. The category "epidemic fevers" is therefore not a clinical
description but a measure of the number of simultaneous deaths on a single ship.
17. Bryson, *Principal Diseases,* pp. 177–78.
18. PP, 1850 (Lords), xxiv (35), appendix, p. 221.

Annual average mortality of the West African squadron,
1858–1867[19]   2.2 %

Mortality of fever victims

Gallinas Raid (1840): 130 men, 7 days up river; 23 fever cases
3 deaths[20]

Niger Expedition (1841): European personnel only[21]
  Albert: 64 days up river, 62 men; 55 fever cases, 23 deaths.
  Wilberforce: 45 days up river, 56 men; 48 fever cases, 7 deaths.
  Soudan: 40 days up river, 27 men; 27 fever cases, 10 deaths.

19. PP, 1867–1868, lxiv (158), p. 7.
20. R. R. Madden, Commissioner's Report, PP, 1842, xii (551), p. 226.
21. J. O. M'William, *Medical History of the Expedition to the Niger During the Years 1841–42* . . . (London, 1843), p. 126.

The sources for a work of this kind have no clear limits. Ideally, it should be based on a careful reading of every work concerned in any way with West Africa, on all the periodical literature, the newspapers—all the archives of the missionary societies, the merchant houses, and the governments. Perfection would demand a similar knowledge of the German, French, and American works on Africa, but the demands of perfection meet practical limitations. I have followed leads into the European and American literature, when works from abroad seemed to have a peculiar importance for the development of British thought. Printed books and articles published in Britain have been covered more thoroughly, and Chapters 1, 8, and 13 are in part bibliographical essays.

Among the non-specialist journals, special attention has been paid to the *Anti-Jacobin Review*, the *Eclectic Review*, the *Westminster Review*, the *Quarterly Review*, the *New Monthly Magazine*, and *Blackwood's Magazine* as broadly representative of the kind of journal the educated middle class without a special interest in Africa might have read. More specialized journals are discussed in the bibliographical chapters.

Archival sources and the personal papers of key authorities are also too extensive to be used exhaustively. They have been consulted with special reference to key periods of changing policy. At these times the official correspondence often went beyond problems of day to day administration, into those of theory and planning. Among the more important manuscript sources have been those of the Public Record Office, London, the National Archives of Sierra Leone, the National Archives of Ghana, the Nigerian National Archives, the Clarkson papers in the British Museum, the archives of the Church Missionary Society, the Archives of the Methodist Missionary Society, the papers of the Anti-Slavery Society and the Aborigines Protection Society.

Special attention has been paid to the government correspondence which was printed for Parliament, partly because it was available to the public and partly because it included the important suggestions and statements of policy. Where possible, citations have indicated the more readily available Parliamentary Papers, even when a document may have been consulted in the archives.

INDEX

Abd Shabeeny, El Hage, 200–201
Abeokuta: growth of, 156, 313; foreign relations, 314–15, 464; mentioned, 478
Aberdeen, Earl of: reference, 362
Abo, 462, 464, 465, 468
Abomey, 31, 155
Aborigines: theories about extinction of, 372–75, 376, 381, 420; legal status of, 474–75
Aborigines Committee. *See* Commons, House of
The Aborigines Friend, 339
Aborigines protection movement, 299, 375
Aborigines Protection Society: foundation of, 329–30; legal studies of, 417–18; archives of, 489; mentioned, 266, 339, 374; reference, 330, 428
Acclimatization: recognition of, 82–83; artificial acquisition of, 83, 191–92; promoters' reaction to, 178
Accra, 9, 169, 307, 312
Acculturation. *See* Culture change
Acherknecht, E. H.: reference, 81, 182, 195
Adam and Eve: racial nature of, 40
Adamawa, 201, 311
Adams, C. D.: reference, 12
Adams, H. G.: reference, 386

Adams, Capt. John: strategic views, 163; commercial guide, 200; on slave trade, 255, 271; reference, 12, 163, 200, 211, 254, 255, 271
Adams, Rev. John, 24
Adams, Robert: pretended trip to Timbuctu, 164; reference, 165
Adangme: ethnographic report on, 329
Adanson, Michel: in history of botany, 12*n*; investigations in Senegal, 15–16, 220; mentioned, 23, 59; reference, 12
Adelung, J. C.: linguistic studies of, 222
Administration, colonial: discussions of 1808–1821, 159–64; discussions of 1800–1830, 277–79; problems of, in informal empire, 470–71
Admiralty: sponsors exploration, 151, 172, 200, 311–12; scientific investigations of, 334; mentioned, 162; reference, 468. *See also* Navy
Africa: relation to West Africa, 292–93; British trade with (1829–1852), 294
African Agricultural Association: reference, 451
African Association: foundation of, 17; expeditions of, 17–18, 144–46, 151; and geographical scholarship, 22, 199; and belief in healthy interior, 86–87; 87*n*;